The Public Trust Doctrine in Environmental and Natural Resources Law

The Public Trust Doctrine in Environmental and Natural Resources Law

SECOND EDITION

Michael C. Blumm
JEFFREY BAIN FACULTY SCHOLAR AND PROFESSOR OF LAW
LEWIS & CLARK LAW SCHOOL

Mary Christina Wood
PHILIP H. KNIGHT PROFESSOR OF LAW
UNIVERSITY OF OREGON SCHOOL OF LAW

CAROLINA ACADEMIC PRESS
Durham, North Carolina

ISBN 978-1-61163-723-6
LCCN 2015940829

Carolina Academic Press
700 Kent Street
Durham, North Carolina 27701
Telephone (919) 489-7486
Fax (919) 493-5668
www.cap-press.com

Printed in the United States of America

Dedication

Throughout the ages, the public trust has come to life as a result of extraordinary vision and courage on the part of jurists, lawyers, and scholars. We dedicate this book to all of the pioneers, past and present, with particular recognition of the contributions of Justinian,[1] Sir Matthew Hale,[2] Justice Andrew Kirkpatrick,[3] Justice Stephen J. Field,[4] Justice Stanley Mosk,[5] Justice Alan Broussard,[6] Justice Paula Nakayama,[7] Justice Presbitero Valasco, Jr.,[8] Judge Gisela Triana,[9] Justice Ronald Castille,[10] and of course Professor Joseph Sax.[11] And, too, we dedicate it to our own children, all children on Earth, and to future generations — all of whom have a stake in the legal evolution of a doctrine that advances their inalienable rights to a balanced and healthy ecology.

---

1. For his influential code, the Institutes of Justinian, *see* J. INST. (T. Sandars trans., 4th ed. 1867).

2. For his treatise, *De Jure Maris, reprinted in* STUART MOORE, A HISTORY OF THE FORESHORE AND THE LAW RELATING THERETO (3rd ed. 1888).

3. For *Arnold v. Mundy,* 6 N.J.L. 1 (N. J. 1821).

4. For *Illinois Central R.R. Co. v. Illinois,* 146 U.S. 387 (1892).

5. For *City of Berkeley v. Superior Court of Alameda County,* 606 P.2d 362 (Cal. 1980).

6. For the "Mono Lake" opinion, *National Audubon Soc. v. Superior Court of Alpine Cty.,* 33 Cal.3d 419, 189 Cal.Rptr. 346, 658 P.2d 709 (1983).

7. For the "Waiahole Ditch" opinion, *In re Water Use Permit Applications,* 9 P.3d 409 (Haw. 2000).

8. For *Metropolitan Manila Development Authority v. Concerned Citizens of Manila Bay,* 574 S.C.R.A. 661 (Phil. S. Ct. 2008).

9. For a decision recognizing atmosphere as a trust asset, *Angela Bonser-Lain, et al. v. Texas Commission on Environmental Quality,* No. D-1-GN-11-002194 (201st Judicial District Court, Tx., Aug. 2, 2012).

10. For his scholarly opinion in *Robinson Township v. Commonwealth,* 83 A.2d 901 (Pa. 2013).

11. For his path-breaking article, *The Public Trust Doctrine in Natural Resource Law: Effective Judicial Intervention,* 68 Mich. L. Rev. 471 (1970).

Summary of Contents

Detailed Table of Contents

Table of Cases

The principal cases are in bold type. Cases cited or discussed in the text are in roman type. References are to pages. Cases cited in principal cases and within other quoted materials are not included.

Table of Secondary Sources

40 Am. Jur. 2d, *Highways, Streets, and Bridges* § 313 (2014), **23**

Kristina Alexander, *Congressional Research Service, The 2010 Oil Spill: Natural Resource Damage Assessment Under the Oil Pollution Act* (Sept. 8, 2010), www.fas.org/sgp/crs/misc/R41396.pdf, **239**

Jerry Anderson, *Britain's Right to Roam: Redefining the Landowner's Bundle of Sticks,* 19 Geo. Int. Envtl. L. Rev. 375 (2007), **325, 360**

William D. Araiza, *Democracy, Distrust, and the Public Trust: Process-Based Constitutional Theory, the Public Trust Doctrine, and the Search for a Substantive Environmental Value,* 45 UCLA L. Rev. 385 (1997), **159, 434**

———, *The Public Trust Doctrine as an Interpretive Canon,* 45 U.C. Davis L. Rev. 693 (2012), **293**

Argument of the United States, *Fur Seal Arbitration* (U.S. v. Gr. Brit. 1893), *reprinted in* 9 Fur Seal Arbitration: Proceedings of the Tribunal of Arbitration (Gov't Printing Office 1895); also reprinted in 1 John Bassett Moore, History and Digest of the International Arbitrations to Which the United States Has Been a Party 755, 813–14 (1898), **371**

Craig Anthony (Tony) Arnold, *Working Out an Environmental Ethic: Anniversary Lessons from Mono Lake,* 4 Wyo. L. Rev. 1 (2004), **398**

———, *The Reconstitution of Property: Property as a Web of Interests,* 26 Harv. Envtl. L. Rev. 281, 349–50 (2002), **146**

———, *Water Privatization Trends in the United States: Human Rights, National Security, and Public Stewardship,* 33 Wm. & Mary Envtl. L. & Pol'y Rev. 785 (2009), **208**

Hope M. Babcock, *The Public Trust Doctrine: What a Tall Tale They Tell,* 61 S.C. L. Rev. 393 (2009), **17, 401**

Maude Barlow, Blue Covenant: The Global Water Crisis and the Coming Battle for the Right to Water 91 (New Press 2007), **207**

———, *Advice for Water Warriors,* YES Magazine, Nov. 8, 2010, http://www.yesmagazine.org/planet/advice-for-water-warriors, **359**

Maude Barlow & Tony Clarke, *Who Owns the Water?* The Nation, Sept. 2, 2002, **207, 215**

Anthony D. Barnosky et al., *Approaching a State Shift in Earth's Biosphere,* 486 Nature 52, 52 (2012), http://www.ecoearth.info/shared/docfeed/biosphere_state_shift_nature.pdf, **376**

Paul A. Barresi, *Mobilizing the Public Trust Doctrine in Support of Publicly Owned Forests as Carbon Dioxide Sinks in India and the United States,* 23 Colo. J. Int'l Envtl. L. & Pol'y 39 (2012), **188–89, 312**

Authors' Note

We edited the case law liberally throughout for readability, eliminating redundant citations and sometimes creating paragraphs. Any footnotes are numbered consecutively throughout chapters; we did not retain the original footnote numbers.

Case citations in the text, the footnotes of judicial opinions, and the writings of commentators have been omitted without so specifying. Footnotes in judicial opinions and articles are also omitted without specifying. Asterisks and brackets are used to designate omissions from the original materials.

Excerpts from the following books and articles appear with the kind permission of the copyright holders (in order of appearance in this text):

DAVID C. SLADE ET. AL, PUTTING THE PUBLIC TRUST DOCTRINE TO WORK (Coastal States Org. 2d ed. 1997). Reprinted by permission of David C. Slade.

HARRISON C. DUNNING, WATERS AND WATER RIGHTS (Amy K. Kelley ed., 3d ed. 2013). Reprinted by permission of Matthew Bender & Company, Inc., a part of LexisNexis. Copyright 2013. All rights reserved.

Joseph L. Sax, *The Public Trust Doctrine in Natural Resource Law: Effective Judicial Intervention,* Mich. L. Rev. 68, no. 3 (1970): 471–566. Reprinted by permission of Joseph L. Sax and the Michigan Law Review.

Robin Kundis Craig, *A Comparative Guide to the Eastern Public Trust Doctrines: Classification of States, Property Rights, and State Summaries,* 16 Penn. St. L. Rev. 1, 16–18 (2007). Reprinted by permission of Robin Kundis Craig and the Penn. State Law Review.

Charles F. Wilkinson, *The Headwaters of the Public Trust, Some Thoughts on the Source and Scope of the Traditional Doctrine,* 19 Envtl. L. 425 (1989). Reprinted by permission of Charles F. Wilkinson.

Michael C. Blumm, *The Public Trust Doctrine—A Twenty-First Century Concept,* 14 Hastings W-Nw. J. Envtl. L. & Policy 105 (2005). Reprinted by permission of Michael C. Blumm and the Hastings West Northwest Journal of Environmental Law & Policy.

Alexandra B. Klass & Ling-Yee Huang, *Restoring the Public Trust Water Resources and the Public Trust Doctrine: A Manual for Advocates* (Center for Progressive Reform Report #908, 2009). Reprinted by permission of Alexandra B. Klass, Ling-Yee Huang, and the Center for Progressive Reform.

EarthJustice Press Release, *Hawai'i Water Commission Splits Over Waiahole Water Case.* Reprinted by permission of EarthJustice.

Craig Anthony (Tony) Arnold, *Water Privatization Trends in the United States: Human Rights, National Security, and Public Stewardship*, 37 Wm. & Mary Envtl. Law & Pol'y Rev. 785–849 (2009). Reprinted by permission of Tony Arnold and the William & Mary Environmental Law & Policy Review.

Michael C. Blumm & Lucus Ritchie, *The Pioneer Spirit and the Public Trust: The American Rule of Capture and State Ownership of Wildlife*, 35 Envtl. L. 673 (2005). Reprinted by permission of Michael C. Blumm and Lucus Ritchie.

Mary Christina Wood, *Advancing the Sovereign Trust of Government to Safeguard the Environment for Present and Future Generations (Part I): Ecological Realism and the Need for a Paradigm Shift*, 39 Envtl. L. 43 (2009). Reprinted by permission of Mary Christina Wood.

Carol M. Rose, *The Comedy of the Commons: Custom, Commerce, and Inherently Public Property*, 53 U. Chi. L. Rev. 711 (1986). Reprinted by permission of the Copyright Clearance Center.

Michael C. Blumm, *The Public Trust Doctrine and Private Property: The Accommodation Principle*, 27 Pace Envtl. L. Rev. 649 (2010). Reprinted by permission of Michael C. Blumm and the Pace Environmental Law Review.

Robin Kundis Craig, *A Comparative Guide to the Western Public Trust Doctrines: Classification of States, Property Rights, and State Summaries*, By permission from Robin Kundis Craig and the Regents of the University of California. © 2010 by the Regents of the University of California. Reprinted from 37 Ecology L. Q. 53 (2010).

David Takacs, *The Public Trust Doctrine. Environmental Human Rights, and the Future of Private Property*, 16 N.Y.U. Envtl. L. Rev. 711 (2008). Reprinted by permission of David Takacs and the N.Y.U. Environmental Law Journal.

Ved P. Nanda & William K. Ris, Jr., *The Public Trust Doctrine: A Viable Approach to International Environmental Protection*, Reprinted by permission of Ved P. Nanda, William K. Ris, Jr. and the Regents of the University of California. © 1975–1976 by the Regents of the University of California Reprinted from 5 Ecology L. Q. 291.

Peter H. Sand, *Sovereignty Bounded: Public Trusteeship for Common Pool Resources?*, in Global Environmental Politics, vol. 4, no. 1, Feb. 2004, pp. 47–71, MIT Press Journals. Reprinted by permission of Peter H. Sand and MIT Press Journals.

Edith Brown Weiss, *The Planetary Trust: Conservation and Intergenerational Equity*, Reprinted by permission of Edith Brown Weiss and the Regents of the University of California. © 1983–84 by the Regents of the University of California, reprinted from 11 Ecology L.Q. 495.

Mary Christina Wood, *Atmospheric Trust Litigation Across the World*, in KEN COGHILL, CHARLES SAMFORD & TIM SMITH, FIDUCIARY DUTY AND THE ATMOSPHERIC TRUST (Farnham: Ashgate 2011) pp. 317–328. Reprinted by permission from Mary Christina Wood and Ashgate Publishing.

Casey Jarman, *The Public Trust Doctrine In The Exclusive Economic Zone*, 65 Ore. L. Rev. 1 (1986). Reprinted by permission of Casey Jarman and the Oregon Law Review.

Hope M. Babcock, *The Public Trust Doctrine: What a Tall Tale They Tell*, 61 S.C. L. Rev. 393 (2009). Reprinted by permission of Hope M. Babcock and the South Carolina Law Review.

Mary Turnipseed et al., *The Silver Anniversary of the United States' Exclusive Economic Zone: Twenty-Five Years of Ocean Use and Abuse and the Possibility of a Blue Water Public Trust Doctrine,* 36 Ecology L. Q. 1 (2009). Reprinted by permission of Mary Turnipseed.

Mary Christina Wood, *"You Can't Negotiate with a Beetle": Environmental Law for a New Ecological Age,* 50 Nat. Res. J. 167 (2010). Reprinted by permission of Mary Christina Wood.

Gail Osherenko, *New Discourses on Ocean Governance: Understanding Property Rights and the Public Trust,* 21 J. Envtl. L. & Litig. 317 (2006). Reprinted by permission of Gail Osherenko and the Journal of Environmental Law & Litigation.

Patrick S. Ryan, *Application of the Public-Trust Doctrine and Principles of Natural Resource Management to Electromagnetic Spectrum,* Mich. Telecomm. & Tech. L. Rev. 10, no. 2: (2004) 285–372. Reprinted by permission of Patrick S. Ryan and the Michigan Telecommunications & Technology Law Review.

Kristen A. Carpenter, *A Property Rights Approach to Sacred Sites Cases: Asserting a Place for Indians as Nonowners,* 52 U.C.L.A. L.Rev. 1061 (2005). Reprinted by permission of Kristen A. Carpenter and the University of California at Los Angeles Law Review.

Patty Gerstenblith, *Identity and Cultural Property: The Protection of Cultural Property in the United States,* 75 B.U. L. Rev. 559 (1995). Reprinted by permission of Patty Gerstenblith.

Richard A. Epstein, *Congress's Copyright Giveaway,* Wall Street Journal (Dec. 21, 1998). Reprinted by permission of Richard A. Epstein.

William B. Araiza, *Democracy, Distrust, and the Public Trust: Process-Based Constitutional Theory, the Public Trust Doctrine, and the Search for a Substantive Environmental Value,* 45 UCLA L. Rev. 385 (1997). Reprinted by permission of William B. Araiza.

DAVID C. SLADE, THE PUBLIC TRUST DOCTRINE IN MOTION (2008). Reprinted by permission of David C. Slade.

Preface to the Second Edition

Our goal in publishing the first edition of this casebook a couple of years ago was to create a systematic approach to the study of the public trust doctrine (PTD), and we think our book has helped to begin the institutionalization of the doctrine in law study.

In this second edition, we have included several significant developments in what is a rapidly evolving body of law. The most notable new decision is *Robinson Township v. Commonwealth* (p. 82), a decision of the Pennsylvania Supreme Court which has quickly become a foundational decision. We have also included the Wisconsin Supreme Court's opinion in *Rock-Koshkonong Lake District v. Department of Natural Resources* (p. 147), in which the court narrowly interpreted the scope of that state's PTD, arguably misinterpreting that court's seminal decision of *Just v. Marinette County* (p. 141) in the process. A case which may expand the scope of the PTD in California to groundwater is *Environmental Law Foundation v. State Water Resources Control Board* (p. 184), although whether California will join states like Hawaii and Vermont that recognize groundwater as a trust resource awaits whether the environmental claimants can prove a link between groundwater pumping and the surface flows of the navigable Scott River.

There have been a considerable number of developments in the cluster of cases that seek to recognize the atmosphere as a trust resource, and we discuss these developments in some detail in chapter 11 (pp. 365–405). A steady stream of case law also continues to arise out of efforts of members of the public to access trust resources, mostly in the context of waterways experiencing monopoly control (chapter 3, pp. 95–138). We also have updated the text to expand our consideration of the PTD abroad to include considerable case law from Indonesia (p. 352), a constitutional amendment in Norway (p. 359), and statutory developments in Britain and the Nordic countries (p. 360).

There are other changes as well. The above summary reflects only a snapshot of developments in this rapidly expanding area of law. We expect the pace of change to accelerate in the near future, and we pledge to try to keep current with it.

We continue to believe that this course is an ideal upper-level course in environmental law. It offers a common-law-based approach to environmental decision making, a contrast in a field dominated by statutes and administrative regulations. Although there is a role for statutory and regulatory interpretations of the PTD, there is little doubt that the vibrant center of the PTD lies in a judiciary that understands the importance of trust resources to both present and future generations. That in turn requires courts that are schooled in the doctrine's history, its evolution in other jurisdictions, and the fundamental anti-monopolistic purposes it has always served and continues to serve, including intergenerational equity.

We hope this effort contributes to the evolution of the PTD in the 21st century by educating the next generation of lawyers who must convince judges of the role the PTD can play in a world that is becoming increasingly crowded, experiencing the diminishment of trust resources, and threatened with climate change which will imperil trust resources first.

MCB
MCW
February 2015

Preface to the First Edition

The public trust doctrine (PTD) is an ancient doctrine of property law that governs sovereign stewardship of natural resources. First surfacing in Roman law through the Justinian Code, it was revived in medieval England largely through the efforts of Sir Mathew Hale and became entrenched in American law in the nineteenth century through the process of statehood. In the twentieth century, the doctrine became a favorite of the law professoriate and the environmental community for its potential to recognize public rights in private property. The doctrine both promotes public access to trust resources and justifies government protection of them. It also equips the public—the beneficiaries of the trust—with the right to challenge government on the management of their ecological assets. This doctrine, remarkable for its endurance through the ages, now brings populist overtones and human rights underpinnings to the modern fields of environmental law and property law.

We offer the first casebook on public trust law. In it, we have endeavored to capture the rich history and considerable diversity of the field. Although the PTD is often characterized as a doctrine of state law, we think the perception is erroneous because the PTD is an inherent attribute of sovereignty and, accordingly, should apply to both the federal and state governments. The origins of the American PTD lie in bilateral federal-state agreements admitting states to the Union, but the doctrine is also recognized in countries as far-flung as India, the Philippines, Kenya, and Brazil. We survey the PTD's application from the local to global level.

The wellspring of the American PTD lies in a distinctive antimonopoly sentiment that, widespread in the nineteenth century, continues to inspire a vibrant body of case law concerning public access to trust resources. That case law—as well as state constitutions and statutes—has expanded the scope of trust assets from lands submerged beneath navigable waters to wetlands, beaches, parklands, wildlife, air, and groundwater. Internationally, the doctrine has advanced concepts of sustainable development and the precautionary principle, and thus is frequently linked to the public's right to life, health, and environmental protection. There are ongoing efforts to use the PTD to combat climate change by applying it to curb carbon emissions.

While the origins of the PTD date to Roman times, the PTD carries enormous importance today, as many statutory systems fail in their basic purpose of protecting public resources from private exploitation. A course in public trust law allows students to break out of the narrow confines of statutory law and immerse themselves in fundamental principles that provide a fulcrum for sustainable environmental management. The course can, and we think should, delve into the most basic questions of constitutionalism and the role of the judiciary, legislatures, and courts in allocating natural resources.

At less than 500 pages, we think this book is ideal for an advanced course or seminar in environmental, natural resources, or property law. The casebook is accompanied by a teachers' manual as well. We have designed the text not only as a set of teaching materials, but also as a research platform for further inquiry into public trust law. We have relied heavily on the rich scholarship in public trust law and have tried to supplement it. Students in our classes have produced multiple summaries of state public trust law as well as law review notes and articles analyzing some of the most intriguing questions generated by the doctrine. We encourage you to send us cases and materials and as well as your contributions to the law of the public trust, which we will use in new editions of this text and in a treatise on the subject.

MCB
MCW
December 2012

Acknowledgments

Three stellar Lewis and Clark Law research assistants, Serena Liss '15, Angela Ostrowski '15, and Lynn Schaffer LL.M '15, were indispensable to the creation of the Second Edition. Lisa Frenz again managed to cover up our mistakes with her word processing wizardry.

The Rocky Mountain Mineral Law Foundation provided research assistant support for the first edition, for which we remain grateful.

The Public Trust Doctrine in Environmental and Natural Resources Law

Chapter 1

Introduction

The public trust doctrine (PTD), an ancient doctrine governing the management of natural resources, first surfaced in Roman law, reemerged in medieval England, and then was transported across the Atlantic to the United States in the early nineteenth century. Functioning as a public property doctrine, the PTD imposes limits on governmental action and provides public access rights to trust resources. In the United States, the doctrine's reach expanded from coastal areas affected by the tides to large inland waterways in the nineteenth century; it also evolved from a mechanism promoting navigation and commercial fishing to one protecting recreation and ecological integrity. Some commentators see the potential of the PTD to continue to evolve into an organizing principle for natural resources management in the twenty-first century.

Many environmental law classes focus on statutory law to address environmental issues. But the enduring PTD long predates all modern statutes, having roots in United States law in court opinions from over a century ago. Although the legislature's police power underlies statutes, the PTD emanates from property law. The doctrine posits the government as a trustee of selected natural resources that must be managed for the long-term benefit of the public. A trust is a type of ownership in which one party manages property for the benefit of another party. The trust bifurcates ownership between the *trustee*, who holds legal title, and the *beneficiary* who holds beneficial ownership. The assets in the trust make up the *res* or *corpus* of the trust. The trustee is under a fiduciary obligation to manage the assets for the sole benefit of the beneficiaries.

Trusts are well-established in the private law context. The basic construct, as well as many of the same principles, applies also to the sovereign context. In the case of the public trust, the beneficiaries are the citizens, both present and future generations. As a foundational property law principle, this doctrine aims to ensure that government safeguards and makes publicly accessible natural resources which are necessary for public welfare and survival.

The doctrine has attracted widespread attention from the legal academy and legal practitioners for its potential to force government protection of environmental resources. Professor Harrison Dunning has called the doctrine a "fundamental doctrine of American property law."[1] Professor Gerald Torres has described the PTD as "the law's DNA."[2] The public property right to trust resources ranks so fundamental that some scholars and courts characterize it as a natural right or human right. As Professor Joseph Sax suggested

---

1. Harrison C. Dunning, *A Fundamental Doctrine of American Property Law*, 19 Envtl. L. 515 (1989).
2. Gerald Torres, *The Public Trust: The Law's DNA*, Keynote Address at the University of Oregon School of Law (Feb. 23, 2012).

over four decades ago in a landmark article, the public trust responsibility underpins democracy itself, demarcating a society of "citizens rather than of serfs."[3]

The PTD requires governmental trustees to manage the resources that are in the corpus of the trust as a long-term steward for the benefit of both present and future generations. The doctrine thus interjects notions of sustainable development and intergenerational equity into the decision-making calculus. And because application of the doctrine encourages active judicial review of resource allocation, it provides a counterweight to a tradition of judicial deference to agency decision making which has come to characterize statutory environmental law.

For all of these reasons, the PTD is attractive conceptually to those concerned about sustainable natural resource use in the twenty-first century, particularly where statutes have failed to achieve their protective aims. However, the doctrine suffers from fragmentation. Each jurisdiction has its own interpretation of the doctrine. Some jurisdictions have quite active versions; some have PTDs that have been seldom used. This variety has hindered widespread use of the doctrine, as neither practitioners nor students nor professors have ready access to analysis of the PTD in their particular jurisdictions or to a systematic comparison of PTD themes across jurisdictions.[4]

As interest in the public trust surges both in the United States and internationally, the PTD becomes ever more a doctrine "in motion," as David Slade has put it.[5] This book assembles court cases, scholarly articles, and other materials to provide coherence to this emerging field. As you read through the materials, you should consider the future evolution of the doctrine as much as its history and current interpretation. In particular, the following structure and themes weave through all of the book's chapters, posing both practical and theoretical questions about the PTD's role in protecting environmental resources.

The Origin and Character of the Trust—As the following materials elaborate, the origins of the trust date to at least ancient Roman law. However, in the United States, the doctrine is often characterized as a state law doctrine. This characterization reflects the fact that most public trust cases arise in state courts. But although the PTD is undoubtedly a state doctrine, is it exclusively that? In other words, do its origins suggest that it applies only to the U.S. states? Surely not, as the PTD surfaces in many countries throughout the world. Reflecting its deep origins, some scholars and courts have described the doctrine as an attribute of sovereignty applicable to all sovereigns, not just states in America. In one landmark case, *Geer v. State of Connecticut*, the U.S. Supreme Court referred to the trust over wildlife as an "attribute of government" and traced the doctrine back "through all vicissitudes of governmental authority."[6] Some modern decisions consider the doctrine as inherent in the sovereign structure. For example, in *In re Water Use Permit Applications* (often called the *Waiahole Ditch* case), the Hawai'i Supreme Court stated, "[H]istory and precedent have established the public trust as an inherent attribute of sovereign authority…."[7] In another case, a federal district court described the trust as a limitation on sovereignty that "can only be destroyed by the destruction of the sovereign."[8]

---

3. Joseph L. Sax, *The Public Trust Doctrine in Natural Resource Law: Effective Judicial Intervention*, 68 Mich. L. Rev. 471, 484 (1970).

4. Professor Blumm's students have been compiling state-by-state analyses of individual state PTDs. By early 2015, they had evaluated 45 states. See Michael C. Blumm (ed), *The Public Trust Doctrine in 45 States*, available at http://ssrn.com/abstract=2235329.

5. David C. Slade, The Public Trust Doctrine in Motion, 1997–2008 (2008).

6. *Geer v. State of Connecticut*, 161 U.S. 519, 525–28 (1896).

7. *In re Water Use Permit Applications*, 9 P.3d 409, 443–44 (Haw. 2000).

8. *United States v. 1.58 Acres of Land*, 523 F. Supp. 120, 124 (D. Mass. 1981).

Professor Karl Coplan has claimed, "The idea that public trust limits and powers inhere in the very nature of sovereignty is one consistent thread in public trust cases.... Public trust principles have been described as an essential attribute of sovereignty across cultures and across millennia,"[9] and one of the editors has likewise noted, "The trust attribute of sovereignty ... is fundamentally one of limitation, not power, organically comprised as a central principle of governance itself."[10]

The trust has been incorporated into many state constitutions and statutes in the U.S. as well as in the constitutions and statutes of other countries. It is important to recognize, however, that the trust pre-exists such enactments. For example, in *Esplanade Properties v. City of Seattle*, the Ninth Circuit declared, "It is beyond cavil that 'a public trust has always existed in Washington'" and noted that the doctrine is "partially encapsulated in the language of" the state constitution as well as reflected in the state shoreline management act.[11] The Philippines Supreme Court gave the matter poetic force in *Oposa v. Factoran*, when it characterized the right of future generations to "a balanced and healthful ecology," which had been incorporated expressly in the Philippines 1987 Constitution. The Court noted:

> Such a right belongs to a different category of rights altogether for it concerns nothing less than self-preservation and self-perpetuation— ... the advancement of which may even be said to predate all governments and constitutions. As a matter of fact, these basic rights need not even be written in the Constitution for they are assumed to exist from the inception of humankind. If they are now explicitly mentioned in the fundamental charter, it is because of the well-founded fear of its framers that unless the right to a balanced and healthful ecology and to health are mandated as state policies by the Constitution itself ... the day would not be too far when all else would be lost not only for the present generation, but also for those to come— generations which stand to inherit nothing but parched earth incapable of sustaining life.[12]

An important question is whether the public trust has constitutional force in those instances where it has not been incorporated explicitly into a constitution of a state or nation. Doctrines of constitutional character take precedence over contrary statutes, whereas judge-made common law alone does not carry such trump force. Although the U.S. PTD is often characterized as common law, some scholars have located implicit constitutional underpinnings as well. For example, Professor Doug Grant viewed the American doctrine as embedded in the constitutional reserved powers doctrine, a concept we explore in chapters 2 and 12.[13]

The Trustees— The PTD characterizes the government as trustee. Each branch plays a role according to its constitutional position in the structure of government. As the primary governing branch of the sovereign, the legislature is the principal trustee of the

9. Karl S. Coplan, *Public Trust Limits on Greenhouse Gas Trading Schemes: A Sustainable Middle Ground?*, 35 Colum. J. Envt'l L. 287, 311 (2010).

10. Mary Christina Wood, *Advancing the Sovereign Trust of Government to Safeguard the Environment for Present and Future Generations (Part I): Ecological Realism and the Need for a Paradigm Shift*, 39 Envtl. L. 43, 71 (2009).

11. *Esplanade Properties, LLC. v. City of Seattle*, 307 F. 3d 978, 985 (9th Cir. 2002) (quoting *Rettkowski v. Dep't of Ecology*, 858 P.2d 232, 239 (Wash. 1993); *Orion Corp. v. State*, 747 P.2d 1062, 1072 (Wash. 1987)).

12. *Oposa v. Factoran*, 224 S.C.R.A. 792 (S.C. 1993) (Phil.).

13. Douglas L. Grant, *Underpinnings of the Public Trust Doctrine: Lessons from Illinois Central Railroad*, 33 Ariz. St. L.J. 849, 879–80 (2001).

public's assets. Agencies in the executive branch act as "agents" of the legislature and are encumbered by trust obligations as well (although some jurisdictions require an explicit conferral of trust authority by the legislature to impose trust duties on administrative agencies). Generally, the agencies with authority to regulate the harm in question are the ones subject to a trust duty.[14] Finally, the courts act as enforcers of the trust, just as they do in the private trust world.

State governments are well-established trustees under the PTD. Historically, states took the primary role in managing environmental and natural resources, so most PTD conflicts involved states instead of the federal government. With the enactment of major environmental statutes in the 1970s, however, the federal government assumed primacy in much environmental regulation (although many statutes allow states to develop programs implementing federal statutes). This active federal role brings to the forefront the question of whether the federal legislature and agencies are trustees along with the states. Few cases have considered the issue, but over 50 law professors signed an amicus brief claiming that the federal government is indeed a trustee,[15] a matter we explore in chapter 11.

If the federal government is not a trustee, what is its role with respect to the public property it controls? Surely the federal government must act to protect the public from whom it gains its power. If we view the trust as an attribute of sovereignty, is there any reason to distinguish the federal and state governments? Professor Coplan has suggested that "[i]f ... the public trust is essential to the nature of sovereignty and encompasses rights reserved to the people generally, then the doctrine applies equally to the sovereign federal government as it does to the sovereign state governments."[16]

What would be the ramifications of applying the PTD to the federal government? The case that considered the matter most thoroughly (and found the PTD applicable to the federal government) is *United States v. 1.58 Acres of Land* (p. 367).[17] One of the editors has characterized the federal government as a "co-trustee" of resources along with the states, concluding, "Within the United States, layered sovereign interests in natural resources arise from the constitutional configuration of states and the federal government. Where the federal government has a national interest in the resource, it is a co-trustee along with the states."[18]

How have other countries dealt with this issue? Are federal agencies and legislatures in other nations subject to the PTD? One of the editors co-authored a study examining PTD case law from a dozen other countries and found that several nations applied the public trust to their national government.[19] We take up the PTD abroad in chapter 10.

---

14. See *Center for Biological Diversity v. FPL Group, Inc.*, 83 Cal. Rptr. 3d 588, 603, 607 (Cal. Ct. App. 2008) (applying the trust duty to "agencies that are responsible for regulating [the harmful] activities" and noting a right held by the public "to insist that the state, through its appropriate subdivisions and agencies, protect and preserve public trust property").

15. See *Alec L.* ex rel. *Loorz v. McCarthy*, 561 Fed. Appx. 7 (Mem) (D.C. Cir. 2014), *cert. denied*, 135 S. Ct. 774 (2014). Brief for Law Professors as Amici Curiae in Support of Granting Writ of Certiorari, Alec L. *ex rel.* Loorz v. McCarthy, 561 Fed. Appx. 7 (Mem) (No. 14-405), 2014 U.S. S. Ct. Briefs LEXIS 3897. *See* Michael C. Blumm & Lynn Schaffer, *The Federal Public Trust Doctrine: A Law Professors' Amicus Brief* (November 6, 2014), Lewis & Clark Law School Legal Studies Research Paper No. 2014-18, available at SSRN: http://ssrn.com/abstract=2518260.

16. Coplan, above note 9, at 313.

17. 523 F. Supp. 120 (D. Mass. 1981), see p. 367.

18. *See* Wood, above note 10, at 85.

19. Michael C. Blumm & Rachel D. Guthrie, *Internationalizing the Public Trust Doctrine: Natural Law and Constitutional and Statutory Approaches to Fulfilling the Saxion Vision*, 45 U.C. Davis L. Rev. 741, 763 (2012).

The Beneficiaries—Courts have repeatedly emphasized that the beneficiaries of the trust are both the present and future generations of citizens. Professor John Davidson has observed that this feature gives a dual quality to the PTD, protecting both *intra-generational* and *inter-generational* interests.[20] Much of the trust literature and case law has focused on present-day disputes between different classes of citizens. In an article excerpted later in this chapter, for example, Professor Joseph Sax called attention to the disparity between a "diffuse majority" and a "concerted minority" in natural resources law, noting that the trust can serve as a tool of "democratization" to protect the rights of citizens.[21] Other scholars, such as Edith Brown Weiss, have focused on the question of intergenerational equity, which stands threatened when the consumptive needs of the present citizens deprive future beneficiaries of their natural trust inheritance.[22]

The Assets in the Trust—The materials in this first chapter focus on what is generally thought of as the "traditional public trust," which concerns primarily submerged lands and navigable waterways. But the trust has expanded greatly beyond the navigability confines in many states. As Professor Lazarus reported, the doctrine has been applied to water resources, wildlife, parklands, a battlefield, and other important areas.[23] As this field evolves, a primary question concerns the scope of the *res*: What assets are considered public trust assets? Although some scholars tend to focus narrowly on the historical precedent, increasingly resources beyond streambeds play an equally important societal role, a fact recognized by many courts in jurisdictions beyond the U.S.[24] If the PTD is to maintain relevance in a changing world, courts must continue to recognize an expanding group of trust resources, which the Supreme Court defined over a century ago to mean those "of public concern."[25]

Some statutes and constitutions specify that all natural resources fall within the *res* of the trust. For example, Article XI, section 1 of the Hawai'i Constitution declares that "All public natural resources are held in trust by the State for the benefit of the people."

Is there any good reason—beyond historical—to treat submerged lands in the trust and not, say, the atmosphere and public drinking water supplies? As you read the materials, ask what factors led a court to treat a resource as a public trust asset and examine whether that logic could be extrapolated to other natural resources that have equal importance to society. One of the editors, for example, has argued for an expansion of the scope of the trust to a full "ecological res."[26]

Fiduciary Duties—Every trustee has fiduciary duties to ensure management of the asset in accordance with the purposes of the trust. In the private law context, these duties are both procedural and substantive, enforced strictly by courts. Substantive duties ensure protection of the assets of the trust, while procedural duties attempt to ensure that the

---

20. *See* John Davidson, *Taking Posterity Seriously: Intergenerational Justice*, Climate Legacy Initiative Research Forum of Vermont Law School (Jan. 28, 2008), https://vlscli.wordpress.com/2008/01/28/taking-posterity-seriously-intergenerational-justice/.

21. Joseph L. Sax, *The Public Trust Doctrine in Natural Resource Law: Effective Judicial Intervention*, 68 Mich. L. Rev. 471, 560–61 (1970) excerpted on p. 23.

22. Edith Brown Weiss, *The Planetary Trust: Conservation and Intergenerational Equity*, 11 Ecology L.Q. 495 (1984).

23. Richard J. Lazarus, *Changing Conceptions of Property and Sovereignty in Natural Resources: Questioning the Public Trust Doctrine*, 71 Iowa L. Rev. 631 (1986).

24. *See* Blumm & Guthrie, above note 19, at 760–807 (explaining the public trust doctrines in India, Pakistan, Philippines, Uganda, Kenya, Nigeria, South Africa, Brazil, Ecuador, and Canada).

25. *Illinois Central R.R. Co. v. Illinois*, 146 U.S. 387, 455 (1892).

26. *See* Wood, above note 10, at 78–84.

trustee acts in the sole interest of the beneficiary. The trustee's duty of loyalty, for example, ranks highest in the category of procedural duties.

In the public law trust context, ask yourself what fiduciary duty the courts seem to apply in a given circumstance. Some courts have derived the standard of "substantial impairment" from the landmark *Illinois Central* case (p. 68) as a substantive standard by which to evaluate government action with respect to trust assets. For example, in the *Waiahole Ditch* case, the Hawai'i Supreme Court noted:

> As commonly understood, the trust protects public waters and submerged lands against irrevocable transfer to private parties ... or "substantial impairment," whether for private or public purposes.... In this jurisdiction, our decisions ... and the plain meaning and history of the term "protection" [in the State's constitution] establish that the state has a comparable duty to ensure the continued availability and existence of its water resources for present and future generations.[27]

Another intriguing aspect of the public trust fiduciary duty is its relationship to statutory mandates. Can a legislature, for example, allow damage to a public trust asset by statute? Do statutes affecting trust assets supplant the PTD? These issues raise a number of separation of powers issues between the legislature and the courts.

Applications of the Trust—The PTD tends to arise in five different contexts, which are becoming more distinct as this field advances.

1) Government conveyance of public trust assets to private parties. Much early case law for example, focused on privatization issues, for example, the circumstances in which a state could permissibly convey its tidelands to private parties. Modern cases state appropriation of water rights to private parties might be considered as part of this category as well.

2) Government management of trust assets. Increasingly, modern agencies fail to protect public resources, and citizens look to the PTD to provide more effective action by requiring fiduciary action. For example, an ongoing legal campaign known as atmospheric trust litigation, discussed in chapter 11, seeks to force government action to curtail carbon pollution, since the Clean Air Act has largely failed.

3) The duties of private owners on land previously held in trust (such as tidelands), and then conveyed into private ownership. The PTD conceptually divides trust assets into two (as does a private trust): a *jus privatum*, subject to the private owner's prerogative and a *jus publicum*, subject to the sovereign's prerogative. The upshot is that the owner of the *jus privatum* may not be able to impair public uses by, for example, filling wetlands which remain subject to the *jus publicum*.

4) The PTD as a defense to constitutional takings claims. The PTD functions as a "background principle" of property law, and therefore, where applicable, means that there is no private property upon which to base a Fifth Amendment claim of a taking of private property for public use.

5) Government's right to obtain damages from those destroying or damaging trust assets. Several statutes, for example, provide for natural resource damages, but the duty to collect damages preceded the statutes and exists independently of the statutes as a common law remedy for trustees.

As you consider these materials, ask what principles transfer from one context to another? What contexts are underdeveloped, and why?

---

27. *In re Water Use Permit Applications*, 9 P.3d 409, 451 (Haw. 2000).

Enforcing the Trust—Without effective enforcement of fiduciary obligations, there is no real trust, and the trustee is left with enormous power over the trust assets. Thus, enforcement remains a crucial part of the PTD. In the private law context, trusts are rigorously enforced to protect the trust beneficiaries. In the public law context, however, such enforcement sometimes gives rise to separation of powers issues. Normally a court will defer to the legislative intent expressed in a statute, but courts have occasionally overturned legislation as a violation of the PTD,[28] suggesting the PTD as a constitutional principle. Professor Dunning once wrote of the PTD, "More indicative of the doctrine's fundamental nature, however, is the way the courts, the originators of the doctrine in this country, have in some states concluded that the doctrine is so entrenched as to be immune from legislative abolition. In those states the public trust doctrine has assumed the character of an implied constitutional doctrine...."[29] But courts have been less than clear about the precise underpinnings of public trust authority.

In Arizona, the courts blocked a legislative attempt to relinquish public ownership of navigable riverbeds on both public trust and state constitutional grounds.[30] What is the rationale for such a judicial "veto" of legislative action that violates the trust? Under what circumstances should courts be deferential, and under what circumstances should they insist on the trustee fulfilling its trust obligations? Does it matter whether the legislative action risks irrevocable harm? Consider this statement of the Arizona court: "The beneficiaries of the public trust are not just present generations but those to come. The check and balance of judicial review provides a level of protection against improvident dissipation of an irreplaceable res."[31] Is deference more appropriate when there is time and opportunity to prevent irrevocable loss to the trust?

These are some of the intriguing unanswered questions concerning the PTD field. As citizens increasingly turn to the PTD to try to force government action when statutes fail to protect a resource, courts will encounter defenses raised by government trustees involving preemption and displacement of the public trust. Resolution of these issues will depend in large part upon whether one views the trust as an inherent constitutional obligation or a common law obligation, the latter susceptible to being trumped by statute.

The Private/Public Property Rights Link—Although law students spend a significant part of their first-year curriculum studying private property rights, the PTD presents public property rights that are often overlooked. Courts dealing with the PTD endeavor to demarcate the appropriate balance between privatization and public property rights. Depending on the circumstances, the trust might be thought of as imposing an easement (allowing public access along tidelands, for example) or a servitude (preventing an owner from damaging a trust resource).

The PTD right, held originally by the people and exercised through government, runs antecedent to any private property right later acquired. Accordingly, it plays a unique role in the constitutional takings doctrine arising under the Fifth Amendment, which calls for compensation when government "takes" private property for public purposes. Public trust theory holds that the assertion of public trust rights does not deprive the property owner of any rights he or she ever had, because a landowner's title was always

---

28. See p. 77.
29. Harrison C. Dunning, *The Public Trust: A Fundamental Doctrine of American Property Law,* 19 Envtl. L. 515, 516 (1989).
30. *Arizona Center for Law in the Public Interest v. Hassell,* 837 P.2d 158 (Ariz. Ct. App. 1991) (interpreting the gift clause of the state constitution).
31. *Id.* at 169.

encumbered by the "background principle" of public trust. Although the PTD can defeat private takings claims, as one of the editors described in reviewing the doctrine's relationship with private property rights, the PTD is fundamentally an accommodation
doctrine.[32] Both public and private property uses often coexist in the same tract. The
public's *jus publicum* combines with the private *jus privatum* to make up "title" to the
tract. We explore the public/private synthesis in chapter 9.

Flexibility to Respond to Changing Conditions—The PTD is notable for its capacity to
change in response to the emerging needs of society. As the New Jersey Supreme Court
long ago observed, "[W]e perceive the public trust doctrine not to be 'fixed or static,' but
one to 'be molded and extended to meet changing conditions and needs of the public it
was created to benefit.'"[33] In a similar vein, the California Supreme Court emphasized, "In
administering the trust the state is not burdened with an outmoded classification favoring one mode of utilization over another."[34] But despite many courts' embrace of change,
in some jurisdictions the doctrine has remained closely linked to its traditional application to streambeds of navigable waters. What is the function of precedent in molding a
doctrine to new circumstances? In an article later in this chapter, Professor Sax noted,

> [I]t is clear that the judicial techniques developed in public trust cases need not
> be limited either to [the] conventional interests or to questions of disposition of
> public properties ... [but] would be equally applicable and equally appropriate
> in controversies involving air pollution, the dissemination of pesticides, the lo-
> cation of rights of way for utilities, and strip mining or wetland filling on pri-
> vate lands in a state where governmental permits are required.[35]

As you read through the materials in this book, consider whether and how the doctrine
should expand to meet modern exigencies.

The following treatments of the PTD introduce the doctrine and explain its importance.

Putting the Public Trust Doctrine to Work

David C. Slade
Coastal States Org. (2d ed. 1997)

The public trust doctrine provides that public trust lands, waters and living resources
in a state are held by the state in trust for the benefit of all of the people, and establishes
the right of the public to fully enjoy public trust lands, waters and living resources for a
wide variety of recognized public uses. The doctrine also sets limitations on the states, the
public, and private owners, as well as establishing the responsibilities of the states when
managing these public trust assets.

In general, public trust waters are the "navigable waters" in a state, and public trust lands
are the lands beneath these waters, up to the ordinary high water mark. The living resources (*e.g.*, the fish and aquatic plant and animal life) inhabiting these lands and waters are also subject to the public trust doctrine.

---

32. *See* Michael C. Blumm, *The Public Trust Doctrine and Private Property: The Accommodation Principle*, 27 Pace Envtl. L. Rev. 649 (2010).

33. *Raleigh Avenue Beach Ass'n v. Atlantis Beach Club, Inc.*, 879 A.2d 112, 121 (N.J. 2005) (quot-ing *Matthews v. Bay Head Improvement Ass'n*, 471 A.2d 355, 365 (N.J. 1984)) (pp. 265, 261).

34. *Marks v. Whitney*, 491 P.2d 374, 380 (Cal. 1971).

35. Sax, above note 3, at 556–57, excerpted on p. 23.

* * *

Public trust lands are special in nature. They are generally unsuitable for commercial agriculture or permanent structures. Because of the "public" nature of trust lands, the title to them is not a singular title in the manner of most other real estate titles. Rather, public trust land is vested with two titles: the *jus publicum*, the public's right to use and enjoy trust lands and waters for commerce, navigation, fishing, bathing and other related public purposes, and the *jus privatum*, or the private proprietary rights in the use and possession of trust lands.

Whenever a state exercises its public trust authority, it does so immediately adjacent to some of the most expensive real estate in America—waterfront property. Given the strong property (riparian) interests of private upland owners, coupled with the confusion over riparian "rights" and how the public trust doctrine applies, coastal managers need to be keenly aware that their actions under the doctrine may be met with strong resistance.

A. The Public Trust Doctrine: Why is it Important?

In 1820, a New Jersey man was collecting oysters along the shores when he was challenged as a trespasser by the upland property owner. The dispute reached the New Jersey Supreme Court, where a justice expressed surprise that the taking of:

> a few bushels of oysters should involve in it questions, so momentous in their nature, as well as in their magnitude; ... affecting the rights of all our citizens, and embracing ... the laws of Nations and of England, the relative rights of sovereign and subjects, as well as the municipal regulations of our own country.[36]

If the taking of a few oysters raises such fundamental questions affecting the rights of all citizens, then clearly the building of private docks, industrial wharves, marinas, or the dredging of ship channels, among the countless other activities within the purview of coastal managers, merit close attention. In each instance, from oysters to ports, the public trust doctrine applies. Whenever a state exercises its authority under the public trust doctrine, the rights of all citizens are involved.

Generally speaking, all navigable waters and the lands beneath these waters are subject to the public trust doctrine. In the United States, there are 79,481 square miles of inland navigable waters, 74,364 square miles of coastal waters, and an estimated 37,500 square miles of ocean waters within the jurisdiction of the coastal states. This totals to approximately 191,000 square miles of navigable waters within the boundaries of the states—roughly equal in size to Maryland, Virginia, North Carolina, South Carolina and Georgia combined—most of which is subject to the public trust doctrine. Further, there are 88,633 miles of tidelands and 10,031 miles of Great Lakes shoreline, for a total of 98,664 miles of trust shoreland. Along this tremendous length of shoreline, over 90 percent of the adjacent uplands are privately owned, raising difficulties for the public to access the trust shorelands below the ordinary high water mark.

The public trust doctrine is a very important part of the body of law that applies to this tremendous and special area of lands and waters. To effectively manage the countless activities that take place within these 191,000 square miles of navigable waters, including the lands beneath and the living resources inhabiting them, a coastal manager must be familiar with the public trust doctrine.

---

36. *Arnold v. Mundy*, 6 N.J.L. 1, 95 (1821) (Rossell, J., concurring opinion).

B. The Public Trust Doctrine: What Is It?

The public trust doctrine provides that public trust lands, waters and living resources in a state are held by the state in trust for the benefit of all of the people, and establishes the right of the public to fully enjoy public trust lands, waters and living resources for a wide variety of recognized public uses. The public trust doctrine is applicable whenever navigable waters or the lands beneath are altered, developed, conveyed, or otherwise managed or preserved. It applies whether the trust lands are publicly or privately owned. The doctrine articulates not only the public rights in these lands and waters. It also sets limitations on the states, the public, and private owners, as well as establishing duties and responsibilities of the states when managing these public trust assets. The public trust doctrine has been recognized and affirmed by the United States Supreme Court, the lower federal courts and state courts from the beginning days of this country to the present.

The "trust" referred to is a real trust in the legal sense of the word. There are trust assets, generally in the form of navigable waters, the lands beneath these waters, the living resources therein, and the public property interests in these trust assets. The trust has a clear and definite beneficiary: the public, which includes "not just present generations but those to come."[37] There are trustees: the state legislatures, which often delegate their trust powers and duties to state coastal commissions, land commissions, or similar state agencies, as well as municipalities. These trustees have a duty to protect the trust. There is a clear purpose for the trust: to preserve and continuously assure the public's ability to fully use and enjoy public trust lands, waters and resources for certain public uses.[38]

In the United States, each state has the authority and responsibility for applying the public trust doctrine to trust lands and waters "within its borders according to its own views of justice and policy."[39] As a result, there is really no single "public trust doctrine." Rather, there are over fifty different applications of the doctrine, one for each state, Territory or Commonwealth, as well as the federal government. Nonetheless, a common core of principles remains, forming the foundation for how the Doctrine is applied in each state, Commonwealth or Territory.

C. Origins of the Public Trust Doctrine

It is often stated that the public trust doctrine dates back to the sixth century Institutes of Justinian and the accompanying Digest, which collectively formed Roman civil law, codified under the reign of the Roman Emperor Justinian between 529 and 534 A.D. The sixth century Institutes of Justinian, however, were based, often verbatim,[40] upon the second century Institutes and Journal of Gaius,[41] an eminent Roman jurist, who codified the

---

37. *Arizona Center for Law in the Public Interest v. Hassell*, 837 P.2d 158, 169 (Ariz. Ct. App. 1991).

38. *Idaho Forest Industries, Inc. v. Hayden Lake Watershed Improvement District*, 733 P.2d 733, 738 (Idaho 1987) ("The public trust doctrine is based upon common law equitable principles. That is, the administration of land subject to the public trust is governed by the same principles applicable to the administration of trusts in general.") (citing Bogert & Bogert, Law of Trusts, §6 (1973)); *Slocum v. Borough of Belmar*, 569 A.2d 312, 316–17, (N.J. Super. Ct. Law. Div. 1989) (The Borough of Belmar, as a municipality chartered by the state, is trustee over the public trust resources within its jurisdiction. As trustee, it has a duty of "loyalty," "disclosure," and "to keep clear and adequate records of accounts.... When the trustee fails to keep proper accounts, all doubts are resolved against him.").

39. *Shively v. Bowlby*, 152 U.S. 1, 26 (1894).

40. "Over one-half of the Institutes of Justinian is borrowed bodily from the text of Gaius." Charles Phineas Sherman, Roman Law in the Modern World 121, 122 (3rd. ed. 2012).

41. J. Inst., Proemium, 4, 5, 6 (T. Sandars trans., 4th ed. 1867).

natural law of Greek philosophers. The sixth century Romans who wrote the Institutes must have regarded the Institutes of Justinian as the re-codification of ancient law.

Ancient in their own right, as well as a recodification of even more ancient law, the Institutes of Justinian remain the touchstone of today's public trust doctrine. The public's right to full use of the seashore emanates from a commonly quoted section of Book II of the Institutes that described the public nature of rivers, ports, and the seashore:

> By the law of nature these things are common to all mankind — the air, running water, the sea, and consequently the shores of the sea. No one, therefore, is forbidden to approach the seashore, provided that he respects habitations, monuments, and the buildings, which are not, like the sea, subject only to the law of nations.[42]

Specific public rights in the use of the seashore were delineated in the Institutes and the Digest, such as:

> "Any person is at liberty to place on it a cottage, to which he may retreat, or to dry his nets there, and haul them from the sea."[43]

> "The right of fishing in the sea from the shore belongs to all men."[44]

> "Everyone has a right to build on the shore, or, by piles, upon the sea, and retain the ownership of the construction so long as it lasts, but when it falls into ruins, the soil reverts to its former status as *res communis*."[45]

> "The public use of the banks of a river is part of the law of nations, just as is that of the river itself. All persons, therefore, are as much at liberty to bring their vessels to the bank, to fasten ropes to the trees growing there, and to place any part of their cargo there, as to navigate the river itself. But the banks of a river are the property of those whose land they adjoin; and consequently the trees growing on them are also the property of the same persons."[46]

Roman civil law eventually influenced the jurisprudence of all Western European nations. Most important to American jurisprudence, Roman civil law was adopted in substance (with modifications) by English common law after the Magna Carta. English common law in turn recognized the special nature of the tidelands and waters, giving them protection in the king's name for all English subjects. From England to the American colonies, through the American Revolution to the thirteen original states, tempered by the United States Constitution and the evolution of modern society, the public trust doctrine survives in the United States as "one of the most important and far-reaching doctrines of American property law."[47]

D. The Special Nature of Public Trust Lands

Public trust lands, generally speaking, are those lands below navigable waters, with the upper boundary being the ordinary high water mark. Tidelands, shorelands of navigable lakes and rivers, as well as the land beneath the oceans, lakes and rivers, are usually considered public trust lands.

---

42. *Id.* 2.1.1.
43. *Id.* 2.1.5.
44. Dig. 1.8.4 (W.A. Hunter, A Systematic and Historical Exposition of Roman Law in the Order of a Code (J. Ashton Cross trans., 4th ed. 1903)).
45. *Id.*
46. J. Inst. 2.1.4 (T. Sandars trans., 4th ed. 1867).
47. Glenn J. MacGrady, *The Navigability Concept in the Civil and Common Law: Historical Development, Current Importance, and Some Doctrines that Don't Hold Water*, 3 Fla. St. U. L. Rev. 511 (1975).

The Romans recognized the special status of the seashore: "The shores are not under-stood to be property of any man, but are compared to the sea itself, and to the sand or ground which is under the sea."[48] English common law viewed these shorelands as use-less for cultivation or other improvement and considered their natural and primary uses— navigation, commerce and fishing—to be public in nature.

Under American law, the public nature of shorelands is well recognized. Tidelands, as well as the shorelands of navigable freshwaters, are generally unsuitable for commercial agriculture. The action of the wind, waves, tide and salt make any type of commercial farm-ing impossible. Navigable waters have long been recognized as the equivalent of high-ways, being vast corridors for water-borne commerce.[49] In the early days of the country, the immediate shores of these waters were needed in order to conduct that commerce. Sailors tied their boats to trees for the night. Fishermen hoisted their skiffs far up the beach for the night, and dried or repaired their nets on the beach. In short, the uses to which these lands were put were public in nature. The public trust doctrine "is founded upon the ne-cessity of preserving to the public the use of navigable waters free from private interrup-tion and encroachment."[50]

The public character of trust lands has been noted by the United States Supreme Court as well as several state supreme courts. For example, the United States Supreme Court noted that tidelands are "unfit for cultivation, the growth of grasses or other uses to which upland is applied."[51] State courts have similar descriptions of trust shorelands. "Through-out history, the shores of the sea have been recognized as a special form of property of unusual value; and therefore subject to different rules from those which apply to inland property."[52] "Beaches are a unique resource and are irreplaceable."[53] "Oceanfront property is uniquely suitable for boating and other recreational activities. Because it is unique and highly in demand, there is growing concern about the reduced 'availability to the public of its priceless beach areas.'"[54] For these reasons, the title to public trust land is:

> a title different in character from that which the state holds in lands intended
> for sale. It is different from the title the United States holds in the public lands
> which are open to pre-emption and sale. It is a title held in trust for the people

---

48. J. Inst. 2.1.5 (T. Sandars trans., 4th ed. 1867).

49. *Packer v. Bird*, 137 U.S. 661, 667 (1891) ("It is, indeed, the susceptibility to use as highways of commerce which gives sanction to the public right of control over navigation upon [navigable wa-terways.]").

50. *Illinois Central R.R. Co. v. Illinois*, 146 U.S. 387, 436 (1892). *See also Phillips Petroleum Co. v. Mississippi*, 484 U.S. 469, 488 (1988) (O'Connor, J., dissenting).

51. *City & County of San Francisco v. LeRoy*, 138 U.S. 656, 672 (1890). *See also United States v. 1.58 Acres of Land*, 523 F. Supp. 120, 122–23 (1981) ("For centuries, land below the low water mark has been recognized as having a peculiar nature, subject to varying degrees of public demand for rights of navigation, passage, portage, commerce, fishing, recreation, conservation and aesthetics. Histor-ically, no developed western civilization has recognized absolute rights of private ownership in such land as a means of allocating this scarce and precious resource among the competing public demands. Though private ownership was permitted in the Dark Ages, neither Roman Law nor the English com-mon law as it developed after the signing of the Magna Carta would permit it."); *Kaiser Aetna v. United States*, 444 U.S. 164, 183 (1979) (The "geographical, chemical and environmental" qualities makes lands beneath tidal waters unique) (Blackmun, J., dissenting); *Shively v. Bowlby*, 152 U.S. 1, 57 (1894) ("Lands under tide waters are incapable of cultivation or improvement in the manner of lands above high water mark.").

52. *Boston Waterfront Development Co. v. Commonwealth*, 378 Mass. 629, 631 (1979).

53. *Matthews v. Bay Head Improvement Ass'n.*, 471 A.2d. 355, 364 (N.J. 1984).

54. *Lusardi v. Curtis Point Property Owners Ass'n.*, 430 A.2d 881 (N.J. 1981) (quoting *Van Ness v. Borough of Deal*, 78 N.J. 174, 180 (1978)).

of the state that they may enjoy the navigation of the waters, carry on commerce over them, and have liberty of fishing therein freed from the obstruction or interference of private parties.[55]

Although trust lands have long been considered suitable for public purposes, this does not mean that a state is powerless to convey any interest in trust land to private ownership. To the contrary, states do have this power, and several of them have conveyed tremendous amounts of acreage of trust lands into private ownership. But because of the special nature of trust lands for public uses, conveyance from the state to private ownership does not by itself terminate the public's right to continue to use those lands for certain purposes. In order to convey trust lands, while preserving the public's rights to use them, the law resorts to a legal fiction of splitting the title to trust lands in two: a proprietary title, the *jus privatum*, and the public's equitable title, held by the state in trust, the *jus publicum*.

E. The Jus Privatum *and* Jus Publicum *in Public Trust Land*

Because of their special and public nature, the title to public trust lands is not a singular title in the manner of most other real estate titles. Rather, public trust land is vested with two titles, one dominant and the other subservient, a concept necessary to understand in order to apply the public trust doctrine. The dominant title is the *jus publicum*, simply described as the bundle of trust rights of the public to fully use and enjoy trust lands and waters for commerce, navigation, fishing, bathing and other related public purposes. The subservient title is the *jus privatum*, or the private proprietary rights in the use and possession of trust lands. The distinction between the two titles is often cited by the courts when they define a state's authority to convey public trust land to private ownership, and when describing the rights of the public remaining in public trust land that has been so conveyed.

In most states, the upland owner's boundary is the "ordinary high water mark." In these "high water" states, the state is the "fee simple absolute" owner of public trust land, owning both interests—the private (*jus privatum*) and public (*jus publicum*) titles.[56] The state has the proprietary rights of a private landowner, which include the right to possess and convey the property, under its *jus privatum* interests. At the same time, the state holds the separate *jus publicum* title, the "trust" title, derived from its basic sovereign obligation to act in the best interests of its citizens. From this obligation derives the state's power to

---

55. *Illinois Central R.R. Co. v. Illinois*, 146 U.S. 387, 452 (1892); *Coxe v. State*, 144 N.Y. 396, 405–06 (1895) ("The title of the state to the seacoast and shores of tidal rivers is different from the fee simple which an individual holds to an estate in lands. It is not a proprietary, but a sovereign right, and it has been frequently said that a trust is engrafted upon this title for the benefit of the public of which the state is powerless to divest itself."); *Boston Waterfront Development Corp. v. Commonwealth*, 393 N.E.2d 356, 358 (Mass. 1979) (Different legal rules apply to public trust lands beneath navigable waters as compared to state-held title in other land); *State of Vermont and City of Burlington v. Central Vermont Railway, Inc.*, 571 A.2d 1128 (Vt. 1989) ("The character of this title is distinctive as compared to state-held title in other lands ... and different legal rules therefore apply.").

56. *Orion Corporation v. State*, 747 P.2d 1062, 1072 (Wash. 1987) ("State ownership of [trust] property has two aspects, the private property interest, which reflects the State's title to the property, and the public authority interest, which reflects the State's sovereignty and dominion."), *cert. denied* 108 S.Ct. 1996 (1988); *Caminiti v. Boyle*, 732 P.2d 989, 992 (Wash. 1987) ("it is clear that the state's ownership of tidelands and shore lands is not limited to the ordinary incidents of legal title, but is comprised of two distinct aspects."); *United States v. 1.58 Acres of Land*, 523 F. Supp 120, 124 (D. Mass. 1981) ("When the federal government takes such property by eminent domain ... [it] obtains the fullest fee that may be had in land of this peculiar nature; the *jus privatum* and the *jus publicum*.").

govern, manage and protect the public's trust rights in lands and water subject to the public trust doctrine.[57]

In several states, the upland owner's boundary is the "ordinary low water mark" or some other line seaward of the ordinary high water mark. In these "low water" states, the upland owner holds the *jus privatum* title in the tidelands, while the state retains the *jus publicum* title. Thus, even though the upland owner "owns" the beach or submerged lands, that ownership is still subject to several paramount rights of the public to use those trust lands for public trust purposes. Both the *jus publicum* and the *jus privatum* are property interests. Although both procedural and substantive limitations exist, a state can convey the *jus privatum* interest into private ownership. On the other hand, a state cannot convey the *jus publicum* interest into private ownership, nor can it abdicate its trust responsibilities. In certain limited situations, a state can terminate the *jus publicum* in small parcels of trust lands.

Limited exception [handwritten margin note]

F. Takings, Expectations, Taxes and the Public Trust Doctrine

A central strength of using the public trust doctrine as a management tool for coastal resources is that the state holds a continuing property interest, the *jus publicum*, in the trust lands, waters and living resources, regardless of whether the *jus privatum* is held by the state or private owner. This allows the state to manage these resources as a property owner without having to exercise either its regulatory police powers or its powers of eminent domain. At the same time, whenever a state exercises its public trust authority, it does so immediately adjacent to some of the most expensive real estate in America—waterfront property. Waterfront (riparian) property owners justifiably can harbor strong opinions about their riparian property interests, especially if they also own the *jus privatum* rights in the adjacent public trust land.

Usually a private *jus privatum* owner of public trust land pays property taxes on the trust lands, lending a certain credence to the private owner's perception that she has sole possession and control of the property, exclusive of the public. Adding to the confusion, boundary descriptions in deeds and property titles of waterfront property often are silent as to any *jus publicum* retained by the state, giving the landowner the further expectation that she has exclusive rights of possession and use of the land. Boundary descriptions may simply state that the property extends "to the water" or even to the "low water mark," or some similar phrase. Waterfront property owners commonly regard their property as extending to where the water level is, or to the low water mark, unaware that the state has a reserved *jus publicum* interest up to the "ordinary high water mark"—a boundary line that presents difficult factual determination problems. It is also very common for a commercial upland owner, such as a resort or marina owner, to have a strong economic interest in the use of adjacent publicly owned trust lands and waters.

Given the strong property interests of private upland owners, coupled with the confusion over riparian "rights" as well as the distinction of the *jus publicum* and *jus privatum* in trust lands and how the public trust doctrine applies, coastal managers need to be keenly aware that their actions under the doctrine may be met with strong resistance. Claims of private property "takings" and charges of governmental interference in private property rights can, and should, be expected.

---

57. *Lane v. Harbor Commission*, 40 A. 1058 (Conn. 1898) ("The State has the *jus publicum*, or right of governing its shores and navigable waters for the protection of public rights."); *State of Vermont and City of Burlington v. Central Vermont Railway*, 571 A.2d 1128 (Vt. 1989) (comparing the 1874 and 1827 Acts, court concluded that legislature meant to convey only the "legal title" while recognizing that the beneficial title to the public trust lands at issue was vested in the public).

When acting under the authority of the public trust doctrine, however, the state and state agencies are in a strong position to defend against "takings" claims. Public trust land has been held by the state in trust for the benefit of the public since statehood. Therefore, public trust land that has been conveyed to private ownership has always been burdened by the public's trust rights. Given this, a state's management of the public's trust assets should be less vulnerable to, although not totally immune from, takings challenges. Because the owner received the trust land already burdened by the public's trust rights, a private owner's argument that she had unfettered investment-backed expectations is far more tenuous.

Notes

1. This edition of the book (the original was published in 1990) was followed by DAVID C. SLADE, THE PUBLIC TRUST IN MOTION: THE EVOLUTION OF THE DOCTRINE, 1997–2008 (2008), a volume filled with anecdotes about how the public trust doctrine has helped to resolve a number of disputes over resources along the land-water margin. An excerpt from that book concludes this casebook.

2. The figure Mr. Slade cites about the vast extent of the public trust doctrine — 191,000 square miles, about the equivalent of the size of Maryland, Virginia, North and South Carolina, and Georgia combined — is surely an underestimate, since the estimate includes only traditionally navigable coastal and inland waters. Many state public trust doctrines include waters (and indeed, lands) beyond traditionally navigable waters, as this text makes clear.

3. Slade emphasizes the relevance of the PTD as a principle to guide management of coastal resources. How would you advise a coastal commission or agency of its duties and powers under the trust?

4. Of what legal relevance is the fact that the public trust doctrine is of such a vintage origin? Does its history add to the legitimacy of the doctrine? To its effect on private property rights? For an attempt to de-legitimize the doctrine's ancient historical pedigree, see James L. Huffman, *Speaking of Inconvenient Truths: A History of the Public Trust Doctrine*, 18 Duke Envtl. L. & Pol'y F. 1 (2007), an article containing no original historical research, alleging that the Roman and English versions of the doctrine were more limited than its supporters claim. Professor Huffman is particularly skeptical of the role played by Sir Matthew Hale in the evolution of the public trust doctrine, claiming that his treatise described the doctrine as he wished it were, not as it existed in medieval England. *Id.* at 8. Hale is discussed in the following excerpt by Professor Dunning. Early public trust doctrine cases like *Arnold v. Mundy* (p. 57) and *Shively v. Bowlby* (p. 77) relied on Hale's treatise. For a vigorous rebuttal to Professor Huffman's article, see Hope M. Babcock, *The Public Trust Doctrine: What a Tall Tale They Tell*, 61 S.C. L. Rev. 393 (2009); see also Michael C. Blumm & J.B. Ruhl, *Background Principles, Takings, and Libertarian Property: A Reply to Professor Huffman*, 37 Ecology L.Q. 805 (2010).

5. Note that the banks of waterways subject to the public trust doctrine are largely private. This poses significant access problems that will be discussed in chapter 3.

6. Federal public lands represent a unique category of public ownership, one that raises important questions about the applicability of trust principles. Note that a primary concern in managing traditional public trust lands has been prevention of private monopoly, but throughout the nineteenth and early twentieth centuries the privatization of federal public lands was overriding federal policy. *See generally* GEORGE C. COGGINS ET AL., FEDERAL

PUBLIC LAND AND RESOURCES LAW 58–108 (7th ed. 2014). We consider the question of whether the public trust doctrine applies to retained federal lands in chapter 8.

7. The following except, part of a comprehensive treatise on water law, contains perhaps the most thorough recent explanation of the origins of the doctrine in England.

Waters and Water Rights
Harrison C. Dunning
Lexis Nexis/Matthew Bender 3rd ed., Amy K. Kelly, ed. (2013)

§ 29.01 Introduction.

The public right to use water in place is one with ancient roots. *Arnold v. Mundy*, the foundational public trust doctrine decision in the United States, relied upon a "great principle of the common law," albeit one that was in England "in ancient times ... gradually encroached upon and broken down," only to be restored by Magna Carta. That principle is rooted in the English law on the ownership of land under water.

§ 29.02 The English Common Law.

(a) Ownership of Land Under Water.

The original source of most land titles in England is a grant from the Crown. And so, titles to land on the seashore go back to such grants, nearly all of them as far back as the reign of King John, which ended in 1216. These early grants were commonly in Latin and often lacked the precision and the niceties later developed within the law of conveyancing. The common law develops in response to problems that have arisen; at this early date in England the initial grants of coastal land presented no great problems, so it is not surprising that the grants were imprecise and incomplete, particularly in their lack of description of the seaward boundary of the coastal grants. As might be expected, the grantee of land along the coast came to look upon the property as extending right into the sea. This suited the grantee's interest and convenience. Either the Crown acquiesced in that view or, as seems at least as plausible, there were matters more interesting to the Crown, or more pressing, than the use of the barren seacoasts. Private use and occupancy of the tidelands was not challenged until the latter part of the sixteenth century; until then it had not occurred to the Crown to be specific about seacoast boundaries in its conveyances either.

In 1568–69, Thomas Digges, a mathematician, engineer, astronomer, and lawyer, wrote a short treatise asserting that the tidelands had not been included in grants of the seacoasts by the Crown. The Crown brought only a few actions based upon this thesis over a considerable period of time. But Digges' thesis appeared again in 1670 in the very influential treatise *De Jure Maris* by Sir Matthew Hale. The impact of this treatise was such that the burden of proof was placed upon the subject to show that private ownership extended to the low-water mark. In the absence of proof of a specific grant of the tidelands, placement of the burden of proof could be decisive.

That was the state of English law at the time England colonized the eastern coastline of North America. The presumption of ownership in the Crown, or in a state or the people as successor to the Crown, and against private ownership, is a part of the heritage that the United States received from England.

(b) Public Use of Water.

Although the references to water problems in early English legal literature are sparse because of the plentiful supply of water in relation to the human need, public rights to water uses have been recognized from the earliest times. Bracton clearly recognized both a common right and a right in the Crown to the fresh waters of the great rivers. The Ancient Indictments and the Coram Rege Rolls at the end of the fourteenth century prove that the large rivers were subject to a public right of navigation and that the Crown prosecuted those responsible for interference with that right. Interference with the flow or navigability of these streams was a purpresture encroaching upon the prerogatives of the Crown and also was a public nuisance to the extent that it interfered with the common right of passage. In either situation, the Crown could prosecute those responsible. Clause 33 of Magna Carta commands the King to remove kydells, or weirs, from the Thames and the Medway and throughout all England except the seacoasts, so as to clear the streams for the free passage of both people and fish.

The right of fishery was originally an exclusively royal right based on the King's dominion over the territorial seas, their inland reaches, the beds of these seas, and the tidal reaches of the rivers. The public succeeded to this right on the theory that the King held the rights in tidal waters in trust for the use of the people. The public right of fishery remained distinct from the right of navigation and did not include fresh-water rivers whose beds and banks were in private riparian ownership.

The beds and banks of fresh-water rivers were thought to be usable by the public, according to Bracton, but probably very little use of this soil was made by the public in his time. Four centuries later, by the time of Sir Matthew Hale in the seventeenth century, the legal presumption was that the riparian owners along fresh-water rivers had the exclusive right to use the beds and banks. But that presumption was subject to a public right to use the bed and banks for purposes incidental to navigation where the public had acquired that right by prescription or custom. Where the public had need, the beds and banks of navigable rivers were used by the public, as a matter of right, for anchoring, for mooring, and for towing vessels along the banks. The right to those uses was thus established.

The one clear right of the public in the use of water was for travel. In medieval England, the general public exerted few other demands for water use, and water was so sufficiently plentiful that there were but few conflicts in its use. Where there was conflict with the public right of navigation, the right of navigation prevailed. In short, medieval common law recognized the only substantial public demand for water use that was exerted.

The maturing of the common law concerning inland waterways is rather like the maturing cycle in the life of an anadromous fish. The salmon grows and takes on substance in the open sea, then moves to coastal waters and finally to inland waterways that are navigable to it. The common law of inland waterways has been dependent upon doctrines that came from the law concerning coastal waters, and coastal waters, in turn, owe their debt to the law of the sea itself. This extension of legal doctrines inland may be accounted for in part by the fact that there was so little indigenous growth in the common law concerning inland water use and rights throughout the Middle Ages and even through the earlier stages of the industrial revolution. Because the laws regarding ownership and use of the sea influenced the law of other navigable waters, it is desirable to include a brief discussion of the law of the sea.

Our law concerning the sea has its origins in a time when the Mediterranean Sea was *the* sea, and when, for lack of any serious challenge, it was a Roman sea. Thus, in Justinian's statement that the seas are common to all, the word "all" is to be taken in a Pickwickian sense; he meant "all Romans." Imperial Rome depended upon overseas supplies of food, notably grain from Egypt, and Rome controlled trade, shipping, and the sea.

After the decline of Rome, the infant nations bordering on the Atlantic Ocean could not use the sea beyond strictly local fishing ventures because the art of shipbuilding during the Dark Ages had not developed ships capable of ocean voyages. In the Middle Ages these countries improved the art of shipbuilding, and it was the demand for fish that stimulated that improvement.

The Roman concept of the one-nation sea could not survive the proliferation of national power and complicated commercial interests that had developed [in northern Europe in the sixteenth and seventeenth centuries]. During the eighteenth century the United States added to the complexity of world trade in which all European countries were participating. It came to be in the interest of those nations who could best compete for trade to advocate free trade, freedom of the seas, and the abolition of restrictive national monopolies. Therefore, British theory was brought into conformity with her own trade practices.

Justinian's dictum that the high seas are common to all is true today, but the meaning has been expanded to include non-Romans. The law has conformed to the human need; the seas are free for navigation by water and air, and for fishing and other public purposes for which there is any substantial demand.

§ 29.03 The Civil Law.

In addition to the English common law, *Arnold v. Mundy* [the first American public trust doctrine case] rested its pronouncements on the public right to use water in place on the civil law, although *Arnold* did not include an analysis of civilian sources as it did for the common law. Civilian sources have, however, been relied upon to support the public use right by state courts in those parts of the country once under Spanish rule.

Las Siete Partidas,[58] a treatise regarded as a major source of civilian norms in Spain, included a law that explicitly adopts general principles even broader than those widely recognized today in the United States:

> Rivers, harbors, and public highways belong to all persons in common, so that parties from foreign countries can make use of them, just as those who live or dwell in the country where they are situated. And although the banks of rivers are, so far as their ownership is concerned, the property of those whose lands include them, nevertheless, every man has a right to use them, by mooring his vessels to the trees, by repairing his ships and his sails upon them, and by landing his merchandise there; and fishermen have the right to deposit their fish and sell them, and dry their nets there, and to use said banks for every other purpose like these which appertain to the calling and the trade by which they live.

Las Siete Partidas is itself a compilation drawn from the Roman law. While there is great dispute about the correct interpretation of Roman law with regard to the public right to use water in place and the related question of the property rights regime for land under navigable waters, the Institutes of Justinian do contain the following celebrated statement: "By natural law the air, flowing water, the sea, and therefore the shores of the sea are common to all."

* * *

---

58. The Castilian Statutory Code compiled between the years 1256 and 1265, during the reign of King Alfonso X of Castile.

§ 30.02 The Public Trust Doctrine.

(a) Association with State Sovereign Ownership.

Historically, the public trust doctrine in natural resources law has been associated closely with the state sovereign ownership doctrine, [which] holds as a matter of federal law that when states achieve sovereignty within the union, one consequence is immediate state ownership of certain lands and waters previously owned by the British Crown or the federal government. These natural resources are viewed as being held by the state in a fiduciary capacity, for the benefit of members of the general public, and indeed, the "public trust doctrine" could be regarded as simply the law on the fiduciary aspect of state sovereign ownership.

Reasons exist, however, for maintaining a distinction between the doctrine of state sovereign ownership and that of the public trust. For one thing, the federal courts, as a matter of federal law, have been heavily involved in developing the state sovereign ownership doctrine, whereas the public trust doctrine has been developed almost entirely in the law of the various states. Also important is the fact that in some jurisdictions the public trust doctrine has outgrown its original direct association with state sovereign ownership. In Ohio and California, for example, the public trust doctrine has been used with regard to water resources that apparently have never been subject to sovereign ownership. In New Jersey the doctrine has been applied to land owned by a subdivision of the state in a non-sovereign capacity, notably the "dry sand" portions of beaches. And in Massachusetts it arguably has been used for state-owned parklands. But an attempt to apply the public trust doctrine to retroactive extension of copyright protection was summarily rejected by a federal trial court.

(b) Development a Matter of State Law.

Although it is a principle of federal law that title to sovereign lands and waters generally resides in the states at the inception of their statehood, what happens thereafter so far as the public trust doctrine is concerned is up to the law of each state. Some states, generally ones with a seacoast, have a highly developed body of law on the public trust doctrine; others have practically nothing. Most states have restated and, often, reinforced the state fiduciary obligation. A few have disregarded it. Although arguments have been made that federal law somehow constrains these state law choices, in practice to date the states have been free to shape their public trust doctrine law as they wish.

The state law basis for the public trust doctrine was emphasized by the Supreme Court in 1926 in *Appleby v. City of New York.* In *Appleby*, pursuant to state statutes, New York City had granted two parcels, including land below the high-water mark of the Hudson River, to Appleby and another person in the 1850s. Subsequently, the city built piers into the river at the ends of streets crossing or adjacent to the granted parcels, leased space for vessels at its piers, and dredged the area to enhance navigation. The city filed a condemnation action with regard to the privately owned land, but it was discontinued after twenty years.

Appleby sued on the theory there had been state impairment of the obligation of a contract in violation of the federal constitution. No one questioned that, by virtue of state sovereign ownership and transactions between the city and both prerevolutionary governors and the State of New York, the city had held title to the land in question prior to the 1850s. But a key question was the proper construction and effect of the land grants, and the Court said that "the extent of the power of the State and city to part with property under navigable waters to private persons ... is a state question."

* * *

(c) The Fiduciary Obligation of the State.

At the core of the public trust doctrine is the fiduciary obligation of the state to hold state sovereign resources for the benefit of the general public. Indeed, it is the public interest in public use of navigable water that serves to justify the doctrine of state sovereign ownership in the first place. State sovereign ownership and the public trust doctrine are "founded upon the necessity of preserving to the public the use of navigable waters from private interruption and encroachment." This point was made forcefully in 1821 in *Arnold v. Mundy,* the foundation case for the public trust doctrine in the United States, as follows:

> [B]y the law of nature, which is the only true foundation of all the social rights ... by the civil law, which formerly governed almost the whole civilized world ... by the common law of England ... the navigable rivers in which the tide ebbs and flows, the ports, the bays, the coasts of the sea, including both the water and the land under the water, for the purposes of passing and repassing, navigation, fishing, fowling, sustenance, and all other uses of the water and its products (a few things excepted), are common to all the citizens, and ... each has a right to use them according to his necessities, subject only to the laws which regulate that use; ... the property, indeed, strictly speaking, is vested in the sovereign, but it is vested in him, not for his own use, but for the use of the citizen; that is, for his direct and immediate enjoyment.

[6 N.J.L. at 76–77.]

The state generally has great discretion to determine the direction that management of state sovereign resources for public benefit should take. To enhance commercial navigation, for example, the state may provide for the development of the shallow waters of a bay into a harbor. The project may include establishment of a bulkhead line, construction of wharves and building of warehouses on state sovereign lands. Such development, however, is subject to limits to ensure that the rights of the public are not prejudiced unduly. The most important of the limitations is the principle recognized in most states that grantees of state sovereign lands ordinarily take title subject to the same public right that bound the state.

Where the state has not approved impairment of state sovereign resources, private encroachment upon public use of the resources is treated as a public nuisance and is subject to abatement.

Notes

1. *Arnold v. Mundy* is set forth below (p. 57). The decision was largely responsible for linking the public trust doctrine to the Magna Carta, a matter discussed in some detail by Professor Dunning.

2. The pertinent language of Justinian is: "Things common to mankind by the law of nature, are the air, running water, the sea, and consequently the shores of the sea; no man therefore is prohibited from approaching any part of the seashore, whilst he abstains from damaging farms, monuments, edifices, [] which are not in common as the sea is." J. Inst. 2.1.1. (Thomas Cooper trans. 1841). The Institutes of Justinian also anticipated the need to draw a line between public and private rights: "All that tract of land, over which the greatest winter flood extends itself, is the sea-shore." J. Inst. 2.1.3. (Thomas Cooper trans. 1841). The Institutes elaborated on the public uses that may be made of the seashore as follows:

> The use of the sea-shore, as well as of the sea, is also public by the law of nations; and therefore any person may erect a cottage upon it, to which he may resort to dry his nets, and hawl them from the water; for the shores are not understood to be property in any man, but are compared to the sea itself, and to the sand or ground which is under the sea.

J. INST. 2.1.4. (Thomas Cooper trans. 1841).

3. Professor Dunning mentioned purprestures, which are encroachments on navigable waterways or public highways. At common law, purprestures were controlled by public nuisance doctrine, guarding against substantial and unreasonable interferences with public rights. The common law employed nuisance doctrine, not trespass, against docks impeding vessels on waterways or overhangs from buildings that blocked highway traffic because nuisance allowed for more nuanced decisions and promoted multiple uses of public waters and highways. *See* THOMAS W. MERRILL & HENRY E. SMITH, PROPERTY: PRINCIPLES AND POLICIES 307 (2nd ed. 2012). Permanent, fixed, stationary encroachments — as opposed to temporary obstructions — which "unreasonably and unnecessarily interferes with public travel, or which endangers the safety of travelers constitutes a public nuisance per se." 40 AM. JUR. 2d, *Highways, Streets, and Bridges* § 313 (2014).

4. Notice Professor Dunning's linkage of the public trust doctrine with the concept of state sovereign ownership of certain natural resources, a subject explored in some detail in chapter 6, on the wildlife trust doctrine. Since the public trust doctrine has been traditionally thought of as a doctrine inherited from the English sovereign, the interpretation and application of the doctrine have varied widely from state to state.

The public trust doctrine, an ancient precept dating as far back as Roman law and inherited from English common law, historically provided a surprising counterpoise to Anglo-American law's preference for private property. First recognized by the New Jersey Supreme Court in 1821 in *Arnold v. Mundy* (p. 57) as a kind of anti-monopolization doctrine, giving the public fishing rights in tidal waters and later adopted by the U.S. Supreme Court in 1842 in *Martin v. Waddell* (p. 63), the doctrine grew by the late 19th century to include inland waters that were navigable. Then, a half-century later, in 1892, in a landmark decision in *Illinois Central Railroad v. Illinois* (p. 68), the U.S. Supreme Court interpreted the doctrine to impose a limit on sovereign alienation of public rights, effectively announcing a preference for public ownership of lands submerged by navigable waters. Four years later, the Court announced that wildlife was also owned by the sovereign in trust for the public in *Geer v. Connecticut* (p. 221).

In the late 20th century, the public trust doctrine became a vehicle for environmental protection. How that came to be was partly due to one of the most consequential law review articles in the history of environmental law. That remarkable article, written by Professor Joseph Sax, then of the University of Michigan, follows.

The Public Trust Doctrine in Natural Resource Law: Effective Judicial Intervention

Joseph L. Sax

68 Mich. L. Rev. 471 (1970)

Public concern about environmental quality is beginning to be felt in the courtroom. Private citizens, no longer willing to accede to the efforts of administrative agencies to protect the public interest, have begun to take the initiative themselves. One dramatic result is a proliferation of lawsuits in which citizens, demanding judicial recognition of their rights as members of the public, sue the very governmental agencies which are supposed to be protecting the public interest. While this Article was being written, several dozen such suits were initiated to enforce air and water pollution laws in states where public agencies have been created for that purpose; to challenge decisions of the Forest Service about the use of public land under its control; to question the Secretary of the Interior's regulation of federal offshore oil leases; and, in a myriad of cases against state and local officials, to examine airport extensions, highway locations, the destruction of parklands, dredging and filling, oil dumping, and innumerable other governmental decisions dealing with resource use and management.

* * *

Of all the concepts known to American law, only the public trust doctrine seems to have the breadth and substantive content which might make it useful as a tool of general application for citizens seeking to develop a comprehensive legal approach to resource management problems. If that doctrine is to provide a satisfactory tool, it must meet three criteria. It must contain some concept of a legal right in the general public; it must be enforceable against the government; and it must be capable of an interpretation consistent with contemporary concerns for environmental quality.

I. The Nature Of The Public Trust Doctrine

A. The Historical Background

* * *

As carried over to American law, this history has produced great confusion. Our system has adopted a dual approach to public property which reflects both the Roman and the English notion that certain public uses ought to be specially protected. Thus, for example, it has been understood that the seashore between high and low tide may not be routinely granted to private owners as was the general public domain under the Homestead Act and similar laws. It has rather been a general rule that land titles from the federal government run down only to the high water mark, with title seaward of that point remaining in the states, which, upon their admission to the Union, took such shorelands in "trusteeship" for the public.

Whether and to what extent that trusteeship constrains the states in their dealings with such lands has, however, been a subject of much controversy. If the trusteeship puts such lands wholly beyond the police power of the state, making them inalienable and unchangeable in use, then the public right is quite an extraordinary one, restraining government in ways that neither Roman nor English law seems to have contemplated. Conversely, if the trust in American law implies nothing more than that state authority must be exercised consistent with the general police power, then the trust imposes no restraint on government beyond that which is implicit in all judicial review of state action—the challenged conduct, to be valid, must be exercised for a public purpose and must not merely be a gift of public property for a strictly private purpose.

The question, then, is whether the public trust concept has some meaning between the two poles; whether there is, in the name of the public trust, any judicially enforceable right which restrains governmental activities dealing with particular interests such as shorelands or parklands, and which is more stringent than are the restraints applicable to governmental dealings generally.

Three types of restrictions on governmental authority are often thought to be imposed by the public trust: first, the property subject to the trust must not only be used for a public purpose, but it must be held available for use by the general public; second, the property may not be sold, even for a fair cash equivalent; and third, the property must be maintained for particular types of uses. The last claim is expressed in two ways. Either it is urged that the resource must be held available for certain traditional uses, such as navigation, recreation, or fishery, or it is said that the uses which are made of the property must be in some sense related to the natural uses peculiar to that resource. As an example of the latter view, San Francisco Bay might be said to have a trust imposed upon it so that it may be used for only water-related commercial or amenity uses. A dock or marina might be an appropriate use, but it would be inappropriate to fill the bay for trash disposal or for a housing project.

* * *

C. An Outline of Public Trust Doctrine

One who searches through the reported cases will find many general statements which seem to imply that a government may never alienate trust property by conveying it to a private owner and that it may not effect changes in the use to which that property has been devoted. In one relatively old case, for example, the Supreme Court of Ohio said that:

> [t]he state as trustee for the public cannot by acquiescence abandon the trust property or enable a diversion of it to private ends different from the object for which the trust was created. If it is once fully realized that the state is merely the custodian of the legal title, charged with the specific duty of protecting the trust estate and regulating its use, a clearer view can be had. An individual may abandon his private property, but a public trustee cannot abandon public property.[59]

Similarly, the Supreme Court of Florida said:

> The trust in which the title to the lands under navigable waters is held is governmental in its nature and cannot be wholly alienated by the States. For the purpose of enhancing the rights and interests of the whole people, the States may by appropriate means, grant to individuals limited privileges in the lands under navigable waters, but not so as to divert them or the waters thereon from their proper uses for the public welfare....[60]

But a careful examination of the cases will show that the excerpts just quoted, and almost all other such statements, are dicta and do not determine the limits of the state's legitimate authority in dealing with trust lands. Unfortunately, the case law has not developed in any way that permits confident assertions about the outer limits of state power. Nonetheless, by examining the diverse and often loosely written opinions dealing with public lands, one may obtain a reasonably good picture of judicial attitudes.

The first point that must be clearly understood is that there is no general prohibition against the disposition of trust properties, even on a large scale. A state may, for example, recognize private ownership in tidelands and submerged lands below the high water mark; indeed, some states have done so and have received judicial approval. Still, courts do not look kindly upon such grants and usually interpret them quite restrictively, and apply a more rigorous standard than is used to analyze conveyances by private parties. In this connection, courts have held that since the state has an obligation as trustee which it may not lawfully divest, whatever title the grantee has taken is impressed with the public trust and must be read in conformity with it. It is at this point that confusion sets in,

---

59. State v. Cleveland & Pittsburgh R.R. Co., 113 N.E. 677, 682 (Ohio 1916).
60. *Brickell v. Trammel*, 82 So. 221, 226 (Fla. 1919).

for the principle, while appealing, simply states a conclusory rule as to the very matter that is in question—what, exactly, are the limitations which must be read into such grants? In attempting to answer that question, one can do no more than cite some illustrations which suggest the content of the principle as courts have come to understand it.

In the old Massachusetts case of *Commonwealth v. Alger*,[61] the court examined the validity of state grants to private persons of tidelands below the high water mark. The court recognized that such grants were lawful even though they permitted grantees to fill or to build in the submerged lands and thereby to terminate the public's free right of passage across those areas. A question was raised, however, as to the limits of the principle which had been expressed in an earlier Massachusetts case, that "the riparian proprietor has an absolute right under the colony law, so to build to low water mark and exclude all mankind."[62] It was apparently argued in *Alger* that the implication of that rule, if sustained, would permit a holder of such riparian rights to thwart all navigation or, through his economic power, to bend navigation to his will. The court made clear that no such meaning could, or should, be read into the language of the earlier case:

> No qualification ... to the general rule was expressed ... not even the condition not to hinder the passage of boats and vessels.... This judgment must be construed according to the subject matter, which was, the right to flats then in controversy, belonging to land adjoining the Charles River ... where the river was broad, and where the channel or deep part of the river was quite wide, and afforded abundant room for any boats or vessels to pass along the river and to other men's houses and lands. Had the court been giving an opinion in regard to flats differently situated, there is no reason to doubt that they would have qualified it by stating the proper conditions and limitations.[63]

A similar concern, and limitation, was noted by the Ohio Supreme Court in *State v. Cleveland and Pittsburgh Railway*.[64] In that case a railroad which owned riparian upland on Lake Erie successfully tested its right to build a wharf upon submerged lands that were said to belong to the state of Ohio; no grant had been made, and the state itself was the plaintiff. The court found that a wharf could be built, without regard to the title question, out to an area where ships could come. But as in the Massachusetts case, the extreme implications of the case were suggested by counsel, and the court made it clear that wharves which interfered with navigation would not be allowed and that no rights which would permit that result were obtainable. The state's trusteeship existed

> to secure the rights of the public and prevent interference with navigation.... It must be remembered that [the littoral owner's] right ... is one that can be exercised only in aid of navigation and commerce, and for no other purpose. What he does is therefore in furtherance of the object of the trust, and is permitted solely on that account.[65]

As these cases make clear, the courts have permitted the transfer of some element of the public trust into private ownership and control, even though that transfer may exclude or impair certain public uses. In both of the cases just cited, private entrepreneurs were permitted to enhance their own rights by excluding the public from a part of the trust property which was formerly open to all. Thus, what one finds in the cases is not a niggling

---

61. 61 Mass. (7 Cush.) 53, 74–75 (1851).
62. *Id.* at 75 (quoting *Austin v. Carter*, 1 Mass. 231 (1804)).
63. *Id.*
64. 113 N.E. 677 (1916).
65. *Id.* at 681.

preservation of every inch of public trust property against any change, nor a precise maintenance of every historical pattern of use. The Wisconsin court put the point succinctly when it permitted a segment of Milwaukee harbor land on Lake Michigan to be granted to a large steel company for the building of navigation facilities:

> It is not the law, as we view it, that the state, represented by its legislature, must forever be quiescent in the administration of the trust doctrine, to the extent of leaving the shore of Lake Michigan in all instances in the same condition and contour as they existed prior to the advent of the white civilization in the territorial area of Wisconsin.[66]

These traditional cases suggest the extremes of the legal constraints upon the states: no grant may be made to a private party if that grant is of such amplitude that the state will effectively have given up its authority to govern, but a grant is not illegal solely because it diminishes in some degree the quantum of traditional public uses.

D. The Lodestar in American Public Trust Law: Illinois Central Railroad Company v. Illinois

The most celebrated public trust case in American law is the decision of the United States Supreme Court in *Illinois Central Railroad Company v. Illinois.*[67] In 1869 the Illinois legislature made an extensive grant of submerged lands, in fee simple, to the Illinois Central Railroad. That grant included all the land underlying Lake Michigan for one mile out from the shoreline and extending one mile in length along the central business district of Chicago—more than one thousand acres of incalculable value, comprising virtually the whole commercial waterfront of the city. By 1873 the legislature had repented of its excessive generosity, and it repealed the 1869 grant; it then brought an action to have the original grant declared invalid.

The Supreme Court upheld the state's claim and wrote one of the very few opinions in which an express conveyance of trust lands has been held to be beyond the power of a state legislature. It is that result which has made the decision such a favorite of litigants. But the Court did not actually prohibit the disposition of trust lands to private parties; its holding was much more limited. What a state may not do, the Court said, is to divest itself of authority to govern the whole of an area in which it has responsibility to exercise its police power; to grant almost the entire waterfront of a major city to a private company is, in effect, to abdicate legislative authority over navigation.

But the mere granting of property to a private owner does not ipso facto prevent the exercise of the police power, for states routinely exercise a great deal of regulatory authority over privately owned land. The Court's decision makes sense only because the Court determined that the states have special regulatory obligations over shorelands, obligations which are inconsistent with large-scale private ownership. The Court stated that the title under which Illinois held the navigable waters of Lake Michigan is

> different in character from that which the state holds in lands intended for sale.... It is a title held in trust for the people of the state that they may enjoy the navigation of the waters, carry on commerce over them, and have liberty of fishing therein freed from the obstruction or interferences of private parties.[68]

With this language, the Court articulated a principle that has become the central substantive thought in public trust litigation. When a state holds a resource which is avail-

---

66. *City of Milwaukee v. State*, 214 N.W. 820, 830 (1927).
67. 146 U.S. 387 (1892).
68. *Id.* at 452.

able for the free use of the general public, a court will look with considerable skepticism upon *any* governmental conduct which is calculated *either* to reallocate that resource to more restricted uses *or* to subject public uses to the self-interest of private parties.

The Court in *Illinois Central* did not specify its reasons for adopting the position which it took, but the attitude implicit in the decision is fairly obvious. In general, governments operate in order to provide widely available public services, such as schools, police protection, libraries, and parks. While there may be good reasons to use governmental resources to benefit some group smaller than the whole citizenry, there is usually some relatively obvious reason for the subsidy, such as a need to assist the farmer or the urban poor. In addition, there is ordinarily some plainly rational basis for the reallocative structure of any such program — whether it be taxing the more affluent to support the poor or using the tax base of a large community to sustain programs in a smaller unit of government. Although courts are disinclined to examine these issues through a rigorous economic analysis, it seems fair to say that the foregoing observations are consistent with a general view of the function of government. Accordingly, the court's suspicions are naturally aroused when they are faced with a program which seems quite at odds with such a view of government.

In *Illinois Central*, for example, everything seems to have been backwards. There appears to have been no good reason for taxing the general public in order to support a substantial private enterprise in obtaining control of the waterfront. There was no reason to believe that private ownership would have provided incentives for needed developments, as might have been the case with land grants in remote areas of the country; and if the resource was to be maintained for traditional uses, it was unlikely that private management would have produced more efficient or attractive services to the public. Indeed, the public benefits that could have been achieved by private ownership are not easy to identify.

Although the facts of *Illinois Central* were highly unusual and the grant in that case was particularly egregious — the case remains an important precedent. The model for judicial skepticism that it built poses a set of relevant standards for current, less dramatic instances of dubious governmental conduct. For instance, a court should look skeptically at programs which infringe broad public uses in favor of narrower ones. Similarly, there should be a special burden of justification on government when such results are brought into question. But *Illinois Central* also raises more far-reaching issues. For example, what are the implications for the workings of the democratic process when such programs, although ultimately found to be unjustifiable, are nonetheless promulgated through democratic institutions? Furthermore, what does the existence of those seeming imperfections in the democratic process imply about the role of the courts, which, *Illinois Central* notwithstanding, are generally reluctant to hold invalid the acts of co-equal branches of government?

II. The Contemporary Doctrine of the Public Trust: An Instrument for Democratization

A. The Massachusetts Approach

The *Illinois Central* problem has had its most significant modern exegesis in Massachusetts. In that state, the Supreme Judicial Court has shown a clear recognition of the potential for abuse which exists whenever power over public lands is given to a body which is not directly responsive to the electorate. To counteract the influence which private interest groups may have with administrative agencies and to encourage policy decisions to be made openly at the legislative level, the Massachusetts court has developed a rule that a change in the use of public lands is impermissible without a clear showing of legislative approval.

1. Gould v. Greylock Reservation Commission

In *Gould v. Greylock Reservation Commission,*[69] the Supreme Judicial Court of Massachusetts took the first major step in developing the doctrine applicable to changes in the use of lands dedicated to the public interest. Because *Gould* is such an important case in the development of the public trust doctrine, and because the implications of the case are so far-reaching, it is important to have a clear understanding of both the facts of the case and the court's decision.

Mount Greylock, about which the controversy centered, is the highest summit of an isolated range which is surrounded by lands of considerably lower elevation. In 1888 a group of citizens, interested in preserving the mountain as an unspoiled natural forest, promoted the creation of an association for the purpose of laying out a public park on it. The state ultimately acquired about 9,000 acres, and the legislature enacted a statute creating the Greylock Reservation Commission and giving it certain of the powers of a park commission. By 1953 the reservation contained a camp ground, a few ski trails, a small lodge, a memorial tower, some TV and radio facilities, and a parking area and garage. In that year, the legislature enacted a statute creating an Authority to construct and operate on Mount Greylock an aerial tramway and certain other facilities, and it authorized the original Commission to lease to the Authority "any portion of the Mount Greylock Reservation."

For some time the Authority was unable to obtain the financing necessary to go forward with its desire to build a ski development, but eventually it made an arrangement for the underwriting of revenue bonds. Under that arrangement the underwriters, organized as a joint venture corporation called American Resort Services, were to lease 4,000 acres of the reservation from the Commission. On that land, the management corporation was to build and manage an elaborate ski development, for which it was to receive forty per cent of the net operations revenue of the enterprise. The underwriters required these complex and extensive arrangements so that the enterprise would be attractive for potential purchasers of bonds.

After the arrangements had been made, but before the project went forward, five citizens of the county in which the reservation is located brought an action against both the Greylock Reservation Commission and the Tramway Authority. The plaintiffs brought the suit as beneficiaries of the public trust under which the reservation was said to be held, and they asked that the court declare invalid both the lease of the 4,000 acres of reservation land and the agreement between the Authority and the management corporation. They asked the court to examine the statutes authorizing the project, and to interpret them narrowly to prevent both the extensive development contemplated and the transfer of supervisory powers into the hands of a profit-making corporation. The case seemed an exceedingly difficult one for the plaintiffs, both because the statutes creating the Authority were phrased in extremely general terms, and because legislative grants of power to administrative agencies are usually read quite broadly. Certainly, in light of the statute, it could not be said that the legislature desired Mount Greylock to be preserved in its natural state, nor could the legislature be said to have prohibited leasing agreements with a management agency. Nonetheless, the court held both the lease and the management agreement invalid on the ground that they were in excess of the statutory grant of authority.

Gould cannot be considered merely a conventional exercise in legislative interpretation. It is, rather, a judicial response to a situation in which public powers were being

---

69. 215 N.E.2d 114 (1966).

used to achieve a most peculiar purpose. Thus, the critical passage in the decision is that in which the court stated:

> The profit sharing feature and some aspects of the project itself strongly suggest a commercial enterprise. In addition to the absence of any clear or express statutory authorization of as broad a delegation of responsibility by the Authority as is given by the management agreement, we find no express grant to the Authority of power to permit use of public lands and of the Authority's borrowed funds for what seems, in part at least, a commercial venture for private profit.[70]

In coming to this recognition, the court took note of the unusual developments which led to the project. What had begun as authorization to a public agency to construct a tramway had developed into a proposal for an elaborate ski area. Since ski resorts are popular and profitable private enterprises, it seems slightly odd in itself that a state would undertake such a development. Furthermore, the public authority had gradually turned over most of its supervisory powers to a private consortium and had been compelled by economic circumstances to agree to a bargain which heavily favored the private investment house.

It hardly seems surprising, then, that the court questioned why a state should subordinate a public park, serving a useful purpose as relatively undeveloped land, to the demands of private investors for building such a commercial facility. The court, faced with such a situation, could hardly have been expected to have treated the case as if it involved nothing but formal legal issues concerning the state's authority to change the use of a certain tract of land.

Yet the court was unwilling to invalidate an act of the legislature on the sole ground that it involved a modification of the use of public trust land. Instead, the court devised a legal rule which imposed a presumption that the state does not ordinarily intend to divert trust properties in such a manner as to lessen public uses. Such a rule would not require a court to perform the odious and judicially dangerous act of telling a legislature that it is not acting in the public interest, but rather would utilize the court's interpretive powers in accordance with an assumption that the legislature is acting to maintain broad public uses. Under the Massachusetts court's rule, that assumption is to guide interpretations, and is to be altered only if the legislature clearly indicates that it has a different view of the public interest than that which the court would attribute to it.

Concerns Although such a rule may seem to be an elaborate example of judicial indirection, it is in fact directly responsive to the central problem of public trust controversies. There must be some means by which a court can keep a check on legislative grants of public lands while ensuring that historical uses may be modified to accommodate contemporary public needs and that the power to make such modifications resides in a branch of government which is responsive to public demands. Similarly, while there ought to be available some mechanism by which corrupt legislative acts can be remedied, it will be the rare case in which the impropriety is so patent that, as in the *Illinois Central* case, a court would find it to be outside the broad boundaries of legitimacy. It is to these concerns that the Massachusetts court so artfully addressed itself.

While it will seldom be true that a particular governmental act can be termed corrupt, it will often be the case that the whole of the public interest has not been adequately considered by the legislative or administrative officials whose conduct has been brought into question. In those cases, which are at the center of concern with the public trust, there is a strong, if not demonstrable, implication that the acts in question represent a response

---

70. *Id.* at 126.

to limited and self-interested proponents of public action. It is not difficult to perceive the reason for the legislative and administrative actions which give rise to such cases, for public officials are frequently subjected to intensive representations on behalf of interests seeking official concessions to support proposed enterprises. The concessions desired by those interests are often of limited visibility to the general public so that public sentiment is not aroused; but the importance of the grants to those who seek them may lead to extraordinarily vigorous and persistent efforts. It is in these situations that public trust lands are likely to be put in jeopardy and that legislative watchfulness is likely to be at the lowest levels. To send such a case back for express legislative authority is to create through the courts an openness and visibility which is the public's principal protection against overreaching, but which is often absent in the routine political process. Thus, the court should intervene to provide the most appropriate climate for democratic policy making.

Sneaky

Gould v. Greylock Reservation Commission is an important case for two reasons. First, it provides a useful illustration that it is possible for rather dubious projects to clear all the legislative and administrative hurdles which have been set up to protect the public interest. Second, and more significantly, the technique which the court used to confront the basic issues suggests a fruitful mode for carrying on such litigation. Moreover, *Gould is* not unique; it is one of a line of exceedingly important cases in which the Massachusetts court has produced a remarkable body of modern public trust interpretation by using the technique which it developed in that case.

*   *   *

As a result of *Gould* and the cases which followed it, the situation is considerably better in Massachusetts. That state's supreme judicial court has penetrated one of the very difficult problems of American government—inequality of access to, and influence over, administrative agencies. It has struck directly at low-visibility decision-making, which is the most pervasive manifestation of the problem. By a simple but ingenious flick of the doctrinal wrist, the court has forced agencies to bear the burden of obtaining specific, overt approval of efforts to invade the public trust.

The court has accomplished that result by extending the application of a well-established rule designed to mitigate traditional conflicts between public agencies arising when one agency seeks to condemn land held by another. Under that established rule, one agency cannot take land vested in another agency without explicit authorizing legislation; otherwise the two agencies "might successively try to take and retake the property ad infinitum."[71] Clearly, that principle evolved as a judicial means of avoiding conflict between agencies. The Massachusetts court has turned it into an affirmative tool for private citizens to use against governmental agencies which are assertedly acting contrary to the public interest.[72]

*   *   *

... [P]ublic trust law is not so much a substantive set of standards for dealing with the public domain as it is a technique by which courts may mend perceived imperfections in the legislative and administrative process. The public trust approach which has been developed in Massachusetts and the exercise in applying that approach * * * situations in Mary-

---

71. *Commonwealth v. Massachusetts Turnpike Authority*, 191 N.E.2d 481, 484 (1963).

72. The court has made this shift knowingly and explicitly: "That decision [*Commonwealth v. Massachusetts Turnpike Authority*, 191 N.E.2d 481 (1963)] does not rest, as the defendant argues, on our inability to determine which of two state agencies was intended by the legislature to have paramount authority over the land in question." *Sacco v. Department of Pub. Works*, 227 N.E.2d 478, 480 (1967).

land and Virginia demonstrate that the public trust concept is, more than anything else, a medium for democratization. To test that proposition further, it is useful to look at developments in those states which have the most amply developed case law in the public trust area—Wisconsin and California. Moreover, to indicate the breadth of the acceptance of responsibility by the courts for guarding public lands, public trust developments in other states will be examined.

* * *

While the general principle of the early cases—that the public trust may not be conveyed to private parties—has never been brought into question, the original application of that principle has been modified by later cases. Although the early cases had held such grants wholly invalid, the court subsequently decided to validate the grants, but to find that they were impressed with the public trust which required the owners to use their land in a manner consistent with the right of the public. As the court stated in the landmark case of *People v. California Fish Company*,[73] the grantee of such lands will not obtain the absolute ownership, but will take "the title to the soil ... subject to the public right of navigation...."[74]

Precisely where this rule leaves the private owners of such tideland grants is not certain. It is clear that so long as the land or water overlying it is still physically suitable for public use, the owner may not exclude the public—he may not fence his land or eject the public as trespassers. It is similarly clear that a private owner may alter the land in a manner that impairs public uses if the alterations are consistent with a public decision authorizing them; such a situation arises when, for example, a harbor line or bulkhead line is set by the state and private owners are permitted to build behind that line. But the acts of private owners in such situations are the product of, and are in harmony with, a larger public plan for the advancement of navigation and commerce. It is a much more difficult question whether a private owner, on his own initiative and for entirely personal purposes, may alter the land in a manner that impairs public uses.

* * *

III. Conclusion

A. The Scope of the Public Trust

It is clear that the historical scope of public trust law is quite narrow. Its coverage includes, with some variation among the states, that aspect of the public domain below the low-water mark on the margin of the sea and the great lakes, the waters over those lands, and the waters within rivers and streams of any consequence. Sometimes the coverage of the trust depends on a judicial definition of navigability, but that is a rather vague concept which may be so broad as to include all waters which are suitable for public recreation. Traditional public trust law also embraces parklands, especially if they have been donated to the public for specific purposes; and, as a minimum, it operates to require that such lands not be used for nonpark purposes. But except for a few cases like *Gould v. Greylock Reservation Commission,* it is uncommon to find decisions that constrain public authorities in the specific uses to which they may put parklands, unless the lands are reallocated to a very different use, such as a highway.

If any of the analysis in this Article makes sense, it is clear that the judicial techniques developed in public trust cases need not be limited either to these few conventional inter-

---

73. 138 P. 79 (1913).
74. *Id.* at 87–88.

ests or to questions of disposition of public properties. Public trust problems are found whenever governmental regulation comes into question, and they occur in a wide range of situations in which diffuse public interests need protection against tightly organized groups with clear and immediate goals. Thus, it seems that the delicate mixture of procedural and substantive protections which the courts have applied in conventional public trust cases would be equally applicable and equally appropriate in controversies involving air pollution, the dissemination of pesticides, the location of rights of way for utilities, and strip mining or wetland filling on private lands in a state where governmental permits are required.

Certainly the principle of the public trust is broader than its traditional application indicates. It may eventually be necessary to confront the question whether certain restrictions, imposed either by courts or by other governmental agencies, constitute a taking of private property; but a great deal of needed protection for the public can be provided long before that question is reached. Thus, for example, a private action seeking more effective governmental action on pesticide use or more extensive enforcement of air pollution laws would rarely be likely to reach constitutional limits. In any event, the courts can limit their intervention to regulation which stops short of a compensable taking.

Finally, it must be emphasized that the discussion contained in this Article applies with equal force to controversies over subjects other than natural resources. While resource controversies are often particularly dramatic examples of diffuse public interests and contain all their problems of equality in the political and administrative process, those problems frequently arise in issues affecting the poor and consumer groups. Only time will reveal the appropriate limits of the public trust doctrine as a useful judicial instrument.

B. The Role of the Courts in Developing Public Trust Law

The principal purpose of this Article has been to explore the role of the courts in shaping public policy with respect to a wide spectrum of resource interests which have the quality of diffuse public uses. The attempt has not been to propose or to identify the particular allocative balance which is appropriate for a wise public policy as to any particular resource problem, but rather to examine an important and poorly understood institutional medium for better obtaining that wisdom which leads to intelligent public policy. Thus, as is usually the wont of lawyers, the author has attended essentially to problems of process rather than to problems of substance. It is hoped, however, that the Article makes clear the futility of any rigid separation between those two elements. It should be obvious that courts operate with an extraordinary degree of freedom and that the procedural devices they employ are very significantly determined by their attitudes about the propriety of the policies which are before them. It is virtually unheard of for a court to rule directly that a policy is illegal because it is unwise; the courts are both too sophisticated and too restrained to adopt such a procedure. Rather, they may effectively overrule a questionable policy decision by requiring that the appropriate agency provide further justification; alternatively, the courts may, in effect, remand the matter for additional consideration in the political sphere, thus manipulating the political burdens either to aid underrepresented and politically weak interests or to give final authority over the matter to a more adequately representative body.

The very fact that sensitive courts perceive a need to reorient administrative conduct in this fashion suggests how insulated such agencies may be from the relevant constituencies. A highway agency, for example, which has a professional bureaucracy, which performs its function within a large geographic area rather than within a particular community, and which is rarely the subject of attack in political campaigns, may feel quite free to hold perfunctory and essentially predetermined public hearings. In such circumstances, the decision-making process may be inadequate even though a proceeding called a public hearing has been held. These realities imply that there is a need for the more searching sort of judicial intervention described above.

Understandably, courts are reluctant to intervene in the processes of any given agency. Accordingly, they are inclined to achieve democratization through indirect means—either by requiring the intervention of other agencies which will serve to represent underrepresented interests or by calling upon the legislature to make an express and open policy decision on the matter in question. The phenomenon of indirect intervention reveals a great deal about the role of the judiciary. The closer a court can come to thrusting decision making upon a truly representative body—such as by requiring a legislature to determine an issue openly and explicitly—the less a court will involve itself in the merits of a controversy. This relationship suggests that democratization is essentially the function which the courts perceive themselves as performing, and that even those courts which are the most active and interventionist in the public trust area are not interested in displacing legislative bodies as the final authorities in setting resource policies.

That self-perception is an appropriate one, for in theory there is no reason that the judiciary should be the ultimate guardian of the public weal. In the ideal world, legislatures are the most representative and responsive public agencies; and to the extent that judicial intervention moves legislatures toward that ideal, the citizenry is well served. Certainly even the most representative legislature may act in highly unsatisfactory ways when dealing with minority rights, for then it confronts the problem of majority tyranny. But that problem is not the one which arises in public resource litigation. Indeed, it is the opposite problem that frequently arises in public trust cases—that is, a diffuse majority is made subject to the will of a concerted minority. For self-interested and powerful minorities often have an undue influence on the public resource decisions of legislative and administrative bodies and cause those bodies to ignore broadly based public interests. Thus, the function which the courts must perform, and have been performing, is to promote equality of political power for a disorganized and diffuse majority by remanding appropriate cases to the legislature after public opinion has been aroused. In that sense, the public interests with which this Article deals differ from the interests constitutionally protected by the Bill of Rights—the rights of permanent minorities. That realization, in turn, lends even greater support for the rejection of claims that public trust problems should be considered as constitutional issues which are ultimately to be resolved by courts even if there is a clear legislative determination.

Not all the situations which have been examined in this Article fit directly into the majority-minority analysis suggested above, but, if properly understood, they do meet the principle of that analysis. For example, in a dispute between advocates of parks and those who would take parkland for highways, it often cannot be said that one group constitutes a majority and the other a minority. It can, however, be said that one interest is at least adequately represented in its access to, and dealings with, legislative or administrative agencies while the other interest tends to face problems of diffuseness and thus tends to be underrepresented in the political process. In such cases, all that is asked of courts is that they try to even the political and administrative postures of the adversaries; if that equalization can be done judicially, the courts may properly withdraw and leave the ultimate decision to a democratized democratic process.

* * *

Having determined that the fundamental function of courts in the public trust area is one of democratization, the next subject for analysis is the means by which courts are to identify the problems which require judicial action. The first step in this process is the search for those situations in which political imbalance exists, and the signal for the existence of that problem is diffusion. Political imbalance is to be found wherever there are interests which have difficulties in organizing and financing effectively enough that they can deal with legislative and administrative agencies. When a claim is made on behalf of diffuse public uses, courts take the first step in the process by withdrawing the usual presumption that all relevant issues have been adequately considered and resolved by routine statutory and administrative processes. That first step is tantamount to a court's acceptance of jurisdiction.

The next critical step is to seek out the indicia which suggest that a particular case, on its own merits, possibly or probably has not been properly handled at the administrative or legislative level. That is the most difficult part of the process, and to cope with it the courts have developed four basic guidelines.

First, has public property been disposed of at less than market value under circumstances which indicate that there is no very obvious reason for the grant of a subsidy? That determination can be relatively simple if it appears that the grant serves a public purpose by aiding the poor, by promoting an important service or technological advance for which no private market has developed, by encouraging population resettlement, or by sustaining a faltering economy which appears unable to sustain itself. These are but a few of the easily verifiable grounds which would suggest to a court that objections are unworthy of further judicial attention. Conversely, if land is being given away to a developer of proposed luxury high-rise apartments, a court would be very much inclined to seek further explanation and to interpose a substantial dose of skepticism. Even in such a case it might be possible to satisfy a court that some rational public policy supports the conduct, but there will be a strong inclination to examine statutory authority with great care and to seek out substantial supporting evidence in order to ensure that all the issues have been made fully public.

Second, has the government granted to some private interest the authority to make resource-use decisions which may subordinate broad public resource uses to that private interest? In the extreme case, that question raises the problem of *Illinois Central*, and a court might appropriately interpose a flat legal prohibition on the ground that the state has divested itself of its general regulatory power over a matter of great public importance. More often, the situation is one in which a court seeks to deal with the ramifications of a private property system in relation to resources which have the element of commonality. A resource like San Francisco Bay, for example, is of such a physical character that the exercise of ordinary private property rights may have very large direct effects on the whole public which has had the use of that bay. In such circumstances courts are inclined to scrutinize with great care claims that private property rights should be found to be superior to the claim of continued public regulatory authority. Indeed, it is unlikely that such rights will be allowed unless they are consistent with a general public plan for regulation of the resource. This issue has arisen in litigation in the San Francisco Bay cases and in several Florida cases.

In such situations, the courts generally purport to be merely interpreting and defining traditional property law rights, but implicit in their analyses is a hesitancy to recognize that any such expansive private rights could have been granted if due consideration had been given to the public interest. Thus, in order to make a retrospective "reformation" of earlier, imperfectly considered governmental decisions, courts may read into patents or grants implied conditions, such as a servitude in favor of the public trust. They would thereby force the private claimant to go before a contemporary administrative tribunal, whose conduct will itself be subject to judicial scrutiny, and there to establish the consistency of his project with the public interest.

Third, has there been an attempt to reallocate diffuse public uses either to private uses or to public uses which have less breadth? This is the most complex of the judicial bench marks. In one respect, it merely reflects judicial concern that any act infringing diffuse public uses is likely to have been made in the absence of adequate representation for the diffuse group, and accordingly the courts are willing to send such decisions back for reaffirmation or more explicit authorization. That procedure is exemplified by the developments in Massachusetts.

In addition, although there is little specific supporting evidence, there seems to be implicit in the cases a feeling that there is something rather questionable about the use of governmental authority to restrict, rather than to spread, public benefits. At the extreme, that attitude is reflected in the judicial rule that government may not act for a purely private purpose. While cases involving such holdings are rare, there are many situations in which benefits are sufficiently narrow that it is difficult to determine what public purpose is meant to be achieved by a particular governmental act. That difficulty is emphasized when the price of providing any such narrow benefit is the withdrawal of a beneficial use which is available to a wide segment of the population.

* * *

This judicial device serves to call attention to the inadequacies in conventional public techniques for evaluating resource decisions involving diffuse public uses. Rarely do the decision-making agencies attempt to make a careful benefit-cost analysis which would provide useful information about the effects of such decisions. What is lost, for example, when a local public beach is closed and the area filled for garbage disposal, highway development, or residential development? Governmental bodies have made little effort to answer such questions; yet they do make decisions that one sort of allocation or another advances the public interest. The courts properly evince reluctance to approve decisions based upon ignorance; and when that factor is joined with the courts' strong feeling that diffuse public uses are both poorly represented and, by their nature, difficult to measure, judicial wariness is inevitably enhanced.

One product of such judicial reluctance is an incentive for decision-making agencies to begin seeking careful and sophisticated measurements of the benefits and costs involved in resource reallocations. To the extent that judicial hesitancy cautions the agencies against making such reallocations without better information on the public record, the courts are deterring ventures into the unknown. And if the relevant facts are unknown, and yet legislatures and administrative agencies show eagerness to go forward, the courts are only reinforced in their over-all suspicion that they are dealing with governmental responsiveness to pressures imposed by powerful but excessively narrow interests.

The fourth guideline that courts use in determining whether a case has been properly handled at the administrative or legislative level is to question whether the resource is being used for its natural purpose—whether, for example, a lake is being used "as a lake." This is perhaps the most specific of the guidelines the courts use, but, as is shown by the Wisconsin cases, it is seldom employed with rigor. In fact it is little more than a variant of the previous guideline, under which courts question the reallocation of resources from broader to narrower uses, for it is very often the case with natural resources that they have their broadest uses when they are left essentially in their natural state. This result is in part a product of the physical fact of commonality, as with a lake, and in part a result of the extraordinary diversity of many natural systems, as with an estuarial area which may contain fishery resources, opportunities for swimming and boating, scenic views, and wildlife. To fill such an area and to build an apartment house on it would eliminate all those uses, which are enjoyed by a wide variety of people, in favor of a use that would benefit a small class of residents. Courts must be persuaded that any such transition promotes a significant public purpose.

Although this guideline could theoretically be subsumed within the third, there are advantages to maintaining it as a separate concept. It applies to particular water resources more clearly and more directly than does the third guideline and thus seems to be useful to the courts. Indeed, it might be helpful if such an approach were attempted with terrestrial resources.

IV. Postscript

This Article has been an extended effort to make the rather simple point that courts have an important and fruitful role to play in helping to promote rational management of our natural resources. Courts have been both misunderstood and underrated as a resource for dealing with resources. It is usually true that those who know the least about the judicial process are often the most ready to characterize the courts as doctrinaire and rigid, and the adversary process as a somewhat sinister game in which neither truth nor intelligent outcome are of importance to the participants. This Article should help to dispel some of those beliefs, for it is demonstrable that the courts, in their own intuitive way—sometimes clumsy and cumbersome—have shown more insight and sensitivity to many of the fundamental problems of resource management than have any of the other branches of government. If lawyers and their clients are willing to ask for less than the impossible, the judiciary can be expected to play an increasingly important and fruitful role in safeguarding the public trust.

Notes

1. The Sax article has proved to be so influential that it is regarded as the foundation of the modern public trust doctrine, having been cited no fewer than 856 times by 2011. Fred R. Shapiro & Michelle Pearse, *The Most Cited Law Review Articles of All Time*, 110 Mich. L. Rev. 1483, 1489 (2012). The word "seminal" captures the impact of Professor Sax's article on the public trust doctrine. Professor Rick Frank considered the article to be the most heavily cited law review article in four decades of environmental law, having a catalytic effect on court cases like the California Supreme Court's decision in *Marks v. Whitney*, 491 P.2d 374 (Cal. 1971) (p. 132); the New Jersey Supreme Court's decision in *Borough of Neptune City v. Borough of Avon-by-the-Sea*, 294 A.2d 47 (N.J. 1972) (p. 257); and *Just v. Marinette County*, 201 N.W.2d 761 (Wis. 1972) (p. 141). Richard M. Frank, *The Public Trust Doctrine: Assessing Its Recent Past & Charting Its Future*, 45 U.C. Davis L. Rev. 665, 667–68 (2012). Sax's article has also proved a beacon for courts of other countries such as India in developing public trust jurisprudence. *See, e.g.*, pp. 335–36, 340.

2. According to Professor Sax, some natural resources have public rights attached to them, restricting governments from privatizing all property rights associated with them. These public rights represent a kind of sovereign easement or servitude, imposing limits on private ownership, at least restricting the uses to which these resources may be put and, in some cases, resisting privatization altogether. The implementation of these limits is often through the courts, which recognize trust obligations on the part of governments to protect and preserve these public rights. The resources to which the public trust

doctrine attached were historically largely water-based, particularly tidal and navigable waters, which were crucial for public navigation, travel, and fishing. But note that Sax also cited to the Massachusetts Supreme Judicial Court's ruling in *Gould v. Greylock* (p. 291) that subjected parklands to public trust scrutiny, so the doctrine apparently is capable of evolving to apply to dry land, a kind of amphibious evolution.

3. At the outset of the article, Sax cited *Commonwealth v. Alger*, 61 Mass. 53 (1851), a decision of the Massachusetts Supreme Judicial Court in which Chief Justice Lemuel Shaw stated:

> We think it is a settled principle, growing out of the nature of well-ordered civil society, that every holder of property, however absolute and unqualified may be his title, holds it under the implied liability that his use of it may be so regulated, that it shall not be injurious to the equal enjoyment of others having an equal right to the enjoyment of their property, nor injurious to the rights of the community. All property in this commonwealth, as well that in the interior as that bordering on tide waters, is derived directly or indirectly from the government, and held subject to those general regulations, which are necessary to the common good and general welfare. Rights of property, like all other social and conventional rights, are subject to such reasonable limitations in their enjoyment, as shall prevent them from being injurious, and to such reasonable restraints and regulations established by law, as the legislature, under the governing and controlling power vested in them by the constitution, may think necessary and expedient.

Id. at 84–85. Chief Justice Shaw's discussion of public and private rights in property anticipated the modern recognition of the distinction between *jus publicum* and *jus privatum* in public trust case law.

4. In *Gould v. Greylock*, 215 N.E.2d 114 (Mass. 1966) (p. 291), examined by Professor Sax, the Massachusetts court employed the public trust doctrine to interpret a statutory grant of authority to the commission. The role of the public trust doctrine in construing statutes and regulations is an often overlooked aspect of the doctrine. *See* Alexandra B. Klass, *Modern Public Trust Principles: Recognizing Rights and Integrating Standards*, 82 Notre Dame L. Rev. 699 (2006); William D. Araiza, *The Public Trust Doctrine as Interpretive Canon*, 45 U.C. Davis L. Rev. 693 (2012).

5. Notice also that the Saxion vision of the public trust doctrine has a large democratization-reinforcing component to it. This perception is no doubt a fallout of *Illinois Central Railroad* (p. 68), a case exhumed by Sax, in which the U.S. Supreme Court ruled that the Illinois legislature could not pass a statute conveying the whole of Chicago Harbor to the railroad, in what appeared to be the product of corruption. The ability of narrowly-focused minorities, such as the railroad lobby in the nineteenth century, to control diffuse majorities in legislatures and administrative bodies prompted a new theory of government around the time that Sax wrote his article. Termed "public choice" analysis, or a capture theory of government, the idea was popularized in influential works like James Buchanan & Gordon Tullock, The Calculus of Consent (1962); Mancur Olson, The Logic of Collective Action (1965); and Phillip Foss, Politics and Grass (1960). In terms of majority vs. minority rights, Sax usefully compares the differences between the role of the public trust doctrine and the role of the Bill of Rights. What is the difference?

6. Note the remedy that Professor Sax suggests when a court finds that the legislature violated the PTD: "[T]he function which the courts must perform, and have been per-

forming, is to promote equality of political power for a disorganized and diffuse majority by remanding appropriate cases to the legislature after public opinion has been aroused." The *legislative remand* allows the court to send the matter back to the legislature for further consideration, theoretically a democracy-forcing measure. By placing the decision back in the hands of the legislature, do courts avoid usurping legislative prerogatives? Increasingly, government defendants raise a "political question" defense, charging that environmental decisions belong to the legislature, not to the courts. Do courts side-step this problem through a legislative remand? Can the remedy in a PTD case strike the right balance in a system demanding separation of powers? Note that in statutory environmental cases courts use the *agency remand*, sending the matter back to the agency to correct the procedural deficiencies of its decision.

7. Also observe that Sax acknowledged that the public trust doctrine in Roman law allowed for some privatization of public trust resources. Without referencing Sax's explanation, Professor Huffman attempted to mount an historical attack on the legitimacy of the public trust doctrine. James L. Huffman, *Speaking of Inconvenient Truths: A History of the Public Trust Doctrine*, 18 Duke L. & Pol'y F. 1 (2007), relying heavily on Glenn J. McGready, *The Navigability Concept in Civil and Common Law: Historical Development, Current Importance, and Some Doctrines That Don't Hold Water*, 3 Fla. St. U. L. Rev. 511 (1975). Whether or not the public trust doctrine was a creation of the imagination of Sir Matthew Hale's treatise in the 1660s, as alleged in Huffman's polemic, it was introduced in American law in the early 1800s and has been a prominent, if misunderstood, feature of American law ever since.

8. Sax explained that in Anglo-American law riparian landowners have the right to extend their wharves out into waterways ("wharfing out"), another example of the public trust doctrine allowing small privatizations of public resources. In a sense, the doctrine requires a kind of balancing between public and private uses. Professor Carol Rose compared this balancing to the riparian rights doctrine in water law, which allows private landowners to consume small amounts of the water of a stream so long as the public's right in the flow of the stream is maintained. *See* Carol M. Rose, *Joseph Sax and the Idea of the Public Trust*, 25 Ecology L.Q. 351 (1998).

9. The article's citation to the California Supreme Court's 1913 decision *People v. California Fish Co.*, 138 P. 79 (Cal. 1913), is noteworthy as an early judicial recognition that a private owner's "title to the soil" in a riverbed was not absolute. Instead, the public had rights — a kind of public easement — that forbade the landowner from excluding the public. Thus, the California Supreme Court construed states purporting to grant tidelands and swamp lands to private parties without mentioning navigation or fishery rights to convey only "naked title" to the lands, subject to the public rights of navigation and fishery that the state continued to hold in trust. *Id.* at 88. The grantee's *jus privatum* was subject to the public's paramount rights unless public authorities, as part of navigation improvement like a seawall, permanently exclude the lands from navigation, as in the case of San Francisco Bay. *Id.* at 87. This early recognition of the public easement characteristic of public trust lands would become a more persistent feature of public trust law in the late 20th and early 21st centuries.

10. In a kind of postscript to the excerpted article, Professor Sax revisited the public trust doctrine a decade later, in Joseph L. Sax, *Liberating the Public Trust from Its Historical Shackles*, 14 U.C. Davis L. Rev. 185 (1980). There he noted that the "essence of property law is respect for reasonable expectations...," and emphasized that expectations are not always reflected in title ownership but are held by the public as well as private owners. *Id.* at 186–87. Sax observed that "one of the most basic and persistent concerns of the

legal system" is a commitment to "evolutionary rather than revolutionary change, for the rate of change and the capacity it provides for transition are precisely what separate continuity and adaptation from crisis and collapse." *Id.* at 188. He argued that the chief purpose of the PTD was to prevent "the destabilizing disappointment of expectations held in common but without formal recognition such as title." *Id.*

This proscription against destabilizing public ecological expectations could arguably prevent developments adversely affecting trust resources like wetland fills, dams, or water diversions. Could it have its greatest impact in the climate context at a time when leading scientists warn that Earth is nearing a tipping point that could alter civilization as we have known it? In a federal climate case advancing the PTD, Dr. James Hansen, head of NASA's Goddard Institute for Space Studies, submitted an amicus brief (in his private capacity) declaring "the urgent need to get beyond fossil fuels before Earth is altered in fundamental respects—including its ability to sustain civilization...." Brief for Dr. James Hansen as Amicus Curiae Supporting Plaintiffs, *Alec L. v. Lisa Jackson*, 2011 WL 8583134 (N.D. Cal. 2011) (No. 4:11-cv-02203 EMC), at 14, available at http://www.ourchildrenstrust.org/sites/default/files/Hansen%20Amicus%20.pdf. Could the PTD force action to reduce carbon pollution where government has thus far failed to respond adequately to the climate threat? The question is taken up in the last chapter.

11. Sax's article began an outpouring of scholarship on the public trust doctrine, some of it of a critical nature, including James L. Huffman, *A Fish Out of Water: The Public Trust Doctrine in a Constitutional Democracy*, 19 Envtl. L. 527 (1989) (contending that the public trust doctrine undermines the democratic choices of public officials); Richard Delgado, *Our Better Natures: A Revisionist View of Joseph Sax's Public Trust Theory of Environmental Protection, and Some Dark Thoughts on the Possibility of Law Reform*, 44 Vand. L. Rev. 1209 (1991) (maintaining that Sax's article quieted more radical approaches to environmental protection suggested by ecofeminism, Native American philosophy, and critical race theory). *See also* Erin Ryan, *Public Trust and Distrust: The Theoretical Implications of the Public Trust Doctrine for Natural Resource Management*, 31 Envtl. L. 477 (2001) (surveying the public trust scholarship). In 1986, Professor Richard Lazarus undertook an extensive survey of the PTD and concluded that its role was no longer necessary in an era dominated by statutes and administrative regulations, which assure greater accountability. *See* Richard J. Lazarus, *Changing Conceptions of Property and Sovereignty in Natural Resources: Questioning the Public Trust Doctrine*, 71 Iowa L. Rev. 631 (1986). But note that his observation was made before many environmental regulatory failures became evident. Some administrations undermine environmental protection. *See* Patrick Parenteau, *Anything Industry Wants: Environmental Policy Under Bush II*, 14 Duke Envtl. L. & Pol'y F. 363 (2004) ("From day one, the Bush Administration has set about the task of systematically and unilaterally dismantling over thirty years of environmental and natural resources law."). Is the PTD truly superfluous, or is it needed now more than ever to infuse environmental agencies with fiduciary obligation? Consider the observation made by one of the editors:

> The ecological crisis of today is largely a result of government's failure to protect natural resources on behalf of its citizens. Under the system of environmental statutory laws enacted in the United States over the past three decades, agencies at every jurisdictional level have gained nearly unlimited authority to manage natural resources and allow their destruction by private interests through permit systems. Although environmental statutes were designed to protect natural resources, most agencies have used permit provisions to allow continual destruc-

tion of natural resources. Though permits often contain mitigation conditions, the overall cumulative effect of agency-permitted damage pursuant to statutory authority is staggering. Nearly every natural resource—including the atmosphere, water, air, wetlands, wildlife, fisheries, soils, marine systems, grasslands, and forests—is seriously degraded, and many are at the brink of collapse. Without a fundamental paradigm shift in the way government manages the environment, government will continue to impoverish natural capital until society will no longer be able to sustain itself.... [T]he public trust doctrine [serves] as the most compelling beacon for a fundamental and rapid paradigm shift towards sustainability.

Mary Christina Wood, *Advancing the Sovereign Trust of Government to Safeguard the Environment for Present and Future Generations (Part I): Ecological Realism and the Need for a Paradigm Shift*, 39 Envtl. L. 43, 44–45 (2009).

————————

Another provocative article was penned by Professor Charles Wilkinson as part of a symposium, *The Public Trust and the Waters of the American West: Yesterday, Today, and Tomorrow*, 19 Envtl. L. 425–735 (1989). Wilkinson explored the origins of the public trust doctrine and found them in surprising sources. His conclusion was that there is a minimum public trust doctrine—a floor—which federal law imposes on the states, but the states have the authority to expand the doctrine as they see fit. The states then set the ceiling of the scope of the public trust doctrine.

The Headwaters of the Public Trust: Some Thoughts on the Source and Scope of the Traditional Doctrine

Charles F. Wilkinson
19 Envtl. L. 425 (1989)

The public trust doctrine is complicated—there are fifty-one public trust doctrines in this country alone; timely—the judicial, legislative and scholarly work on the doctrine is proceeding apace; and arcane—the roots of the public trust doctrine go back literally for millennia. But those factors do not explain why the public trust doctrine is one of the most controversial developments in modern American law, and perhaps the single most controversial development in natural resources law.

There are two basic reasons for the intense debate over the trust. First, the traditional public trust doctrine deals with our coastlines, harbors, and major rivers and lakes, which as a group are among our most valuable natural resources, whether valued in terms of economics, recreation, beauty, or spirituality. Second, the debate evidences, at its quick, a collision between two treasured sets of expectancy interests: those of private landowners who expect their titles to land and water to remain secure, and those of the general public, which expects that most of its rivers will remain rivers, its lakes lakes, and its bays bays.

The public trust doctrine comes in many different forms. To understand the trust, however, it is important to begin with its core, what I refer to as the traditional doctrine. By the traditional doctrine, I mean the trust principles that the United States Supreme Court has applied to those watercourses that are navigable for the purposes of title—those watercourses whose shorelines, beds, and banks pass by implication to states at the time of statehood. Those natural resources were the subject of such leading nineteenth century cases as *Shively v. Bowlby*[75] and *Illinois Central Railroad v. Illinois*.[76] Different courts have since extended the public trust doctrine to many other kinds of resources, but first I want to focus on these particular resources and the traditional doctrine that governs them.

* * *

II. The Public Interest in Major Watercourses

A great many countries have legal rules that, in one fashion or another, give special treatment to major bodies of water. Typically, these rules articulate public concern for the resources and, typically, these disparate concepts have ancient roots. Public values in water can be traced back, for example, to the Roman Institutes of Justinian[77] and the Magna Carta[78] — often cited as historical antecedents for the public trust — and to medieval Spain[79] and France.[80] But these ideas extended far beyond Europe. In the Orient, recognition of public uses of water existed well before the birth of Christ.[81] African nations held similar traditions: "from time immemorial the people of Nigeria have enjoyed the right to fish the sea, with its creeks and arms and navigable rivers within the tides."[82] In Moslem countries, "the fundamentals of Islamic water law purport to ensure to all members of the Moslem community the availability of water."[83] Spanish and Mexican laws and institutions in the New World evinced a powerful tradition that large portions of the water supply must be dedicated to the community good.[84]

This general and nearly universal notion — the reluctance to allow our great watercourses to be subject to wholesale private acquisition — goes back even further on this continent, for most American Indian cultures wholly denied the possibility of ownership of land, air, and water. Tecumseh, the Shawnee Chief, asked rhetorically, "Sell the earth? Why not sell the air, the clouds, the great sea?" Frank Tenorio, Governor of the San Felipe Pueblo, spoke of the community values and spirituality that Indian people traditionally have associated with water.

---

75. 152 U.S. 1 (1894).

76. 146 U.S. 387 (1892).

77. J. INST., 2.1.1–2.1.6 at 55 (P. Birks & G. McLeod trans. 1987) ("The things which are naturally everybody's are: air, flowing water, the sea, and the sea-shore.").

78. MAGNA CARTA reissue, 1225, chapter 23.

79. LAS SIETE PARTIDAS, the thirteenth century codification of King Alfonso X of Castile, is cited as a Spanish antecedent for the public trust doctrine. *See, e.g.*, MICHAEL C. MEYER, WATER IN THE HISPANIC SOUTHWEST 106–09 (1984) (LAS SIETE PARTIDAS "became a major source of Spanish law and indeed formed the basis for much of the legal system later to be introduced in the New World."). *See also* Richard J. Lazarus, *Changing Conceptions of Property and Sovereignty in Natural Resources: Questioning the Public Trust Doctrine*, 71 Iowa L. Rev. 631, 634 (1986).

80. An 11th century statement of regional French law is cited by Professor Sax as a proper source for the modern public trust doctrine. "[T]he public highways and byways, running water and springs, meadows, pastures, forest, heaths and rocks ... are not to be held by lords, ... nor are they to be maintained ... in any other way than that their people may always be able to use them." Joseph L. Sax, *Liberating the Public Trust from Its Historical Shackles*, 14 U.C. Davis L. Rev. 185, 189 (1980) (citing M. BLOCH, FRENCH RURAL HISTORY 183 (1966)).

81. U.N. ECONOMIC COMM'N FOR ASIA & THE FAR EAST, WATER LEGISLATION IN ASIA & THE FAR EAST, at 210, U.N. Sales No. E.69.22.F.6 (1968) [hereinafter U.N. ECONOMIC COMM'N]. Under the earliest Chinese water laws, first codified under the Ch'in dynasty (249–207 B.C.), "private water ownership never appeared and the individual duties in water undertakings would eventually lead to and enhance public welfare." *Id.*

82. T. ELIAS, NIGERIAN LAND LAW 48 (1971) (citation omitted). Elias also relates that "[a]ll the inhabitants of Neigeria also enjoy a right of free navigation in tidal and other large inland waterways." *Id.* at 49.

83. U.N. ECONOMIC COMM'N, above note 81, at 211.

84. *See, e.g.*, MICHAEL C. MEYER, WATER IN THE HISPANIC SOUTHWEST 117–19 (1984).

There has been a lot said about the sacredness of our land which is our body; and the values of our culture which is our soul; but water is the blood of our tribes, and if its life-giving flow is stopped, or it is polluted, all else will die and the many thousands of years of our communal existence will come to an end.[85]

The English, whose common law is the most direct source of our public trust doctrine, saw ownership differently than did American Indian people and generally favored private ownership of natural resources. But the British made an exception for navigable waterways.[86] The common law distinguished between the *privatum*, which the Crown could transfer to individuals in fee ownership, and the *jus publicum*, which the Crown held in trust for the public. The most important areas of these public rights were the coasts and those stretches of rivers affected by the ebb and flow of the tide.

The real headwaters of the public trust doctrine, then, arise in rivulets from all reaches of the basin that holds the societies of the world. These things were articulated in different ways in different times by different peoples. In some cases the waters ran deep, in other places the waters ran shallow. But the idea of a high public value in water seems to have existed in most places in some fashion.

Public values in water certainly existed in America at the time of its founding. Indeed, it is hard to overstate the importance of the major watercourses during the formative years of the United States. To the early settlers, the rivers furnished paths of exploration and avenues for the fur trade and log floats. Due to the density of the forests and the difficulty of road construction, the watercourses provided transportation routes, and their shores afforded logical areas for settlement. Fishing was significant, both for commercial and subsistence purposes. The Revolutionary War and the War of 1812 demonstrated the military necessity of controlling the natural highways. The new nation realized that water had more abstract value as well.

* * *

Article IV of the Northwest Ordinance of 1787, reenacted in 1789 as the eighth law adopted by the First Congress, provided:

> The navigable waters leading into the Mississippi and St. Laurence, and the carrying places between the same, shall be common highways, and forever free, as well to the inhabitants of the said territory, as to the citizens of the United States, and those of any other States that may be admitted into the confederacy, without any tax, impost, or duty therefor.[87]

---

85. American Indian Lawyer Training Program, Indian Water Policy in a Changing Environment 2 (1982).

86. One authority summarized the public uses of river beds and banks in England in the following terms:

> by the time of Sir Matthew Hale in the seventeenth century, the legal presumption was that the riparian owners along fresh-water rivers had the exclusive right to the use of the beds and banks. But that presumption was subject to a public right to use the bed and banks for purposes incidental to navigation where the public had acquired that right by prescription or custom. The beds and banks of navigable rivers were indeed used by the public, as a matter of right, for anchoring, mooring, and towing vessels along the banks; where the public had had need for such uses, the right was thus established.... Where there was conflict with the public right of navigation, the right of navigation prevailed. In short, medieval common law recognized the only substantial public demand for water use that was exerted.

1 R. Clark, Waters and Water Rights 182–83 (1967) (footnotes omitted).

87. Ch. 8, 1 Stat. 50, 52 (1789).

Congressional regulation of commerce on navigable watercourses was a primary area of emphasis during the early years of the Republic. Thomas Jefferson, who envisioned uniting the continent through the watercourses, initiated the Lewis and Clark expeditions in 1803 to "explore the river Missouri, from its mouth to its source, and, crossing the highlands by the shortest portage, to seek the best water communication thence to the Pacific ocean...." Politically, water improvements were popular and commonly appeared in the party platforms of the day.

In an even larger sense, water was a unifying factor for the Nation. Rivers and lakes facilitated trade, allowed immigration to new areas, and established communication lines among the states. The need for one central governing body to oversee water traffic was a key impetus for Congress' primacy under the commerce clause of the Constitution.[88] Chief Justice Marshall explained the significance of the clause and of navigation to the nation as a whole in Gibbons v. Ogden[89] by saying that "[t]he power over commerce, including navigation, was one of the primary objects for which the people of America adopted their government, and must have been contemplated in forming it." Gibbons v. Ogden, one of the first Supreme Court commerce clause decisions, involved a monopoly of the steamboats in New York State; the conflict between steamboat monopolies and free watercourses was of great concern nationally. Marshall, upholding a federal license granted outside of the New York scheme and justifying the need for federal regulation of the waterways, wrote that "deep streams ... pass through the interior of almost every State in the Union, and furnish the means of exercising this right to regulate commerce. If Congress has the power to regulate it, that power must be exercised whenever the subject exists."

Thus, the ribbons of waterways tied the early nation together—economically, politically, and symbolically.

* * *

The Supreme Court, because of the intrinsic importance of these resources and the priority that Congress and the new states placed on them, was asked to rule on a number of major issues relating to navigable watercourses. During the nineteenth century, the Court developed four major doctrines—essentially an integrated package of state prerogatives, state obligations, and federal powers—dealing with these watercourses. The doctrines involve (1) state ownership of the beds and banks of navigable watercourses, (2) congressional regulatory authority over navigable watercourses, (3) the navigation servitude, and (4) the public trust doctrine.

* * *

III. Navigable Watercourses: State Prerogatives

In England, there was no doubt as to the identity of the owner of lands under navigable watercourses. England was not a federal government since all authority emanated from the Crown. In the United States, however, there were two potential owners, the United States and the state within which the navigable watercourse was located. The matter of ownership was not so pressing in the original thirteen states, where lands within state

88. "The Congress shall have Power ... To regulate Commerce with foreign Nations, and among the several States, and with the Indian Tribes." U.S. Const. art. I, § 8, cl. 3. Other constitutional provisions indicating the framers' overriding concern with free navigation include the tonnage duty clause of U.S. Const. art. I, § 10, cl. 3; the import-export clause, U.S. Const. art. I, § 10, cl. 2; the ports and vessels clause, U.S. Const. art. I, § 9, cl. 6; and the admiralty clause, U.S. Const. art. III, § 2, cl. 1.
89. 22 U.S. (9 Wheat.) 1 (1824).

boundaries never passed to the United States; the colonies, now states, held title to lands within their borders before the union was formed and they retained ownership to those lands afterward. The situation was different, however, with respect to the western lands that the United States obtained through treaties with France, England, Spain, Mexico, and Russia. As to public lands not within any state, the United States initially was the owner, and Congress had legislative authority, apparently under the property clause of the Constitution, because it was "the only government which could impose laws upon" public lands before statehood. Nevertheless, the Territorial citizens wanted statehood and eventually state governments were formed.

* * *

The bargaining over the land transfers from the United States to the new states never failed to be heated. Ohio was the first public land state in 1803. Congress finally agreed to grant Ohio, along with other more minor grants, one section (section 16) out of every township; a section is one square mile and each township contains thirty-six sections. In all, Ohio received about four percent of all land within its borders.[90] Over time, Congress became more generous with new states. Later states received two sections in each township. The latest states in the Lower Forty-Eight made even more favorable bargains. Utah, Arizona, and New Mexico each received four sections per township for school lands, and a total of fourteen to sixteen percent of all land within the state. In all cases, states received additional express grants in the statehood acts for various designated purposes. Finally, the United States agreed to transfer to Alaska 103 million acres of the 365 million acres in the state.

* * *

The United States never expressly granted to the new states, either in the statehood acts or in the later land grant statutes, the lands under navigable watercourses. Given the tremendous amount of attention that was trained on land grants at statehood and in subsequent years, it would have been easy for the courts to find that there was no intent to transfer such important property interests out of federal ownership. The standard maxim of construction, *inclusio unius est exclusio alterius* (the inclusion of one is the exclusion of another), seems tailor-made for this situation. With so much express statutory action on the subject, how could there be room for an implied grant? Real property transactions are done by treaty, statute, deed, or patent. To leave a land transfer of such magnitude and complexity to implication is aberrational in the extreme.

Nonetheless, the Supreme Court concluded that lands under navigable watercourses did pass by implication to new states at the time of statehood. The leading cases were Martin v. Waddell[91] in 1842 and *Pollard's Lessee v. Hagan* in 1845.[92] The Court reached

---

90. Paul W. Gates, A History of Public Land Law Development 291 (1968).

91. 41 U.S. (16 Pet.) 367, 410 (1842). Although *Martin v. Waddell* involved a dispute over lands in one of the original 13 states, New Jersey, the case is foundational in the Court's analysis of the equal footing doctrine.

92. 44 U.S. (3 How.) 212 (1845). *Pollard's Lessee* involved a title dispute in the new state of Alabama, which was created from lands ceded to the United States by Georgia and Virginia. *Id.* at 220–22. At issue was title to lands lying below the high watermark of the navigable, freshwater Mobile River. Plaintiffs claimed ownership under a federal patent issued after Alabama's admission to the Union; defendants claimed under a state grant. The Court held that lands below the high watermark of navigable watercourses passed to the states under the equal footing doctrine. The federal patent was therefore inoperative, as Congress had no power to transfer to individuals the title to state-owned lands. *Id.* at 229.

its holding as a matter of constitutional law.[93] The statehood clause, article 4, section 3, clause 1, provides that "New States may be admitted by the Congress into this Union...." The Court, looking to the constitutional phrase "*this* Union,"[94] has developed the equal footing doctrine, requiring that new states enter the Union on a basis of full political equality with all other states. The mid-century Court reasoned that the western states were entitled to own title to lands under navigable watercourses as a matter of equal footing: since the original states retained those lands, the Court reasoned, so too must the western states in order to achieve equality.

* * *

IV. Navigable Watercourses: State Obligations and Federal Prerogatives

Given the national importance of watercourses navigable for title and the circumstances under which they were transferred to the states, it is understandable that the judiciary might structure some limits on the states in their administration of lands under navigable watercourses. Three such limitations have emerged. First, under the commerce clause, Congress has authority to regulate these watercourses. Of course, today the Court has found federal regulatory power over commerce to be nearly unlimited, but the issue of federal supremacy over commerce was hotly disputed during the Marshall years and the issue was decided in the context of navigable watercourses. Second, the navigation

---

93. The *Pollard's Lessee* Court engaged in a lengthy discussion of the authority for its holding in the following passage:

> The compact made between the United States and the state of Georgia, was sanctioned by the Constitution of the United States; by the 3d section of the 4th article of which it is declared, that "New states may be admitted by the Congress into this union; but no new state shall be formed or erected within the jurisdiction of any other state, nor any state be formed by the junction of two or more states or parts of states, without the consent of the legislatures of the states concerned, as well as of Congress." When Alabama was admitted into the union, on an equal footing with the original states, she succeeded to all the rights of sovereignty, jurisdiction, and eminent domain which Georgia possessed at the date of the cession ... Nothing remained to the United States, according to the terms of the agreement, but the public lands.

44 U.S. (3 How.) at 223. The Court further stated, "[t]he right of Alabama and every other new state to exercise all the powers of government, which belong to and may be exercised by the original states of the union, must be admitted, and remain unquestioned...." *Id.* at 224. The Court found that any reservation or exercise of municipal sovereignty within a state by the United States would be "repugnant to the Constitution...." *Id.* Ultimately, the Court held that the rights of states include title to the beds and banks of navigable watercourses: "First, The shores of navigable waters, and the soils under them, were not granted by the Constitution to the United States, but were reserved to the states respectively. Secondly, The new states have the same rights, sovereignty, and jurisdiction over this subject as the original states." *Id.* at 230.

94. *Coyle v. Oklahoma*, 221 U.S. 559, 567 (1911). The Supreme Court refuted suggestions that the political power of states might be diminished by acts of Congress accepted as conditions to statehood, stating:

> "This Union" was and is a union of States, equal in power, dignity and authority, each competent to exert that residuum of sovereignty not delegated to the United States by the Constitution itself. To maintain otherwise would be to say that the Union, through the power of Congress to admit new States, might come to be a union of States unequal in power, as including States whose powers were restricted only by the Constitution, with others whose powers had been further restricted by an act of Congress accepted as a condition of admission. Thus it would result, first, that the powers of Congress would not be defined by the Constitution alone, but in respect to new States, enlarged or restricted by the conditions imposed upon new States by its own legislation admitting them into the Union; and, second, that such new States might not exercise all of the powers which had not been delegated by the Constitution, but only such as had not been further bargained away as conditions of admission.

Id.

servitude applies to navigable watercourses. This allows the United States to condemn land, including state land, up to the high water mark without being required to pay just compensation. This limit on the states' land title is also based on the Constitution: "The Commerce Clause Confers a unique position upon the Government in connection with navigable waters.... 'For this purpose they are the public property of the nation, and subject to all the requisite legislation by Congress.' ... This power to regulate navigation confers upon the United States a 'dominant servitude....'"

The third limitation on state ownership is another servitude—the public trust doctrine. Trust language first appeared in *Martin v. Waddell* in 1842, but the leading case on the traditional public trust doctrine is *Illinois Central Railroad v. Illinois*, Justice Stephen J. Field's opinion that belongs on any short list of great natural resource opinions.

* * *

In 1869, the state of Illinois had granted to the Illinois Central Railroad more than 1000 acres comprising a substantial part of Chicago's waterfront on Lake Michigan, a navigable lake. The grant included submerged lands in Chicago's harbor; the area

> is as large as that embraced by all the merchandise docks along the Thames at London; is much larger than that included in the famous docks and basins at Liverpool; is twice that of the port of Marseilles, and nearly if not quite equal to the pier area along the water front of the city of New York.[95]

Four years later, amid cries of corruption, the state of Illinois revoked its earlier absolute grant.

The Supreme Court recognized that Illinois received title to the harbor by implication at statehood. The state's title, however, was impressed with a public trust in order to keep these waterways open to the public for uses such as navigation, commerce, and fishing. Accordingly, "any grant of the kind is necessarily revocable, and the exercise of the trust by which the property was held by the State can be resumed at any time." The opinion left no doubt that the traditional public trust doctrine imposes obligations on the states:

> A grant of all the lands under the navigable waters of a State has never been adjudged to be within the legislative power; and any attempted grant of the kind would be held, if not absolutely void on its face, as subject to revocation. The State can no more abdicate its trust over property in which the whole people are interested, like navigable waters and soils under them, so as to leave them entirely under the use and control of private parties, except in the instance of parcels mentioned for the improvement of the navigation and use of the waters, or when parcels can be disposed of without impairment of the public interest in what remains, than it can abdicate its police powers in the administration of government and the preservation of the peace.[96]

Thus was the traditional public trust doctrine, the third limitation on states' ownership of the beds and banks of navigable watercourses, explained in a comprehensive way.

V. The Source and Scope of the Traditional Trust

Today, nearly a century later, after all of the words on the subject, two foundational issues concerning the traditional doctrine have still not been decided. The first matter is the source of the trust—where does it come from? The second is the scope and definition of the trust—what law defines the trust and what is the content of the trust?

---

95. *Illinois Cent. R.R. v. Illinois*, 146 U.S. 387, 454 (1892).
96. *Id.* at 453.

The doctrine, as first announced by Justice Field, might be viewed as stemming either from federal law or from the internal law of Illinois. *Illinois Central*, however, seems plainly to have been premised on federal law. The briefs relied upon both federal cases and authority from many different states, of which Illinois was just one. The parties were plainly arguing principles of general applicability, not just Illinois law. The *Illinois Central* opinion itself leaves little doubt that the Court conceived of a general trust that applied to all states. Throughout the opinion, the Court refers to "a state" and employs other phrases of general applicability. In describing the trust, the Court made it clear that the trust derives from federal law and is binding on all states:

> It is the settled law of this country that the ownership of and dominion and sovereignty over lands covered by tide waters, within the limits of the several States, belong to the respective States within which they are found, with the consequent right to use or dispose of any portion thereof, when that can be done without substantial impairment of the interest of the public in the waters, and subject always to the paramount right of Congress to control their navigation so far as may be necessary for the regulation of commerce with foreign nations and among the States.[97]

Later Supreme Court decisions have recognized that states are accorded broad discretion in administering the trust. Nevertheless, the subsequent opinions do not disturb *Illinois Central*'s premise that the public trust doctrine applies on all navigable watercourses as a matter of federal law.

The Court has never explicitly stated the specific source of "the settled law of this country" that mandates the trust in the "several States." There are at least four possibilities. First, the public trust doctrine could be viewed as a matter of federal common law. This source of law, however, is not in favor and is unlikely to be employed in light of the more specific available sources discussed below. Second, the *Illinois Central* Court employed language similar to that commonly used in the guaranty clause cases.[98] The guaranty clause also has fallen into disuse and, again, it is unlikely that a modern court would look to it as a basis for the public trust doctrine.

The other two alternatives—the public trust as the product of congressional preemption resulting from a comprehensive legislative program to keep the major watercourses open and free, or as constitutionally founded in the commerce clause—are both much more consonant with the extensive body of law that has developed around those watercourses that are navigable for title.

A persuasive case can be made that the trust is based on congressional preemption, manifested by implication either through a comprehensive legislative scheme or, more specifically, through the statehood acts. Congress' tradition of mandating that navigable watercourses be kept open to the public runs deep, from the Northwest Ordinance's guarantee in 1787 that such rivers and lakes must be "forever free" through the comprehensive matrix of legislation that Congress has since enacted on the subject of navigation.

---

97. *Id.* at 435.
98. The guaranty clause provides "The United States shall guarantee to every State in this Union a Republican Form of Government...." U.S. CONST. art. IV, §4, cl. 1. Justice Field's assertion that "[t]he State can no more abdicate its trust ... than it can abdicate its police powers in the administration of government and the preservation of the peace," Illinois Cent. R.R. v. Illinois, 146 U.S. 387, 453 (1892), suggests the concept of a minimum level of state authority below which a republican government would not exist. The Supreme Court's initial considerations of the guaranty clause are found in, e.g., *Luther v. Borden*, 48 U.S. (7 How.) 1, 37–46 (1849); *Kies v. Lowrey*, 199 U.S. 233, 239 (1905).

Importantly, the "forever free" language from the Northwest Ordinance, one of this country's most luminous enactments,[99] was expressly included in the statehood acts of all the states in the old Northwest Territory and in the charters of several other states as well. The Supreme Court has recognized Congress' determination to keep the major waterways open in numerous opinions. As Justice Swayne explained in *Gilman v. Philadelphia*, "Commerce includes navigation.... This necessarily includes the power to keep major watercourses open and free from any obstruction to their navigation...."[100]

Since all new states took title to the beds and banks of navigable watercourses at statehood as a matter of implication, and since the public trust applies to the same bodies of water, it is logical to view the trust as an implied condition of statehood—a key adjunct of Congress' general purpose of keeping those watercourses "forever free." Congressional power to impose such a condition, in implementing the commerce authority, is beyond question. This analysis, of course, would mean that the public trust doctrine is not constitutionally mandated. Rather, it is accomplished by preemption, with congressional policy being effected through the statehood acts and the many statutes governing navigation. The approach would be attractive to modern courts because preemption, rather than recognition of constitutional standards, is the preferred method of analysis in constitutional adjudication.

Nevertheless, in the context of the law involving watercourses navigable for title, with its special traditions and heavy overlay of constitutional doctrine, locating the public trust doctrine in the Constitution itself is perhaps more persuasive. The navigation servitude, a limit on state authority on exactly the same watercourses, is an implied component of the commerce clause. The navigation servitude and the public trust doctrine are parallel doctrines, both affording complementary protections to major watercourses—the Court has recently, and correctly, described the public trust as a "servitude." Similarly, the Court has found that the extraordinary implied land transfer to the states upon admission is guaranteed to the states under the Constitution by the equal footing doctrine. It follows that the trust, a "servitude" or "easement" on the underlying land title, is also imposed by the same source, the Constitution. For more than 150 years, the Supreme Court has consistently given a constitutional cast to state and federal prerogatives and obligations with regard to waters navigable for title, due ultimately to the key role of these watercourses in the country's commerce and society and in the formation of the national government. Thus, although the other federal alternatives mentioned above have characteristics that cut in their favor, the fairest and most principled conclusion is that the public trust doctrine is rooted in the commerce clause and became binding on new states at statehood.

---

99. Justice Story called "the famous ordinance" of 1787 "the model of all our territorial governments ... equally remarkable for the brevity and exactness of its text, and for its masterly display of the fundamental principles of civil and religious liberty." 3 J. STORY, COMMENTARIES ON THE CONSTITUTION OF THE UNITED STATES 187 (1833). Story also called the ordinance a "notable and imperishable monument." *Id.* at 190 n.1. Paul Gates remarked on the stature of the Northwest Ordinance, stating:

> The Northwest Ordinance of 1787 was simply an act of the Congress of the Confederation, and therefore subject to whatever revision any later Congress might wish to make. Nevertheless, it became something more because of liberal features written into it and the great prestige it early acquired as part of American democratic traditions.

Gates, above note 90, at 285. The Northwest Ordinance became part of American democratic traditions early; it was re-enacted by the First Congress on August 7, 1789, the eighth statute passed under the new Constitution. 1 Stat. 50 (1789).

100. *Id.* at 724–25. *See also United States v. Coombs*, 37 U.S. (12 Pet.) 72 (1838); *Hobart v. Drogan*, 35 U.S. (10 Pet.) 108 (1836); *Gibbons v. Ogden*, 22 U.S. (9 Wheat.) 1 (1824).

The second unresolved question is whether the substantive standards for administering the trust are defined by state or federal law. There are three possibilities. First, there is language in both old and new cases suggesting that the content of the traditional trust is purely a matter of state law. Thus, for example, the Supreme Court in the 1926 opinion in Appleby v. City of New York[101] stated that "the conclusion reached in *Illinois Central* was necessarily a statement of Illinois law...."[102] United States Supreme Court decisions during the 1980s have not addressed the issue directly but have made repeated references to state prerogatives over lands navigable for title.[103]

A second, and opposite, conclusion is that the trust is defined solely by federal law. Certainly this is the fairest reading of *Illinois Central*. Although the opinion necessarily refers to the state of Illinois occasionally, much of the opinion is written more comprehensively with references to "a State" and with phrases that are plainly of general applicability, such as "any grant of the kind is necessarily revocable...." Suggestions that trust standards are established as a matter of federal law are also found in many other court opinions.

My conclusion, however, is that there is a third approach that provides a middle ground that is more sensitive to the many different factors at work here. Both the implied transfer and the overlying trust in favor of public access are now settled parts of our jurisprudence. There are powerful state interests—powerful enough to induce the implied transfer in the first place—and strong national interests—strong enough to impress an implicit trust on these highly valued natural resources. It does not make sense that a state could abdicate a federally and constitutionally imposed trust completely.[104] As Justice Field put

---

101. 271 U.S. 364, 395 (1926) (state acts of dominion over submerged lands, previously granted by City of New York in fee simple absolute to the plaintiffs' testator, were an unconstitutional impairment of contracts under state law).

102. *Id.* The *Appleby* Court went on to note that "the general principle and the exception [of *Illinois Central*] have been recognized the country over and have been approved in several cases in the State of New York." *Id.* The *Appleby* ruling contains an involved and comprehensive analysis of New York state law and state court decisions, in contrast to the very limited treatment of Illinois authority in Illinois Central. *Compare Illinois Cent. R.R. v. Illinois*, 146 U.S. 387 (1892) *with Appleby v. New York*, 271 U.S. 364 (1926).

103. The most recent Supreme Court cases in this field are *Phillips Petroleum Co. v. Mississippi*, 108 S.Ct. 791 (1988); *Utah Div. of State Lands v. United States*, 482 U.S. 193 (1987); *Summa Corp. v. California ex rel. State Lands Comm'n*, 466 U.S. 198 (1984); *Block v. North Dakota ex rel. Bd. of Univ. & School Lands*, 461 U.S. 273 (1983); *Kaiser Aetna v. United States*, 444 U.S. 164 (1979); *Vaughn v. Vermilion Corp.*, 444 U.S. 206 (1979).

104. This thought is at the core of public trust law. As the Court stated in *Shively v. Bowlby*:
    Lands under tide waters are incapable of cultivation or improvement in the manner of lands above high water mark. They are of great value to the public for the purposes of commerce, navigation, and fishery. Their improvement by individuals, when permitted, is incidental or subordinate to the public use and right. Therefore the title and the control of them are vested in the sovereign for the benefit of the whole people.
152 U.S. 1, 57 (1894). Thus, while the states can relinquish title to trust lands,
    [t]he control of the State for the purposes of the trust can never be lost, except as to such parcels as are used In promoting the interests of the public therein, or can be disposed of without any substantial impairment of the public interest in the lands and waters remaining.
Illinois Central, 146 U.S. at 453. Modern cases have recognized that state "control" for public trust purposes exceeds the scope of state title over navigable waterways. Thus, in *Marks v. Whitney*, 491 P.2d 374 (1971), the California Supreme Court held that submerged lands sold by the state for other than trust purposes continue to be impressed with the public trust, despite their private ownership. Such cases are entirely consistent with the 'no substantial impairment' rule of *Illinois Central*, and with modern treatment of the public trust ... since state title law is a separate issue.

it in *Illinois Central*, if there were no trust at all, such a situation "would place every harbor in the country at the mercy of a majority of the legislature of the State in which the harbor is situated."[105] At the same time, there is plainly broad state discretion; *Illinois Central* recognized the propriety both of state transfers consistent with navigation and of nonnavigation-related transfers that did not substantially impair the trust.[106] Later cases have approved a variety of state transactions of trust lands. Probably the most satisfactory formulation is the standard, set out in *Illinois Central* and reaffirmed in *Shively v. Bowlby*, that the states have extensive leeway but that the purposes of the trust cannot be "substantially impair[ed]."[107] Professor Sax has explained the basic legal rule this way:

> [T]he Court [in *Illinois Central*] articulated a principle that has become the central substantive thought in public trust litigation. When a state holds a resource which is available for the free use of the general public, a court will look with considerable skepticism upon *any* governmental conduct which is calculated *either* to relocate that resource to more restricted uses *or* to subject public uses to the self-interest of private parties.[108]

To be sure, there is language in some cases suggesting that states have unfettered discretion in administering the trust. The most recent opinion, *Phillips Petroleum Co. v. Mississippi*, stated that "ownership of public trust tide lands ... is a question of state law." *Phillips*, however, was only a dispute over real property title to tidelands. It did not involve the right of the public to obtain access to the overlying waters, which is the essence of the public trust doctrine. Indeed, two other recent Supreme Court cases, *Kaiser Aetna v. United States*[109] and *Vaughn v. Vermilion Corp.*[110] were plainly premised on the idea that the public has a right to use the surface of watercourses navigable for title, regardless of relevant state law. State court opinions have also regularly operated on the assumption that states are bound, as a matter of national law, to keep navigable watercourses open to public use. Neither the Supreme Court nor any state courts have disavowed the prohibition of "substantial impairment" of public rights of navigation, commerce, and fishing announced in *Illinois Central* and *Shively v. Bowlby*.

The standards for the trust, then, are best understood as having very broad parameters set as a matter of federal mandate, either by way of congressional preemption or constitutional law; the constitutional rationale is more consonant with the whole body of law. The traditional trust allows the states wide latitude, but the states are federally prohibited from abrogating the public trust entirely.

* * *

VI. Beyond the Traditional Doctrine

Court decisions and legislation in most states have supplemented the traditional federal doctrine, and most of the remaining states are likely to follow eventually. The developments have been many, but the major developments are these. First, some states have extended the coverage of the trust beyond those watercourses navigable for title to

---

105. 146 U.S. at 455. This language has been cited as suggesting that the Court intended a national application of the *Illinois Central* rule.

106. *See* 146 U.S. at 453.

107. *Illinois Central*, 146 U.S. at 453; *Shively*, 152 U.S. at 47.

108. Joseph L. Sax, *The Public Trust Doctrine in Natural Resources Law: Effective Judicial Intervention*, 68 Mich. L. Rev. 471, 490 (1970).

109. 444 U.S. 164 (1979).

110. 444 U.S. 206 (1979).

all, or nearly all, waters of the state. A leading example is Montana, where the courts and legislature have applied the public trust to all waters usable for recreational purposes. Second, cases have extended the trust beyond the traditional purposes of commerce, navigation, and fishing, with the most common "new"purposes being various forms of recreation. Third, various cases have extended the reach beyond watercourses per se. Thus, decisions and state constitutions extend the trust to dry sand beaches, wildlife, and state parks. One recent decision in New Jersey even extended the trust to drinking water in a dispute over the distribution of proceeds from a water supply company.

Last, ... a number of state courts have moved into the area of appropriation of water. These courts hold or suggest that water rights obtained under the prior appropriation doctrine might be curtailed if such appropriations substantially impair watercourses navigable for title. The Mono Lake[111] case and the Bay Delta[112] case, both in California, are the most notable opinions on this point. Variations of this reasoning can be found in Idaho, Alaska, and North Dakota.

* * *

VII. Conclusion

The public trust, as it is applied to the appropriation of water, is based on a set of modest beliefs: a belief that the public benefits mightily from private development, but that the public interest is in fact greater than the sum of the private interests; a belief that property ownership must be profoundly respected but that property rights in water, like rights in land, are not absolute but rather can be regulated and adjusted in reasonable ways for the good of the citizenry as a whole; a belief that wasteful uses of public resources are wrong and are not excused by return flows that return to our rivers not just water but also silt, salts, agrichemicals, and temperature changes; a belief that our rivers and canyons are more than commodities, that they have a trace of the sacred; a belief that words like "trust" ought to be taken seriously.

The public trust is one doctrine, one idea, in a historic reform movement that, slowly but steadily, is reshaping water law and policy in the West. The trust, however, has a special place in that movement because of its ancient roots, because of the context in which it was first announced in this country, because of the dynamic way in which it has been applied to a whole range of resource controversies, and because of the intangible way in which it evokes a sense of dignity and calls out the best and highest in us as a people. The trust, whether invoked by courts or legislatures, can play a principled part in structuring a system that really does reflect the vitality, diversity, and sacredness of both our ever-changing society and our inspiring, magnificent river systems.

Notes

1. Professor Wilkinson points out that there are at least fifty-one different public trust doctrines in the United States. Actually, there are many more than that worldwide, given the international endorsement of the doctrine, as explored in chapter 10.

---

111. *National Audubon Soc'y v. Superior Court (Mono Lake)*, 658 P.2d 709, *cert. denied*, 464 U.S. 977 (1983).
112. *United States v. State Water Resources Control Bd.*, 182 Cal. App. 3d 82 (1986).

2. According to Wilkinson, there is a "core" to the public trust doctrine established through federal law. What is this core? Of what significance is there to such a federally established core?

3. Wilkinson suggested that historically the public trust doctrine focused on maintaining public rights in major bodies of water. Why would the doctrine have concentrated on major waterways in the 19th century? *See* Kris J. Mitchener & Ian W. McLean, *The Productivity of the U.S. States Since 1880*, 8 J. of Econ. Growth 73–114 (Mar. 2003); EMORY R. JOHNSON, INLAND WATERWAYS: THEIR ANNALS OF THE AMERICAN ACADEMY OF POLITICAL AND SOCIAL SCIENCE (1893) (explaining the importance of navigable waters before the advent of railroads in a country with bad roadways). What resources today assume the same importance to society?

4. Wilkinson also cited the constitutional law staple of *Gibbons v. Ogden*, 22 U.S. 1 (1824), Chief Justice John Marshall's historic decision which endorsed a broad view of the scope of the constitution's commerce clause. The effect of that decision was to break up a transportation monopoly. *See* Samuel R. Olken, *Chief Justice John Marshall and the Course of American Constitutional History*, 33 J. Marshall L. Rev. 743 (2000). Is the public trust doctrine similarly anti-monopolistic?

5. Wilkinson suggested several possible sources of the public trust doctrine in American law. For Wilkinson, the individual statehood acts are central to the origins of the public trust doctrine. Why? For details, see Eric Biber, *The Price of Admission: Causes, Effects, and Patterns of Conditions Imposed on States Entering the Union*, 46 Am. J. Legal Hist. 119 (2004).

6. Wilkinson mentioned the navigation servitude, a somewhat mysterious federal doctrine protecting navigation projects from constitutional takings claims by adversely affected landowners. *See* Harrison C. Dunning, *Sources of the Public Right*, *in* 2 WATERS AND WATER RIGHTS, § 30.05 (Amy K. Kelley ed., 3rd ed. 2013). Could this servitude be thought of as an outgrowth of a federal public trust interest? Does it protect public needs and interact with private property rights in much the same way as the public trust?

7. Do declarations of state or public ownership of various resources like water or wildlife, which are commonplace in state law, reflect the existence of the public trust doctrine? Why or why not?

8. Wilkinson spent some time explaining the land grants made by the federal government to states as part of their statehood acts. These grants were made for specific purposes such as supporting schools in the state. They are uniformly deemed to be held in "trust," but their management has traditionally been distinguished from the PTD. Most state lands managers believe their mission is to maximize the revenue from the lands for purposes of raising money for education. Accordingly, the lands are often leased for purposes that undermine ecological values. For an overview and analysis, see PETER W. CULP, DIANE CONRADI & CYNTHIA C. TUELL, TRUST LANDS IN THE AMERICAN WEST: A LEGAL OVERVIEW AND POLICY ASSESSMENT (2005); JON A. SOUDER & SALLY K. FAIRFAX, STATE TRUST LANDS: HISTORY, MANAGEMENT, AND SUSTAINABLE USE (1996).

9. The following article begins to examine the evolution of the doctrine in the states from a comparative perspective. The article was preceded by a comparative study of the PTD in water allocation schemes of the eastern states. *See* Robin Kundis Craig, *A Comparative Guide to the Eastern Public Trust Doctrines: Classifications of States, Property Rights, and State Summaries*, 16 Penn St. L. Rev. 1 (2007) [hereinafter Craig, *A Comparative Guide to the Eastern Public Trust Doctrine*].

A Comparative Guide to the Western States' Public Trust
Doctrines: Public Values, Private Rights, and the
Evolution Toward an Ecological Public Trust

Robin Kundis Craig
37 Ecology L.Q. 53 (2010)

* * *

In some ways, what was true for the eastern states is also true for the western states. A state's public trust doctrine outlines public and private rights in water and submerged lands by delineating five components of those rights: (1) the beds and banks of waters that are subject to state/public ownership; (2) the line or lines dividing private from public title in those submerged lands; (3) the waters subject to public use rights; (4) the line or lines in those waters that mark the limit of public use rights; and (5) the public uses that the doctrine will protect in the waters where the public has use rights.

* * *

Nevertheless, public trust doctrine law in the western states can be differentiated from that in the eastern states in several respects. First, in the eastern states, coastal access, coastal development, and coastal rights have generally been of more pressing concern than public trust rights in fresh waters. Because of the timing of their statehood, many eastern states' public trust doctrines have been influenced in significant ways by the English "ebb and flow" tidal test of navigability for purposes of state title. In addition, many eastern states recognize different public/private title lines along the sea coasts and Great Lakes than they do in fresh water streams, rivers, and lakes and/or protect more extensive sets of public rights in the ocean and Great Lakes. In contrast, most western states became states *after* the U.S. Supreme Court had outlined most of its core principles regarding navigable waters, and far fewer of them are coastal states—only Alaska, California, Hawai'i, Oregon, Texas, and Washington. Partially as a result of this timing and geographical reality, western states, in general, have paid far greater attention than eastern states to public rights in fresh waters.

In addition, western states are more arid than eastern states, resulting in a consciousness of the importance of fresh water that pervades many of these states' public trust doctrines. The Hundredth Meridian, which runs through North Dakota, South Dakota, Nebraska, Kansas, Oklahoma, and Texas, is generally considered the "water divide" of the United States—east of that line, there is generally enough rainfall to support farming without irrigation; west of the line, there generally is not.[113] Survival in the west depends on access to water, and water is generally viewed as being in short supply. As will be discussed, this perception of shortage or potential shortage of fresh water has influenced the public trust doctrine in many western states.

Further, the western states use a different system of water law than the eastern states. Eastern states' water laws are founded on common-law riparianism,[114] although many states have transitioned to regulated riparian systems.[115] Riparianism incorporates no-

---

113. Herbert C. Young, Understanding Water and Conflicts 42 (2d ed. 2003).

114. George A. Gould, *Water Rights Systems*, in Water Rights of the Eastern United States 8–9 (Kenneth R. Wright, ed., 1998).

115. Richard F. Ricci et al., *Battles over Eastern Water*, 21 Nat. Resources & Env't 38, 38 (2006); Jeremy Nathan Jungreis, *"Permit" Me Another Drink: A Proposal for Safeguarding the Water Rights of Federal Lands in the Regulated Riparian East*, 29 Harv. Envtl. L. Rev. 369, 370–71 (2005).

tions of adjustable, correlative rights to water among riparian property owners, with a general expectation—couched originally in terms of a "natural flow" doctrine and more recently in terms of "reasonable use"—that there is enough water to both serve human needs and leave water in the natural system. In contrast, western states (with the notable exception of Hawai'i) base their water law on prior appropriation, including states like California that retain limited riparian rights.[116] Prior appropriation is based on the principle of "first in time, first in right" and acknowledges through its priority system that water supplies from a given source will sometimes—maybe often—be insufficient to meet all needs. Thus, prior appropriation as a legal system acknowledges that fresh water is in short supply. In practice, however, prior appropriation systems have allowed appropriators to drain streams and rivers dry, making obvious the loss of public values such as navigation, fishing and other recreation, aesthetics, species, biodiversity, water quality, ecological health and, more recently, ecosystem services.

Finally, in almost all prior appropriation states, state water law includes a declaration, constitutional or statutory, that the state or the public owns the fresh water itself. Legally, these declarations dissociate control over the water from land ownership, including submerged land ownership. For public trust purposes, therefore, such declarations leave western states free to impress waters with public trust protections entirely independently of state ownership of the beds and banks of navigable waters, extending many state public trust doctrines to non-navigable waters.

All of these features of prior appropriation water law have become relevant to states' public trust doctrines in the West. Indeed, western public trust common law reflects conscious struggles, often lacking in the eastern states, regarding the legal relationship between private appropriative water rights, on the one hand, and public rights and values in water, on the other.

* * *

The western states, ranging from Hawai'i and California on one end of a complex spectrum to Arizona and Colorado on the other, provide a particularly instructive diversity of approaches to the recognition (or not) of public rights in, and the public values of, water and other aspects of the environment. In comparing the public trust doctrines of the western states, moreover, four factors emerge as most important in the evolution of state public trust doctrines. First, the severing of water rights from real property ownership and the riparian rights doctrine freed these states from one set of potentially confining private property rights. Second, subsequent state declarations of public ownership of fresh water allow western states' public trust doctrines to operate independently of state title to submerged lands and federal pronouncements regarding "the" public trust doctrine. Third, perceptions of shortages of fresh water, submerged lands, and environmental amenities have prompted increased interest, compared to the East, in preserving the public values in these resources. Finally, the willingness of most western states to raise water and other environmental issues to constitutional status and/or to incorporate broad public trust mandates into statutes has encouraged their courts to evolve water-based public trust principles into expanding ecological public trust doctrines.

As the most recent cases demonstrate, and despite occasional limiting interventions by states legislatures (as in Idaho), the evolution of western state public trust doctrines is not slowing. Instead, in true common law fashion, state courts are using state public trust doctrines to respond to particular and emerging state needs—the loss of native species

---

116. *Gould*, above note 114, at 7.

and critical need to protect coastal waters in Hawai'i; profound conflicts between appropriators, species, and ecological values in California; and the perhaps climate-change driven appearance of new publicly usable water resources in South Dakota. While such evolutions and expansions complicate the identity—indeed, the very existence—of any unitary, national, perhaps Constitution-based public trust doctrine, they also provide place-based balancing of public and private needs and values in that most basic of natural resources—fresh water—that may better serve the long-term interests of the nation as a whole.

Notes

1. Professor Craig's western study emphasizes the predominance of state ownership of the beds of navigable waters, declarations of public ownership of water, and the emergence of an ecological public trust doctrine in the West. Concerning the latter, she spotlights California and Hawai'i, but also examines decisions from Alaska, Texas, Washington, and North Dakota courts. *Id.* at 80–91. Professor Craig's eastern water study reports that at least six eastern states have interpreted their public trust doctrine to include "evolving public protection": Illinois, Mississippi, New Hampshire, New Jersey, South Carolina, and Vermont. Craig, *A Comparative Guide to the Eastern Public Trust Doctrine*, cited above, note 9, p. 53 at 21–24.

2. Assembling public trust water decisions nationwide, Professor Craig's western study contains a 105-page appendix surveying the public trust doctrines of nineteen western states, and her eastern study includes an 87-page appendix surveying the doctrine in thirty-one eastern states. *See id.* One of the editors and his students have compiled analyses of all but five of the fifty states. *See The Public Trust Doctrine in Forty-Five States* (Michael C. Blumm ed., 2014 ed.), available at http://ssrn.com/abstract=2235329.

Chapter 2

The Foundation Cases

As indicated by both Professors Sax and Wilkinson, the origins of the public trust doctrine lie in Roman law, in the Institutes of Justinian, in the English Magna Carta, and the writings of Sir Matthew Hale. Transported across the Atlantic, the first manifestation of the doctrine occurred in an early 19th century case. In *Carson v. Blazer,* 2 Binn. 475 (Pa. 1810), involving a claim by a riparian owner to exclusive rights to harvest fish to the middle of the Susquehanna River, the Pennsylvania Supreme Court ruled that shoreside landowner had "no exclusive right to fish in the river immediately in front of his lands ... [because] the right to fisheries in [a large freshwater river not subject to tidal influence] is vested in the state, and open to all...." *Id.* at 477. This recognition was one of the earliest from American courts enlarging the scope of public rights from tidal waters to navigable-in-fact waters, which would become the generic American rule in the late 19th century. The case below, decided eleven years after *Carson*, proved influential, as the U.S. Supreme Court relied on it in the 1842 *Martin v. Waddell* decision which follows the case below.

Arnold v. Mundy
Supreme Court of New Jersey
6 N.J.L. 1 (1821)

[In 1818, Benjamin Mundy led a group of oyster boats up the Raritan River to an extremely productive shellfishery that was adjacent to land owned by Robert Arnold, a farmer who claimed he planted the oysters and staked off the area. Mundy and his colleagues proceeded to harvest oysters, and Arnold filed suit. Mundy defended on the ground that because the river was navigable, the public had harvesting rights. At trial, Mundy prevailed, and Arnold appealed.]

JUDGE ANDREW KIRKPATRICK, the Chief Justice of the New Jersey Supreme Court, affirmed in the following opinion:[1]

* * *

The grant of Charles II to the duke of York was not only of territory but of government also. It was made, not with a view to give that territory and that government to the duke, to be enjoyed as a private estate, but with a view to the settlement of it as a great colony, to the enlargement of the British Empire, and the extension of its laws and dominions. In construing this grant, therefore, we ought always to have our eye fixed upon these great objects. If we shall find some things contained in it, which by the laws of England, as well as of all other civilized countries, and even by the very law of nature itself, are declared to be the common property of all men, then, by every fair rule of construction, we are to consider these things as granted to him, as the representative of the sovereign, and

---

1. We have eliminated most italics used by the court. — Eds.

as a trustee to support the title for the common use, and especially so, if we shall find that the king himself had no other dominion over them.

The grant is not only of all lands, but of "all rivers, harbours, waters, fishings, etc. and of all other royalties, so far as the king had estate, right, title, or interest therein, together with full and absolute power and authority to correct, punish, pardon, govern, and rule all such the subjects of the king, his heirs, and successors, as should, from time to time, adventure themselves into the said territory;" and for this purpose to make statutes, ordinances, etc. provided the same should not be contrary to the laws, statutes, and government of England, but saving to the inhabitants, nevertheless, the right of appeal, and to the crown the right of hearing and determining the same. The duke was to govern, but he was to govern, substantially, according to the principles of the British constitution. The colonists were to be governed by him, but, by the very words of the charter, they were to be British subjects, and to enjoy the protection, liberty, and privileges of the British government. In order to accomplish those great objects, the king selected his royal brother, and granted to him all the rights which he himself had, or could exercise in and over this great territory, saving to himself only the right of hearing appeals. Those things, therefore, which were, properly speaking, the subjects of property, and which the king himself could divide and grant severally to the settlers, the duke by virtue of this charter, could also divide and grant; but those things which were not so, and which the king could not grant, but held for the common use, the duke necessarily held for the same use, and in the same way.

Let us see, then, upon what principle the king held the subject matter of this inquiry; what right he had in it, and how far he could dispose of it.

Every thing susceptible of property is considered as belonging to the nation that possesses the country, and as forming the entire mass of its wealth. But the nation does not possess all those things in the same manner. By very far the greater part of them are divided among the individuals of the nation, and become private property. Those things not divided among the individuals still belong to the nation, and are called public property. Of these, again, some are reserved for the necessities of the state, and are used for the public benefit, and those are called "the domain of the crown or of the republic;" others remain common to all the citizens, who take of them and use them, each according to his necessities, and according to the laws which regulate their use, and are called common property. Of this latter kind, according to the writers upon the law of nature and of nations, and upon the civil law, are the air, the running water, the sea, the fish, and the wild beasts. *Vattel lib. i, 20. 2 Black. Com.* 14. But inasmuch as the things which constitute this common property are things in which a sort of transient usufructuary possession, only, can be had; and inasmuch as the title to them and to the soil by which they are supported, and to which they are appurtenant, cannot well, according to the common law notion of title, be vested in all the people; therefore, the wisdom of that law has placed it in the hands of the sovereign power, to be held, protected, and regulated for the common use and benefit. But still, though this title, strictly speaking, is in the sovereign, yet the use is common to all the people. This principle, with respect to rivers and arms of the sea, is clearly maintained in the case of the royal fishery upon the Banne, in Ireland....

In Lord Fitzwalter's case, (1 Mod. 105) it is said, that in an action of trespass for fishing in a river, where the tide flows and reflows, it is a good justification to say, that ... *prima facie*, the fishing is common to all. In *Warren v. Matthews*, (6 Mod. 73) we are told every subject of common right may fish with lawful nets in a navigable river, as well as in the sea, and the king's grant cannot bar him thereof. Same case (Salk. 357). *Carter v. Marcott* (Bun. 2162). In navigable rivers, the fishery is common, it is prima facie in the king, but is public and for the common use.

Nothing can be more clear, therefore, than, that part of the property of a nation which has not been divided among the individuals, and which Vattel calls public property, is divided into two kinds, one destined for the use of the nation in its aggregate national capacity, being a source of the public revenue, to defray the public expense, called the domain of the crown, and the other destined for the common use and immediate enjoyment of every individual citizen, according to his necessity, being the immediate gift of nature to all men, and, therefore, called the common property. The title of both these, for the greater order, and, perhaps, of necessity, is placed in the hands of the sovereign power, but it is placed there for different purposes. The citizen cannot enter upon the domain of the crown and apply it, or any part of it, to his immediate use. He cannot go into the king's forests and fall and carry away the trees, though it is the public property; it is placed in the hands of the king for a different purpose, it is the domain of the crown, a source of revenue; so neither can the king intrude upon the common property, thus understood, and appropriate it to himself, or to the fiscal purposes of the nation, the enjoyment of it is a natural right which cannot be infringed or taken away, unless by arbitrary power; and that, in theory at least, could not exist in a free government, such as England has always claimed to be.

But if this be so it will be asked, how does it happen that in England, whose polity in this respect we are now examining, we find not only navigable rivers, but also arms of the sea, ports, harbours, and certain portions of the main sea itself upon the coasts, and all the fisheries appertaining to them in the hands of individuals. That the fact is so cannot be controverted; but how it became so is not so easy, at this period of time, satisfactorily to [show]. So far as it depends upon royal grant, however, it seems pretty clear that it has always been considered as an encroachment upon the common rights of the people.

* * *

Lord Hale says, "the sea, and the arms of the sea, and the navigable rivers in which the tide ebbs and flows, are of the dominion of the king, as of his proper inheritance; and that this dominion, embraces, also, the shores, litora, the spaces covered with the slime and mud deposited by the water between the high and the low water mark, in the ordinary flow and reflow of the tide; that this dominion consists, first, in the right of jurisdiction which he exercises by his maritime courts; and, secondly, in the right of fishing in the waters; but that though the king is the owner of these waters, and, as consequent of his property, hath the primary right of fishing therein, yet the common people of England have regularly a liberty of fishing in the sea, and the creeks and the arms thereof, as a public common piscary, and may not, without injury to their right, be restrained thereof." This is his general doctrine.

* * *

Then as to the case of the Banne water in Ireland. It was this: the plaintiff had obtained a royal grant for the territory of Rout, adjoining the river Banne.... And the question was, whether this fishery passed by the grant? and it was held, that it did not; not indeed, upon the principle, that the king could not grant in that case, but upon the construction of the grant.

In the discussion of the case, however, it was laid down, "that every navigable river, so far as the tide ebbs and flows, is a royal river, and that the fishery of it is a royal fishery, and belongs to the king by his prerogative; arid the reason is, that the river participates of the nature of the sea, and is said to be a branch of the sea so far as it flows; and the sea is not only under the dominion of the king, but it is also his proper inheritance, and, therefore, he shall have the land gained out of it, and also the grand fishes of the sea, such as whales, sturgeons, etc., which are royal fish, and no subject can have them without the king's special grant; and he shall have the wild swans also, as royal fowls, on the sea and its branches."

* * *

Upon the whole, therefore, I am of opinion, as I was at the trial, that by the law of nature, which is the only true foundation of all the social rights; that by the civil law, which formerly governed almost the whole civilized world, and which is still the foundation of the polity of almost every nation in Europe; that by the common law of England, of which our ancestors boasted, and to which it were well if we ourselves paid a more sacred regard; I say I am of opinion, that by all these, the navigable rivers in which the tide ebbs and flows, the ports, the bays, the coasts of the sea, including both the water and the land under the water, for the purpose of passing and repassing, navigation, fishing, fowling, sustenance, and all the other uses of the water and its products (a few things excepted) are common to all the citizens, and that each has a right to use them according to his necessities, subject only to the laws which regulate that use; that the property, indeed, strictly speaking, is vested in the sovereign, but it is vested in him not for his own use, but for the use of the citizen, that is, for his direct and immediate enjoyment.

I am of opinion, that this great principle of the common law was, in ancient times, in England gradually encroached upon and broken down; that the powerful barons, in some instances, appropriated to themselves these common rights; that the kings themselves, also, in some instances during the same period, granted them out to their courtiers and favourites; and that these seizures and these royal favours are the ground of all the several fisheries in England, now claimed either by prescription or by grant; that the great charter, as it is commonly called, which was nothing but a restoration of common right, though it did not annul, but confirmed, what had been thus tortiously done, yet restored again the principles of the common law, in this as well as in many other respects; and since that time no king of England has had the power of granting away these common rights, and thereby despoiling the subject of the enjoyment of them.

I am of opinion, that when Charles II took possession of this country, by his right of discovery, he took possession of it in his sovereign capacity; that he had the same right in it, and the same power over it, as he had in and over his other dominions, and no more; that this right consisted chiefly in the power of granting the soil to private citizens for the purposes of settlement and colonization, of establishing a government, of appointing a governor, of conveying to him all those things appurtenant to the sovereignty, commonly called royalties, for the benefit of colonists; but that he could not, and never did, so grant what is called the common property as to convert it into private property; that these royalties, therefore, which constitute that common property of which the rivers, bays, ports, and coasts of the sea were part, by the grant of king Charles, passed to the duke of York, the governor of the province exercising the royal authority for the public benefit, and not as the proprietor of the soil, and for his own private use; and that if they passed from the duke of York to his grantees, which is a very doubtful question, then, upon the surrender of the government, as appurtenant thereto, and inseparable therefrom, they reverted to the crown of England.

And I am further of opinion, that, upon the Revolution, all these royal rights became vested in the people of New Jersey as the sovereign of the country, and are now in their hands; and that they, having, themselves, both the legal title and the usufruct, may make such disposition of them, and such regulation concerning them, as they may think fit; that this power of disposition and regulation must be exercised by them in their sovereign capacity; that the legislature is their rightful representative in this respect, and, therefore, that the legislature, in the exercise of this power, may lawfully erect ports, harbours, basins, docks, and wharves on the coasts of the sea and in the arms thereof, and in the navigable rivers; that they may bank off those waters and reclaim the land upon the shores; that they may build dams, locks, and bridges for the improvement of the navigation and the ease of passage; that they may clear and improve fishing places, to increase the product of the fishery; that they may create, enlarge, and improve oyster beds, by planting oysters therein in order to procure a more ample supply; that they may do these things, themselves, at the public expense, or they may authorize others to do it by their own labour, and at their own expense, giving them reasonable tolls, rents, profits, or exclusive and temporary enjoyments; but still this power, which may be thus exercised by the sovereignty of the state, is nothing more than what is called the *jus regium* [i.e., the police power—Eds.], the right of regulating, improving, and securing for the common benefit of every individual citizen. The sovereign power itself, therefore, cannot, consistently with the principles of the law of nature and the constitution of a well ordered society, make a direct and absolute grant of the waters of the state, divesting all the citizens of their common right. It would be a grievance which never could be long borne by a free people.

From this statement, it is seen that, in my opinion, the proprietors, as such, never had, since the surrender of the government, any such right to, interest in, or power over, these waters, or the land covered by them, as that they could convey the same and convert them into private property; and that, therefore, the grant in question is void, and ought not to prevail for the benefit of the plaintiff, and, of course, that the rule to show cause must be discharged.

Notes

1. *Arnold v. Mundy* was a test case, occasioned by a Benjamin Mundy-led fleet of oyster boats up the Raritan River, challenging Robert Arnold's claim of an exclusive fishery based on his ownership of riparian land. Both were eager to "try the right." As Bonnie McCay recounted in OYSTER WARS AND THE PUBLIC TRUST: PROPERTY, LAW, AND ECOLOGY IN NEW JERSEY HISTORY 45–47 (1998), this was a "social action, intended not just to grab a few oysters, but to get the attention of the courts." Arnold proceeded to sue Mundy in local county court, and Mundy defended on the basis that Arnold could not exclude fishers from a navigable river, claiming that everyone had a common right to harvest oysters in a navigable water. The dispute produced the first significant articulation of the public trust doctrine in America.

2. Chief Justice Andrew Kirkpatrick, who served on the New Jersey Supreme Court for over a quarter-century and as Chief Justice for over twenty years, not only upheld Mundy's rights to harvest, he ruled that Arnold didn't own the bed of the Raritan River. Instead, the state owned the riverbed. The assumption was that public riverbed ownership was necessary to public access to the oysters, which might have been due to the fact that oyster beds are attached to the riverbed. But isn't it conceivable that the public might have rights to fish in privately-owned riverbeds, on the theory that the public trust impressed a public easement on the waterway, regardless of bed ownership?

3. The case relied on the Irish case, *Royal Fishery of the Banne*, 80 Eng. Rep. 540, 152, 155 (K.B. 1611), involving rights to fish for salmon on an Irish tidal river, in which the court divided rivers into navigable and non-navigable waters, based on tidal influence. The former were royal rivers belonging to the King; the latter were owned by riparian landown-

ers. The case began the link between public rights to fish and the navigability of the waterway.

4. The decision also mentions Emer de Vattel's treatise, The Law of Nations (1758, English translation, 1760), which reiterated the Justinian claims about the public nature of "the air, the running water, the sea, the fish, and the wild beasts." Vattel, who was influenced by the writings of Gottfried Leibniz and Hugo Grotius, was read widely by the Revolutionary generation, including Benjamin Franklin and George Washington.

5. Justice Kirkpatrick relied heavily on Sir Matthew Hale's treatise in support of his conclusion of the paramount role of public rights. Hale's treatise De Jure Maris, written around 1660, was not published until 1786, thirty-five years before the *Arnold v. Mundy* decision. Hale maintained that although the English King "owned" navigable waters, the public had a right to fish in them—"a public common piscary...." Based largely on Hale, Kirkpatrick concluded that both the water and the bed of navigable waters are publicly held, and that all citizens have the right to navigate and fish in navigable waters, subject to regulation. This public property was, according to Kirkpatrick, vested in the sovereign for use by its citizens.

6. Kirkpatrick acknowledged that the public's property right had been encroached by both kings and barons, and claimed that the Magna Carta was designed to restore the public's rights by limiting the king's power to alienate common property rights.

7. Note that, according to Justice Kirkpatrick, the discovery doctrine gave the king sovereign ownership of New Jersey, which passed to the state after the Revolutionary War. Sovereign ownership gave the king the power to grant "the soil" to individuals and to establish a government. But it did not give the right to convert public property in rivers, bays, ports, and coasts into private property. Although the state legislature could authorize the filling, damming, and reclamation of waterways, it could not make a "direct and absolute grant of the waters of the state," divesting citizens of their common rights consistent with the "law of nature and the constitution of a well ordered society." This latter insight of the limits of the state's sovereign powers—a restraint on alienation—presaged the U.S. Supreme Court's 1892 decision in the *Illinois Central Railroad* decision (p. 68). Justice Kirkpatrick stated that making an absolute grant of the waters of the state would "be a grievance which never could be long borne by a free people." Does this language underscore a sense of popular sovereignty underlying the trust? Does it suggest that the trust ranks fundamental to democracy by protecting public access to resources needed for the citizens' welfare? The statement was quoted in the *Illinois Central Railroad* decision as well. *Illinois Central Railroad Co. v. Illinois*, 146 U.S. 387, 456 (1892).

8. Another adumbration of *Illinois Central* was the distinction Justice Kirkpatrick drew between public lands "destined for the use of the nation in its aggregate national capacity, being a source of the public revenue, to defray the public expense, called the *domain of the crown*, and the other destined for the common use and immediate enjoyment of every individual citizen, according to his necessity, being the immediate gift of nature to all men, and, therefore, called the *common property*." The Supreme Court would endorse this distinction between public property destined to raise revenue, perhaps by sale, and public trust property reserved for common use.

9. Observe that Justice Kirkpatrick upheld the doctrine of common ownership despite recognizing its longtime violation in England prior to the Magna Carta. His approach underscores that a legal doctrine should not be defined by its violation.

10. The *Arnold v. Mundy* opinion repeatedly finds the source of the rule that navigable waters are common property, owned by the sovereign in trust, to be in natural law—

or "the principles of the law of nature and the constitution of a well ordered society." Isn't this another way of saying that the public trust doctrine imposes inherent limits on sovereign powers?

Martin v. Waddell's Lessee

Supreme Court of the United States
41 U.S. (16 Pet.) 367 (1842)

[In 1835, William Waddell's lessee filed suit in federal court seeking to eject Merrit Martin and others from harvesting oysters on one hundred acres of submerged lands allegedly owned by Waddell in Raritan Bay, New Jersey, not far from the site of the conflict in *Arnold v. Mundy*, in an apparent attempt to overturn that decision. Waddell, who traced his title to the lands to 17th century grants from the King of England to the Duke of York, prevailed in the lower court, but the Supreme Court reversed in the opinion by Chief Justice Roger Taney below.]

TANEY, C.J.:

* * *

The questions before us arise upon an action of ejectment instituted by the defendant in error, who was the plaintiff in the court below, to recover one hundred acres of land, covered with water, situated in the Township of Perth Amboy in the State of New Jersey. At the trial in the circuit court, the jury found a special verdict, setting forth, among other things, that the land claimed lies beneath the navigable waters of the Raritan River and Bay, where the tide ebbs and flows. And it appears that the principal matter in dispute is the right to the oyster fishery in the public rivers and bays of East New Jersey.

The plaintiff makes title under the charters granted by Charles II to his brother, the Duke of York, in 1664 and 1674, for the purpose of enabling him to plant a colony on this continent.

* * *

The questions ... are—Whether the dominion and propriety in the navigable waters, and in the soils under them, passed, as a part of the prerogative rights annexed to the political powers conferred on the duke? Whether, in his hands, they were intended to be a trust for the common use of the new community about to be established or private property to be parceled out and sold to individuals for his own benefit? And in deciding a question like this, we must not look merely to the strict technical meaning of the words of the letters patent. The laws and institutions of England, the history of the times, the object of the charter, the contemporaneous construction given to it, and the usages under it for the century and more which has since elapsed are all entitled to consideration and weight. It is not a deed conveying private property, to be interpreted by the rules applicable to cases of that description. It was an instrument upon which was to be founded the institutions of a great political community, and in that light it should be regarded and construed.

Taking this rule for our guide, we can entertain no doubt as to the true construction of these letters-patent. The object in view appears upon the face of them. They were made for the purpose of enabling the Duke of York to establish a colony upon the newly discovered continent, to be governed, as nearly as circumstances would permit, according to the laws and usages of England, and in which the duke, his heirs and assigns, were to stand in the place of the King, and administer the government according to the principles of the British Constitution. And the people who were to plant this colony, and to form the political body over which he was to rule, were subjects of Great Britain, accustomed to be governed according to its usages and laws.

It is said by Hale, in his treatise *de Jure Maris*, Harg. Law Tracts 11, when speaking of the navigable waters, and the sea on the coasts within the jurisdiction of the British Crown,

> that although the King is the owner of this great coast, and as a consequent of his propriety, hath the primary right of fishing in the sea, and creeks and arms thereof, yet the common people of England have regularly a liberty of fishing in the sea or creeks or arms thereof as a public common of piscary, and may not, without injury to their right, be restrained of it unless in such places, creeks or navigable rivers, where either the King or some particular subject hath gained a propriety exclusive of that common liberty.

The principle here stated by Hale, as to "the public common of piscary" belonging to the common people of England, is not questioned by any English writer upon that subject. The point upon which different opinions have been expressed is whether, since Magna Carta, "either the King or any particular subject can gain a propriety exclusive of the common liberty." For undoubtedly, rights of fishery, exclusive of the common liberty, are at this day held and enjoyed by private individuals under ancient grants. But the existence of a doubt as to the right of the King to make such a grant, after Magna Carta, would of itself show how fixed has been the policy of that government on this subject for the last six hundred years, and how carefully it has preserved this common right for the benefit of the public. And there is nothing in the charter before us indicating that a different and opposite line of policy was designed to be adopted in that colony. On the contrary, after enumerating in the clause herein before quoted, some of the prerogative rights annexed to the Crown, but not all of them, general words are used, conveying "all the estate, right, title, interest, benefit, advantage, claim and demand" of the King, in the lands and premises before granted. The estate and rights of the King passed to the duke in the same condition in which they had been held by the Crown, and upon the same trusts. Whatever was held by the King, as a prerogative right, passed to the duke in the same character. And if the word "soils" be an appropriate word to pass lands covered with navigable water, as contended for on the part of the defendant in error, it is associated in the letters patent with "other royalties," and conveyed as such. No words are used for the purpose of separating them from the *jura regalia* [rights of the monarch—Eds.] and converting them into private property, to be held and enjoyed by the duke apart from and independent of the political character with which he was clothed by the same instrument.

Upon a different construction it would have been impossible for him to have complied with the conditions of the grant. For it was expressly enjoined upon him as a duty in the government he was about to establish, to make it as near as might be agreeable in their new circumstances to the laws and statutes of England, and how could this be done if in the charter itself this high prerogative trust was severed from the regal authority? If the shores and rivers and bays and arms of the sea and the land under them, instead of being held as a public trust for the benefit of the whole community, to be freely used by all for navigation and fishery, as well for shellfish as floating fish, had been converted by the charter itself into private property, to be parceled out and sold by the duke for his own individual emolument? There is nothing, we think, in the terms of the letters patent nor in the purposes for which it was granted that would justify this construction. And in the judgment of the court, the lands under the navigable waters passed to the grantee as one of the royalties incident to the powers of government, and were to be held by him in the same manner and for the same purposes that the navigable waters of England, and the soils under them, are held by the Crown.

* * *

[W]hen the people of New Jersey took possession of the reins of government and took into their own hands the powers of sovereignty, the prerogatives and regalities which before belonged either to the Crown or the Parliament became immediately and rightfully vested in the state.

* * *

[T]he right now claimed was not seriously asserted on their part before the case of *Arnold v. Mundy*, which suit was not instituted until the year 1818; and upon that occasion, the supreme court of the state held that the claim made by the proprietors was without foundation.

* * *

The question here depends, not upon the meaning of instruments framed by the people of New Jersey, or by their authority, but upon charters granted by the British crown; under which certain rights are claimed by the state, on the one hand, and by private individuals on the other. And if this court had been of opinion, that upon the face of these letters-patent, the question was clearly against the state, and that the proprietors had been derived at their just rights, by the erroneous judgment of the state court [in *Arnold v. Mundy*]; it would, perhaps, be difficult to maintain, that this decision, of itself, bound the conscience of this court. It is, however, unquestionably, entitled to great weight....

Independently, however, of this decision of the supreme court of New Jersey, we are of opinion that the proprietors are not entitled to the rights in question, and the judgment of the circuit court must, therefore, be reversed.

[Justice Thompson dissented, complaining that "[a] majority of the court seems to have adopted the doctrine of *Arnold v. Mundy*," acknowledging that "title to land under a navigable stream of water must be held subject to certain public rights," but maintaining that the scope of those rights—while including navigation and "the right to fish for floating fish"—did not include the right to harvest shellfish attached to submerged lands.]

Notes

1. This case involves another dispute over oyster harvesting, perhaps not surprising in that interstate oyster wars in the 1780s were one of the precipitating events leading to the Constitutional Convention in Philadelphia in 1787. *See, e.g.*, David O. Stewart, The Summer of 1787: The Men Who Invented the Constitution 1–7 (2007) (describing a dispute between Maryland and Virginia over harvesting rights in the Potomac River culminating in an agreement brokered at George Washington's Mount Vernon estate that declared the river to be a "common highway" for the citizens of both states); *cf.*, Northwest Ordinance, art. IV, July 13, 1787, 1 Stat. 50, 52 (1789) ("The navigable waters leading into the Mississippi and St. Laurence, and the carrying places between the same, shall be common highways, and forever free, as well to the inhabitants of the said territory, as to the citizens of the United States....."). *See generally* Bonnie McCay, Oyster Wars and the Public Trust: Property, Law and Ecology in New Jersey History (1998).

2. In *Martin*, Chief Justice Roger Taney essentially adopted the *Arnold v. Mundy* result as the national rule of submerged lands, relying heavily on Sir Matthew Hale. The decision agreed with *Arnold v. Mundy* that the state of New Jersey was successor to the English king, and the king held submerged lands "in his public and regal character, as the representative of the nation; and in trust for them." Therefore, the landowner, Waddell,

could not exclude the harvester, Martin, just as Robert Arnold could not exclude Benjamin Mundy.

3. *Martin* involved a dispute in one of the original thirteen states, which inherited their sovereignty from Britain. Subsequently admitted states, which generally were federal territories before becoming states, raised issues of federalism that the Supreme Court addressed in the following case.

Pollard v. Hagan

Supreme Court of the United States
44 U.S. (3 How.) 212 (1845)

[Alabama became a state in 1819, from territory that Georgia ceded to the federal government in 1802. Pollard claimed title to submerged land in Mobile Bay from a federal patent under an 1836 Act of Congress. Hagan's claim was based on a prior Spanish grant. The trial court ruled for Hagan, and Pollard appealed.]

MCKINLEY, J.:

* * *

We think a proper examination of this subject will show, that the United States never held any municipal sovereignty, jurisdiction, or right of soil in and to the territory, of which Alabama or any of the new states were formed; except for temporary purposes, and to execute the trusts created by the acts of the Virginia and Georgia legislatures, and the deeds of cession executed by them to the United States, and the trust created by the treaty with the French republic, of the 30th of April, 1803, ceding Louisiana.

* * *

Taking the legislative acts of the United States, and the states of Virginia and Georgia, and their deeds of cession to the United States, and giving to each, separately, and to all jointly, a fair interpretation, we must come to the conclusion that it was the intention of the parties to invest the United States with the eminent domain of the country ceded, both national and municipal, for the purposes of temporary government, and to hold it in trust for the performance of the stipulations and conditions expressed in the deeds of cession and the legislative acts connected with them. To a correct understanding of the rights, powers, and duties of the parties to these contracts, it is necessary to enter into a more minute examination of the rights of eminent domain, and the right to the public lands. When the United States accepted the cession of the territory, they took upon themselves the trust to hold the municipal eminent domain for the new states, and to invest them with it, to the same extent, in all respects, that it was held by the states ceding the territories.

* * *

When Alabama was admitted into the union, on an equal footing with the original states, she succeeded to all the rights of sovereignty, jurisdiction, and eminent domain which Georgia possessed at the date of the cession, except so far as this right was diminished by the public lands remaining in the possession and under the control of the United States, for the temporary purposes provided for in the deed of cession and the legislative acts connected with it. Nothing remained to the United States, according to the terms of the agreement, but the public lands.

* * *

We will now inquire into the nature and extent of the right of the United States to these lands, and whether that right can in any manner affect or control the decision of the case before us. This right originated in voluntary surrenders, made by several of the old states, of their waste and unappropriated lands, to the United States, under a resolution of the old Congress, of the 6th of September, 1780, recommending such surrender and cession, to aid in paying the public debt, incurred by the war of the Revolution The object of all the parties to these contracts of cession, was to convert the land into money for the payment of the debt, and to erect new states over the territory thus ceded; and as soon as these purposes could be accomplished, the power of the United States over these lands, as property, was to cease.

* * *

This right of eminent domain over the shores and the soils under the navigable waters, for all municipal purposes, belongs exclusively to the states within their respective territorial jurisdictions, and they and they only, have the constitutional power to exercise it. To give to the United States the right to transfer to a citizen the title to the shores and the soils under the navigable waters, would be placing in their hands a weapon which might be wielded greatly to the injury of state sovereignty, and deprive the states of the power to exercise a numerous and important class of police powers. But in the hands of the states this power can never be used so as to affect the exercise of any national right of eminent domain or jurisdiction with which the United States have been invested by the Constitution. For, although the territorial limits of Alabama have extended all her sovereign power into the sea, it is there, as on the shore, but municipal power, subject to the Constitution of the United States, "and the laws which shall be made in pursuance thereof."

By the preceding course of reasoning we have arrived at these general conclusions: First. The shores of navigable waters, and the soils under them, were not granted by the Constitution to the United States, but were reserved to the states respectively. Second. The new states have the same rights, sovereignty, and jurisdiction over this subject as the original states. Third. The right of the United States to the public lands, and the power of Congress to make all needful rules and regulations for the sale and disposition thereof, conferred no power to grant to the plaintiffs the land in controversy in this case. The judgment of the Supreme Court of the state of Alabama is, therefore, affirmed.

MR. JUSTICE CATRON dissented [opinion omitted].

Notes

1. The *Pollard* Court used the term "eminent domain" to mean the equivalent of "sovereignty."

2. In affirming the trial court, the Supreme Court ruled in favor of a Spanish land grantee that was later recognized by the territorial government over a subsequent federal land grantee. A couple of decades earlier, in *Johnson v. M'Intosh*, 21 U.S. 543 (1823), the Supreme Court ruled in favor of the federal grantee over a grantee of Indians. Why doesn't the federal grantee prevail in this case?

3. By concluding that the federal government could not transfer title to the shores and soils under navigable waters to a private citizen, didn't the Court in fact recognize and impose a trust on the federal government? The federal government held the lands in trust in a proprietary sense for transfer to the states. But even after such transfer, the federal government maintained certain interests in the property to protect national concerns. The Court made clear, "But in the hands of the states this power can never be used so as

to affect the exercise of any national right...." Doesn't the public trust encumber the federal government in carrying out such national interests?

4. Although the *Pollard* opinion suggests that the federal government would not retain and manage federal lands in new states, that has not proved to be the case. *See* 1 George C. Coggins & Robert L. Glicksman, Public Natural Resources Law ch. 1–2 (2d ed. 2014) (explaining how and why the federal government retains roughly thirty percent of the land ownership of the United States). In *United States v. California*, 332 U.S. 19 (1947), the Supreme Court limited *Pollard* to its facts and ruled that the federal government, not the individual coastal states, owned the submerged lands off the coasts of the United States. However, the states turned to Congress, which in 1953 passed the Submerged Lands Act, 43 U.S.C. §§ 1301–1356a, which conveyed to the coastal states title to lands submerged by coastal waters within three miles offshore (three marine leagues in the case of Texas and Florida). The federal government retained ownership of the remaining offshore, now called the outer continental shelf.

5. Despite state ownership of the beds of navigable waters at statehood, the federal government may claim ownership of the overlying waters to carry out the purposes of federal land reservations under the reserved water rights doctrine. *Arizona v. California*, 373 U.S. 546, 596–97 (1963) (holding that the *Pollard* rule applied only to the ownership of submerged lands, not to other federal lands or the water flowing through them); *see generally* 2 Waters and Water Rights, ch. 37 (Amy K. Kelley ed., 3rd ed. 2014) (explaining the reserved rights doctrine in detail).

6. Professor Robert Emmet Clark once succinctly described the *Pollard* rule that awarded newly admitted states only the beds of navigable waters while leaving the remaining public lands in the hands of the federal government as "ridiculous, but true." 1 Waters and Water Rights 251 (1967).

7. The *Pollard* decision awarded to newly admitted states the beds of navigable waters to put them on an "equal footing" with the original states. States have equal representation in the U.S. Senate, but they are hardly equal in the House of Representatives. They also are equal in ownership of lands submerged beneath navigable waters. Nevertheless, the question of what constitutes a "navigable water" is one of the more complex issues in natural resources law. We take up the navigability concept and its implications in chapter 3.

Illinois Central Railroad Co. v. Illinois

Supreme Court of the United States
146 U.S. 387 (1892)

[In 1869, the Illinois legislature passed a statute granting "all the right and title" of one square mile of submerged lands in Lake Michigan to Illinois Central Railroad to construct wharves, piers, docks, and other facilities in Chicago harbor. In 1873, the legislature repealed the statute and revoked the grant. Ten years later, in 1883, the state attorney general filed suit against the railroad, alleging that the railroad's construction of improvements in Chicago harbor was on submerged lands owned by the state. The railroad defended on the ground that the grant in the 1869 act was valid. The case reached the Supreme Court in 1892, producing the following opinion.]

FIELD, J.:

* * *

The act, if valid and operative to the extent claimed, placed under the control of the railroad company nearly the whole of the submerged lands of the harbor, subject only to the limitations that it should not authorize obstructions to the harbor, or impair the public right of navigation, or exclude the legislature from regulating the rates of wharfage or dockage to be charged. With these limitations, the act put it in the power of the company to delay indefinitely the improvement of the harbor, or to construct as many docks, piers, and wharves and other works as it might choose, and at such positions in the harbor as might suit its purposes, and permit any kind of business to be conducted thereon, and to lease them out on its own terms for indefinite periods. The inhibition against the technical transfer of the fee of any portion of the submerged lands was of little consequence when it could make lease for any period, and renew it at its pleasure; and the inhibitions against authorizing obstructions to the harbor and impairing the public right of navigation placed no impediments upon the action of the railroad company which did not previously exist. A corporation created for one purpose, the construction and operation of a railroad between designated points, is by the act converted into a corporation to manage and practically control the harbor of Chicago, not simply for its own purpose as a railroad corporation, but for its own profit generally.

The circumstances attending the passage of the act through the legislature were on the hearing the subject of much criticism. As originally introduced, the purpose of the act was to enable the city of Chicago to enlarge its harbor, and to grant to it the title and interest of the state to certain lands adjacent to the shore of Lake Michigan, on the eastern front of the city, and place the harbor under its control; giving it all the necessary powers for its wise management. But during the passage of the act its purport was changed. Instead of providing for the cession of the submerged lands to the city, it provided for a cession of them to the railroad company. It was urged that the title of the act was not changed to correspond with its changed purpose, and an objection was taken to its validity on that account. But the majority of the court were of opinion that the evidence was insufficient to show that the requirement of the constitution of the state, in its passage, was not complied with.

The question, therefore, to be considered, is whether the legislature was competent to thus deprive the state of its ownership of the submerged lands in the harbor of Chicago, and of the consequent control of its waters; or, in other words, whether the railroad corporation can hold the lands and control the waters by the grant, against any future exercise of power over them by the state.

That the state holds the title to the lands under the navigable waters of Lake Michigan, within its limits, in the same manner that the state hold title to soils under tide water ... we have already shown; and that title necessarily carries with it control over the waters above them, whenever the lands are subjected to use. But it is a title different in character from that which the state holds in lands intended for sale. It is different from the title which the United States hold in the public lands which are open to pre-emption and sale. It is a title held in trust for the people of the state, that they may enjoy the navigation of the waters, carry on commerce over them, and have liberty of fishing therein, freed from the obstruction or interference of private parties. The interest of the people in the navigation of the waters and in commerce over them may be improved in many instances by the erection of wharves, docks, and piers therein, for which purpose the state may grant parcels of the submerged lands; and, so long as their disposition is made for such purpose, no valid objections can be made to the grants....

But that is a very different doctrine from the one which would sanction the abdication of the general control of the state over lands under the navigable waters of an entire harbor or bay, or of a sea or lake. Such abdication is not consistent with the exercise of that trust which requires the government of the state to preserve such waters for the use of the public. The trust devolving upon the state for the public, and which can only be discharged by the management and control of property in which the public has an interest, cannot be relinquished by a transfer of the property. The control of the state for the purposes of the trust can never be lost, except as to such parcels as are used in promoting the interests of the public therein, or can be disposed of without any substantial impairment of the public interest in the lands and waters remaining....

A grant of all the lands under the navigable waters of a state has never been adjudged to be within the legislative power; and any attempted grant of the kind would be held, if not absolutely void on its face, as subject to revocation. The state can no more abdicate its trust over property in which the whole people are interested, like navigable waters and soils under them, so as to leave them entirely under the use and control of private parties, except in the instance of parcels mentioned for the improvement of the navigation and use of the waters, or when parcels can be disposed of without impairment of the public interest in what remains, than it can abdicate its police powers in the administration of government and the preservation of the peace. In the administration of government the use of such powers may for a limited period be delegated to a municipality or other body, but there always remains with the state the right to revoke those powers and exercise them in a more direct manner, and one more conformable to its wishes. So with trusts connected with public property, or property of a special character, like lands under navigable waters; they cannot be placed entirely beyond the direction and control of the state.

The harbor of Chicago is of immense value to the people of the state of Illinois, in the facilities it affords to its vast and constantly increasing commerce; and the idea that its legislature can deprive the state of control over its bed and waters, and place the same in the hands of a private corporation, created for a different purpose, — one limited to transportation of passengers and freight between distant points and the city, — is a proposition that cannot be defended.

The area of the submerged lands proposed to be ceded by the act in question to the railroad company embraces something more than 1,000 acres, being, as stated by counsel, more than three times the area of the outer harbor, and not only including all of that harbor, but embracing — adjoining submerged lands, which will, in all probability, be hereafter included in the harbor. It is as large as that embraced by all the merchandise docks along the Thames at London; is much larger than that included in the famous docks and basins at Liverpool; is twice that of the port of Marseilles, and nearly, if not quite, equal to the pier area along the waterfront of the city of New York. And the arrivals and clearings of vessels at the port exceed in number those of New York, and are equal to those of New York and Boston combined. Chicago has nearly 25 percent of the lake carrying trade, as compared with the arrivals and clearings of all the leading ports of our great inland seas. In the year ending June 30, 1886, the joint arrivals and clearances of vessels at that port amounted to 22,096, with a tonnage of over 7,000,000; and in 1890 the tonnage of the vessels reached nearly 9,000,000. As stated by counsel, since the passage of the lake front act, in 1869, the population of the city has increased nearly 1,000,000 souls, and the increase of commerce has kept pace with it. It is hardly conceivable that the legislature can divest the state of the control and management of this harbor, and vest it absolutely in a private Corporation. Surely an act of the legislature transferring the title to its submerged lands and the power claimed by the railroad company to a foreign state or nation would be repudiated, without hesitation, as a gross perversion of the trust over the property under which it is held. So would a similar transfer to a corporation of another state. It would not be listened to that the control and management of the harbor of that great city—a subject of concern to the whole people of the state—should thus be placed elsewhere than in the state itself. All the objections which can be urged to such attempted transfer may be urged to a transfer to a private corporation like the railroad company in this case.

Any grant of the kind is necessarily revocable, and the exercise of the trust by which the property was held by the state can be resumed at any time. Undoubtedly there may be expenses incurred in improvements made under such a grant, which the state ought to pay; but, be that as it may, the power to resume the trust whenever the state judges best is, we think, incontrovertible. The position advanced by the railroad company in support of its claim to the ownership of the submerged lands, and the right to the erection of wharves, piers, and docks at its pleasure, or for its business in the harbor of Chicago, would place every harbor in the country at the mercy of a majority of the legislature of the state in which the harbor is situated.

We cannot, it is true, cite any authority where a grant of this kind has been held invalid, for we believe that no instance exists where the harbor of a great city and its commerce have been allowed to pass into the control of any private corporation. But the decisions are numerous which declare that such property is held by the state, by virtue of its sovereignty, in trust for the public. The ownership of the navigable waters of the harbor, and of the lands under them, is a subject of public concern to the whole people of the state. The trust with which they are held, therefore, is governmental, and cannot be alienated, except in those instances mentioned, of parcels used in the improvement of the interest thus held, or when parcels can be disposed of without detriment to the public interest in the lands and waters remaining.

This follows necessarily from the public character of the property, being held by the whole people for purposes in which the whole people are interested....

In *Newton v. Commissioners*, 100 U.S. 548, it appeared that by an act passed by the legislature of Ohio, in 1846, it was provided that upon the fulfillment of certain conditions by the proprietors or citizens of the town of Canfield, the county seat should be permanently established in that town. Those conditions having been complied with, the county seat was established therein accordingly. In 1874 the legislature passed an act for the removal of the county seat to another town. Certain citizens of Canfield thereupon filed their bill, setting forth the act of 1846, and claiming that the proceedings constituted an executed contract, and prayed for an injunction against the contemplated removal. But the court refused the injunction, holding that there could be no contract and no irrepealable law upon governmental subjects, observing that legislative acts concerning public interests are necessarily public laws; that every succeeding legislature possesses the same jurisdiction and power as its predecessor; that the latter have the same power of repeal and modification which the former had of enactment, neither more nor less; that all occupy in this respect a footing of perfect equality; that this is necessarily so in the nature of things; that it is vital to the public welfare that each one should be able, at all times, to do whatever the varying circumstances and present exigencies attending the subject may require; and that a different result would be fraught with evil.

As counsel observe, if this is true doctrine as to the location of a county seat it is apparent that it must apply with greater force to the control of the soils and beds of navigable waters in the great public harbors held by the people in trust for their common use and of common right as an incident to their sovereignty. The legislature could not give away nor sell the discretion of its successors in respect to matters, the government of which, from the very nature of things, must vary with varying circumstances. The legislation which may be needed one day for the harbor may be different from the legislation that may be required at another day. Every legislature must, at the time of its existence, exercise the power of the State in the execution of the trust devolved upon it. We hold, therefore, that any attempted cession of the ownership and control of the State in and over the submerged lands in Lake Michigan, by the act of April 16, 1869, was inoperative to affect, modify or in any respect to control the sovereignty and dominion of the State over the lands, or its ownership thereof, and that any such attempted operation of the act was annulled by the repealing act of April 15, 1873, which to that extent was valid and effective. There can be no irrepealable contract in a conveyance of property by a grantor in disregard of a public trust, under which he was bound to hold and manage it.

* * *

MR. JUSTICE SHIRAS, [with whom concurred MR. JUSTICE GRAY and MR. JUSTICE BROWN] dissenting.

* * *

[We agree that the State cannot part,] by contract, with her sovereign powers. The railroad company takes and holds these lands subject at all times to the same sovereign powers in the state as obtain in the case of other owners of property. Nor can the grant in this case be regarded as in any way hostile to the powers of the general government in the control of harbors and navigable waters.

The able and interesting statement, in the opinion of the majority, of the rights of the public in the navigable waters, and of the limitation of the powers of the state to part with its control over them, is not dissented from. But its pertinency in the present discussion is not clearly seen. It will be time enough to invoke the doctrine of the inviolability of public rights when and if the railroad company shall attempt to disregard them.

Should the state of Illinois see in the great and unforeseen growth of the city of Chicago and of the lake commerce reason to doubt the prudence of her legislature in entering into the contract created by the passage and acceptance of the act of 1869, she can take the rights and property of the railroad company in these lands by a constitutional condemnation of them. So, freed from the shackles of an undesirable contract, she can make, as she expresses in her bill a desire to do, a "more advantageous sale or disposition to other parties," without offense to the law of the land.

* * *

Notes

1. The *Illinois Central* decision was 4–3, with Chief Justice Melvin Fuller recusing himself because, as a counsel to the City of Chicago before his appointment to the Supreme Court, he headed a consortium that also sought to develop the city's outer harbor as a competitor to the railroad. *See* Joseph D. Kearney & Thomas W. Merrill, *The Origins of the American Public Trust Doctrine: What Really Happened in* Illinois Central, 71 U. Chi. L. Rev. 799 (2004) (noting that downstate legislators favored the grant to the railroad because its operations were subject to a seven percent gross receipts tax, but acknowledging the weight of evidence suggests some bribery of legislators).

2. Although not the first U.S. judicial pronouncement on the public trust, *Illinois Central* is widely considered to be the lodestar decision of the field. Particularly important is the Court's view of the public trust as setting limits on legislative sovereignty. Note that the Court emphasized that all legislatures "occupy ... a footing of perfect equality," and that "[t]he legislature could not give away nor sell the discretion of its successors in re-

spect to matters, the government of which, from the very nature of things, must vary with varying circumstances." Note the Court's reliance on *Newton v. Commissioners*, 100 U.S. 548 (1879) (concerning the location of a county seat in Ohio), for this proposition of temporal equal footing of legislatures. Isn't this another way of saying that sovereign power is limited by a concern for future generations?

One of the deeper interpretations of *Illinois Central* was offered by Professor Douglas Grant, who surmised that the origins of the PTD as expressed by Justice Field lie in the federal constitutional reserved power doctrine. Douglas L. Grant, *Underpinnings of the Public Trust Doctrine: Lessons from* Illinois Central Railroad, 33 Ariz. St. L.J. 849 (2001). That doctrine first emerged in an early body of jurisprudence geared toward defining basic duties of government. It allows a legislature to repudiate contracts bargaining away or limiting essential sovereign powers. The *Newton v. Commissioners* case, discussed above, was in that doctrinal lineage.

As Professor Grant explained, the reserved powers doctrine makes clear that essential sovereign powers are implicitly reserved to the legislature in perpetuity, and are inalienable such that they could "'neither be abdicated nor bargained away ... even by express grant.'" *Id.* at 856 (citing *Atl. Coast Line R.R. Co. v. Goldsboro*, 232 U.S. 548, 558 (1914)). This principle prevents one legislature from taking actions that would compromise a future legislature's ability to exercise sovereignty on behalf of its citizens. Because of the crucial public character of submerged lands—described as a "subject of concern to the whole people"—these lands were clothed with sovereign interests and could not be conveyed away by any one legislature under the reserved powers doctrine. Isn't this interpretation consistent with Justice Field's words, "[a] grant of all the lands under the navigable waters of a State has never been adjudged to be within the legislative power...."? Allowing one legislature to privatize submerged lands, Justice Field admonished, "would place every harbor in the country at the mercy of a majority of the legislature of the state in which the harbor is situated." Isn't this tantamount to saying that the public trust doctrine imposes inherent limits on sovereignty?

3. The source of Justice Field's decision has mystified many scholars. He relied on no state law, leaving the implication that the public trust is of federal origin. *See* Charles F. Wilkinson, *The Headwaters of the Public Trust* (p. 41) (noting that *Illinois Central* "seems plainly to have been premised on federal law"). Ensuing Supreme Court decisions, such as *Shively v. Bowlby* (p. 77) and *Appleby v. New York*, 271 U.S. 364 (1926), have assumed that the doctrine is grounded in state law, but the vast majority of state court interpretations of *Illinois Central* consider it to be binding authority. *See* Crystal S. Chase, *The* Illinois Central *Public Trust Doctrine and Federal Common Law: An Unconventional View*, 16 Hastings W-Nw. J. Envtl. L. & Pol'y 113, 151–53 (2010) (of 35 state courts relying on *Illinois Central*, 29 of them treat it as controlling). In addition to the reserved powers basis explained above, other federal sources of authority include federal common law, *see id.* at 141–43; the equal protection clause, *see* Richard A. Epstein, *The Public Trust Doctrine*, 7 Cato J. 411, 422–28 (1987) (explaining that "[w]hen property is conveyed out of public trust for inadequate consideration, some citizens receive disproportionate benefits, while others receive disproportionate losses"); or the commerce clause, as suggested by Professor Wilkinson in his *Headwaters* article (p. 41).

At least as it applies to submerged lands, many have associated the public trust doctrine with *Pollard v. Hagan's* equal footing doctrine, under which the federal government implicitly conveyed to states the ownership of the beds of navigable waters in statehood acts. The equal footing doctrine is constitutionally grounded on the language authorizing new states "into this Union." *Coyle v. Smith*, 221 U.S. 559 (1911) (striking down a provision of the Oklahoma statehood act limiting the state's ability to move its capital from Guthrie to Oklahoma City as violative of equal footing). The implicit conveyance of equal footing lands to the states came with public trust conditions attached, an argument propounded by Professor Wilkinson's article (p. 41). Also noting the close connection of the equal footing and public trust doctrines are James R. Rasband, *The Disregarded Common Parentage of the Equal Footing and Public Trust Doctrines*, 32 Land & Water L. Rev. 1 (1997); and Harrison C. Dunning, *The Public Trust: A Fundamental Doctrine of American Property Law*, 19 Envtl. L. 515, 524 (1989). Are these separate doctrines, or is one a subset of the other?

Or does the public trust doctrine inhere *solely* in the equal footing grants to the states? Would such an interpretation explain the expansion of the PTD to include resources beyond traditionally navigable waters and to serve purposes other than navigation and fishing? If the trust originates as an inherent limit on legislative power, does that explain why the submerged lands conveyed by the equal footing doctrine carry a trust restriction against privatization? Does this interpretation also underscore the PTD as an attribute of sovereignty compatible with the doctrine's manifestation in other countries, such as the case law discussed in chapter 10?

4. Was the result of the decision that the state could not privatize the harbor, or was it that the state could revoke the grant it made earlier without compensation? In other words, was the grant void as beyond the state's sovereign authority, or was it voidable by a subsequent legislature? The Court's opinion suggests both possibilities. There is a difference: the former imposes a limit on sovereign authority; the latter enables the state to take action to rescind unwise grants. The two need not be exclusive if the latter is viewed as a remedy for a grant exceeding legislative authority.

5. Notice that the three-member dissent authored by Justice Shiras did not question "the rights of the public in the navigable waters, and of the limitation of the powers of the state to part with its control over them." But the dissent maintained that there was no ripe controversy and apparently thought the state's means of using its retained sovereign control was through to "a constitutional condemnation." But isn't there a difference between a condemnation and revocation of a grant on the basis that it was invalid? Doesn't it come down to whether the private grantee deserves compensation? Justice Field's opinion clearly indicates that the original title was invalid to begin with, thus giving no basis for compensation. Professor Rasband, interpreting Justice Field's suggestion that the state *should* pay compensation for taking improvements undertaken by Illinois Central, has propounded a theory that all state assertions of the public trust doctrine should be accompanied by what he calls "equitable compensation." *See* James R. Rasband, *Equitable Compensation for Public Trust Takings*, 69 U. Colo. L. Rev. 331 (1998) (calling for compensation under either a mistaken improver theory or a thorough revision of the public trust doctrine). Would this vitiate the force of the public trust doctrine as a check against privatization?

6. What is distinctive about submerged lands warranting public trust protection? Did Justice Field announce any tests? Can you find a "public concern" test emerging from the descriptions of streambeds as property which "is a subject of public concern to the whole people of the state" and "property of a special character"? Did Justice Field indicate that the trust includes *only* submersible lands and waters above them, or was it more inclusive? Are other resources, such as groundwater and atmosphere, subject to equivalent (or even greater) public concern today? Does the rationale of *Illinois Central* reach to those resources? Note that the traditional focus of the trust was for fishing, navigation and commerce, but cases have expanded the interests protected by the trust to include such matters as recreation and aesthetics, as later chapters will show.

7. Note that the prohibition on conveying streambeds is not absolute. Justice Field created two exceptions, which modern courts apply. One is conveyance of "such parcels as are used in promoting the interests of the public therein" and the other is conveyance of parcels that "can be disposed of without any substantial impairment of the public interest in the lands and waters remaining." One persistent question has to do with changed uses on these parcels over time. What if a parcel is conveyed under one of these two exceptions, but the use later changes so as to undermine the public interest or to cause substantial impairment?

8. Justice Field's majority opinion is perhaps best interpreted as anti-monopolistic, refusing to allow the legislature to authorize a private railroad to control Chicago's harbor. But the evidence suggests that the grant to the railroad would have only supplemented existing facilities by creating a new "outer harbor," making the railroad the largest operator in Chicago harbor but not the only one. *See* THOMAS W. MERRILL & HENRY E. SMITH, PROPERTY: PRINCIPLES AND POLICIES 302 (2d ed. 2012) (suggesting that although he was an ardent free-market advocate, Justice Field was opposed to special privileges for corporations). The outer harbor contemplated in the grant to the railroad was never built. Today, the only commercial facility of any significance in Chicago harbor is Navy Pier, now a popular tourist attraction. *Id.* at 322.

9. Stephen J. Field, who was appointed by Abraham Lincoln, served on the Court for thirty-four years (1863–1897), breaking Chief Justice John Marshall's record for longevity. As a westerner from California, he wrote many influential public lands decisions and was also influential in the Court's adoption of the doctrine of substantive due process to reign in state police powers, which might help explain his unwillingness to rely on the state's police power to regulate the railroad in *Illinois Central*. His reasoning in dissent in the *Slaughter-House Cases*, 83 U.S. 36 (1872), and *Munn v. Illinois*, 94 U.S. 113 (1876), eventually became majority opinions after he left the Court in decisions like *Lochner v. New York*, 198 U.S. 45 (1905).

10. Progeny of *Illinois Central* have invalidated other grants of Lake Michigan submerged lands. *See People ex rel. Scott v. Chicago Park Dist.*, 360 N.E.2d 773 (Ill. 1976) (striking down a grant of 194 acres of submerged lands to U.S. Steel for a proposed mill); *Lake Michigan Federation v. U.S. Army Corps of Engineers*, 742 F.Supp. 441 (N.D. Ill. 1990) (striking down a conveyance of 18 acres to Loyola University). *See also Center for Law in the Public Interest v. Hassell*, 837 P.2d 158 (Ariz. Ct. App. 1991) (ruling that the state could not, consistent with the public trust doctrine and the state constitution's gift clause, convey the beds of navigable waters to private landowners); *Lawrence v. Clark County*, 254 P.3d 606 (Nev. 2011) (applying the public trust doctrine to limit the state legislature's ability to alienate trust lands, including the now-dry riverbed and banks of the historic Colorado River).

One of the most significant modern decisions in the lineage of *Illinois Central* is *Lake Michigan Federation*, cited above. In that case, the federal district court of Illinois invalidated a legislative grant of part of the shoreline of Lake Michigan to Loyola University (a private educational non-profit corporation) and enjoined Loyola's planned fill of the shoreline. Interestingly, while the environmental plaintiffs asserted two claims, one based on the public trust, and one based on a wetlands permit requirement in the Clean Water Act, the court chose to base its decision solely on the broader public trust claim. Loyola planned to expand its campus by filling 18.5 acres of Lake Michigan. The plans called for construction of bike and walking paths, and other areas that the public could use in unrestricted manner. Some of the land was to be used for athletic facilities that the public could access subject to Loyola's ownership rights.

While the legislature had acknowledged that it held the lands in trust for the public, it nonetheless conveyed them to Loyola reasoning that the public would benefit from the lakefill and planned development. Squarely holding the conveyance invalid under the *Illinois Central* precedent, the federal court summarized the public trust obligation as follows:

> Three basic principles can be distilled from [the] body of public trust case law. First, courts should be critical of attempts by the state to surrender valuable public resources to a private entity. Second, the public trust is violated when the primary purpose of a legislative grant is to benefit a private interest. Finally, any attempt by the state to relinquish its power over a public resource should be invalidated under the doctrine.
>
> Applying these criteria to the legislative grant of the lakebed to Loyola, it is apparent that the transfer violates the public trust doctrine. First, while the project has some aspects which are beneficial to the public, the primary purpose of the grant is to satisfy a private interest. Loyola sought and received the grant in order to satisfy its desire for a larger campus. [The] inescapable truth is that the lakebed property will be sacrificed to satisfy Loyola's private needs. Under the public trust doctrine, such a sacrifice cannot be tolerated.

Id. at 445 (citations omitted).

The court's ruling is notable because of its requirement that a grant not be made for the "primary purpose" of satisfying a private interest, however laudable that interest might be (such as education). Recognizing that nearly all grants could be justified by a combination of public and private interests, the court refused to defer to the legislature's determination that this grant would be for public benefit. Its language reflects the same suspicion of legislative intent that characterized the *Illinois Central* opinion and is relevant to any inquiry into the separation of powers between the legislature and courts in determining the scope of the public trust:

> Loyola also argues that we should be deferent to the Illinois legislature's determination that the grant at issue did not violate the public trust. In both the debate before the law was passed and in the legislation itself, the legislature acknowledged that it held the lakebed in trust for the public and declared that the grant would not violate this trust because of the project's numerous public benefits. According to Loyola, we should yield to this specific legislative consideration of public interest.
>
> However, this claim is incorrect both as a matter of logic and precedent. The very purpose of the public trust doctrine is to police the legislature's disposition of public lands. If courts were to rubber stamp legislative decisions, as Loyola advocates, the doctrine would have no teeth. The legislature would have unfettered discretion to breach the public trust as long as it was able to articulate some gain to the public. Moreover, Illinois courts have acknowledged that courts are not encumbered by legislative expressions of public interest. Therefore, we find that the legislative determination that the lakefill would serve the public is no obstacle to our conclusion that the grant was in breach of the public trust.

* * *

What we have here is a transparent giveaway of public property to a private entity. The lakebed of Lake Michigan is held in trust for and belongs to the citizenry of the state. The conveyance of lakebed property to a private party—no matter how reputable and highly motivated that private party may be—violates this public trust doctrine.

Id. at 446–47 (citations omitted).

11. At various times, legislatures have tried to restrict the public trust through statute, thus testing the constitutional force of the doctrine. In Arizona, the legislature passed a statute relinquishing the state's interest in nearly all of the state's watercourses, which the Arizona Court of Appeals invalidated in *Arizona Center for Law in the Public Interest v. Hassell*, cited above, on grounds that both the public trust doctrine and the gift clause in the state's constitution limited conveyances of public property. Relying on *Illinois Central* to determine the limits of state legislative power and emphasizing the role of the judiciary in the constitutional separation of powers, the court stated:

> From *Illinois Central*, we derive the proposition that the state's responsibility to administer its watercourse lands for the public benefit is an inabrogable attribute of statehood itself.

> * * *

> The second grounding for an Arizona law of public trust lies in our constitutional commitment to the checks and balances of a government of divided powers.

> * * *

> Judicial review of public trust dispensations complements the concept of a public trust. Our supreme court said in reviewing a disposition of mineral deposits on school trust lands, "The duties imposed upon the state [are] the duties of a trustee and not simply the duties of a good business manager." Just as private trustees are judicially accountable to their beneficiaries for dispositions of the res, so the legislative and executive branches are judicially accountable for their dispositions of the public trust. The beneficiaries of the public trust are not just present generations but those to come. The check and balance of judicial review provides a level of protection against improvident dissipation of an irreplaceable res.

Id. at 168–69 (citations omitted).

The *Hassell* decision led to a series of legislative attempts to eliminate the public trust doctrine, all invalidated by the judiciary, which construed the trust doctrine as an inherent constitutional limit of sovereignty. See *San Carlos Apache Tribe v. Superior Court ex rel. County of Maricopa*, 972 P.2d 179, 199 (Ariz. 1999) (concluding that legislation that eliminated the public trust doctrine from consideration in water rights adjudications was unconstitutional because, "[t]he public trust doctrine is a constitutional limitation on legislative power to give away resources held by the state in trust for its people."); *Defenders of Wildlife v. Hull*, 18 P.3d 722 (Ariz. Ct. App. 2001) (holding that a statute forfeiting state's interest in certain watercourses was unconstitutional under the public trust doctrine and the gift clause). For an analysis of the Arizona public trust doctrine, see Tracey Dickman Zobenica, *The Public Trust Doctrine in Arizona's Streambeds*, 38 Ariz. L. Rev. 1053, 1058 (1996).

Shively v. Bowlby

Supreme Court of the United States
152 U.S. 1 (1894)

[In 1854, John Shively recorded a land claim in the town of Astoria, including tidelands in the Columbia River, under a federal statute applicable to the Oregon Territory. In 1876, after statehood, the state conveyed to John Bowlby the same tidelands. Bowlby filed suit, claiming that the federal pre-statehood grant passed no title to Shively below the high water mark. Bowlby prevailed in state courts, and Shively appealed to the U.S. Supreme Court.]

GRAY, J.:

I. By the common law, both the title and the dominion of the sea, and of rivers and arms of the sea, where the tide ebbs and flows, and of all the lands below high water mark, within the jurisdiction of the Crown of England, are in the King. Such waters, and the lands which they cover, either at all times or at least when the tide is in, are incapable of ordinary and private occupation, cultivation, and improvement, and their natural and primary uses are public in their nature, for highways of navigation and commerce, domestic and foreign, and for the purpose of fishing by all the King's subjects. Therefore the title, *jus privatum*, in such lands, as of waste and unoccupied lands, belongs to the King, as the sovereign, and the dominion thereof, *jus publicum*, is vested in him as the representative of the nation and for the public benefit.

The great authority in the law of England upon this subject is Lord Chief Justice Hale, whose authorship of the treatise De Jure Maris, sometimes questioned, has been put beyond doubt by recent researches. Moore on the Foreshore (3d ed.) 318, 370, 413. [The Court interpreted Lord Hale to recognize that the King owned tidal waters and the right of fishing therein, but "the common people [have] a liberty of fishing in the sea or creeks or arms thereof, as a public common of piscary...." The opinion proceeded to cite *Martin v. Waddell* and its reliance on *Arnold v. Mundy* for the proposition that King's sovereign and proprietary rights in navigable waters passed in "trust for the common use of the ... community" to the states, "to be freely used by all for navigation and fishery ... not as private property to be parceled out and sold...."]

* * *

III. The governments of the several colonies, with a view to induce persons to erect wharves for the benefit of navigation and commerce, early allowed to the owners of lands bounding on tidewaters greater rights and privileges in the shore, below high-water mark, than they had in England; but the nature and degree of such rights and privileges differed in the different colonies, and in some were created by statute, while in others they rested upon usage only.

* * *

The foregoing summary of the laws of the original states shows that there is no universal and uniform law upon the subject, but that each state has dealt with the lands under the tidewaters within its borders according to its own views of justice and policy, reserving its own control over such lands or granting rights therein to individuals or corporations, whether owners of the adjoining upland or not, as it considered for the best interests of the public. Great caution therefore is necessary in applying precedents in one state to cases arising in another.

* * *

As has been seen, by the law of England, the title in fee, or *jus privatum*, of the king or his grantee, was, in the phrase of Lord Hale, "charged with and subject to that *jus publicum* which belongs to the king's subjects," or, as he elsewhere puts it, "is clothed and superinduced with a *jus publicum*, wherein both natives and foreigners in peace with this kingdom are interested by reason of common commerce, trade, and intercourse." Harg. Law Tracts, 36, 84. In the words of Chief Justice Taney, "the country" discovered and settled by Englishmen "was held by the king, in his public and regal character, as the representative of the nation, and in trust for them;" and the title and the dominion of the tide waters, and of the soil under them, in each colony, passed by the royal charter to the grantees as "a trust for the common use of the new community about to be established," and, upon the American Revolution, vested absolutely in the people of each state, "for their own common use, subject only to the rights since surrendered by the constitution to the general government." *Martin v. Waddell's Lessee*, 16 Pet. 367, 409–11. As observed by Mr. Justice Curtis, "This soil is held by the state, not only subject to, but in some sense in trust for, the enjoyment of certain public rights." *Smith v. Maryland*, 18 How. 71, 74. "The title to the shore and lands under tide water," said Mr. Justice Bradley, "is regarded as incidental to the sovereignty of the state, a portion of the royalties belonging thereto, and held in trust for the public purposes of navigation and fishery." *Hardin v. Jordan*, 140 U.S. 371, 381. And the territories acquired by congress, whether by deed of cession from the original states, or by treaty with a foreign country, are held with the object, as soon as their population and condition justify it, of being admitted into the Union as states, upon an equal footing with the original states in all respects; and the title and dominion of the tide waters, and the lands under them, are held by the United States for the benefit of the whole people, and, as this court has often said, in cases above cited, "in trust for the future states." *Pollard's Lessee v. Hagan*, 3 How. 212, 221, 222; *Weber v. Commissioners*, 18 Wall. 57, 65; *Knight v. Association*, 142 U.S. 161, 183.

* * *

The [Oregon Supreme Court] thus stated its final conclusion:

> From all this, it appears that when the State of Oregon was admitted into the union, the tidelands became its property, and subject to its jurisdiction and disposal; that in the absence of legislation or usage, the common law rule would govern the rights of the upland proprietor, and by that law the title to them is in the state; that the state has the right to dispose of them in such manner as she might deem proper, as is frequently done in various ways, and whereby sometimes large areas are reclaimed and occupied by cities and are put to public and private uses, state control and ownership therein being supreme, subject only to the paramount right of navigation and commerce. The whole question is for the state to determine for itself. It can say to what extent it will preserve its rights of ownership in them or confer them on others. Our state has done that by the legislation already referred to, and our courts have declared its absolute property in and dominion over the tidelands and its right to dispose of its title in such manner as it might deem best, unaffected by any 'legal obligation to recognize the rights of either the riparian owners, or those who had occupied such tidelands' other than it chose to resign to them, subject only to the paramount right of navigation and the uses of commerce. From these considerations it results, if we are to be bound by the previous adjudications of this Court, which have become a rule of property, and upon the faith of which important rights and titles have become vested, and large expenditures have been made and incurred, that the defendants have no rights or interests in the lands in question.

* * *

The conclusions from the considerations and authorities above stated may be summed up as follows:

[1.] Lands under tidewaters are incapable of cultivation or improvement in the manner of lands above high water mark. They are of great value to the public for the purposes of commerce, navigation, and fishery. Their improvement by individuals, when permitted, is incidental or subordinate to the public use and right. Therefore the title and the control of them are vested in the sovereign for the benefit of the whole people.

[2.] At common law, the title and the dominion in lands flowed by the tide were in the King for the benefit of the nation. Upon the settlement of the colonies, like rights passed to the grantees in the royal charters, in trust for the communities to be established. Upon the American Revolution, these rights, charged with a like trust, were vested in the original states within their respective borders, subject to the rights surrendered by the Constitution to the United States.

[3.] Upon the acquisition of a territory by the United States, whether by cession from one of the states, or by treaty with a foreign country, or by discovery and settlement, the same title and dominion passed to the United States for the benefit of the whole people and in trust for the several states to be ultimately created out of the territory.

The new states admitted into the union since the adoption of the Constitution have the same rights as the original states in the tidewaters and in the lands under them, within their respective jurisdictions. The title and rights of riparian or littoral proprietors in the soil below high water mark therefore are governed by the laws of the several states, subject to the rights granted to the United States by the Constitution.

[4.] The United States, while they hold the country as a territory, having all the powers both of national and of municipal government, may grant, for appropriate purposes, titles or rights in the soil below high water mark of tidewaters. But they have never done so by general laws, and, unless in some case of international duty or public exigency, have acted upon the policy, as most in accordance with the interest of the people and with the object for which the territories were acquired, of leaving the administration and disposition of the sovereign rights in navigable waters and in the soil under them to the control of the states, respectively, when organized and admitted into the Union.

Grants by Congress of portions of the public lands within a territory to settlers thereon, though bordering on or bounded by navigable waters convey, of their own force no title or right below high water mark, and do not impair the title and dominion of the future state, when created, but leave the question of the use of the shores by the owners of uplands to the sovereign control of each state, subject only to the rights vested by the Constitution in the United States.

The donation land claim, bounded by the Columbia River, upon which the plaintiff in error relies includes no title or right in the land below high water mark, and the statutes of Oregon under which the defendants in error hold are a constitutional and legal exercise by the State of Oregon of its dominion over the lands under navigable waters. [Consequently, the Supreme Court affirmed the state court decision in favor of the state grantee.]

Notes

1. In *Shively*, the Court had to interpret the scope of a federal land grant under the Oregon Donation Act of 1850, a predecessor to the federal Homestead Act of 1862. Shively staked his claim to both uplands and submerged lands in 1854, when Oregon was still a federal territory. Pre-statehood grants of submerged lands could defeat a state's equal footing lands recognized in *Pollard v. Hagan* (p. 66). How does the Court interpret the scope of the grant under the 1850 Act?

2. The Court suggests that pre-statehood federal grants could be upheld in the case of "international duty" or "public exigency." Some pre-statehood conveyances have been upheld if they meet the Supreme Court's standard of clearly expressed intention. *See, e.g.,* *Utah Div. of State Lands v. United States,* 482 U.S. 193 (1987) (concluding that two pre-statehood statutes did not meet this standard); *United States v. Alaska,* 521 U.S. 1 (1997) (deciding that a Department of Interior withdrawal of lands to create the Arctic National Wildlife Refuge included submerged lands, preventing them from passing to the state at statehood); *Idaho v. United States,* 533 U.S. 262 (2001) (ruling that an Indian reservation that included part of Lake Coeur d'Alene met the standard).

3. *Shively* is sometimes cited as precedent for the proposition that the public trust doctrine has its roots in state, not federal law. Is this accurate? Doesn't it have its roots in the national law of England? Like the decision in *Arnold v. Mundy,* this one clearly articulates the origin of the doctrine as tracing to English law (noting that the *jus publicum* vested in the King "as the representative of the nation and for the public benefit"). It then shows the lineage of the doctrine in the United States, applying initially to the colonies, then to the states and to the federal government when it held land in trust for the states. Given this origin, wouldn't it be more appropriate to call this trust a "sovereign" doctrine rather than a "state" doctrine? Does the public trust arise under federal law or state law, or both? Is it significant that two of the landmark public trust opinions came from the U.S. Supreme Court (*Shively v. Bowlby* and *Illinois Central Railroad v. Illinois*)? Did these opinions just apply the law of the involved states, or did they apply a general doctrine that became, as a matter of federal law, reflected in those states as an attribute of sovereignty?

4. Notice that the Court distinguished the *jus privatum* from the *jus publicum* in tidelands and relied heavily on Sir Matthew Hale's treatise. Hale's book, DE JURE MARIS, discussed earlier (p. 62), was written in the 1660s but not published until 1786, explained the public's "liberty of fishing" which could be displaced "where the King has gained a propriety exclusive of that common liberty." Otherwise, there was a *prima facie* right in the King for the common good.

5. Two years after *Shively,* the Court again applied trust principles in articulating the concept of state sovereign ownership of wildlife. In *Geer v. Connecticut,* 161 U.S. 519, 529 (1896) (p. 221), the Court stated that "the power or control [over wildlife] lodged in the State, resulting from this ownership, is to be exercised, like all other powers of government, as a trust for the benefit of the people, and not as a prerogative for the advantage of the government as distinct from the people, or the benefit of private individuals as distinguished from the public good." Thus, within four years the Supreme Court found trust principles to govern cases involving ownership of the beds of inland navigable waters and coastal tidal waters as well as wildlife.

* * *

The previous foundational cases were all decided in the 19th century. In December 2013, public trust jurisprudence took an extraordinary leap forward when Chief Justice Ronald Castille of the Supreme Court of Pennsylvania articulated foundational principles that explained the sovereign constitutional basis of the trust and the fiduciary duties of the legislature. In a pioneering opinion that represents the most modern comprehensive judicial treatment of the trust, the Court struck down as unconstitutional a statute passed by the Pennsylvania Legislature in 2012 to promote natural gas extraction and "fracking."

The enacted amendments to the Oil and Gas Act ("Act 13") addressed the permitting, funding and fee collection for unconventional gas wells in the Marcellus Shale, a natural gas reservoir beneath the state's surface. Extraction techniques include hydraulic frac-turing or slick-water "fracking." Fracking is a highly controversial process because of its environmental hazards and adverse effects on nearby property owners. It involves pump-ing a mixture of sand, water, and chemicals at high pressure into the rock until the rock breaks, releasing the gas. Each well uses several million gallons of water. Act 13, described by the court as a statute designed to create a "maximally favorable environment" for the natural gas industry to exploit Pennsylvania's resources, prohibited any local regulation of oil and gas operations and required statewide uniformity in local zoning of oil and gas resources. The Act also included waivers of mandatory setbacks, which would have sep-arated gas wells from sensitive water sources.

Citizens and local governments sued the state ("Commonwealth"), seeking an in-junction prohibiting the application of Act 13. They argued that the statute violated the Pennsylvania Constitution, which includes an Environmental Rights Amendment (Arti-cle 1, Section 27) that sets forth public trust duties. The lower court (the Commonwealth Court) found the statute unconstitutional in part, but rejected the citizens' claims that Act 13 violated the Environmental Rights Amendment. On appeal, a majority of the Supreme Court concluded that Act 13 violated the Pennsylvania Constitution. The Court first ad-dressed the issues of standing and justiciability, finding in favor of the citizen plaintiffs on both questions. It specifically rejected the argument that the litigation posed a polit-ical question inappropriate for judicial resolution. The Chief Justice then wrote a plural-ity opinion, joined by two other justices, expounding on the public trust doctrine and holding that Act 13 violated the Environmental Rights Amendment. A fourth justice, Justice Baer, expressed no disagreement with Justice Castille's lead opinion, but wrote separately be-cause he determined that Act 13 violated the state's constitutional due process protection of private property.

Robinson Township v. Pennsylvania

Supreme Court of Pennsylvania
83 A.3d 901 (2013)

[Act 13 was, according to the state, an exercise of its police powers as a "comprehensive reform of the oil and gas laws" of the state in order to promote the development of its "vast natural gas reserves...," while creating jobs and energy self-sufficiency, providing "impact fees" to local governments where drilling occurs, ensuring uniformity of local zoning or-dinances, and "updating" the state's environmental regulation of the oil and gas industry. Amici business groups emphasized that the Marcellus Shale deposit holds "trillions of cubic feet of natural gas," with the capability of meeting present and future demands for natural gas at affordable prices. Robinson Township and the citizens alleged that Act 13 violated the Pennsylvania Constitution, particularly its Environmental Rights Amendment.]

CASTILLE, C.J.:

* * *

3. The Applicable Constitutional Paradigm

The General Assembly derives its power from the Pennsylvania Constitution in Arti-cle III, Sections 1 through 27. The Constitution grants the General Assembly broad and flexible police powers embodied in a plenary authority to enact laws for the purposes of promoting public health, safety, morals, and the general welfare....

[A]lthough plenary, the General Assembly's police power is not absolute; this distinc-tion matters. Legislative power is subject to restrictions enumerated in the Constitution and to limitations inherent in the form of government chosen by the people.... Specifically, ours is a government in which the people have delegated general powers to the General Assembly, but with the express exception of certain fundamental rights reserved to the people in Article I of our Constitution....[2]

Article I is the Commonwealth's Declaration of Rights, which delineates the terms of the social contract between government and the people that are of such "general, great and essential" quality as to be ensconced as "inviolate." P. Const. art. I, Preamble & § 25; *see also* P. Const. art. I, § 2 ("All power is inherent in the people, and all free governments are founded on their authority and instituted for their peace, safety and happiness."). The Declaration of Rights assumes that the rights of the people articulated in Article I of our Constitution—vis-à-vis the government created by the people—are inherent in man's nature and preserved rather than created by the Pennsylvania Constitution....[3]

The first section of Article I "affirms, among other things, that all citizens 'have certain inherent and indefeasible rights.'" *Pap's*, 812 A.2d at 603 (quoting Pa. Const. art. I, § 1). Among the inherent rights of the people of Pennsylvania are those enumerated in Section 27, the Environmental Rights Amendment:

> The people have a right to clean air, pure water, and to the preservation of the natural, scenic, historic and esthetic values of the environment. Pennsylvania's public natural resources are the common property of all the people, including generations yet to come. As trustee of these resources, the Commonwealth shall conserve and maintain them for the benefit of all the people.

PA. Const. art. I, § 27 (Natural resources and the public estate).

* * *

4. Plain Language

Initially, we note that the Environmental Rights Amendment accomplishes two primary goals, via prohibitory and non-prohibitory clauses: (1) the provision identifies protected rights, to prevent the state from acting in certain ways, and (2) the provision establishes a nascent framework for the Commonwealth to participate affirmatively in the development and enforcement of these rights. Section 27 is structured into three mandatory clauses that define rights and obligations to accomplish these twin purposes; and each clause mentions "the people."

A legal challenge pursuant to Section 27 may proceed upon alternate theories that either the government has infringed upon citizens' rights or the government has failed in its trustee obligations, or upon both theories, given that the two paradigms, while serving different purposes in the amendatory scheme, are also related and overlap to a sig-

---

2. A majority of the members of the Court agreed with this construction in *Commonwealth v. Nat'l Gettysburg Battlefield Tower, Inc.*, 311 A.2d 588 (1973) (*Gettysburg*), the first case decided by this Court involving the Environmental Rights Amendment. Mr. Justice Roberts wrote that the Commonwealth, prior to the adoption of Article I, Section 27, "possessed the inherent sovereign power to protect and preserve for its citizens the natural and historic resources now enumerated in Section 27. The express language of the constitutional amendment merely recites the 'inherent and independent rights' of mankind relative to the environment which are 'recognized and unalterably established' by Article I, Section 1 of the Pennsylvania Constitution." *Id.* at 595 (Roberts, J., concurring, joined by Manderino, J.)....

3. The Court's recent decision in *Driscoll v. Corbett*, 69 A.3d 197 (2013) recognized that, in Pennsylvania, "the concept that certain rights are inherent to mankind, and thus are secured rather than bestowed by the Constitution, has a long pedigree in Pennsylvania that goes back at least to the founding of the Republic." *Id.* at 208....

nificant degree. Facing a claim premised upon Section 27 rights and obligations, the courts must conduct a principled analysis of whether the Environmental Rights Amendment has been violated.

* * *

I. First Clause of Section 27 — Individual Environmental Rights

According to the plain language of Section 27, the provision establishes two separate rights in the people of the Commonwealth. The first ... is the declared "right" of citizens to clean air and pure water, and to the preservation of natural, scenic, historic and esthetic values of the environment. This clause affirms a limitation on the state's power to act contrary to this right. While the subject of the right certainly may be regulated by the Commonwealth, any regulation is "subordinate to the enjoyment of the right ... [and] must be regulation purely, not destruction"; laws of the Commonwealth that unreasonably impair the right are unconstitutional.

The terms "clean air" and "pure water" leave no doubt as to the importance of these specific qualities of the environment for the proponents of the constitutional amendment and for the ratifying voters. Moreover, the constitutional provision directs the "preservation" of broadly defined values of the environment, a construct that necessarily emphasizes the importance of each value separately, but also implicates a holistic analytical approach to ensure both the protection from harm or damage and to ensure the maintenance and perpetuation of an environment of quality for the benefit of future generations.

Although the first clause [of Section 27] does not impose express duties on the political branches to enact specific affirmative measures to promote clean air, pure water, and the preservation of the different values of our environment, the right articulated is neither meaningless nor merely aspirational. The corollary of the people's Section 27 reservation of right to an environment of quality is an obligation on the government's behalf to refrain from unduly infringing upon or violating the right, including by legislative enactment or executive action. [E]ach branch of government [must] consider in advance ... the environmental effect of any proposed action on the constitutionally protected features. The failure to obtain information regarding environmental effects does not excuse the constitutional obligation because the obligation exists *a priori* to any statute purporting to create a cause of action.

Moreover, as the citizens argue, the constitutional obligation binds all government, state or local, concurrently....

Also apparent from the language of the constitutional provision are the substantive standards by which we decide a claim for violation of a right protected by the first clause of Section 27. The right to "clean air" and "pure water" sets plain conditions by which government must abide. We recognize that, as a practical matter, air and water quality have relative rather than absolute attributes. Furthermore, state and federal laws and regulations both govern "clean air" and "pure water" standards and, as with any other technical standards, the courts generally defer to agency expertise in making a factual determination whether the benchmarks were met. Accord 35 P.S. § 6026.102(4) (recognizing that General Assembly "has a duty" to implement Section 27 and devise environmental remediation standards). That is not to say, however, that courts can play no role in enforcing the substantive requirements articulated by the Environmental Rights Amendment in the context of an appropriate challenge. Courts are equipped and obliged to weigh parties' competing evidence and arguments, and to issue reasoned decisions regarding constitutional compliance by the other branches of government. The benchmark for decision is the express purpose of the Environmental Rights Amendment to be a bulwark against actual or likely degradation of, *inter alia,* our air and water quality. Accord *Montana Env'l Info. Ctr. v. Dep't of Env'l Quality*, 988 P.2d 1236, 1249 (Mont. 1999) (constitutional "inalienable ... right to a clean and healthful environment" did not protect merely against type of environmental degradation "conclusively linked" to ill health or physical endangerment and animal death, but could be invoked to provide anticipatory and preventative protection against unreasonable degradation of natural resources).

Section 27 also separately requires the preservation of "natural, scenic, historic and esthetic values of the environment." Pa. Const. art. I, § 27. By calling for the "preservation" of these broad environmental values, the Constitution again protects the people from governmental action that unreasonably causes actual or likely deterioration of these features. The Environmental Rights Amendment does not call for a stagnant landscape; nor, as we explain below, for the derailment of economic or social development; nor for a sacrifice of other fundamental values. But, when government acts, the action must, on balance, reasonably account for the environmental features of the affected locale, as further explained in this decision, if it is to pass constitutional muster.

* * *

II. The Second and Third Clauses of Section 27 — The Public Trust

The second right reserved by Section 27 is the common ownership of the people, including future generations, of Pennsylvania's public natural resources. On its terms, the second clause ... applies to a narrower category of "public" natural resources than the first clause of the provision. The drafters, however, left unqualified the phrase public natural resources, suggesting that the term fairly implicates relatively broad aspects of the environment, and is amenable to change over time to conform, for example, with the development of related legal and societal concerns. At present, the concept of public natural resources includes not only state-owned lands, waterways, and mineral reserves, but also resources that implicate the public interest, such as ambient air, surface and ground water, wild flora, and fauna (including fish) that are outside the scope of purely private property. See, e.g., 30 Pa. C.S. § 721 (fish: acquisition of property by Commonwealth); 34 Pa. C.S. § 103(a) (Commonwealth's ownership of game or wildlife); 71 P.S. § 1340.302(a) (acquisition and disposition of Commonwealth-owned forests). See also 35 P.S. §§ 691.1, 691.501, 691.503 (pollution of [state] waters, as broadly defined by act, is public nuisance; protection required); 35 P.S. § 1451 (public interest in quantity of water; authorizes immediate action by governor to conserve natural resources threatened by drought and forest fire); 35 P.S. §§ 4003, 4013 (violation of Air Pollution Control Act and related regulations, orders, permits is public nuisance); 35 P.S. §§ 4501, 4502 (immunity for shooting ranges in public nuisance suits for noise pollution; assumes noise pollution regulated at local level).

* * *

The third clause of Section 27 establishes the Commonwealth's duties with respect to Pennsylvania's commonly-owned public natural resources, which are both negative (*i.e.,* prohibitory) and affirmative (*i.e.,* implicating enactment of legislation and regulations). The provision establishes the public trust doctrine with respect to these natural resources (the corpus of the trust), and designates "the Commonwealth" as trustee and the people as the named beneficiaries. The terms of the trust are construed according to the intent of the settlor which, in this instance, is "the people." *See Estate of Sykes,* 383 A.2d 920, 921 (Pa. 1978) ("To ascertain this intent, a court examines the words of the instrument and, if necessary, the scheme of distribution, the circumstances surrounding execution of the [instrument] and other facts bearing on the question.").

"Trust" and "trustee" are terms of art that carried legal implications well developed at Pennsylvania law at the time the amendment was adopted. The statement offered in the General Assembly in support of the amendment explained the distinction between the roles of proprietor and trustee in these terms:

> Under the proprietary theory, government deals at arms['] length with its citizens, measuring its gains by the balance sheet profits and appreciation it realizes from its resources operations. Under the trust theory, it deals with its citizens as a fiduciary, measuring its successes by the benefits it bestows upon all its citizens in their utilization of natural resources under law.

1970 Pa. Legislative Journal-House at 2273. See also *Nat'l Audubon Soc'y v. Superior Court*, 658 P.2d 709, 724 (Cal. 1983) ("[P]ublic trust is more than an affirmation of state power to use public property for public purposes. It is an affirmation of the duty of the state to protect the people's common heritage of streams, lakes, marshlands and tidelands, surrendering that right of protection only in rare cases when the abandonment of that right is consistent with the purposes of the trust."). The trust relationship does not contemplate a settlor placing blind faith in the uncontrolled discretion of a trustee; the settlor is entitled to maintain some control and flexibility, exercised by granting the trustee considerable discretion to accomplish the purposes of the trust. . . .

* * *

As trustee, the Commonwealth is a fiduciary obligated to comply with the terms of the trust and with standards governing a fiduciary's conduct. The explicit terms of the trust require the government to "conserve and maintain" the corpus of the trust. The plain meaning of the terms conserve and maintain implicates a duty to prevent and remedy the degradation, diminution, or depletion of our public natural resources. As a fiduciary, the Commonwealth has a duty to act toward the corpus of the trust—the public natural resources—with prudence, loyalty, and impartiality.

As the parties here illustrate, two separate Commonwealth obligations are implicit in the nature of the trustee-beneficiary relationship. The first obligation arises from the prohibitory nature of the constitutional clause creating the trust, and is similar to other negative rights articulated in the Declaration of Rights. Stated otherwise, the Commonwealth has an obligation to refrain from performing its trustee duties respecting the environment unreasonably, including via legislative enactments or executive action. As trustee, the Commonwealth has a duty to refrain from permitting or encouraging the degradation, diminution, or depletion of public natural resources, whether such degradation, diminution, or depletion would occur through direct state action or indirectly, *e.g.*, because of the state's failure to restrain the actions of private parties. In this sense, the third clause of the Environmental Rights Amendment is complete because it establishes broad but concrete substantive parameters within which the Commonwealth may act. This Court perceives no impediment to citizen beneficiaries enforcing the constitutional prohibition in accordance with established principles of judicial review.

The second obligation peculiar to the trustee is, as the Commonwealth recognizes, to act affirmatively to protect the environment, via legislative action. Accord *Geer v. Connecticut*, 161 U.S. at 534 (trusteeship for benefit of state's people implies legislative duty "to enact such laws as will best preserve the subject of the trust, and secure its beneficial use in the future to the people of the state"). The General Assembly has not shied from this duty; it has enacted environmental statutes. . . . As these statutes (and related regulations) illustrate, legislative enactments serve to define regulatory powers and duties, to describe prohibited conduct of private individuals and entities, to provide procedural safeguards, and to enunciate technical standards of environmental protection. These administrative details are appropriately addressed by legislation because, like other "great ordinances" in our Declaration of Rights, the generalized terms comprising the Environmental Rights Amendment do not articulate them. The call for complementary legislation, however, does not override the otherwise plain conferral of rights upon the people.

Of course, the trust's express directions to conserve and maintain public natural resources do not require a freeze of the existing public natural resource stock; rather ... the duties to conserve and maintain are tempered by legitimate development tending to improve upon the lot of Pennsylvania's citizenry, with the evident goal of promoting sustainable development.

Within the public trust paradigm of Section 27, the beneficiaries of the trust are "all the people" of Pennsylvania, including generations yet to come. The trust's beneficiary designation has two obvious implications: first, the trustee has an obligation to deal impartially with all beneficiaries and, second, the trustee has an obligation to balance the interests of present and future beneficiaries. Dealing impartially with all beneficiaries means that the trustee must treat all equitably in light of the purposes of the trust. Here, the duty of impartiality implicates questions of access to and distribution of public natural resources, including consumable resources such as water, fish, and game. The second, cross-generational dimension of Section 27 reinforces the conservation imperative: future generations are among the beneficiaries entitled to equal access and distribution of the resources, thus, the trustee cannot be shortsighted. Moreover, this aspect of Section 27 recognizes the practical reality that environmental changes, whether positive or negative, have the potential to be incremental, have a compounding effect, and develop over generations. The Environmental Rights Amendment offers protection equally against actions with immediate severe impact on public natural resources and against actions with minimal or insignificant present consequences that are actually or likely to have significant or irreversible effects in the short or long term.

5. Other considerations

[The Court then described the ecological exploitation that prompted passage of the Environmental Rights Amendment in 1971.] The decision to affirm the people's environmental rights in a Declaration or Bill of Rights, alongside political rights, is relatively rare in American constitutional law....

That Pennsylvania deliberately chose a course different from virtually all of its sister states speaks to the Commonwealth's experience of having the benefit of vast natural resources whose virtually unrestrained exploitation, while initially a boon to investors, industry, and citizens, led to destructive and lasting consequences not only for the environment but also for the citizens' quality of life. Later generations paid and continue to pay a tribute to early uncontrolled and unsustainable development financially, in health and quality of life consequences, and with the relegation to history books of valuable natural and esthetic aspects of our environmental inheritance. The drafters and the citizens of the Commonwealth who ratified the Environmental Rights Amendment, aware of this history, articulated the people's rights and the government's duties to the people in broad and flexible terms that would permit not only reactive but also anticipatory protection of the environment for the benefit of current and future generations. Moreover, public trustee duties were delegated concomitantly to all branches and levels of government in recognition that the quality of the environment is a task with both local and statewide implications, and to ensure that all government neither infringed upon the people's rights nor failed to act for the benefit of the people in this area crucial to the well-being of all Pennsylvanians.

* * *

B. The Relevant Provisions of Act 13

[The Court then turned to Act 13.] Reviewing the amended Act, few could seriously dispute how remarkable a revolution is worked by this legislation upon the existing zoning regimen in Pennsylvania, including residential zones.... The displacement of prior planning, and derivative expectations, regarding land use, zoning, and enjoyment of property is unprecedented.

* * *

C. Article I, Section 27 Rights in Application

... The Commonwealth suggests that Act 13 is an enactment based on valid legislative objectives and, therefore, falls properly within its exclusive discretionary policy judgment.

In contrast, the citizens construe the Environmental Rights Amendment as protecting individual rights and devolving duties upon various actors within the political system; and they claim that breaches of those duties or encroachments upon those rights is, at a minimum, actionable. According to the citizens, this dispute is not about municipal power, statutory or otherwise, to develop local policy, but it is instead about compliance with constitutional duties. Unless the Declaration of Rights is to have no meaning, the citizens are correct.

[The] Environmental Rights Amendment ... delineates limitations on the Commonwealth's power to act as trustee of the public natural resources. [This] constitutional provision speaks on behalf of the people, to the people directly, rather than through the filter of the people's elected representatives to the General Assembly. See Pa. Const. art. I, §§ 25, 27.

The Commonwealth's obligations as trustee to conserve and maintain the public natural resources for the benefit of the people, including generations yet to come, create a right in the people to seek to enforce the obligations....

* * *

The type of constitutional challenge presented today is as unprecedented in Pennsylvania as is the legislation that engendered it. But, the challenge is in response to history seeming to repeat itself: an industry, offering the very real prospect of jobs and other important economic benefits, seeks to exploit a Pennsylvania resource, to supply an energy source much in demand. The political branches have responded with a comprehensive scheme that accommodates the recovery of the resource. By any responsible account, the exploitation of the Marcellus Shale Formation will produce a detrimental effect on the environment, on the people, their children, and future generations, and potentially on the public purse, perhaps rivaling the environmental effects of coal extraction. The litigation response was not available in the nineteenth century, since there was no Environmental Rights Amendment. The response is available now.

The challenge here is premised upon that part of our organic charter that now explicitly guarantees the people's right to an environment of quality and the concomitant expressed reservation of a right to benefit from the Commonwealth's duty of management of our public natural resources. The challengers here are citizens—just like the citizenry that reserved the right in our charter. They are residents or members of local legislative and executive bodies, and several localities directly affected by natural gas development and extraction in the Marcellus Shale Formation. Contrary to the Commonwealth's characterization of the dispute, the citizens seek not to expand the authority of local government but to vindicate fundamental constitutional rights that, they say, have been compromised by a legislative determination that violates a public trust. The Commonwealth's efforts to minimize the import of this litigation by suggesting it is simply a dispute over public policy voiced by a disappointed minority requires a blindness to the reality here and to Pennsylvania history, including Pennsylvania constitutional history; and, the position ignores the reality that Act 13 has the potential to affect the reserved rights of every citizen of this Commonwealth now, and in the future....

* * *

2. Section 3304

* * *

We have explained that, among other fiduciary duties under Article I, Section 27, the General Assembly has the obligation to prevent degradation, diminution, and depletion of our public natural resources, which it may satisfy by enacting legislation that adequately restrains actions of private parties likely to cause harm to protected aspects of our environment. We are constrained to hold that [the statute] falls considerably short of meeting this obligation....

* * *

... Act 13 simply displaces development guidelines, guidelines which offer strict limitations on industrial uses in sensitive zoning districts; instead, Act 13 permits industrial oil and gas operations as a use "of right" in *every zoning district throughout the Commonwealth*, including in residential, commercial, and agricultural districts.... [T]he provision compels exposure of otherwise protected areas to environmental and habitability costs associated with this particular industrial use.... The entirely new legal regime alters existing expectations of communities and property owners and substantially diminishes natural and esthetic values of the local environment, which contribute significantly to a quality of environmental life in Pennsylvania.... In constitutional terms, the Act degrades the corpus of the trust....

A second difficulty arising from [the] requirement that local government permit industrial uses in all zoning districts is that some properties and communities will carry much heavier environmental and habitability burdens than others. This disparate effect is irreconcilable with the express command that the trustee will manage the corpus of the trust for the benefit of "all the people." Pa. Const. art. I, § 27. A trustee must treat all beneficiaries equitably in light of the purposes of the trust.... Act 13's blunt approach fails to account for this constitutional command at all.... Imposing statewide environmental and habitability standards appropriate for the heaviest of industrial areas in sensitive zoning districts lowers environmental and habitability protections for affected residents and property owners below the existing threshold and permits significant degradation of public natural resources. The outright ban on local regulation of oil and gas operations (such as ordinances seeking to conform development to local conditions) that would mitigate the effect, meanwhile, propagates serious detrimental and disparate effects on the corpus of the trust.

To be sure, the Commonwealth and its *amici* make compelling policy arguments that Pennsylvania's populace will benefit from the exploitation of the natural gas found in the Marcellus Shale Formation....

If economic and energy benefits were the only considerations at issue, this particular argument would carry more weight.... [But] [t]o comply with the constitutional command, the General Assembly must exercise its police powers to foster sustainable development in a manner that respects the reserved rights of the people to a clean, healthy, and esthetically-pleasing environment.

For these reasons, we are constrained to hold that the degradation of the corpus of the trust and the disparate impact on some citizens sanctioned by ... Act 13 are incompatible with the express command of the Environmental Rights Amendment. We recognize the importance of this legislation, and do not question the intentions behind it; we recognize, too, the urgency with which the political branches believe they must act to secure the benefits of developing the unconventional natural gas industry. By any measure, this legislation is of sweeping import. But, in that urgency, it is apparent that ... constitutional commands have been swept aside. Act 13's unauthorized use of the public trust assets is unprecedented and constitutionally infirm, even assuming that the trustee believes it is acting solely and in good faith to advance the economic interests of the beneficiaries.

Notes

1. The *Robinson Township* opinion represents the most detailed judicial pronouncement on the PTD in modern times. One of its most important aspects is the characterization of environmental rights as constitutional. Note that while Pennsylvania has a trust provision in its constitution, Justice Castille began his public trust discussion by describing the "applicable constitutional paradigm," including the Environmental Rights Amendment as part of Article I's more basic affirmation of "'inherent and indefeasible rights.'" See Pa. Const. art. I, § 1 (setting forth "Inherent Rights of Mankind" to include "certain inherent and indefeasible rights"); *Robinson*, 83 A.3d at 948 (plurality opinion). These rights, Justice Castille emphasized, arise from the social contract between people and their government. Such rights are "of such 'general, great and essential' quality as to be ensconced as 'inviolate.'" *Id.* at 947–48 (citing Pa. Const. art. I, pmbl.; art. I, § 25).

The opinion makes clear that the 1971 Environmental Rights Amendment (art. I, § 27) did not create new rights, but rather enumerated the pre-existing rights that the people had reserved to themselves in creating government. Might the *Robinson Township* plurality's constitutional characterization of the public trust apply to other states without express trust amendments to their constitutions? Many other states have similar declarations of inherent rights forming the constitutional paradigm upon which the plurality opinion in *Robinson* relies.[4] Even in states lacking such declarations of inherent rights, aren't the democratic understandings underlying government authority fairly equal across the states? Does the *Robinson Township* plurality opinion, with its focus on inherent rights of citizens, illuminate Professor Joseph Sax's famous statement that the public trust demarcates a society of "citizens rather than of serfs"? *See* Joseph L. Sax, *The Public Trust Doctrine in Natural Resource Law: Effective Judicial Intervention*, 68 Mich. L. Rev. 471, 484 (1970)).[5]

---

4. *See, e.g.*, Or. Const. art. I, § 1 (entitled "Natural rights inherent in people," declaring "that all power is inherent in the people, and all free governments are founded on their authority, and instituted for their peace, safety, and happiness...."); Cal. Const. art. I, § 1 ("All people are by nature free and independent and have inalienable rights."); Haw. Const. art. I, § 2 ("Rights of Individuals. All persons are free by nature and are equal in their inherent and inalienable rights."); Kan. Const. Bill of Rights § 1 ("Equal Rights. All men are possessed of equal and inalienable natural rights...."); N.D. Const. art. I, § 1 ("All individuals are by nature equally free and independent and have certain inalienable rights, among which are those of enjoying and defending life and liberty....").

5. In the federal atmospheric trust litigation case against the Obama administration, thirty-three law professors, including Joseph Sax, submitted an amicus brief iterating the constitutional basis of the federal public trust doctrine. *See* Brief of Law Professors as *Amicus Curiae* Supporting Plaintiffs-Appellants Seeking Reversal, *Alec L. v. Gina McCarthy*, USCA Case #13-5192 (filed D.C. Circuit 2013), at 2, available at http://www.ourchildrenstrust.org/sites/default/files/FiledLawProfAmicus.pdf ("The constitutional reserved powers doctrine in conjunction with the public trust prevents any one legis-

2. In a non-excerpted but important part of the opinion (Part II), a majority of the court held unequivocally that the political question doctrine did not bar judicial review. *Robinson*, 83 A.3d at 925–30. Typically, government attorneys defending legislative action against trust claims assert the political question doctrine as a procedural bar, claiming that the legislature, not the judiciary, has the last word on policy. *See id.* at 925 (characterizing the government's argument in the following terms: "According to the [government], the [court] interfered with the exercise of the General Assembly's constitutional police powers by 'revisiting' and 'second-guessing' legislative choices"). In the *Robinson* case, the government emphasized the highly politicized context of fracking to insinuate that the judiciary should stay out of the fray. The court noted that the defense called into question the separation of powers between the branches. It unequivocally held that it is within the province of the judiciary to decide constitutional questions—and hold legislatures accountable where citizen's rights are at stake:

> Responsive litigation rhetoric raising the specter of judicial interference with legislative policy does not remove a legitimate legal claim from the Court's consideration; the political question doctrine is a shield and not a sword to deflect judicial review. Furthermore, a statute is not exempt from a challenge brought for judicial consideration simply because it is said to be the General Assembly's expression of policy rendered in a polarized political context.... As the U.S. Supreme Court has stated:
>
>> The idea that any legislature, state or federal, can conclusively determine for the people and for the courts that what it enacts in the form of law, or what it authorizes its agents to do, is consistent with the fundamental law, is in opposition to the theory of our institutions. The duty rests upon all courts, federal and state, ... to see to it that no right secured by the supreme law of the land is impaired or destroyed by legislation. This function and duty of the judiciary distinguishes the American system from all other systems of government. The perpetuity of our institutions, and the liberty which is enjoyed under them, depend, in no small degree, upon the power given the judiciary to declare null and void all legislation that is clearly repugnant to the supreme law of the land (citation omitted).

Id. at 928–29, quoting *Smyth v. Ames*, 169 U.S. 466, 527–28 (1898). Other courts have emphasized the court's role in enforcing the trust. As the Hawai'i Supreme Court has emphasized, it is decidedly the role of courts to prevent "improvident disposition of an irreplaceable *res*" held in public trust. *In re Water Use Permit Applications*, 9 P.3d 409, 455 (Haw. 2000). Does it matter whether citizens, in bringing trust claims, characterize the trust as a constitutional or a common law doctrine?

3. Note the expansive *res* of the trust as characterized by the *Robinson* plurality: "At present, the concept of public natural resources includes not only state-owned lands, waterways, and mineral reserves, but also resources that implicate the public interest, such as ambient air, surface and ground water, wild flora, and fauna (including fish) that are outside the scope of purely private property." Does the opinion essentially follow the public concern test of *Illinois Central*? Does the approach mark a move away

---

lature from depriving a future legislature of the natural resources necessary to provide for the well-being and survival of its citizens.... Through the [public trust doctrine], the Constitution governs for the perpetual preservation of the Nation.") (The *Alec L.* litigation is discussed in chapter 11 (p. 389)). For another analysis of the constitutional underpinnings of the public trust doctrine, *see* Gerald Torres & Nathan Bellinger, *The Public Trust: The Law's DNA*, 4 Wake Forest J.L. & Pol'y 281 (2014).

from antebellum characterizations of trust assets as primarily limited to streambeds? One of the main resources impacted by the fracking operations in Pennsylvania is groundwater, which communities rely on for domestic drinking water supplies. Should there be any question as to whether groundwater is included in the trust? For treatment of groundwater under the public trust, see Jack Tuholske, *Trusting the Public Trust: Application of the Public Trust Doctrine to Groundwater Resources*, 9 Vt. J. Envtl. L. 189 (2008).

4. The *Robinson* plurality opinion iterates a broad array of fiduciary duties. Which are procedural in nature, and which are substantive? When elaborating on fiduciary duties, the opinion frequently refers to standards applicable to private trustees, as set forth in the RESTATEMENT OF TRUSTS. See *Robinson*, 83 A.3d at 957. Specifically, the court cited the RESTATEMENT (SECOND) OF TRUSTS § 174 (stating that the "duty of prudence generally requires trustees to exercise ordinary skill, prudence, and caution in managing corpus of trust); RESTATEMENT (SECOND) OF TRUSTS § 170 (stating that the trustee has duty of loyalty to administer the trust solely in beneficiary's interest and not his own); RESTATEMENT (SECOND) OF TRUSTS § 232 (setting forth trustee's duty of impartiality). The standards of a private trustee are well-established and quite detailed. Is the court essentially saying that the same basic standards apply to public trustees, and also that such standards provide an adequate basis for judicial review? How do they add to existing statutory standards?

5. In a non-excerpted portion of Justice Castille's opinion, the court describes the extensive history of environmental damage to Pennsylvania's striking natural resources— damage that includes decades of clearcut logging and coal mining. 83 A.3d at 960–61. The opinion seems to portray the state's history as being unique and uses it to explain the strong intent behind the Environmental Rights Amendment. But is the history unique? Hasn't every area of the United States suffered environmental damage, as evidenced by extinct salmon runs in the Pacific Northwest, clearcut rainforests in Alaska, and the lost wetlands of the Florida Everglades? Wouldn't such damage form a backdrop and justification for any modern trust approach that provides increased protection?

6. The *Robinson* plurality emphasized the fiduciary duty to treat all beneficiaries with impartiality. The pro-fracking legislation challenged in the case seemed to favor natural gas interests at the expense of residents who suffered severe environmental degradation. Indeed, the lead opinion by the Chief Justice, albeit in the context of the Environmental Rights provision of the Pennsylvania Constitution, Article I, Section 27, recognized inequalities associated with the "uniform application" of Act 13 statewide:

> A second difficulty arising from Section 3304's requirement that local government permit industrial uses in all zoning districts is that some properties and communities will carry much heavier environmental and habitability burdens than others. This disparate effect is irreconcilable with the express command that the trustee will manage the corpus of the trust for the benefit of "all the people."

83 A.3d at 1007.

What political incentives provoke legislators to favor business interests even when doing so harms communities? Could the fiduciary duty of impartiality be a game changer in governmental permit processes? Could it give legs to the notion of environmental justice? And how could the duty of loyalty, also mentioned in the opinion, change the current legislative approach? The opinion also underscores the duty to future generations. How should the legislature balance the needs of present and future generations? In which ways are they compatible, and in which ways are they at odds with each other?

7. Much of Justice Castille's opinion focuses on private property rights threatened by fracking. As he notes, the groundwater and air contamination impairs the basic habitability of communities. The opinion demonstrates how the public trust secures the natural infrastructure necessary for enjoyment of private property rights. The interrelationship of private property rights and public trust rights is further explored in chapter 9.

8. The *Robinson Township* decision generated considerable interest in Pennsylvania's Environmental Rights Amendment. Prior to the opinion, the amendment had not carried much weight in curbing legislative or agency action. A few other state trust constitutional provisions have suffered the same fate. But as the *Robinson Township* plurality shows, the trust represents a formidable and timeless principle; and courts can breathe new life into the trust despite adverse or weak precedent. Professor John Dernbach, whose scholarship on the Amendment was cited several times by the court, has compiled the legislative history of Article I, Section 27, available at http://papers.ssrn.com/sol3/papers.cfm?abstract_id=2474660. For his analysis of the *Robinson* decision and its impact across public trust law, see John Dernbach, Robinson Township *and the Role of the Public Trust Doctrine in State Constitutions*, 45 Envtl. L. (forthcoming 2015). For an analysis of other state constitutional trust provisions, see page 434 below.

Note on the Source of the Public Trust Doctrine, According to Justice Kennedy

1. Is the public trust a legitimate exercise of state judicial or legislative power? The first step in legitimation is to ground the trust in the federal constitution or in common law. In *Idaho v. Coeur d'Alene Tribe*, 521 U.S. 261, 283–87 (1997), Justice Kennedy offered this analysis of the constitutional basis for the doctrine:

> The Court from an early date has acknowledged that the people of each of the Thirteen Colonies at the time of independence "became themselves sovereign; and in that character hold the absolute right to all their navigable waters and the soils under them for their own common use, subject only to the rights since surrendered by the Constitution to the general government." *Martin v. Lessee of Waddell*, 16 Pet. 367, 410 (1842). Then, in *Lessee of Pollard v. Hagan*, 44 U.S. 212 (1845), the Court concluded that States entering the Union after 1789 did so on an "equal footing" with the original States and so have similar ownership over these "sovereign lands." In consequence of this rule, a State's title to these sovereign lands arises from the equal footing doctrine and is "conferred not by Congress but by the Constitution itself." *Oregon ex rel. State Land Bd. v. Corvallis Sand & Gravel Co.*, 429 U.S. 363, 374 (1977). The importance of these lands to state sovereignty explains our longstanding commitment to the principle that the United States is presumed to have held navigable waters in acquired territory for the ultimate benefit of future States and "that disposals by the United States during the territorial period are not lightly to be inferred, and should not be regarded as intended unless the intention was definitely declared or otherwise made very plain." [*United States v. Holt State Bank*, 270 U.S. 49 (1926).]

> The principle which underlies the equal footing doctrine and the strong presumption of state ownership is that navigable waters uniquely implicate sovereign interests. The principle arises from ancient doctrines. See, e.g., INSTITUTES OF JUSTINIAN, Lib. 11, Tit. I, §2 (T. Cooper transl. 2d ed. 1841) ("Rivers and ports are public; hence the right of fishing in a port, or in rivers are in common"). The special treatment of navigable waters in English law was recognized in Brac-

ton's time. He stated that "all rivers and ports are public, so that the right to fish therein is common to all persons. The use of river banks, as of the river itself, is also public." 2 H. Bracton. DE LEGIBUS ET CONSUETUDINIBUS ANGLIAE 40 (S. Thorne trans. 1968). The Magna Carta provided that the Crown would remove "all fish-weirs ... from the Thames and the Medway and throughout all England, except on the sea coast." M. Evans & R. Jack, SOURCES OF ENGLISH LEGAL AND CONSTITUTIONAL HISTORY 53 (1984); see also *Martin v. Waddell* (p. 63) (tracing tidelands trusteeship back to Magna Carta).

2. The Court in *Shively v. Bowlby*, 152 U.S. 1, 13 (1894), summarizing English common law, stated:

> In England, from the time of Lord Hale, it has been treated as settled that the title in the soil of the sea, or of arms of the sea, below ordinary high water mark, is in the King; except so far as an individual or a corporation has acquired rights in it by express grant, or by prescription or usage ... and that this title, *jus privatum*, whether in the King or in a subject, is held subject to the public right, *jus publicum*, of navigation and fishing.

3. Justice Kennedy elaborated on the source of the public trust doctrine in *PPL Montana v. Montana*, 132 S.Ct. 1215, 1234–35 (2012):

> The public trust doctrine is of ancient origin. Its roots trace to Roman civil law and its principles can be found in the English common law on public navigation and fishing rights over tidal lands and in the state laws of this country. *See Coeur d'Alene*, 521 U.S., at 284–286; *Illinois Central R.R. Co. v. Illinois*, 146 U.S. 387, 458 (1892); D. Slade, PUTTING THE PUBLIC TRUST DOCTRINE TO WORK 3–8, 15–24 (1990); *see, e.g., National Audubon Soc. v. Superior Court of Alpine Cty.*, 658 P.2d 709, 718–724 (1983); *Arnold v. Mundy*, 6 N.J.L. 1, 9–10 (1821). Unlike the equal-footing doctrine, however, which is the constitutional foundation for the navigability rule of riverbed title, the public trust doctrine remains a matter of state law, see *Coeur d'Alene*, 521 U.S. at 285 (*Illinois Central*, a Supreme Court public trust case, was "'necessarily a statement of Illinois law'"); *Appleby v. City of New York*, 271 U.S. 364, 395 (1926) (same), subject as well to the federal power to regulate vessels and navigation under the Commerce Clause and admiralty power. While equal-footing cases have noted that the State takes title to the navigable waters and their beds in trust for the public, see *Shively*, 152 U.S., at 49, the contours of that public trust do *not* depend upon the Constitution. Under accepted principles of federalism, the States retain residual power to determine the scope of the public trust over waters within their borders, while federal law determines riverbed title under the equal-footing doctrine.

The statement that "the public trust doctrine remains a matter of state law," remains dictum, as there was no issue raised in the case concerning the validity of federal public trust law. Nevertheless, the statement is bound to be cited by federal defendants resisting any public trust obligation. Chapter 11 considers whether Justice Kennedy has properly interpreted *Illinois Central* as a statement of state law, and whether the doctrine should apply to the federal sovereign as well as state sovereigns.

Chapter 3

Navigability and Its Evolution

One of the first questions in public trust law concerns the scope of the *res*. How are natural resources defined as assets falling within the trust held by government for the people? In the past, courts turned to navigability as the test for waterways falling within the reach of the trust. Originally, the prerequisite to public rights was a determination of tidal influence, presumably because coastal, tidal waters were important for defense, and therefore under the control of the Crown and its successors, the states. In England, there were no large, commercially important streams that were not tidal, but in America that was not true, as rivers like the Ohio, the Mississippi, and the Potomac—as well as the Great Lakes—were essential transportation hubs, the privatization of which would create expensive monopolies. Thus, well before the end of the nineteenth century, public rights evolved to include waterways that, although not tidal, were navigable-in-fact. Without the demarcation of tidal influence, the scope of public rights in navigable waters was contested. Issues included whether recreational use was sufficient to reflect navigability, and whether waters created by artificial improvements (like dams and stream channelization projects) could be navigable and contain public rights.

The evolution in the geographic scope of the public trust largely, although not exclusively, in the nineteenth century, was matched in the late twentieth century by an evolution in the purposes served by the public trust doctrine—to include recreation and ecological functions, among other purposes. The effect of the public trust doctrine on private property was also refined in the late twentieth century to insulate government actions protective of trust resources from claims of takings of private property rights.

This chapter explores these issues as well as introduces the U.S. Supreme Court's recent view of the public trust doctrine and its source (which has been of particular interest to Justice Kennedy, the key swing vote on the current Supreme Court). The chapter shows that the doctrine has been an evolving one for more than a century—and will likely continue to evolve in the future.

Note on Navigability

Historically, navigability formed the talisman of public trust law, defining what lands and waters fell within the trust *res*. Navigability is a confusing concept, perhaps deliberately so, since the confusion separates lawyers from the general public. There are at least four distinct definitions of navigability, all serving different purposes.

First, navigability determines the extent of admiralty jurisdiction, which is not relevant to a public trust inquiry. *See* Thomas J. Schoenbaum, 1 Admiralty & Maritime Law §§ 3-3 (5th ed., 2011).

Second, navigable waters often serve as a surrogate for federal statutory jurisdiction (and underlying commerce clause jurisdiction). *See, e.g.,* the Clean Water Act, 33 U.S.C. §502(7) (2006) (defining navigable waters as "waters of the United States"). *See also United States v. Riverside Bayview Homes,* 474 U.S. 121 (1985) (holding that wetlands adjacent to navigable waters were within federal Clean Water Act jurisdiction); *Solid Waste Agency of Northern Cook County v. U.S. Army Corps of Engineers,* 531 U.S. 159 (2001) (deciding that wetlands not hydrologically connected to navigable waters were not within Clean Water Act jurisdiction); *Rapanos v. United States,* 547 U.S. 715 (2006) (Kennedy, J., concurring) (waters within Clean Water Act jurisdiction must have significant nexus to navigable waters).

Third, as in *Arnold* and *Pollard*, navigability serves as a boundary between public and private land ownership. This is called title navigability, and it is a federal rule, imposing a uniform test on the states, announced by the Supreme Court in 1926:

> [S]treams or lakes which are navigable in fact must be regarded as navigable in law; that they are navigable in fact when they are used, or susceptible of being used, in their natural and ordinary condition, as highways for commerce, over which trade and travel are or may be conducted in the customary modes of trade and travel on water; and further that navigability does not depend on the particular mode in which such use is or may be had—whether by steamboats, sailing vessels or flatboats—nor on an absence of occasional difficulties in navigation, but on the fact, if it be a fact, that the stream in its natural and ordinary condition affords a channel for useful commerce.

United States v. Holt State Bank, 270 U.S. 49, 56 (1926). These issues are still lively; see *PPL Montana v. Montana*, 132 S.Ct. 1215 (2012), discussed at p. 94.

Fourth, states have their own definitions of navigability which they use to delineate the scope of "public waters." This state-defined navigability concept is most relevant for the public trust doctrine, since it imposes public rights in waterways flowing over private property. These public rights often take the form of easements, not public ownership, a phenomenon taken up in the materials that follow.

In *Oregon v. Riverfront Protection Ass'n,* 672 F.2d 792 (9th Cir. 1982), the Ninth Circuit reversed a district court decision and ruled that the bed of the McKenzie River was navigable because it was navigable at statehood, using post-statehood log drives as evidence. The court distinguished the navigability test for statehood from other navigability tests as follows:

> Navigability for title to riverbeds differs in three important respects from navigability for federal regulatory jurisdiction over power plants under the Commerce Clause. The former must exist at the time the State is admitted into the Union. Also it must exist in the river's ordinary condition, *see United States v. Utah*, 283 U.S. 64, 75–76 (1931); it cannot occur as a result of reasonable improvements. This is not the case in federal power plant licensing. *See United States v. Appalachian Electric Power Co.*, 311 U.S. 377 (1940). Finally, to support federal regulatory jurisdiction over power plants the river must by statute be, or have been, "suitable for use for the transportation of persons or property in interstate or foreign commerce." 16 U.S.C. §796(8) (1976). No such "in interstate or foreign commerce" requirement exists when the issue is navigability for title.

Id. at 794 n.1.

A. The Evolving Geographic Scope of Navigability

Phillips Petroleum Co. v. Mississippi
Supreme Court of the United States
484 U.S. 469 (1988)

Justice WHITE delivered the opinion of the Court.

The issue here is whether the State of Mississippi, when it entered the Union in 1817, took title to lands lying under waters that were influenced by the tide running in the Gulf of Mexico, but were not navigable in fact.

I

As the Mississippi Supreme Court eloquently put it: "Though great public interests and neither insignificant nor illegitimate private interests are present and in conflict, this in the end is a title suit." *Cinque Bambini Partnership v. State*, 491 So.2d 508, 510 (1986). More specifically, in question here is ownership of 42 acres of land underlying the north branch of Bayou LaCroix and 11 small drainage streams in southwestern Mississippi; the disputed tracts range from under one-half acre to almost 10 acres in size. Although the waters over these lands lie several miles north of the Mississippi Gulf Coast and are not navigable, they are nonetheless influenced by the tide, because they are adjacent and tributary to the Jourdan River, a navigable stream flowing into the Gulf. The Jourdan, in the area involved here, is affected by the ebb and flow of the tide. Record title to these tracts of land is held by petitioners, who trace their claims back to prestatehood Spanish land grants.

The State of Mississippi, however, claiming that, by virtue of the "equal-footing doctrine," it acquired at the time of statehood and held in public trust all land lying under any waters influenced by the tide, whether navigable or not, issued oil and gas leases that included the property at issue. This quiet title suit, brought by petitioners, ensued.

The Mississippi Supreme Court, affirming the Chancery Court with respect to the lands at issue here, held that by virtue of becoming a State, Mississippi acquired "fee simple title to all lands naturally subject to tidal influence, inland to today's mean high water mark...." *Ibid.* Petitioners' submission that the State acquired title to only lands under navigable waters was rejected.

We granted certiorari to review the Mississippi Supreme Court's decision, 479 U.S. 1084 (1987), and now affirm the judgment below.

II

As petitioners recognize, the "seminal case in American public trust jurisprudence is *Shively v. Bowlby*, 152 U.S. 1 (1894)." Reply Brief for Petitioners 11. The issue in *Shively v. Bowlby*, 152 U.S. 1 (1894), was whether the State of Oregon or a prestatehood grantee from the United States of riparian lands near the mouth of the Columbia River at Astoria, Oregon, owned the soil below the high-water mark. Following an extensive survey of this Court's prior cases, the English common law, and various cases from the state courts, the Court concluded:

> At common law, the title and dominion in lands flowed by the tide water were in the King for the benefit of the nation.... Upon the American Revolution, these rights, charged with a like trust, were vested in the original States within their respective borders, subject to the rights surrendered by the Constitution of the United States.

* * *

The new States admitted into the Union since the adoption of the Constitution have the same rights as the original States in the tide waters, and in the lands under them, within their respective jurisdictions. [*Shively*, 152 U.S. at 57.]

Shively rested on prior decisions of this Court, which had included similar, sweeping statements of States' dominion over lands beneath tidal waters. *Knight v. United States Land Association*, 142 U.S. 161, 183 (1891), for example, had stated that "[i]t is the settled rule of law in this court that absolute property in, and dominion and sovereignty over, the soils under the tidewaters in the original States were reserved to the several States, and that the new States since admitted have the same rights, sovereignty and jurisdiction in that behalf as the original States possess within their respective borders." On many occasions, before and since, this Court has stated or restated these words from *Knight* and *Shively*.[1]

Against this array of cases, it is not surprising that Mississippi claims ownership of all of the tidelands in the State. Other States have done as much.[2] The 13 original States, joined by the Coastal States Organization (representing all coastal States), have filed a brief in support of Mississippi, insisting that ownership of thousands of acres of tidelands under nonnavigable waters would not be disturbed if the judgment below were affirmed, as it would be if petitioners' navigability-in-fact test were adopted. *See* Brief for 13 Original States *as Amici Curiae* 3–5, 26–27.

Petitioners rely on early state cases to indicate that the original States did not claim title to nonnavigable tidal waters. *See* Brief for Petitioners 23–29. But it has been long established that the individual States have the authority to define the limits of the lands held in public trust and to recognize private rights in such lands as they see fit. *Shively v. Bowlby*, 152 U.S. at 26. Some of the original States, for example, did recognize more private interests in tidelands than did others of the 13 — more private interests than were recognized at common law, or in the dictates of our public trusts cases. Because some of the cases which petitioners cite come from such States (*i.e.*, from States which abandoned the common law with respect to tidelands), they are of only limited value in understanding the public trust doctrine and its scope in those States which have not relinquished their claims to all lands beneath tidal waters.

Finally, we note that several of our prior decisions have recognized that the States have interests in lands beneath tidal waters which have nothing to do with navigation. For example, this Court has previously observed that public trust lands may be used for fishing — for both "shell-fish [and] floating fish." *See, e.g., Smith v. Maryland*, 18 How. 71, 75 (1855). On several occasions the Court has recognized that lands beneath tidal waters may be reclaimed to create land for urban expansion. *E.g., Hardin v. Jordan*, 140 U.S. 371, 381–82 (1891). Because of the State's ownership of tidelands, restrictions on the plant-

---

1. *E.g., Borax Consolidated, Ltd. v. Los Angeles*, 296 U.S. 10, 15 (1935); *Appleby v. City of New York*, 271 U.S. 364, 381 (1926); *Illinois Central R. Co. v. Illinois*, 146 U.S. 387, 435 (1892); *Hardin v. Jordan*, 140 U.S. 371, 381 (1891); *McCready v. Virginia*, 94 U.S. 391, 394 (1877); *Weber v. Harbor Comm'rs*, 18 Wall. 57, 65 (1873); *Goodtitle v. Kibbe*, 9 How. 471, 477–78 (1850).

2. *See, e.g., Wright v. Seymour*, 10 P. 323, 324–26 (Cal. 1886), which held that the State of California owned the bottom of the Russian River as far as the tide affected it, even where the River was not navigable in fact. Earlier, the Connecticut Supreme Court had held that the tidal flats adjoining an arm of the sea were in public ownership. *Simons v. French*, 25 Conn. 346, 352–53 (1856). The South Carolina Supreme Court reached a similar conclusion concerning "salt marshes." *State v. Pinckney*, 22 S.C. 484, 507–09 (1885). Both of these cases, and many others like them, recognize state dominion over lands beneath nonnavigable tidal waters.

ing and harvesting of oysters there have been upheld. *McCready v. Virginia*, 94 U.S. 391, 395–97 (1877).[3] It would be odd to acknowledge such diverse uses of public trust tidelands, and then suggest that the sole measure of the expanse of such lands is the navigability of the waters over them.

Consequently, we reaffirm our longstanding precedents which hold that the States, upon entry into the Union, received ownership of all lands under waters subject to the ebb and flow of the tide. Under the well-established principles of our cases, the decision of the Mississippi Supreme Court is clearly correct: the lands at issue here are "under tide-waters," and therefore passed to the State of Mississippi upon its entrance into the Union.

III

Petitioners do not deny that broad statements of public trust dominion over tidelands have been included in this Court's opinions since the early 19th century. Rather, they advance two reasons why these previous statements of the public trust doctrine should not be given their apparent application in this case.

* * *

B

Petitioners ... contend that, even if the common law does not support their position, subsequent cases from this Court developing the *American* public trust doctrine make it clear that navigability—and not tidal influence—has become the *sine qua non* of the public trust interest in tidelands in this country.

It is true that *The Genesee Chief*, 12 How. 443, 456–57 (1852), overruled prior cases of this Court which had limited admiralty jurisdiction to waters subject to tidal influence. *Cf. The Thomas Jefferson*, 10 Wheat. 428, 429 (1826). The Court did sharply criticize the "ebb and flow" measure of admiralty inherited from England in *The Genesee Chief*, and instead insisted quite emphatically that the different topography of America— in particular, our "thousands of miles of public navigable water[s] ... in which there is no tide"—required that "jurisdiction [be] made to depend upon the navigable character of the water, and not upon the ebb and flow of the tide." 12 How. at 457. Later, it came to be recognized as the "settled law of this country" that the lands under navigable freshwater lakes and rivers were within the public trust given the new States upon their entry into the Union, subject to the federal navigation easement and the power of Congress to control navigation on those streams under the Commerce Clause. *Barney v. Keokuk*, 94 U.S. 324, 338 (1877). *See also Illinois Central R. Co. v. Illinois*, 146 U.S. 387, 435–36 (1892).

That States own freshwater river bottoms as far as the rivers are navigable, however, does not indicate that navigability is or was the prevailing test for state dominion over tidelands. Rather, this rule represents the American decision to depart from what it understood to be the English rule limiting Crown ownership to the soil under tidal waters. In *Oregon ex rel. State Land Board v. Corvallis Sand & Gravel Co.*, 429 U.S. 363, 374 (1977), after recognizing the accepted doctrine that States coming into the Union had title to all lands under the tidewaters, the Court stated that *Barney v. Keokuk* had "extended the doctrine to waters which were nontidal but nevertheless navigable, consistent with [the Court's] earlier extension of admiralty jurisdiction."

---

3. These cases lead us to reject the dissent's assertion that "the fundamental purpose of the public trust is to protect commerce"....

This Court's decisions in *The Genesee Chief* and *Barney v. Keokuk* extended admiralty jurisdiction and public trust doctrine to navigable freshwaters and the lands beneath them. But we do not read those cases as simultaneously withdrawing from public trust coverage those lands which had been consistently recognized in this Court's cases as being within that doctrine's scope: *all* lands beneath waters influenced by the ebb and flow of the tide. *See Mann v. Tacoma Land Co.,* 153 U.S. 273 (1894).

* * *

We are skeptical of the suggestions by the dissent, *post* at 484 U.S. 485, 493, that a decision affirming the judgment below will have sweeping implications, either within Mississippi or outside that State. The State points out that only one other case is pending in its courts which raises this same issue. Tr. of Oral Arg.19. And as for the effect of our decision today in other States, we are doubtful that this ruling will do more than confirm the prevailing understanding—which in some States is the same as Mississippi's, and in others is quite different. As this Court wrote in *Shively v. Bowlby,* 152 U.S. at 26, "there is no universal and uniform law upon the subject; but ... each State has dealt with the lands under the tide waters within its borders according to its own views of justice and policy."

Consequently, our ruling today will not upset titles in all coastal States, as petitioners intimated at argument. Tr. of Oral Arg. 32. As we have discussed *supra,* at 484 U.S. 475–76, many coastal States, as a matter of state law, granted all or a portion of their tidelands to adjacent upland property owners long ago. Our decision today does nothing to change ownership rights in States which previously relinquished a public trust claim to tidelands such as those at issue here.

Indeed, we believe that it would be far more upsetting to settled expectations to reverse the Mississippi Supreme Court decision. As *amici* note, *see, e.g.,* Brief for State of California et al. as *Amici Curiae* 19, many land titles have been adjudicated based on the ebb-and-flow rule for tidelands—we cannot know how many titles would have to be adjusted if the scope of the public trust was now found to be limited to lands beneath navigable tidal waters only. If States do not own lands under nonnavigable tidal waters, many state land grants based on our earlier decisions might now be invalid. *Cf. Hardin v. Jordan,* 140 U.S. at 381–82. Finally, even where States have given dominion over tidelands to private property owners, some States have retained for the general public the right to fish, hunt, or bathe on these lands. These long-established rights may be lost with respect to nonnavigable tidal waters if we adopt the rule urged by petitioners.

The fact that petitioners have long been the record title holders, or long paid taxes on these lands does not change the outcome here. How such facts would transfer ownership of these lands from the State to petitioners is a question of state law. Here, the Mississippi Supreme Court held that under Mississippi law, the State's ownership of these lands could not be lost via adverse possession, laches, or any other equitable doctrine. 491 So.2d at 521. *See* Miss. Const., Art. 4, § 104; *Gibson v. State Land Comm'r,* 374 So.2d 212, 216–17 (Miss. 1979); *City of Bay St. Louis v. Board of Supervisors of Hancock County,* 80 Miss. 364, 371–72 (1902). We see no reason to disturb the "general proposition [that] the law of real property is, under our Constitution, left to the individual States to develop and administer." *Hughes v. Washington,* 389 U.S. 290, 295 (1967) (Stewart, J., concurring). *See Davies Warehouse Co. v. Bowles,* 321 U.S. 144, 155 (1944); *Borax Consolidated, Ltd. v. Los Angeles,* 296 U.S. 10, 22 (1935). Consequently, we do not believe that the equitable considerations petitioners advance divest the State of its ownership in the disputed tidelands.

V

Because we believe that our cases firmly establish that the States, upon entering the Union, were given ownership over all lands beneath waters subject to the tide's influence, we affirm the Mississippi Supreme Court's determination that the lands at issue here became property of the State upon its admission to the Union in 1817. Furthermore, because we find no reason to set aside that court's state-law determination that subsequent developments did not divest the State of its ownership of these public trust lands, the judgment below is Affirmed.

[Justice Kennedy took no part in this case. Justice O'Connor wrote a dissent, which Justices Stevens and Scalia joined, that argued that the public trust doctrine should "properly extend[] only to land underlying navigable bodies of water and their borders, bays, and inlets." She maintained that "[n]avigability, not tidal influence, ought to be acknowledged as the universal hallmark of the public trust."]

Notes

1. Why isn't the majority concerned about upsetting the reasonable expectations of landowners who thought they owned the non-navigable but tidal-influenced bayou land lying several miles north of the Gulf of Mexico?

2. The Court stated that once a state takes title to submerged lands under the equal footing doctrine, the state has the authority to recognize private rights in trust lands "as they see fit." How then did the Illinois legislature overstep its authority in the *Illinois Central* decision? Is there a common floor of federal doctrine that the states must respect while still having latitude to administer the trust in the interests of their citizens?

3. The notion that the public trust doctrine is "necessarily a statement of state law" was first articulated in *Appleby v. City of New York,* 271 U.S. 364, 395 (1926). But what state law governed in *Illinois Central*? Is the *Appleby* statement a revision of the *Illinois Central* holding? *See* Crystal Chase, *The* Illinois Central *Public Trust Doctrine and Federal Common Law: An Unconventional View,* 16 Hastings W.-NW. J. Envtl. L. & Pol'y 113 (2010) (arguing that the Supreme Court misinterpreted *Illinois Central* in both *Appleby* and *Phillips Petroleum*); see also Michael C. Blumm & Lynn S. Schaffer, *The Federal Public Trust Doctrine: Misinterpreting Justice Kennedy and* Illinois Central Railroad, 45 Envtl. L. (forthcoming 2015). For further discussion, see chapter 11 (p. 393).

4. Under *Pollard*, states gain title to streambeds along navigable waterways. Thus, the navigability question is key to determining what riverbeds are owned by the state. Surprisingly, this question is still fiercely disputed in modern times. In *PPL Montana v. Montana,* 132 S.Ct. 1215 (2012), the state of Montana asserted ownership of streambeds along the Missouri, Madison, and Clark Fork Rivers. PPL Montana, LLC, a private power company, had used the riverbeds for years for its hydroelectric facilities without paying the state any money. The state claimed ownership of the riverbeds and sought some $40 million for PPL's use from 2000 through 2007. Although the Supreme Court of Montana held that the riverbeds were owned by the state under the federal test for navigability, the U.S. Supreme Court reversed in a unanimous opinion by Justice Kennedy. The Court ruled that the state court had misapplied the federal test by failing to judge navigable conditions on a segment-by-segment basis, and that segments which are so obstructed to require portages likely make a river non-navigable for title purposes. The Court also reiterated that the relevant test for title navigability was whether the waterway was "susceptible to being used" in its natural condition for commercial navigation at the time of statehood (in

Montana's case, 1889), so a river need not be actually commercially navigated at statehood. But unlike state navigability rules employing the "pleasure boat" test (*see* p. 118), use by recreational watercraft post-statehood would not generally meet the federal test for title navigability. Modern recreational boating is relevant only if it is not materially different from the watercraft used for commercial purposes at statehood and if the river's condition has not materially changed since statehood. *Id.* at 1233–34.

5. The *PPL Montana* decision also distinguished the federal question of title navigability from the public trust doctrine, which the Court again described as a state law doctrine securing "public access to the waters above [river]beds for purposes of navigation, fishing, and other recreational uses." *Id.* at 1234. Justice Kennedy did not mention that in many states the public trust doctrine also includes ecosystem function.

6. Justice White's opinion in *Phillips* contained a useful review of the public trust case law, emphasizing *Shively* and mid-nineteenth-century cases like *The Genesee Chief*, 53 U.S. 443 (1851); and *Barney v. Keokuk*, 94 U.S. 324 (1877), that extended the reach of public rights beyond tidal waters to include navigable-in-fact waterways.

7. One of the editors commented on the evolving scope of the public trust doctrine throughout history in the following terms:

The Public Trust Doctrine: A Twenty-First Century Concept
Michael C. Blumm
16 Hastings W.-Nw. J. Envtl. L. & Pol'y 105 (2010)

The public trust, an ancient legal precept of public ownership of important natural resources, has traditionally been moored to navigable waters. But the doctrine has been continuously evolving since it was introduced to American law in the landmark case of *Arnold v. Mundy*. As explained in a recent text, the public trust doctrine is "in motion," a dynamic vehicle protecting both public access to natural resources and to decisionmakers with the authority to allocate those resources. The doctrine's central purpose may be to serve as a vehicle to avoid monopolization of resources with important public values.

The evolution of the public trust doctrine was evident in mid-nineteenth century America, when the Supreme Court refused to limit the scope of the federal navigation power to tidal waters, as had been the case in England. In *The Genesse Chief*, the Court used the advent of steam power, which opened up inland waterways to commercial navigation, as a reason to expand the scope of the navigation power, noting that the United States had "thousands of miles of public navigable water, including lakes and rivers in which there is no tide" [53 U.S. 443, 457 (1851)]; therefore, the English standard of navigability did not fit the American continent, with its great rivers and lakes. Thus, over a century-and-a-half ago, navigability—central to the historic public trust doctrine, evolved from a coastal to an inland, upriver concept.

The public trust doctrine's evolution proceeded apace in the twentieth century, both in terms of its scope of applicability and its purposes. The navigability tether was gradually eroded, as numerous courts extended the scope of public rights to all waters suitable for recreation. The California Supreme Court specifically extended the public trust doctrine to include water rights and to non-navigable waters affecting navigable waters. The Hawaiian Supreme Court not only agreed that the doctrine burdened water rights, but extended its scope to groundwater. The New Jersey Supreme Court showed that the doctrine could be amphibious, ruling that it applied to dry sand beaches. The California Supreme Court ruled that the purposes of the public trust extended beyond the traditional purposes of navigation and fishing to include recreation and ecological preservation. The expanded purposes seemed only logical, as the fishing purpose would be undermined if the doctrine could not protect fishable waters.

People ex rel. Baker v. Mack

Court of Appeal of California
97 Cal. Rptr. 448 (1971)

BRAY, J.

Questions Presented

1. In California the sole test of navigability of a stream is not whether it is or can be used for commercial purposes.

* * *

1. The Test of Navigability

The main issue in the case is whether or not Fall River, in the area of defendants' properties, is in fact or in law a navigable stream. If it is navigable, then a public right of navigation exists and any obstruction of a navigable stream is a public nuisance. (Civ. Code, § 3479.) On the other hand, if it is not navigable, the owners of riparian properties have the right to obstruct the use of the river as they own the stream, banks and bed.

Defendants contend that the test of navigability is whether the stream is susceptible to a useful commercial purpose. The evidence in the instant case shows that Fall River probably does not meet this test although some 50 years past logs were floated down the river. (*See* 65 C.J.S., Navigable Waters, § 5, pp. 75–76, to the effect that streams that are merely floatable and useful for logging purposes are considered navigable. However, see *American River Water Co. v. Amsden*, 6 Cal. 443, 446 (1856), holding that a stream which can only float logs is not navigable.)

Plaintiffs contend and the court determined that the test of navigability is met if the stream is capable of boating for pleasure.

In addition to considerable testimony proving that the river is capable of use by boating for pleasure and is so used (except when prevented by defendants), court and counsel observed the river from the air and in a 14-foot aluminum flat-bottom boat with a 5 horsepower motor traversed the portion of the river involved herein.

* * *

It hardly needs citation of authorities that the rule is that a navigable stream may be used by the public for boating, swimming, fishing, hunting and all recreational purposes. (*Munninghoff v. Wisconsin Conservation Com.* 38 N.W.2d 712, 714–16 (Wis. 1949); *Willow River Club v. Wade,* 76 N.W. 273 (Wis. 1898); *see Diana Shooting Club v. Husting,* 145 N.W. 816 (Wis. 1914), which pointed out that at common law the rights of hunting and fishing were held to be incident to the right of navigation.)

The modern tendency in several other states, as well as here, to hold for use of the public any stream capable of being used for recreational purposes is well expressed in *Lamprey v. State (Metcalf)* 53 N.W. 1139, 1143 (Minn. 1893), where the court said: "But if, under present conditions of society, bodies of water are used for public uses other than mere commercial navigation, in its ordinary sense, we fail to see why they ought not to be held to be public waters, or navigable waters, if the old nomenclature is preferred. Certainly, we do not see why boating or sailing for pleasure should not be considered navigation, as well as boating for mere pecuniary profit." *Lamprey* points out that there are innumerable waters—lakes and streams—which will never be used for commercial purposes but which have been, or are capable of being used, "for sailing, rowing, fishing, fowling, bathing, skating" and other public purposes, and that it would be a great wrong upon the public for all time to deprive the public of those uses merely because the waters are either not used or not adaptable for commercial purposes. (Cases from other states which cite with approval the test in *Lamprey v. State, supra,* include *Coleman v. Schaeffer,* 126 N.E.2d 444, 446 (Ohio 1955); *Hillebrand v. Knapp,* 274 N.W. 821, 822 (S.D. 937); *Roberts v. Taylor,* 181 N.W. 622, 625–26 (N.D. 1921); *see Muench v. Public Service Com.,* 53 N.W.2d 514, 519, 55 N.W.2d 40 (Wis. 1952), wherein a Wisconsin statute now makes a stream navigable in fact which is capable of floating *any* boat, skiff or canoe, of the shallowest draft used for recreational purposes.)

* * *

[I]n California "all waters are deemed navigable which are really so." [Churchill Co. v. Kingsbury, 174 P. 329, 330 (Cal. 1918).] (*See City and County of San Francisco v. Main,* 137 P. 281, 281 (Cal. Ct. App. 1913).)

"... The right of the public to use navigable waters, however, is not limited to any particular type of craft. Pleasure yachts and fishing boats are used for navigation...." (*Miramar Co. v. City of Santa Barbara,* 143 P.2d 1, 3 (Cal. 1943).)

* * *

The failure of the Legislature to designate Fall River in the list of navigable waters in Harbors and Navigation Code sections 101–106, is of no consequence. In *City of Los Angeles v. Aitken,* 52 P.2d 585 (Cal. Dist. Ct. App. 1935), the court held Mono Lake navigable although it was not so declared in Harbors and Navigation Code. *Newcomb v. City of Newport Beach,* 60 P.2d 825 (Cal. 1936), held Newport Bay a navigable waterway even though at that time it was not so designated in the code. The state acquired sovereignty in all navigable streams in 1850. The Legislature's failure to include a water course within its listing of waterways did not and cannot cede such waterways into private ownership. (*See People v. California Fish Co.,* 138 P. 79 (Cal. 1913).) The state acquired title by its sovereignty upon its creation in 1850. (*Le Roy v. Dunkerly,* 54 Cal. 452 (1880).)

* * *

The streams of California are a vital recreational resource of the state. The modern determinations of the California courts, as well as those of several of the states, as to the test of navigability can well be restated as follows: members of the public have the right to navigate and to exercise the incidents of navigation in a lawful manner at any point below high water mark on waters of this state which are capable of being navigated by oar or motor-propelled small craft.

The attention of this court has been directed to the recent case of *Utah v. United States,* 403 U.S. 9, 10 (1971), wherein the Supreme Court in determining the navigability of Salt Lake reiterated the federal test of navigability as the use of the waters "as highways for commerce, over which trade and travel are or may be conducted in the customary modes of trade and travel on water...." However, as pointed out by amici curiae the federal test of navigability involving as it does property title questions, has always been much more restrictive than state tests dealing with navigability for purposes of the right of public passage. (*See Youngstown Mines Corp. v. Prout,* 124 N.W.2d 328, 341–42 (Minn. 1963); *State v. Bollenbach,* 63 N.W.2d 278, 287–88 (Minn. 1954).) The federal test of navigation does not preclude a more liberal state test establishing a right of public passage whenever a stream is physically navigable by small craft.

Judgment is affirmed.

Notes

1. The *Baker* court cited *Lamprey v. Metcalf*, 53 N.W. 1139 (Minn. 1893), an early, influential PTD case in which the Minnesota Supreme Court indicated that the distinction between navigable and non-navigable waters divided publicly accessible waters from private waters, and that the definition of navigable waters for this purpose was a matter of state law. The *Lamprey* court ruled that the inland lakes in the state were navigable under state law, and thus subject to public access rights, if they were floatable for recreation. The court wrote:

> To hand over all these lakes to private ownership, under any old or narrow test of navigability, would be a great wrong upon the public for all time, the extent of which cannot, perhaps, be now even anticipated.

Id. at 1143. The case illustrates judicial protection of the rights and interests of future generations — interests that would be foreclosed by full privatization. The court looked beyond present uses to a broader set of uses to which the waters are "capable of being put," arising "as population increases, and towns and cities are built up in their vicinity." *Id.* The Minnesota court announced that the public's navigation uses of water included "sailing, rowing, fishing, fowling, bathing, skating, taking water for domestic, agricultural, and even city purposes, cutting ice, and other public purposes *which cannot now be enumerated or even anticipated.*" *Id.* (emphasis added).

2. The Oregon Supreme Court relied on *Lamprey* in *Guilliams v. Beaver Lake Club*, 175 P. 437, 442 (Or. 1918), to extend public rights beyond those rivers in which the state owned the bed under the equal footing doctrine, to include all waterways capable of recreational boating. The court eschewed restrictive definitions of navigability that required strict commercial use of the waters, emphasizing (like the *Lamprey* court) that the public usage over time changes and noting also that commercial use includes recreation. The court reasoned:

> The Columbia River, in a legal sense, was just as navigable a century ago when it "heard no sound save its own dashing," as it is with the commerce of three states being borne upon its waters.... Even confining the definition of navigability, as many courts do, to suitability for the purposes of trade and commerce, we fail to see why commerce should not be construed to include the use of boats and vessels for the purposes of pleasure. The vessel carrying a load of passengers to a picnic is in law just as much engaged in commerce as the one carrying grain or other merchandise.

Id. at 441. *See also Luscher v. Reynolds*, 56 P.2d 1158, 1162 (Or. 1936) (holding that the public has the right to use privately owned lakes, stating, "[r]egardless of the ownership of the bed, the public has the paramount right to the use of the waters ... for the purpose of transportation and commerce," including transportation for pleasure).

3. Cases such as *Lamprey, Baker,* and *Guilliams* help bring into focus a doctrinal dilemma faced by courts in deciding public trust cases. Should courts define the scope of the trust according to a full, but yet unrealized, set of public uses to which a trust asset (like a waterway) might be susceptible, or should they lock in the scope of the interests

Courts choose the more expansive form [handwritten marginal note]

to the particular usages common at the time the case arises? The judicial proclivity in these cases is, resoundingly, to reserve legal space for public uses that have not yet come into being. In *Guilliams*, the Oregon Supreme Court emphasized the underlying capacity of a waterway to support public uses. *Guilliams*, 175 P.2d at 441 ("The test of navigability of a stream ... is the capacity to ... enable boats and vessels to make successful progress through its waters, rather than circumstances involving the present right of approach to its banks. The latter are changeable and subject to the will of man; the former is a *physical condition dependent upon nature*" (emphasis added).) Bear in mind that this approach, which allows expansion of the public rights (sometimes called the *jus publicum*) over time, necessarily condones a concomitant restriction over time of the private rights of the property owner upon whose land the waterway is situated.

4. Does the term "navigability" continue to offer guidance in these public use cases? Do you sense that the courts are trying to fit a fast-expanding set of new interests into an outdated legal concept? Consider the statement of the *Lamprey* court along these lines:

> If the term "navigable" is not capable of a sufficiently extended meaning to preserve and protect the rights of the people to all beneficial public uses of these inland lakes, to which they are capable of being put, we are not prepared to say that it would not be justifiable, within the principles of the common law, to discard the old nomenclature, and adopt the classification of public waters and private waters.

Lamprey, 53 N.W. at 1143–44.

As you will see in cases below, modern courts have increasingly gravitated towards the term "public waters" to describe waterways over which the public has rights of access.

Parks v. Cooper

Supreme Court of South Dakota
676 N.W.2d 823 (2004)

KONENKAMP, J.

The dispute in this appeal centers on three bodies of water located in Day and Clark counties in South Dakota, known as Long Lake, Parks Slough, and Schiley Slough. Because of unseasonably wet years, the water has accumulated into large lakes. They have attracted the interest of the public looking for sporting and recreational opportunities. Landowners with property interests in one or more of these three areas sought a declaratory judgment on their property rights and an injunction against the State and the public from using these lakes. In deciding in favor of the landowners, the circuit court held both the land and the water to be private property and enjoined public access. On appeal, the State raises multiple legal issues for our consideration, but ultimately, we conclude that all water in South Dakota belongs to the people in accord with the public trust doctrine and as declared by statute and precedent, and thus, although the lake beds are mostly privately owned, the water in the lakes is public and may be converted to public use, developed for public benefit, and appropriated, in accord with legislative direction and state regulation. Thus, we reverse and remand.

I.

Over the past several years, rainfall and snowmelt have flooded and enlarged all three areas into large bodies of water. On appeal, the question is whether the lakebeds of Long Lake, Parks Slough, and Schiley Slough and the water on the lakebeds can be declared separate properties, the land, private, and the water, public....

* * *

During the past 125 years, depending on weather patterns, these areas were either dry or marshy or covered with water at varying depths. Only recently has the land been continuously covered with deep water. For more than seventy years, the areas at issue have been consistently used to pasture cattle and raise crops. Many of the areas now several feet under water had large mature trees growing on them. In their current state, these bodies of water are capable of being used for fishing, hunting, trapping, and other recreational purposes.

* * *

The trial court concluded that the three bodies of water were not "meandered," i.e. not plotted out as lakes, when the federal government surveyed the land before statehood, thus the waters were not "navigable" and the State did not receive title to the beds in question under the equal footing doctrine. Further, the court reasoned that in South Dakota some bodies of water may be deemed "navigable" under the State legal test for navigability, but still remain private. Ultimately, the trial court declared Long Lake, Parks Slough, and Schiley Slough to be private bodies of water and enjoined the State from providing public access to them. Of course, South Dakota was free to open any state owned land to the public if it was adequately marked so that the existing property boundaries under the water could be determined with specificity. On appeal, the State raises the following issues: (1) Whether the public trust doctrine recognizes water as a unique natural resource held in trust by the public for use by the public. (2) Whether the recreational use of water bodies controls public access. (3) Whether the federal "navigability for title" test is applicable to this case.

* * *   *US, navigability outright*

A. Applicable Navigability Test

Since the decision in *Illinois Central Railroad* [*v. Illinois*, 146 U.S. 387 (1892)], it is commonly accepted that states hold navigable waters, as well as lands beneath them, in trust for the public. Here, we must first determine which navigability test applies—the federal navigability for title test or the state navigability test. Under the federal test, the question is whether the water body was "navigable in fact" at the time the state entered the Union....

* * *

Relying on *Lamprey v. Metcalf*, 53 N.W. 1139 (Minn. 1893), this Court assumed that it had the jurisdiction to design its own test of navigability for title and applied the "pleasure boat" test to find the lake navigable.... However, the United States Supreme Court has made clear that the navigability for title test is one of federal law. *United States v. Utah*, 283 U.S. 64, 75 (1931) (The question of navigability is a federal question and state laws cannot affect titles vested in the United States.)....   *ok got it but state test applies where?*

Applying the federal navigability for title test to the lakebeds here, we conclude that the title to these beds lies with the landowners. A review of the record reveals no evidence tending to establish navigability in fact or a use of the water for commercial purposes at the time of statehood. In fact, the survey records reveal that there was little, if any, water on these lands at the time the land was surveyed. Therefore, the circuit court properly applied the federal test of navigability, finding that the beds were owned by those holding the federal patent to the property. But we are still left with the question of water ownership as a separate asset.

* * *

C. Water as a Separate Public Trust Asset.

The landowners here do not claim a vested interest through prior usage or appropriation of the water in the lakes on their land. Their claim is that because they own the land underlying the lakes, they own the water as well. Yet, notwithstanding private ownership of beds underlying water bodies, a number of state courts have recognized the application of the public trust doctrine to their water resources, holding that where a body of water is suitable for public use according to state law standards, a public right to use that water will be recognized.

[An extensive review of case law from other states followed.]

* * *

[I]n 1955, our Legislature reconfirmed that all water is public property and abolished the previous rule that standing water belonged to landowners. The following South Dakota statutes, in the Water Resources Act (SDCL ch 46-1), depart from common law notions of private water ownership, and, although they regulate the appropriative and consumptive uses of water, they reflect an aspect of the public trust doctrine, requiring the State to preserve water for public use.

SDCL 46–1–1:

It is hereby declared that the people of the state have a paramount interest in the use of all the water of the state and that the state shall determine what water of the state, surface and underground, can be converted to public use or controlled for public protection.

SDCL 46–1–2:

It is hereby declared that the protection of the public interest in the development of the water resources of the state is of vital concern to the people of the state and that the state shall determine in what way the water of the state, both surface and underground, should be developed for the greatest public benefit.

SDCL 46–1–3:

It is hereby declared that all water within the state is the property of the people of the state, but the right to the use of water may be acquired by appropriation as provided by law.

The landowners acknowledge the limitations imposed on them by the Water Resources Act, but argue that the Act does not deprive them of their ownership of the water. Although we agree that this Act certainly displaces common law rules of water use where effective, it does not override the public trust doctrine or render it superfluous. History and precedent have established the public trust doctrine as an inherent attribute of sovereign authority. *See Illinois Cent. R.R. Co.*, 146 U.S. at 455 ("[S]uch property is held by the State, by virtue of its sovereignty, in trust for the public."). The doctrine exists independent of any statute. *See, e.g., Nat'l Audubon Soc'y v. Superior Ct. Of Alpine County,* 658 P.2d 709, 728 n.27 (Cal. 1983) ("Aside from the possibility that statutory protections can be repealed, the noncodified public trust doctrine remains important both to confirm the state's sovereign supervision and to require consideration of public trust uses in cases filed directly in the courts...."), *cert. denied,* 464 U.S. 977 (1983); *Kootenai Envtl. Alliance v. Panhandle Yacht Club, Inc.,* 671 P.2d 1085, 1095 (Idaho 1983) ("[M]ere compliance by [agencies] with their legislative authority is not sufficient to determine if their actions comport with the requirements of the public trust doctrine. The public trust doctrine at all times forms the outer boundaries of permissible government action with respect to public trust resources.").

Thus, while we regard the public trust doctrine and Water Resources Act as having shared principles, the Act does not supplant the scope of the public trust doctrine. The Water Resources Act evinces a legislative intent both to allocate and regulate water resources. In part, this Act codifies public trust principles. The first three sections of the Act embody the core principles of the public trust doctrine—"the people of the state have a paramount interest in the use of all the water of the state," SDCL 46–1–1; "the state shall determine in what way the water of the state, both surface and underground, should be developed for the greatest public benefit," SDCL 46–1–2; and "all water within the state is the property of the people of the state." SDCL 46–1–3. *See Caminiti v. Boyle*, 732 P.2d 989, 995 (Wash. 1987) (stating Shoreline Management Act complied with the requirements of the constitutional public trust), *cert. denied*, 484 U.S. 1008 (1988).

From our examination of the statutes and precedent, we conclude that the State of South Dakota retains the right to use, control, and develop the water in these lakes as a separate asset in trust for the public. Accordingly, we align ourselves with the Idaho, Iowa, Minnesota, New Mexico, Montana, North Dakota, Oregon, Utah, and Wyoming decisions that have recognized the public trust doctrine's applicability to water, independent of bed ownership. As our Court stated in 1964, "South Dakota is largely a semi-arid state. The Legislature was fully justified in finding that the public welfare requires the maximum protection and utilization of its water supply." *Knight v. Grimes*, 127 N.W.2d 708, 711 (S.D. 1964). Moreover, we find the public trust doctrine manifested in the South Dakota's Environmental Protection Act, authorizing legal action to protect "the air, water and other natural resources and the public trust therein from pollution, impairment or destruction." SDCL 34A-10-1. This Court has previously recognized the public trust doctrine and applied it to navigable waters and their beds. *Flisrand v. Madson*, 152 N.W. 796, 800 (S.D. 1915) ("State holds the title to such lake bed in trust for the benefit of the public."); *Hillebrand v. Knapp*, 274 N.W. 821, 822–23 (S.D. 1937) ("State holds title to the bed ... not in a proprietary capacity, but in trust for the people that they may enjoy the use of navigable waters for fishing, boating, and other public purposes freed of interference of private parties[.]"); *South Dakota Wildlife Fed'n v. Water Mgmt. Bd*, 382 N.W.2d 26 (S.D. 1986). Today we acknowledge, in accord with the State's sovereign powers and the legislative mandate, that all waters within South Dakota, not just those waters considered navigable under the federal test, are held in trust by the State for the public.

D. Extent of Public's Right to Use Water.

Having determined that the waters in question are public waters held in trust for the people, the more narrow inquiry is whether the public has a right to use these waters for recreation. As previously mentioned, some states have recognized that the public trust extends to recreational use of public waters independent of bed or adjacent land ownership. *Southern Idaho Fish and Game Ass'n v. Picabo Livestock, Inc.*, 528 P.2d 1295 (Idaho 1974) (navigable creek); *State v. Sorensen*, 436 N.W.2d 358 (Iowa 1989) (land adjacent to Missouri River); *Montana Coalition for Stream Access v. Hildreth*, 684 P.2d 1088 (Mont. 1984) (navigable stream flowing over possibly private land); *Montana Coalition for Stream Access v. Curran*, 682 P.2d 163 (Mont. 1984) (navigable stream flowing over private land); *Day v. Armstrong*, 362 P.2d 137 (Wyo. 1961) (regardless of whether it was navigable or non-navigable river channel open for recreational use); *Orion Corp. v. State*, 747 P.2d 1062 (Wash. 1987), *cert. denied* 486 U.S. 1022 (1988) (owner purchased tidelands subject to requirements of public trust doctrine).

In interpreting statutes similar to our Water Resources Act, the Utah Supreme Court held in *J.J.N.P. Co. v. State*, 655 P.2d 1133, 1136, 1137 (Utah 1982):

> Although "navigability" is a standard used to determine title to waterbeds ... it does not establish the extent of the State's interest in the waters of the State.... Section 73–1–1 states: "All waters in this state, whether above or under the ground

are *hereby declared to be the property of the public,* subject to all existing rights to the use thereof."

* * *

Private ownership of the land underlying natural lakes and streams does not defeat the State's power to regulate the use of the water or defeat whatever right the public has to be on the water. *Irrespective of the ownership of the bed and navigability of the water, the public, if it can obtain lawful access to a body of water, has the right to float leisure craft, hunt, fish, and participate in any lawful activity when utilizing that water* (internal citations omitted) (emphasis added).

Yet, it must be noted, the lake in *J.J.N.P. Co.* and the waters considered in the cases cited in the previous paragraph do not compare with the lakes at issue here. In *J.J.N.P. Co.*, the lake was "natural" and permanent. In the cases cited in the previous paragraph, the waters were permanent in nature, being flowing streams, rivers, or tidewaters. Here, the trial court found that during the past 125 years the land on which the lakes now exist had been completely dry, marshy, or covered by shallow, seasonal waters. This land in the past seventy years had been used to pasture cattle and raise crops. It has only been in the last five or six years that the land has been continuously covered by water far deeper than previously experienced.

Furthermore, although state law in both South and North Dakota makes all water public property, neither state has gone so far as to hold that non-meandered lakes navigable under the state test are open for public recreational uses. *Flisrand*, 152 N.W. 796 (meandered lake); *Hillebrand*, 274 N.W. 821 (meandered lake); *Roberts v. Taylor*, 181 N.W. 622 (N.D. 1921) (meandered lake). It is true, as the State contends, that our standard for determining public use is "whether the water is *capable* of use by the public for public purposes." *Flisrand*, 152 N.W. at 800 (meandered lake) (emphasis added). SDCL 43–17–2. "Public purposes" are defined in SDCL 43–17–21 as "including, but not limited to boating, fishing, swimming, hunting, skating, picnicking and similar recreational pursuits." This test is derived from the "pleasure boat" test for navigability in *Flisrand*, *Hillebrand*, and *Lamprey*. Nonetheless, this test has only been applied to areas where the State owns both the lake and the bed. We face a more unique question here.

In abolishing private ownership of "standing water," the Legislature did not necessarily intend that such waters would become open for recreation. On the contrary, in the very Act that abolished this provision, our Legislature appears to have provided reasonable limits respecting vested rights. Thus in eliminating ownership of standing water by private parties, the intent was to preserve water for specific "beneficial" uses. The Water Resources Act states that "Beneficial use is the basis, the measure and the limit of the right to the use of waters described in this title." SDCL 46–1–8....

The Water Resources Act does not explicitly grant to the Water Management Board the responsibility to determine recreational use of public waters. Nonetheless, because the Water Resources Act (SDCL 46) and the Water Resources Management Act (SDCL 46A) are the provisions governing public water lying on or under private property, the Department of Environment and Natural Resources is the agency at present given oversight of these lakes. It is the clear intent of our Legislature to provide for the "general health, welfare and safety of the people" through "the conservation, development, management, and optimum use of all this state's water resources." To balance these multiple uses, the Legislature and Governor formulate policies in the public interest to "be carried out through a coordination of all state agencies and resources." *Id*; SDCL 46A–1–10. Therefore, it is not for us now to proclaim the highest and best use of these public waters in the interest of the "general health, welfare and safety of the people." *Id.* Decisions on beneficial use belong ultimately to the Legislature. SDCL 46–2–11. Deciding how these waters and immediate shorelines should be managed and what constitutes a proper use goes beyond the scope of this opinion. The trial court erred in declaring these waters to be private and in granting an injunction on that basis. In the meantime, in the interest of maintaining the status quo, we leave the injunction intact until such time as, on remand, the trial court has the opportunity to consider the positions of the parties, the state agencies, and the public and grant such relief as it deems appropriate, in light of this opinion.

* * *

In conclusion, the public trust doctrine imposes an obligation on the State to preserve water for public use. It provides that the people of the State own the waters themselves, and that the State, not as a proprietor, but as a trustee, controls the water for the benefit of the public. In keeping with its responsibility, the Legislature has designated the Department of Environment and Natural Resources to manage our public water resources. However, it is ultimately up to the Legislature to decide how these waters are to be beneficially used in the public interest.

Reversed and remanded.

Notes

1. A non-excerpted portion of the case contains a robust inventory of state court cases dealing with water as a separate public trust asset. *Parks v. Cooper,* 676 N.W.2d 823, 835–37 (S.D. 2004).

2. This court, like many others, underscored the essential character of the public trust as an "inherent attribute of sovereign authority." It also described the public trust as a doctrine independent of statutory law, while noting that the water statutes codify the doctrine in part. In a legal context heavily dominated by statutory law, government officials often claim the trust has been subsumed by statute, but as the *Parks* case demonstrates, this is not the case.

3. Notice that the court declared the water over private lands as a public trust asset but left the question of their appropriate use to the legislature. Does this contrast with other decisions that find a public trust right to recreational use of public waters? The court made clear that the public trust "exists independent of any statute," so why did it leave the question of use to the legislature?

4. The lands in question had been dry for at least periods of time until a recent period of "unseasonably wet" years. As climate change alters precipitation patterns, do you think that more courts will be faced with questions of ownership and public use on newly inundated lands? For discussion of climate and precipitation, see Mohammed H.I. Dore, *Climate Change and Changes in Global Precipitation Patterns: What Do We Know?* 31 Environment International 1167–1181 (Oct. 2005).

5. For analysis of the *Parks* case, see Janice Holmes, *Following the Crowd: The Supreme Court of South Dakota Expands the Scope of the Public Trust Doctrine to Non-navigable, Non-meandered Bodies of Water* in Parks v. Cooper, 38 Creighton L. Rev. 1317 (2005). For commentary on the public trust in South Dakota, also see Bradley P. Gordon, *The Emergence of the Public Trust Doctrine as a Public Right to Environmental Preservation in South Dakota,* 29 S.D. L. Rev. 496 (1984).

Wilbour v. Gallagher

Supreme Court of Washington
462 P.2d 232 (1969)

HILL, J.

We are here concerned with the uses to which privately owned land can be put, which for "thirty-five years" has been submerged each year by waters of a navigable lake. The submergence at its maximum depth (3 to 15 feet) was for approximately 3 months, June 15 to September 15 each year.

* * *

Lake Chelan is a glacial gorge in Chelan County, approximately 55 miles in length, and with a width, generally speaking, of from 1 to 2 miles. Its navigability is conceded. Prior to 1927, it lay in its natural state with the level of its waters at 1,079 feet above sea level. By 1891 the land involved in this action had passed into private ownership being included in the "Plat of the Town of Lake Park." The platter dedicated and quitclaimed all streets and alleys therein to the use of the public forever. All of the platted property subsequently became a part of the town of Lakeside, and is now a part of the town of Chelan....

* * *

It should be noted that the public is the beneficiary of the grant in perpetuity of "* * * the right of access * * * over the lands included within the boundaries of those portions of the vacated streets and alleys hereinafter described, to Lake Chelan, at all stages of water * * *."

The Chelan Electric Company constructed a dam, pursuant to a permit by the Federal Power Commission, which permitted the annual raising of the level of the lake to 1,100 feet above sea level, with the requirement that it reach that level by June 15 each year. Thereafter in May of each year the dam was closed and the waters gradually rose to the 1,100 foot level, presumably by June 15th. They are maintained at that level until September when the dam was opened and the waters gradually subsided to the natural 1,079 foot level.

We come now to a consideration of the right claimed by the defendants, Norman G. Gallagher and Ruth I. Gallagher, his wife, to fill their land below the 1,100 foot level to a height 5 feet above that level, and thus prevent its being submerged and making it available for use at all times. (Certain fills have now been completed.)

The claimed right is challenged by the plaintiffs ([Wilbour, et al.]) who brought a class action on behalf of themselves and the public asking that the fills be removed, and asking for damages to their own properties caused by the fills.

* * *

The trial court found that for 35 years prior to the trial (July and September 1965) and except for the filling by the defendants, commenced in 1961, the waters of Lake Chelan

> covered the lands of Defendants in Blocks 2 and 3, Lake Park, including the streets and alleys in and adjacent to said Blocks 2 and 3 for a period each year from late spring through September, to a depth of three feet to fifteen feet.

And that for the same period

> the general public, including Plaintiffs and their respective predecessors in interest, have used the waters covering the portions of Blocks 2 and 3, Plat of Lake Park, now owned by the Defendants, as well as the water covering portions of the streets and alleys adjacent thereto, for fishing, boating, swimming and for gen-

eral recreational use and that said use was open adverse, notorious and uninterrupted for said period, during the period of each year when water covers the
said portions of Block 2 and 3 and the adjacent streets and alleys.

The trial court ultimately concluded (based upon estoppel) that the defendants
should not be compelled to remove their fills, but awarded the plaintiffs damages, finding that the value of the Wilbour property had been lessened $8,500, and the value of
the Green property had been lessened $11,000 by reason of the fills established by the
defendants.

* * *

This lessening of value was predicated principally on the loss of view, but also on inability to use the water over the filled land for navigation, fishing, swimming, boating
and general recreational uses; and because, in consequence of the defendants' fill, "algae
has become an increasing problem, which has created an unsightly situation on Plaintiffs' beaches."

From this judgment the defendants appealed, urging that they were simply making
their own property usable and that any damages sustained by the plaintiffs were damnum
absque injuria.

The plaintiffs have cross-appealed urging that the defendants' fills should have been abated.

The importance of this litigation transcends the consideration it has received from the
public authorities. If every owner of property between the 1,079 foot and the 1,100 foot
level around Lake Chelan has the right the defendants claim, the public's right in the navigable waters of that lake above the 1,079 foot level would be practically nil.

The property owners could make any use, not prohibited by law, of their properties—from fills for trailer parks close to the highways to high-rise apartments close to
the lake.

Unless the laws applicable to the use of navigable waters apply to this annual artificial
extension of the water of Lake Chelan, to preserve the status quo, it would seem that
everybody is on his own.

The plaintiffs have made an excellent case on the basis of prescriptive rights. The
filling of the vacated streets and alleys by the defendants cannot be sustained on any
basis, since they had acquired no title to them and, in any event, the public had the
right of access over the lands included within the boundaries of the vacated streets and
alleys to Lake Chelan at all stages of water. Further, the obvious purpose of the contemporaneous vacation and the grant to the public of the right of access was to enable
the Chelan Electric Company to acquire the right to submerge the streets and alleys
and yet to preserve to the public the right of access over them to the lake "at all stages
of water."

However, it is unnecessary to rely on prescriptive rights, or on the rights of the public to use the land within the vacated streets and alleys for access to the lake. We prefer to
rest our decision on the proposition that the fills made by the defendants constitute an
obstruction to navigation.

While this is a matter of first impression and no exactly comparable case has been
found, our holding represents the logical extension of establish[ed] law in somewhat
comparable situations.

There was no private ownership of the land under Lake Chelan in its natural state,
and no right to obstruct navigation.

It is well settled that if the level of the lake had been raised to the 1,100 foot level and had been maintained constantly at that level for the prescriptive period, the 1,100 foot level would be considered the natural level of the lake with the submerged lands being converted into part of the lake bed and to state ownership. The public would have the right to use all of the water of the lake up to the 1,100 foot level. *State v. Malmquist*, 40 A.2d 534 (Vt. 1944); *Village of Pewaukee v. Savoy*, 79 N.W. 436 (Wis. 1899).

We have here, however, not only the raising of the lake level by artificial means, but the distinctive features that the level does not remain constant and that the owners of the land between the 1,079 and the 1,100 foot level can occupy their property during most of the year.

We find a somewhat comparable situation in those navigable lakes which have a natural or seasonal fluctuation in extent, and have a recognized high water line and low water line. However, in those cases the problems involved usually hinge on the rights accorded riparian owners (whose titles go to the low water mark) in the areas between the high and low water marks.

The law is quite clear that where the level of a navigable body of water fluctuates due to natural causes so that a riparian owner's property is submerged part of the year, the public has the right to use all the waters of the navigable lake or stream whether it be at the high water line, the low water line, or in between. *Doemel v. Jantz*, 193 N.W. 393 (Wis. 1923); *Diana Shooting Club v. Husting*, 145 N.W. 816 (Wis. 1914). In such situations the riparian owners whose lands are periodically submerged are said to have the right to prevent any trespass on their land between the high and the low marks when not submerged. However, title between those lines is qualified by the public right of navigation and the state may prevent any use of it that interferes with that right....

Thus, in the situation of a naturally varying water level, the respective rights of the public and of the owners of the periodically submerged lands are dependent upon the level of the water. As the level rises, the rights of the public to use the water increase since the area of water increases; correspondingly, the rights of the landowners decrease since they cannot use their property in such a manner as to interfere with the expanded public rights. As the level and the area of the water decreases, the rights of the public decrease and the rights of the landowners increase as the waters drain off their land, again giving them the right to exclusive possession until their lands are again submerged.

When the circumstance of an artificial raising of navigable waters to a temporary higher level is synthesized with the law dealing with navigable waters having a naturally fluctuating level, the logically resulting rule for the protection of the public interest is that, where the waters of a navigable body are periodically raised and lowered by artificial means, the artificial fluctuation should be considered the same as a natural fluctuation with the rights of the public being the same in both situations, i.e., the public has the right to go where the navigable waters go, even though the navigable waters lie over privately owned lands.

* * *

Following the reasoning of these cases we hold that when the level of Lake Chelan is raised to the 1,100 foot mark (or such level as submerges the defendants' land), that land is subjected to the rights of navigation, together with its incidental rights of fishing, boating, swimming, water skiing, and other related recreational purposes generally regarded as corollary to the right of navigation and the use of public waters. *Nelson v. DeLong*, 7 N.W.2d 342 (Minn. 1942). When the level of the lake is lowered so that the defendants' land is no longer submerged, then they are entitled to keep trespassers off their land, and may do with the land as they wish consistent with the right of navigation when it is submerged.

It follows that the defendants' fills, insofar as they obstruct the submergence of the land by navigable waters at or below the 1,100 foot level, must be removed. The court cannot authorize or approve an obstruction to navigation.

* * *

NEILL, J. (dissenting in part).

* * *

The majority opinion reaches the conclusion that the fill on defendants' lots is to be removed on the basis that this fill constitutes an obstruction to navigation. Analogizing from the rule that the public has the right to the use of navigable water at both high levels and low levels, subject to the right of littoral owners to reasonably obstruct them with "aids to navigation" such as docks, wharfs, etc., the majority holds that fluctuations of water levels which are artificially created are no different than fluctuations created by nature.

The difficulty, as I view it, is that under the majority's holding there is a taking of defendants' property right for public use without just compensation. Defendants (through their antecedents in the chain of title) have a full fee title diminished *only* by the right of the power company to periodically inundate their lands to a specific elevation. I see no reason in law or equity for preventing such an owner from protecting his land against such inundation by raising the grade of the land.

The periodic flooding involved here is entirely different from a natural raising and lowering of the lake level by reason of rains, seasonal runoff, and drought. In the latter instance, the littoral owner's rights to the foreshore lands between high and low water, whatever these rights may be, are subject to the public's navigation rights. Here, the defendants' lots, *all of which lie above natural high water*, are not subject to public navigation rights unless there has been a voluntary conveyance, eminent domain proceedings, estoppel, or loss through prescription.[4] Unless precluded by one of the aforementioned reasons, defendants have the right to use their lots, including the right to change the grade thereof, in order to make any lawful use thereof. Accordingly, I do not agree that the fill on defendants' lots is unlawful. They should not be required to remove it.

* * *

Notes

1. Prior to *Wilbour*, the late Professor Ralph Johnson concluded that state case law meant that, in Washington, landowner riparian rights on navigable waters gave way to public rights managed by the state. Ralph W. Johnson, *Riparian and Public Rights to Lakes and Streams*, 35 Wash. L. Rev. & St. B. J. 580 (1960).

2. The court indicated that the case could have been decided in the same way on the basis of using prescriptive rights gained by the public. Yet it preferred to rest its decision on the basis of obstructing navigation. Why? What effect did the decision have as precedent on the other properties around the lake that are inundated during the same period of the year? If the court had relied on the prescriptive rights basis, would that have resolved title questions as to these other properties?

3. The court ruled that public rights increase when a natural lake like Lake Chelan is artificially enlarged. For other decisions extending public rights due to damming streams

---

4. Emphasis in original.

inundating private lands, see *State v. Head*, 498 S.E.2d 389 (S.C. Ct. App. 1997); *Bohn v. Albertson*, 238 P.2d 128 (Cal. Dist. Ct. App. 1951); *Diversion Lake Club v. Heath*, 86 S.W.2d 441 (Tex. 1935); *State v. Superior Court*, 625 P.2d 256 (Cal. 1981) (where a lake is navigable, increasing its size via a dam or levee subjects the additional submerged acres to the public trust). For a decision extending the public trust doctrine to artificially created waters, see *McQueen v. South Carolina Coastal Council* (p. 159); *cf. Golden Feather Community Ass'n v. Thermalito Irrigation Dist.*, 199 Cal.App.3d 402 (1988) (no trust duty to maintain lake levees for fish in a wholly non-navigable, artificial reservoir).

4. The court recognized that the case presented an issue of "first impression," and that "no exactly comparable case has been found." It considered its decision to be a "logical extension of establish[ed] law in somewhat comparable situations." As public trust cases encounter a new set of issues brought on by biodiversity loss, climate change, water depletion, and the like, courts will be asked to formulate rules in many cases of first impression.

Arkansas River Rights Committee v. Echubby Lake Hunting Club

Court of Appeals of Arkansas
126 S.W.3d. 738 (2003)

STROUD, C.J.

[Due to the U.S. Army Corps of Engineers' McClellan-Kerr Navigation project on the Arkansas River, which made the river navigable from the Mississippi River to Tulsa, certain areas that had been uplands became accessible to recreational boaters and hunters after 1968. In 2001, the Echubby Lake Hunting Club bought the Echubby areas and sought to deny the public access to these now inundated areas. The Arkansas River Rights Committee, a group of hunters and fishers, challenged the club's right to exclude on grounds of both prescription and navigability. The landowner prevailed in the lower court, but the Arkansas Supreme Court reversed. After ruling that the public could obtain a prescriptive right to hunt and fish after seven years of use without the landowner's consent if the newly inundated areas had a new discernible high-water mark, the court turned to the navigability issue.]

* * *

Navigability

Determining the navigability of a stream is essentially a matter of deciding if it is public or private property. *State v. McIlroy*, 595 S.W.2d 659 (Ark. 1980), *cert. denied*, 449 U.S. 843 (1980). If a body of water is navigable, it is considered to be held by the State in trust for the public. *See Hayes v. State*, 496 S.W.2d 372 (Ark. 1973); 9 Powell on Real Property §65.11[2][a] (2003). Navigability is a question of fact. *Goforth v. Wilson*, 184 S.W.2d 814 (Ark. 1945).

Arkansas law has defined navigability as follows:

> The true criterion is the dictate of sound business common sense, and depends on the usefulness of the stream to the population of its banks, as a means of carrying off the products of their fields and forests, or bringing to them articles of merchandise. If, in its natural state, without artificial improvements, it may be prudently relied upon and used for that purpose at some seasons of the year, recurring with tolerable regularity, then in the American sense, it is navigable....

McIlroy, 595 S.W.2d at 663 (quoting *Lutesville Sand & Gravel Co. v. McLaughlin*, 26 S.W.2d 892 (Ark. 1930)). In 1980, this definition was expanded by the supreme court to include consideration of the water's recreational use as well as its commercial use in determining navigability. In *McIlroy*, the court was asked to determine whether a stream that had considerable recreational value for boating and fishing was navigable, even though it lacked the commercial adaptability that was the hallmark of traditional navigability. The case involved the Mulberry River, described in the opinion as an intermediate stream at least 100 feet wide at some points, that for fifty to fifty-five miles of its length could be and often was floated by canoes or flat-bottomed boats. The Mulberry was designated by the state Department of Parks and Tourism as Arkansas's finest whitewater float stream. In 1838, it was "meandered" by surveyors, which is prima facie evidence of navigability. Based on these facts, the supreme court held that "there is no doubt that the segment of the Mulberry River that is involved in this lawsuit can be used for a substantial portion of the year for recreational purposes. Consequently, we hold that it is navigable...." *McIlroy*, 595 S.W.2d at 665.

Under *McIlroy*, it is apparent that navigability may be established by recreational usefulness as well as commercial usefulness. In the present case, the Selvey affidavit filed by appellant shows that the Echubby areas have at least some recreational usefulness. Selvey stated that, in the past seven years, he and other fishermen have boated over the entire surface of Pool 2, which includes the Echubby areas, and further that water covers the areas year round. Admittedly, there is nothing in the record at this point to show that the level of recreational use in the Echubby areas compares with the extensive use of the Mulberry River in *McIlroy*, and obviously, the occasional foray by a fisherman into an area does not render it navigable; if that were so, every creek and pond in the state would be navigable. However, we believe that the Selvey affidavit is sufficient to create a fact question as to the Echubby areas' navigability. Therefore, summary judgment was improper on this issue.

Appellee contends that the areas' present-day navigability is not relevant; rather, navigability must solely be determined as of the date of Arkansas's statehood because each state, upon entry into the union, took title to the navigable waters within its borders. *See generally Utah v. United States*, 403 U.S. 9 (1971); *Anderson v. Reames*, 161 S.W.2d 957 (Ark. 1942). We disagree that the concept of navigability for the purpose of determining the public's right to use water is that static. Although navigability to fix ownership of a river bed or riparian rights is determined as of the date of the state's entry into the union, navigability for other purposes may arise later. *See, e.g., United States v. Appalachian Elec. Power Co.*, 311 U.S. 377 (1940); *Hitchings v. Del Rio Woods Recreation & Park Dist.*, 55 Cal.App.3d 560, 568 (1976) ("navigability for purposes of a public navigational easement need not be evaluated as of the date of statehood; it may later arise"); *Bohn v. Albertson*, 238 P.2d 128, 132 (Cal. Dist. Ct. App. 1951) ("if the evidence showed the creation of a new channel of the river, the fact that there was no such channel [at statehood] would not prevent the assertion by proper public authority of the right to use that channel for navigation and fishing"); 65 C.J.S. Navigable Waters § 12 at 68 (2000). This point can be illustrated by the fact that, in the following cases, the Arkansas Supreme Court did not address navigability for the purpose of public usage in terms of whether the water was navigable at the time of statehood but whether the water was currently navigable. *See State v. McIlroy*; *Hayes v. State*; *Five Lakes Outing Club, Inc. v. Horseshoe Lake Protective Ass'n*, 288 S.W.2d 942 (Ark. 1956); *McGahhey v. McCollum*, 179 S.W.2d 661 (Ark. 1944). One case phrased the question of navigability as "whether the lake is susceptible of public servitude as a means of transportation *either now or within the foreseeable future*...." *Parker v. Moore*, 262 S.W.2d 891, 893 (Ark. 1953). Thus, we do not believe that an area's navigability, in the sense that the public may use it, is conclusively established by that area's status in 1836.

Appellee also contends that navigability should be determined by the condition of the area in its natural state, without improvements. It bases its argument on the oft-repeated adage that a waterway is navigable "if, in its natural state, without artificial improvements, it may be prudently relied upon and used for that purpose." *See Lutesville Sand & Gravel Co. v. McLaughlin*, 26 S.W.2d 892, 893 (Ark. 1930). Appellee claims that, because the level of the water in the Echubby areas was artificially raised by the lock and dam, the areas cannot be navigable. First of all, there were no improvements made to the Echubby areas themselves; the inundation of water occurred as the result of improvements on another waterway, the Arkansas River. Second, we have found no Arkansas case, and appellee has cited none, in which the courts have held that a body of water should be closed to the public simply because it was rendered navigable through improvements made to another body of water. We therefore decline to affirm the summary judgment on this basis.

* * *

Notes

1. The cases above introduce some strange terms. A "littoral" owner is the functional equivalent of a riparian or shoreside landowner, except that littoral owners are usually lakeside or oceanside, not riverside. Also, a "meandered" stream is one so designated in an early survey and it is *prima facie* evidence of navigability.

2. The *Arkansas River Rights* decision illustrates the importance of the definition of navigable waters to the scope of public trust rights. The matter can be confusing, because navigability is used to define different sets of public rights. One definition of navigability is federal and used for purposes of determining title to streambeds. Title navigability is decided under the so-called federal equal footing doctrine (*see Pollard v. Hagen*, p. 66). It is, of course, related to the public trust doctrine, since the implicit conveyance of lands submerged beneath navigable waters in Statehood Acts came with the conditions recognized by the Supreme Court in *Illinois Central* (*see* p. 68). But another type of navigability, at issue in the *Arkansas* case, determines whether the public can use the surface of waterways for recreation or other means. This is a matter of state law. The court distinguished between the two types when it said, "Although navigability to fix ownership of a river bed or riparian rights is determined as of the date of the state's entry into the union, navigability for other purposes may arise later." The scope of the public trust doctrine, which limits private rights to exclude the public, is not confined to the submerged lands conveyed to the state by equal footing, as the *Arkansas* court makes clear. How would you describe the public rights affirmed by the *Arkansas* court? Is it a servitude to use surface waters and submerged lands for recreational purposes?

3. The court relied heavily on one of its earlier decisions, *State v. McIlroy*, 595 S.W.2d 659 (Ark. 1980), a case in which the court changed the state definition of navigability to include all waterways suitable for regular recreational use, a question of fact. The decision expanded public rights in those waterways while reducing the ability of adjacent landowners to exclude the public. This evolution of the definition of state navigability has actually been going on for some time. For example, in the nineteenth century, many states broadened their definitions of navigability (and thereby expanded public rights) by adopting the "log float" test. *See* Harrison C. Dunning, 2 WATERS AND WATER RIGHTS, § 32.02 (Amy K. Kelley, ed., 3rd ed. 2014). *McIlroy* is emblematic of twentieth century cases that adopt what has been called the "pleasure boat" test. *Id.* § 32.03.

4. *Arkansas River Rights* expands the *McIlroy* result by making navigability adaptable to physical changes to waterways. The common law doctrines of accretion and reliction accommodated physical changes that were gradual by adjusting land titles accordingly.

See id. § 603(b)(2). This decision, however, went beyond a gradual change to accommodate a physical change that could be more than gradual—in this case, due to a man-made water project. Other courts have also interpreted state navigable waters to reflect physical changes produced by artificial means. *See, e.g., Parks v. Cooper* (p. 106) (state navigability not limited to waters that were navigable at the time of statehood, so rising water levels increase public rights); *McQueen v. South Carolina Coastal Council*, 580 S.E.2d 116 (S.C. 2003) (applying the public trust doctrine to wetlands created by a man-made canal).

5. The court also observed that public rights can be gained through open and notorious use for the statutorily defined prescriptive period. However, in many states public prescriptive rights are disfavored and construed narrowly. *See, e.g., Carnahan v. Moriah Property Owners Ass'n*, 716 N.E.2d 437 (Ind. 1999) (rejecting a public prescriptive right for recreation), *citing* 25 Am. Jur. 2d *Easements and Licenses* § 45, at 615 (1996, 1999 Supp.).

6. The upshot of cases like *Arkansas River Rights* and *McIlroy* is that some landowners lose the right to exclude the public from newly declared navigable waters. Do these redefinitions amount to a taking of landowner rights? Or, alternatively, does the public trust amount to a basic encumbrance that is considered antecedent to privately acquired rights, even though the *scope* of the trust may expand with changing public needs? If the public trust is a pre-existing easement on private property, is it one that inherently incorporates flexibility to expand? What are the limits to that expansion? Consider these questions as you read through other cases in later chapters.

7. The scope of public rights in tidal areas is usually the mean high tide line, meaning that the public has a right to access intertidal areas between the low and high tide lines. Concerning inland waters, the scope of public rights is usually thought of as the "ordinary high water mark." The following case defines that term.

Glass v. Goeckel

Supreme Court of Michigan
703 N.W.2d 58 (2005)

CORRIGAN, J.

The issue presented in this case is whether the public has a right to walk along the shores of the Great Lakes where a private landowner ostensibly holds title to the water's edge. To resolve this issue we must consider two component questions: (1) how the public trust doctrine affects private littoral title; and (2) whether the public trust encompasses walking among the public rights protected by the public trust doctrine.

Despite the competing legal theory offered by Justice Markman, our Court unanimously agrees that plaintiff does not interfere with defendants' property rights when she walks within the area of the public trust. Yet we decline to insist, as do Justices Markman and Young, that submersion at a given moment defines the boundary of the public trust. Similarly, we cannot leave uncorrected the Court of Appeals award to littoral landowners of a "right of exclusive use" down to the water's edge, which upset the balance between private title and public rights along our Great Lakes and disrupted a previously quiet status quo.

Plaintiff Joan Glass asserts that she has the right to walk along Lake Huron. Littoral landowners defendants Richard and Kathleen Goeckel maintain that plaintiff trespasses on their private land when she walks the shoreline. Plaintiff argues that the public trust doctrine, which is a legal principle as old as the common law itself, and the Great Lakes

Submerged Lands Act (GLSLA), MCL 324.32501 *et seq.*, protect her right to walk along the shore of Lake Huron unimpeded by the private title of littoral landowners. Plaintiff contends that the public trust doctrine and the GLSLA preserve public rights in the Great Lakes and their shores that limit any private property rights enjoyed by defendants.

Although we find plaintiff's reliance on the GLSLA misplaced, we conclude that the public trust doctrine does protect her right to walk along the shores of the Great Lakes. American law has long recognized that large bodies of navigable water, such as the oceans, are natural resources and thoroughfares that belong to the public. In our common-law tradition, the state, as sovereign, acts as trustee of public rights in these natural resources. Consequently, the state lacks the power to diminish those rights when conveying littoral property to private parties. This "public trust doctrine," as the United States Supreme Court stated in *Illinois Central R. Co. v. Illinois*, 146 U.S. 387, 435 (1892) (*Illinois Central I*), and as recognized by our Court in *Nedtweg v. Wallace*, 208 N.W. 51 (Mich. 1926), applies not only to the oceans, but also to the Great Lakes.

* * *

[After discussing that history of the public trust doctrine and The Great Lakes Submerged Lands Act, the court turned to the application of the public trust doctrine to the Great Lakes.]

In applying the public trust doctrine to the oceans, courts have traditionally held that rights protected by this doctrine extend from the waters themselves and the lands beneath them to a point on the shore called the "ordinary high water mark." *See, e.g., Shively v. Bowlby*, 152 U.S. 1 (1894); *Hardin v. Jordan*, 140 U.S. 371, 381 (1891); *see also* Hargrave's Law Tracts 11, 12, quoted in *Shively, supra* at 12 ("'The shore is that ground that is between the ordinary high water and low water mark [and this ground belongs to the sovereign.]'"). The United States Supreme Court described this common-law concept of the "high water mark" in *Borax Consolidated, Ltd. v. Los Angeles*, 296 U.S. 10, 22–23 (1935):

> The tideland extends to the high water mark. This does not mean ... a physical mark made upon the ground by the waters; it means the line of high water as determined by the course of the tides. By the civil law, the shore extends as far as the highest waves reach in winter. But by the common law, the shore "is confined to the flux and reflux of the sea at ordinary tides." It is the land "between ordinary high and low-water mark, the land over which the daily tides ebb and flow. When, therefore, the sea, or a bay, is named as a boundary, the line of ordinary high-water mark is always intended where the common law prevails" [citations omitted].

An "ordinary high water mark" therefore has an intuitive meaning when applied to tidal waters. Because of lunar influence, ocean waves ebb and flow, thus reaching one point on the shore at low tide and reaching a more landward point at high tide. The latter constitutes the high water mark on a tidal shore. The land between this mark and the low water mark is submerged on a regular basis, and so remains subject to the public trust doctrine as "submerged land." *See, e.g., Illinois Central R. Co. v. Chicago*, 176 U.S. 646, 660 (1900) (*Illinois Central II*) ("But it is equally well settled that, in the absence of any local statute or usage, a grant of lands by the State does not pass title to *submerged lands below [the] high water mark*....") (citations omitted; emphasis added).

Michigan's courts have adopted the ordinary high water mark as the landward boundary of the public trust. For example, in an eminent domain case concerning property on a bay of Lake Michigan, we held that public rights end at the ordinary high water mark.

Peterman v. Dep't of Natural Resources, 521 N.W.2d 499 (Mich. 1994).[5] Thus, we awarded damages for destruction of the plaintiff's property above the ordinary high water mark that resulted from construction by the state (which occurred undisputedly in the water and within the public trust). *Id.* Similarly, in an earlier case where the state asserted its control under the public trust doctrine over a portion of littoral property, the Court also employed the high water mark as the boundary of the public trust. *State v. Venice of America Land Co.*, 125 N.W. 770, 778–79 (Mich. 1910).

Our court has previously suggested that Michigan law leaves some ambiguity regarding whether the high or low water mark serves as the boundary of the public trust. *See People v. Broedell*, 112 N.W.2d 517, 518–19 (Mich. 1961). But the established distinction in public trust jurisprudence between public rights (*jus publicum*) and private title (*jus privatum*) resolves this apparent ambiguity. Cases that seem to suggest, at first blush, that the public trust ends at the low water mark actually considered the boundary of the littoral owner's private property (*jus privatum*) rather than the boundary of the public trust (*jus publicum*). Because the public trust doctrine preserves public rights separate from a landowner's fee title, the boundary of the public trust need not equate with the boundary of a landowner's littoral title. Rather, a landowner's littoral title might extend past the boundary of the public trust. Our case law nowhere suggests that private title necessarily ends where public rights begin. To the contrary, the distinction we have drawn between private title and public rights demonstrates that the *jus privatum* and the *jus publicum* may overlap.

* * *

Our public trust doctrine employs a term, "the ordinary high water mark," from the common law of the sea and applies it to our Great Lakes. While this term has an obvious meaning when applied to *tidal* waters with regularly recurring high and low tides, its application to *nontidal* waters like the Great Lakes is less apparent.... Notwithstanding some prior imprecision in its use, a term such as "ordinary high water mark" attempts to encapsulate the fact that water levels in the Great Lakes fluctuate. This fluctuation results in temporary exposure of land that may then remain exposed above where water currently lies. This land, although not immediately and presently submerged, falls within the ambit of the public trust because the lake has not permanently receded from that point and may yet again exert its influence up to that point.... Our sister state, Wisconsin, defines the ordinary high water mark as:

> the point on the bank or shore up to which the presence and action of the *Lakes* water is so continuous as to leave a distinct mark either by erosion, destruction of terrestrial vegetation, or other easily recognized characteristic. And where the bank or shore at any particular place is of such a character that is impossible or difficult to ascertain where the point of ordinary high-water mark is, recourse may be had to other places on the bank or shore of the same stream or lake to determine whether a given stage of water is above or below ordinary high-water mark.

* * *

III. The Public Trust Includes Walking Within Its Boundaries

We have established thus far that the private title of littoral landowners remains subject to the public trust beneath the ordinary high water mark. But plaintiff, as a member

---

5. This decision relied not simply on a "navigational servitude" unique to that case, but rooted that "navigational servitude" in the public trust doctrine. *See id.* at 508 n. 22, citing *Collins v. Gerhardt*, 211 N.W. 115, 117 (Mich. 1926); *Venice of America Land Co.*, 125 N.W. 770 (Mich. 1910); *Nedtweg v. Wallace*, 211 N.W. 647 (Mich. 1927). 208 N.W. 51, 52–53.

of the public, may walk below the ordinary high water mark only if that practice receives the protection of the public trust doctrine. We hold that walking along the shore, subject to regulation (as is any exercise of public rights in the public trust) falls within the scope of the public trust.

* * *

In order to engage in these activities specifically protected by the public trust doctrine, the public must have a right of passage over land below the ordinary high water mark. Indeed, other courts have recognized a "right of passage" as protected with their public trust. *See Town of Orange v. Resnick*, 109 A. 864 (Conn. 1920) (listing as public rights "fishing, boating, hunting, bathing, taking shellfish, gathering seaweed, cutting sedge and … passing and repassing"); *Arnold v. Mundy*, 6 N.J.L. 1, 12 (1821) (reserving to the public the use of waters for "purposes of passing and repassing, navigation, fishing, fowling, [and] sustenance").

We can protect traditional public rights under our public trust doctrine only by simultaneously safeguarding activities inherent in the exercise of those rights. *See, e.g., Attorney General, ex rel. Director of Conservation v. Taggart*, 11 N.W.2d 193 (Mich. 1943) (permitting wading in a stream pursuant to the public trust doctrine). Walking the lakeshore below the ordinary high water mark is just such an activity, because gaining access to the Great Lakes to hunt, fish, or boat required walking to reach the water. Consequently, the public has always held a right of passage in and along the lakes.

Even before our state joined the Union, the Northwest Ordinance of 1787, art. IV, protected our Great Lakes in trust: "The navigable waters leading into the Mississippi and St. Lawrence, and the carrying places between the same, shall be common highways and forever free…." *See* Northwest Ordinance of 1787, art. IV. Given that we must protect the Great Lakes as "common highways," *see id.*, we acknowledge that our public trust doctrine permits pedestrian use — in and of itself — of our Great Lakes, up to and including the land below the ordinary high water mark.

* * *

We must conclude with two caveats. By no means does our public trust doctrine permit every use of the trust lands and waters. Rather, this doctrine protects only limited public rights, and it does not create an unlimited public right to access private land below the ordinary high water mark. *See Ryan v. Brown*, 18 Mich. 196, 209 (1869). The public trust doctrine cannot serve to justify trespass on private property. Finally, any exercise of these traditional public rights remains subject to criminal or civil regulation by the Legislature.

* * *

Notes

1. The practical effect of this decision is to recognize public rights to walk along Michigan's Great Lakes shorelines below the ordinary high water mark, which means that the public is not restricted to areas currently inundated by water. The court defined the ordinary high water mark as the point on the bank or shore on which the presence of water leaves a distinct mark. A two-member dissent would have restricted public trust rights to inundated lands. *Glass*, 703 N.W.2d at 79.

Extending the principal decision throughout the Great Lakes states and provinces is the aim of a proposed Great Lakes Trail that would link some 10,000 miles of coastline and would establish the longest walking trail in the world. See Melissa K. Scanlan, *Blueprint for the Great Lakes Trail,* 4 Mich. J. Envtl. & Admin. L. 61 (2014) (contending that getting people to use their public trust rights in walking the coasts of the Great Lakes will engage them in actively seeing the importance of the Great Lakes as an ecological, political, economic, and cultural asset, a precursor to developing and implementing cooperative Great Lakes governance structures).

2. In *Merrill v. Ohio Dep't of Natural Resources,* 955 N.E.2d 935 (Ohio 2011), the Ohio Supreme Court agreed that the state's public trust doctrine burdens the submerged lands of Lake Erie. But the court was unwilling to expressly recognize the upland boundary of the public trust as the ordinary high water mark, instead ruling that the limit was the "natural shoreline," a term of uncertain scope.

3. In the so-called "Ice Mountain controversy," Nestle Waters North America, the world's largest producer of bottled water (with about one-third of the global market), began pumping groundwater in 2002 from the Sanctuary Springs aquifer in Mecosta County, Michigan, after being rebuffed in Wisconsin due to public concern over adverse effects on trout streams. Michigan Citizens for Water Conservation challenged the pumping, claiming adverse effects on the local hydrology and the public trust. After a lower court enjoined the pumping, the Michigan Court of Appeals affirmed based on an unreasonable use of groundwater and riparian rights claims. Earlier in the case, the lower court dismissed a public trust doctrine claim, and the Court of Appeals affirmed, on the ground that the pumping adversely affected only a non-navigable stretch above the navigable portion of the stream. *Michigan Citizens for Water Conservation v. Nestle Waters North America, Inc.,* 709 N.W.2d 174, 218–20 (Mich. Ct. App. 2005), *aff'd in part, rev'd in part,* 737 N.W.2d 447 (Mich. 2007), *rehearing denied,* 739 N.W.2d 332 (Mich. 2007) (rejecting the argument that public trust doctrine applied to non-navigable tributary waters, relying on *Bott v. Comm'n of Natural Resources,* 327 N.W.2d 838, 846 (Mich. 1982) (denying any connection between non-public trust and public trust waters, such as that recognized by the California Supreme Court in *National Audubon Society v. Superior Court of Alpine County,* 658 P.2d 709, 727 (Cal. 1983))).

When the case reached the Michigan Supreme Court, that court ruled that citizens lacked standing to sue under the Michigan Environmental Protection Act (MEPA) to address damage to wetlands located on private property in which the plaintiffs had no proprietary interest. *Michigan Citizens for Water Conservation v. Nestle Waters North America, Inc.,* 737 N.W.2d 447 (Mich. 2007) (ruling that citizens had standing to maintain a MEPA suit only where they could establish a concrete and particularized proprietary injury). Nestle subsequently settled the case in 2009, agreeing to cut its pumping roughly in half; the company then proceeded to expand its bottled water operations from a municipal well dedicated to it by the City of Evart, located on the Muskegon River.

The standing analysis in *Nestle* was explicitly overruled by a 4–3 Michigan Supreme Court in *Lansing Schools Educ. Ass'n v. Lansing Bd. of Educ.,* 792 N.W.2d 686 (Mich. 2010) (holding that teachers had standing to sue a school board to compel expulsion of students who assaulted them and explaining that statutes granting standing should be applied as written). In a subsequent environmental case, *Anglers of the AuSable v. Dep't of Envtl. Quality,* 793 N.W.2d 596, 603 (Mich. 2010) (applying the public trust doctrine to a wastewater dumping proposal), the court followed its decision in *Lansing* and held that landowners and an anglers association had standing to sue the state Department of Environmental Quality for violating MEPA. The *Anglers* court ruled that the statute "should be applied as written" and concluded that MEPA clearly supported standing for plaintiffs by specifying that "any person may maintain an action ... against any person for the protection of the air, water, and other natural resources and the public trust in these resources from pollution, impairment, or destruction." *Id.* But after a change in the composition of the court, in another 4–3 decision, the Michigan Supreme Court vacated its earlier decision because the discharger had abandoned the pollution discharge permit under challenge in *Anglers of the AuSable v. Dep't of Envtl. Quality*, 796 N.W.2d 240 (Mich. 2011) (also vacating the decision of the Court of Appeals, leaving the lower court decision in place; that court ruled that the wastewater discharges would interfere with riparian rights and cause adverse effects in violation of MEPA).

A useful source on Great Lakes law is Professor Noah Hall's blog, available at http://www.greatlakeslaw.org/blog; *see also* James Olson, *All Aboard: Navigating the Course for Universal Adoption of the Public Trust Doctrine*, 15 Vt. J. Envtl. L. 135 (2014).

4. In *McGarvey v. Whittredge*, 28 A.3d 620 (Me. 2011), the Maine Supreme Court ruled that the public had the right to access lands between low and high waters, even those lands owned by Maine landowners.

5. The Great Lakes Compact of 2008, ratified by all eight Great Lakes states and approved by Congress, Act of Oct. 3, 2008, Pub. L. No. 110-342, 122 Stat. 3739, regulates out-of-basin diversions and withdrawals and defines groundwater as a trust resource. However, the Compact also disclaims any intent to affect state common law, and none of the eight Great Lakes states' public trust doctrines extend to non-navigable waters. Thus, courts will be called upon to reconcile the Compact's inclusion of groundwater as a public trust resource and the state pre-existing common law. *See* Bridget Donegan, *The Great Lakes Compact and the Public Trust Doctrine: Beyond Michigan and Wisconsin Common Law*, 24 J. Envtl. L. & Litig. 455 (2009) (arguing that the Compact established a separate "Compact public trust doctrine" governing groundwater). *See also* James M. Olson, *Navigating the Great Lakes Compact: Water, Public Trust, and International Trade Agreements*, 2006 Mich. St. L. Rev. 1103 (2006); Noah D. Hall, *Toward a New Horizontal Federalism: Interstate Water Management in the Great Lakes Region*, 77 U. Colo. L. Rev. 405 (2006).

Montana Coalition for Stream Access, Inc. v. Curran

Supreme Court of Montana
682 P.2d 163 (Mont. 1984)

HASWELL, C.J.

The District Court held that the public have a right to use waters and the streambed of the Dearborn River up to the high water mark as it flows through Curran's property and that the State of Montana owns the streambed between the low water marks. The District Court also dismissed Curran's counterclaim for inverse condemnation. We affirm.

The Dearborn River is approximately sixty-six miles long and originates along the east slope of the Continental Divide in west-central Montana. The river flows generally in a southeasterly direction from its source near Scapegoat Mountain, approximately thirty miles southwest of Augusta, Montana, to the Missouri River.

* * *

Curran and Curran Oil Co., of which he is a principal stockholder, have extensive land holdings in Lewis and Clark and Cascade Counties. Curran also holds leases to some state lands through which the Dearborn flows. Approximately six to seven miles of the Dearborn flows through property owned or controlled by Curran. About four and one-half sections of Curran's land on the Dearborn are immediately upstream from the point at which

U.S. Highway 287 crosses the Dearborn and about six and one-half sections, including one isolated section, are downstream from Highway 287.

Curran claims title to the banks and streambed of a portion of the Dearborn River and claims to have the right, as an owner of private property, to restrict its use.

The District Court essentially held that the Dearborn River is in fact navigable for recreation purposes under Montana law; that recreation access to it is determined by state law according to one criterion — namely, navigability for recreation purposes; and that the question of recreational access is to be determined according to state, not federal, law.

[The court ruled that the Dearborn River met the federal test for title navigability because it was used for log drives prior to statehood.]

Of further importance to the issue of navigability for title is the Public Trust Doctrine. The theory underlying this doctrine can be traced from Roman Law through Magna Carta to present day decisions.

The Public Trust Doctrine was first clearly defined in *Illinois Central Railroad v. Illinois*, 146 U.S. 387 (1892). In this case the United States Supreme Court was called upon to determine whether the State of Illinois had the right to convey, by legislative grant, a portion of Chicago's harbor on Lake Michigan to the Illinois Central Railroad....

In summary, the "equal-footing" doctrine as set forth in *Pollard's Lessee*, 44 U.S. 212 (1845), which held that the federal government retained title to navigable waters so that all states entering the Union subsequent to the original thirteen would enter on an "equal footing" and the Public Trust Doctrine, which provides that states hold title to navigable waterways in trust for the public benefit and use are two important doctrines to be considered in determining a navigability-for-title question. In this matter, the log-floating test was properly applied and the State found to hold title to the riverbed of the Dearborn. In this matter, where title to the bed of the Dearborn rests with the State, the test of navigability for *use* and not for title, is a test to be determined under state law and not federal law.

* * *

III

[Another] issue is whether the District Court erred in determining that recreational use and fishing make a stream navigable. We find no error.

The concept of determining navigability based upon public recreational use is not new. One of the earlier cases, decided in 1893, held:

> ... The division of waters into navigable and nonnavigable is but a way of dividing them into public and private waters, — a classification which, in some form, every civilized nation has recognized; the line of division being largely determined by its conditions and habits. In early times, about the only use — except, perhaps, fishing, — to which the people of England had occasion to put public waters, and about the only use to which such waters were adapted, was navigation, and the only waters suited to that purpose were those in which the tide ebbed and flowed. Hence, the common law very naturally divided waters into navigable and nonnavigable, and made the ebb and flow of the tide the test of navigability. In this country, while still retaining the common-law classification of navigable and nonnavigable, we have, in view of our changed conditions, rejected its test of navigability, and adopted in its place that of navigability in

fact; and, while still adhering to navigability as the criterion whether waters are public or private, yet we have extended the meaning of that term so as to declare all waters public highways which afford a channel for any useful commerce, including small streams, merely floatable for logs at certain seasons of the year. Most of the definitions of "navigability" in the decided cases, while perhaps conceding that the size of the boats or vessels is not important, and, indeed, that it is not necessary that navigation should be by boats at all, yet seem to convey the idea that the water must be capable of some commerce of pecuniary value, as distinguished from boating for mere pleasure. *But if, under present conditions of society, bodies of water are used for public uses other than mere commercial navigation, in its ordinary sense, we fail to see why they ought not to be held to be public waters, or navigable waters, if the old nomenclature is preferred. Certainly, we do not see why boating or sailing for pleasure should not be considered navigation, as well as boating for mere pecuniary profit.* Many, if not the most, of the meandered lakes of this state, are not adapted to, and probably will never be used to any great extent for, commercial navigation; but they are used—and as population increases, and towns and cities are built up in their vicinity, will be still more used—by the people for sailing, rowing, fishing, fowling, bathing, skating, taking water for domestic, agricultural, and even city purposes, cutting ice, and other public purposes which cannot now be enumerated or even anticipated. *To hand over all these lakes to private ownership, under any old or narrow test of navigability, would be a great wrong upon the public for all time, the extent of which cannot, perhaps, be now even anticipated....* (emphasis added). *Lamprey v. State* (Metcalf), 53 N.W. 1139, 1143 (Minn. 1893).

Since 1893, the concept expressed in *Lamprey* has been followed and the idea of navigability for public recreational use has spread to numerous other jurisdictions. According to Albert W. Stone, a professor of Law at the University of Montana and an acknowledged expert in the field of Water Law, there is a tendency in adjudicated cases from other jurisdictions to abandon the tool of defining "navigability" and simply directing the inquiry to whether the water is susceptible to public use. Under this concept, the question of title to the underlying streambed is irrelevant. A.W. Stone, *Montana Water Law for the 1980's* (1981). Thus, the issue becomes one of use, not title.

Navigability for use is a matter governed by state law. It is a separate concept from the federal question of determining navigability for title purposes....

* * *

In essence, the question is whether the waters owned by the State under the Constitution are susceptible to recreational use by the public. The capability of use of the waters for recreational purposes determines their availability for recreational use by the public. Streambed ownership by a private party is irrelevant. If the waters are owned by the State and held in trust for the people by the State, no private party may bar the use of those waters by the people. The Constitution and the public trust doctrine do not permit a private party to interfere with the public's right to recreational use of the surface of the State's waters.

* * *

In sum, we hold that, under the public trust doctrine and the 1972 Montana Constitution, any surface waters that are capable of recreational use may be so used by the public without regard to streambed ownership or navigability for nonrecreational purposes.

* * *

X

We add the cautionary note that nothing herein contained in this opinion shall be construed as granting the public the right to enter upon or cross over private property to reach the State-owned waters hereby held available for recreational purposes.

The limit to the public's right to use these waters is, under normal circumstances, the high water mark of the waters.

... Therefore, we hold that the public has a right to use the state-owned waters to the point of the high water mark except to the extent of barriers in the waters. In case of barriers, the public is allowed to portage around such barriers in the least intrusive way possible, avoiding damage to the private property holder's rights.

* * *

Notes

1. Notice how the court gravitated to public use in defining the scope of the public's ownership rights: "The capability of use of the waters for recreational purposes determines their availability for recreational use by the public." Doesn't this emphasis reflect the core concern in *Illinois Central Railroad Co. v. Illinois* (p. 68)? Recall there that the Supreme Court described the shoreline of Lake Michigan as "property in which the whole people are interested." But at that time, in the nineteenth century, waters and shorelines were used for three primary purposes: fishing, navigation, and commerce. Clearly, modern recreational uses have stretched the public interests protected by the public trust doctrine. Can you imagine other resources, such as drinking water sources and valuable aquifers, which might gain public trust protection in the future? Underground water is not in any way navigable, but is navigability really the core concept in these public trust cases, or is navigability merely a surrogate for public need and interest? Some courts, such as the Hawai'i Supreme Court in *Waiahole Ditch* (p. 189) have extended public trust protection to groundwater.

2. Only a month after the *Curran* decision, the Montana Supreme Court decided *Montana Coalition for Stream Access v. Hildreth*, 684 P.2d 1088 (Mont. 1984). In that case, a citizens' coalition filed suit against a property owner, asserting a right to float on a river running through the private parcel. The court reiterated that the public had the right of access to streams capable of use for recreational purposes regardless of who owns the streambeds, that no landowner has the right to control the use of such streams as they flow through his property, and that the public may portage around stream barriers on private lands, so long as it does so in the least intrusive manner possible, avoiding damage to private property.

3. In *Galt v. State Dep't of Fish, Wildlife and Parks*, 731 P.2d 912 (Mont. 1987), the Montana Supreme Court ruled unconstitutional a statute that allowed the building of duck blinds, boat moorages, and overnight camps on the beds and banks of waterways so long as not within sight of or 500 yards from of an occupied dwelling, and that imposed the cost of establishing portage routes on the landowner. The court stated:

> The public trust doctrine in Montana's Constitution grants public ownership in water not in beds and banks of streams. While the public has the right to use the water for recreational purposes and minimal use of underlying and adjoining real estate essential to enjoyment of its ownership in water, there is no attendant right that such use be as convenient, productive, and comfortable as possible.

The public has a right of use up to the high water mark, but only such use as is necessary to utilization of the water itself. We hold that any use of the bed and banks must be of minimal impact.

* * *

We reaffirm well established constitutional principles protecting property interests from confiscation. Landowners, through whose property a water course flows as defined in *Curran* and *Hildreth*, have their fee impressed with a dominant estate in favor of the public. This easement must be narrowly confined so that impact to beds and banks owned by private individuals is minimal. Only that use which is necessary for the public to enjoy its ownership of the water resource will be recognized as within the easement's scope. The real property interests of private landowners are important as are the public's property interest in water. Both are constitutionally protected. These competing interests, when in conflict, must be reconciled to the extent possible.

Id. at 915–16.

4. In *Public Lands Access Ass'n v. Madison County*, 321 P.3d 38 (Mont. 2014), the Montana Supreme Court added to its public trust jurisprudence regarding streambeds. There, Kennedy, the private owner of a streambed along a non-navigable river, tried to fence off public access to the streambed from a public bridge. The court affirmed the public's right of access between the high water marks of each side of the river. It held that such right, ensconced in Montana's constitution, did not effectuate a taking of Kennedy's private property. In so holding, however, the court seemed to frame the public's right not as a pre-existing property right in the streambed, as is typically the characterization, but as an ancillary access interest (associated with the use of publicly-owned waters):

Our decisions in *Curran* and *Hildreth*, as codified, protect the public's right to recreationally use its non-navigable waters, free from interference by private landowners.... The public has a broad use right to surface waters and private landowners may not place obstacles that impede the public's exercise of its right. This use right is not a property right, or an interest in the landowners' property. Rather, it amounts to a recognition of the physical reality that in order for the public to recreationally use its water resource, some "minimal" contact with the banks and beds of rivers is generally necessary.

* * *

It is settled law in Montana that public recreational use of State-owned waters is not a taking because title to non-navigable riverbeds does not pass to the public.... Some insignificant use of the riverbeds and river banks is, and always has been, necessary to the public's use and enjoyment of its resource. That use does not amount to an easement or any other "interest" in land.... [N]o taking of private property occurs in public use of beds and banks of waters up to the high water mark because title does not pass with the use right. As observed by the United States District Court in *Madison v. Graham*, no private property right is "being extracted" from Kennedy: "In fact, the public has no interest at all in the private streambed *per se*, but only in the publicly-owned surface waters that traverse the streambed." *Madison v. Graham*, 126 F.Supp.2d 1320, 1324 (D. Mont. 2001).

... Kennedy never owned a property right that allowed him to exclude the public from using its water resource, including the riverbed and banks up to the high water mark. Nothing has been taken from him.

Id. at 52–53.

Isn't the court's approach to river access somewhat unorthodox? The public didn't have a pre-existing right in the private lands, but Kennedy, the landowner—who lost the right to exclude—doesn't have a takings claim? Does it fit with other characterizations (such as in *Galt*, note 3) depicting the public's right in the streambed as an "easement"? Note that the *Galt* decision also described the fee held by private landowners in streambeds as "impressed with a dominant estate in favor of the public." Isn't such an estate, or easement, a form of property ownership?

5. Recent public trust access cases include *City of Montpelier v. Barnett*, 49 A.3d 120 (Vt. 2012), in which the Vermont Supreme Court ruled that the city lacked authority to prohibit recreational boating, fishing, and swimming on Berlin Pond, a roughly 250-acre natural lake and source of the city's water supply. Although the city had excluded such uses for generations, the court ruled that these public trust uses could be regulated only by the state, which had neither prohibited recreational use of the pond nor delegated that authority to the city. The court did suggest that the city could exclude recreationalists from trespassing on city-owned lands surrounding the pond, but the city did not own all the surrounding land. *Id.* at 142–43.

In *Friends of Thayer Lake v. Brown*, 1 N.Y.S. 3d 504 (N.Y. App. Div. 2015), the court concluded that Mud Pond Waterway, which includes private lands, is navigable-in-fact by small recreational watercraft in ordinary water, except for several passages requiring portages (including one along a privately created and maintained path), where necessary to avoid impassable rapids. Therefore, the court agreed with canoeists and the state that local landowners could not maintain a trespass cause of action and ruled that the landowners created a public nuisance by placing obstructions to navigation and posting no-trespassing signs.

In another New York decision, the Supreme Court decided that the city of New York violated the public trust doctrine by fencing off 20 acres of Spring Creek Park, a dedicated (but unimproved) waterfront park, for construction of a solid waste management facility. The city thereby unlawfully obstructed the public from accessing the site for fishing, crabbing, biking, and other recreational activities. *Raritan Baykeeper v. City of New York*, 984 N.Y.S.2d 634 (N.Y. Sup. Ct. 2013) (p. 298).

In a case involving the only allegedly private lake in the Portland, Oregon, metropolitan area, residents challenged the city of Lake Oswego's exclusion of the public from accessing the eponymous Oswego Lake for swimming, fishing, and recreational boating. Unlike in the Thayer Lake case, where the state of New York intervened on the side of the recreationalists, the state of Oregon intervened on the side of the city. A lower court upheld the denial of public access, and the case is now before the Oregon Court of Appeals. Over 30 law professors signed an amicus brief in support of the recreationalists. *See* Brief of Amici Curiae Law Professors and Willamette Riverkeeper in *Kramer v. City of Lake Oswego*, Case No. CV12100913 (filed July 1, 2014), available at http://papers.ssrn.com/sol3/papers.cfm?abstract_id=2563331.

6. States recognizing the public's rights to use water independent of ownership of the underlying river or lakebed include Minnesota, *State v. Kuluvar*, 123 N.W.2d 699 (Minn. 1963); New Mexico, *State ex rel. Game Comm'n v. Red River Valley Co.*, 182 P.2d 421 (N.M. 1945); Wyoming, *Day v. Armstrong*, 362 P.2d 137 (Wyo. 1961); Idaho, *Southern Idaho Fish and Game Ass'n v. Picabo Livestock, Inc.*, 528 P.2d 1295 (Idaho 1974); South Dakota, *Parks v. Cooper*, 676 N.W.2d 823 (S.D. 2004) (p. 106); and Oregon, *Guilliams v. Beaver Lake Club*, 175 P. 437, 441 (Or. 1918). *Contra People v. Emmert*, 597 P.2d 1025 (Colo. 1979); *State ex rel. Meek v. Hays*, 785 P.2d 1356 (Kan. 1990).

7. In addition to ensuring public access rights to water bodies in Montana, the *Curran* decision provided grounds for asserting public rights to water quantity. In *Adjudication of the Existing Rights to Use of all Water in the Missouri River Drainage Area*, 55 P.3d 396 (Mont. 2002), the Montana Supreme Court cited the *Curran* decision in deciding that the state could assert nonstatutory instream claims to water rights prior to the enactment of the state's instream flow law in 1973. The court reasoned that "the public trust doctrine which dates back to Montana's statehood" gave "the public ... an instream, non-diversionary right to the recreational use of the State's navigable surface waters." *Id.* at 340.

B. Purposes of Navigability

Munninghoff v. Wisconsin Conservation Commission

Supreme Court of Wisconsin
38 N.W.2d 712 (1949)

[Munninghoff sought a state license to farm muskrats, a beaver-like, wetland-dependent species valuable for its pelts, on submerged lands he owned beneath a navigable river, which became navigable due to a dome erected by a paper company in 1906. Somewhat surprisingly, the state commission refused the request, on the ground that it had no authority under state statutes to issue such a license affecting navigable waters. Munninghoff prevailed in the lower court, and the state commission appealed. The Wisconsin Supreme Court determined that the state had the authority to license the muskrat farm and then considered whether muskrat farming was a use incident to navigation.]

MARTIN, J.

It is admitted that the lands upon which Munninghoff desires to operate a muskrat farm are his own lands, and are located under the navigable waters of the Wisconsin [R]iver. These waters became navigable by the erection by the Rhinelander Paper Company of a dam in the year 1906, which dam flooded the land in question and it has been flooded since that time.

* * *

[Under Wisconsin law, it] is not essential to the public easement that the capacity for navigation be continuous throughout the year to make it navigable or public. It is sufficient that a stream has periods of navigable capacity ordinarily recurrent from year to year and continuing long enough to make the stream usable as a highway. *Willow River Club v. Wade*, 76 N.W. 273 (Wis. 1898). The capacity for floating logs to market during the spring freshets which normally lasts six weeks was held to make a stream navigable. *Falls Mfg. Co. v. Oconto River Imp. Co. et al.*, 58 N.W. 257 (Wis. 1894).

* * *

... Krenz v. Nichols, 222 N.W. 300, 303 (Wis. 1928), ... stated:

> The state, under its police power, and to carry out its trust, passed the [muskrat licensing] statute in question. So far as it affects the public, the statute is reasonable, and is not contrary to any provision of the federal or state Constitution. Nor do we think it is contrary to the decision of this court in *Diana Shooting Club v. Husting*, 156 Wis. 261, 145 N.W. 816, Ann.Cas.1915C, 1148. In that case the court upheld the right of a citizen of the state to hunt from a boat in the navigable inland streams of the state, notwithstanding that the boat should be

on the waters over the lands of a private owner. The court there said that was a right incident to the right of navigation, and that the right of navigation was free to all the citizens of the state upon such waters, by virtue of the Ordinance of 1787, the Enabling Act of the state Constitution, and the constitutional provision there to.

NW Ord.

* * *

In Wisconsin the owner of the banks of the stream is the owner of the bed, regardless of whether the stream is navigable or non-navigable. The owner of the submerged soil of a running stream does not own the running water, but he does have certain exclusive rights to make a reasonable use of the water as it passes over or along his land. For instance, he may erect a pier for navigation; he may pump part of the water out of the stream to irrigate his crops; his cattle may be permitted to drink of it; and his muskrats may use it to gather vegetation for the construction of muskrat houses or for food.

!!

It is not within the power of the state to deprive the owner of submerged land of the right to make use of the water which passes over his land, or to grant the use of it to a non-riparian. The riparian's exclusive right to use the water arises directly from the fact that non-riparians have no access to the stream without trespass upon riparian lands.

Riparian exclusive way.

In the present case the respondent would make use of the water flowing over or past his land in permitting the muskrats to swim in the water, gather feed found in the water or in the bed of the river, build muskrat houses on the bed where the water is shallow, and dig runways in the banks from underneath the surface of the water to their burrows in the banks above the water line.

In general, the rights of the public to the incidents of navigation are boating, bathing, fishing, hunting, and recreation. *See Doemel v. Jantz*, 193 N.W. 393 (Wis. 1923). Trapping is not included for it is an incident of land use. *See Johnson v. Burghorn*, 179 N.W. 225, 228 (Mich. 1920). Appellant asserts that float trapping does not require the use of the bottom. However, floats for float trapping are always anchored to the bottom and any method of anchoring or securing a float would, of necessity, require the use of the land or the bottom. The right to use the running water or the bed for float trapping is not included in the easement of navigation. To float trap in navigable water constitutes a trespass upon the submerged land for which the trespasser may be prosecuted by the owner of the soil and enjoined from using the public water for that purpose.

PTD

Trps not PTD and is a TPASS

The muskrats on a muskrat farm have been bought and paid for by the licensee. They are his personal property whether they are swimming in the waters above his lands or running along on the dry land within the limits of his licensed premises. The presence of the muskrats in a navigable stream covering privately owned lands does not entitle a trespasser to take them any more than a trespasser would be entitled to seize domestic ducks in the same stream. But if a muskrat should leave a licensed area, he becomes ferae naturae, and is legitimate prey for a neighboring trapper. *See* 2 Am. Jur., *Property, Ratione Soli* § 12, at 699.

Appellant also asserts that the right of navigation includes the incidental use of the bottom. This is true where the use of the bottom is connected with navigation, such as walking as a trout fisherman does in a navigable stream, boating, standing on the bottom while bathing, casting an anchor from a boat in fishing, propelling a duck boat by poling against the bottom, walking on the ice if the river is, frozen, etc. These have nothing in common with trapping because the latter involves the exercise of a property right in the land or the bottom.

* * *

The conservation department has authority to issue the license applied for.

Notes

1. Under Wisconsin law, a landowner adjacent to a navigable water owns the bed of the water to the middle of the stream. But that ownership is not determinative of public rights to use the waterway, as the riparian landowner must accommodate public rights. An ensuing Wisconsin decision referred to riparian landowners' ownership of lands beneath navigable waters as "qualified title," and the state's interest as "paramount title." *Town of Ashwaubenon v. Public Service Comm'n*, 125 N.W.2d 647, 653 (Wis. 1963). If a riparian landowner in Wisconsin cannot exclude the public from the stream, of what use is ownership of the streambed?

2. What is the scope of the public rights in Wisconsin navigable waters ("incidents of navigation")? Do those include bathing, hunting, and fishing? What about walking while bathing, hunting, and fishing? What about dropping an anchor while boating? What about trapping? What is the basis of the distinction? Compare the results involving shellfish in *Arnold v. Mundy* (p. 57), and *Martin v. Waddell* (p. 63). *See also State v. Sorenson*, 436 N.W.2d 358 (Iowa 1989) (public use rights not limited to navigation and commerce); *State ex rel. Thompson v. Parker*, 200 S.W. 1014 (Ark. 1917) (public rights to fish and hunt); *Conatser v. Johnson*, 194 P.3d 897 (Utah 2008) (right to float, hunt, and fish on state waters, including the right to touch the bed of waters where incidental to recreational activities).

For a case ruling that navigation rights in Louisiana included the right to boat on seasonally inundated bayous but not the right to fish from recreational boats, see *Parm v. Shumate*, 2006 WL 2513921 (W.D. La. 2006), *aff'd*, 513 F.3d 135 (5th Cir. 2007).

3. Some states recognize rights to use private uplands for portaging around barriers in navigable waters, so long as the use is the "least intrusive way possible." *Montana Coalition for Stream Access v. Curran*, 682 P.2d 163, 172 (Mont. 1984); *Galt v. State Dep't of Fish, Wildlife and Parks*, 731 P.2d 912, 913, 924 (Mont. 1987) (no right to build duck blinds and engage in big-game hunting above the high-water mark because public use rights are limited to those necessary to use the water itself).

4. Under the law of wild animals, if a landowner captured a wild animal and then released it to the wild, the animal would no longer be privately owned. How does the *Munninghoff* court interpret the Wisconsin licensing statute to affect the law of wild animals in the state?

Marks v. Whitney

Supreme Court of California
491 P.2d 374 (1971)

[Marks, a landowner along Tomales Bay, owned tidelands conveyed to his predecessor under an 1874 patent from the state. A portion of his tidelands ran along almost the entire shoreline of his neighbor Whitney's upland property. Marks sought to fill these tidelands for development. Whitney opposed the development, maintaining that it would interfere with his littoral rights and his rights as a member of the public. As to the latter, he claimed that Marks' title was burdened with a public trust easement. The trial court rejected Whitney's argument, ruling that Whitney had no standing to raise the public trust issue.]

McCOMB, J.

* * *

Regardless of the issue of Whitney's standing to raise this issue the court may take judicial notice of public trust burdens in quieting title to tidelands. This matter is of great public importance, particularly in view of population pressures, demands for recreational property, and the increasing development of seashore and waterfront property. [T]he title of Marks in these tidelands is burdened with a public easement....

... The trial court found that the portion of Marks' lands here under consideration constitutes a part of the [t]idelands of Tomales Bay....

* * *

... [T]his court decided in *People v. California Fish Co.*, 138 P. 79, 87 (Cal. 1913), that ... "Our opinion is that * * * the buyer of land [via] statutes receives the title to the soil, the *jus privatum*, subject to the public right of navigation, and in subordination to the right of the state to take possession and use and improve it for that purpose, as it may deem necessary...."

The tidelands ... extend from the Oregon line to Mexico and include the shores of bays and navigable streams as far up as tide water goes and until it meets the lands made swampy by the overflow and seepage of fresh water streams.... The state holds tidelands in trust for public purposes, traditionally delineated in terms of navigation, commerce and fisheries....[6] They are, therefore, subject to a reserved easement in the state for trust purposes.

Public trust easements are traditionally defined in terms of navigation, commerce and fisheries. They have been held to include the right to fish, hunt, bathe, swim, to use for boating and general recreation purposes the navigable waters of the state, and to use the bottom of the navigable waters for anchoring, standing, or other purposes. The public has the same rights in and to tidelands.

The public uses to which tidelands are subject are sufficiently flexible to encompass changing public needs. In administering the trust the state is not burdened with an outmoded classification favoring one mode of utilization over another. There is a growing public recognition that one of the most important public uses of the tidelands—a use encompassed within the tidelands trust is the preservation of those lands in their natural state, so that they may serve as ecological units for scientific study, as open space, and as environments which provide food and habitat for birds and marine life, and which favorably affect the scenery and climate of the area. It is not necessary to here define precisely all the public uses which encumber tidelands.

* * *

The power of the state to control, regulate and utilize its navigable waterways and the lands lying beneath them, when acting within the terms of the trust, is absolute, except as limited by the paramount supervisory power of the federal government over navigable waters. We are not here presented with any action by the state or the federal government modifying, terminating, altering or relinquishing the *jus publicum* in these tidelands or in the navigable waters covering them. Neither sovereignty is a party to this action. This court takes judicial notice, however, that there has been no official act of either sovereignty to modify or extinguish the public trust servitude upon Marks' tidelands....

... In the absence of state or federal action the court may not bar members of the public from lawfully asserting or exercising public trust rights on this privately owned tidelands.

---

6. The preceding sentence appeared in footnote 5 of the court's opinion.

There is absolutely no merit in Marks' contention that as the owner of the *jus priva-tum* under this patent he may fill and develop his property, whether for navigational purposes or not; nor in his contention that his past and present plan for development of these tidelands as a marina have caused the extinguishment of the public easement. Reclamation with or without prior authorization from the state does not *ipso facto* terminate the public trust nor render the issue moot.

* * *

The relief sought by Marks resulted in taking away from Whitney rights to which he is entitled as a member of the general public....

Members of the public have been permitted *to bring* an action to enforce a public right to use a beach access route, *to bring* an action to quiet title to private and public easements in a public beach, and *to bring* an action to restrain improper filling of a bay and secure a general declaration of the rights of the people to the waterways and wildlife areas of the bay. Members of the public have been allowed *to defend* a quiet title action by asserting the right to use a public right of way through private property. They have been allowed to assert the public trust easement for hunting, fishing and navigation in privately owned tidelands *as a defense* in an action to enjoin such use, and to navigate on shallow navigable waters in small boats.

Whitney had standing to raise this issue. The court could have raised this issue on its own.... Where the interest concerned is one that, as here, constitutes a public burden upon [private] land..., that servitude should be explicitly declared.

* * *

Notes

1. *Marks* is a celebrated public trust doctrine case, widely known for its expansion of the PTD from the traditional purposes of navigation, commerce, and fishing to include recreational and ecological purposes. One of the more remarkable aspects of *Marks v. Whitney* is the almost casual way in which the court announced that "[t]he public uses to which tidelands are subject are sufficiently flexible to encompass changing public needs" and that "preservation of those lands in their natural state" is "one of the most important public uses" of trust lands. The decision went far beyond upholding the public's right of access across tidelands. It underscored the public's right to protect the natural state of the tidelands, noting their importance in their "natural state, so that they may serve as ecological units" for scientific study, fish and wildlife habitat, scenery, and climate. This decision is among a handful of pioneering cases that recognize ecosystem services in the array of public values and interests protected by the trust. Preservation also figures prominently in the ensuing *Mono Lake* case (p. 173). Both cases may signal an important direction of the public trust.

2. Trust protection of ecosystem services may prove vital as society faces increased industrialized pressure. Scientists stress the importance of "myriad life support functions" provided by ecosystems, "without which human civilizations could not thrive."[7] Comprehensive reports such as the United Nations 2005 Millennium Ecosystem Assessment

---

7. NAT'L RESEARCH COUNCIL, VALUING ECOSYSTEM SERVICES: TOWARD BETTER ENVIRONMENTAL DECISION-MAKING 17 (2004).

inventory many vital ecosystem services.[8] These include climate regulation, flood risk reduction, waste decomposition, water provision, water purification, food production, storm buffering, plant pollination, seed dispersal, flood water control, ground water recharge, erosion control, regulation of disease, medicinal production, aesthetic and recreational services, nutrient recycling, animal habitat, pest control, maintenance of biodiversity, and a full suite of others. One leading report places a global worth of $30 trillion per year for seventeen major ecosystem services.[9] Although many of the public trust assets recognized by case law (waterways, tidelands, wildlife, and the like) provide such ecosystem services, even modern courts have tended to keep their focus on the navigability values that were the prime concern a century ago.

reluctance.

Sustaining vital ecosystem services will require protection of all of nature's component parts, beyond just the recognized "traditional" public trust assets. As conservation biologist Reed Noss has explained, "Disruption of the characteristic processes of any ecosystem will likely lead to biotic impoverishment."[10] In view of this ecological reality, should the public trust doctrine expand its conception of the *res* to include *ecosystems* rather than simply isolated assets such as tidelands, waters, wildlife, and such? Stated another way, should the trust doctrine continue to hold its anchor in traditional navigability concepts, or should modern concepts such as ecosystem services drive the doctrine's evolution? Would broad recognition of ecosystem services fit within the "changing public needs" that the *Marks* court emphasized?

how to bridge the gap...

If courts use the reasoning of the U.S. Supreme Court in *Illinois Central Railroad v. Illinois* (p. 68) that recognized public trust protection to submerged lands because they were a matter of "public concern," is there any less reason to accord trust protection to full ecosystems? Are ecosystem services matters of "public concern" today, just as navigability was a matter of overriding public concern in the last century? Did the *Marks* decision point in this direction? And will the public trust doctrine continue to have relevance for environmental problems if courts *fail* to move beyond navigability as the legal nomenclature defining public trust interests? How would such expansion affect the doctrine's role in mediating between public and private property rights? How would it affect the realm of environmental statutory law? These questions have generated considerable scholarship. Professors J.B. Ruhl and James Salzman have pointed out that an emphasis on ecosystem services fits well within the utilitarian approach of public trust law and the doctrine's "traditional sensibilities."[11]

3. Notice that although the *Marks* court recognized ecological interests held by the public, it fit such interests in the "reserved easement" traditionally used for navigation, com-

---

8. Millennium Ecosystem Assessment, Ecosystems and Human Well-Being: Synthesis (2005); *see also* Nature's Services: Societal Dependence on Natural Ecosystems (Gretchen Daily ed., 1997).

9. Robert Costanza et al., *The Value of the World's Ecosystem Services and Natural Capital*, 387 Nature 253, 253–54 (1997).

10. Reed F. Noss, *Some Principles of Conservation Biology, as They Apply to Environmental Law*, 69 Chi.-Kent L. Rev. 893, 906 (1994).

11. J.B. Ruhl & James Salzman, *Ecosystem Services and the Public Trust Doctrine: Working Change from Within*, 15 Southeastern Envtl. L.J. 223, 232–38 (2006) ("[W]e propose integrating natural capital and ecosystem services within the public trust doctrine's utilitarian core to make it more ecological on its surface."); *see also* Mary Christina Wood, *Advancing the Sovereign Trust of Government to Safeguard the Environment for Present and Future Generations (Part I): Ecological Realism and the Need for a Paradigm Shift*, 39 Envtl. L. 43, 78–84 (2009) (arguing for an "ecological res" concept under the public trust).

merce, and fisheries, clarifying that the scope of protected public use encompasses fishing, hunting, bathing, swimming, boating, recreational uses, and using the submerged lands for "anchoring, standing, or other purposes." Courts (such as *Munninghoff*, p. 130) tend to define these permitted uses as "incidents of navigation." If the public trust continues to expand to include ecological interests held by the public, should courts abandon the approach of describing such interests as related to navigation? Should they rule that "navigation" is a surrogate for "public concern" that forms the central focus of prior cases?

4. Aside from its language emphasizing the flexibility of the public trust, the *Marks* decision was also important for its language affirming Whitney's standing to sue Marks for a public trust violation, not merely as a neighboring landowner but as a member of the public. The excerpted portion of the case concerned a conflict between Marks' private property rights and Whitney's public property rights under the trust. The trial court had held that Whitney lacked standing to raise the public trust issue. The California Supreme Court reversed the trial court, resoundingly affirming the right of a citizen to enforce public trust rights. The court also noted that, regardless of standing, a court can take judicial notice of the public trust burdening tidelands.

One might think that any member of the public would have standing to sue to enforce the public trust doctrine, but that position has not been universally accepted in all states. In some states, members of the public seeking to enforce trust rights must show "special injury" or "special damage," a concept imported from public nuisance law. *See, e.g., Neuse River Found. v. Smithfield Foods, Inc.*, 574 S.E.2d 48 (N.C. Ct. App. 2002) (denying environmental organizations' trust claim for damages to public waters resulting from hog farm's water pollution, finding that the plaintiffs showed no "special damage" and that "[t]he state is the sole party able to seek non-individualized, or public, remedies for alleged harm to public waters" under the public trust). In other states, public standing to enforce the trust is available only through statutory permission, such as a state administrative procedure act. *Robinson v. Kunach*, 251 N.W.2d 449, 455 (Wis. 1977) ("Our court has clearly held that the public trust doctrine in this state does not *per se* provide an affirmative cause of action in addition to those causes of action recognized by the state. Rather, '[t]he public trust doctrine merely establishes standing for the state, or any person suing in the name of the state for the purpose of vindicating the public trust, to assert a cause of action recognized by the existing law of Wisconsin.'") (citing *State v. Deetz*, 224 N.W.2d 407, 413 (Wis. 1974)).

5. The standing issue was addressed in *Center for Biological Diversity v. FPL Group*, 83 Cal.Rptr.3d 588 (Cal. Ct. App. 2008), a decision excerpted in chapter 6 (p. 244). There, the court denied standing to environmentalists who asserted the public trust to challenge wind generators whose projects inflicted high bird mortalities. While affirming a broad public right to enforce the public trust, the appeals court decided that the appropriate recourse for plaintiffs was to challenge the government agencies that had issued the permits to the generators rather than suing the generators themselves for harm to trust wildlife assets. The court explained:

> The defect in the present complaint is not that it seeks to enforce the public trust, but that it is brought against the wrong parties.... Under traditional trust concepts, plaintiffs, viewed as beneficiaries of the public trust, are not entitled to bring an action against those whom they allege are harming trust property. The trustee charged with the responsibility to implement and preserve the trust alone has the right to bring such an action.... Thus, analogizing this action to the enforcement of a traditional trust agreement, the action must be brought against the appropriate representative of the state as the trustee of the public trust.

Id. at 602. The case may be distinguished from *Marks* on the ground that it involved both the application of a comprehensive regulatory scheme of a trust asset (birds), and the fact that the plaintiffs were not seeking to exercise their rights of access to a trust asset. These distinctions emphasize the importance of recognizing the different contexts in which public trust cases arise.

6. The *Marks* court observed that the state's authority to act under the public trust is "absolute," but subject to the federal navigation power. The federal government's authority under the so-called navigation servitude not only preempts state public trust law, it exempts the federal government from paying compensation for taking of private property. *See* Harrison C. Dunning, *Sources of the Public Right*, 2 WATERS AND WATER RIGHTS § 30.05 (Amy K. Kelley, ed., 3rd ed. 2014). In this sense, the federal navigation servitude operates very much like the public trust, creating an encumbrance on private property. Does this servitude represent an application of the public trust to the federal government? One federal court has found that it does. In *United States v. 1.58 Acres of Land*, 523 F.Supp. 120, 122 (D. Mass. 1981), a decision excerpted in chapter 11 (p. 367), the court held that the public trust "is administered by both the federal and state sovereigns" and follows the division of sovereignty between the two. The court elaborated:

> [T]hose aspects of the public interest ... that relate to the commerce and other powers delegated to the federal government are administered by Congress in its capacity as trustee of the *jus publicum*, while those aspects of the public interest ... reserved to local regulation by the states are administered by state legislatures in their capacity as co-trustee of the *jus publicum*.... An explicit power of the federal government ... is its dominant navigational servitude.

Id. at 123, n. 4.

7. According to the *Marks* decision, a private landowner may not extinguish the public trust by filling tidelands, even if for a navigation purpose. Instead, the court ruled that there must be an "official act of ... sovereignty to modify or extinguish the public servitude upon Marks' tidelands." However, even a legislative act to privatize tidelands may not permanently terminate public rights. The *Marks* case grew out of the state of California's large-scale conveyances of tidelands in the nineteenth century, which included most of San Francisco Bay. Two statutes, passed in 1868 and 1870, authorized the filling of some eighty-eight square miles of the bay. In 1915, the California Supreme Court ruled that the statutes conveyed fee interests that were freed from the public trust. *Knudson v. Kearney*, 152 P. 541 (Cal. 1915). Later, however, the California Supreme Court partially overruled *Knudson* in *Berkeley v. Superior Court of Alameda County*, 606 P.2d 362, 363 (Cal. 1980). There the court ruled that tidal lands conveyed to private parties by the statutes remained subject to the trust unless the tidelands had been already filled, making them no longer useable for trust purposes, reasoning that "it would be more injurious to the public interest to perpetuate the error of *Knudson*" than to overturn the decision. *Id.* at 373. Acknowledging the effect of recognizing continued trust interests on private property rights that had been affirmed under prior decisions, the court confronted the issue of whether to give its decision full retroactive effect. It settled on a middle course:

> We could ... declare that all grants made under the 1870 act are subject to the public trust, or we could hold that our decision is prospective only. We reject both these alternatives. The first would reduce the value of investments that may have been made in reliance on the decisions we overturn, without necessarily promoting the purposes of the trust; while the second would render our holding in this case an academic exercise, because the grants were made more than a century ago.

We choose, instead, an intermediate course: the appropriate resolution is to balance the interests of the public in tidelands conveyed pursuant to the 1870 act
against those of the landowners who hold property under these conveyances. In
the harmonizing of these claims, the principle we apply is that the interests of the
public are paramount in property that is still physically adaptable for trust uses,
whereas the interests of the grantees and their successors should prevail insofar
as the tidelands have been rendered substantially valueless [through fill] for those
purposes.

Id. at 373. The next year, the court extended the *Berkeley* ruling to non-tidal waters conveyed to private parties. *State v. Superior Court of Lake County*, 172 Cal.Rptr. 696 (Cal.
1981) (reaffirming that submerged land between the low and high water mark was subject to the public trust, even if it was in private ownership). *See also State ex rel. Sprynczy-
natyk v. Mills*, 523 N.W.2d 537 (N.D. 1994) (same). By achieving, in substantial measure,
a retroactive affirmation of public trust interests, the essence of these decisions is that the
public trust lies latent in private property. On the relationship of the public trust to private property, see chapter 9; Michael C. Blumm, *The Public Trust Doctrine and Private Property: The Accommodation Principle*, 27 Pace Envtl. L. Rev. 649 (2010).

8. In another California case, *Summa Corp. v. California ex rel. State Lands Comm'n*,
466 U.S. 198, 209 (1984), the U.S. Supreme Court reversed a California Supreme Court
ruling that unfilled tidelands ceded by Mexico under the Treaty of Guadalupe Hidalgo
were subject to the public trust doctrine. The circumstances in that case were distinguishable from those in *Berkeley* because the tidelands in question had been granted by
the Mexican government to private individuals in 1839, before the lands had even become part of the United States as a result of the 1848 Treaty of Guadalupe Hidalgo. The
state of California nevertheless asserted a public trust interest in those lands, alleging that
it gained such interest upon its admission to the union pursuant to the equal footing doctrine. The Supreme Court disagreed, deciding that under the treaty, the United States
"undertook to protect the property rights of Mexican landowners." *Id.* at 202. To this end,
Congress passed a statute in 1851 setting up a land claims settlement procedure that allowed the federal government to issue patents to Mexican landowners. The patent in
question made no mention of public trust interests held by the state. Whereas the Court
acknowledged that an "ordinary federal patent purporting to convey tidelands located
within a State to a private individual is invalid, since the United States holds such tidelands only in trust for the State" under the *Pollard v. Hagan* ruling, a different result obtained where the federal government issued patents pursuant to its authority to discharge
an international duty, such as that encompassed by the Treaty of Guadalupe Hidalgo. The
patent process implementing the treaty "served an overriding purpose of providing repose
to land titles that originated with Mexican grants." *Id.* at 206. The case reflected the supremacy of federal interests in public trust lands—one of which concerns the duty to
carry out international obligations.

Chapter 4

Wetlands

Wetlands—also known as swamps, marshes, fens, and bogs—were once considered tantamount to public nuisances, since they were mosquito habitat, undevelopable, and impediments to travel. *See, e.g., Leovy v. United States*, 177 U.S. 621, 636 (1900) ("[T]he police power is never more legitimately exercised than in removing such nuisances."). The federal government encouraged draining of wetlands through land grant programs, such as the Swamp Lands Act of 1850, which helped lead to destruction of more than one-half of the nation's original wetland acreage in the lower forty-eight states. *See* NAT'L RESEARCH COUNCIL COMM. ON CHARACTERIZATION OF WETLANDS, WETLANDS: CHARACTERIZATION AND BOUNDARIES (1995). In the late twentieth century, however, scientists began to recognize wetlands as vital ecosystems, providing some of the most biologically productive acres on earth, sheltering and feeding fish and waterfowl, and providing important ecosystem services like pollution filters, flood control, and storm barriers.[1]

But since they lie at the intersection of uplands and waters, wetlands provide attractive sites for development, and therefore, despite their ecological value, wetlands remain under sustained attack. Each year in the U.S., roughly 300,000 wetland acres are filled for development. Since 1972, when Congress enacted the modern Clean Water Act, wetland development has been regulated under section 404, but that permit program suffers from ambivalent administration and curtailed jurisdiction (see p. 96). Typically, agencies face enormous political pressure from developers to issue permits to fill wetlands. One study found that, out of 85,000 permits the Corps processes each year, it denies less than 0.3% of them.[2] Many states also have permit programs governing wetland fills, but those are inconsistent in their vigor.

When agencies deny wetlands permits, private landowners often attack the denial as an unconstitutional interference with property rights. Such claims invoke the regulatory takings doctrine under the Fifth Amendment of the Constitution (and similar state constitutional provisions), which says: "nor shall private property be taken for public use, without just compensation." Although it has always been clear that government has the right and duty to regulate harmful uses of property, property owners assert regulatory takings by claiming that the regulation has gone "too far" in reducing the value of their property. The federal regulatory takings doctrine made its debut in 1922 in *Pennsylvania Coal Company v. Mahon*, when Justice Holmes famously said, "while property may be

---

1. *See* USDA NATURAL RES. CONSERVATION SERV., RESTORING AMERICA'S WETLANDS: A PRIVATE LANDS CONSERVATION SUCCESS STORY 2, available at www.nrcs.usda.gov/Internet/FSE_DOCUMENTS/stelprdb1045079.pdf ("Wetlands are among the most biologically productive ecosystems in the world, comparable to tropical rainforests and coral reefs in the diversity of species they support," and noting that "up to one-half of all North American bird species feed or nest in wetlands, more than one-third of Endangered and Threatened species rely on them.").

2. JEFFREY A. ZINN & CLAUDIA COPELAND, CRS ISSUE BRIEF FOR CONGRESS: WETLAND ISSUES, at CRS-6 (2006).

regulated to a certain extent, if regulation goes too far it will be recognized as a taking." *Penn. Coal Co. v. Mahon*, 260 U.S. 393, 415 (1922). Since that time, the Court has struggled with drawing the line between permissible regulation and regulation that is so severe as to amount to a taking. As Justice Holmes himself emphasized in *Mahon*, most regulation will not trigger compensation because "[g]overnment hardly could go on" if it had to pay every owner for diminishment in property value. *Id.*

Regulatory takings jurisprudence has produced a convoluted body of judicial decisions, probably because the Fifth Amendment property clause begs the question of what exactly is the "property" that cannot be taken without compensation. The public trust doctrine shapes a response. By delineating the rights and responsibilities embedded in private title, the doctrine largely defines what can be considered "property" that, if taken, affords a right of compensation. As the cases below show, modern courts have found some private property encumbered by a reserved trust easement or servitude held by the people through their government. In other words, in these cases, the private landowner did not acquire the full "bundle" of rights when the government first conveyed title. It follows that the Fifth Amendment provides no compensation when government steps in to limit landowner activities that interfere with a right the public has held all along. As courts emphasize, "[P]arties acquiring rights in trust property generally hold those rights subject to the trust, and can assert no vested right to use those rights in a manner harmful to the trust." *Nat'l Audubon Soc'y v. Superior Court of Alpine Cnty.*, 658 P.2d 709, 721 (Cal. 1983). One of the editors has concluded that the public trust can form "an absolute defense" to a takings claim.[3]

The cases that follow involve landowners seeking constitutional compensation for restrictions imposed by government on their wetlands-fill projects. The court opinions consider the role of the public trust as a government defense to regulatory takings. This role represents one of the five primary contexts in which the PTD arises, as explained in the introduction to this textbook. In these cases, the courts enter the public trust field through a back door of takings law. Such cases do not involve a claim against government trustees seeking protection of public trust assets, but rather the opposite: takings claims challenge government regulatory protection. The governmental defendants in these cases assert the PTD to defeat the takings claims seeking compensation. In this context, the PTD is a "shield" rather than a "sword" that might be brought by citizens to force government protection of their public trust assets. But as you read the cases, consider whether some of the rules and reasoning could apply in a context where citizens invoke the PTD as a "sword" against recalcitrant trustees that are not protecting wetlands (or other trust resources), perhaps by issuing permits under statutory law. The latter context takes on increasing importance as statutory permitting systems continue to allow damage to society's vital natural resources.

Although the framework of regulatory takings is riddled with complexity, the Supreme Court basically uses two alternative tests to determine if a property owner has suffered a regulatory taking. The traditional regulatory takings rule amounts to an ad-hoc, factual inquiry. Often called the "*Penn Central* test" (after the case that summarized it most cogently), three factors combine into a balancing test to evaluate a takings claim: 1) the economic impact of the regulation; 2) its interference with reasonable investment backed expectations of the property owner; and 3) the character of the government action (whether

---

3. Michael C. Blumm & Lucus Ritchie, *Lucas's Unlikely Legacy: The Rise of Background Principles as Categorical Takings Defenses*, 29 Harv. Envtl. L. Rev. 321, 327 (2005).

the regulation confers a benefit to the public or prevents a harm to the public, the latter generally not warranting compensation). *See Pennsylvania Central Transportation Co. v. City of New York*, 438 U.S. 104 (1978) (upholding historic preservation law against takings challenge). In 1992, however, in *Lucas v. South Carolina Coastal Council*, 505 U.S. 1003 (1992), the Court carved out an exception to the circumstances in which the *Penn Central* test applies, concluding that where a regulation denies the property owner of all "economically viable use" of property, there is a *per se* compensation requirement unless the regulatory restrictions "inhere" in the title to the property by virtue of the state's "background principles" of nuisance and property. *Id.* at 1029.

The public trust works its way into both regulatory takings tests. In the *Penn Central* test, the public trust becomes relevant to determining the "reasonable" expectations of a landowner and also the "character" of the government action (specifically whether it seeks to secure a benefit for the public or to prevent a harm). In the *Lucas* test, the PTD forms a background principle of property law that can "inhere" in the property owner's title and defeat a takings claim. In either case, since the application of the doctrine forms the basis for concluding whether or not there is "property" that the government has taken, it is usually one of the first issues litigated in a takings case.

The following case is a celebrated decision establishing a so-called "natural use" doctrine flowing from public trust analysis. The case was decided at the dawn of modern wetland regulation, the same year Congress established the federal permit program.

Just v. Marinette County
Supreme Court of Wisconsin
201 N.W.2d 761 (1972)

HALLOWS, C.J.

[Marinette County, Wisconsin, adopted a shoreland zoning ordinance in 1967 which places a 36-acre parcel of land owned by the Justs in a "conservancy district," requiring a permit to fill, drain, or dredge wetlands.]

The land owned by the Justs is designated as swamps or marshes on the United States Geological Survey Map and is located within 1,000 feet of the normal high-water elevation of the lake. Thus, the property is included in a conservancy district and, by § 2.29 of the ordinance, classified as "wetlands." Consequently, in order to place more than 500 square feet of fill on this property, the Justs were required to obtain a conditional-use permit from the zoning administrator of the county and pay a fee of $20 or incur a forfeiture of $10 to $200 for each day of violation.

In February and March of 1968, six months after the ordinance became effective, Ronald Just, without securing a conditional-use permit, hauled 1,040 square yards of sand onto this property and filled an area approximately 20-feet wide.... More than 500 square feet of this fill was upon wetlands located contiguous to the water and which had surface drainage toward the lake. The fill within 300 feet of the lake also was more than 2,000 square feet on a slope less than 12 percent. It is not seriously contended that the Justs did not violate the ordinance and the trial court correctly found a violation.

The real issue is whether the conservancy district provisions and the wetlands-filling restrictions unconstitutional because they amount to a constructive taking of the Justs' land without compensation. Marinette [C]ounty and the [S]tate of Wisconsin argue the restrictions of the conservancy district and wetlands provisions constitute a proper exercise of the police power of the state and do not so severely limit the use or depreciate the value of the land as to constitute a taking without compensation.

To state the issue in more meaningful terms, it is a conflict between the public interest in stopping the despoilation of natural resources, which our citizens until recently have taken as inevitable and for granted, and an owner's asserted right to use his property as he wishes. The protection of public rights may be accomplished by the exercise of the police power unless the damage to the property owner is too great and amounts to a confiscation. The securing or taking of a benefit not presently enjoyed by the public for its use is obtained by the government through its power of eminent domain. The distinction between the exercise of the police power and condemnation has been said to be a matter of degree of damage to the property owner. In the valid exercise of the police power reasonably restricting the use of property, the damage suffered by the owner is said to be incidental. However, where the restriction is so great the landowner ought not to bear such a burden for the public good, the restriction has been held to be a constructive taking even though the actual use or forbidden use has not been transferred to the government so as to be a taking in the traditional sense.... Whether a taking has occurred depends upon whether "the restriction practically or substantially renders the land useless for all reasonable purposes."... The loss caused the individual must be weighed to determine if it is more than he should bear. "... [I]f the damage is such as to be suffered by many similarly situated and is in the nature of a restriction on the use to which land may be put and ought to be borne by the individual as a member of society for the good of the public safety, health or general welfare, it is said to be a reasonable exercise of the police power, but if the damage is so great to the individual that he ought not to bear it under contemporary standards, then courts are inclined to treat it as a 'taking' of the property or an unreasonable exercise of the police power."

Many years ago, Professor Freund stated in his work on The Police Power, §511, at 546–47, "It may be said that the state takes property by eminent domain because it is useful to the public, and under the police power because it is harmful ... From this results the difference between the power of eminent domain and the police power, that the former recognises a right to compensation, while the latter on principle does not." Thus the necessity for monetary compensation for loss suffered to an owner by police power restriction arises when restrictions are placed on property in order to create a public benefit rather than to prevent a public harm.

This case causes us to reexamine the concepts of public benefit in contrast to public harm and the scope of an owner's right to use of his property. In the instant case we have a restriction on the use of a citizens' property, not to secure a benefit for the public, but to prevent a harm from the change in the natural character of the citizens' property. We start with the premise that lakes and rivers in their natural state are unpolluted and the pollution which now exists is man made. The [S]tate of Wisconsin under the trust doctrine has a duty to eradicate the present pollution and to prevent further pollution in its navigable waters. This is not, in a legal sense, a gain or a securing of a benefit by the maintaining of the natural *status quo* of the environment. What makes this case different from most condemnation or police power zoning cases is the interrelationship of the wetlands, the swamps and the natural environment of shorelands to the purity of the water and to such natural resources as navigation, fishing, and scenic beauty. Swamps and wetlands were once considered wasteland, undesirable, and not picturesque. But as the people became more sophisticated, an appreciation was acquired that swamps and wetlands serve a vital role in nature, are part of the balance of nature and are essential to the purity of the water in our lakes and streams. Swamps and wetlands are a necessary part of the ecological creation and now, even to the uninitiated, possess their own beauty in nature.

Is the ownership of a parcel of land so absolute that man can change its nature to suit any of his purposes? The great forests of our state were stripped on the theory man's ownership was unlimited. But in forestry, the land at least was used naturally, only the natural fruit of the land (the trees) were taken. The despoilage was in the failure to look to the future and provide for the reforestation of the land. An owner of land has no absolute and unlimited right to change the essential natural character of his land so as to use it for a purpose for which it was unsuited in its natural state and which injures the rights of others. The exercise of the police power in zoning must be reasonable and we think it is not an unreasonable exercise of that power to prevent harm to public rights by limiting the use of private property to its natural uses.

This is not a case where an owner is prevented from using his land for natural and indigenous uses. The uses consistent with the nature of the land are allowed and other uses recognized and still others permitted by special permit. The shoreland zoning ordinance prevents to some extent the changing of the natural character of the land within 1,000 feet of a navigable lake and 300 feet of a navigable river because of such land's interrelation to the contiguous water. The changing of wetlands and swamps to the damage of the general public by upsetting the natural environment and the natural relationship is not a reasonable use of that land which is protected from police power regulation. Changes and filling to some extent are permitted because the extent of such changes and fillings does not cause harm. We realize no case in Wisconsin has yet dealt with shoreland regulations and there are several cases in other states which seem to hold such regulations unconstitutional; but nothing this court has said or held in prior cases indicate that destroying the natural character of a swamp or a wetland so as to make that location available for human habitation is a reasonable use of that land when the new use, although of a more economical value to the owner, causes a harm to the general public.

Wisconsin has long held that laws and regulations to prevent pollution and to protect the waters of this state from degradation are valid police-power enactments.... The active public trust duty of the [S]tate of Wisconsin in respect to navigable waters requires the state not only to promote navigation but also to protect and preserve those waters for fishing, recreation, and scenic beauty. *Muench v. Public Service Comm.*, 53 N.W.2d 514, 55 N.W.2d 40 (Wis. 1952). To further this duty, the legislature may delegate authority to local units of the government, which the state did by requiring counties to pass shoreland zoning ordinances. *Menzer v. Elkhart Lake*, 186 N.W.2d 290 (Wis. 1971).

This is not a case of an isolated swamp unrelated to a navigable lake or stream, the change of which would cause no harm to public rights. Lands adjacent to or near navigable waters exist in a special relationship to the state. They have been held subject to special taxation and are subject to the state public trust powers.... (citations omitted).

Cases wherein a confiscation was found cannot be relied upon by the Justs. In *State v. Herwig*, 117 N.W.2d 335 (Wis. 1962), a "taking" was found where a regulation which prohibited hunting on farmland had the effect of establishing a game refuge and resulted in an unnatural, concentrated foraging of the owner's land by waterfowl. In *State v. Becker*, 255 N.W. 144 (Wis. 1934), the court held void a law which established a wildlife refuge (and prohibited hunting) on private property....

* * *

It seems to us that filling a swamp not otherwise commercially usable is not in and of itself an existing use, which is prevented, but rather is the preparation for some future use which is not indigenous to a swamp. Too much stress is laid on the right of an owner to change commercially valueless land when that change does damage to the rights of the public. It is observed that a use of special permits is a means of control and accomplishing the purpose of the zoning ordinance as distinguished from the old concept of providing for variances. The special permit technique is now common practice and has met with judicial approval, and we think it is of some significance in considering whether or not a particular zoning ordinance is reasonable.

A recent case sustaining the validity of a zoning ordinance establishing a flood plain district is *Turnpike Realty Company v. Town of Dedham*, 284 N.W.2d 891 (Mass. 1972). The court held the validity of the ordinance was supported by valid considerations of public welfare, the conservation of "natural conditions, wildlife and open spaces." The ordinance provided that lands which were subject to seasonal or periodic flooding could not be used for residences or other purposes in such a manner as to endanger the health, safety or occupancy thereof and prohibited the erection of structures or buildings which required land to be filled. This case is analogous to the instant facts. The ordinance had a public purpose to preserve the natural condition of the area. No change was allowed which would injure the purposes sought to be preserved and through the special-permit technique, particular land within the zoning district could be excepted from the restrictions.

The Justs argue their property has been severely depreciated in value. But this depreciation of value is not based on the use of the land in its natural state but on what the land would be worth if it could be filled and used for the location of a dwelling. While loss of value is to be considered in determining whether a restriction is a constructive taking, value based upon changing the character of the land at the expense of harm to public rights is not an essential factor or controlling.

We are not unmindful of the warning in *Pennsylvania Coal Co. v. Mahon*, 260 U.S. 393 (1922):

> … We are in danger of forgetting that a strong public desire to improve the public condition is not enough to warrant achieving the desire by a shorter cut than the constitutional way of paying for the change.

This observation refers to the improvement of the public condition, the securing of a benefit not presently enjoyed and to which the public is not entitled. The shoreland zoning ordinance preserves nature, the environment, and natural resources as they were created and to which the people have a present right. The ordinance does not create or improve the public condition but only preserves nature from the despoilage and harm resulting from the unrestricted activities of humans.

* * *

The Judgment in case number 106, dismissing the Justs' action, is modified to set forth the declaratory adjudication that the shoreland zoning ordinance of respondent Marinette County is constitutional; that the Justs' property constitutes wetlands and that particularly the prohibition in the ordinance against the filling of wetlands is constitutional; and the judgment, as so modified, is affirmed.

Notes

1. The *Just* case is well known for its "natural use" doctrine, elaborated in the court's statement that: "An owner of land has no absolute and unlimited right to change the es-

sential natural character of his land so as to use it for a purpose for which it was unsuited in its natural state and which injures the rights of others." The court concluded that property owners have the right to use their property for "indigenous" uses to which their property is naturally suited. This view deflates any abstract "right to develop," often asserted by permit applicants in regulatory proceedings and responds to one factor that plays heavily in takings analysis: the property's diminished economic value as a result of the regulation. The court essentially found that economic value for purposes of takings analysis should not include the anticipated worth resulting from an unnatural change to the land, where the development would cause public harm. Does this rule strike an appropriate balance between public and private property rights? *See also Graham v. Estuary Properties, Inc.*, 399 So.2d 1374 (Fla. 1981) (no absolute right to change the natural character of land).

2. The *Just* case recognized the ecological value of public trust assets, and their importance to society. The court characterized wetlands as "a necessary part of the ecological creation" and recognized the "vital role" they serve in protecting the purity of water and sustaining the "balance of nature." Does this decision move public trust jurisprudence into a broader realm where courts might recognize a full ecological *res* consisting of all of nature's component parts? Given that the multiple components of ecosystems are inextricably interconnected and mutually reliant for full functioning, should other natural resources that play an equally significant role in the balance of nature be similarly protected under the people's trust? Note, however, the court's inclination not to stray too far from navigable waters (stating that "This is not a case of an isolated swamp unrelated to a navigable lake or stream, the change of which would cause no harm to public rights. Lands adjacent to or near navigable waters exist in a special relationship to the state.").

3. *Just* was heralded as an early landmark decision in environmental law, favoring natural uses over development and possibly establishing a new environmental ethic. Arthur Savage & Joseph Sierchio, *The Adirondack Park Agency Act: A Regional Land Use Plan Confronts "The Taking Issue,"* 40 Alb. L. Rev. 447, 475–76 (1976); Comment, *Developments in the Law-Zoning*, 91 Harv. L. Rev. 1427, 1620–21 (1978). However, one critic thought the precedential effect of the decision was virtually nothing. David Bryden, *A Phantom Doctrine: The Origins and Effects of* Just v. Marinette County, 3 Law & Soc. Inquiry 397 (1978), although that article was written before the Wisconsin Supreme Court's *Zealy* decision (p. 155).

4. The *Just* court adopted Professor Freund's harm/benefit dichotomy to distinguish a reasonable exercise of the police power (which would not require just compensation) from inverse condemnation (which would require compensation). How useful is this distinction? Justice Brennan, writing for the majority in *Penn Central Transportation Co. v. New York*, 438 U.S. 104 (1978), questioned the wisdom of the distinction, suggesting that the so-called "noxious use" cases preventing alleged harm "are better understood as resting not on any supposed 'noxious' quality of the prohibited uses but rather on the ground that the restrictions were reasonably related to the implementation of a policy [that was] expected to produce a widespread public benefit and applicable to all similarly situated property." *Id.* at 133, n.30. In *Lucas v. South Carolina Coastal Council*, 505 U.S. 1003 (1992), Justice Scalia also criticized the harm/benefit distinction as a driving factor in regulatory takings analysis. The regulation there involved a coastal protection ordinance that prevented a property owner from constructing homes on two lots. *Id.* at 1006–07. Justice Scalia stated:

[T]he distinction between "harm-preventing" and "benefit-conferring" regulation is often in the eye of the beholder. It is quite possible, for example, to describe in *either* fashion the ecological, economic, and esthetic concerns that inspired the South Carolina Legislature in the present case. One could say that imposing a servitude on Lucas's land is necessary in order to prevent his use of it from "harming" South Carolina's ecological resources; or, instead, in order to achieve the "benefits" of an ecological preserve.... Whether one or the other of the competing characterizations will come to one's lips in a particular case depends primarily upon one's evaluation of the worth of competing uses of real estate....

Id. at 1024–25.

Do you agree with Justice Scalia's dismissal of the harm/benefit distinction? Does the "natural use" approach of *Just* clarify the harm/benefit distinction by finding its reference in the natural conditions of the property? From a trust perspective, couldn't you objectively characterize the natural wetlands on property as part of the "wealth" in the public trust? If the public trust holds assets for present and future generations, would protection of such assets be a conferral of an added "benefit" to the public any more than protection of cash in a private bank account would confer an added "benefit" to the account holder? Isn't any deprivation of the wealth in a trust account considered a loss to the beneficiary? Is that what the *Just* court was saying?

Increasingly, wetlands are recognized for their enormous value in providing a barrier to storms, thought to be growing in intensity due to climate change.[4] Given this role, which is the more compelling characterization of regulatory wetland protection: conferring a benefit to the public, or preventing a harm to the public?

5. Notice that the court described the public trust doctrine in terms of a state duty: "The active public trust duty of the state of Wisconsin in respect to navigable waters requires the state not only to promote navigation but also to protect and preserve those waters for fishing, recreation, and scenic beauty." What are the parameters of an "active duty"? How is such a duty enforced? Where would courts look to find fiduciary standards for judging performance of this duty? How does the active duty relate to today's massive environmental problems like climate change, nuclear contamination, biodiversity loss, ocean acidification, and a multitude of others that seemingly require bold leadership by government?

6. For commentary on the role of the *Just* case in regulatory takings law, see Craig Anthony Arnold, *The Reconstitution of Property: Property as a Web of Interests*, 26 Harv. Envtl. L. Rev. 281, 349–50 (2002). Some analysts thought that the U.S. Supreme Court's decision in *Lucas v. South Carolina Coastal Council*, 505 U.S. 1003 (1992), implicitly overruled *Just* by recognizing that regulations that wiped out all economically viable uses worked a *per se* taking. *See, e.g.*, Joseph L. Sax, *Property Rights and the Economy of Nature: Understanding* Lucas v. South Carolina Coastal Council, 45 Stan. L. Rev. 1433, 1438–39 (1993). But that prediction was also made before *Zealy* and several other decisions relying on *Just*. *See, e.g.*, Michael C. Blumm & Lucus Ritchie, *Lucas's Unlikely Legacy: The Rise of Background Principles as Categorical Takings Defenses*, 29 Harv. Envtl. L. Rev. 321, 345 (2005) (listing six states following *Just* as part of a survey of case law recognizing background principles of property law).

---

4. Louisiana's Governor Bobby Jindal has explained the value of wetlands "as part of the hurricane protection system" to protect his state from storm damage. *See* State of Louisiana, Governor Bobby Jindal, *Louisiana's Coast: Ecosystem Restoration and Flood Protection*:

If there is one area that exemplifies what is at stake in the Louisiana coastal region, it is the state's storm protection value. Storm protection refers to the function of wetlands in reducing storm energy and storm-generated water surges that cause flooding. This ecosystem service is very important to residents of the Mississippi Delta, the Gulf of Mexico and U.S. Eastern Seaboard.

7. The same year as the *Just* decision, Congress enacted the modern Clean Water Act, including a section 404 permit program governing discharges of dredged or fill material, which now serves as the basic federal wetlands protection program. State approval of discharges is largely a prerequisite to a federal 404 permit, however, so state wetland programs remain important. Moreover, the Clean Water Act authorizes states with federal approval of their programs to displace federal permit requirements. *See* Oliver A. Houck & Michael Rowland, *Federalism in Wetlands Regulation: A Consideration of Delegation of Clean Water Act Section 404 and Related Programs to the States*, 54 Md. L. Rev. 1242 (1995). State programs can also be more comprehensive than the federal program, which employs general permits widely instead of individual permits, *see* Steven G. Davison, *General Permits Under Section 404 of the Clean Water Act*, 26 Pace Envtl. L. Rev. 35 (2009); does not regulate wetland drainage that is unconnected with discharges of fills, *Save Our Community v. EPA*, 971 F.2d 1155 (5th Cir. 1992); and has suffered jurisdictional cutbacks due to the U.S. Supreme Court's decision in *Rapanos v. United States*, 547 U.S. 715 (2006) (requiring either surface connection between wetlands and adjacent navigable waters or a "substantial nexus" between them, which effectively excludes so-called "isolated waters" from the reach of the federal program).

The U.S. Army Corps of Engineers, the agency that implements the scheme, rarely denies permits, and the program has led to the cumulative eradication of wetlands over time. The experience underscores the public trust doctrine as a possible legal avenue to force government protection of wetlands. The *Just* court's emphasis of an active trust duty of protection seemingly sets the stage for challenging a permit that allows damage to wetlands. Although the trust was used as a "shield" in *Just* to protect against a takings claim, could it also be used as a "sword" to hold agencies to trust standards when carrying out their regulatory programs? Many courts have emphasized that compliance with statutory standards does not equate to satisfying trust standards.

8. The *Just* case remained undisturbed as precedent in Wisconsin until 2013 when a fractured Wisconsin Supreme Court handed down the following 4–3 decision in which it re-interpreted *Just* as involving police power regulation of wetlands, not the public trust doctrine. A vigorous dissent disagreed.

Rock-Koshkonong Lake Dist. v. State Dept. of Natural Resources

Supreme Court of Wisconsin
833 N.W.2d 800 (2013)

[The case involved a challenge by the Lake District to a decision by the Wisconsin Department of Natural Resources (DNR) to not raise the level of a navigable lake. The DNR contended that raising the lake level would harm the lake's adjacent private wetlands by eroding shoreline and degrading water quality. DNR claimed it had a public trust duty to protect such wetlands, which were located above the ordinary high water mark (OHWM) of the lake. The state's decision was affirmed administratively and in the lower courts, but the Wisconsin Supreme Court reversed.]

PROSSER, J.

This case, involving a dispute about the water levels on Lake Koshkonong, presents fundamental questions about the authority of the Wisconsin Department of Natural Resources (the DNR), and the criteria it uses in regulating the level of water in navigable waters that are affected by dams.

* * *

B. The DNR'S Consideration of Impacts on Wetlands Adjacent to Navigable Waters

The District contends that the DNR, in making a water level determination ... "in the interest of public rights in navigable waters," exceeded its authority when it considered impacts on private wetlands adjacent to Lake Koshkonong that are above the OHWM. The District is also concerned about the application of the public trust doctrine to any wetlands that are not navigable in fact unless those wetlands are below the OHWM. The District asserts that the DNR's position significantly expands the scope of the DNR's public trust jurisdiction.

* * *

Article IX, Section 1 of the Wisconsin Constitution commands that the state hold navigable waters in trust for the public:

> The state shall have concurrent jurisdiction on all rivers and lakes bordering on this state so far as such rivers or lakes shall form a common boundary to the state and any other state or territory now or hereafter to be formed, and bounded by the same; and the river Mississippi and the navigable waters leading into the Mississippi and St. Lawrence, and the carrying places between the same, shall be common highways and forever free, as well to the inhabitants of the state as to the citizens of the United States, without any tax, impost or duty therefor.

Wis. Const. art. IX, § 1.

This court has long held that the public trust in navigable waters "should be interpreted in the broad and beneficent spirit that gave rise to it in order that the people may fully enjoy the intended benefits." *Diana Shooting Club v. Husting*, 145 N.W. 816, 820 (Wis. 1914); *Lake Beulah Mgmt. Dist. v. State Dep't of Natural Res.*, 799 N.W.2d 73, 83 (Wis. 2011). Broadly interpreting the public trust has resulted in recognition of more than just commercial navigability rights. Protection now extends to "purely recreational purposes such as boating, swimming, fishing, hunting, ... and ... preserv[ing] scenic beauty." *R.W. Docks & Slips v. State*, 628 N.W.2d 781, 788 (Wis. 2001) (citations omitted).

Because the public trust doctrine is rooted in Article IX, Section 1, however, it is important to understand its history and its core principles so that it is properly interpreted....

* * *

The public trust doctrine is premised upon the existence of "navigable waters." ...

The DNR's position seeks to extend its public trust jurisdiction beyond navigable waters to non-navigable waters and land. Wetlands are often not "navigable in fact." Non-navigable land is by definition not navigable and may not be marshy or "wet." Eliminating the element of "navigability" from the public trust doctrine would remove one of the prerequisites for the DNR's *constitutional basis* for regulating and controlling water and land. Applying the public trust doctrine to non-navigable land above the OHWM would eliminate the rationale for the doctrine. The ramifications for private property owners could be very significant.

The public trust doctrine vests the ownership of land *under lakes*—i.e., lake beds—in the state. By contrast, the public trust doctrine in Wisconsin gives riparian owners along navigable streams a qualified title in the stream beds to the center of the stream, while the state holds the navigable waters in trust for the public. In reality, the state effectively controls the land under navigable streams and rivers without actually owning it.

* * *

Contemplating the question of ownership is important because the public trust doctrine implicates state ownership or virtual state ownership—by virtue of its trust responsibility—of *land* under navigable waters. If the public trust were extended to cover wetlands that are not navigable, it would create significant questions about ownership of and trespass on private land, and it would be difficult to cabin expansion of the state's new constitutionally based jurisdiction over private land.

* * *

There is no constitutional foundation for *public trust* jurisdiction over land, including non-navigable wetlands, that is not below the OHWM of a navigable lake or stream. Applying the state's police power to land above or beyond the OHWM of navigable waters—to protect the public interest *in navigable waters*—is different from asserting public trust jurisdiction over non-navigable land and water.

The public trust doctrine entails public rights in navigable waters, including noncommercial "sailing, rowing, canoeing, bathing, fishing, hunting, skating, and other public purposes." *Nekoosa Edwards Paper Co. v. R.R. Comm'n*, 228 N.W. 144, 147 (Wis. 1929). The state's public trust duty "requires the state not only to promote navigation but also to protect and preserve *its waters* for fishing, hunting, recreation, *and scenic beauty*." *Wis.'s Envtl. Decade v. Dep't of Natural Res.*, 271 N.W.2d 69, 72 (Wis. 1978) (emphasis added)....

* * *

In sum, we believe the District has raised legitimate concerns about the DNR's reliance upon the public trust doctrine as authority for some of its regulation in this case.

2. Police Power as a Basis for Protecting Water Resources

This review of the constitutionally based public trust doctrine does not disarm the DNR in protecting Wisconsin's valuable water resources. For instance, the DNR has broad statutory authority grounded in the state's police power to protect wetlands and other water resources. *See Just v. Marinette Cnty.*, 201 N.W.2d 761, 764–65 (Wis. 1972). This police power is sometimes buttressed by requirements imposed by federal law. Moreover, the agency has explicit statutory authority in this case to consider the impact of the water levels of Lake Koshkonong on public and private wetlands adjacent to the lake, Wis. Stat. § 31.02(1), because it has police power authority to "protect ... property."

The *Just* case is a textbook example of using the state's police power to support legislation "to protect navigable waters and the public rights therein from the degradation and deterioration which results from uncontrolled use and development of shorelands." 201 N.W.2d at 765. The Wisconsin Legislature approved the Water Quality Act of 1965 by Chapter 614, Laws of 1965. The Act authorized the passage of shoreland zoning ordinances by counties, subject to certain requirements. Marinette County passed such an ordinance. It later prosecuted Ronald Just for filling in wetlands on his shoreland property without a required permit. *Id.* at 766–67.

* * *

The court's emphasis on the state's police power is evident in the following passages:

[Ed's note: due to length, some passages have been omitted.] Wisconsin has long held that laws and regulations to prevent pollution and to protect the waters of this state from degradation are valid police-power enactments. *Id.* at 768.

If there is any question that the court was not relying on the public trust doctrine to sustain the shoreland zoning ordinance and its authorizing legislation, the court noted that the Marinette County ordinance applied to "lands within 1,000 feet of the normal high-

Scope of PTD defined

R.

water elevation of navigable lakes, ponds, or flowages and 300 feet from a navigable river or stream." *Id.* at 764. These dimensions far exceed the geographic limitations of public trust jurisdiction. It should be obvious that the state does not have *constitutional public trust jurisdiction* to regulate land a distance of more than three football fields away from a navigable lake or pond.

The police power is potent, and legislation grounded in the state's police power is presumed constitutional and will be sustained unless it is deemed unconstitutional beyond a reasonable doubt. Nonetheless, as *Just* makes clear, the distinction between the DNR's constitutionally based public trust authority and the DNR's police power-based statutory authority is that the latter is subject to constitutional and statutory protections afforded to property, may be modified from time to time by the legislature, and requires some balancing of competing interests in enforcement.

* * *

The DNR properly considered the impact of the Petition's proposed water levels on public and private wetlands in and adjacent to Lake Koshkonong. However, the DNR inappropriately relied on the public trust doctrine for its authority to protect non-navigable land and non-navigable water above the ordinary high water mark. The DNR has broad statutory authority grounded in the state's police power to protect non-navigable wetlands and other non-navigable water resources. Thus, the DNR may consider the water level impact on all adjacent property under Wis. Stat. §31.02(1).

* * *

CROOKS, J. (dissenting).

This case presents a question that the majority can—indeed does—answer by interpreting Wis. Stat. §31.02(1) (2009–10). Yet the majority unnecessarily reaches out to the constitutional principle of the public trust doctrine from the Wisconsin Constitution, constricting the doctrine and misreading this court's precedent, especially the well-settled law articulated in *Just v. Marinette County*, 201 N.W.2d 761 (Wis. 1972). Wisconsin's long and robust history of protecting the public trust is widely acknowledged and respected. The public trust doctrine imposes on the state, as trustee, the affirmative duty to protect, preserve, and promote the public's right to Wisconsin's waters.

The majority opinion attempts to undermine this court's precedent, recharacterize its holdings, and rewrite history. Instead of limiting itself to addressing only what must be addressed, the majority seizes this opportunity to limit the public trust doctrine in an unforeseen way, transforming the state's affirmative duty to protect the public trust into a legislative choice. It needlessly unsettles our precedent and weakens the public trust doctrine that is enshrined in the Wisconsin Constitution. This represents a significant and disturbing shift in Wisconsin law.

* * *

I. Wisconsin Courts Have Aggressively Protected the Public Trust Doctrine.

To understand the significance and to see the potential implications of the majority's novel interpretation of the *Just* case, it is necessary to appreciate how settled the public trust doctrine has been in Wisconsin until now. This court highlighted the constitutional basis of the public trust doctrine in *Muench v. Public Service Comm'n,* 53 N.W.2d 514 (Wis. 1952). In that case, the court traced the history of the public trust doctrine to the Northwest Ordinance of 1787.

* * *

Early on, this court declared that the public trust not only required preservation of the trust, it also required promotion of it. *City of Milwaukee v. State*, 214 N.W. 820 (Wis. 1927) ("The equitable title to these submerged lands vests in the public at large, while the legal title vests in the state, restricted only by the trust, and the trust, being both active and administrative, *requires the lawmaking body to act in all cases where action is necessary, not only to preserve the trust, but to promote it*" (emphasis added)).

In *Diana Shooting Club v. Husting*, this court described the state's responsibilities under the public trust doctrine:

> The wisdom of the policy which, in the organic laws of our state, steadfastly and carefully preserved to the people the full and free use of public waters cannot be questioned. *Nor should it be limited or curtailed by narrow constructions*. It should be interpreted in the *broad and beneficent spirit* that gave rise to it in order that the people may fully enjoy the intended benefits.

Diana Shooting Club, 145 N.W. at 820 (emphasis added).

* * *

This court in *Just v. Marinette County* further interpreted the doctrine while upholding a shoreland zoning statute enacted pursuant to the state's public trust duty. The court stated:

> The active public trust duty of the state of Wisconsin in respect to navigable waters *requires the state not only to promote navigation but also to protect and preserve those waters* for fishing, recreation, and scenic beauty. *To further this duty,* the legislature may delegate authority to local units of the government, which the state did by requiring counties to pass shoreland zoning ordinances.

Just, 201 N.W.2d at 768–69 (emphasis added) (citations omitted). This court explained that the purpose of the statute at issue in that case was to "protect navigable waters and the public rights therein from the degradation and deterioration which results from uncontrolled use and development of shorelands." *Id.* at 765. We noted that the stated purpose of the shoreland regulation program is to "aid in the fulfillment of the state's role as trustee of its navigable waters and to promote public health, safety, convenience and general welfare." *Id.*

Since then this court has consistently reiterated the purpose and the significance of the public trust doctrine in its cases. For example, *Wisconsin's Environmental Decade, Inc. v. DNR (Environmental Decade 1978)*, described the duties of the state under the public trust as "not only to promote navigation but also to protect and preserve its waters for fishing, hunting, recreation, and scenic beauty." *Envtl. Decade 1978*, 271 N.W.2d 69, 72 (Wis. 1978). We described the state's responsibility as long-acknowledged and highlighted the legislature's delegation of water management to the DNR in furtherance of "the state's affirmative obligations as trustee." *Id.* at 72–73.

Recently, this court reiterated these principles in *Lake Beulah Management District v. DNR*, holding that under the applicable statutes and the public trust duties, the DNR can and must consider whether an inland well would harm waters of the state before issuing a permit for the well. *Lake Beulah*, 799 N.W.2d 73, 76 (Wis. 2011). This court explained jurisprudence on the public trust doctrine:

> We reaffirmed this maxim in *Muench v. Public Service Commission* in our examination of the history and evolution of the public trust doctrine, which indicated a "*trend to extend* and protect the rights of the public to the recreational

enjoyment of the navigable waters of the state." We have further explained, "*The trust doctrine is not a narrow or crabbed concept of lakes and streams.*"

Id. at 83 (emphasis added) (citations omitted).

Our cases demonstrate that the scope of the public trust doctrine is such that the state holds title to the land between the ordinary high water marks, and state regulation consistent with the public trust doctrine extends to surrounding areas. The ownership of land was emphasized in *Diana Shooting Club,* which was a case about trespass. In that case, there was no trespass because the hunter was hunting between the ordinary high water marks, land that was held in trust for the public. *Diana Shooting Club,* 145 N.W. at 820. In contrast, regulation consistent with the public trust doctrine was at issue in *Just* because the shoreland zoning statute extended well beyond the ordinary high water mark, and the court held that it could be regulated pursuant to the public trust doctrine. *Just,* 201 N.W.2d at 766, 768.

In furtherance of the state's trustee responsibilities, the legislature has enacted statutes to discharge its duties. As the court explained in *Environmental Decade 1978,* several chapters of the Wisconsin statutes, including Chapter 31, which is at issue in this case, were enacted "[i]n furtherance of the state's affirmative obligations as trustee of navigable waters." 271 N.W.2d at 73. We dealt with a similar situation in this court's unanimous decision in *Lake Beulah,* where the legislature had used a statute to implement its public trust duties. This court stated, "[W]e conclude that, through Wis. Stat. § 281.11 and § 281.12, the legislature has *delegated the State's public trust duties* to the DNR in the context of its regulation of high capacity wells and their potential effect on navigable waters such as Lake Beulah." 799 N.W.2d at 84 (emphasis added). That decision dealt with non-navigable water, and explained its relationship to the public trust doctrine. The statutes created to preserve and promote the public trust doctrine allowed the regulation of non-navigable waters because of the potential effects non-navigable waters have on navigable waters.

Connectal? [handwritten marginalia]

II. The Majority Unnecessarily Undermines Well-Settled Law on Wisconsin's Public Trust Doctrine

The heart of the public trust doctrine lies in protecting, preserving, and promoting the public's right to Wisconsin's waters, and this court has vigilantly guarded these rights. The public trust doctrine entrusts to the state the duty to protect, preserve, and promote the public trust. The majority untethers our constitutional jurisprudence from its foundation and attempts to transform 165 years of constitutional precedent into a mere legislative exercise of the state's police power. The citizens of Wisconsin may rightly wonder why the majority is limiting the protection of Wisconsin's waters and reaching a constitutional question that is not essential to its holding. I refuse to unnecessarily constrict our holdings on this important constitutional doctrine, especially in a case that should be decided on statutory grounds.

The central issue in this case is one of statutory interpretation—namely, whether the DNR can consider wetlands above the ordinary high water mark when determining water levels under Wis. Stat. § 31.02(1). Wisconsin Stat. § 31.02(1) states in relevant part: "The department, in the interest of public rights in navigable waters or to promote safety and protect life, health and property[,] may regulate and control the level and flow of water in all navigable waters...." Both the majority and the petitioner agree that a simple reading of § 31.02(1) demonstrates that the statute allows for consideration of private wetlands. In fact, the majority states: "The District acknowledges that 'privately owned wetlands are entitled to consideration as "property" to be protected in establishing a water level order.' There can be no dispute that the DNR can 'consider' water level impact on all adjacent property under Wis. Stat. § 31.02(1)." Because that interpretation is dispositive of the issue, I would stop the analysis there.

... The majority reaches a constitutional issue that it is not required to reach, and it engages in a strained analysis to bolster its holding. [T]he long-settled public trust doctrine support[s] a consideration of the impact on wetlands adjacent to Lake Koshkonong when regulating water levels pursuant to the public trust doctrine.

To support its holding, the majority misconstrues *Just v. Marinette County.* The majority calls the *Just* case "a textbook example of using the state's police power [as opposed to using the constitutional public trust doctrine] to support legislation 'to protect navigable waters and the public rights therein....'"

The clear language of *Just* rebuts the majority's conclusion that it was only a police power case. The thrust of the *Just* opinion showed that the court believed it was relying on the public trust doctrine. The court explicitly held that land above the ordinary high water mark is subject to the public trust doctrine. *Just,* 201 N.W.2d at 768–69 ("Lands *adjacent to* or *near* navigable waters exist in a special relationship to the state. They have been held subject to special taxation and *are subject to the state public trust powers....*" (emphasis added) (citations omitted)).

In an attempt to circumvent the clear language of the *Just* case, the majority makes a circular argument. The majority imports its conclusion from earlier in the opinion— that the public trust does not extend beyond the ordinary high water mark—and applies it to support its subsequent conclusion. Regarding *Just,* it states:

> If there is any question that the court was not relying on the public trust doctrine to sustain the shoreland zoning ordinance and its authorizing legislation, the court noted that the Marinette County ordinance applied to "lands within 1,000 feet of the normal high-water elevation of navigable lakes, ponds, or flowages and 300 feet from a navigable river or stream." These dimensions far exceed the geographic limitations of public trust jurisdiction.

The majority's only apparent support for its conclusion about the dimensions of the public trust jurisdiction comes from its own earlier analysis. The *Just* case establishes the opposite conclusion—that the DNR pursuant to the public trust doctrine may consider the impact on land above the ordinary high water mark.

Not only does an appropriate interpretation of *Just* rebut the majority's conclusions, this court has repeatedly interpreted the public trust doctrine more broadly than the majority does today, and there is no compelling reason presented in this case to change that interpretation. The case law indicates that the state has the power to regulate lands beyond the ordinary high water mark in discharging the duties entrusted to it under the public trust doctrine. *See, e.g., Lake Beulah,* 799 N.W.2d at 84. Likewise, the cases demonstrate that the legislature has an affirmative duty as trustee to protect and promote the public trust. *See, e.g., City of Milwaukee,* 214 N.W. 820.

One explanation for the majority's puzzling holding is that it appears to confuse the concepts of ownership of (or title to) the land with regulation pursuant to the public trust doctrine. In the cases the majority cites to support its position that public trust jurisdiction is confined to limited geographic areas, the idea of *ownership* of the land was paramount, but here, ownership of the private wetlands is not at issue. The issue is only whether the DNR has the authority under the public trust doctrine to consider the impact on those adjacent wetlands consistent with its duties under the public trust doctrine....

Allowing the trustee to discharge its public trust duties by considering things that affect navigable waters is consistent with our precedent. If it could not, how then would the state discharge its extensive duties "not only to promote navigation but also to protect and preserve its waters for fishing, hunting, recreation, and scenic beauty"? *Envtl. Decade 1978*, 271 N.W.2d at 72 (citations omitted). Therefore, the DNR did not err in relying on its public trust power to consider the impact of raising the water levels on adjacent private wetlands even when the wetlands are above the ordinary high water mark. The conclusion the majority reaches is a novel interpretation that cannot be squared with the extensive public trust doctrine case law.

* * *

Notes

1. The majority opinion seemed to confine the PTD to navigable waters below the high water mark. As the dissent pointed out, that approach disregarded established precedent in Wisconsin. For example, the Wisconsin Supreme Court had, just two years prior to this case, interpreted the public trust to extend to groundwater that affected navigable water in *Lake Beulah Management District v. DNR* (p. 412). Apart from the conflict with existing precedent, is the majority's approach superficial? How can the state have the trust duty to protect navigable waters, yet not have the public trust authority to control activities affecting such waters outside of the ordinary high water mark? Is the court's approach tied to an outdated view of ecology, developed during a time when judges simply didn't understand the interconnectedness of wetlands and waterways? Moreover, is the opinion likely to hold in the future? Can a later court reject the majority's approach just as the majority rejected prior case law? The apparent trajectory of the PTD points towards judicial expansion of the trust consistent with ecological reality of interconnectedness of resources. For discussion of the importance of adjacent wetlands to water quality, see Envtl. Protection Agency, *Connectivity of Streams & Wetlands to Downstream Waters: A Review & Synthesis of the Scientific Evidence* (Jan. 2015), *available at* http://cfpub.epa.gov/ncea/cfm/recordisplay.cfm?deid=296414#Download.

2. The dissent criticized the majority for confusing ownership of streambeds with regulation under the PTD, which seems to be a justified criticism. The majority traced the PTD to the constitutional equal footing doctrine. That doctrine, discussed in chapter 3, provided states with ownership of lands submerged beneath the high water mark of navigable waters at statehood; these lands were conveyed by the federal government to the states at statehood under reasoning of the Supreme Court's *Pollard v. Hagen* decision (p. 66). The PTD, a public use and control concept, has often reached to areas well beyond the submerged lands, as prior chapters have explained.

3. As made clear by both the majority and the dissent, the resolution of this case did not actually require PTD analysis, as both the general police power and express statutory language supported regulation of adjacent wetlands. Why, then, did the majority spend so much time stating that the PTD did not support regulation in this instance?

4. The majority characterized *Just* as an opinion that dealt with the police power, not the public trust doctrine. But the dissent, backed by a full body of commentary interpreting *Just* over the years, characterized the *Just* decision as a significant interpretation of the public trust doctrine. Why did the majority opinion attempt to recharacterize *Just* and ignore that court's emphasis on the public trust (particularly the statement that wet-

lands "adjacent to or near navigable waters exist in a special relationship to the state. They ... are subject to the state public trust powers." *Just*, 201 N.W.2d at 769)?

5. If the police power supported the regulation, why did it matter so much to the dissent to find a public trust basis as well? How are the police power and public trust different? Interestingly, both the majority and dissent agree about how different the two bases for regulation are. Consider the majority's statement: "[A]s *Just* makes clear, the distinction between the DNR's constitutionally based public trust authority and the DNR's police power-based statutory authority is that the latter is subject to constitutional and statutory protections afforded to property, may be modified from time to time by the legislature, and requires some balancing of competing interests in enforcement." Does the public trust *require* protection of the public's natural assets while the police power simply provides *discretion* to protect such assets? Does the government have a defense to a takings claim when its regulation is carried out pursuant to the public trust, and does it lack such a defense when it acts pursuant to its police power?

6. For an analysis of the *Rock-Koshkonong* decision, see Christian Eickelberg, Note, *Rock-Koshkonong Lake District and the Surprising Narrowing of Wisconsin's Public Trust Doctrine*, 16 Vt. J. Envtl. L. 38 (2014); Melissa K. Scanlan, *It's Not Open Season on Wetlands*, Milwaukee Journal-Sentinel, July 22, 2013 (maintaining that the public trust language in *Rock-Koshkonong* was dicta).

7. Even though *Rock-Koshkonong* seemed to reinterpret *Just*, the Wisconsin Court of Appeals later found *Just* to be "instructive" in *Murr v. State*, 859 N.W.2d 628 at ¶ 27 (Wis. Ct. App. 2014). The Murrs unsuccessfully challenged a county ordinance that prohibited the development or sale of their two adjacent lots with less than one acre of net project area in an effort to limit environmental damage. The court stated that "*Just* establishes that because of the strong public interest in preventing degradation of the natural environment, property owners advancing takings claims based on environmental legislation have a much more difficult time showing they were deprived of all or substantially all practical use of their property." *Id.*

8. In *Zealy v. City of Waukesha*, 548 N.W.2d 528 (Wis. 1996), the Wisconsin Supreme Court declined an opportunity to overrule *Just's* suggestion that the state shoreline regulation aimed to protect natural uses of the land in the wake of the U.S. Supreme Court's decision in *Lucas v. South Carolina Coastal Council*, 505 U.S. 1003 (1992), which established that a land regulation leaving an owner with no economically valuable use was a categorical taking warranting payment of just compensation. Some thought that *Lucas* implicitly overruled *Just*, but not the Wisconsin court, which stated:

> [The landowners] argue their property has been severely depreciated in value. But this depreciation of value is not based on the use of the land in its natural state but on what the land would be worth if it could be filled and used for the location of a dwelling. While loss of value is to be considered in determining whether a restriction is a constructive taking, value based upon changing the character of the land at the expense of harm to public rights is not an essential factor or controlling.

Id. at 534, quoting *Just*, 201 N.W.2d at 771. Consequently, the court ruled that a wetlands conservancy district regulation that denied Zealy's plans to develop 8.2 acres (of an original 250-acre tract) for residences, which Zealy claimed cost him $200,000, was not a taking warranting just compensation because it did not affect the historic use of the property for farming, and it left his 2.2 acres of uplands unregulated. The court held that the *Lucas* categorical taking rule did not apply because Zealy retained economically viable uses of his land and expressly reaffirmed *Just:* "Nothing in this opinion limits our holding in *Just* and cases following its rule." *Id.* at 534. The court also endorsed *Just*'s view of the importance of wetlands as "part of the balance of nature" and essential to sustaining the purity of lakes, rivers, and streams. *Id.* at 535. The court continued: "Wisconsin has a long history of protecting its water resources, its lakes, rivers, and streams, which depend on wetlands for their proper survival. As stated in *Just,* 201 N.W.2d at 768:

> Swamps and wetlands were once considered wasteland, undesirable, and not picturesque. But as the people became more sophisticated, an appreciation was acquired that swamps and wetlands serve a vital role in nature, are part of the balance of nature and are essential to the purity of the water in our lakes and streams. Swamps and wetlands are a necessary part of the ecological creation and now, even to the uninitiated, possess their own beauty in nature.

Id. at 535.

9. The *Zealy* decision depicted the conflict as one between the public interest in wetlands protection and the private interest in filling wetlands for development. The Maine Supreme Court adopted this dichotomy in *State v. Johnson*, 265 A.2d 711 (Me. 1970), deciding that the state restrictions on wetlands fills were compensable because they were creating public benefits the costs of which should be socially borne, raising again the public benefit vs. public harm dichotomy discussed previously. Although the Maine court characterized wetlands protection as conferring benefits to the public, doesn't that ignore substantial private harms inflicted on neighbors from the filling of wetlands? Costs that can include loss of flood control and pollution filtering that would be borne disproportionately by neighboring landowners? Shouldn't those private costs figure into the equation, so that both the public and private costs of wetlands fills are relevant?

Palazzolo v. Rhode Island

Supreme Court of the United States
533 U.S. 606 (2001)

[Anthony Palazzolo owned land bordering Long Island Sound in Westerly, Rhode Island, most of which (but not all) was designated as coastal wetlands under state law. He wanted to fill tidelands for residential development. The state denied relevant permits, and Palazzolo claimed the denial worked on unconstitutional taking. The Rhode Island courts rejected Palazzolo's claim, and he appealed to the U.S. Supreme Court. The Court reversed the state court on two issues, ruling that 1) Palazzolo's claim was ripe for judicial review, because he had twice been denied the requisite fill permit from the state; and 2) Palazzolo could challenge the state regulation, even though it pre-dated his acquisition of the property. But the Court rejected Palazzolo's claim that the regulation resulted in a taking by depriving him of all economically beneficial use because his 20-acre tract included two acres of developable uplands, worth about $200,000, which the Court concluded provided him with "substantial" value. Thus he could not claim a categorical economic wipeout, a presumptive taking under the Court's *Lucas* decision.

The Court remanded the case to the state courts to determine whether the regulation worked a taking under the so-called multi-factor takings test laid out by the Court's decision in *Penn Central v. New York*, 438 U.S. 104 (1978) (establishing a three-factor balancing test calling for "*ad hoc* factual inquiries" into the economic effect of the regulation on the claimant; the extent to which the regulation interferes with distinct investment-backed expectations; and the character of the government action).]

Palazzolo v. State

Superior Court of Rhode Island
No. WM 88-0297, 2005 WL 1645974
July 5, 2005

GALE, J.

* * *

On writ of certiorari, the United States Supreme Court found the case ripe for decision, reversed the holding of the Rhode Island Supreme Court, and remanded the case for the purpose of a *Penn Central* analysis. *Palazzolo v. Rhode Island,* 533 U.S. 606 (2001). The Rhode Island Supreme Court entered an Order, dated June 24, 2002, remanding the case to the Superior Court with express guidelines....

* * *

The State ... contends that a strong Public Trust Doctrine in Rhode Island must result in a finding that the subject parcel is not capable of being developed economically. This is because, the State maintains, approximately one-half of Plaintiffs property lies below the mean high water mark and is, therefore, not Plaintiff's to develop, at least in contravention to the wishes of the state. Plaintiff disagrees, contending that the survey does not establish the mean high water mark with sufficient precision to allow this Court to accept the survey as establishing the mean high water mark for Plaintiff's property. Plaintiff also contends that Winnapaug Pond is not a tidal pond for purposes of the Public Trust Doctrine and, therefore, Plaintiff's property rights should not be limited by such doctrine.

* * *

II. Public Trust Doctrine

Lucas v. South Carolina, 505 U.S. 1003 (1992) makes clear that, for purposes of takings analysis, the title one takes to property is subject to background principles of state law. *Lucas* states that the government need not compensate the property owner if the regulated or prohibited use was "not part of his title to begin with." *Id.* at 1027. State nuisance doctrine has been discussed above and it would bar Plaintiff's takings claim in this Court's view.

A second significant issue is to what extent the Public Trust Doctrine would have limited the title originally acquired by Plaintiff and his predecessor in interest, Shore Gardens, Inc. (SGI). Succinctly stated, the State contends that because of the Public Trust Doctrine and trial evidence proving that one-half of the site is below mean high water, Plaintiff could not have expected to develop his subdivision absent the consent of the state.

Plaintiff counters by contending that the State's survey is erroneous, claiming that substantially more than one-half of the site is above the 1986 mean high water mark. Moreover, Plaintiff now claims that because the pond is subject to periodic closing of its breachway, it is not truly a tidal pond and thus, is not subject to the Public Trust Doctrine. Thirdly, Plaintiff contends that Winnapaug Pond and other similar coastal ponds are not subject to the Public Trust Doctrine.

After receiving voluminous evidence on the issue, this Court finds that Winnapaug Pond is a tidal body of water. This Court likewise finds that the survey filed with the Court (Ex. CCCCC) is accurate and establishes a mean high water line as of 1986, proving that almost exactly 50% of Plaintiff's property is below mean high water. Thus, the pond and Plaintiff's adjacent property are subject to the Public Trust Doctrine.

In *Shively v. Bowlby*, 152 U.S. 1 (1894), the United States Supreme Court expounded in great detail concerning the history and application of what is now commonly referred to as the Public Trust Doctrine.[5] The Court concluded in general that

> Lands under tide waters are incapable of cultivation or improvement in the manner of lands above high water mark. They are of great value to the public for the purposes of commerce, navigation and fishery. Their improvement by individuals, when permitted, is incidental or subordinate to the public use and right. Therefore the title and the control of them are vested in the sovereign for the benefit of the whole people.
>
> ...
>
> The title and rights of riparian or littoral proprietors in the soil below high water mark, therefore, are governed by the laws of several *States*, subject to the rights granted to the United States by the Constitution. *Id.* at 57–58 (emphasis added).

Shively established beyond question a nationwide Public Trust Doctrine which is to be applied based upon *state* law.

There can be no doubt that the doctrine remains viable law in Rhode Island. Not only was the Public Trust Doctrine incorporated into the Rhode Island Constitution, R.I. Const. art. 1, Section 17, but as recently stated by our Supreme Court, "[a]ny system of regulation of tidal land in Rhode Island must be viewed in the context of [the] ancient and still vital doctrine [ ] of ... the public trust doctrine...." *Champlin's Realty Assocs., L.P. v. Tillson*, 823 A.2d 1162, 1165 (R.I. 2003) (quoting *Town of Warren v. Thornton-Whitehouse*, 740 A.2d 1255, 1259 (R.I. 1999)).

Restated, the Public Trust Doctrine dictates that, "the state holds title to all land below the high-water mark in a proprietary capacity for the benefit of the public." *Greater Providence Chamber of Commerce v. Rhode Island*, 657 A.2d 1038, 1041 (R.I. 1995). "Such common law is in force in Rhode Island 'except as it has been changed by local legislation or custom.'" *Id.* at 1042 (quoting *City of Providence v. Comstock*, 65 A. 307, 308 (R.I. 1906)).

A limitation to the Public Trust Doctrine exists when there has been a legislative decree, such as when the legislature transfers property or grants rights to control or regulate property below mean high water to cities or municipalities. *Thornton-Whitehouse*, 740 A.2d at 1259–60. The State may likewise cede its ownership interest while retaining its rights and powers under the public trust doctrine. *Champlin's Realty Assocs., L.P.*, 823 A.2d at 1167.

As to Winnapaug Pond in general and Plaintiff's property specifically, there has been no express legislative transfer of the state's public trust rights. *Cf. Greater Providence Chamber of Commerce v. Rhode Island*, 657 A.2d at 1040–41. Palazzolo has not shown any such legislative action in relation to the property in question. Nor has there been either express or implied state approval or acquiescence to the filling of tidal waters upon which the Plaintiff has relied to his detriment.[6] Palazzolo has not filled and improved his

---

5. Even before *Shively*, the Rhode Island Supreme Court recognized the public trust doctrine. *See Bailey v. Burges*, 11 R.I. 330, 331 (1876).

6. In *Greater Providence Chamber of Commerce*, landowners who filled along the shore line with acquiescence or express or implied approval of the State and then improved upon that land in reliance on the state's approval were able to establish free and clear title. Those are not the facts in the case before this Court. The state has in no way expressly or impliedly granted permission for filling. Nor has Palazzolo improved the property in reliance on such state approval.

property with the permission or acquiescence of the State. Accordingly, this Court finds that as a result of Rhode Island's Public Trust Doctrine, neither Plaintiff nor SGI has ever had a right to fill or develop that portion of the site which is below mean high water. Thus, as against the State, Palazzolo has gained title and the corresponding property rights to only one-half of the parcel in question. Although the Public Trust Doctrine cannot be a total bar to recovery as to this takings claim, it substantially impacts Plaintiff's title to the parcel in question and has a direct relationship to Plaintiff's reasonable investment-backed expectations....

* * *

Notes

1. Notice that the Rhode Island court interpreted *Shively* to establish "beyond question a nationwide Public Trust Doctrine which is to be applied based upon state law." This seems to indicate that the court believed that the doctrine has federal origins.

2. The court also observed that the public trust doctrine in Rhode Island is constitutionally entrenched, although it also refers to the trust as being a common law doctrine that could be changed by "local legislation or custom." In other states, the trust doctrine also has a constitutional basis. *See* William D. Araiza, *Democracy, Distrust, and the Public Trust: Process-Based Constitutional Theory, the Public Trust Doctrine, and the Search for a Substantive Environmental Value*, 45 UCLA L. Rev. 385 (1997). Of what significance is there to constitutional adoption of the public trust doctrine? See chapter 12 (p. 434).

3. In Rhode Island, the public trust doctrine is alienable through a state legislative act to cities or municipalities, *Town of Warren v. Thornton-Whitehouse*, 740 A.2d 1255, 1259–60 (R.I. 1999). In addition, as in *Marks v. Whitney*, the state may alienate the *jus privatum* to private parties so long as it retains the *jus publicum. Champlin's Realty Assocs., L.P. v. Tillson*, 823 A.2d 1162, 1167 (R.I. 2003). What did the court say about Palazzolo's ownership rights to the half of the parcel lying below the mean high water mark? Does Palazzolo have *any* property interest in that? Does he have *jus privatum*, while the state maintains *jus publicum*? Consider the court's statement, "Thus, as against the State, Palazzolo has gained title and the corresponding property rights to only one-half of the parcel in question."

4. What is the effect of the public trust doctrine on Palazzolo's claim that the state's denial of a permit to fill his coastal wetlands constituted a taking? Why? Of what relevance is the Supreme Court's decision in *Lucas v. South Carolina Coastal Council*, 505 U.S. 1003 (1992)?

McQueen v. South Carolina Coastal Council
Supreme Court of South Carolina
580 S.E.2d 116 (2003)

MOORE, J.

This regulatory takings case is before us on remand from the United States Supreme Court to reconsider our previous decision in light of *Palazzolo v. Rhode Island*, 533 U.S. 606 (2001).

In the early 1960's, respondent McQueen purchased two non-contiguous lots located on manmade saltwater canals in the Cherry Grove section of North Myrtle Beach. He paid $2,500 in 1961 for a lot on 53rd Avenue and $1,700 in 1963 for a lot on 48th Avenue. Since then, both lots have remained unimproved. The lots surrounding McQueen's are improved and have bulkheads or retaining walls.

In 1991, McQueen filed applications with petitioner Office of Ocean and Coastal Resource Management (OCRM) to build bulkheads on his lots. After an administrative delay, he reapplied in 1993 requesting permits to backfill his lots and build bulkheads. In January 1994, a hearing was held at which the following facts were put into evidence.

At the time of the hearing, the majority of both lots had reverted to tidelands or critical area saltwater wetlands. This reversion was caused by "continuous" erosion, although little change had occurred since the permits were originally sought in 1991. The 53rd Avenue lot is inundated regularly by tidal flow all the way up to the street. The 48th Avenue lot has less tidal flow but contains more critical area wetland vegetation. On both lots, only some irregular portions of high ground remain.

The proposed backfill would permanently destroy the critical area environment on these lots. Without the backfill and bulkheads, the property does not have enough high ground to be developed. Eventually tidal water will reach the roads bordering these lots which will require bulkheads to protect the public roads.

In October 1994, a final decision was issued denying both permits based on OCRM's evaluation of McQueen's lots as predominantly critical area wetlands. McQueen then commenced this action seeking compensation for a regulatory taking. The master-in-equity found the denial of the permits deprived McQueen of all economically beneficial use of the lots and awarded him $50,000 per lot as just compensation.

OCRM appealed. By a divided court, the Court of Appeals affirmed the finding of a taking because McQueen was deprived of all economically beneficial use of his property. The majority held: "The definitive issue is what rights McQueen possessed when he purchased the lots and … the right to add a bulkhead and fill were McQueen's at the time of purchase." *McQueen v. South Carolina Coastal Council*, 496 S.E.2d 643, 647 (S.C. Ct. App. 1998). The Court of Appeals found the evidence insufficient, however, to support the amount of compensation awarded by the master and the case was remanded. OCRM then sought a writ of certiorari in this Court which was granted.

On review of the Court of Appeals' decision, we reversed. We found it was uncontested that McQueen was deprived of all economically beneficial use of his property but found he had no reasonable investment-backed expectations because of pre-existing wetlands regulations, therefore no taking had occurred. *McQueen v. South Carolina Coastal Council*, 530 S.E.2d 628 (S.C. 2000). The United States Supreme Court then granted McQueen's petition for a writ of certiorari, summarily vacated our opinion, and remanded for further consideration in light of the recent *Palazzolo* decision.

Palazzolo involved a partial taking of property including wetlands. The Rhode Island Supreme Court found the landowner had not been deprived of all economically beneficial use of his property and, even if he had, the right to fill wetlands was not part of his ownership estate because regulations prohibiting such activity were enacted before he acquired title. *Palazzolo v. State*, 746 A.2d 707 (2000). On writ of certiorari, the United States Supreme Court reversed holding that pre-existing regulation was not dispositive in itself, either in the context of determining ownership rights under background principles of state law or in determining the investment-backed expectation factor in a partial taking. *Palazzolo*, 533 U.S. at 626 & 629–30.

Issue

Do background principles of South Carolina property law absolve the State from compensating McQueen?

Discussion

First, we accept as uncontested that McQueen's lots retain no value and therefore a total taking has occurred. When there has been a total deprivation of all economically beneficial use, the threshold issue in determining whether compensation is due is whether the landholder's rights of ownership are "confined by limitations on the use of land which 'inhere in the title itself.'" *Palazzolo*, 533 U.S. at 629 (quoting *Lucas*, 505 U.S. at 1029); *see also Rick's Amusement, Inc. v. State*, 570 S.E.2d 155 (S.C. 2001), *cert. denied* 535 U.S. 1053 (2002) (threshold inquiry in regulatory taking is whether the property interest affected is inherent in the plaintiff's ownership rights). Background principles of State property and nuisance law inform this inquiry. *Palazzolo*, 533 U.S. at 629. Where the proscribed use is not part of the owner's title to begin with, no compensatory taking has occurred. *Lucas*, 505 U.S. at 1027.

Public Trust Doctrine

As a coastal state, South Carolina has a long line of cases regarding the public trust doctrine in the context of land bordering navigable waters. Historically, the State holds presumptive title to land below the high water mark. As stated by this Court in 1884, not only does the State hold title to this land in *jus privatum*, it holds it in *jus publicum*, in trust for the benefit of all the citizens of this State. *State v. Pacific Guano Co.*, 22 S.C. 50, 84 (1884); *see also State v. Hardee*, 193 S.E.2d 497 (S.C. 1972); *Rice Hope Plantation v. South Carolina Pub. Serv. Auth.*, 59 S.E.2d 132 (S.C. 1950), *overruled on other grounds, McCall v. Batson*, 329 S.E.2d 741 (S.C. 1985).[7]

The State has the exclusive right to control land below the high water mark for the public benefit, *Port Royal Mining Co. v. Hagood*, 9 S.E. 686 (S.C. 1889), and cannot permit activity that substantially impairs the public interest in marine life, water quality, or public access. *Sierra Club v. Kiawah Resort Assocs.*, 456 S.E.2d 397 (S.C. 1995); *see also Heyward v. Farmers' Min. Co.*, 19 S.E. 963 (S.C. 1884) (public trust land cannot be placed entirely beyond direction and control of the State); *Cape Romain Land & Improvement Co. v. Georgia-Carolina Canning Co.*, 146 S.E. 434 (S.C. 1928) (protected public purposes of trust include navigation and fishery). The State's presumptive title applies to tidelands. *State v. Yelsen Land Co.*, 216 S.E.2d 876 (S.C. 1975).

Significantly, under South Carolina law, wetlands created by the encroachment of navigable tidal water belong to the State. *Coburg Dairy, Inc. v. Lesser*, 458 S.E.2d 547 (S.C. 1995). Proof that land was highland at the time of grant and tidelands were subsequently created by the rising of tidal water cannot defeat the State's presumptive title to tidelands. *State v. Fain*, 259 S.E.2d 606 (S.C. 1979).

As described above, each of McQueen's lots borders a man-made tidal canal. At the time the permits were denied, the lots had reverted to tidelands with only irregular portions of highland remaining. This reversion to tidelands effected a restriction on McQueen's property rights inherent in the ownership of property bordering tidal water.

The tidelands included on McQueen's lots are public trust property subject to control of the State. McQueen's ownership rights do not include the right to backfill or place bulkheads on public trust land and the State need not compensate him for the denial of

---

7. The State's presumptive title may be overcome only by showing a specific grant from the sovereign which is strictly construed against the grantee. *Hobonny Club, Inc. v. McEachern*, 252 S.E.2d 13 (S.C. 1979). *Cf. City of Folly Beach v. Atlantic House Props., Ltd.*, 458 S.E.2d 426 (S.C. 1995) (without considering public trust, compensation was ordered where it was uncontested plaintiff was "owner of record" of land below high water mark).

permits to do what he cannot otherwise do. *Accord Esplanade Props., Inc. v. City of Seattle*, 307 F.3d 978 (9th Cir. 2002) (finding no taking where state public trust doctrine precludes dredging and filling tidelands). Any taking McQueen suffered is not a taking effected by State regulation but by the forces of nature and McQueen's own lack of vigilance in protecting his property.

We find no compensation is due. After reconsideration in light of *Palazzolo*, we reach the same conclusion we originally reached in this case and reverse the Court of Appeals.

Reversed.

Notes

1. In its earlier opinion in the *McQueen* case, 530 S.E.2d 628 (S.C. 2000), the South Carolina Supreme Court overruled an earlier decision that relied on *Just v. Marinette County*, to deny a takings claim in the context of wetland filling. *Carter v. S.C. Coastal Council*, 314 S.E.2d 327 (S.C. 1984). The 2000 court thought that the Supreme Court's decision in *Lucas v. S.C. Coastal Council*, 505 U.S. 1003 (1992), implicitly overruled the *Just* rationale by recognizing that landowners had the right to an economically beneficial use of their land. Does this decision endorse that view?

2. Note that *McQueen* involved coastal wetlands created by tidal water carried through artificial, man-made canals. Do these "created wetlands" become subject to public trust limitations? If so, the public trust doctrine moves geographically to accommodate changes in waterbodies, whether accomplished by natural or artificial means. Other decisions have granted public trust rights over waterbodies that are artificially enlarged. *See Wilbour v. Gallagher* (p. 112) (artificially enlarged lake); *Arkansas River Rights Committee* (p. 116) (new freshwaters created by dams); *Parks v. Cooper* (p. 106) (extending public rights to newly inundated areas, even if the underlying bed was privately owned).

3. Does the *McQueen* court give a standard for judging a trustee's fiduciary protection of the resource? The court says that the state "cannot permit activity that substantially impairs the public interest in marine life, water quality, or public access." The origin of the substantial impairment test traces back to the language of *Illinois Central* in which the U.S. Supreme Court said, "The control of the state for the purposes of the trust can never be lost, except as to such parcels as are used in promoting the interests of the public therein, or can be disposed of without any substantial impairment of the public interest in the lands and waters remaining." *Illinois Central*, 146 U.S. at 453. Although the test surfaces in the context of a takings case, could the substantial impairment test also be used as a standard in a case in which citizens sue their trustee for failure to protect an asset? Stated another way, is it an applicable standard when the PTD operates as a sword to hold the agency accountable to fiduciary duties (as distinguished from use of the PTD as a shield to protect the trustee from takings claims when the trustee has carried out fiduciary duties through protective regulation)?

4. Although the *McQueen* case did involve artificial canals, the court frankly noted that the "rising of tidal water" through "forces of nature" caused formerly upland portions of the lot to become tideland. The court seemed to leave no doubt that the state's public trust title moved upland with the rising tides. As climate change swells ocean waters and melts ice masses on the planet, rising seas are becoming a major concern for coastal states and those private property owners along coastlines who will suffer nature's own condemnations. *See* Justin Gillis, *Rising Sea Levels Seen as Threat to Coastal U.S.*,

N.Y. Times, March 13, 2012, *available at* http://www.nytimes.com/2012/03/14/science/earth/study-rising-sea-levels-a-risk-to-coastal-states.html.

What are the public trust duties triggered by rising tides and changing mean high water marks? Given the *Just* court's statement that the public trust imposes an *active duty*, should coastal trustees anticipate sea level rise and begin prohibiting damaging activities in zones that will be inundated within the next century or two? Is it wise to continue to allow industrial and residential uses in areas that will be flooded? Should trustees proactively begin a process of moving present oil and gas refineries, nuclear power plants, and chemical manufacturing plants out of the zone of sea level rise? Would they have to pay compensation for condemnations, or is there an anticipatory public trust defense to any takings? Does this question turn in part on the scientific projections as to the pace of sea level rise?

In Boston, Massachusetts, The Boston Harbor Association, a non-profit organization, issued a report called *The Rising Tide* that makes recommendations on proactive actions the city and other public agencies should take to prepare for an anticipated sea level rise of two feet by 2050 and six feet by 2100. *See* Press Release, Bos. Harbor Ass'n, *Report Identifies Risk, Helps Boston Property Owners Prepare for Sea Level Rise, Coastal Flooding* (Feb. 5, 2013) (reporting that "Once sea level rises five feet—which could possibly occur before 2100—Boston will experience this '100-year coastal flood' as the twice-daily high tide," which means that even a "moderate storm surge" of 2.5 feet would flood 30 percent of the city).

In North Carolina, an opposite inclination prevails among lawmakers. In response to a major report warning of accelerating sea level rise (the fastest rate in the world) along the stretch of coastline from North Carolina to Massachusetts, state lawmakers passed a law prohibiting state agencies from making plans or laws for the next four years based on accelerated sea level rise predictions. An earlier version of the law banned state agencies from using exponential extrapolation in models predicting sea-level rise, requiring them to use linear projections based on historical data instead. *See* Jane J. Lee, *Update: Revised North Carolina Sea Level Rise Bill Goes to Governor*, Sci. Insider, July 3, 2012; Leigh Phillips, *North Carolina Sea Level Rises Despite State Senators*, Sci. American, June 27, 2012.

5. Some coastal states undertake beach "renourishment" projects to replace sand lost along coastlines due to rising seas and increased storm intensity. These projects pose vexing questions for property ownership, because waterfront property owners suddenly find a strip of newly replaced sand between their lots and the ocean. The question becomes, who owns this restored beach—the state or the upland property owner? In *Stop the Beach Renourishment, Inc. v. Florida Department of Environmental Protection*, 560 U.S. 702 (2010), local governments and a state agency in Florida restored a beach area by dumping sand seaward of the high water mark, effectively moving the high water mark towards the ocean. Owners of waterfront property brought a takings claim because the state-provided new beach came with a public access requirement. The Supreme Court unanimously held that under Florida law, the state gained title to the new sand area, the previous high water mark remained the boundary between the property owners and the state, and that no takings occurred because the project amounted to an "avulsion" (a sudden event that can either expose land or submerge land). After an avulsive event, the prior property boundary remains intact (whereas under common law, gradual change caused by an "accretion" will generally move the property boundary). The Court stated:

> Two core principles of Florida property law intersect in this case. First, the State
> as owner of the submerged land adjacent to littoral property has the right to fill

that land, so long as it does not interfere with the rights of the public and the rights of littoral landowners. Second, as we described, if an avulsion exposes land seaward of littoral property that had previously been submerged, that land belongs to the State even if it interrupts the littoral owner's contact with the water. The issue here is whether there is an exception to this rule when the State is the cause of the avulsion. Prior law suggests there is not.

Id. at 2611 (citations omitted).

For scholarship addressing the relationship between the public trust doctrine and the takings doctrine in the context of government actions to prepare coastlines for rising sea levels, see Tim Eichenberg, Sean Bothwell, & Darcy Vaughn, *Climate Change and the Public Trust Doctrine: Using an Ancient Doctrine to Adapt to Rising Sea Levels in San Francisco Bay*, 3 Golden Gate U. Envtl. L.J. 243 (2010). On the Florida case, and what it might mean for takings by court decisions, see Michael C. Blumm & Elizabeth B. Dawson, *The Florida Beach Case and the Road to Judicial Takings*, 35 Wm. & Mary Envtl. L. & Pol'y Rev. 713 (2011).

Esplanade Properties, LLC v. City of Seattle
United States Court of Appeals, Ninth Circuit
307 F.3d 978 (2002)

FLETCHER, J.

Plaintiff Esplanade Properties, LLC ("Esplanade") challenges the legality of the City of Seattle's ("the City's") denial of its application to develop shoreline property on Elliot Bay in Seattle, Washington. Esplanade contends that the City's action resulted in a complete deprivation of economic use of its property, constituting an inverse condemnation in violation of federal and state constitutional law, and violating both federal and state substantive due process. Specifically, plaintiff appeals three decisions of the district court which, *in toto*, resulted in the dismissal of its claims against the defendant, *to wit*, granting summary judgment to the defendant on plaintiff's takings claim, granting summary judgment to the defendant on plaintiff's federal substantive due process claim, and dismissing plaintiff's state substantive due process claim. We have jurisdiction under 28 U.S.C. § 1291 and we affirm.

I. Background

In 1992, Esplanade began a long, and ultimately unsuccessful, process of attempting to secure permission to construct single-family residential housing on and over tidelands located below Magnolia bluff, near both a large city park and a large marina. The property is classified as first class tide-land, and is submerged completely for roughly half of the day, during which time it resembles a large sand bar.

Esplanade purchased the property for $40,000 in 1991, and quickly retained a development team to design and secure permits for nine waterfront homes, each to be constructed on platforms supported by pilings. In June of 1992, Esplanade applied for building permits, as well as various use permits, variance permits, and special use permits. None of these applications were ever approved.

* * *

[After rejecting Esplanade's federal and state substantive due process claims, the court turned to the company's takings claim.]

C. Esplanade's Takings Claim

The Takings Clause of the Fifth Amendment prohibits the government from taking "private property ... for public use, without just compensation." U.S. Const. amend. V. This clause prohibits "Government from forcing some people alone to bear public burdens which, in all fairness and justice, should be borne by the public as a whole." *Penn. Cent. Transp. Co. v. City of New York*, 438 U.S. 104, 123 (1978) (quoting *Armstrong v. United States*, 364 U.S. 40, 49 (1960)). In addition to instances of physical invasion or confiscation, the Supreme Court has long held that "if regulation goes too far it will be recognized as a taking." *Penn. Coal Co. v. Mahon*, 260 U.S. 393, 415 (1922).

"Courts have had little success in devising any set formula for determining when government regulation of private property amounts to a regulatory taking," *Tahoe-Sierra Preserv. Council, Inc. v. Tahoe Reg'l Planning Agency*, 216 F.3d 764, 771–72 (9th Cir. 2000), affirmed by *Tahoe-Sierra Preserv. Council, Inc. v. Tahoe Reg'l Planning Agency*, 535 U.S. 302 (2002). However, it is clear that under the "categorical" takings doctrine articulated in *Lucas*, "when the owner of real property has been called upon to sacrifice *all* economically beneficial uses in the name of the common good, that is, to leave his property economically idle, he has suffered a taking." *Lucas*, 505 U.S. at 1019; *see also Palazzolo v. Rhode Island*, 533 U.S. 606, 617 (2001). Where a regulation "denies all economically beneficial or productive use of land," the multi-factor analysis established in *Penn Central* is not applied, and a compensable taking has occurred *unless* "the logically antecedent inquiry into the nature of the owner's estate shows that the proscribed use interests were not part of his title to begin with." *Lucas*, 505 U.S. at 1027. In other words, for a government entity to avoid liability, any "law or decree" depriving the property owner of all economically beneficial use of her property "must inhere in the title itself, in the restrictions that background principles of the State's law of property and nuisance already place upon land ownership." *Id.* at 1029.

Here, the district court found no taking of plaintiff's property for two reasons. First, the court found that the City's interpretation of the SSMP and its ultimate cancellation of Esplanade's development applications were not the proximate cause of Esplanade's alleged damages. Second, the court found that the background principles of Washington law, specifically the public trust doctrine, burdened plaintiff's property and precluded Esplanade from prevailing in a takings action against the City.

* * *

1. Background Principle: Washington's Public Trust Doctrine

As discussed above, a deprivation by the government of all beneficial uses of one's property results in a taking unless, *inter alia*, the "background principles" of state law already serve to deprive the property owner of such uses. *Lucas*, 505 U.S. at 1029. In *Lucas*, subsequent to plaintiff's purchase of two residential lots of shoreline property, the state of South Carolina passed a statute having the "direct effect of barring petitioner from erecting any permanent structures on his two parcels," rendering them "valueless." 505 U.S. at 1007. In response, the plaintiff sued, alleging that the government effected a complete deprivation of his property. The Court held that "[a]ny limitation so severe cannot be newly legislated or decreed (without compensation), but must inhere in the title itself, in the restrictions that background principles of the State's law of property and nuisance already place upon land ownership," and remanded for a determination of whether such "background principles" would have prevented the proposed use of plaintiff's property. *Id.*, 505 U.S. at 1029.

In this case, the "restrictions that background principles" of Washington law place upon such ownership are found in the public trust doctrine. As the Washington Supreme

Court recently explained, the "state's ownership of tidelands and shorelands is comprised of two distinct aspects—the *jus privatum* and the *jus publicum*." *State v. Longshore*, 5 P.3d 1256, 1262 (Wash. 2000). Relevant here, the "*jus publicum*, or public trust doctrine, is the right 'of navigation, together with its incidental rights of fishing, boating, swimming, water skiing, and other related recreational purposes generally regarded as corollary to the right of navigation and the use of public waters.'" *Id.* (quoting *Caminiti v. Boyle*, 732 P.2d 989, 994 (Wash. 1987) (internal quotation marks and citation omitted)). The "doctrine reserves a public property interest, the *jus publicum*, in tidelands and the waters flowing over them, despite the sale of these lands into private ownership." *Weden v. San Juan County*, 958 P.2d 273, 283 (Wash. 1998), (citing Ralph W. Johnson et al., *The Public Trust Doctrine and Coastal Zone Management in Washington State*, 67 Wash. L. Rev. 521, 524 (1992)). "The state can no more convey or give away this *jus publicum* interest than it can 'abdicate its police powers in the administration of government and the preservation of the peace.'" *Caminiti*, 732 P.2d at 994 (quoting *Illinois Cent. R.R. v. Illinois*, 146 U.S. 387, 453 (1892)). Instead, the state may only divest itself of interests in the state's waters in a manner that does not substantially impair the public interest. *Id.* at 993–95.

It is beyond cavil that "a public trust doctrine has always existed in Washington." *Orion Corp. v. State*, 747 P.2d 1062, 1072 (Wash. 1987) (citing *Caminiti*, 732 P.2d at 994). The doctrine is "partially encapsulated in the language of [Washington's] constitution which reserves state ownership in 'the beds and shores of all navigable waters in the state.'" *Rettkowski v. Dep't of Ecology*, 858 P.2d 232, 239 (Wash. 1993) (quoting Wash. Const. art. 17, § 1). The doctrine is also reflected in Washington's Shoreline Management Act ("SMA"), adopted in 1971. RCW §§ 90.58.010–.930.[8] Following a long history "favoring the sale of tidelands and shorelands," resulting in the privatization of approximately 60 percent of the tidelands and 30 percent of the shorelands originally owned by the state, *Caminiti*, 732 P.2d at 996, the Washington legislature found that the SMA was necessary because "unrestricted construction on the privately owned or public owned shorelines ... is not in the best public interest." RCW 90.58.020.

The public trust doctrine, reflected in part in the SMA, unquestionably burdens Esplanade's property.

We agree with the district court that the Washington Supreme Court's decision in *Orion* controls the outcome of this case, and that Washington's public trust doctrine ran with the title to the tideland properties and alone precluded the shoreline residential development proposed by Esplanade.

In *Orion*, the plaintiff corporation, prior to the enactment of the SMA, purchased tideland property in Padilla Bay, the "most diverse, least disturbed, and most biologically productive of all major estuaries on Puget Sound." *Id.*, 747 P.2d at 1065. Orion Corp. proposed dredging and filling of the Bay to create a significant residential community. *Id.* In addressing plaintiff's challenge to subsequent local and state environmental regulations, which it alleged combined to completely deprive it of all economically viable use of its property, the court decided that the tidelands of the Bay were burdened by the public trust doctrine prior to the enactment of the SMA. *Id.* at 1072. At the time of Orion's

---

8. The district court erred in stating that "whatever public trust doctrine existed prior to the enactment of the SMA has been superceded and the SMA is now the declaration of that doctrine." The doctrine itself is reflected *in* the SMA, but is not superseded *by* it, as made clear by the Washington Supreme Court in *Orion*, 747 P.2d at 1073 n.11 ("We have [ ] observed that trust principles are *reflected* in the SMA's underlying policy....") (emphasis added).

purchase, "Orion could make no use of the tidelands which would substantially impair the [public] trust." *Id.* at 1073. Specifically, "Orion never had the right to dredge and fill its tidelands, either for a residential community or farmlands [s]ince a property right must exist before it can be taken, neither the SMA nor the SCSMMP effected a taking ..." *Id.* (internal quotation marks and citation omitted).

We find that the development proposed by Esplanade would suffer the same fate under the public trust doctrine as the project proposed by Orion Corp.

Esplanade's argument that *Orion* lacks authority, following the Court's decision in *Lucas*, is without merit. *Lucas*, while articulating an expansive concept of what constitutes a regulatory taking, effectively recognized the public trust doctrine:

> Any [regulation that prohibits all economically beneficial use of land] ... must inhere in the title itself, in the restrictions that background principles of the State's law of property and nuisance already place upon land ownership. A law or decree with such an effect must, in other words, do no more than duplicate the result that could have been achieved in the courts—by adjacent landowners (or other uniquely affected persons) under the State's law of private nuisance, or by the State under its complementary power to abate nuisances that affect the public generally, or otherwise.... The principal "otherwise" that we have in mind is litigation absolving the State (or private parties) of liability for the destruction of "real and personal property, in cases of actual necessity, to prevent the spreading of a fire" or to forestall other grave threats to the lives and property of others.

505 U.S. at 1029 & n. 16 (internal citations omitted). *Lucas* does nothing to disturb *Orion's* application of Washington's public trust doctrine.

Esplanade's contention that the proposed development *was* consistent with the SMA at the time his project vested in 1992 is similarly without merit. As the City concedes, at the time of the purchase, the SMA, theoretically, permitted single-family dwellings to be constructed on the property. As the district court noted, however, "[t]here are numerous limitations that the SMA places on developments of shorelines, even if those developments, like Esplanade's, are not categorically prohibited." (citing, *e.g.*, RCW 90.58.020(2) (requiring that shoreline developments "[p]reserve the natural character of the shoreline"), and RCW 90.58.020(4) (requiring that "[p]rojects protect the resources and ecology of the shoreline")). In this case, because Esplanade's tideland property is navigable for the purpose of public recreation (used for fishing and general recreation, including by Tribes), and located just 700 feet from Discovery Park, the development would have interfered with those uses, and thus would have been inconsistent with the public trust doctrine. Therefore, Esplanade's development plans never constituted a legally permissible use.

As the district court correctly noted, "Esplanade ... took the risk," when it purchased this large tract of tidelands in 1991 for only $40,000, "that, despite extensive federal, state, and local regulations restricting shoreline development, it could nonetheless overcome those numerous hurdles to complete its project and realize a substantial return on its limited initial investment. Now, having failed..., it seeks indemnity from the City." The takings doctrine does not supply plaintiff with such a right to indemnification.

IV. Conclusion

Esplanade's proposal to construct concrete pilings, driveways and houses in the navigable tidelands of Elliot Bay, an area regularly used by the public for various recreational and other activities, was inconsistent with the public trust that the State of Washington is obligated to protect.

For the reasons given, we affirm.

Notes

1. The *Esplanade* court fits the public trust doctrine squarely within the holding of the Supreme Court's decision in *Lucas v. South Carolina Coastal Council*, 505 U.S. 1003 (1992). *Lucas* announced a new *per se* categorical takings rule for land regulations working complete economic wipeouts on landowners, but it carved out a significant exception for regulations that merely forbade uses prohibited by "background principles of the State's law of property and nuisance" that inhere in land titles. *Id.* at 1029. In other words, under the state's law of property or nuisance, if a property owner could not put the property to a certain use, the owner could not succeed in a regulatory takings claim where a regulation prevented that use, even if it caused complete deprivation of economic use of the property. Like the Rhode Island court in *Palazzolo*, the *Esplanade* court identified the public trust doctrine as a "background principle" of Washington property law defeating Esplanade's takings claim. (For other "background principles" cases, see chapter 9, pp. 325–32.) Note that the public trust also works its way into takings analysis under the *Penn Central* traditional three-part test. The overriding rationale, as stated by the *Esplanade* court, controls all takings contexts: "The 'doctrine reserves a public property interest, the *jus publicum*, in tidelands and the waters flowing over them, despite the sale of these lands into private ownership.'" 307 F.3d at 985 (quoting *Weden v. San Juan County*, 958 P.2d 273, 283 (Wash. 1998)).

2. The *Esplanade* case (and the *Orion* case on which it relied) made clear that the public trust limitation operates quite apart from any statutory law and has always existed as an encumbrance on private title. Although Washington passed its Shoreline Management Act (SMA) in 1971, the Ninth Circuit emphasized that the public trust existed prior to the enactment of the SMA. The court stated that the public trust doctrine "is reflected *in* the SMA, but is not superseded *by* it...." *Esplanade*, 307 F.3d at 986 n. 8. This recognition of the PTD as an independent source of legal obligation apart from statutory law becomes increasingly important in view of the dominance of statutory schemes in environmental law. Often, the public trustees use their statutory authority to allow damage to the resource, arguably in contravention of their trust responsibility to both present and future generations. If courts find the trust responsibility readily subsumed by statutory expressions, the doctrine will lose force as a protective doctrine and may ultimately become superfluous to statutory law. Recall that the Supreme Court in *Illinois Central* (p. 68) underscored the need for judicial trust enforcement against legislative abdications of the trust. In the modern context, don't some statutory permitting schemes amount to abdications of the trust as well?

3. Like the last case, *McQueen,* the Ninth Circuit in *Esplanade* voiced the substantial impairment test. Notably, in *Orion Corp. v. State*, the Washington Supreme Court observed that the public trust "resembles 'a covenant running with the land (or lake or marsh or shore) for the benefit of the public and the land's dependent wildlife,'" and determined, "[A]t the time it purchased its tidelands, Orion could make no use of the tidelands which would *substantially impair* the trust." 747 P.2d 1062, 1072–73 (Wash. 1987) (citation omitted) (emphasis added). In essence, the *Orion* court took what *Illinois Central* announced as a fiduciary standard and embedded it into the private property owner's title to define ownership prerogatives (and specifically, development rights). The court's method showed

how a standard governing one context of the PTD (fiduciary behavior of government) may also prove determinative in another context (landowner duty to protect private property). Moreover, the *Orion* court's interpretation of the substantial impairment test suggests a servitude that expands to match public need. The court explained:

> Recognizing modern science's ability to identify the public need, state courts have extended the doctrine beyond its navigational aspects. We have had occasion to extend the doctrine beyond navigational and commercial fishing rights to include "incidental rights of fishing, boating, swimming, water skiing, and other related recreational purposes ..." Resolution of this case does not require us to decide the total scope of the doctrine.... Orion had no right to make any use of its property that would substantially impair the public rights of navigation and fishing, as well as incidental rights and purposes recognized previously by this court.

Id. at 641 (citations omitted).

If the public trust servitude (or "covenant," as the *Orion* court called it) expands to meet new public needs over time (such as a new form of recreation), does it protect the property rights of landowners who may not have anticipated the full burden of such public use when they bought the property? Is the answer informed by recognition that private title to trust property does not amount to full title in the first place, but only *jus privatum*?

4. *Esplanade* was somewhat unusual because a federal court interpreted a state's public trust doctrine under diversity jurisdiction. For other federal court decisions, see *United States v. 1.58 Acres of Land*, 523 F.Supp. 120 (D. Mass. 1981) (p. 367) (ruling that when the federal government condemned state trust land below the low water mark of Boston Harbor for a Coast Guard facility, it took title subject to the limitations imposed by the public trust doctrine); *Lake Michigan Federation v. U.S. Army Corps of Engineers*, 742 F.Supp. 441 (N.D. Ill. 1990) (striking down a conveyance of 18 acres of Lake Michigan shoreline to Loyola University).

Chapter 5

Water Rights

Water represents a quintessential public trust resource, vital to human survival. As Justice Holmes recognized long ago, the rivers are "a necessity of life."[1] Groundwater supplies are especially crucial, as groundwater provides about half of the drinking water of the United States (nearly all of the drinking water for farm communities).[2] Justinian referred to water as a public trust resource, and the Supreme Court has repeatedly expressed a public trust over waters. *See, e.g., Illinois Central Railroad Co. v. Illinois*, 146 U.S. 387, 455 (1892) ("The ownership of the navigable waters of the harbor, and of the lands under them, is a subject of public concern to the whole people of the state. The trust with which they are held, therefore, is governmental, and cannot be alienated....."). Many of the cases in chapter 3 affirm a public trust right to use the surface of waters for navigation, fishing, commerce, recreation and other uses. But while these cases focus on the public's surface use rights, another aspect of public trust law concerns the rights of the public to maintain instream levels of water. The latter set of cases is primarily concerned with the ecological functioning of water bodies to support fish, wildlife, aesthetics, and a host of other important ecological and economic functions. Both surface use and in-stream protection are beneficial uses of the public trust. Another trust use of water is implicated by increasing international attention focused on preserving scarce public drinking water supplies and resisting their privatization by monopolies, a matter we take up at the end of this chapter.

In the United States, states manage their surface waters (usually through permit systems) for multiple out-of-stream uses, granting usufructuary water rights for agricultural, municipal, domestic, and industrial purposes. In many river basins (particularly in the western U.S.), cities, farmers, industries, recreationalists, and species compete for an overtaxed supply of water. Large water withdrawals can de-water the streams, unraveling aquatic ecosystems and pushing fisheries towards extinction.

As the materials in this chapter show, diverting or pumping water for private uses raises challenging public trust questions. As climate change reallocates water, some areas are going to experience drought.[3]

In the U.S., two systems of water law prevail (some states have a mix of the two). In the Eastern U.S., states employ some variant of the common law rule of riparian water rights, which considers a reasonable use of waters adjacent to land to be an incidental right

---

1. *New Jersey v. New York*, 283 U.S. 336, 342 (1931).
2. *See* Yee Huang, Ctr. for Progressive Reform, *Protecting the Invisible: The Public Trust Doctrine and Groundwater*, CPR Blog (July 24, 2009), http://www.progressivereform.org/CPRBlog.cfm?id Blog=897E966E-C8F9-131C-E12ABAA7E9BF8A60.
3. *See* Maggie Fox, *Climate Change Drying Up Big Rivers, Study Finds*, Reuters (Apr. 21, 2009), *available at* http://www.reuters.com/article/2009/04/21/us-climate-rivers-idUSTRE53K4MR20090421 (reporting overall water loss in a third of the world's largest rivers).

to having fee simple ownership. A riparian landowner has the right to make "reasonable use" of the water, although about half of riparian jurisdictions have adopted a system of "regulated riparianism." *See* Joseph W. Dellapenna, *Regulated Riparianism, in* 1 WATERS AND WATER RIGHTS, ch. 9 (Amy K. Kelley ed., 3rd ed. 2014). Riparian rights are contextual, correlative rights; their scope (i.e., what can be considered "reasonable") is a function of how other landowners are using water and the condition of the stream from which the water is drawn. There do not appear to have been significant conflicts between riparian rights and the public trust doctrine, and therefore are no cases on the issue.

The same cannot be said for water rights in the West, which are governed by what is called the prior appropriation system. This system developed from a simple first-come, first-serve approach that governed mining camps in the mid-nineteenth century. Historically, prior appropriation water rights went only to "appropriators" diverting water out-of-stream and putting it to "beneficial use": traditionally, mining, irrigation, or municipal purposes. Those who diverted first (or whose predecessors diverted first) have priority over those who diverted water later in time (the "first in time, first in right" principle). Western rivers consequently have a series of water rights prioritizing senior appropriators and junior appropriators according to their date of first use and amount of use. Appropriators must make use of the water or forfeit their rights (the "use it or lose it" principle), which sometimes encourages the continuation of wasteful and inefficient diversion methods and technology. The prior appropriation system has de-watered many streams. The public trust doctrine might serve as an antidote to Western water's focus on temporal priority.

Professor Robin Craig has conducted an extensive study of the public trust as it applies to water rights regimes in both the eastern and western United States. *See* Robin Kundis Craig, *A Comparative Guide to the Eastern Public Trust Doctrines: Classifications of States, Property Rights, and State Summaries*, 16 Penn St. L. Rev. 1 (2007); Robin Kundis Craig, *A Comparative Guide to the Western States' Public Trust Doctrines: Public Values, Private Rights, and the Evolution Toward an Ecological Public Trust*, 37 Ecology L.Q. 53 (2010). The following report captures some of the possibilities of applying the public trust doctrine to water rights. The case following this report represents a landmark opinion applying the public trust doctrine to a water appropriation scheme in California.

Restoring the Public Trust: Water Resources and the Public Trust Doctrine, A Manual for Advocates
Alexandra B. Klass & Ling-Yee Huang
Center for Progressive Reform White Paper #908 (2009)

The very concept of the public trust doctrine captures the imagination with its ideas of guardianship, responsibility, and community. Its well-established legal history invites use by judges and lawmakers, and its succinct encapsulation of environmental and other public values deserves greater notice by water advocacy groups. The public trust doctrine is as much a legal tool as an environmental paradigm, a principle that use of critical water resources must "ultimately proceed with due regard for certain enduring public rights."

A public trust doctrine narrative is persuasive because of its deep legal roots: It is a well-established doctrine that courts have used since the founding of the United States. Judicial opinions that involve the public trust doctrine nearly all begin by elaborating on its historical context. In water resource disputes, state courts are becoming receptive to the doctrine, affirming its importance and relevance. For example, in 2004, the South

Dakota Supreme Court declared that "history and precedent have established the public trust doctrine as an inherent attribute of sovereign authority."[4] In Idaho, the state supreme court has stated that "the public trust doctrine at all times forms the outer boundaries of permissible government action with respect to public trust resources,"[5] demonstrating both the broad gap-filling role of the doctrine and its power to color government action.

The doctrine is also persuasive because it captures timeless values that are being rediscovered by the public in this current environmental reawakening. As one practitioner in Michigan commented: "The beauty of the doctrine is that it makes old values new again; it is the wisdom of the ages applied to modern challenges. Its power in advocacy is that it is an old, entrenched doctrine."[6]

The idea that the state must manage water resources for the benefit of *present and future generations* captures the idea of *sustainability* and reflects our extended connection to those who succeed us. For judges who favor fair and equitable outcomes, the public trust champions the underrepresented or inchoate interests—such as the public at large or future generations—against specialized, minority interests. The ability to harness the rhetorical power of the doctrine may prove to be a tipping point in water resources litigation.

National Audubon Society v. Superior Court of Alpine County ("*Mono Lake*" Decision)

Supreme Court of California
658 P.2d 709 (1983)

BROUSSARD, J.:

Mono Lake, the second largest lake in California, sits at the base of the Sierra Nevada escarpment near the eastern entrance to Yosemite National Park. The lake is saline; it contains no fish but supports a large population of brine shrimp which feed vast numbers of nesting and migratory birds. Islands in the lake protect a large breeding colony of California gulls, and the lake itself serves as a haven on the migration route for thousands of Northern Phalarope, Wilson's Phalarope, and Eared Grebe. Towers and spires of tufa on the north and south shores are matters of geological interest and a tourist attraction.

Although Mono Lake receives some water from rain and snow on the lake surface, historically most of its supply came from snowmelt in the Sierra Nevada. Five freshwater streams—Mill, Lee Vining, Walker, Parker and Rush Creeks—arise near the crest of the range and carry the annual runoff to the west shore of the lake. In 1940, however, the Division of Water Resources, the predecessor to the present California Water Resources Board, granted the Department of Water and Power of the City of Los Angeles (hereafter DWP) a permit to appropriate virtually the entire flow of four of the five streams flowing into the lake. DWP promptly constructed facilities to divert about half the flow of these streams into DWP's Owens Valley aqueduct. In 1970, DWP completed a second diversion tunnel, and since that time has taken virtually the entire flow of these streams.

As a result of these diversions, the level of the lake has dropped; the surface area has diminished by one-third; one of the two principal islands in the lake has become a peninsula, exposing the gull rookery there to coyotes and other predators and causing the gulls

---

4. *Parks v. Cooper*, 676 N.W.2d 823 (S.D. 2004).

5. *Kootenai Envtl. Alliance v. Panhandle Yacht Club*, 671 P.2d 1085, 1095 (Idaho 1983).

6. Telephone Interview with Chris Bzdok, Principal, Olson, Bzdok, & Howard P.C., in Traverse City, Mich. (Feb. 12, 2009).

to abandon the former island. The ultimate effect of continued diversions is a matter of intense dispute, but there seems little doubt that both the scenic beauty and the ecological values of Mono Lake are imperiled.

Plaintiffs filed suit in the superior court to enjoin the DWP diversions on the theory that the shores, bed and waters of Mono Lake are protected by the public trust....

This case brings together for the first time two systems of legal thought: the appropriative water rights system which since the days of the gold rush has dominated California water law, and the public trust doctrine which, after evolving as a shield for the protection of tidelands, now extends its protective scope to navigable lakes. Ever since we first recognized that the public trust protects environmental and recreational values (*Marks v. Whitney* 491 P.2d 374 (Cal. 1971)), the two systems of legal thought have been on a collision course. (Johnson, *Public Trust Protection for Stream Flows and Lake Levels* 14 U.C. Davis L. Rev. 233 (1980).) They meet in a unique and dramatic setting which highlights the clash of values. Mono Lake is a scenic and ecological treasure of national significance, imperiled by continued diversions of water; yet, the need of Los Angeles for water is apparent, its reliance on rights granted by the board evident, the cost of curtailing diversions substantial.

Attempting to integrate the teachings and values of both the public trust and the appropriative water rights system, we have arrived at certain conclusions which we briefly summarize here. In our opinion, the core of the public trust doctrine is the state's authority as sovereign to exercise a continuous supervision and control over the navigable waters of the state and the lands underlying those waters. This authority applies to the waters tributary to Mono Lake and bars DWP or any other party from claiming a vested right to divert waters once it becomes clear that such diversions harm the interests protected by the public trust. The corollary rule which evolved in tideland and lakeshore cases barring conveyance of rights free of the trust except to serve trust purposes cannot, however, apply without modification to flowing waters. The prosperity and habitability of much of this state requires the diversion of great quantities of water from its streams for purposes unconnected to any navigation, commerce, fishing, recreation, or ecological use relating to the source stream. The state must have the power to grant nonvested usufructuary rights to appropriate water even if diversions harm public trust uses. Approval of such diversion without considering public trust values, however, may result in needless destruction of those values. Accordingly, we believe that before state courts and agencies approve water diversions they should consider the effect of such diversions upon interests protected by the public trust, rind attempt, so far as feasible, to avoid or minimize any harm to those interests.

The water rights enjoyed by DWP were granted, the diversion was commenced, and has continued to the present without any consideration of the impact upon the public trust. An objective study and reconsideration of the water rights in the Mono Basin is long overdue. The water law of California—which we conceived to be an integration including both the public trust doctrine and the board-administered appropriative rights system—permits such a reconsideration; the values underlying that integration require it.

* * *

The board's decision states that:

> [i]t is indeed unfortunate that the City's proposed development will result in decreasing the aesthetic advantages of Mono Basin but *there is apparently nothing that this office can do to prevent it.* The use to which the City proposes to put the water under its Applications ... is defined by the Water Commission Act as the

highest to which water may be applied and to make available unappropriated water for this use the City has, by the condemnation proceedings described above, acquired the littoral and riparian rights on Mono Lake and its tributaries south of Mill Creek. This office therefore has *no alternative but to dismiss all protests based upon the possible lowering of the water level in Mono Lake and the effect that the diversion of water from these streams may have upon the aesthetic and recreational value of the Basin.*

(Div. Wat. Resources Dec. 7053, 7055, 8042 & 8043 (Apr. 11, 1940), at 26 (emphasis added by court).)

* * *

Plaintiffs predict that the lake's steadily increasing salinity, if unchecked, will wreak havoc throughout the local food chain. They contend that the lake's algae, and the brine shrimp and brine flies that feed on it, cannot survive the projected salinity increase. To support this assentation, plaintiffs point to a 50 percent reduction in the shrimp hatch for the spring of 1980 and a starling 95 percent reduction for the spring of 1981. These reductions affirm experimental evidence indicating that brine shrimp populations diminish as the salinity of the water surrounding them increases. DWP admits these substantial reductions, but blames them on factors other than salinity.

DWP's diversions also present several threats to the millions of local and migratory birds using the lake. First, since many species of birds feed on the lake's brine shrimp, any reduction in the shrimp population allegedly caused by rising salinity endangers a major avian food source. The Task Force Report considered it "unlikely that any of Mono Lake's major bird species ... will persist at the lake if populations of invertebrates disappear." Second, the increasing salinity makes it more difficult for the birds to maintain osmotic equilibrium with their environment.

* * *

2. The Public Trust Doctrine in California

"By the law of nature these things are common to mankind—the air, running water, the sea and consequently the shores of the sea." (Institutes of Justinian 2.1.1.) From this origin in Roman law, the English common law evolved the concept of the public trust, under which the sovereign owns "all of its navigable waterways and the lands lying beneath them 'as trustee of a public trust for the benefit of the people.'" (*Colberg. Inc. v. State of California ex rel. Dept. Pub. Wks.*, 432 P.2d 3, 8 (Cal. 1967)) The State of California acquired title as trustee to such lands and waterways upon its admission to the union (*City of Berkeley v. Superior Court* 606 P.2d 362 (Cal. 1980) and cases there cited); from the earliest days its judicial decisions have recognized and enforced the trust obligation.

Three aspects of the public trust doctrine require consideration in this opinion: the purpose of the trust; the scope of the trust, particularly as it applies to the nonnavigable tributaries of a navigable lake; and the powers and duties of the state as trustee of the public trust. We discuss these questions in the order listed.

(a) The purpose of the public trust.

The objective of the public trust has evolved in tandem with the changing public perception of the values and uses of waterways. As we observed in *Marks v. Whitney,*

> [p]ublic trust easements [were] traditionally defined in terms of navigation, commerce and fisheries. They have been held to include the right to fish, hunt bathe, swim, to use for boating and general recreation purposes the navigable wa-

ters of the state, and to use the bottom of the navigable waters for anchoring, standing, or other purposes.

491 P.2d 374 (Cal. 1974). We went on, however, to hold that the traditional triad of uses—
navigation, commerce and fishing—did not limit the public interest in the trust res....

Mono Lake is a navigable waterway. (*City of Los Angeles v. Aitken*, 52 P.2d 585 (Cal.
Ct. App. 1935).) It supports a small local industry which harvests brine shrimp for sale
as fish food, which endeavor probably, qualifies the lake as a "fishery" under the traditional
public trust cases. The principal values plaintiffs seek to protect, however, are recreational
and ecological—the scenic views of the lake and its shore, the purity of the air, and the
use of the lake for nesting and feeding by birds. Under *Marks v. Whitney*, it is clear that
protection of these values is among the purposes of the public trust.

(b) Scope of the public trust.

* * *

Mono Lake is, as we have said, a navigable waterway. The beds, shores and waters of
the lake are without question protected by the public trust. The streams diverted by DWP,
however, are not themselves navigable. Accordingly, we must address in this case a question not discussed in any recent public trust case—whether the public trust limits conduct affecting nonnavigable tributaries to navigable waterways.

* * *

DWP points out that *People v. Gold Run D. & M. Co.*, 4 P. 1152 (Cal. 1884), decision
did not involve diversion of water, and that in *People v. Russ*, 64 P. 111 (Cal. 1901), there
had been no finding of impairment to navigation. But the principles recognized by those
decisions apply fully to a case in which diversions from a nonnavigable tributary impair
the public trust in a downstream river or lake. "If the public trust doctrine applies to constrain *fills* which destroy navigation and other public trust uses in navigable waters, it
should equally apply to constrain *extraction* of water that destroys navigation and other
public interested. Both actions result in the same damage to the public interest."

We conclude that the public trust doctrine, as recognized and developed in California decisions, protects navigable waters from harm caused by diversion of nonnavigable tributaries.[7]

(c) Duties and powers of the state as trustee.

In the following review of the authority and obligations of the state as administrator
of the public trust, the dominant theme is the state's sovereign power and duty to exercise continued supervision over the trust. One consequence, of importance to this and many
other cases, is that parties acquiring rights in trust property generally hold those rights
subject to the trust, and can assert no vested right to use those rights in a manner harmful to the trust.

As we noted recently in *City of Berkeley v. Superior Court*, 606 P.2d at 365, the decision
of the United States Supreme Court in *Illinois Central Railroad Company v. Illinois*, 146
U.S. 387 (1892) "remains the primary authority even today, almost nine decades after it
was decided." The Illinois Legislature in 1886 had granted the railroad in fee simple 1,000

---

7. In view of the conclusion stated in the text, we need not consider the question whether the
public trust extends for some purposes—such as protection of fishing, environmental values, and
recreation interests—to nonnavigable streams. For discussion of this subject, see Walston, *The Public Trust Doctrine in the Water Rights Context: The Wrong Environmental Remedy*, 22 Santa Clara L. Rev.
63, 85 (1982).

acres of submerged lands, virtually the entire Chicago waterfront. Four years later it sought to revoke that grant. The Supreme Court upheld the revocatory legislation. Its opinion explained that lands under navigable waters conveyed to private parties for wharves, docks, and other structures in furtherance of trust purposes could be granted free of the trust because the conveyance is consistent with the purpose of the trust. But the legislature, it held, did not have the power to convey the entire city waterfront free of trust, thus freeing all future legislatures from protecting the public interest....

* * *

[I]n our recent decision in *City of Berkeley v. Superior Court*, 606 P.2d 362 (Cal. 1980) we considered whether deeds executed by the Board of Tidelands Commissioners pursuant to an 1870 act conferred title free of the trust. Applying the principles of earlier decisions, we held that the grantees' title was subject to the trust, both because the Legislature had not made clear its intention to authorize a conveyance free of the trust and because the 1870 act and the conveyances under it were not intended to further trust purposes.

Once again we rejected the claim that establishment of the public trust constituted a taking of property for which compensation was required....

In summary, the foregoing cases amply demonstrate the continuing power of the state as administrator of the public trust, a power which extends to the revocation of previously granted rights or to the enforcement of the trust against lands long thought free of the trust (see *City of Berkeley v. Superior Court*). Except for those rare instances in which a grantee may acquire a right to use former trust property free of trust restrictions, the grantee holds subject to the trust, and while he may assert a vested right to the servient estate (the right of use subject to the trust) and to any improvements he erects, he can claim no vested right to bar recognition of the trust or state action to carry out its purposes.

* * *

Thus, the public trust is more than an affirmation of state power to use public property for public purposes. It is an affirmation of the duty of the state to protect the people's common heritage of streams, lakes, marshlands and tidelands, surrendering that right of protection only in rare cases when the abandonment of that right is consistent with the purposes of the trust.

3. The California Water Rights System.

* * *

Our recent decision in *People v. Shirokow*, 605 P.2d 859 (Cal. 1980), described the early history of the appropriative water rights system in California. We explained that "California operates under the so-called dual system of water rights which recognizes both the appropriation and the riparian doctrines...."

* * *

In 1926, however, a decision of this court led to a constitutional amendment which radically altered water law in California and led to an expansion of the powers of the board. In *Herminghaus v. South California Edison Co.*, 252 P. 607 (Cal. 1926), we held not only that riparian rights took priority over appropriations authorized by the Water Board, a point which had always been clear, but that as between the riparian and the appropriator, the former's use of water was not limited by the doctrine of reasonable use. *Id.* at 100–01. That decision led to a constitutional amendment which abolished the right of a riparian to devote water to unreasonable uses, and established the doctrine of reasonable use as an overriding feature of California water law.

* * *

This amendment does more than merely overturn *Herminghaus*—it establishes state water policy. All uses of water, including public trust uses, must now conform to the standard of reasonable use.

* * *

Thus, the function of the Water Board has steadily evolved from the narrow role of deciding priorities between competing appropriators to the charge of comprehensive planning and allocation of waters. This change necessarily affects the board's responsibility with respect to the public trust....

4. The relationship between the Public Trust Doctrine and the California Water Rights System.

[T]he public trust doctrine and the appropriative water rights system administered by the Water Board developed independently of each other. Each developed comprehensive rules and principles which, if applied to the full extent of their scope, would occupy the field of allocation of stream waters to the exclusion of any competing system of legal thought. Plaintiffs, for example, argue that the public trust is antecedent to and thus limits all appropriative water rights, an argument which implies that most appropriative water rights in California were acquired and are presently being used unlawfully. Defendant DWP, on the other hand, argues that the public trust doctrine as to stream waters has been "subsumed" into the appropriative water rights system and, absorbed by that body of law, quietly disappeared; according to DWP, the recipient of a board license enjoys a vested right in perpetuity to take water without concern for the consequences to the trust.

We are unable to accept either position. In our opinion, both the public trust doctrine and the water rights system embody important precepts which make the law more responsive to the diverse needs and interests involved in the planning and allocation of water resources. To embrace one system of thought and reject the other would lead to an unbalanced structure, one which would either decry as a breach of trust appropriations essential to the economic development of this state, or deny any duty to protect or even consider the values promoted by the public trust. Therefore, seeking an accommodation which will make use of the pertinent principles of both the public trust doctrine and the appropriative water rights system, and drawing upon the history of the public trust and the water rights system, the body of judicial precedent, and the views of expert commentators, we reach the following conclusions:

a.   The state as sovereign retains continuing supervisory control over its navigable waters and the lands beneath those waters. This principle, fundamental to the concept of the public trust, applies to rights in flowing waters as well as to rights in tidelands and lakeshores; it prevents any party from acquiring a vested right to appropriate water in a manner harmful to the interests protected by the public trust.

b.   As a matter of current and historical necessity, the Legislature, acting directly or through an authorized agency such as the Water Board, has the power to grant usufructuary licenses that will permit an appropriator to take water from flowing streams and use that water in a distant part of the state, even though this taking does not promote, and may unavoidably harm, the trust uses at the source stream. The population and economy of this state depend upon the appropriation of vast quantities of water for uses unrelated to in-stream trust values. California's Constitution (see art. X, § 2), its statutes (see Cal. Water Code §§ 100, 104), decisions, and Commentators all emphasize the need to make efficient use of California's limited water resources: all recognize, at least implicitly, that efficient use requires diverting water from in-stream uses. Now that the economy and population centers of this state have developed in reliance upon appropriated water, it would be disingenuous to hold that such appropriations are and have always been improper to the extent that they harm public trust uses, and can be justified only upon theories of reliance or estoppel.

c.   The state has an affirmative duty to take the public trust into account in the planning and allocation of water resources, and to protect public trust uses whenever feasible. Just as the history of this state shows that appropriation may be necessary for efficient use of water despite unavoidable harm to public trust values, it demonstrates that an appropriative water rights system administered without consideration of the public trust may cause unnecessary and unjustified harm to trust interests. As a matter of practical necessity the state may have to approve appropriations despite foreseeable harm to public trust uses. In so doing, however, the state must bear in mind its duty as trustee to consider the effect of the taking on the public trust (see *United Plainsmen v. N.D. State Water Cons. Commission* 247 N.W.2d 457, 462–63 (N.D. 1976)), and to preserve, so far as consistent with the public interest, the uses protected by the trust.

Once the state has approved an appropriation, the public trust imposes a duty of continuing supervision over the taking and use of the appropriated water. In exercising its sovereign power to allocate water resources in the public interest, the state is not confined by past allocation decisions which may be incorrect in light of current knowledge or inconsistent with current needs.

The state accordingly has the power to reconsider allocation decisions even though those decisions were made after due consideration of their effect on the public trust. The case for reconsidering a particular decision, however, is even stronger when that decision failed to weigh and consider public trust uses. In the case before us, the salient fact is that no responsible body has ever determined the impact of diverting the entire flow of the Mono Lake tributaries into the Los Angeles Aqueduct. This is not a case in which the Legislature, the Water Board, or any judicial body has determined that the needs of Los Angeles outweigh the needs of the Mono Basin, that the benefit gained is worth the price. Neither has any responsible body determined whether some lesser taking would better balance the diverse interests. Instead, DWP acquired rights to the entire flow in 1940 from a water board which believed it lacked both the power and the duty to protect the Mono Lake environment, and continues to exercise those rights in apparent disregard for the resulting damage to the scenery, ecology, and human uses of Mono Lake.

It is clear that some responsible body ought to reconsider the allocation of the waters of the Mono Basin. No vested rights bar such reconsideration. We recognize the substantial concerns voiced by Los Angeles—the city's need for water, its reliance upon the 1940 board decision, the cost both in terms of money and environmental impact of obtaining water elsewhere. Such concerns must enter into any allocation decision. We hold only that they do not preclude a reconsideration and reallocation which also takes into account the impact of water diversion on the Mono Lake environment.

* * *

This opinion is but one step in the eventual resolution of the Mono Lake controversy. We do not dictate any particular allocation of water. Our objective is to resolve a legal conundrum in which two competing systems of thought—the public trust doctrine and the appropriative water rights system—existed independently of each other, espousing principles which seemingly suggested opposite results. We hope by integrating these two doctrines to clear away the legal barriers which have so far prevented either the Water Board or the courts from taking a new and objective look at the water resources of the Mono Basin. The human and environmental uses of Mono Lake—uses protected by the public trust doctrine—deserve to be taken into account. Such uses should not be destroyed because the state mistakenly thought itself powerless to protect them.

* * *

Notes

1. *Mono Lake* was not the first state court decision to apply the public trust doctrine to water rights. In *United Plainsmen Ass'n v. North Dakota State Water Conservation Comm'n*, 247 N.W.2d 457 (N.D. 1976), the North Dakota Supreme Court ruled that the trust required state water officials to ascertain the effects of a proposed diversion for a coal-fired power plant on existing and future water supplies and to institute water conservation measures, if necessary. Although some commentators predicted that the *Mono Lake* decision would encourage other Western states to apply the public trust doctrine to water rights, *see, e.g.,* Michael C. Blumm & Thea Schartz, *Mono Lake and the Evolving Public Trust in Western Water*, 37 Ariz. L. Rev. 701 (1995), largely that has not occurred. Cases have been sparse, though the Hawai'i Supreme Court's opinion in the case following this represents a landmark decision applying the trust to water resources.

The public trust clearly applies to the state's control of water resources, as noted at the outset of this chapter. The lack of public trust cases guiding water appropriations in many western states is perplexing. Do states have the latitude to dismiss trust obligations when allocating water to private interests and municipalities? Although the Supreme Court in *Phillips Petroleum Co.* (p. 97) gave states considerable autonomy in administering the trust by saying, "[I]t has been long established that the individual States have the authority to define the limits of the lands held in public trust and to recognize private rights in such lands as they see fit…," does this mean that states are at liberty to ignore trust obligations towards basic resources such as water? Could a state find there is no public trust limitation on the allocation of water given that such allocation represents an alienation of a recognized trust resource? Does it make sense that water would receive trust protection in one state and not another? Water is water, whether found in California or Texas, isn't it? Perhaps the *Phillips Petroleum Co.* Court was trying to say that each state has latitude to prioritize the beneficial uses of the trust according to the local circumstances and needs of its population. Clearly states face differing policy concerns and practical exigencies in deciding upon appropriate beneficial uses of the trust. Affording states latitude in that respect, however, is altogether different from allowing them to dismiss altogether a basic trust obligation with respect to water.

2. The Idaho Supreme Court endorsed applying the public trust doctrine to water rights in *Kootenai Environmental Alliance, Inc. v. Panhandle Yacht Club, Inc.*, 671 P.2d 1085, 1094 (Idaho 1983), stating:

> The public trust doctrine takes precedent even over vested water rights. Grants, even if purporting to be in fee simple, are given subject to the trust and to action by the state necessary to fulfill its trust responsibilities. Grants to individuals of public trust resources will be construed as given subject to the public trust doctrine unless the legislature explicitly provides otherwise.

But the Idaho legislature subsequently eliminated the application of the public trust doctrine to water rights. Idaho Code § 58-1203. Although some have questioned the effectiveness of this declaration of non-applicability, see Michael C. Blumm, Harrison C. Dunning & Scott W. Reed, *Renouncing the Public Trust Doctrine: An Assessment of the Validity of Idaho House Bill 794*, 24 Ecology L.Q. 461 (1997), there have been no challenges to the state's action. In Arizona, the legislature passed a statute to exclude public trust considerations from a water rights adjudication, but the Supreme Court of Arizona would have none of it, stating:

> The public trust doctrine is a constitutional limitation on legislative power to give away resources held by the state in trust for its people. *See Arizona Ctr. for Law in the Public Interest v. Hassell*, 837 P.2d 158, 166–68 (Ariz. Ct. App. 1991) (applying both the separation of powers doctrine and the gift clause, article 9, section 7 of the Arizona Constitution). The Legislature cannot order the courts to make the doctrine inapplicable to these or any proceedings. While the issue has been raised before the master, we do not yet know if the doctrine applies to all, some, or none of the claims. That determination depends on the facts before a judge, not on a statute. It is for the courts to decide whether the public trust doctrine is applicable to the facts. The Legislature cannot by legislation destroy the constitutional limits on its authority. *See id.* at 168–71.

San Carlos Apache Tribe v. Superior Court ex. rel. County of Maricopa, 972 P.2d 179, 199 (Ariz. 1999).

3. *Mono Lake* involved a significant expansion in the scope of the public trust doctrine in California, but it did not unmoor the doctrine from navigable waters. Why did the court conclude that the mountain feeder streams to Mono Lake are subject to the public trust? Is the doctrine concerned about the condition of the feeder streams or the condition of the lake? Notice that this case continued the emphasis on ecological values expressed by the court in *Marks v. Whitney* (p. 132). The court made clear that the trust has among its purposes the protection of "the scenic views of the lake and its shore, the purity of the air, and the use of the lake for nesting and feeding by birds." Assuming the court understood the ecological nexus between tributary streams and the lake, do you think it would also protect the lake from pollution (either waterborne or airborne, such as mercury)? Does it make sense to protect water levels of a water body but not the water *quality* of the water body? Natural resources law is notorious for artificially partitioning problems that are, in fact, inextricably connected as a matter of ecological function. Could the public trust provide a more integrated approach to management of a resource?

4. The Los Angeles DWP, invoking the Western water law doctrine of temporal priority (first in time, first in right), argued that its 1940 priority date for its diversions insulated it from public trust interference. Why wasn't the result of this case a violation of the "first in time, first in right" principle of Western water law? How did the court integrate public property (trust) rights into a system of private rights governed by prior appropriation?

5. *Mono Lake* was especially controversial because, by emphasizing that no water rights could vest against the public trust, it undermined the security of private rights to divert water for irrigation, municipal, and other purposes. The opinion is consistent with the many cases that apply the public trust retrospectively on privately owned tidelands. Collectively, these decisions underscore the antecedent and superior nature of public trust rights to private title or interests. At the same time, however, the doctrine in the water rights context operates as a doctrine of accommodation, similar to its role in delineating private and public rights in land parcels. *See Mono Lake*, 658 P.2d at 727 (seeking "an accommodation which will make use of the pertinent principles of both the public trust doctrine and the appropriative water rights system....."). The effect of the decision was evident

fairly quickly, as the California Court of Appeal ruled, in *United States v. State Water Resources Control Bd.*, 227 Cal. Rptr. 161 (Cal. Ct. App. 1986), that the public trust doctrine enabled the state to modify water rights if necessary to preserve water quality.

6. Observe how the role of the court in this and other major public trust cases differs from the judicial posture in a statutory context. Statutory interpretation tends to focus on narrow and often quite technical issues of law. Courts give substantial deference to agencies and legislatures on matters of statutory law. By contrast, many of the leading public trust cases involve judicial decision making in a very broad context. Public trust cases often require judges to create new principles of common law adapted to the issues at hand, using the reasoning of past cases to guide them. The court in *Mono Lake*, for example, observed that the case brought "together for the first time two systems of legal thought: the appropriative water rights system ... and the public trust doctrine...." These two broad areas of law were headed on a collision course over issues such as those arising over Mono Lake and its tributaries. The court proceeded to establish a set of principles to reconcile both legal doctrines, drawing upon "the history of the public trust and the water rights system, the body of judicial precedent, and the views of expert commentators...."

7. One important aspect of this case involved the relationship between the water board regulations governing appropriation (which implemented state constitutional provisions) and the trust. The DWP argued that the constitutional provisions of reasonable and beneficial use and the state water board's regulations implementing them "subsumed" the trust. The court rejected this argument, concluding that both the trust and the appropriation system form an integrated water rights management regime. The court's opinion is instructive for other public trust cases, as most involve the interaction between statutory law and trust law. Government defendants characteristically assert that statutory regimes subsume the trust, but as the *Mono Lake* case (and the *Waiahole Ditch* case that follows) show, courts may conclude otherwise. Does this judicial inclination to protect the trust from being assimilated into statutes and regulations point to the fundamental role of the trust as providing a restraint on legislative power, as articulated in many of the cases in chapter 2?

8. What must the state do to discharge its trust responsibility? Must it keep Mono Lake from drying up? The court suggested some fiduciary principles to guide water appropriation in accordance with trust values. First, it made clear that water management agencies have an "affirmative duty to take the public trust into account in the planning and allocation of water resources" (and where this has not happened, agencies "ought to reconsider the allocation of the waters" in view of trust purposes). Second, the trust imposed on the state a duty of continuing supervision over waters with the authority (and, impliedly, the duty) to revoke permits that "may be incorrect in light of current knowledge or inconsistent with current needs." Third, although the state has the power to issue permits that do "not promote, and may unavoidably harm, the trust uses at the source stream...," the state also has the duty "to protect public trust uses whenever feasible" and "to preserve, so far as consistent with the public interest, the uses protected by the trust."

The court refrained from dictating any "particular allocation" of water, leaving it instead to the water management agencies. Did the court give enough guidance to the water agencies in fulfilling their fiduciary obligation? What does it mean to preserve trust uses "so far as consistent with the public interest" and "whenever feasible"? Doesn't the fiduciary standard require some sort of inquiry into the character of the water use in order to determine whether the use justifies harm to ecological trust values? Since water is a public resource, shouldn't an authorized water use serve some sort of compelling public need in order to justify a harmful withdrawal impairing trust values? For example, would a water agency be more justified in issuing a permit for municipal drinking water as opposed to a permit to supply water to a water-slide park or a golf course? The next case explores fiduciary obligations in more detail.

9. As to the duty of the state to "exercise continued supervision over the trust...," the court made clear that changing public needs trigger a duty to reexamine allocations. This continued duty of supervision operates in tandem with the part of the opinion holding that water rights do not vest against the public trust. *See Mono Lake*, 658 P.2d at 728 ("In exercising its sovereign power to allocate water resources in the public interest, the state is not confined by past allocation decisions which may be incorrect in light of current knowledge or inconsistent with current needs."). Do rapidly changing climate conditions and threats of long-term drought create a fiduciary responsibility to reassess allocation schemes? As Justice Holmes famously stated, the law responds to the "felt necessities of the time...."[8]

10. The *Mono Lake* case induced the California Water Resources Board to fulfill its trust responsibilities through a 1994 administrative decision that amended DWP's water rights to allow the lake to eventually reach a level of 6,392 feet above sea level, some 25 feet less than the pre-diversion lake level. But in early 2015, the lake was still thirteen vertical feet below that goal.[9] In 2013, the Mono Lake Committee, CalTrout, California Department of Fish and Wildlife, and DWP reached an agreement in which DWP committed to modernizing aqueduct infrastructure for the purpose of increasing inflow to Mono Lake.[10] The agreement also deferred the state water board's hearing on DWP's water licenses, which was to take place in 2014, until 2020. The state water board has hardly been a vigorous implementer of the public trust doctrine outside of the Mono Lake Basin. *See* Dave Owen, *The* Mono Lake *Case, the Public Trust Doctrine, and the Administrative State*, 45 U.C. Davis L. Rev. 1099 (2012). Is that because the court did not provide enough guidance on the fiduciary obligation to protect water assets in the public trust?

11. In ensuing litigation affecting Mono Lake, in *California Trout v. Superior Court*, 266 Cal. Rptr. 788 (Cal. App. 1989), the state court of appeal interpreted a provision of the California Fish and Game Code to require maintenance and reestablishment of fish life in the Mono Lake feeder streams, in effect leading to the establishment of minimum flows for the streams and providing more stringent restrictions on the diversions than the *Mono Lake* decision did. The California Supreme Court later relied on the *California Trout* decision in announcing that in California there were distinct statutory and common law public trust doctrines. *Environmental Protection Information Center v. California Dep't of Forestry & Fire Protection*, 187 P.3d 888, 926 (Cal. 2008).

12. Notice that the state resisted the application of the public trust doctrine to the Mono Lake situation, with the state attorney general arguing in support of DWP. How then did this case get before the courts? *Compare Marks v. Whitney* (p. 132), allowing a neighboring landowner to employ the doctrine against a private tideland fill.

13. For more on the public trust in water, see Carole Necole Brown, *Drinking from a Deep Well: The Public Trust and Western Water Law*, 34 Fla. St. L. Rev. 1 (2006). The most

---

8. OLIVER WENDELL HOLMES, THE COMMON LAW 1 (Empire Books 2012).

9. In February 2015, the lake's level was 6,379.0 feet, only 7 feet above its lowest level of 6,372 feet in 1981 and 1982. Mono Lake Committee, TODAY AT MONO LAKE, http://www.monolake.org/today/water; Mono Basin Clearinghouse, MONO LAKE LEVELS 1979–PRESENT, http://www.monobasinresearch.org/data/levelmonthly.php.

10. Mono Lake Committee, *Groundbreaking Agreement Gives Los Angeles Aqueduct New Purpose*, TODAY AT MONO LAKE: THE MONO-LOGUE (Aug. 24, 2013), http://www.monolake.org/today/2013/08/24/groundbreaking-agreement-gives-los-angeles-aqueduct-new-purpose-healing-streams/.

prominent current controversies concerning the public trust in water involve whether the doctrine supplies a defense to the application of limitations imposed by the federal Endangered Species Act (ESA) works a taking warranting just compensation. *See Tulare Lake Basin Water Storage Dist. v. United States*, 49 Fed. Cl. 313 (2001) (finding a taking as a result of ESA restrictions); *Casitas Mun. Water Dist. v. United States*, 102 Fed. Cl. 443 (2011) (no taking because under state law a claimant has a compensable interest only when it puts the water to actual beneficial use, which does not include diverting for storage). *See* John D. Echeverria, *The Public Trust Doctrine as a Background Principles Defense in Takings Litigation*, 45 U.C. Davis L. Rev. 931 (2012) (discussing both *Tulare Lake* and *Casitas*).

The *Mono Lake* case's adoption of the scope of the PTD to extend to non-navigable waters affecting navigable waters opens the door to applying the doctrine to other water resources with such an effect. Consider the following decision concerning groundwater in California.

Environmental Law Foundation v. State Water Resources Control Board

Superior Court of California
Case No. 34-2010-80000583, July 15, 2014

SUMNER, J.:

* * *

Introduction

Petitioners, the Environmental Law Foundation, Pacific Coast Federation of Fishermen's Associations, and Institute for Fisheries Resources bring this an action against Respondents County of Siskiyou ("County") and the State Water Resources Board ("Board") raising an issue of first impression: Does the public trust doctrine apply to groundwater hydrologically connected to a navigable river? Petitioners seek a declaration it does. They also seek a writ of mandate or injunction compelling the County to stop issuing well drilling permits until it complies with its duties under the public trust doctrine....

* * *

The Scott River located in Siskiyou County is a navigable waterway used for boating and fishing. In the past two decades the Scott River experienced decreased flows caused in part by groundwater pumping.... Petitioners use the terms "interconnected groundwater" to refer to groundwater so hydrologically connected to the Scott River that its pumping causes decreased flows in the river. According to Petitioners, at times almost every gallon of groundwater pumped decreases the flow of the Scott River by the same amount.

As a result of these decreased flows, the Scott River is often "dewatered" in the summer and early fall. The river is then reduced to a series of pools. This, in turn, has injured the river's fish populations. Although not explicitly alleged, it is implicit this also impacts the Scott River's navigability, rendering it less suitable for boating and other recreational activities.

The County is responsible for issuing permits for wells used to pump groundwater. Petitioners allege the County does not consider the effect groundwater pumping will have on the Scott River when it issues its permits. Petitioners believe the public trust doctrine requires the County to consider those effects when issuing permits to pump groundwater....

* * *

Analysis

I. The public trust doctrine protects navigable waters from harm caused by the extraction of groundwater

A. The public trust doctrine

* * *

The nature of the State's title imposes fiduciary-like obligations: The State has a duty to supervise and administer the trust so the public may continue to use navigable waterways for trust purposes....

[The California Supreme Court in *National Audubon Society v. Superior Court of Alpine County* explained,] "[a]s a matter of practical necessity the state may have to approve appropriations despite foreseeable harm to public trust uses. In so doing, however, the state must bear in mind its duty as trustee to consider the effect of the taking on the public trust ... and to preserve, so far as consistent with the public interest, the uses protected by the trust." (658 P.2d 709, 728.)

* * *

... The issue is whether the public trust doctrine applies to *groundwater* so connected to a navigable river that its extraction harms trust uses of the river. Relying primarily on *National Audubon*, Petitioners argue the public trust doctrine applies. The court concludes they are correct.

B. Under National Audubon *the public trust doctrine applies to the facts alleged here*

* * *

Although the facts alleged here are different [from those in *National Audubon*], it is a difference without a legal distinction. *National Audubon* involved extraction of water from non-navigable surface streams. This case involves extraction of underground water. But the result is allegedly the same — decreasing the flow of navigable waters harming public trust uses.

The public trust doctrine would prevent pumping directly out of the Scott River harming public trust uses. So too under *National Audubon* the public trust doctrine would prevent pumping a non-navigable tributary of the Scott River harming public trust uses of the river. The court finds no reason why the analysis of *National Audubon* would not apply to the facts alleged here. The court thus finds the public trust doctrine protects navigable waters from harm caused by extraction of groundwater, where the groundwater is so connected to the navigable water that its extraction adversely affects public trust uses.

This formulation is slightly different than the declaration Petitioners seek. Petitioners request a declaration groundwater hydrologically connected to navigable surface flows is protected by the public trust doctrine. However, the court does not find *groundwater* itself is a resource protected by the public trust doctrine. (*Cf. In re Water Use Permit Applications*, 9 P.3d 409, 445–47 (Haw. 2000).) California case law has applied the public trust doctrine to protect *navigable waters*; groundwater is not navigable. (*State of California v. Superior Court (Lyon)*, 625 P.2d 239, 250 (Cal. 1981) ["it is navigability which is the touchstone in determining whether or not the public trust applies"]; *Santa Teresa Citizen Action Group* v. *City of San Jose*, 114 Cal. App. 4th 689, 709 (Cal. Dist. Ct. App. 2003) [public trust doctrine "has no direct application to groundwater resources."].) The court thus finds only that the public trust doctrine applies when the extraction of groundwater causes harm to navigable waters harming the public's right to use those navigable waters for trust purposes.

As applied to the facts alleged here, the public trust doctrine protects the Scott River and the public's right to use the Scott River for trust purposes, including fishing, rafting and boating. It also protects the public's right to use, enjoy and preserve the Scott River in its natural state and as a habitat for fish. If the extraction of groundwater near the Scott River adversely affects those rights, the public trust doctrine applies.

The County argues the public trust doctrine does not apply to groundwater, because groundwater is not navigable. This is true, but not dispositive. Again, the court does not hold the public trust doctrine applies to groundwater itself. Rather, the public trust doctrine applies if extraction of groundwater adversely impacts a navigable waterway to which the public trust doctrine does apply.

* * *

The County argues *extraction* of groundwater is not a *diversion*. Perhaps. But the County does not explain why the difference between extracting as opposed to diverting water changes the analysis. The end result is the same—less water in a navigable river harming public trust uses. The County also ignores the fact the Court in *National Audubon* explained it was not limiting its holding to *diversion* of water, but also encompassed extraction: "the public trust doctrine ... should equally apply to constrain the *extraction* of water that destroys navigation and other public interests." (658 P.2d at 720 [emphasis in original].)

* * *

If pumping groundwater impairs the public's right to use a navigable waterway for trust purposes, there is no sound reason in law or policy why the public trust doctrine should not apply.

2. The Legislature has not released the County from its obligations under the public trust doctrine

... The County argues even if the public trust doctrine applies to extraction of groundwater as alleged here, the doctrine does not impose any specific duty on the County.

Petitioners seek a writ of mandate or injunction compelling the County to stop issuing permits to drill wells for groundwater in the Scott River basin until it complies with its duties under the public trust doctrine. Again, Petitioners do not assert what the County's duty may be. The County nevertheless argues it has no duty to regulate groundwater under the public trust doctrine because the Legislature has given it complete discretion to decide whether to regulate groundwater. Accordingly, neither mandate nor injunctive relief will lie to compel the County to exercise its discretion. The court is not persuaded.

The County relies on Water Code section 10750 et seq., where the Legislature declared "groundwater is a valuable natural resource in California" and should be managed accordingly. To help manage this resource the Legislature authorized local agencies, such as the County, to adopt groundwater management plans to manage groundwater resources within their jurisdictions.

From this grant of authority to adopt a groundwater management plan, the County makes a big leap: Because the Legislature did not require the County to implement a groundwater management plan, the County cannot be required to regulate groundwater under the public trust doctrine. This argument fails for several reasons.

First, section 10750 et seq. does not subsume the public trust doctrine, rendering it inapplicable to groundwater. As our Supreme Court instructs, the public trust doctrine and California's statutory water rights system co-exist; neither occupies the field to the exclusion of the other. (*National Audubon*, 658 P.2d at 727) ... The court ... finds no evidence the Legislature, in enacting section 10750 et seq., intended to *preclude* the County from applying the public trust doctrine where necessary.

Second, there is no conflict between authorizing the County to adopt a groundwater management plan, and requiring it to comply with the public trust doctrine. The public trust doctrine applies when the extraction of groundwater harms navigable waters and the public's use for trust purposes. If the County's issuance of well permits will result in extraction of groundwater adversely affecting the public's right to use the Scott River for trust purposes, the County must take the public trust into consideration and protect public trust uses when feasible. Such a requirement does not conflict with the County's discretion to decide whether or not to implement an overall groundwater management plan.

Third, while the County has discretion whether to adopt a groundwater management plan, it does not have discretion to ignore its duties under the public trust doctrine. Although administration of the public trust rests primarily with the State as sovereign, the County is a subdivision of the State. (CAL. CONST. art XI, §I, subd. (a) ["The State is divided into counties which are legal subdivisions of the State."].) As a subdivision of the State, the County "shares responsibility" for administering the public trust. (See *Center for Biological Diversity, Inc. v. FPL Group, Inc.*, 166 Cal. App. 4th 1349, 1370, n.19 (Cal. Ct. App. 2008) ["the county, as a subdivision of the state, shares responsibility for protecting our natural resources and may not approve of destructive activities without giving due regard to the preservation of those resources."].) The State cannot abdicate its duties under the public trust doctrine. (*Illinois Central*, 146 U.S. at 452 ["The State can no more abdicate its trust over property in which the whole people are interested ... than it can abdicate its police powers"]; *National Audubon*, 658 P.2d at 721 [trust property "is a subject of public concern to the whole people of the State" and thus "cannot be alienated"].) Neither can the County.

As the Court explained in *National Audubon*, the Legislature may grant licenses to appropriate water. (658 P.2d at 727.) When it does so, the Legislature, or its authorized agent, has "an affirmative duty to take the public trust into account ... and to protect public trust uses whenever feasible." (*Id.*) Thus as a legal subdivision of the State, the County has an affirmative duty to consider the public trust when it issues permits to appropriate groundwater.

* * *

Notes

1. Note how the California courts tied the trust to navigable waters. The Supreme Court of Wisconsin also linked the trust to navigable waters. *Lake Beulah Mgmt. Dist. v. State Dep't of Natural Res.*, 799 N.W.2d 73, 92–93 (Wis. 2011) (concluding that under the PTD, the Wisconsin Department of Natural Resources had "the authority and a general duty" to consider the affects of groundwater pumping on navigable waters) (p. 412). Is this focus too narrow? The California court was obviously constrained by prior case law that had depicted navigability as the "touchstone" of the public trust. *See Lyon*, 625 P.2d at 250. Some courts have declined to include groundwater in the trust because it is not "navigable." *See, e.g., Michigan Citizens for Water Conservation v. Nestle Waters North America, Inc.*, 709 N.W.2d 174, 218–20 (Mich. Ct. App. 2005), *aff'd* in part, *rev'd* in part 737 N.W.2d 447 (Mich. 2007); *Rettkowski v. Dep't of Ecology*, 858 P.2d 232 (Wash. 1993) On the other hand, the Hawai'i Supreme Court and a plurality of the Pennsylvania

Supreme Court have both recognized groundwater as squarely within the public trust (discussed further in note 2 below). *See In re Water Use Permit Applications*, 9 P.3d 409, 445 (Haw. 2000) (p. 189); *Robinson Township v. Pennsylvania*, 83 A.3d 901 (Pa. 2013) (p. 82). Should those courts that still cling to the concept of navigability explore the rationale for why the trust applied to navigable waters over a century ago, then extrapolate that rationale to other resources such as groundwater? Is their failure to do so a sign of judicial timidity, or is it a sign of judicial fidelity to precedent?

In the modern era, in which planetary heating has caused extreme drought and scarcity of drinking water supplies, isn't groundwater just as important as surface navigable waters in fulfilling society's needs? Can you imagine a Wisconsin or California court in the future departing from navigability altogether and concluding that groundwater is inherently part of the public trust because it serves a vital function in supporting human survival and other needs? Couldn't such a court dismiss the navigability rule saying the practical context has changed dramatically? The Arizona court of appeals in *Jamie Lynn Butler* (p. 411) stated that its precedent applying the public trust doctrine to waters did not preclude an extension of the doctrine to air. For analysis of the PTD's application to groundwater, see Yee Huang, Ctr. for Progressive Reform, *Protecting the Invisible: The Public Trust Doctrine and Groundwater*, CPR BLOG (July 24, 2009), *available at* http://www.progressivereform.org/CPRBlog.cfm?idBlog=897E966E-C8F9-131C-E12ABAA7E 9BF8A60.

2. In *Waiahole Ditch* (p. 189), the Supreme Court of Hawai'i held that the public trust *res* includes both groundwater and water—indeed, "all water resources without exception or distinction," reasoning, "[m]odern science and technology have discredited the surface-ground dichotomy." The court emphasized that the trust demands "maintenance of ecological balance." *In re Water Use Permit Applications*, 9 P.3d 409, 445 (Haw. 2000). What about other natural resources beyond groundwater which also are essential to human survival and well-being? Consider, for example, large forests. Scientists point out their crucial role in storing carbon dioxide, a paramount concern as climate crisis intensifies. Climate, in turn, affects navigable waterways (a traditional trust asset) because, as the planet heats, rivers lose water to evaporation. Forests also regulate watershed hydrology and provide habitat for fish and wildlife. Clearcutting forests can destroy fisheries, a quintessential public trust resource, by adding sediment to the streams. Can the navigable waters be protected without protecting the atmosphere? Can the atmosphere be protected without protecting the forests? Can fisheries be protected without safeguarding the forests and the atmosphere? Nature's weave is intricate, and all resources have synergistic functions that contribute to overall ecological sustainability.

Are these links between forests and fisheries, or between forests and atmosphere, any more tenuous than the link between groundwater and navigable surface water, recognized by the *Environmental Law Foundation* court? Has science advanced to the point that there is no longer a rational basis for extending trust protection to navigable waters but not other assets of nature that affect such waters? Should courts simply recognize a full ecological *res* that reflects nature's own organization and relationships? In *Robinson Township v. Pennsylvania*, 83 A.3d 901 (Penn. 2013) (p. 82), a plurality of the Supreme Court of Pennsylvania determined that the trust *res* included a broad realm of resources. *See id.* at 955 ("At present, the concept of public natural resources includes not only state-owned lands, waterways, and mineral reserves, but also resources that implicate the public interest, such as ambient air, surface and ground water, wild flora, and fauna (including fish) that are outside the scope of purely private property."). For an argument that the public trust extends to forests, see Paul A. Barresi, *Mobilizing the Public Trust Doctrine in*

Support of Publicly Owned Forests as Carbon Dioxide Sinks in India and the United States, 23 Colo. J. Int'l Envtl. L. & Pol'y 39 (2012).

3. Some state constitutional expressions of public trust refer to all natural resources, including air and groundwater, as being in the trust. *See, e.g.*, HAW. CONST. art. XI, § 1 (declaring, "All public natural resources are held in trust by the State for the benefit of the people," and "the State and its political subdivisions shall conserve and protect Hawai'i's ... natural resources, including land, water, air, minerals and energy resources"). Could these expressions be persuasive to courts of other states, since air and groundwater have the same characteristics no matter where located? For a discussion of the role of the public trust doctrine as it appears in constitutions, legislation, and administrative regulations, see Alexandra B. Klass, *Modern Public Trust Principles: Recognizing Rights and Integrating Standards*, 82 Notre Dame L. Rev. 699 (2006).

4. In *Robinson Township v. Pennsylvania*, cited above in note 2, a plurality of justices of the Pennsylvania Supreme Court applied the public trust to groundwater and held unconstitutional a law that facilitated fracking. If this opinion proves influential, could it be a game-changer as to fracking, which threatens drinking water sources and air quality? Recall that the PTD forbids "substantial impairment" to trust resources. At present, state regulation is inconsistent and federal regulation virtually nonexistent. *See, e.g.*, Dusty Horwitt, Environmental Working Group, *Drilling Around the Law*, *available at* http://www.ewg.org/sites/default/files/report/EWG-2009drillingaroundthelaw.pdf; Neil Zussman, *Fracking: Gas Drilling and the Marcellus Shale*, (2010), http://frack.mixplex.com/fracking.

5. Note that the *Environmental Law Foundation* court applied the PTD to the county as a subdivision of the state. The *Robinson Township* plurality also applied the PTD to local entities. Given that local agencies hold enormous power in regulating land use and resource extraction, does this application greatly broaden the potential impact of the PTD?

6. Notice the deference given to the legislature by California courts, as evident in the *Environmental Law Foundation* opinion. Is such deference warranted? Isn't the whole purpose of the PTD to provide a check on legislative action? The *Robinson* court felt it was, holding that fracking statute passed by the legislature was unconstitutional under the PTD and the due process clause of the Pennsylvania Constitution. As more judges and scholars consider the constitutional underpinnings of the PTD, do you expect courts to give less deference to legislative action that irreparably harms public trust resources?

———————

The court in *Environmental Law Foundation* applied the "affects test" to extend the PTD to protect groundwater that affects navigable waters. Consider the following case in which the Supreme Court of Hawai'i considers whether groundwater is a PTD resource.

In re Water Use Permit Applications, Petitions for Interim Instream Flow Standard Amendments, and Petitions for Water Reservations for The Waiahole Ditch (*"Waiahole Ditch"* Decision)

Supreme Court of Hawai'i
9 P.3d 409 (Haw. 2000)

[From 1913 to 1995, the Waiahole Ditch collected surface water and dike-impounded groundwater and transported it from the windward to the leeward side of Oahu to irrigate a sugar plantation. After the plantation was discontinued, the Waiahole Irrigation Company (WIC) filed water rights applications with the Hawai'i Water Rights Commission on behalf of existing water users. The combined filings exceeded the capacity of the ditch. A group of so-called "Windward Parties" sought to return diverted flows to the streams to restore native stream and estuarine life to protect customary Native Hawaiian practices and traditional small family farming. Large agricultural and development interest, joined by the state, sought to continue the flow of windward water to leeward lands for golf course irrigation, agriculture, and housing development. The Commission initially ordered WIC to stop disposing of wastewater into central Oahu ditches and to release the surplus water to restore depleted windward streams. This experiment in ecosystem management was successful; the flows flushed out exotic species and experts predicted that native species could be reintroduced and thrive in the streams. After a contested hearing, the Commission concluded that it had a public trust duty to establish instream flow standards. The standards could only be established after a long-term research and monitoring program but the precautionary principle required the standards to err on the side of in-stream flow protection. The Commission apportioned the stream by requiring that 6.97 million gallons per day (mgd) be released into windward streams as an interim instream flow, 14.51 mgd be set aside for off-stream leeward uses, primarily for diversified agriculture, and 1.29 mgd be allocated to a state prison, a cemetery and two golf courses but ordered them to seek available alternative sources. The Commission designated the instream flow standards as interim and announced that it would revise them periodically. The net effect of the allocations was to confine instream flows to water not otherwise allocated to off-stream uses. Existing users and landowners argued that the state's 1992 water allocation superseded any common law public trust duties. The Court held otherwise.]

NAKAYAMA, J.:

* * *

Having established the public trust doctrine's independent validity, we must define its basic parameters with respect to the water resources of this state. In so doing, we address: a) the "scope" of the trust, or the resources it encompasses; and b) the "substance" of the trust, including the purposes or uses it upholds and the powers and duties it confers on the state.

a. Scope of the Trust

The public trust doctrine has varied in scope over time and across jurisdictions. In its ancient Roman form, the public trust included "the air, running water, the sea, and consequently the shores of the sea." J. Inst. 2.1.1. Under the English common law, the trust covered tidal waters and lands. *See Shively v. Bowlby*, 152 U.S. 1, 11 (1894). Courts in the United States have commonly understood the trust as extending to all navigable waters and the lands beneath them irrespective of tidality. *See Illinois Central*, 146 U.S. 387 (1892); *Phillips Petroleum Co. v. Mississippi*, 484 U.S. 469 (1988) (confirming that the public trust still applies to tidal waters, whether navigable or not). In Hawai'i, this court has recognized, based on founding principles of law in this jurisdiction, a distinct public trust encompassing all the water resources of the state. *See Robinson*, 658 P.2d 287, 310 (Haw. 1982). The Hawai'i Constitution declares that "all public resources are held in trust by the state for the benefit of its people," Haw. Const. art. XI, § 1, and establishes public trust obligation "to protect, control, and regulate the use of Hawai'i's water resources for the benefit of its people," Haw. Const. art. XI, § 7.

We need not define the full extent of article XI, section 1's reference to "all public resources" at this juncture. For the purposes of this case, however, we reaffirm that, under article XI, sections 1 and 7 and the sovereign reservation, the public trust doctrine applies to all water resources without exception or distinction. [Kamehameha Schools Bishop Estate (KSBF)] and [Castle and Cooke, Inc. (Castle)] advocate for the exclusion of ground waters from the public trust. Their arguments, first, contradict the clear import of the constitutional provisions, which do not differentiate between categories of water in mandating the protection and regulation of water resources for the common good.[11] The convention's records confirm that the framers understood "water resources" as "includ[ing] ground water, surface water and all other water." Debates, in 2 Proceedings, at 861 (statement by Delegate Fukunaga).

We are also unpersuaded by the contention of KSBE and Castle that the sovereign reservation does not extend to ground waters. Their position rests almost entirely on one decision, *City Mill Co., Ltd. v. Honolulu Sewer & Water Comm'n*, 30 Haw. 912 (1929). Discussing the effect of the Mahele, the *City Mill* court observed that "'all mineral or metallic mines' were reserved to the Hawaiian government, but there was no reservation whatever of the subterranean waters." *Id.* at 934. Nowhere in the opinion, however, does the court address the reservation of sovereign prerogatives and its surrounding historical and legal context. This fatal oversight, common to other cases subsequently invalidated by this court, discounts the precedential value of *City Mill* concerning the public trust. *See Robinson*, 658 P.2d at 306, 306 n.25.

* * *

Even more fundamentally, just as ancient Hawaiian usage reflected the perspectives of that era, the common law distinctions between ground and surface water developed without regard to the manner in which "both categories represent no more than a single integrated source of water with each element dependent upon the other for its existence." *Reppun v. Board of Water Supply*, 656 P.2d 57, 73 (Haw. 1982). Modern science and technology have discredited the surface-ground dichotomy. *See id.* (describing the "modern scientific approach" of acknowledging "the unity of the hydrological cycle"); A. Dan Tarlock, LAW OF WATER RIGHTS AND RESOURCES § 4:5 (2000). Few cases highlight more plainly its diminished meaning and utility than the present one, involving surface streams depleted by ground water diversions and underground aquifers recharged by surface water applications. In determining the scope of the sovereign reservation, therefore, we see little sense in adhering to artificial distinctions neither recognized by the ancient system nor borne out in the present practical realities of this state.

Water is no less an essential "usufruct of lands" when found below, rather than above, the ground. In view of the ultimate value of water to the ancient Hawaiians, it is inescapable that the sovereign reservation was intended to guarantee public rights to all water, regardless of its immediate source. Whatever practices the ancients may have observed in their time, therefore, we must conclude that the reserved trust encompasses any usage developed in ours, including the "ground water" uses proposed by the parties in the instant case. The public trust, by its very nature, does not remain fixed for all time, but must conform to changing needs and circumstances. *See, e.g., Reppun*, 656 P.2d at 72 (acknowledging that "the continued satisfaction of the framers' intent requires that the [riparian] doctrine be permitted to evolve in accordance with changing needs and cir-

---

11. With respect to article XI, section 1, KSBE contends that the provision's reference to "public natural resources" indicates an intent to exclude "privately owned" waters from the public trust. This argument misses the point; at least in the water resources context, we have maintained that, apart from any private rights that may exist in water, "there is, as there always has been, a superior public interest in this natural beauty." *Robinson*, 658 P.2d at 312.

cumstances"); *Matthews v. Bay Head Improvement Ass'n*, 471 A.2d 855 (N.J. 1984) (extending the trust to privately owned beaches, in recognition of the "increasing demand for our State's beaches and the dynamic nature of the public trust doctrine"); *People ex rel. Baker v. Mack*, 97 Cal. Rptr. 448, 451–53 (Cal. Ct. App. 1971) (expanding the "narrow and outmoded" definition of "navigability" in recognition of modern recreational uses); *cf. Phillips Petroleum*, 484 U.S. at 483 (noting, with respect to the tidelands trust, that "there is no universal and uniform law on the subject; but … each State has dealt with the lands under the tide waters within its borders according to its own views of justice and policy" (quoting *Shively*, 152 U.S. at 26) (ellipsis in original)).

In sum, given the vital importance of all waters to the public welfare, we decline to carve out a ground water exception to the water resources trust. Based on the plain language of our constitution and a reasoned modern view of the sovereign reservation, we confirm that the public trust doctrine applies to all water resources, unlimited by any surface-ground distinction.

b. Substance of the Trust

The public trust is a dual concept of sovereign right and responsibility. Previous decisions have thoroughly reviewed the sovereign authority of the state under the trust. The arguments in the present appeal focus on the state's trust duties. In its decision, the Commission stated that, under the public trust doctrine, "the State's first duty is to protect the fresh water resources (surface and ground) which are part of the public trust res," a duty which it further described as "a categorical imperative and the precondition to all subsequent considerations." The public trust, the Commission also ruled, subjects offstream water uses to a "heightened level of scrutiny." Commission on Water Resource Management, Conclusions of Law 10 (Dec. 24, 1997).

In *Illinois Central*, the United States Supreme Court described the state's interest in its navigable waters as "title," not in a proprietary sense, but "title held *in trust for the people of the State that they may enjoy* the navigation of *the waters*, carry on commerce over them, and have liberty of fishing therein *freed from the obstruction or interference of private parties*." 146 U.S. at 452 (emphases added). The trust, in the Court's simplest terms, "requires the government of the State to *preserve such waters for the use of the public*." *Id.* at 453 (emphasis added).

Based on this formulation, other courts have sought to further define the requirements of the public trust doctrine. The rules developed in order to protect public water bodies and submerged lands for public access and use, however, *see, e.g., State v. Public Serv. Comm'n*, 81 N.W.2d 71, 74 (Wis. 1957) (prohibiting substantial destruction of navigable waters through land reclamation); *People ex rel. Webb v. California Fish Co.*, 138 P. 79, 88 (Cal. 1913) (holding that a grantee of submerged lands gains "naked title," subject to the "public easement" in the waters above), do not readily apply in the context of water resources valued for consumptive purposes, where competing uses are more often mutually exclusive. This court recognized as much in *Robinson*, stating that "[t]he extent of the state's trust obligation over all waters of course would not be identical to that which applies to navigable waters." 658 P.2d at 310. Keeping this distinction in mind, we consider the substance of the water resources trust of this state, specifically, the purposes protected by the trust and the powers and duties conferred on the state thereunder.

i. Purposes of the Trust

In other states, the "purposes" or "uses" of the public trust have evolved with changing public values and needs. The trust traditionally preserved public rights of navigation, commerce, and fishing. *See Illinois Central*, 146 U.S. at 452, 13 S. Ct. 110. Courts have further identified a wide range of recreational uses, including bathing, swimming, boating, and scenic viewing, as protected trust purposes. *See, e.g., Neptune City v. Avon-By-The-Sea*, 294 A.2d 47, 54–55 (N.J. 1972).

As a logical extension from the increasing number of public trust uses of waters in their natural state, courts have recognized the distinct public interest in resource protection. As explained by the California Supreme Court:

> [O]ne of the most important public uses of the tidelands—a use encompassed within the tidelands trust—*is the preservation of those lands in their natural state,* so that they may serve as ecological units for scientific study, as open space, and as environments which provide food and habitat for birds and marine life, and which favorably affect the scenery and climate of the area.

National Audubon Society v. Superior Court of Alpine County, 658 P.2d 709, 719 (Cal. 1983) (quoting *Marks v. Whitney*, 491 P.2d 374, 380 (Cal. 1971)) (emphasis added)....

This court has likewise acknowledged resource protection, with its numerous derivative public uses, benefits, and values, as an important underlying purpose of the reserved water resources trust. *See Robinson*, 658 P.2d at 310–11 (upholding the public interest in the "purity and flow," "continued existence," and "preservation" of the waters of the state). The people of our state have validated resource "protection" by express constitutional decree. *See* Haw. Const. art. XI, §§ 1, 7. We thus hold that the maintenance of waters in their natural state constitutes a distinct "use" under the water resources trust. This disposes of any portrayal of retention of waters in their natural state as "waste." *See Reppun*, 656 P.2d at 76 n.20 (citing article XI, section 1 as an acknowledgment of the public interest in "a free-flowing stream for its own sake").

Whether under riparian or prior appropriation systems, common law or statute, states have uniformly recognized domestic uses, particularly drinking, as among the highest uses of water resources. *See, e.g.,* Restatement (Second) of Torts § 850A cmt. c (1979) [hereinafter Restatement (Second)] (preference for domestic, or "natural," uses under riparian law); Cal. Water Code § 1254 (West 1971) ("domestic use is the highest use"); Minn. Stat. Ann. § 103G.261(a)(1) (West 1997) (domestic use given first priority). This jurisdiction presents no exception. In granting individuals fee simple title to land in the Kuleana Act, the kingdom expressly guaranteed: "The people shall ... have a right to drinking water, and running water...." Enactment of Further Principles of 1850 § 7, Laws of 1850 at 202 (codified at HRS § 7-1 (1993)). *See also McBryde Sugar Co. v. Robinson*, 504 P.2d 1330, 1341–44 (Haw. 1973) (comparing section 7 of the Kuleana Act with authority in other jurisdictions recognizing riparian rights to water for domestic uses); *Carter v. Territory*, 24 Haw. 47, 66 (1917) (granting priority to domestic use based on riparian principles and section 7 of the Kuleana Act). And although this provision and others, including the reservation of sovereign prerogatives, evidently originated out of concern for the rights of native tenants in particular, we have no doubt that they apply today, in a broader sense, to the vital domestic uses of the general public. Accordingly, we recognize domestic water use as a purpose of the state water resources trust. *Cf. Clifton v. Passaic Valley Water Comm'n*, 539 A.2d 760, 765 (N.J. Super. Ct. Law Div. 1987) (holding that the public trust "applies with equal impact upon the control of drinking water reserves").

In acknowledging the general public's need for water, however, we do not lose sight of the trust's "original intent." As noted above, review of the early law of the kingdom reveals the specific objective of preserving the rights of native tenants during the transition to a western system of private property. Before the Mahele, the law "Respecting Water for Irrigation" assured native tenants "their equal proportion" of water. Subsequently, the aforementioned Kuleana Act provision ensured tenants' rights to essential incidents of land beyond their own kuleana, including water, in recognition that "a little bit of land even with allodial title, if they be cut off from all other privileges would be of very little value," 3B Privy Council Records 713 (1850). *See also Reppun*, 656 P.2d at 69–70 (analogizing riparian rights under section 7 of the Kuleana Act to water rights of Indian reservations in *Winters v. United States*, 207 U.S. 564, (1908)); *cf. Peck v. Bailey*, 8 Haw. 658, 661 (1867) (recognizing "appurtenant rights" to water based on "immemorial usage"). In line with this history and our prior precedent, *See Kalipi v. Hawaiian Trust Co.*, 656 P.2d 745 (Haw. 1982); *Public Access Shoreline Hawai'i v. Hawai'i Planning Comm'n*, 903 P.2d 1246, 1259–68 (Haw. 1995), *cert. denied*, 517 U.S. 1163 (1996), and constitutional mandate, *See* Haw. Const. art. XII, §7, we continue to uphold the exercise of Native Hawaiian and traditional and customary rights as a public trust purpose.

[Land Use Research Foundation (LURF)] asserts that the public trust in Hawai'i encompasses private use of resources for "economic development," citing, *inter alia*, *Territory v. Liliuokalani*, 14 Haw. 88 (1902) (grants of tidal lands to private individuals), *Haalelea v. Montgomery*, 2 Haw. 62 (1858) (konohiki fishing rights), and the Admissions Act, Act of Mar. 18, 1959, Pub. L. 83-3, 73 Stat. 4, §5(f) (designating "development of farm and home ownership" as one of the purposes of the state ceded lands trust). While these examples generally demonstrate that the public trust may allow grants of private interests in trust resources under certain circumstances, they in no way establish private commercial use as among the public purposes *protected* by the trust.

Although its purpose has evolved over time, the public trust has never been understood to safeguard rights of exclusive use for private commercial gain. Such an interpretation, indeed, eviscerates the trust's basic purpose of reserving the resource for use and access by the general public without preference or restriction....

                                    * * *

We hold that, while the state water resources trust acknowledges that private use for "economic development" may produce important public benefits and that such benefits must figure into any balancing of competing interests in water, it stops short of embracing private commercial use as a protected "trust purpose." We thus eschew LURF's view of the trust, in which the "'public interest' advanced by the trust is the sum of competing private interests" and the "rhetorical distinction between 'public trust' and 'private gain' is a false dichotomy." To the contrary, if the public trust is to retain any meaning and effect, it must recognize enduring public rights in trust resources separate from, and superior to, the prevailing private interests in the resources at any given time. *See Robinson*, 658 P.2d at 312 ("[U]nderlying every private diversion and application there is, as there always has been, a superior public interest in this natural bounty.").

ii. Powers and Duties of the State under the Trust

This court has described the public trust relating to water resources as the authority and duty "to maintain the *purity and flow* of our waters for future generations *and* to assure that the waters of our land are put to *reasonable and beneficial uses*." *Id.* at 310 (emphases added). Similarly, article XI, section 1 of the Hawai'i Constitution requires the state both to "protect" natural resources *and* to promote their "use and development." The state water resources trust thus embodies a dual mandate of 1) protection and 2) maximum reasonable and beneficial use.

The mandate of "protection" coincides with the traditional notion of the public trust developed with respect to navigable and tidal waters. As commonly understood, the trust protects public waters and submerged lands against irrevocable transfer to private parties, see, e.g., *Illinois Central*, 146 U.S. 387 (1892), or "substantial impairment," whether for private or public purposes....

In this jurisdiction, the water resources trust also encompasses a duty to promote the reasonable and beneficial use of water resources in order to maximize their social and economic benefits to the people of this state. Post-Mahele water rights decisions ignored this duty, treating public water resources as a commodity reducible to absolute private ownership, such that "no limitation ... existed or was supposed to exist to [the owner's] power to use the ... waters as he saw fit," *Hawaiian Commercial & Sugar Co. v. Wailuku Sugar Co.*, 15 Haw. 675, 680 (1904). *See Reppun*, 656 P.2d at 63–69. Based on founding principles of the ancient Hawaiian system and present necessity, this court subsequently reasserted the dormant public interest in the equitable and maximum beneficial allocation of water resources.

* * *

[W]e seek to define the trust's essential parameters in light of this state's legal and practical requirements and its historical and present circumstances. To this end, we hold that the state water resources trust embodies the following fundamental principles:

Under the public trust, the state has both the authority and duty to preserve the rights of present and future generations in the waters of the state. *See Robinson*, 658 P.2d at 310; *see also State v. Central Vt. Ry.*, 571 A.2d 1128, 1132 (Vt. 1989) ("The state's power to supervise trust property in perpetuity is coupled with the ineluctable duty to exercise this power."), *cert. denied*, 495 U.S. 931 (1990). The continuing authority of the state over its water resources precludes any grant or assertion of vested rights to use water to the detriment of public trust purposes. *See Robinson*, 658 P.2d at 312; *see also National Audubon*, 658 P.2d at 727; *Kootenai*, 671 P.2d at 1094 ("The public trust doctrine takes precedent even over vested water rights."); *cf. Karam v. Department of Envtl. Protection*, 705 A.2d 1221, 1228 (N.J. Super. Ct. App. Div. 1998) ("The sovereign never waives its right to regulate the use of public trust property."), *aff'd*, 157 N.J. 187, 723 A.2d 943, cert. denied, 528 U.S. 814 (1999). This authority empowers the state to revisit prior diversions and allocations, even those made with due consideration of their effect on the public trust. *See National Audubon*, 658 P.2d at 728.

The state also bears an "affirmative *duty* to take the public trust into account in the planning and allocation of water resources, and to protect public trust uses whenever feasible[12]." *Id.* (emphasis added). Preliminarily, we note that this duty may not readily translate into substantive results. The public has a definite interest in the development and use of water resources for various reasonable and beneficial public and private offstream purposes, including agriculture, *see generally* Haw. Const. art. XI, § 3. Therefore, apart from the question of historical practice, reason and necessity dictate that the public trust may have to accommodate offstream diversions inconsistent with the mandate of protection, to the unavoidable impairment of public instream uses and values. See *National Audubon*, 658 P.2d at 727. As discussed above, by conditioning use and development on resource "conservation," article XI, section 1 does not preclude offstream use, but merely requires that all uses, offstream or instream, public or private, promote the best economic and social interests of the people of this state. In the words of another court, "the result ... is a controlled development of resources rather than no development."

---

12. Read narrowly, the term "feasible" could mean "capable of achievement," apart from any balancing of benefits and costs. *See Industrial Union Dept., AFL-CIO v. American Petroleum Inst.*, 448 U.S. 607, 718–19, (1980) (Marshall, J., dissenting). The *National Audubon* court apparently did not use "feasible" in this strict sense, and neither do we in this case.

Payne v. Kassab, 312 A.2d 86, 94 (Pa. Cmwlth. Ct. 1973), *aff'd*, 323 A.2d 407 (1974), *aff'd*, 361 A.2d 263 (Pa. 1976).

We have indicated a preference for accommodating both instream and offstream uses where feasible. *See Reppun*, 656 P.2d at 71–72, 73–78 & n.20 (allowing ground water diversions short of "actual harm" to surface uses); *Robinson*, 658 P.2d at 310 (describing the trust as "authority to assure the continued existence and beneficial application of the resource for the common good" (emphasis added)). In times of greater scarcity, however, the state will confront difficult choices that may not lend themselves to formulaic solutions. Given the diverse and not necessarily complementary range of water uses, even among public trust uses alone, we consider it neither feasible nor prudent to designate absolute priorities between broad categories of uses under the water resources trust. Contrary to the Commission's conclusion that the trust establishes resource protection as "a categorical imperative and the precondition to all subsequent considerations," we hold that the Commission inevitably must weigh competing public and private water uses on a case-by-case basis, according to any appropriate standards provided by law. *See Robinson*, 658 P.2d at 312; *see also Save Ourselves v. Louisiana Environmental Control Comm'n*, 452 So.2d 1152, 1152 (La. 1984) (reading the constitution to establish a "rule of reasonableness" requiring the balancing of environmental costs and benefits against economic, social, and other factors).

Having recognized the necessity of a balancing process, we do not suggest that the states public trust duties amount to nothing more than a restatement of its prerogatives, *see Robinson*, 658 P.2d at 310 n.31, nor do we ascribe to the constitutional framers the intent to enact laws devoid of any real substance and effect. Rather, we observe that the constitutional requirements of "protection" and "conservation," the historical and continuing understanding of the trust as a guarantee of public rights, and the common reality of the "zero-sum" game between competing water uses demand that any balancing between public and private purposes begin with a presumption in favor of public use, access, and enjoyment. *See, e.g., State v. Zimring*, 566 P.2d 725, 735 (Haw. 1977) ("The State as trustee has the duty to protect and maintain the trust [resource] and regulate its use. Presumptively, this duty is to be implemented by devoting the [resource] to actual public uses, e.g., recreation."). Thus, insofar as the public trust, by nature and definition, establishes use consistent with trust purposes as the norm or "default" condition, we affirm the Commission's conclusion that it effectively prescribes a "higher level of scrutiny" for private commercial uses such as those proposed in this case.[13] In practical terms, this means that the burden ultimately lies with those seeking or approving such uses to justify them in light of the purposes protected by the trust.

The constitution designates the Commission as the primary guardian of public rights under the trust. Haw. Const. art. XI, section 7. As such, the Commission must not relegate itself to the role of a mere "umpire passively calling balls and strikes for adversaries appearing before it," but instead must take the initiative in considering, protecting, and advancing public rights in the resource at every stage of the planning and decisionmak-

---

13. It is widely understood that the public trust assigns no priorities or presumptions in the balancing of public trust purposes. *See National Audubon*, 658 P.2d at 723; Jan S. Stevens, *The Public Trust: A Sovereign's Ancient Prerogative Becomes the People's Environmental Right*, 14 U.C. Davis L. Rev. 195, 223–225 (1980). Such balancing, nevertheless, must be reasonable, *see, e.g., State v. Public Serv. Comm'n*, 81 N.W.2d at 73–74 (noting that no one public use would be destroyed or greatly impaired and that the benefit to public use outweighed the harm), and must conform to article XI, section 1's mandate of "conservation." The Commission, in other words, must still ensure that all trust purposes are protected to the extent feasible.

ing process. Specifically, the public trust compels the state duly to consider the cumulative impact of existing and proposed diversions on trust purposes and to implement reasonable measures to mitigate this impact, including the use of alternative sources. The trust also requires planning and decisionmaking from a global, long-term perspective. In sum, the state may compromise public rights in the resource pursuant only to a decision made with a level of openness, diligence, and foresight commensurate with the high priority these rights command under the laws of our state.

c. Standard of Review under the Trust

Finally, the special public interests in trust resources demand that this court observe certain qualifications of its standard of review. As in other cases, agency decisions affecting public trust resources carry a presumption of validity....

The public trust, however, is a state constitutional doctrine. As with other state constitutional guarantees, the ultimate authority to interpret and defend the public trust in Hawai'i rests with the courts of this state. *See State v. Quitog*, 85 938 P.2d 559, 561 n.3 (1997) (recognizing the Hawai'i Supreme Court as the "ultimate judicial tribunal with final, unreviewable authority to interpret and enforce the Hawai'i Constitution").

> Judicial review of public trust dispensations complements the concept of a public trust.... Just as private trustees are judicially accountable to their beneficiaries for dispositions of the res, so the legislative and executive branches are judicially accountable for the dispositions of the public trust. The beneficiaries of the public trust are not just present generations but those to come. The check and balance of judicial review provides a level of protection against improvident dissipation of an irreplaceable res.

Arizona Cent. for Law in Pub. Interest v. Hassell, 837 P.2d 158, 168–69 (Ariz. App. 1991) (brackets and citation omitted). Nevertheless, as the Idaho Supreme Court elaborated:

> This is not to say that this court will supplant its judgment for that of the legislature or agency. However, it does mean that this court will take a "*close look*" at the action to determine if it complies with the public trust doctrine and it will not act merely as a rubber stamp for agency or legislative action.

Kootenai, 671 P.2d at 1092 (emphasis added).

* * *

The Commission made numerous findings regarding the current lack of scientific knowledge and the inability of the experts to quantify the correlation between stream flows and environmental benefits. We decline to substitute our judgment for the Commission's concerning its ultimate ruling that there was insufficient evidence to support a more conclusive assessment of instream flow requirements. Such a mixed determination of law and fact lies within the Commission's designated expertise and sound discretion, and the evidence in this case does not demonstrate it to be clearly erroneous. *See Ko'olau Agricultural Co. v. Commission on Water Resource Management*, 927 P.2d 1367, 1376 (Haw. 1996) (according deference to the Commission's expertise in the designation of water management areas); *Camara v. Agsalud*, 685 P.2d 794, 797 (Haw. 1984) ("In deference to the administrative agency's expertise and experience in its particular field, the courts should not substitute their own judgment for that of the administrative agency where mixed questions of fact and law are presented.").

We must emphasize, however, that the Commission's present disposition largely defeats the purpose of the instream use protection scheme set forth in HRS § 174C-71. Every concession to immediate offstream demands made by the Commission increases the risk of unwarranted impairment of instream values, ad hoc planning, and arbitrary distribution. A number of parties object to the Commission's conclusion that:

> Where scientific evidence is preliminary and not yet conclusive regarding the management of fresh water resources which are part of the public trust, it is prudent to adopt "*precautionary principles*" in protecting the resource. That is, where there are present or potential threats of serious damage, lack of full scientific certainty should not be a basis for postponing effective measures to prevent environmental degradation. "Awaiting for certainty will often allow for only reactive, not preventive, regulatory action." *Ethyl Corp. v. EPA*, 541 F.2d 1, 25, 5–29 (D.C. Cir. 1976), *cert. denied*, 426 U.S. 941 (1976). In addition, where uncertainty exists, a trustee's duty to protect the resource mitigates in favor of choosing presumptions that also protect the resource. *Lead Indus. Ass'n v. EPA*, 647 F.2d 1130, 1152–56 (D.C. Cir. 1976), *cert. denied*, 449 U.S. 1042 (1980).

Commission on Water Resource Management, Conclusions of Law 33 (Dec. 24, 1997) (emphasis added). The "precautionary principle" appears in diverse forms throughout the field of environmental law. *See, e.g., Ethyl Corp.*, 541 F.2d at 20–29;[14] *Lead Industries*, 647 F.2d at 1154–55 (relying on the statutory "margin of safety" requirement in rejecting argument that agency could only authorize standards designed to protect "clearly harmful health effects"); *Les v. Reilly*, 968 F.2d 985 (9th Cir. 1992) (confirming that agency has no discretion under statute to permit use of carcinogenic food additives, regardless of degree of risk), cert. denied, 507 U.S. 950 (1993); *see generally* Gregory D. Fullem, Comment, *The Precautionary Principle: Environmental Protection in the Face of Scientific Uncertainty*, 31 Willamette L. Rev. 495 (1995). As with any general principle, its meaning must vary according to the situation and can only develop over time. In this case, we believe the Commission describes the principle in its quintessential form: at minimum, the absence of firm scientific proof should not tie the Commission's hands in adopting reasonable measures designed to further the public interest.

So defined, the precautionary principle simply restates the Commission's duties under the constitution and Code. Indeed, the lack of full scientific certainty does not extinguish the presumption in favor of public trust purposes or vitiate the Commission's affirmative duty to protect such purposes wherever feasible. Nor does present inability to fulfill the instream use protection framework render the statute's directives any less mandatory. In requiring the Commission to establish instream flow standards at an early planning stage, the Code contemplates the designation of the standards based not only on scientifically proven facts, but also on future predictions, generalized assumptions, and policy judgments. Neither the constitution nor Code, therefore, constrains the Commission to wait for full scientific certainty in fulfilling its duty towards the public interest in minimum instream flows.

* * *

---

14. Judge J. Skelly Wright's majority opinion [from *Ethyl Corp.*] ...:
Questions involving the environment are particularly prone to uncertainty.... *Yet the statutes — and common sense — demand regulatory action to prevent harm*, even if the regulator is less than certain that harm is otherwise inevitable. Undoubtedly, certainty is the scientific ideal — to the extent that even science can be certain of its truth.... *Awaiting certainty[, however,] will often allow for only reactive, not preventative, regulation.* Petitioners suggest that anything less than certainty, that any speculation, is irresponsible. But when statutes seek to avoid environmental catastrophe, can preventative, albeit uncertain, decisions legitimately be so labeled?
Id. at 24–25 (citation and footnote omitted) (emphasis added).

... Thus, pursuant to its duties as trustee, and in the interest of precaution, the Commission should consider providing reasonable "margins of safety" for instream trust purposes when establishing instream flow standards. The Commission, however, should not concern itself with allocations to a "buffer" at the outset. Rather, the Commission should incorporate any allowances for scientific uncertainty into its initial determination of the minimum standard. Any flows in excess of this standard shall remain in the stream until permitted and actually needed for offstream use, in keeping with the policy against waste and in recognition that the standard merely states an absolute minimum required under any circumstances. These unallocated flows, however, will not constitute a distinct category or quantity, but will fluctuate according to variations in supply and demand.

* * *

Notes

1. *Waiahole Ditch* is a landmark public trust opinion that has had an influential effect on the modern development of public trust law. For full discussion, see Symposium, *Managing Hawaii's Public Trust Doctrine*, 24 U. Hawai'i L. Rev. 1 (2001). The case arose out of a background of land tenure unique to Hawai'i. The Mahele (also called the Great Mahele), mentioned by the court, was a land redistribution scheme proposed by King Kamehameha III in the 1830s and enacted in 1848. Guided by foreign advisors, the king divided lands that had formerly been held in common and administered by chiefs and their konohiki, or overseers. The Mahele allocated 23 percent of land in the Islands to the king (called crown lands); 40 percent to konohiki lands, divided among 245 chiefs; and 37 percent to government lands, awarded to commoners who worked the land as active tenants. An appointed Land Commission and Court of Claims administered the land division. The Mahele was followed in 1850 by the Kuleana Act, which established fee simple ownership of land. Historical land tenants were required to document their claims to specific parcels in order to gain permanent title. Once granted, a kuleana plot was entirely independent of the traditional ahupua'a tract in which it was situated, and it could also be sold to parties with no historical ties to the area.

2. In an ensuing decision, *In re Water Use Permit Applications*, 93 P.3d 643 (Haw. 2004), after the state water commission set a new interim instream flow standard and issued water permits, including a permit for system losses, the Hawai'i Supreme Court reversed, ruling that it would not merely rubberstamp the decision of the agency but would "take a close look" to determine if its decision complied with the public trust doctrine. The court also indicated that the commission could only compromise public trust rights with "openness, diligence, and foresight commensurate with the high priority these rights command under law[]...." The court ruled that the Commission failed to make sufficient findings based on evidence in the record to support its ruling, faulting the Commission's decision to set the instream flow standard at half the historic flow because the evidence did not suggest that instream values would be protected "to the extent practicable." The court ordered the Commission to reconsider the amount of water the windward streams need to support native stream life and community uses. In a later decision, *In re Water Use Permit Applications*, 147 P.3d 836 (Haw. 2006), the Hawai'i Supreme Court, interpreting a 2004 statute, directed further appeals to be filed initially in the intermediate appellate court.

3. Unlike the *Mono Lake* decision, which declared the source of the California public trust doctrine to be in the common law, the Hawai'i Supreme Court found the doctrine embedded in the state's constitution. Moreover, in a non-excerpted portion of the opin-

ion, the court discussed the origin of the trust as "an inherent attribute of sovereign authority that the government ought not, and ergo, … cannot surrender." *Waiahole Ditch*, 9 P.3d at 443 (quotation omitted). Did the source of the public trust doctrine influence its judicial articulation? Like the California Supreme Court's approach in the *Mono Lake* case, the *Waiahole Ditch* court clearly established the public trust as a source of obligation independent of statutory law embodied in the State Water Code (referred to as "the Code" below), stating:

> Other state courts, without the benefit of such constitutional provisions, have decided that the public trust doctrine exists independently of any statutory protections supplied by the legislature.…
>
> The Code and its implementing agency, the Commission, do not override the public trust doctrine or render it superfluous. Even with the enactment and any future development of the Code, the doctrine continues to inform the Code's interpretation, define its permissible 'outer limits,' and justify its existence. To this end, although we regard the public trust and Code as sharing similar core principles, we hold that the Code does not supplant the protections of the public trust doctrine.

Id. at 444–45 (citations omitted).

4. The *Waiahole Ditch* court also embraced (as did the California Supreme Court) the notion that members of the public have standing to assert the trust against the state. Note the court's description of the judicial relationship to the legislature: "Just as private trustees are judicially accountable to their beneficiaries for dispositions of the res, so the legislative and executive branches are judicially accountable for the dispositions of the public trust." Under this view, could a trust really be a "trust" without the beneficiaries having the capacity to sue their trustees for breach of fiduciary duty? Do states that don't recognize citizen standing to enforce the public trust doctrine fundamentally change the trust construct?

5. The *Waiahole Ditch* decision went beyond *Mono Lake* by unlinking the scope of the public trust doctrine to navigable waters and applying the doctrine to groundwater diversions. Notice the court's statement, "we see little sense in adhering to artificial distinctions" between groundwater and surface water. Why do so many other courts adhere to such distinctions? In California, waters that do not affect state navigable waters are not subject to the trust doctrine. *Golden Feather Community Ass'n v. Thermalito Irrigation Dist.*, 257 Cal. Rptr. 836 (Cal. Ct. App. 1989). Do you think that, as groundwater supplies diminish further in many communities (or become contaminated), this resource too will come into the fold of public trust protection to meet public needs? Vermont applies its public trust doctrine to groundwater, Vt. Stat. Ann. tit 10, § 1390 (5) (West 2009), as interpreted by the Vermont Environmental Court, in *In re Omya Solid Waste Facility Final Certification*, Docket No. 96-6-10 Vtec, Decision and Order on Motion for Summary Judgment (Feb. 28, 2011). *See generally* Jack Tuholske, *Trusting the Public Trust: Application of the Public Trust Doctrine to Groundwater Resources*, 9 Vt. J. Envtl. L. 189 (2009) (discussing the doctrine's extension to groundwater in other states). We consider groundwater as part of the public trust "frontier" in chapter 12 (pp. 412–18); we take up trust protection for drinking water later in this chapter.

6. The Hawai'i Supreme Court took care to clearly set forth the purposes of the public trust, as factors to guide trustees in management decisions. The court adopted the *Mono Lake* court's vision of the public trust doctrine as evolving to embrace changing public values and needs, meaning that its scope and purposes of the Hawaiian public

trust are not tethered to traditional notions of navigable waters. The trust purposes listed by the court include: 1) traditional uses of fishing, navigation, and commerce; 2) an expanded set of recreational and scenic public uses (as recognized by other courts); 3) ecological protection of waters in their natural state (which justifies decisions to keep water instream); 4) domestic water use (with particular emphasis on drinking water supplies); and 5) exercise of Native Hawaiian traditional and customary rights. The court framed its iteration of purposes by emphasizing (as have other courts) that public trust purposes evolve over time.

Diversionary interests argued that one of the purposes of the public trust was to promote "economic development," but the court rejected it outright, stating, "While ... the public trust may allow grants of private interests in trust resources under certain circumstances, they in no way establish private commercial use as among the public purposes *protected* by the trust." The court emphasized that "enduring public rights in trust resources [are] separate from, and superior to, the prevailing private interests in the resources at any given time."

Private permit applicants typically argue that their proposed projects will bring jobs to a community and increase the tax base, thereby providing public benefit. But in the *Mono Lake* case, the California Supreme Court said that basing public trust decisions on claims of general economic benefit would "in practical effect ... impose no restrictions on the state's ability to allocate trust property." *National Audubon Society*, 658 P.2d at 723. Drawing from its tidelands trust precedent, the court declared, "no one could contend that the state could grant tidelands free of the trust merely because the grant served some public purpose, such as increasing tax revenues, or because the grantee might put the property to a commercial use." *Id.* at 24. Similarly, the Hawai'i Supreme Court in *Waiahole Ditch* subjected private uses to a "higher level of scrutiny" and stated that "[t]he burden ultimately lies with those seeking or approving such uses to justify them in light of the purposes protected by the trust."

7. Note that the Hawai'i Supreme Court articulated the fiduciary obligation more precisely than did the California Supreme Court in the *Mono Lake* case, listing the following specific duties (framed by the purposes of the trust elaborated above): 1) "promote the reasonable and beneficial use of water resources in order to maximize their social and economic benefits to the people of this state"; 2) "preserve the rights of present and future generations in the waters of the state"; 3) fulfill the "affirmative duty to take the public trust into account in the planning and allocation of water resources, and to protect public trust uses whenever feasible." (citing *National Audubon*, 658 P.2d at 728, among other cases).

Of course, as the court recognized, water appropriations represent a "zero-sum" game between competing water uses, and the court stops short of creating a firm list of priorities for water allocations. However, the court clearly called for a fiduciary process of balancing competing interests with the public trust in mind. It stated, "Having recognized the necessity of a balancing process ... any balancing between public and private purposes [must] begin with a presumption in favor of public use, access, and enjoyment." In such a balancing process, should the agencies look at the benefit to the public associated with the water withdrawal, the alternatives to consumptive withdrawals, the effects on the waterway, and whether such effects are temporary or result in irrevocable loss to future generations? Did the court's emphasis on the need for supplying domestic and drinking water supplies indicate the need to rank public benefits (served by competing water uses) in terms of public necessity? Could a trustee rationally "maximize" the social and economic benefits to the beneficiaries (both present and future) while ignoring these factors? Reflecting on the actual circumstances of the *Waiahole Ditch* case, how do withdrawals for golf courses rank against these factors?

The court explained that instream and offstream uses are competing uses that the commission must balance when allocating water resources: "[B]y conditioning use and development on resource 'conservation,' article XI, section 1 [of the Hawaiian constitution] does not preclude offstream use, but merely requires that all uses, offstream or instream, public or private, promote the best economic and social interests of the people of this state." Similarly, the Montana Supreme Court in *Adjudication of the Existing Rights to Use of all Water in the Missouri River Drainage Area*, 55 P.3d 396 (Mont. 2002), concluded that the state could assert instream claims to water rights to ensure the quantity of water remaining instream was adequate for public use. The court relied on the public trust doctrine and held "that Montana recognized fish, wildlife and recreation uses as beneficial and that valid instream and inlake appropriations of water existed in Montana prior to [the enactment of Montana's instream flow law in 1973] where the intended beneficial use did not require diversion...." *Id.* at 407.

8. Notice that the Hawai'i Supreme Court incorporated the so-called "precautionary principle" into the state's public trust doctrine. This principle instructs that the burden of scientific proof should not be placed on the public challenging the state's allocation of trust resources. The principle parallels a steadfast rule in the private trust realm requiring a trustee to exercise reasonable caution in managing the trust assets. In the case of a financial *res*, for example, a trustee must avoid investment in "speculative or hazardous ventures" and new ventures of which he has little knowledge.[15]

Application of the precautionary principle led the court to instruct the water commission to establish instream flow standards wherever feasible, "based not only on scientifically proven facts, but also future predictions, generalized assumptions, and policy judgments" without waiting for scientific certainty. Erroneous applications of the burden of proof have led to other successful public trust doctrine challenges in Hawai'i. *See In re Wai'ola O Moloka'i*, 83 P.3d 664 (Haw. 2004) (finding a trust violation to native Hawaiians in groundwater application on the island of Moloka'i, but allowing the use of groundwater on non-overlying land under the Hawaiian water code); *In re Kukui*, 174 P.3d 320 (Haw. 2007) (finding a trust violation in granting a groundwater permit on Moloka'i for failing to consider the practical availability of alternative water sources).

Consider how revolutionary the precautionary principle would be if broadly applied to environmental law through the trust doctrine. Would it not put a halt to chemical and pesticide registrations that were not proven safe? How would the principle affect government's duty in climate crisis? The United Nations Framework Convention on Climate Change (to which the United States is a party) states: "The Parties should take precautionary measures to anticipate, prevent or minimize the causes of climate change and mitigate its adverse effects. Where there are threats of serious or irreversible damage, lack of full scientific certainty should not be used as a reason for postponing such measures...." United Nations Framework Convention on Climate Change, art. 3 (Mar. 21, 1994). For a full discussion of the precautionary approach in environmental law, *see* PRECAUTIONARY TOOLS FOR RESHAPING ENVIRONMENTAL POLICY (Nancy J. Myers & Carolyn Raffensperger eds., 2006).

9. The Hawai'i system of water rights incorporates obligations unique to native Hawaiians. In other states, tribes have recognized property rights to water as well. Indian reser-

---

15. *See In re Hall*, 164 N.Y. 196, 199, 200 (1900); *see also* GEORGE BOGERT, THE LAW OF TRUSTS AND TRUSTEES § 102, at 366–67 (2d ed. 1980).

vations generally carry an implied water right, and some tribes have an instream water right to support treaty fisheries. *See United States v. Adair*, 723 F.2d 1394, 1414 (9th Cir. 1984). These rights are held in trust for the tribes by the federal government, but the Indian trust obligation is distinct from the public trust duty, as the tribes rather than the general public are the beneficiaries of the Indian trust. *See Dep't of Interior v. Klamath Water Users Protective Ass'n*, 532 U.S. 1, 11 (2001) (describing, in a case involving Klamath Tribe's water rights, "the United States as trustee, the Indian tribes ... as beneficiaries, and the property and natural resources managed by the United States as the trust corpus"). Nevertheless, many principles of protection surface in both trust contexts. *See Fort Mojave Indian Tribe v. United States*, 23 Cl. Ct. 417, 426 (1991), *aff'd* 64 F.3d 677 (Fed. Cir. 1995) (stating, in a case involving Indian water rights, "[w]here a trust relationship exists, 'the trustee has a duty to protect the trust property against damage or destruction. He is obligated to the beneficiary to do all acts necessary for the preservation of the trust res which would be performed by a reasonably prudent man employing his own like property for purposes similar to those of the trust'") (citing George Bogert, The Law of Trusts and Trustees § 582 (2d ed. 1980)).

10. The public trust offers citizens a vocabulary quite different from highly technical statutory regimes to use in advocating for protection of natural resources. Two attorneys in the Hawai'i water litigation commented on this aspect of the trust claim, noting that the citizens coalition took its message beyond the courts to the public arena: "The trust has given the [coalition] a cause with a powerful message: they are fighting not for 'their' water, but for water belonging to all, including generations unborn." The attorneys reported that the coalition "fully internalized and frequently deployed" trust terminology (words such as trustee, beneficiaries, fiduciary duty, and present and future generations), and observed, "The layperson or legislator may not know or care about an 'interim flow standard,' but can appreciate the certain gravity carried by the words 'public trust.'" By invoking the public trust in the policy realm along with litigation, the trust found its way into the "consciousness and working vocabulary" of public officials, the press, and the broader public. D. Kapua'ala Sproat & Isaac H. Moriwake, *Ke Kalo Pa'a O Waiahole: Use of the Public Trust as a Tool for Environmental Advocacy, in* Creative Common Law Strategies for Protecting the Environment 247, 280–81 (Clifford Rechtschaffen & Denise Antolini eds., 2007). Is it important to frame environmental claims in such a way that the public and legislators find compelling? Should environmental advocates worry about how the public and legislators respond to the cases they bring in court? Do trust claims hold an advantage in this regard, as observed by the Hawai'i public interest attorneys?

11. Despite this pathbreaking opinion from the Hawai'i Supreme Court, six years later (in the 13th year of litigation), the state water commission seemingly continued a business-as-usual approach. The summary below was prepared by one of the environmental groups advocating for instream flows. As you sort through the details of the commission's decision, ask whether the decision meets the fiduciary standards set forth in the court's opinion.

Hawai'i Water Commission Splits Over Waiahole Water Case

Earthjustice, July 14, 2006 (press release)

Honolulu, HI—The Hawai'i State Commission on Water Resource Management issued a split decision in the latest development in the landmark water rights litigation over the stream flows diverted by the Waiahole Ditch System on O'ahu. Four members of the Commission, led by Commissioner Lawrence Milke, voted to largely maintain the allocations the Commission approved in its original 1997 decision, including extensive diversions for leeward uses, such as corporate agriculture and golf courses. However, two Commissioners—Peter Young, Commission Chair and Director of the state Department of Land and Natural Resources, and Chiyome Fukino, state Department of Health Director—issued a forceful dissent criticizing the majority for failing to give more protection to windward stream resources and uses.

Specifically, the dissent challenged the majority's refusal to include almost 2.5 million gallons a day ("mgd") of unallocated water in the instream flow standard, which is the minimum flow necessary to support instream uses such as ecological protection, Hawaiian practices, recreation, and scenic values. The dissent criticized the majority for treating this water "as some commodity awaiting future permitting to some offstream use." Quoting the Hawai'i Supreme Court's decisions from earlier phases of this case, the dissent urged that this "unpermitted" water be included in the instream flow standard to provide "margins of safety under our public trust duties and the precautionary principle."

Young and Fukino also objected to the issuance of a water use permit to the now-defunct golf course Pus u Makakilo Inc. ("PMI"), which has not used any water from the Waiahole Ditch in nearly two years. The dissent criticized the majority for ignoring "changed circumstances," including "PMI's razing of the golf clubhouse, PMI's public statement that the property is unsuitable for use as a golf course, and the contrast between usage under PMI's interim permit and its apparent need."

This decision is the Commission's third attempt to resolve this case after twice being reversed by the Hawai'i Supreme Court for not adequately protecting windward streams. The case is now in its 13th year, but has developed an additional subplot of the Commission defending its original 1997 allocation in the face of the Court's repeated reversals. The author of the majority decision, Commissioner Milke, participated in the original Commission hearings, then served as the Hearing Officer in the second and third round of hearings. He also drafted the Commission's second decision in 2001, after which he published a book on Hawai'i water law defending the decision, which was on appeal at that time.

The dissent marks the first time that the Commission has split over any decision in this case. Such controversy has rarely, if ever, occurred on the Commission, which over the years has drawn fire from public trust advocates as well as the Hawai'i Supreme Court for its lack of initiative and vision. Now, two Commissioners have joined the chorus of criticism.

"We're disappointed that after 13 years and two appeals to the Hawai'i Supreme Court, a majority of the Water Commission still refuses to give our streams the protection that the law requires," said Waiahole taro farmer Charlie Reppun. "Regrettably, the problem appears to be less about the needs of streams and rural communities and more about the Commission justifying itself against the Court. We're grateful that Chair Young and Commissioner Fukino embrace their public trust duties and the Court's exhortations and seek to fulfill both the letter and spirit of our laws," explained Reppun.

"Our state Water Code mandates that this Commission restore streams where practicable, not treat our public trust resources as convenient reservoirs for speculators who are banking their land for future development," pointed out Earthjustice attorney Kapua Sproat. "This is about far more than the streams and communities affected by the Waiahole Ditch. This is a quality of life issue that will shape Hawai'i's future. Will we have streams and other public trust resources for local people to enjoy? Or will the beauty of our islands and quality of life be lost forever?"

* * *

Yesterday's decision again divided the water between windward streams and leeward users. Out of an annual average flow in the ditch system of 27 mgd, 12 mgd was split between 4 different windward streams: Waiahole, Waianu, Waikane and Kahana. 12.57 mgd was permitted for immediate offstream use in leeward O'ahu. The remaining flow (2.43 mgd) was temporarily restored to the streams, but is available for future agricultural or other off-stream uses.

This decision is notable not just because the Commission again gave more water to leeward users than it restored to windward streams, but also because it essentially rehashed the Commission's 2001 decision. The majority granted a water use permit to every applicant that sought one, including over 2 mgd to the operator of the Waiahole Ditch (Agribusiness Development Corporation) for waste that leaks out of the system, and almost 1 mgd to PMI, a defunct golf course whose club house was torn down, whose own executive conceded that "[t]he area isn't suitable for a golf course" and who hasn't used water from the Waiahole Ditch for nearly two years.

Notes

1. It is not unusual for principles set forth in a judicial decree to be thwarted by the implementing agencies. What institutional factors are to blame for this? Does the problem have to do with the politically-charged nature of water allocation and, more broadly, natural resources management? In the Hawai'i water context, do you suppose developers and golf course owners exert pressure on the agencies behind the scenes, causing principles set forth in a state supreme court judgment to wash downriver when it comes time to make actual allocation decisions?

2. What remedies might be available to supervise recalcitrant agencies and hold them to public trust obligations? In other contexts such as school funding reform, prison reform, and treaty fishing rights disputes, courts maintain on-going jurisdiction over intractable disputes so that they can exercise continued supervision over the agencies. *See, e.g., McCleary v. State*, 269 P.3d 227, 248 (Wash. 2012) (on-going jurisdiction in school funding case); *Coleman v. Schwarzenegger*, 922 F. Supp. 2d 882 (E.D. Cal. & N.D. Cal. 2009) (special judicial panel overseeing prison reform in California and maintaining on-going jurisdiction); *United States v. Oregon*, 302 F. Supp. 899 (D. Or. 1969) (on-going jurisdiction in treaty fishing dispute, now in its fifth decade of court supervision). Although judges may not welcome a direct supervisory role over agencies, it has proved necessary in a variety of settings involving recalcitrant agencies, and courts have many tools at their disposal to effectuate their rulings.

In this sort of "institutional litigation," courts often issue structural injunctions to monitor and control the actions of the agency in implementing the court decree; in this respect, the court assumes quasi-administrative functions. Structural injunctions characteristically set firm benchmarks to rein in the discretion of the implementing agency, and often the court appoints a special master to make sure the agency abides by the legal principles set forth in the decree on remand. Treaty fishing rights litigation in the Pacific Northwest used this judicial approach. In the 1970s, agencies in Washington State refused to implement the decree of a federal district court allocating approximately half of the share of harvestable fish to the tribes. This refusal gave rise to extraordinary judicial involvement that positioned the court as a "fishmaster" over the river for a period of years. *See Puget Sound Gillnetters Ass'n v. United States*, 573 F.2d 1123, 1126 (9th Cir. 1978)

("The state's extraordinary machinations in resisting [Judge Boldt's] decree have forced the district court to take over a large share of the management of the state's fishery in order to enforce its decrees.... [The litigants] offered the court no reasonable choice."), *aff'd Washington v. Wash. State Commercial Passenger Fishing Vessel Ass'n*, 443 U.S. 658, 660, 696 (1979) ("[T]he District Court may assume direct supervision of the fisheries if state recalcitrance or state-law barriers should be continued."); *see also United States v. Washington*, 520 F.2d 676, 693 (9th Cir. 1975) (Burns, J., concurring) ("[T]o affirm [the Boldt opinion] also involves ratification of the role of the district judge as a 'perpetual fishmaster.'"). For commentary, *see* Michael C. Blumm & Brett M. Swift, *The Indian Treaty Piscary Profit and Habitat Protection in the Pacific Northwest: A Property Rights Approach*, 69 U. Colo. L. Rev. 407, 456–57 (1998) (discussing fishmaster role of court in treaty litigation); Mary Christina Wood, *The Tribal Property Right to Wildlife Capital (Part II): Asserting a Sovereign Servitude to Protect Habitat of Imperiled Species*, 25 Vt. L. Rev. 355 (2001) (discussing structural injunctions in context of wildlife habitat cases). On the implementation of treaty fishing rights in the Northwest generally, see MICHAEL C. BLUMM, SACRIFICING THE SALMON: A LEGAL AND POLICY HISTORY OF THE DECLINE OF COLUMBIA BASIN SALMON 69–86, 249–77 (2002).

For scholarship on institutional litigation, see Judith Resnik, *Managerial Judges*, 96 Harv. L. Rev. 374, 424–25 (1982); Theodore Eisenberg & Stephen C. Yeazell, *The Ordinary and the Extraordinary in Institutional Litigation*, 93 Harv. L. Rev. 465 (1980); Michael C. Blumm & Aurora Paulsen, *The Role of the Judge in ESA Implementation: District Judge James Redden and the Columbia Basin Salmon Saga*, 32 Stan. Envtl. L. Rev. 87 (2013).

3. The above excerpt is a press release. Is it written in such a way as to galvanize the public beneficiaries to object to the decision of the Commission? Could you re-write it to draw more upon public trust terminology and reasoning?

4. In 2014, the Hawai'i Supreme Court issued an opinion that further solidified its public trust jurisprudence. In *Kauai Springs, Inc. v. County of Kaua'i*, 324 P.3d 951 (Haw. 2014), a county planning commission denied an application for permits that would allow continued operation of a water bottling facility. The court confirmed that the PTD applied to the planning commission as a subdivision of the state and imposed an affirmative duty on the agency to "take the initiative in considering, protecting, and advancing public rights in the resource at every stage of the planning and decision-making process." *Id.* at 983. The court continued:

> To assist agencies in the application of the public trust doctrine, the court provided a clear iteration of applicable fiduciary standards:
>
> a. The agency's duty and authority is to maintain the purity and flow of our waters for future generations and to assure that the waters of our land are put to reasonable and beneficial use.
>
> b. The agency must determine whether the proposed use is consistent with the trust purposes:
>
> > i. the maintenance of waters in their natural state;
> >
> > ii. the protection of domestic water use;
> >
> > iii. the protection of water in the exercise of Native Hawaiian and traditional and customary rights; and
> >
> > iv. the reservation of water enumerated by the State Water Code.
>
> c. The agency is to apply a presumption in favor of public use, access, enjoyment, and resource protection.

d. The agency should evaluate each proposal for use on a case-by-case basis, recognizing that there can be no vested rights in the use of public water.

e. If the requested use is private or commercial, the agency should apply a high level of scrutiny.

f. The agency should evaluate the proposed use under a "reasonable and beneficial use" standard, which requires examination of the proposed use in relation to other public and private uses.

Applicants have the burden to justify the proposed water use in light of the trust purposes.

a. Permit applicants must demonstrate their actual needs and the propriety of draining water from public streams to satisfy those needs.

b. The applicant must demonstrate the absence of a practicable alternative water source.

c. If there is a reasonable allegation of harm to public trust purposes, then the applicant must demonstrate that there is no harm in fact or that the requested use is nevertheless reasonable and beneficial.

d. If the impact is found to be reasonable and beneficial, the applicant must implement reasonable measures to mitigate the cumulative impact of existing and proposed diversions on trust purposes, if the proposed use is to be approved.

Id. at 984–85. Read the test carefully. How should an agency respond to an applicant whose main argument in favor of the permit is that no evidence yet exists suggesting harm from the proposed use?

———

Increasingly, the public right to access water is framed as a human right protected by the public trust doctrine. The impetus for this characterization arises from a fast-growing movement to privatize crucial water supplies. As Maude Barlow, an internationally known water expert, observed in her book, *Blue Covenant*, "[T]he world is moving toward a corporate-controlled freshwater cartel, with private companies, backed by governments and global institutions, making fundamental decisions about who has access to water and under what conditions."[16]

In an influential article published in *The Nation*, Barlow and co-author Tony Clarke explained that the growing number of "hot stains" on the planet—places where water is increasingly scarce—has created a huge and profitable water industry that treats water as a commodity and seeks privatization of the resource: "Price water, they say in chorus; put it up for sale and let the market determine its future."[17] These transnational corporations, which find backing by huge international institutions such as the World Bank, the International Monetary Fund, and the United Nations, are "aggressively taking over the management of public water services in countries around the world, dramatically raising the price of water to the local residents and profiting especially from the Third World's desperate search for solutions to its water crisis." The corporate water campaign, they pointed out, treats waters as a human "need," not a human "right." The difference between the two is basic, Barlow and Clarke assert: "No one can sell a human right."

16. Maude Barlow, Blue Covenant: The Global Water Crisis and the Coming Battle for the Right to Water 91 (2007).
17. Maude Barlow & Tony Clarke, *Who Owns the Water?*, The Nation, Sept. 2, 2002.

The question of who controls water strikes at the heart of the public trust, a doctrine that fundamentally limits the privatization of crucial resources needed by the public. The following materials explore the threat to drinking water supplies, both in the United States and elsewhere, and suggest a response shaped by the public trust doctrine.

Water Privatization Trends in the United States: Human Rights, National Security, and Public Stewardship

Craig Anthony (Tony) Arnold
33 Wm. & Mary Envtl. L. & Pol'y Rev. 785 (2009)

... The Article [focuses] on water privatization trends in the United States, discuss[ing] three aspects of water privatization in the U.S.: 1) the privatization of public water services, 2) private property rights in water, and 3) water as a consumer commodity. These trends arise in the context of global water privatization trends and the opposition of human rights advocates and environmentalists to private corporate exploitation of water for profit. They arise in the context of the legal and socio-cultural history of private property rights in the United States. They arise in the context of tensions between the private and public nature of water; economic efficiency and social equity; globalization and local control; resource development and resource conservation; and the meaning of water as an economic good and as the ecological, ethical, religious, and social meanings of water.

For example, the water woes of the state of Georgia illustrate the power of water privatization and commodification forces in U.S. society and their deleterious effects. In recent years, Georgia has had at least eleven public water systems operated by private water companies.... Water often had to be boiled due to insufficient water pressure, ran a rusty brown color, and did not even reach many customers for lengthy periods due to backlogged work orders.

The water problems of Atlanta and Georgia have extended far beyond poorly-run municipal systems to problems of water scarcity and conflict. Once considered to be water abundant, the U.S. Southeast now struggles with drought, relentless and growing demand for water, depleting water sources, and persistent conflicts among major water users. Georgia has found itself in water crisis due to legal and political institutions' accommodation of consumer demand for both water and energy produced by water: a growing population particularly in the sprawling Atlanta metropolitan area, recreational users of water, agricultural irrigators, power generators, and industries like pulp and paper mills, textiles, chemical manufacturing facilities, and the mining industry. For example, Georgia's population grew by over 140% between 1950 and 2000, and its agricultural withdrawals from the Apalachicola-Chattahoochee-Flint ("ACF") River System increased by 1320% just between 1970 and 1990.

However, the state and local governments have done little to constrain sprawl, mandate water-conservation techniques in design and development, or manage growth based on sustainable and secure water supplies. In addition, Georgia's statutes regulating riparian rights to water through permits for water allocation have largely exempted agricultural water users, the largest category of water use in the state. Instead, Georgia has attempted to satisfy its diverse and powerful interest groups' water demands by increasing withdrawals from the ACF system—primarily though increased withdrawals from Lake Lanier, to the detriment of its neighbors, Alabama and Florida—and the ecology of the system. Georgia also is seeking to redraw its boundary with Tennessee so that it can obtain rights to water in the Tennessee River, which currently does not cross into Georgia.

The Georgia state government finally adopted the state's first statewide comprehensive water management plan in February 2008 — only after experiencing sustained drought and losing to Alabama and Florida in an action enjoining Georgia's additional withdrawals from Lake Lanier. The Georgia Department of Natural Resources issued a draft of a water conservation plan in December 2008. The Georgia Chamber of Commerce, however, has insisted that any comprehensive water planning for Georgia recognize that water rights in Georgia are private property with which the legislature cannot interfere and should be freely transferable by the owner. In fact, the new state water plan allows for interbasin transfers while relying on soft study and planning techniques, instead of hard allocations. Atlanta's recent metropolitan plans for water conservation are modest at best. Georgia's persistent treatment of water as a private consumer good, instead of a necessary public resource, is especially remarkable considering that Governor Sonny Perdue declared a state of emergency in northern Georgia in October 2007 when dangerously low levels of water in Lake Lanier put area residents arguably within 90 days of running out of water.

This Article argues that privatization of water and public water systems pose underappreciated risks to both public rights and national security in the United States. All life depends on water. Therefore, all communities, social and political systems, and economies depend on this finite resource for survival and vitality. However, both human rights and national security protections are inadequate to guarantee that all people will receive sufficient quantities of good quality water to meet basic human needs. These inadequacies result from the deeply entrenched conceptualization of rights in the United States, the fact that human rights and national security policies are not self-implementing, and the particular characteristics of water. Individual rights to water or protections against terrorist threats to water supplies do not necessarily achieve water conservation, sustainable management of water and watersheds, or long-term planning and investment.

Instead, the United States needs legislation and legal doctrines that limit private control over water sources and systems and that regulate privatization processes in order to protect the integrity and security of individuals, communities, and the nation. Even more importantly, the United States needs comprehensive principles of public stewardship of water resources to support human life and national security. Public stewardship principles are premised on the concept that the government is a trustee of water resources for the public, a fiduciary obligation not limited to the traditional public trust doctrine, but based in the many public characteristics of water in the United States, as well as the social and human necessities of a complex society. However, each member of the public would not only be a beneficiary but would also owe duties to his, her, or its co-beneficiaries, the other members of the public. Public stewardship principles would require long-range place-based planning with transparency and public participation, public investment, water conservation, watershed protection, water quality controls, full-cost pricing with subsidies to those unable to pay full costs, and heightened security measures.

* * *

I. Water Privatization in the United States

* * *

A. Privatization of Public Water Services

* * *

The United States is experiencing a controversial trend towards privatization of public water services. The amount of all public water services in the United States provided by privately-owned water suppliers is relatively small. They serve about 15% of U.S. water customers (measured in volume of water handled).... Nonetheless, private operation, control, or ownership of local water supply systems has increased dramatically since the 1980s. The increased interest in privatizing public water services is an outgrowth of political forces and public policies favoring privatization of public services generally, and water resources specifically. A growing number of contracts to privatize public water services is an indicator that privatization has become increasingly attractive to many public water institutions....

* * *

[P]rivatization of public water supplies and infrastructure is a global trend, appearing prominently in developing countries and creating intense conflicts over human rights, community vitality, ecological sustainability, and national security. In 2000 alone, ninety-three countries had municipalities that underwent some form of privatization. Financially-strapped developing nations are turning to large multinational water corporations to invest in, build, and operate water systems that will supply potable drinking water to large populations currently lacking access to water. In addition, world economic institutions, such as the International Monetary Fund and the World Bank, are pressuring developing nations to turn to privatized water systems, and even conditioning loans to developing nations on water privatization.

Worldwide, over 1 billion people, mostly in developing countries, lack access to adequate supplies of safe drinking water for basic human needs.... Governments of developing nations, however, typically lack the financial resources required to make the major investments in water development, management, and distribution systems needed to ensure safe water supplies.

Large multinational water corporations have capital to invest in water systems worldwide in exchange for ownership or control of these systems and the (estimated) substantial profits from these water ventures. These corporations have specialized in water development, management, and distribution, seeing a globally unmet need that will be increasingly profitable, and they aggressively seek out investment and ownership opportunities in water service systems worldwide. [One corporation] operates in over 100 countries and provides water services to 110 million people, [another] operates in 130 countries and provides water services to 115 million people; and [yet another] provides water services to over 70 million people. The combined revenue potential of these three dominant multinational water corporations is close to $3 trillion.

Water privatization in the developing world has been met with public opposition and conflict, as opponents argue that water is a human right and that global corporations are exploiting the needs of the world's poor for profit. In Cochabamba, Bolivia, the government, under pressure from the World Bank, granted a 40-year concession to a private consortium, ... to operate the municipal water system. The municipal water system had failed to meet local need, with over forty percent of the area residents lacking access to a water supply network. After only four months, water prices had increased as much as 400% and workers were spending over one-quarter of their income on water. The government cancelled the contract after anti-privatization protests of 15,000 to 20,000 people from a diverse cross-section of Bolivian society resulted in hundreds of injuries, $20 million in property damage, and the death of a 17-year-old boy from confrontations between the protesters and police. The consortium filed a $25 million claim against Bolivia, but eventually dropped it in the face of worldwide public outrage. The controversy also produced the Cochabamba Declaration, a nonbinding assertion that "[w]ater is a fundamental human right and a public trust to be guarded by all levels of government, therefore, it should not be commodified, privatized or traded for commercial purposes."

* * *

B. Private Property Rights in Water

Beyond private ownership and control of public water supply systems, privatization is also about the recurring and relentless efforts in the United States to treat interests in water as private property rights, akin to private ownership of land. Water is different than other objects of private ownership and rights, and as such, it has always had both strong public characteristics and strong private characteristics. Therefore, the legal system's treatment of water as a private property right has been more about a reiterative tension than about a linear trend.

* * *

[P]ublic rights and interests in water may be a theoretical starting point from which private rights and interests in water emerge, but as a practical matter, private rights in water have primacy, subject to a few key public interest limitations. Several doctrines define the public interests in water. The "state ownership doctrine" holds that ownership of navigable waters and their submerged lands passed from the federal government into state ownership upon the state's admission to the Union. The "public trust doctrine" limits the ability to of the state government to convey navigable waters and their submerged lands if such conveyances would be contrary to the public's equitable interest in these resources for navigation, fishing, recreation, and possibly ecological value....

* * *

C. Water as a Consumer Commodity

Even more broadly than embracing privatized public water systems and private water rights, American society and public policy are increasingly framing water solely as a consumer commodity. In this mindset, the primary purpose of water is to satisfy consumer demand for it, regardless of whether the consumers are agricultural irrigators receiving federally subsidized water, commercial or industrial enterprises that expect localities to provide abundant supplies and up-to-date infrastructure to support their private profit-making ventures, or members of residential households who feel entitled to fill their pools, keep their non-native lawns looking lush, take long showers, and have ready access to bottled water. Conservation is inconvenient. Remarkably, many homeowners in Las Vegas expressed defiance towards government limits on lawn watering in a climate that receives three to five inches of rainfall per year. They insisted that they were entitled to grassy lawns in the desert.

Moreover, scarcity and competition increase pressures to get water now from any available source, regardless of where it is or regardless of the long-term ecological impacts. Water markets and trans-basin transfers have become popular policy proposals in order to satisfy consumer demand. As a result, water has become disconnected conceptually and politically from its places of origin: particular watersheds, ecosystems, and landscapes. Even some attempts to protect the environmental features of water, such as private water trusts and monetary valuation of ecosystem services, are seeking to rely on the economic value of water and watersheds and on consumer demand for healthy environment. Public policy is framed in terms of satisfying private consumer interest. Indeed, one of the problems of modernity is that social institutions and government regimes are themselves engines of consumerism and the "growth imperative," responding to public dependence on perpetual growth by supporting and facilitating uses of natural resources beyond nature's carrying capacity.

* * *

IV. Public Stewardship of Water

A. The Harms of Privatization and Commodification of Water

Private control and commodification of water in the United States pose large-scale and long-term risks and harms of which human rights concerns and national security risks are only parts. Private control and commodification of water threaten the integrity and sustainability of waters, water systems, and watersheds in interconnected human and natural systems.

Privatization and commodification of water fail to achieve ecological integrity and sustainability, because water is treated as disaggregated into discrete units of private control and consumption, instead of being considered part of interdependent human and natural communities. A private commodity concept of water fails to see the sustainability of human life as integrally tied to the sustainability of entire ecosystems, biodiversity and biological life, and nature's hydrology. For example, private development of wetlands eliminates critical natural biodiversity, filtration, and absorption functions, contributing to disasters like the flooding of New Orleans after Hurricane Katrina. Over-pumping of groundwater sources, whether by private landowners, water bottling companies, or sprawling cities meeting consumer demand, leads to adverse alterations of interconnected groundwater-surface water hydrology (e.g., saltwater intrusion, dropping aquifer levels) and landscapes (e.g., subsidence, loss of native vegetation). Private water companies calculate the value of source water protection lands in trade-offs between potential treatment costs savings and potential revenues from sale or development, without considering their other ecological and human values. Water diversions for consumption, dams, and other "replumbing" water works for water supplies take away instream flows that sustain aquatic species, alter basic stream hydrology and composition, and facilitate invasive species.

* * *

B. A Case for Reconceptualization

The problems posed by water privatization in the United States require a reconceptualization of the public and private nature of water in the U.S....

We are in the midst of dramatically changing social conditions with respect to water and its control and management. Scarcity in particular locations and at particular times has become a major problem, not only in the traditionally arid West but also in the traditionally humid East. Population growth, sprawl, and consumption patterns create increasing demands for water, change the locations at which and the purposes for which water is sought, and degradation of watershed lands. Climate change will contribute substantially to increasing water stress and scarcity. Terrorism poses risks to water supplies and infrastructure. Extraction and exports of both groundwater and surface water increasingly harm source waters, watersheds or aquifers, and communities. Inter-jurisdictional conflicts over water have proven persistently unresolved under current dispute resolution and inter-jurisdictional allocation methods. Our water consumption practices are unsustainable, and public policies and norms to protect natural and human environments increasingly conflict with water rights and use....

* * *

C. The Principles and Duties of Public Stewardship of Water

Therefore, I propose a reconceptualization of water, which I call "public stewardship of water." It has three core principles. First, water and water services should be under public ownership and control, yet subject to recognized private interests that are usufructuary in nature and regulated by the government for the public interest. Second, because of the unique characteristics of water, private property rights in water should be characterized as property interests in water that are part of interconnected webs of interests. Third, the government should have fiduciary stewardship responsibilities to the public for management and governance of water, water systems, and watersheds: a broadly based trustee role facilitated by all members of the public—the beneficiaries of this trust—having correlative duties or responsibilities to their fellow beneficiaries in the public at large.

* * *

… The public trust doctrine imposes fiduciary duties on the state government to hold, manage, and regulate navigable and tidal waters and their submerged lands for the benefit of the public, who hold an equitable interest in these resources. Grounded in ancient Roman law doctrines that came to the U.S. from English legal tradition, the public trust doctrine serves as a significant inherent limit on private property interests in water and aquatic land, as well as a source of authority for the government to regulate private property without owing just compensation. The California Supreme Court has extended the public trust doctrine to the state's ongoing fiduciary obligation to balance water appropriation and use rights with the public's enduring interest in the ecological conditions of flowing waters in their natural water courses. The Hawai'i Supreme Court has extended the public trust doctrine to groundwater. [A New Jersey court] has limited the public transfer of public water supplies based on the public trust in public water supplies. The public trust doctrine has proven capable of evolution.

However, the public trust doctrine, as it is currently defined, is far too limited to ensure the kind of government stewardship of water, water supplies and systems, and watershed functions for the public that we now need. In many states, there are substantial limitations on the waters and, lands to which it applies, the scope and enforceability of government duties, the specific public trust purposes or rights that the public enjoys under the doctrine, and the doctrine's impact on private rights and interests in water or land….

… I urge a broadly defined public trustee responsibility for water, water supplies and systems, and other aquatic resources, emerging out of both the public trust doctrine and emergent and urgent social needs, but not unduly limited by the parameters of the public trust doctrine as applied historically in the United States. In fact, the concept of the government as a trustee of resources for the public is not confined to the public trust doctrine and water-related resources. Courts treat the government as trustee of public streets, parks, and sidewalks for the benefit of the public and its expressive activities…. John Locke's compact theory of government, influential in U.S. political theory, conceives of the government as a trustee with obligations to the public.

* * *

In particular, the government's fiduciary duties with respect to water should include six duties: 1) the duty of security; 2) the duty of conservation; 3) the duty of sustainability; 4) the duty of equity; 5) the duty of investment; and 6) the duty of long-range, place-based planning….

First, the government should have the duty to maintain the security of waters and water supplies and infrastructure. This duty should, of course, include the government's responsibility for measures to safeguard the public's water supplies and infrastructure from acts and risks of terrorism….

Second, the government should have a duty to conserve water resources and to induce consumers' conservation of water....

* * *

Third, the government should have a duty to control and manage water for the long-term sustainability of all human life, biological life generally, watersheds and hydrologic processes, local communities, and society. The core of this duty is the concept that all life depends on water for survival....

* * *

Fourth, the government should have a duty of equity with respect to water control, management, and allocation. This duty requires that water policies meet basic principles of social justice. Three particular principles are especially important. The first is the principle that every person in the United States should receive enough water to meet the basic needs of life, regardless of ability to pay. This could be accomplished by public water suppliers, through the imposition of a fiduciary duty, and by private water suppliers, through utility regulation....

Fifth, the government should have a duty to invest resources in the development, management, maintenance, security, sustainability, and conservation of water supplies, water distribution infrastructure, and the restoration and preservation of waterways and critical watershed features....

Finally, the government should have a duty to engage in long-range, place-based planning for the sustainability, security, and conservation of water supplies and watersheds....

These six duties identify the government as the entity with fiduciary responsibility to act on them. However, unlike typical trusts, these duties must also be shared by every member of the public and the public as a whole. While each of us is a beneficiary of the government's ownership, control, management, allocation, conservation, and stewardship of water, each of us also profoundly affects how the government's responsibility for water is effectuated by the ways we use water, influence water decisions, demand water, and affect water quality and watersheds through a myriad of activities. We are co-beneficiaries but we are also co-trustees or co-managers of waters, water supplies and systems, and watersheds. The term "public stewardship" aims to capture this sense in which the government and the public share responsibility for being good and wise stewards of limited water resources that are essential to life, society, and nature.

Notes

1. Professor Arnold envisions an expanded public trust to address the problem of water privatization. What does the public trust offer as a legal and conceptual tool that could be applied to this situation? His article outlined in detail modern circumstances that compel public trust protection of water supplies. To what extent would courts be persuaded to justify expanding the public trust based on these changing needs of society?

2. As Arnold noted, some courts (like the Hawai'i Supreme Court) already recognize a trust over all water including groundwater. The New Jersey decision he referenced is *City of Clifton v. Passaic Valley Water Comm'n*, 539 A.2d 760 (N.J. Super. 1987). Although the case concerned financial issues surrounding municipal water supply agreements, the court underscored the public trust in drinking water supplies at the outset of its opinion, stating:

Water is an essential commodity which all of nature requires for survival. Our food supply is derived through water which combines with nutrients and minerals to form the fruits and vegetables which become part of our daily diet. The plants of the soil, nurtured by water and consumed by animals, provide our main staple of meat. Like the plants and animals, we too must be nurtured by water.

Potable water, then, is an essential commodity which every individual requires in order to sustain human existence. Frequently, residents in rural areas have individual wells and thus become somewhat self-sufficient and independent with respect to their water supply. However, residents in urban and suburban areas are dependent upon the agency or institution which supplies potable water.

While the original purpose of the public trust doctrine was to preserve the use of the public natural water for navigation, commerce and fishing, it is clear that since water is essential for human life, the public trust doctrine applies with equal impact upon the control of our drinking water reserves. The Supreme Court has determined that "It is appropriate to consider the unique nature of water." Ultimate ownership rests in the people and this precious natural resource is held by the state in trust for the public benefit.

Id. at 765 (citations omitted). Wouldn't the court's reasoning apply in any jurisdiction? Isn't drinking water a vital life source, wherever located? Does it make any sense that groundwater would escape public trust protection in other states? Would you expect courts to recognize the groundwater trust as public needs for water intensify?

3. Professor Arnold outlined six fiduciary duties that should govern public trustees of water supplies. Don't some or all of these obligations reflect fiduciary duties articulated by the *Mono Lake* and *Waiahole Ditch* courts? Can you find specific language in those cases to support any or all of these duties?

4. As a general matter, does water commodification violate the principles announced by the Hawai'i Supreme Court in *Waiahole Ditch* that place public rights above private gain? Under the Hawai'i approach, private profit is not a legitimate purpose protected by the trust. How would a private bottling company justify its application for water appropriation from a groundwater source in a jurisdiction following the *Waiahole Ditch* precedent? Does it matter whether the bottled water products are designed for emergency response (such as in the aftermath of hurricanes when public water supplies may be interrupted), or for high school vending machines?

5. As Professor Arnold detailed in his article, governmental agencies in many states (and in other countries) have already issued permits for water privatization. Are these permits revocable under the public trust? Is that one of the strengths of the public trust in this situation?

6. Water is increasingly viewed as a commodity, as Professor Arnold pointed out. What is the danger in that? Consider the statement of water experts Maude Barlow and Tony Clarke:

If we allow the commodification of the world's freshwater supplies, we will lose the capacity to avert the looming water crisis. We will be allowing the emergence of a water elite that will determine the world's water future in its own interest. In such a scenario, water will go to those who can afford it and not to those who need it.[18]

---

18. Maude Barlow & Tony Clarke, *Who Owns the Water?*, THE NATION, Sept. 2, 2002.

Barlow and Clarke advocate characterizing water as a public trust asset, and access to water as a core human right:

> Water must be declared and understood for all time to be the common property of all. In a world where everything is being privatized, citizens must establish clear perimeters around those areas that are sacred to life and necessary for the survival of the planet.... No one has the right to appropriate [water] for profit. Water must be declared a public trust....[19]

7. As part of the rush to profit from water, some corporations are proposing bulk transport of fresh water across the globe to serve markets in water-deprived areas. In 2010, for example, a U.S. company announced plans to draw huge quantities of water from Blue Lake in Alaska (about 90 miles southwest of Juneau) for shipment to a water hub located in India, using sea vessels that can hold 50 million gallons. *See* Lisa Song, *US Company Plans to Ship Fresh Water from Alaska to India*, THE GUARDIAN, Sept. 6, 2010, http://www.guardian.co.uk/environment/2010/sep/06/ship-fresh-water-alaska-india. Such withdrawals would undoubtedly require water appropriation permits from a state agency. What is the public trust obligation of the agency in considering such a proposal? Does it matter that citizens of India are not the legal beneficiaries of a public trust in Alaska? Is it a per se violation of the trust to allow transfers of water out of the state, much less the country? What about some of the transfers Professor Arnold wrote about in which cities in one state take water from sources located in another state? Does that violate the trust in the same way, or could one argue that all Americans are beneficiaries, jointly, of all water supplies?

---

19. *Id.*

Chapter 6

The Wildlife Trust

The original public trust doctrine cases in the United States—*Arnold v. Mundy* (p. 57) and *Martin v. Waddell* (p. 63)—involved oyster harvesting, and therefore might have been thought to establish a public trust in wildlife. Actually, a predecessor case from Britain, *The Royal Fishery of Banne*, 80 Eng. Rep. 540 (K.B. 1611), also concerned wildlife: salmon. But the *Arnold* and *Martin* decisions emphasized ownership of submerged lands because oysters were attached to the beds. *Banne*, on the other hand, did not involve a fish attached to a riverbed, yet the King's Bench—some two centuries before *Arnold*—also ruled that fishing rights to the salmon presumptively belong to the owner of the submerged land, in this case the English king, since the river was tidal, and therefore a navigable "royal river." Thus, in all three cases the right to fish was presumptively an incident of submerged lands ownership. For details on the English history, see DALE D. GOBLE & ERIC T. FREYFOGLE, WILDLIFE LAW: CASES AND MATERIALS 244–54 (2d ed. 2010).

Another English case described an alternative path to deciding who owned the wildlife, involving birds instead of fish. In *The Case of the Swans*, 77 Eng. Rep. 435 (K.B. 1592), the King's Bench, over a decade before its *Banne* decision, ruled that wild, unmarked white swans belonged to the king "by his prerogative" because, just as "whales and sturgeons [were r]oyal fish," swans were "royal fowls." *Id.* at 438. This decision was not a product of land ownership but instead a consequence of the character of the wildlife. Thus, while marked swans, or domesticated animals, could be privately owned, the *Swans* decision upheld royal ownership for certain kinds of wildlife and laid the foundation for the modern state ownership doctrine.

But across the Atlantic, in post-Revolutionary America, courts were deciding rights to wildlife through the rule of capture in cases like the celebrated decision in *Pierson v. Post*, 3 Caines 175 (N.Y. 1805), in which the New York Supreme Court decided ownership of a fox based on first capture, or at least mortal wounding, on what the court considered to be "wild," unowned land. As the 19th century progressed, first capture became the wildlife ownership rule, with little or no consideration of sovereign prerogatives, *see, e.g., Ghen v. Rich*, 8 F. 159 (D. Mass. 1881) (involving a harpooned whale). The rule of capture led to widespread overharvesting of wildlife and extinctions of species like the passenger pigeon, which perished due to the rise of "market hunting" in the post-Civil War era. *See* DALE D. GOBLE & ERIC T. FREYFOGLE, WILDLIFE LAW: CASES AND MATERIALS 25–29 (2d ed. 2010).

Wildlife extinctions and near-extinctions prompted a reaction, the Progressive conservation movement of the late 19th century, which began as a wildlife protection effort on the state level. The states, as successors of the royal king, claimed the authority to regulate wildlife harvests through sovereign ownership of wildlife, and their claims were largely upheld in court decisions, some of which are discussed below. These decisions formed the genesis of a well-established wildlife trust. The corpus of such trust is *ferae naturae*, a Latin term that means wildlife in its natural free state.

More recently, since the Endangered Species Act was passed in 1973, actions affecting wildlife listed under the Act have been subject to federal regulation with mixed success. Threats to wildlife have magnified over the last few decades; ecosystem collapse and climate change now eclipse the traditional threats of overharvesting and poaching that gave rise to early trust decisions. In 2014, IUCN listed over 22,000 species as threatened — and of those, 2,119 were critically endangered. IUCN, THE IUCN RED LIST OF THREATENED SPECIES, Version 2014.3, tbls.1 & 2, http://www.iucnredlist.org/ (last visited Feb. 14, 2015). IUCN estimated that approximately 26% of mammals, 13% of birds, and 41% of amphibians were threatened as of late 2014. *Id.* at tbl.1. The situation will likely worsen as temperatures rise; scientists predict that an increase in global temperature of 3°C will result in "extensive biodiversity loss." UNITED NATIONS INTERGOVERNMENTAL PANEL ON CLIMATE CHANGE, CLIMATE CHANGE 2014: SUMMARY FOR POLICYMAKERS 12 box.1 (Fifth Assessment, 2014). In light of these monumental ecological threats to the wildlife species, ask yourself what role can the public trust doctrine play in a legal regime now heavily dominated by statutes such as the ESA? What principles established in the cases excerpted in this chapter can adapt to modern exigencies to protect the wildlife trust?

The Pioneer Spirit and the Public Trust:
The American Rule of Capture and State Ownership of Wildlife
Michael C. Blumm & Lucus Ritchie
35 Envtl. L. 673 (2005)

* * *

The vigorous capture rules fostered by early America's pioneer spirit resulted in the extinction of many species in the New World and the depletion of populations of many more. State legislators sought to maintain a sustainable food supply for their citizens, but their power to curb the rule of capture remained questionable. To ensure that capturers did not exploit North American wildlife to extinction, several state courts upheld legislation to stop overharvesting by looking to English law. Although American courts rejected the English class-based restrictions on arms and hunting, they did not erase all remnants of the king's sovereign prerogative. Instead, American courts transformed the English concept of prerogative ownership and fashioned a uniquely American justification for regulation: the state "ownership" doctrine, also known as the wildlife trust. Professor Goble has aptly referred to this transition as "republicanizing" the royal prerogative.[1] By the late 1800s, many states had employed a sovereign ownership theory to regulate the use of fishing grounds, restrict hunting by seasons or outright prohibitions, and terminate certain commerce in wildlife altogether.

A. The Foundation of the American Wildlife Trust

The foundation for nineteenth-century wildlife regulation was laid by several state and U.S. Supreme Court decisions supporting state ownership of public resources in trust for all citizens. Development of an American public trust doctrine began with the 1821 New Jersey Supreme Court decision *Arnold v. Mundy*. In *Arnold*, Chief Justice Kilpatrick ruled that under English common law, New Jersey's navigable waters and the lands submerged beneath them were "common to all the citizens, and … the property is … vested in the sovereign … not for his own use, but for the use of the citizens." The court explained that

---

1. Dale D. Goble, Three Cases/Four Tales: Commons, Capture, the Public Trust, and Property in Land, 35 Envtl. L. 807, 831–33 (2005).

this ownership interest, once the English king's prerogative, transferred to New Jersey as a result of the revolution and provided the state inherent authority to regulate the resource for the benefit of its citizenry.

... [T]he Supreme Court adopted the New Jersey approach in the 1842 case of *Martin v. Waddell*.... The Court proceeded to hold that "when the Revolution took place, the people of each state became themselves sovereign; and in that character hold the absolute right to all their navigable waters and the soils under them for their own common use." *Arnold* and *Martin* became the cornerstones of the public trust in navigable waters and submerged lands, and they also figured prominently in the evolution of another line of cases concluding that public trust principles extended beyond the beds and banks of navigable waterways to wildlife.

In 1855, in *Smith v. Maryland*[, 59 U.S. 71, 75 (1855)], the Supreme Court ruled that Maryland's proprietary interest in submerged lands conferred upon the state the authority to regulate the taking of oysters embedded within its tidelands. As explained by Justice Curtis: "This power results from the ownership of the soil, from the legislative jurisdiction of the State over it, and from the duty to preserve unimpaired those public uses for which the soil is held." [*Id.* at 76.] Also in 1855, the Supreme Judicial Court of Massachusetts upheld a statute prohibiting the use of purse seines within a mile of the Nantucket shore, declaring that swimming fish, as well as shellfish, belonged to the state in trust for its citizens. [*Dunham v. Lamphere*, 69 Mass. 268 (1855).] Similarly, the U.S. Supreme Court, in the 1891 case of *Manchester v. Massachusetts*[, 139 U.S. 240 (1891)], validated a Massachusetts regulation restricting the lawful methods for catching menhaden—a bait fish that served as the primary food source for larger, commercially valuable fish—under the theory that the state had a proprietary interest in all fish within the state's inland and coastal waters. Following English common law, which treated fish the same as terrestrial animals, the public trust doctrine announced by the Supreme Court in *Martin* and broadened in *Smith* and *Manchester* eventually became amphibious, ultimately extending to all animals *ferae naturae*.

B. Early Wildlife Cases: Correcting the Market Hunting Problem

In the latter half of the nineteenth century, state legislatures began to regulate wildlife taking in order to preserve a food supply decimated by market hunters. The earliest regulations imposed bag limits and shortened or closed hunting seasons in an attempt to prevent excessive slaughter of fowl and other game. Although market hunters challenged limits that restricted their right to capture wildlife, courts routinely upheld the laws using public trust principles. Just as the king owned all wildlife at common law, so the states, by the transfer of royal authority, maintained a proprietary interest in the wild animals within their borders, which provided them authority to limit the taking of game. As explained by the Supreme Court of Illinois in 1881:

> The ownership being in the people of the State—the repository of the sovereign authority—and no individual having any property rights to be affected, it necessarily results that the legislature, as the representative of the people of the State, may withhold or grant to individuals the right to hunt and kill game, or qualify and restrict it, as, in the opinion of its members, will best serve the public welfare.

[*Magner v. People*, 97 Ill. 320, 333–34 (1881).]

* * *

Nineteenth-century courts employed state ownership of animals *ferae naturae* to justify limiting the taking of wildlife because the enactment of market restrictions occurred at a time when courts held a narrow view of the scope of the state police power. In the late nineteenth and early twentieth centuries, the U.S. Supreme Court interpreted the Due Process Clause of the Fourteenth Amendment to impose significant limits on state economic regulation. During this era, the Court basically elevated freedom of contract to a fundamental right with which the state could interfere only to control significant public health, safety, or moral problems.

State game laws completely withholding the right to sell certain species may have foundered under this turn-of-the-century judicial view of the police power. To avoid due process-imposed limits on economic regulation, courts viewed marketing laws not as a regulation enforced on a hunter's property after capture, but instead as a restriction on the property right the hunter could obtain in wild animals in the first instance. As owner of all *ferae naturae* within its borders, the state had the power to determine which rights were included in the private ownership of wildlife. The state ownership doctrine thus enabled courts to avoid difficult inquiries into the limits of the state's sovereign authority to regulate trade in wild animals.

Legislation restricting the possession and sale of wildlife and wildlife products within particular states dramatically reduced hunters' exploitation of certain game, especially fowl. Often, however, if a state set rigorous restrictions on selling game species, market hunters would simply poach game in the regulated state and transport the carcasses into a neighboring, less-regulated state for sale. This development was encouraged by the new technology of efficient cold storage in the 1870s and 1880s, allowing eastern markets to be regularly supplied animals taken in the West. Some cities, like Boston and Washington, D.C.—because of their extended sale periods—became known as "dumping grounds" for game killed in other states. The Massachusetts Fish and Game Protective Association estimated in 1896 that ninety to ninety-five percent of the game sold in Boston originated outside Massachusetts. To close such loopholes, states began to enact legislation prohibiting the shipment of game out-of-state, even where the game had been lawfully harvested. Hunters resisted the new regulations, filing suits in which they argued that these protectionist laws violated the federal Commerce Clause['s] prohibition against disrupting interstate commerce.

Notes

1. A decision that epitomized late 19th century judicial thinking on the state level was *State v. Rodman*, 59 N.W. 1098 (Minn. 1894), in which the Minnesota Supreme Court upheld the conviction of a hunter who possessed game after the state closed the hunting season, even though the harvest took place during the hunting season:

> We take it to be the correct doctrine in this country that the ownership of wild animals, so far as they are capable of ownership, is in the state, not as proprietor, but in its sovereign capacity, as the representative, and for the benefit, of all its people in common. The preservation of such animals as are adapted to consumption as food, or to any other useful purpose, is a matter of public interest; and it is within the police power of the state, as the representative of the people in their united sovereignty, to enact such laws as will best preserve such game, and secure its beneficial use in the future to the citizens, and to that end it may adopt any reasonable regulations, not only as to time and manner in which such game may be taken and killed, but also imposing limitations upon the right of property in such game after it has been reduced to possession. Such limitations deprive no person of his property, because he who takes or kills game had no pre-

vious right of property in it, and, when he acquires such right by reducing it to possession, he does so subject to such conditions and limitations as the legislature has seen fit to impose.

Id. at 1099.

2. A similar Connecticut statute, forbidding interstate transportation of wildlife after capture, was at issue in the following landmark decision of the U.S. Supreme Court, which characterized the state's sovereign ownership descending from the royal prerogative as a trust.

Geer v. Connecticut

United States Supreme Court
161 U.S. 519 (1896)

[The defendant, Geer, was found guilty of possessing "with the wrongful and unlawful intent to procure transportation beyond the limits of the state" woodcock, ruffed grouse, and quail. He appealed, arguing that the statutes prohibiting the transportation of game birds out of the state were unconstitutional. The Connecticut Supreme Court rejected his argument and concluded that the state had the power to regulate the transport of taken wildlife. The case reached the U.S. Supreme Court in 1896.]

WHITE, J.:

... [T]he sole issue which the case presents is, was it lawful, under the Constitution of the United States (section 8, Article I[, the Commerce Clause]), for the state of Connecticut to allow the killing of birds within the state during a designated open season, to allow such birds, when so killed, to be used, to be sold, and to be bought for use, within the state, and yet to forbid their transportation beyond the state? Or, to state it otherwise, had the state of Connecticut the power to regulate the killing of game within her borders so as to confine its use to the limits of the state, and forbid its transmission outside of the state?

* * *

From the earliest traditions, the right to reduce animals *ferae naturae* to possession has been subject to the control of the law-giving power.

* * *

Among other subdivisions, things were classified by the Roman law into public and common. The latter embraced animals *ferae naturae*, which, having no owner, were considered as belonging in common to all the citizens of the state....

* * *

... In the feudal as well as the ancient law of the continent of Europe, in all countries, the right to acquire animals *ferae naturae* by possession was recognized as being subject to the governmental authority and under its power, not only as a matter of regulation, but also of absolute control....

* * *

In tracing the origin of the classification of animals ferae naturae, as things common, Pothier[,[2] in his treatise on property,] says:

---

2. Robert Joseph Pothier wrote a treatise on property, TRAITÉ DU DROIT DE DOMAINE DE PROPRIÉTÉ, in 1772. Pothier "helped to revive the Roman law approach to property as a monolithic entity, rather than the medieval system of fractionalized interests among different holders." JOHN G. SPRANKLING, THE INTERNATIONAL LAW OF PROPERTY 326 (2014). [Eds].

The first of mankind had in common all those things which God had given to the human race.... The human race having multiplied, men partitioned among themselves the earth and the greater part of those things which were on its surface. That which fell to each one among them commenced to belong to him in private ownership, and this process is the origin of the right of property. Some things, however, did not enter into this division, and remain therefore to this day in the condition of the ancient and negative community.

Referring to those things which remain common, or in what he qualified as the negative community, this great writer says:

These things are those which the jurisconsults [persons learned in law, Eds.] called res communes. Marcien[3] refers to several kinds—the air, the water which runs in the rivers, the sea and its shores.... As regards wild animals, *ferae naturae*,[4] they have remained in the ancient state of negative community.

* * *

The common law of England also based property in game upon the principle of common ownership, and therefore treated it as subject to governmental authority.

Blackstone, while pointing out the distinction between things private and those which are common, rests the right of an individual to reduce a part of this common property to possession, and thus acquire a qualified ownership in it, on no other or different principle from that upon which the civilians based such right. 2 WILLIAM BLACKSTONE, COMMENTARIES ON THE LAWS OF ENGLAND *1, *12.

Referring especially to the common ownership of game, he says:

But, after all, there are some few things which, notwithstanding the general introduction and continuance of property, must still unavoidably remain in common, being such wherein nothing but an usufructuary property is capable of being had; and therefore they still belong to the first occupant during the time he holds possession of them, and no longer. Such (among others) are the elements of light, air, and water, which a man may occupy by means of his windows, his gardens, his mills, and other conveniences. Such, also, are the generality of those animals which are said to be *ferae naturae* or of a wild and untamable disposition, which any man may seize upon or keep for his own use or pleasure.

Id. at *14.

A man may lastly have a qualified property in animals *ferae naturae—propter privilegium*, that is, he may have the privilege of hunting, taking, and killing them in exclusion of other persons. Here he has a transient property in these animals usually called "game" so long as they continue within his liberty, and he may restrain any stranger from taking them therein; but, the instant they depart into another liberty, this qualified property ceases.... A man can have no absolute permanent property in these, as he may in the earth and land; since these are of a vague and fugitive nature, and therefore can only admit of a precarious and qualified ownership, which lasts so long as they are in actual use and occupation, but no longer.

---

3. Marcien (also spelled Marcian) was a 3d century Roman jurist. The Institutes of Justinian quoted the passage referenced by the Court. J. INST. 2.1.1. [Eds].

4. The Court used the term feroe nature, which we have amended to reflect modern spelling. [Eds].

Id. at *394.

In stating the existence and scope of the royal prerogative, Blackstone further says:

> There still remains another species of prerogative property, founded upon a very different principle from any that have been mentioned before, — the property of such animals, *ferae naturae, as* are known by the denomination of "game," with the right of pursuing, taking, and destroying them, which is vested in the king alone, and from him derived to such of his subjects as have received the grants of a chase, a park, a free warren, or free fishery.... In the first place, then, we have already shown, and indeed it cannot be denied, that, by the law of nature, every man, from the prince to the peasant, has an equal of pursuing and taking to his own use all such creatures as are *ferae naturae*, and therefore the property of nobody, but liable to be seized by the first occupant, and so it was held by the imperial law as late as Justinian's time.... But it follows from the very end and constitution of society that this natural right, as well as many others belonging to man as an individual, may be restrained by positive laws enacted for reasons of state or for the supposed benefit of the community.

Id. at *410.

The practice of the government of England from the earliest time to the present has put into execution the authority to control and regulate the taking of game.

Undoubtedly, this attribute of government to control the taking of animals *ferae naturae*, which was thus recognized and enforced by the common law of England, was vested in the colonial governments, where not denied by their charters, or in conflict with grants of the royal prerogative. It is also certain that the power which the colonies thus possessed passed to the states with the separation from the mother country, and remains in them at the present day, in so far as its exercise may be not incompatible with, or restrained by, the rights conveyed to the federal government by the constitution....

The adjudicated cases recognizing the right of the states to control and regulate the common property in game are numerous. In *McCready v. Virginia*, 94 U.S. 391 (1876), the power of the state of Virginia to prohibit citizens of other states from planting oysters within the tide waters of that state was upheld by this court. In *Manchester v. Massachusetts*, 139 U.S. 240 (1891), the authority of the state of Massachusetts to control and regulate the catching of fish within the bays of that state was also maintained. [The Court then cited several cases in which state supreme courts found that the state had the authority to regulate game.]

While the fundamental principles upon which the common property in game rest have undergone no change, the development of free institutions had led to the recognition of the fact that the power or control lodged in the state, resulting from this common ownership, is to be exercised, like all other powers of government, as a trust for the benefit of the people, and not as a prerogative for the advantage of the government as distinct from the people, or for the benefit of private individuals as distinguished from the public good. Therefore, for the purpose of exercising this power, the state, as held by this court in *Martin v. Waddell*, 41 U.S. (16 Pet.) 367 (1842), represents its people, and the ownership is that of the people in their united sovereignty. The common ownership, and its resulting responsibility in the state, is thus stated in a well-considered opinion of the Supreme Court of California:

> The wild game within a state belongs to the people in their collective, sovereign capacity. It is not the subject of private ownership, except in so far as the peo-

ple may elect to make it so; and they may, if they see fit, absolutely prohibit the taking of it, or traffic and commerce in it, if deemed necessary for its protection or preservation, or the public good.

Ex parte Maier, 37 P. 402, 483 (Cal. 1894).

The same view has been expressed by the supreme court of Minnesota, as follows:

We take it to be the correct doctrine in this country that the ownership of wild animals, so far as they are capable of ownership, is in the state, not as proprietor, but in its sovereign capacity, as the representative and for the benefit of all its people in common.

State v. Rodman, 59 N.W. 1098, 1099 (Minn. 1894).

The foregoing analysis of the principles upon which alone rests the right of an individual to acquire a qualified ownership in game, and the power of the state, deduced therefrom, to control such ownership for the common benefit, clearly demonstrates the validity of the statute of the state of Connecticut here in controversy. The sole consequence of the provision forbidding the transportation of game killed within the state, beyond the state, is to confine the use of such game to those who own it, — the people of that state. The proposition that the state may not forbid carrying it beyond her limits involves, therefore, the contention that a state cannot allow its own people the enjoyment of the benefits of the property belonging to them in common, without at the same time permitting the citizens of other states to participate in that which they do not own.

It was said in the discussion at bar, although it be conceded that the state has an absolute right to control and regulate the killing of game as its judgment deems best in the interest of its people, inasmuch as the state has here chosen to allow the people within her borders to take game, to dispose of it, and thus cause it to become an object of state commerce, as a resulting necessity such property has become the subject of interstate commerce; hence controlled by the provisions of article 1, §8, of the constitution of the United States. But the errors which this argument involves are manifest. It presupposes that, where the killing of game and its sale within the state are allowed, it thereby becomes "commerce" in the legal meaning of that word. In view of the authority of the state to affix conditions to the killing and sale of game, predicated, as is this power, on the peculiar nature of such property and its common ownership by all the citizens of the state, it may well be doubted whether commerce is created by an authority given by a state to reduce game within its borders to possession, provided such game be not taken, when killed, without the jurisdiction of the state.

The common ownership imports the right to keep the property, if the sovereign so chooses, always within its jurisdiction for every purpose. The qualification which forbids its removal from the state necessarily entered into and formed part of every transaction on the subject, and deprived the mere sale or exchange of these articles of that element of freedom of contract and of full ownership which is an essential attribute of commerce. Passing, however, as we do, the decision of this question, and granting that the dealing in game killed within the state, under the provision in question, created internal state commerce, it does not follow that such internal commerce became necessarily the subject-matter of interstate commerce, and therefore under the control of the Constitution of the United States. The distinction between internal and external commerce and interstate commerce is marked, and has always been recognized by this court....

* * *

The fact that internal commerce may be distinct from interstate commerce destroys the whole theory upon which the argument of the plaintiff in error proceeds. The power of the state to control the killing of and ownership in game being admitted, the commerce in game which the state law permitted was necessarily only internal commerce, since the restriction that it should not become the subject of external commerce went along with the grant, and was a part of it. All ownership in game killed within the state came under this condition, which the state had the lawful authority to impose; and no contracts made in relation to such property were exempt from the law of the state consenting that such contracts be made, provided only they were confined to internal, and did not extend to external, commerce.

* * *

> ... It is, perhaps, accurate to say that the ownership of the sovereign authority is in trust for all the people of the state; and hence, by implication, it is the duty of the legislature to enact such laws as will best preserve the subject of the trust, and secure its beneficial use in the future to the people of the state....

Magner, 97 Ill. at 334....

* * *

Aside from the authority of the state, derived from the common ownership of game and the trust for the benefit of its people which the state exercises in relation thereto, there is another view of the power of the state in regard to the property in game, which is equally conclusive. The right to preserve game flows from the undoubted existence in the state of a police power to that end, which may be nonetheless efficiently called into play, because by doing so interstate commerce may be remotely and indirectly affected. Indeed, the source of the police power as to game birds (like those covered by the statute here called into question) flows from the duty of the state to preserve for its people a valuable food supply. *Phelps v. Racey*, 60 N.Y. 10 (1875); *Ex parte Maier,* 37 P. 402 (Cal.1894); *Magner*, 97 Ill. 320 (1881). The exercise by the state of such power therefore comes directly within the principle of *Plumley v. Massachusetts*, 155 U.S. 461 (1894). The power of the state to protect by adequate police regulation, its people against the adulteration of articles of food (which was in that case maintained), although, in doing so, commerce might be remotely affected, necessarily carries with it the existence of a like power to preserve a food supply which belongs in common to all the people of the state, which can only become the subject of ownership in a qualified way, and which can never be the object of commerce except with the consent of the state, and subject to the conditions which it may deem best to impose for the public good.

Judgment affirmed.

BREWER and PECKHAM, J.J., not having heard the argument, took no part in the decision of this cause.

FIELD, J., dissenting:

* * *

When any animal, whether living in the waters of the state or in the air above, is lawfully killed for the purposes of food or other uses of man, it becomes an article of commerce, and its use cannot be limited to the citizens of one state to the exclusion of citizens of another state....

* * *

I do not doubt the right of the state, by its legislation, to provide for the protection of wild game, so far as such protection is necessary for their preservation, or for the comfort, health, or security of its citizens, and does not contravene the power of Congress in the regulation of interstate commerce. But I do deny the authority of the state, in its legislation for the protection and preservation of game, to interfere in any respect with the paramount control of Congress in prescribing the terms by which its transportation to another state, when killed, shall be restricted to such conditions as the state may impose. The absolute control of Congress in the regulation of interstate commerce, unimpeded by any state authority, is of much greater consequence that any regulation the state may prescribe with reference to the place where its wild game, when killed, may be consumed.

* * *

HARLAN, J., dissenting:

* * *

I do not question the power of the state to prescribe a period during which wild game within its limits may not be lawfully killed. The state, as we have seen, does not prohibit the killing of game altogether, but permits hunting and killing of woodcock, quail, ruffled grouse, and gray squirrels between the 1st day of October and the 1st day of January. The game in question having been lawfully killed, the person who killed it and took it into his possession became the rightful owner thereof.... To hold that the person receiving personal property from the owner may not receive it with the intent to send it out of the state is to recognize an arbitrary power in the government which is inconsistent with the liberty belonging to every man, as well as with the rights which inhere in the ownership of property. Such a holding would also be inconsistent with the freedom of interstate commerce which has been established by the Constitution of the United States....

* * *

Notes

1. The Court described the state's ownership as a "trust for the benefit of the people," and found a duty on the part of the legislature to preserve the wildlife for the future citizens ("'[B]y implication, it is the duty of the legislature to enact such laws as will best preserve the subject of the trust, and secure its beneficial use in the future to the people of the state.'" (quoting *Magner*)). The Court also referred to "common ownership, and its resulting responsibility in the state...." Perhaps this suggests that wildlife is owned in common by the people, who (implicitly) conveyed that ownership in trust to the state. Such an interpretation would make the people the settlors of the trust, the state the trustee, and the people the beneficiaries. But under traditional trust law the settlor of the trust and the beneficiaries are separate entities. GEORGE GLEASON BOGERT, GEORGE TAYLOR BOGERT AND AMY MORRIS HESS, THE LAW OF TRUSTS & TRUSTEES § 1 Terminology and Classification (3d. ed. 2014).

Were the settlors of the American trust, in effect, the original founding fathers who wrote the constitution that granted power to a new government? Did they characterize the beneficiaries as a class of present and future generations of citizens described as "ourselves and our Posterity" in the preamble to the U.S. Constitution?

2. Note that the Court cited both its *Martin v. Waddell* decision, involving ownership in trust of the beds of navigable waters, and the Minnesota Supreme Court's *State v. Rodman*, involving deer killed during hunting season but possessed more than five days after the season ended, suggesting that the Court meant to apply public trust principles equally to navigable water beds and wildlife, including terrestrial wildlife.

3. The Court traced the origins of property law back to early legal thinkers, such as Pothier and Marcien, for the proposition that certain things remain in a state of "negative community" and are classified as *res communes* belonging to the people. These resources included not only wildlife, but also air, waters, the sea and its shores. If the Court recognized sovereign ownership of wildlife based on this ancient classification, doesn't the rationale also pertain to air? Isn't air equally a trust asset belonging to the public? For an argument that it is, see Gerald Torres, *Who Owns the Sky?*, 18 Pace Envtl. L. Rev. 227, 234–35 (2001) ("The atmosphere has not, historically, been thought of as a natural resource that was subject to private ownership.... Because it could not be reduced to exclusive possession, it was generally categorized within that class of assets that were invested with a public character. To the extent that there was a property interest in the sky, it was as *res communes*.").

4. The majority opinion clearly distinguished between sovereign and individual property ownership in wildlife. The sovereign owns *ferae naturae* (species in their pre-possessory, free state) in trust for the people. Government, and government alone, can grant property rights (licenses or permits) to individuals to take individual fish or animals. The *Pierson v. Post* rule of capture applies on the individual level to determine which of two competing hunters or fishermen acquire private rights in the prey. Sovereign trust ownership of wildlife parallels other contexts. Recall that the state owns title to streambeds but can, subject to certain trust limitations, alienate title to individuals, granting private ownership subject to *jus publicum*. Recall also how, in the water context, the *Mono Lake* (p. 173) and *Waiahole Ditch* (p. 189) courts made clear that the states own the water resource in trust, but can convey usufructuary rights to individuals through water appropriation permits.

Both dissents in *Geer*, however, seemed to infer that private ownership of wildlife can be created by private actions independent of the state. But isn't property a state-created institution, and don't all property rights originate in the state? If the state doesn't recognize asserted property rights, how will such alleged rights be enforced? Without state involvement, wouldn't trespassers invade with impunity? Professor Eric Freyfogle has concluded, "It is simply not the case that private rights exist apart from law ... or exist as a form of private power that is independent of public power." Eric T. Freyfogle, *Goodbye to the Public-Private Divide*, 36 Envtl. L. 7, 15 (2006).

5. The *Geer* opinion made two assertions. One involved the state trusteeship of wildlife. The other concerned the commerce clause. As to the latter, the Court decided that prohibiting transportation of killed game out of state, "entered into and formed part of every transaction on the subject," essentially keeping the game out of the realm of interstate commerce. 161 U.S. at 530, 532 ("[T]he restriction that [the game] should not become the subject of external commerce went along with the grant, and was part of it.").

Hughes v. Oklahoma, 441 U.S. 322 (1979), overruled the second part of the opinion's reading of the commerce clause. Facing circumstances similar to *Geer*, the *Hughes* Court ruled that an Oklahoma statute prohibiting the shipping of Oklahoma minnows out-of-state violated the commerce clause. In striking this part of the *Geer* opinion, the *Hughes* Court made clear that the state's sovereignty is conditioned on constitutional restrictions that protect a national framework of economic unity. *See Hughes*, 441 U.S. at 325 ("[I]n order to succeed, the new Union would have to avoid the tendencies toward economic Balkanization that had plagued relations among the Colonies and later among the States under the Articles of Confederation."). If *Hughes* means that wildlife are articles of commerce governed by the commerce clause, why do most state attorney generals maintain that their state owns the wildlife within their borders? For a list of 47 separate state claims of state ownership of wildlife, see Michael C. Blumm & Aurora Paulsen, *The Public Trust in Wildlife*, 2013 Utah. L. Rev. 1437 app. (2013).

6. Despite the overruling of *Geer's* commerce clause holding, the Court's announcement of the wildlife trust remains in force. In his opinion for the *Hughes* Court, Justice Brennan recognized that

> the whole [state] ownership theory, in fact, is now generally regarded as but a fiction expressive in legal shorthand of the importance to its people that a State have power to preserve and regulate the exploitation of an important resource. And there is no necessary conflict between that vital policy and the constitutional command that the State exercise that power ... so as not to discriminate without reason against citizens of other States.

441 U.S. at 334 (quoting *Toomer v. Witsell*, 334 U.S. 385, 402 (1948)). Brennan proceeded to maintain that "the general rule we adopt in this case makes ample allowance for preserving, in ways not inconsistent with the Commerce Clause, the legitimate state concerns for conservation and protection of wild animals underlying the 19th-century legal fiction of state ownership." *Id.* at 335–36. For discussion, see Mary Christina Wood, *The Tribal Property Right to Wildlife Capital (Part I): Applying Principles of Sovereignty to Protect Imperiled Wildlife Populations*, 37 Idaho L. Rev. 1, 60–64 (2000) ("In rejecting the state ownership doctrine in cases of conflict with the Constitution, the Supreme Court neither overruled the sovereign trusteeship underlying the doctrine nor precluded its use in other contexts of sovereign wildlife ownership which do not conflict with the Constitution.").

Elsewhere, the Supreme Court has declared that states "unquestionably" have broad trustee powers over wildlife. *See Kleppe v. New Mexico*, 426 U.S. 529, 545 (1976). Courts continue to refer to the state trusteeship over wildlife, and some explicitly note that *Hughes* did not overrule that aspect of the *Geer* decision. *See, e.g., State v. Fertterer*, 841 P.2d 467, 470–71 (Mont. 1992), *partially overruled by State v. Gatts*, 928 P.2d 114 (Mont. 1996) (observing that *Hughes* "expressly abandoned the title ownership theory as promulgated in *Geer*...," but holding that the state continues to have an ownership interest in wild game "held by it in its sovereign capacity for the use and benefit of the people"); *Owsichek v. State, Guide Licensing and Control Bd.*, 763 P.2d 488, 495 n.12 (Alaska 1988) (noting that, after *Hughes*, statements regarding state ownership are "technically incorrect," but, "[n]evertheless, the trust responsibility that accompanied state ownership remains.") (p. 239); *see also Attorney General v. Hermes*, 339 N.W.2d 545, 550 (Mich. Ct. App. 1983) (recognizing that "the state is 'public trustee' of these resources, which are held in trust for all the people of the state in their collective capacity.").

7. The *Geer* Court clearly characterized the control over *ferae naturae* as an "attribute of government" that followed the sovereign lineage descending from England to the colonial governments, and then to the American states. In England, the ownership of *ferae naturae* was decidedly national in character, vested in the King. Elsewhere in the *Geer* opinion, the Court cited Pothier's treatise on property law to trace sovereign control of wildlife to France and all of the nations in Europe. *See Geer*, 161 U.S. at 523 ("'In France, as well as in all other civilized countries of Europe, the civil law has restrained the liberty which the pure law of nature gave to every one to capture animals who ... belong to no person in particular. The sovereigns have reserved to themselves, and to those to whom they judge proper to transmit it, the right to hunt all game, and have forbidden hunting to

other persons.'" (quoting Robert Joseph Pothier, Traité du Droit de Domaine de Propriété Nos. 27–28 (1772))).

If the trust is an attribute of government with origins applicable to national sovereigns such as England and "all civilized countries of Europe," wouldn't the wildlife trust apply to the federal government (in addition to the states) in its management of wildlife? While most of the cases dealing with the wildlife trust arise on the state level, at least one federal court explicitly applied the wildlife trust to the federal government. *See In Re Steuart Transportation Co.*, 495 F. Supp. 38, 40 (E.D. Va. 1980) (allowing federal government to seek damages for injury to migratory waterfowl under common law trust theory) (p. 372); *see also Kleppe v. New Mexico*, 426 U.S. 529, 537 (1976) (noting a possible federal property interest in horses and burros on federal lands "superior to" that of the State of New Mexico, but not deciding the matter); *Palila v. Haw. Dep't of Land & Natural Res.*, 471 F.Supp. 985, 995 n.40 (D. Haw. 1979) *aff'd*, 639 F.2d 495 (9th Cir. 1981) ("[W]here endangered species are concerned, national interests come into play.... The importance of preserving such a national resource may be of such magnitude as to rise to the level of a federal property interest.").

8. Note how the *Geer* Court distinguished between the trust and the police power. The Court explained that "there is another view of the power of the State in regard to the property in game, which is equally conclusive. The right to preserve game flows from the undoubted existence in the State of a police power to that end...." *See also Illinois Central*, 146 U.S. 387, 454 (1892) ("The State can no more abdicate its trust over property in which the whole people are interested ... than it can abdicate its police powers in the administration of government and the preservation of the peace.") (p. 68). The police power, also an attribute of government, is distinct from the trust. *See* Jan G. Laitos, Sandra B. Zellmer & Mary C. Wood, Natural Resources Law 326 (2d ed. 2012) ("Because the public trust doctrine emanates from property ownership on behalf of the public, the duties and powers to preserve the trust are distinct from the states' legislative police powers."); *Center for Biological Diversity, Inc. v. FPL Group, Inc.*, 83 Cal. Rptr. 3d 588, 600–01 (Cal. Ct. App. 2008) (distinguishing police power and public trust, noting the latter is not "superfluous" to statutes). Can you identify key differences between how these attributes of sovereignty operate? Consider the class of citizens served by each. Is the public trust doctrine unique in protecting the interests of future generations?

9. One commentator has described a state's public trust doctrine, like a state's police power, as grounded in the Tenth Amendment of the U.S. Constitution, noting that it is sometimes difficult to ascertain which power of the state's reserved powers it is invoking but observing that, under *Illinois Central Railroad v. Illinois* (p. 68), a state can abdicate neither. Moreover,

> the distinction between a state exercising its police power and acting as a trustee under the public trust doctrine is profound in the area of fifth amendment 'takings.' When a state acts under its police powers, it is regulating private property, and thus opens itself to 'takings' claims. But when a state acts under its public trust authority it is managing its own trust assets, and thus is sheltered from 'takings' claims because a state cannot unconstitutionally 'take' what it already owns in trust....
>
> ... The fact that a state's public trust authority is an aspect of state sovereignty—that the public trust authority is a core *sovereign power*—is not commonly acknowledged.

David C. Slade, The Public Trust Doctrine in Motion, 1997–2008, at 47–48 (2008).

Cawsey v. Brickey

Supreme Court of Washington

144 P. 938 (1914)

ELLIS, J.:

Action to enjoin the enforcement of an order creating a game preserve in Skagit county. The plaintiffs constitute a gun club, and have leased for a term of years certain lands as a shooting preserve, including lands of the interveners, and have for a long time maintained thereon a gun club, and have expended considerable sums in equipment. The defendants are the sheriff, prosecuting attorney, game warden, and the three members of the game commission, of Skagit county, appointed under the Game Code. Acting under section 4 of that law, the game commission selected certain lands as a game preserve, including the lands covered by the plaintiffs' lease as well as those owned by the interveners. The injunction was denied. The plaintiffs and interveners have appealed.

The appellants attack the law of 1913, and particularly subdivision 7, of section 4, claiming that it is unconstitutional ... because [it] deprives the appellants of valuable property rights and privileges without due process of law, bears unequally on different persons and communities, and is class legislation....

* * *

Subdivision 7, section 4, of the act reads as follows:

> The county game commission in their respective counties shall have the power and authority ... to set aside certain parts or portions of their respective counties as game preserves wherein no game bird or game animal or game fish can be caught or killed within the boundaries thereof, for such time and so long as they may see fit and proper....

Do these provisions tend to deprive any one of property rights or vested privileges? We think not. Under the common law of England all property right in animals *ferae naturae* was in the sovereign for the use and benefit of the people. The killing, taking, and use of game was subject to absolute governmental control for the common good. This absolute power to control and regulate was vested in the colonial governments as a part of the common law. It passed with the title to game to the several states as an incident of their sovereignty, and was retained by the states for the use and benefit of the people of the states, subject only to any applicable provisions of the federal Constitution. *Geer v. Connecticut*, 161 U.S. 519, 527, 528 (1896); *Harper v. Galloway*, 51 So. 226, 228 (Fla.1910); *State v. Snowman*, 46 A. 815 (Me.1900); *Smith v. State*, 58 N.E. 1044 (Ind. 1900); *Ex parte Maier*, 37 P. 402 (Cal. 1894); *Magner v. People*, 97 Ill. 320 (1881); *State v. Hume*, 95 P. 808 (Or. 1908); *Sherwood v. Stephens*, 90 P. 345 (Idaho 1907); *Hornbeke v. White*, 76 P. 926 (Colo. Ct. App. 1904); FREUND, POLICE POWER § 418. There is no private right in the citizen to take fish or game, except as either expressly given or inferentially suffered by the state. *State v. Tice*, 125 P. 168 (Wash. 1912). Section 21 of the Game Code provides:

> No person shall at any time or in any manner acquire any property in, or subject to his dominion or control, any of the game birds, game animals, or game fish, or any parts thereof, of the game birds, game animals or game fish herein mentioned, but they shall always and under all circumstances be and remain the property of the state.

This is but declaratory of the common law. Whatever special or qualified rights or, more correctly speaking, privileges, a landowner may have as to game, while it is on his own land, though protected by the laws of trespass as against other persons, have no protection, because they have no existence, as against the state. Since the title to game is in the state for the common good, the state's right to control, regulate, or prohibit the taking of game wheresoever found and on whosesoever land is an inherent incident of the police power of the state. TIEDEMAN'S LIMITATIONS OF POLICE POWER § 121(f). It may be exercised *ad libitum* so long as the regulation or prohibition bears equally on all persons similarly situated with reference to the subject-matter and purpose to be served by the regulation. *Portland Fish Co. v. Benson*, 108 P. 122 (Or. 1910).

Does the act here in question bear unequally on persons similarly situated so as to be obnoxious to the constitutional inhibition against class legislation? We think not. It is the universality of the operation of a law on all persons of the state similarly situated with reference to the subject-matter that determines its validity as a general and uniform law, not the extent of territory in which it operates. That its operation may not be at all times coextensive with the territorial limits of the state is usually an immaterial circumstance. The owner of land which from its location and character is peculiarly suited for a game preserve is not situated similarly to other landowners with reference to the subject-matter and purpose of a law creating a preserve. The subject-matter and purpose is protection and preservation of game. It is so declared in the title of the act. One whose land is thus peculiarly suited to meet those purposes obviously occupies a different relation to the purpose of the law from that occupied by one whose land is not so suited. When, therefore, the state authorizes the setting apart of his land for a game preserve and deprives him and all others of the privilege of taking game thereon, the law operates equally on all persons similarly situated, and is a proper exercise of the police power.

In this phase the case here is not distinguishable from *Hayes v. Territory*, 5 P. 927 (Wash. Terr. 1884), where a territorial law restricted hunting in only five counties. Obviously owners of land in those counties were subjected to restricted hunting on their own land, while owners of land in other counties could hunt on their own land without restriction. The law was assailed as invalid on the ground that it granted special privileges. The Territorial Supreme Court, through Greene, C.J., tersely and soundly disposed of the question as follows:

> The game law in question restricted hunting in five counties only. It is contended that, for this reason, it is inconsistent with that inhibition in the Organic Act, which forbids the Legislature from granting special privileges. But the provisions of this game law fall without distinction upon all inhabitants of the territory. All are forbidden to hunt at certain seasons within the counties named. There is no special privilege, unless it be in favor of the brute life of the specified area, or those of human kind who are so happy as to be alive at the hunting season.

In both the *Hayes Case* and this case the circumscribed geographical operation of the law makes the difference in the relation of those owning land within and those owning land without the circumscribed area. Barring this difference, the law is absolutely uniform in its operation on all persons. No one can hunt or take game or fish within that area.

*   *   *

... We hold that the section complained of deprives the appellants of no property right, bears equally upon all persons similarly situated, and is not void as class legislation.

*   *   *

Notes

1. *Cawsey* illustrates the result of the state ownership doctrine: hunting, even on one's own land, is a privilege which the state may grant, condition, or withhold—not a prop-

erty right incident to land ownership. This represents the dominant American view. *See, e.g., State v. Herwig*, 117 N.W.2d 335 (Wis. 1962); *Collopy v. Wildlife Comm'n*, 625 P.2d 994 (Colo. 1981); *see also Democko v. Iowa Dep't of Natural Res.*, 840 N.W.2d 281, 293–94 (Iowa 2013) (upholding an Iowa statute restricting hunting by non-resident landowners because under the statute "a landowner ha[d] no title to or interest in wildlife within the state borders, even if the wildlife is on the landowner's property").

2. On the other hand, there are a few cases indicating that a landowner has a right to hunt on her own land independent of state sanction. *See, e.g., Alford v. Finch*, 155 So.2d 790 (Fla. 1963) (explaining that a right to hunt is inherent in fee simple ownership, so the state could not classify his land as a wildlife refuge); *Allen v. McClellan*, 405 P.2d 405 (N.M. 1965) (concluding that a state attempt to designate private land as a wildlife preserve violated the landowner's right to hunt game on his property).

3. *Cawsey* reflects a judicial sensitivity to the contextual nature of property rights. The gun club's right to hunt was cabined by the natural features of the land—in this case, its value as wildlife habitat. A more abstract, less contextual perspective might have produced a judicial conclusion that the state had taken the club's property rights. Instead, the court concluded that the environmentally sensitive nature of the land was a legitimate reason to restrict the gun club and similarly situated landowners' rights. In *Penn Central Transp. Co. v. City of New York*, 438 U.S. 104, 132 (1978), the Supreme Court rejected an attack on the city's historic landmarks ordinance, ruling that although it affected only selected properties, it ensured against unfairness or arbitrary application through "a comprehensive plan to preserve structures of historic or aesthetic interest wherever they might be found in the city...."

Barrett v. State

New York Court of Appeals
116 N.E. 99 (1917)

ANDREWS, J.:

At one time beaver were very numerous in this state. So important were they commercially that they were represented upon the seal of the New Netherlands and upon that of the colony as well as upon the seals of New Amsterdam and of New York. Because of their value, they were relentlessly killed, and by the year 1900 they were practically exterminated. But some 15 animals were left scattered through the southern portion of Franklin county. In that year the Legislature undertook to afford them complete protection, and there has been no open season for beaver since the enactment of chapter 20 of the Laws of 1900.

In 1904 it was further provided that:

> No person shall molest or disturb any wild beaver or the dams, houses, homes or abiding places of same.

This is still the law, although in 1912 the forest, fish, and game commission was authorized to permit protected animals which had become destructive to public or private property to be taken and disposed of.

By the act of 1904, $500 was appropriated for the purchase of wild beaver to restock the Adirondacks, and in 1906 $1,000 more was appropriated for the same purpose. The commission, after purchasing the animals, was authorized to liberate them. Under this authority 21 beaver have been purchased and freed by the commission. Of these 4 were placed upon Eagle creek, an inlet of the Fourth Lake of the Fulton Chain. There they seem to have remained and increased.

Beaver are naturally destructive to certain kinds of forest trees. During the fall and winter they live upon the bark of the twigs and smaller branches of poplar, birch, and alder. To obtain a supply they fell even trees of large size, cut the smaller branches into suitable lengths, and pull or float them to their houses. All this it must be assumed was known by the Legislature as early as 1900.

The claimants own a valuable tract of woodland upon Fourth Lake bounded in the rear by Eagle creek. Their land was held by them for building sites and was suitable for that purpose. Much of its attractiveness depended upon the forest grown upon it. In this forest were a number of poplar trees. In 1912 and during two or three years prior thereto 198 of these poplars were felled by beaver. Others were girdled and destroyed. The Court of Claims has found, upon evidence that fairly justifies the inference, that this destruction was caused by the four beaver liberated on Eagle creek and their descendants, and that by reason thereof the claimants have been damaged in the sum of $1,900. An award was made to them for that sum, and this award has been affirmed by the Appellate Division. To sustain it the respondents rely upon three propositions. It is said: First, that the state may not protect such an animal as the beaver which is known to be destructive; second, that the provision of the law of 1904 with regard to the molestation of beaver prohibits the claimants from protecting their property, and is therefore an unreasonable exercise of the police power; and, third, that the state was in actual physical possession of the beaver placed on Eagle creek, and that its act in freeing them, knowing their natural propensity to destroy trees, makes the state liable for the damage done by them.

We cannot agree with either of these propositions.

As to the first, the general right of the government to protect wild animals is too well established to be now called in question. Their ownership is in the state in its sovereign capacity, for the benefit of all the people. Their preservation is a matter of public interest. They are a species of natural wealth which without special protection would be destroyed. Everywhere and at all times governments have assumed the right to prescribe how and when they may be taken or killed. As early as 1705, New York passed such an act as to deer. A series of statutes has followed protecting more or less completely game, birds, and fish.

> The protection and preservation of game has been secured by law in all civilized countries, and may be justified on many grounds.... The measures best adapted to this end are for the Legislature to determine, and courts cannot review its discretion. If the regulations operate, in any respect, unjustly or oppressively, the proper remedy must be applied by that body.

Phelps v. Racey, 60 N.Y. 10, 14 (1875).

Wherever protection is accorded, harm may be done to the individual. Deer or moose may browse on his crops; mink or skunks kill his chickens; robins eat his cherries. In certain cases the Legislature may be mistaken in its belief that more good than harm is occasioned. But this is clearly a matter which is confided to its discretion. It exercises a governmental function for the benefit of the public at large, and no one can complain of the incidental injuries that may result.

It is sought to draw a distinction between such animals and birds as have ordinarily received protection and beaver, on the ground that the latter are unusually destructive and that to preserve them is an unreasonable exercise of the power of the state.

The state may exercise the police power

wherever the public interests demand it, and in this particular a large discretion is necessary vested in the Legislature to determine, not only what the interest of the public require, but what measures are necessary for the protection of such interests.... To justify the state in thus interposing its authority in behalf of the public, it must appear, first, that the interests of the public generally, as distinguished from those of a particular class, require such interference; and, second, that the means are reasonably necessary for the accomplishment of the purpose, and not unduly oppressive upon individuals.

Lawton v. Steele, 152 U.S. 133, 136 (1894).

The police power is not to be limited to guarding merely the physical or material interests of the citizen. His moral, intellectual, and spiritual needs may also be considered. The eagle is preserved, not for its use, but for its beauty.

The same thing may be said of the beaver. They are one of the most valuable of the fur-bearing animals of the state. They may be used for food. But apart from these considerations, their habits and customs, their curious instincts and intelligence, place them in a class by themselves. Observation of the animals at work or play is a source of never-failing interest and instruction. If they are to be preserved experience has taught us that protection is required. If they cause more damage than deer or moose, the degree of the mischief done by them is not so much greater or so different as to require the application of a special rule. If the preservation of the former does not unduly oppress individuals, neither does the latter.

In the determination of what is a reasonable exercise of the powers of the government, the acts of other governments under similar circumstances have some bearing. In Wyoming, Utah, North Dakota, Wisconsin, Maine, Colorado, and Vermont, beaver are absolutely protected. In Michigan, they are protected except between November 1st and May 15th of each year. In South Dakota, except between November 15th and April 2d. In Quebec, for a number of years there was no open season. Lately there has been an open season for a short time in the autumn.

We therefore reach the conclusion that in protecting beaver the Legislature did not exceed its powers. Nor did it so do in prohibiting their molestation. It is possible that were the interpretation given by the respondents to this section right a different result might follow. If the claimants, finding beaver destroying their property, might not drive them away, then possibly their rights would be infringed. In *Aldrich v. Wright*, 53 N.H. 398 (1873), it was said in an elaborate opinion, although this question we do not decide, that a farmer might shoot mink even in the closed season should he find them threatening his geese.

But such an interpretation is too rigid and narrow. The claimants might have fenced their land without violation of the statute. They might have driven the beaver away, were they injuring their property. The prohibition against disturbing dams or houses built on or adjoining water courses is no greater or different exercise of power from that assumed by the Legislature when it prohibits the destruction of the nests and eggs of wild birds even when the latter are found upon private property.

The object is to protect the beaver. That object as we decide is within the power of the state. The destruction of dams and houses will result in driving away the beaver. The prohibition of such acts, being an apt means to the end desired, is not so unreasonable as to be beyond the legislative power.

We hold therefore that the acts referred to are constitutional....

Somewhat different considerations apply to the act of the state in purchasing and liberating beaver. The attempt to introduce life into a new environment does not always result happily. The rabbit in Australia, the mongoose in the West Indies, have become pests. The English sparrow is no longer welcome. Certain of our most troublesome *weeds* are foreign flowers.

Yet governments have made such experiments in the belief that the public good would be promoted. Sometimes they have been mistaken. Again, the attempt has succeeded. The English pheasant is a valuable addition to our stock of birds. But whether a success or failure, the attempt is well within governmental powers.

If this is so with regard to foreign life, still more is it true with regard to animals native to the state, still existing here, when the intent is to increase the stock upon what the Constitution declares shall remain forever wild forest lands. If the state may provide for the increase of beaver by prohibiting their destruction, it is difficult to see why it may not attain the same result by removing colonies to a more favorable locality or by replacing those destroyed by fresh importations.

Nor are the cases cited by the respondents controlling. It is true that one who keeps wild animals in captivity must see to it at his peril that they do no damage to others. But it is not true that whenever an individual is liable for a certain act the state is liable for the same act. In liberating these beaver the state was acting as a government. As a trustee for the people and as their representative, it was doing what it thought best for the interests of the public at large. Under such circumstances, we cannot hold that the rule of such cases as those cited is applicable.

We reach the conclusion that no recovery can be had under this claim....

The judgment of the Appellate Division and the determination of the Court of Claims must be reversed, and the claim dismissed, with costs in Appellate Division and in this court.

Notes

1. In *Lucas v. South Carolina Coastal Council*, 505 U.S. 1003 (1992), in the process of finding a taking of a landowner's property due to a development restriction, the Supreme Court, per Justice Scalia, stated that development restrictions that wiped out all landowner value would nevertheless not be a constitutional taking if they merely replicated "background principles" of state property law. Does the *Barrett* result fall within the *Lucas* takings exception for "background principles"?

2. The *Barrett* case presents the overwhelming majority rule. *See Mountain States Legal Foundation v. Hodel*, 799 F.2d 1423, 1429 (10th Cir. 1986) (collecting cases in the process of denying a takings claim brought by ranchers complaining that federally protected wild horses consumed grass on the rancher's land, which were checker-boarded with federal land). These cases make clear that a property owner has no entitlement to harm wildlife on his or her privately owned land without authority of the state, which owns the wildlife in trust. *See Mountain States Legal Foundation*, 799 F.2d at 1426 ("[I]t is well settled that wild animals are not the private property of those whose land they occupy, but are instead a sort of common property whose control and regulation are to be exercised 'as a trust for the benefit of the people'" (quoting *Geer v. Connecticut*, 161 U.S. at 528–29)). Does this rule, in effect, reflect another aspect of the public's reserved *jus publicum* easement on private land? Recall the streambed cases that relied on the *jus publicum* to uphold public access over privately owned tidelands. The wildlife cases make clear that wildlife access must be protected anywhere on private property, indicating that this aspect of the sovereign's reserved property interest is not confined to tidelands (the conventional focus of public trust cases).

3. Apart from protecting actual species located on private land, does the wildlife trust doctrine protect their habitat on private land? The question has gained paramount importance, as 75% of species listed under the Endangered Species Act (ESA) occur on private land. *See* U.S. Department of Agriculture, U.S. Forest Service (Northeastern Area), *Threatened and Endangered Species and the Private Landowner*, http://www.na.fs.fed.us/ spfo/pubs/wildlife/endangered/endangered.htm. The law upheld in *Barrett* protected not only the beavers themselves but their "dams, houses, homes or abiding places of same...," which implicates habitat. In another classic case, *State v. Sour Mountain Realty, Inc.*, 714 N.Y.S.2d 78, 84 (2000), the court relied in part on the wildlife trust doctrine to uphold (against a takings claim) a requirement protecting rattlesnakes' access to their habitat. The landowner in that case wished to use his property for mining purposes. When a den of rattlesnakes (a threatened species in New York) was found a few hundred feet off his property, the landowner constructed a "snake proof" fence that prevented their entry onto his property. Because the rattlesnakes would have naturally foraged on the private property, the court granted the Department of Environmental Conservation's motion for a preliminary injunction requiring removal of the fence.

In a comprehensive article exploring the wildlife trust and constitutional takings claims, Professor John Echeverria and Julie Lurman compiled cases that sustain habitat protection requirements (many arising outside the context of the ESA) against constitutional challenge. *See* John D. Echeverria & Julie Lurman, *"Perfectly Astounding" Public Rights: Wildlife Protection and the Takings Clause*, 16 Tulane Envtl. L.J. 331 (2003). They concluded:

> Older, non-ESA cases support the conclusion that the public ownership argument should cover activities which indirectly kill or injure wildlife....
>
> While modern wildlife laws often involve more extensive restrictions on private land use than older wildlife laws, public sovereign rights should continue to be recognized. The basic nature of public rights in wild animals remains the same as in past centuries, and the doctrine should continue to apply with the same force even if the nature of the threats to wildlife has changed somewhat. The Supreme Court in *Lucas* famously observed that the meaning and scope of background principles must evolve as "changed circumstances or new knowledge may make what was previously permissible no longer so." No extravagant extension of earlier precedent is required to apply the public ownership argument in today's circumstances. Property owners never had a protected right to destroy wildlife present on their land and modern wildlife laws simply continue the implementation of this long-standing principle.

Id. at 382–83.

State Department of Fisheries v. Gillette

Court of Appeals of Washington
621 P.2d 764 (1980)

REED, C.J.:

Defendants Cyril and Sharon Gillette appeal a verdict and judgment awarding damages to the Washington State Department of Fisheries for loss of salmon caused when the Gillettes reconstructed the bank of a stream bordering their property....

[Defendants farmed property bordering a salmon spawning stream. When flooding deposited soil and gravel on their pasture, one of Gillettes' employees was directed to rebuild the bank. The employee testified that, using a tractor with an attached blade, he drove back and forth through the stream and pushed material from the creek bed and the adjacent field to construct a dike that rose as much as 20 feet above the creek.]

RCW 75.20.100 provides that anyone wishing to construct a hydraulic project that will interfere with any river or stream bed must obtain written approval from both the Director of Fisheries and the Director of Game. The statute's purpose is to ensure that such projects include adequate protection for the fish life involved. Violation of the statute is a gross misdemeanor. Being unaware of the statute's requirements, the Gillettes did not obtain the necessary hydraulics project permit.

Representatives of both the Department of Game and the Department of Fisheries responded to reports of the construction and inspected the scene. The Department of Fisheries then filed this action in negligence for damages for the loss to the salmon fishery caused by the project. At the close of the evidence, the court granted Fisheries a directed verdict on the issue of liability. The jury thus considered only proximate cause and damage issues and awarded the State $3,150. Defendants appeal.

Capacity and Standing

* * *

The second prong of defendants' argument opposing Department of Fisheries' standing raises a more significant question. Does the Department of Fisheries, or the State of Washington for that matter, have standing to bring a civil action for damage to fish, absent specific legislative authorization? Although no Washington cases have addressed this question, and other jurisdictions have divided on the issue, we believe our statutes and court decisions provide the guidance necessary for its resolution.

First, the legislature has specifically charged the Department of Fisheries with the duty "to preserve, protect, perpetuate and manage the food fish and shellfish in the waters of the state.... [T]he department shall seek to maintain the economic well-being and stability of the commercial fishing industry in the state of Washington." RCW 75.08.012. Our courts have long recognized the rule that "when a statute contains a grant of authority to achieve a lawful objective there is included in the grant by implication the doing of such acts as are reasonably necessary to properly attain such objective." *State v. Melton*, 248 P.2d 892 (Wash. 1952). There is no question that the Hydraulics Act furthers the lawful objectives outlined in RCW 75.08.012. Nor does it seem unreasonable for the Department to protect the fish in its charge through a damage action when individuals have caused a loss to the fishery.

Second, the state's proprietary interest in animals *ferae naturae* dates at least from the common law of England. *See* 2 WILLIAM BLACKSTONE, COMMENTARIES *403. Our courts have incorporated this concept in cases upholding the state's authority to regulate fish and game. *State Department of Fisheries v. Chelan County P.U.D. 1*, 588 P.2d 1146 (Wash. 1979), and cases cited therein. Washington courts have emphasized that the food fish of the state are the sole property of the people and that the state, acting for the people, is dealing with its own property, "over which its control is as absolute as that of any other owner over his property." *State ex rel. Bacich v. Huse*, 59 P.2d 1101 (Wash. 1936). In addition to recognizing the state's proprietary interest in its fish, our courts have also held that the state holds its title as trustee for the common good. *Id.*

In bringing this action, the Department of Fisheries specifically relied on its capacity as trustee and its responsibilities under RCW Title 75 to protect the state's fisheries.... Representing the people of the state—the owners of the property destroyed by violation of the statute—the Department of Fisheries thus has a right of action for damages. In addition, the state, through the Department, has the fiduciary obligation of any trustee to seek damages for injury to the object of its trust. We note in passing that if the state were denied a right of recovery for the damage which the jury found this construction did to the state's fishery, no one would have standing to recover for the injury. *Department of Environmental Protection v. Jersey Central Power & Light Co.*, 336 A.2d 750, 759 (N.J. Super. Ct. Ap. Div. 1975), *rev'd on other grounds*, 351 A.2d 337 (N.J. 1976) (questionable whether, absent special interest, anyone but state is proper party to sue for damages to environment). We therefore hold that where the violation of a statute designed to protect the state's property causes injury to that property, the state or a responsible executive agency of the state has standing to seek compensation for the injury.

* * *

Affirmed.

Notes

1. The *Gillette* decision allowed the state to sue for damages to wildlife habitat. On what basis? There was no statute explicitly authorizing a suit for damages. This case is instructive for pointing out the authority and duty emanating from the realm of trust law as opposed to statutory law. The court emphasized that, as trustee, the Department held a right of action for damages to the asset. Other cases have found the same authority supported by common law. *See, e.g., State v. City of Bowling Green*, 313 N.E.2d 409, 411 (Ohio 1974) ("The state's right to recover exists simply by virtue of the public trust property interest which is protected by traditional common law....").

2. The court indicates that the state must have the power to sue for damages, since no one else could do so. *But see Columbia River Fishermen's Protective Union v. City of St. Helens*, 87 P.2d 195, 197–98 (Or. 1939) (allowing licensed fisherman to sue for damage to their equipment and for interference with their fishing livelihoods as a result of municipal and industrial pollution discharges, noting that the fishermen's interests were "distinct from the public" and that "this suit is not brought for the purpose of obtaining the salmon but to protect the right of fishermen to pursue their vocation of fishing").

3. Notice that the court apparently believes that the state, as trustee, not only has the authority but also the duty to seek damages (the state "has the fiduciary obligation of any trustee to seek damages for injury to the object of its trust"). *See also In re Steuart Transportation Co.*, 495 F. Supp. 38, 40 (E.D. Va. 1980) (state and federal government have "the right and the duty ... to preserve the public's interest" in wildlife by seeking damages resulting from an oil spill). In *City of Bowling Green*, above, the court explained the duty, stating:

> The common law in Ohio has consistently recognized the trust doctrine and that it is predicated upon the property interest which the state holds in such wildlife as a trustee for all citizens.

> We conclude that where the state is deemed to be the trustee of property for the benefit of the public it has the obligation to bring suit not only to protect the corpus of the trust property but also to recoup the public's loss occasioned by the negligent acts of those who damage such property....

> An action against those whose conduct damages or destroys such property, which is a natural resource of the public, must be considered an essential part of a trust doctrine, the vitality of which must be extended to meet the changing societal needs.

313 N.E.2d at 411.

Do these cases mean that if a state does not file an action for damages, citizens may sue the state to compel it to do so? Trust logic assumes they should be able to. As one treatise explains, a trustee "is obligated to the beneficiary to do all acts necessary for the preservation of the trust res...." GEORGE GLEASON BOGERT, GEORGE T. BOGERT & AMY MOR-RIS HESS, THE LAW OF TRUSTS & TRUSTEES § 582 (3d ed. 2014). Recognizing the danger of recalcitrant trustees, private trust law allows beneficiaries to sue an indolent trustee who neglects to bring a suit for damage to trust property (and a beneficiary may even sue the third-party wrongdoer where the trustee fails to do so, as long as the suit also names the trustee as a defendant). *Id.* § 871.

4. The *Gillette* case and others like it form a body of public trust jurisprudence that focuses on "natural resource damages," otherwise known as NRDs. While lodged in common law, authority for seeking NRDs exists in federal statutes as well, such as the Oil Pollution Act (OPA) and the Comprehensive Environmental Response Cleanup Liability Act (CERCLA). These statutes make clear that, in addition to states, the federal government and tribes stand as sovereign trustees authorized to recoup damages to natural resources. *See* CERCLA, 42 U.S.C. § 9607(f)(1) (stating liability for natural resources "shall be to the United States Government and to any State ... and to any Indian tribe for natural resources belonging to, managed by, controlled by, or appertaining to such tribe, or held in trust for the benefit of such tribe."); OPA, 33 U.S.C. § 2706(a) (similar). For discussion of natural resource damages, see Carter H. Strickland, Jr., *The Scope of Authority of Natural Resource Trustees*, 20 Colum. J. Envtl. L. 301 (1995). A recent high-profile NRD settlement involved the BP oil spill. *See* KRISTINA ALEXANDER, CONG. RESEARCH SERV., R41396, THE 2010 OIL SPILL: NATURAL RESOURCE DAMAGE ASSESSMENT UNDER THE OIL POLLUTION ACT (2010), *available at* www.fas.org/sgp/crs/misc/R41396.pdf.

5. Note that the *Gillette* court describes the state's interest in wildlife as "proprietary" and says "the state, acting for the people, is dealing with its own property, 'over which its control is as absolute as that of any other owner over his property.'" 621 P.2d at 767. What the court undoubtedly meant was that the state, as trustee, held all of the powers of a private party in protection of the asset and, like a private owner, could sue for damage to property. The court could not have literally meant that the state's ownership is as "absolute" as other private property owners, for a trust comes with strict fiduciary obligations that do not bind standard property owners. A trust bifurcates ownership between the trustee (legal owner) and the beneficiaries, and imposes an unwavering duty on the trustee to manage the property in the interests of the beneficiaries. The court was quick to clarify, "In addition to recognizing the state's proprietary interest in its fish, our courts have also held that the state holds its title as trustee for the common good." *Id.* Early cases, like the *Rodman* case (and *Geer,* which quoted it), were more careful in their use of ownership terminology. *See State v. Rodman,* 59 N.W. 1098, 1099 (Minn. 1894) ("We take it to be the correct doctrine in this country that the ownership of wild animals, so far as they are capable of ownership, is in the state, not as proprietor, but in its sovereign capacity, as the representative, and for the benefit, of all its people in common."). The proprietary language comes up frequently in cases dealing with federal public lands, causing significant confusion in that realm, as explored further in the next chapter.

Owsichek v. State, Guide Licensing and Control Bd.

Supreme Court of Alaska
763 P.2d 488 (1988)

RABINOWITZ, C.J.:

We are called upon to decide whether two statutes, AS 08.54.040(a)(7) & .195, comport with article VIII, section 3 of the Alaska Constitution. These statutes authorize the

Guide Licensing and Control Board to grant hunting guides "exclusive guide areas," [(EGAs)] geographic areas in which only the designated guide may lead hunts and from which all other guides are excluded. Licensed hunters, including other guides, may hunt recreationally in these areas, but only the holder of the exclusive guide area may lead hunts professionally.

* * *

... Owsichek submitted an application for EGAs in Units 17 and 19 before the November 1, 1976, deadline established by the Board. The Board considered applications for EGAs in Units 17 and 19 in its December 1977 meeting. Owsichek's application was denied on the ground that he had not submitted "evidence of contracts for guided hunts in the area for two of the five years preceding the application."

* * *

We observe initially that, in guaranteeing people "common use" of fish, wildlife and water resources, the framers of the constitution clearly did not intend to prohibit all regulation of the use of these resources. Licensing requirements, bag limits, and seasonal restrictions, for example, are time-honored methods of conserving the resources that were respected by delegates to the constitutional convention. Questions presented by this case concern the type and extent of permissible regulation consistent with common use.

* * *

We begin by examining constitutional history to determine the framers' intent in enacting the common use clause. This was a unique provision, not modeled on any other state constitution. Its purpose was anti-monopoly. This purpose was achieved by constitutionalizing common law principles imposing upon the state a public trust duty with regard to the management of fish, wildlife and waters.

The framers' reliance on historic principles regarding state management of wildlife and water resources is evident from a written explanation in the committee materials for the term "reserved to the people for common use." This discussion also highlights an intent to prohibit "exclusive grants or special privilege[s]."

> Ancient traditions in property rights have never recognized that a private right and title can be acquired by a private person to wildlife in their natural state or to water in general. The title remained with the sovereign, and in the American system of government with its concept of popular sovereignty this title is reserved to the people or the state on behalf of the people. *The expression "for common use" implies that these resources are not to be subject to exclusive grants or special privilege as was so frequently the case in ancient royal tradition.* Rather rights to use are secured by the general laws of the state. In all English and American legal systems ownership of water cannot be asserted, rights acquire only to the *use* of water. Once wildlife is captured and removed from their natural state possessory right accrues to the captor, provided that the wildlife was captured in conformity with provisions of law.

Alaska Constitutional Convention Papers, Folder 210, paper prepared by Committee on Resources entitled "Terms" (emphasis added, except to "use"). Because an EGA is clearly a type of monopoly, "exclusive grant," or at least a "special privilege," this history strongly suggests that the statutes at issue here are unconstitutional. However, this history also states that "rights to use are secured by the general laws of the state," clearly giving the legislature some leeway in regulating use of the resources.

* * *

In a discussion about fishing in lakes, the Constitutional Convention underscored its intent that the public retain broad access to fish, wildlife and water resources, and that these resources not be the subject of private grants. In floor debates, a question arose about the status of a natural lake falling within the boundaries of someone's private property. The delegates agreed that the common use clause guaranteed the public's right to use the lake for fishing, although it did not authorize a trespass across the landowner's property to get to the lake. 4 Proceedings of the Alaska Constitutional Convention 2460 (Jan. 17, 1956). The Convention made it clear that only fish in small private ponds may be owned free of the public's right of access. *See id.* at 2460–61; 6 Proceedings of the Alaska Constitutional Convention app. V, at 98 (Commentary on Article on State Lands and Natural Resources, Jan. 16, 1956). This confirms the view of the common use clause and the public trust expressed in *CWC Fisheries v. Bunker,* 755 P.2d 1115 (Alaska 1988), holding that a grant of a fee interest in tidelands remains impressed with a public trust easement. It also reinforces our conclusion that grants of exclusive rights to harvest natural resources listed in the common use clause should be subjected to close scrutiny.

As we have noted, the drafters of the common use clause apparently intended to constitutionalize historic common law principles governing the sovereign's authority over management of fish, wildlife and water resources. A review of the history of wildlife law will therefore shed further light on the central issue in this case.

The Supreme Court traced the history of wildlife law from its roots in ancient Rome through its English common law development and transfer to this country in *Geer v. Connecticut,* 161 U.S. 519, 522–29 (1896). In that case, the Court affirmed the defendant's conviction, upholding a state statute forbidding transportation of certain game birds killed in Connecticut across state lines. The Court noted that in England, the right to hunt and fish "[was] vested in the King alone and from him derived to such of his subjects as [had] received the grants of a chase, a park, a free warren, or free fishery." *Id.* at 527 (quoting 2 W. Blackstone, *Commentaries* *410). As a recent authority explains: "Stripped of its many formalities, the essential core of English wildlife law on the eve of the American Revolution was the complete authority of the king and Parliament to determine what rights others might have with respect to the taking of wildlife." Michael J. Bean, The Evolution of National Wildlife Law 12 (2d ed. 1983).

The *Geer* court asserted that this authority to regulate taking of wildlife passed to the states upon separation from England. 161 U.S. at 528. However, unlike the authority vested in the King, the authority of the states, with their guarantees of democratic government, was not plenary.

> Whilst the fundamental principles upon which the common property in game rests have undergone no change, the development of free institutions has led to the recognition of the fact that the power or control lodged in the state, resulting from this common ownership, is to be exercised like all other powers of government *as a trust for the benefit of the people,* and not as a prerogative for the advantage of the government as distinct from the people, *or for the benefit of private individuals as distinguished from the public good.*

Id. at 529 (emphasis added). The Court held that the state's "ownership" of wildlife, in trust for the people, authorized the statute at issue in that case. *Id.*

The framers of the common use clause probably relied heavily on *Geer.* The following statement from the constitutional papers, as quoted above, closely tracks the reasoning of *Geer:*

The title remained with the sovereign, and in the American system of government with its concept of popular sovereignty this title is reserved to the people or the state on behalf of the people. The expression "for common use" implies that these resources are not to be subject to exclusive grants or special privilege as was so frequently the case in ancient royal tradition.

Alaska Constitutional Convention Papers, Folder 210, paper prepared by Committee on Resources entitled "Terms."

Thus, common law principles incorporated in the common use clause impose upon the state a trust duty to manage the fish, wildlife and water resources of the state for the benefit of all the people.[5] We have twice recognized this duty in our prior decisions. In *Metlakatla Indian Community, Annette Island Reserve v. Egan*, 362 P.2d 901 (Alaska 1961), *aff'd*, 369 U.S. 45 (1962), we stated: "These migrating schools of fish, while in inland waters, are the property of the state, *held in trust for the benefit of all the people of the state*, and the obligation and authority to equitably and wisely regulate the harvest is that of the state." *Id.* at 915 (emphasis added). Similarly, in *Herscher v. State, Department of Commerce*, 568 P.2d 996 (Alaska 1977), we noted that the state acts "as trustee of the natural resources for the benefit of its citizens." *Id.* at 1003.

The extent to which this public trust duty, as constitutionalized by the common use clause, limits a state's discretion in managing its resources is not clearly defined. The state argues that it imposes no limit at all. While acknowledging that the common use clause constitutionalizes the state's trust duty, the state asserts, "The sovereign's power to allow and control use of the resources is broad, and restricted only by other constitutional limitations such as equal protection." This assertion clearly overstates the extent of the state's authority under the public trust duty and the common use clause.

First, as noted above, this court has stated in at least four cases that the common use clause is intended to provide independent protection of the public's access to natural resources. *See Johns v. Commercial Fisheries Entry Comm'n*, 758 P.2d 1256, 1266 & n.12 (Alaska 1988); *CWC Fisheries v. Bunker*, 755 P.2d 1115, 1120 (Alaska 1988); *State v. Ostrosky*, 667 P.2d 1184, 1189, 1191 (Alaska 1983), *appeal dismissed*, 467 U.S. 1201 (1984); *Werberg v. State*, 516 P.2d 1191, 1198–99 (Alaska 1973); *see also Ostrosky*, 667 P.2d at 1196 (Rabinowitz, J., dissenting).

Second, under the state's interpretation, the common use clause would be a nullity. "It is a well-accepted principle of judicial construction that, whenever reasonably possible, every provision of the Constitution should be given meaning and effect, and related provisions should be harmonized." *Park v. State*, 528 P.2d 785, 786–87 (Alaska 1974). To give meaning and effect to the common use clause, it must provide protection of the public's use of natural resources distinct from that provided by other constitutional provisions.

Third, the history of the common use clause, as noted above, reveals an anti-monopoly intent to prohibit "exclusive grants" and "special privilege[s]," wholly apart from the limits imposed by other constitutional provisions.

---

5. The Court overruled *Geer*'s state ownership doctrine in *Hughes v. Oklahoma*, 441 U.S. 322 (1979).... Nothing in the opinion, however, indicated any retreat from the state's public trust duty discussed in Geer. Indeed, the Court stated, "[T]he general rule we adopt in this case makes ample allowance for preserving, in ways not inconsistent with the Commerce Clause, the legitimate state concerns for conservation and protection of wild animals underlying the 19th century legal fiction of state ownership." Id. at 335–36.

Finally, cases applying the public trust doctrine in navigable waters have frequently struck down state actions in violation of the trust without any reference to either federal or state constitutions. A good example is the lodestar of American public trust law, *Illinois Central Railroad Co. v. Illinois*, 146 U.S. 387 (1892). In that case, the Illinois legislature purported to grant to a railroad more than 1,000 acres of land underlying Lake Michigan in the harbor of Chicago. The Court applied the doctrine of the public trust in navigable waters to uphold the legislature's later revocation of the grant:

> A grant of all the lands under the navigable waters of a State has never been adjudged to be within the legislative power; and any attempted grant of the kind would be held, if not absolutely void on its face, as subject to revocation. The State can no more abdicate its trust over property in which the whole people are interested ... than it can abdicate its police powers in the administration of government and the preservation of the peace.

Id. at 453.

In light of this historical review we conclude that the common use clause was intended to engraft in our constitution certain trust principles guaranteeing access to the fish, wildlife and water resources of the state. The proceedings of the Constitutional Convention, together with the common law tradition on which the delegates built, convince us that a minimum requirement of this duty is a prohibition against any monopolistic grants or special privileges. Accordingly, we are compelled to strike down any statutes or regulations that violate this principle.

We conclude that exclusive guide areas and joint use areas fall within the category of grants prohibited by the common use clause. These areas allow one guide to exclude all other guides from leading hunts professionally in "his" area. These grants are based primarily on use, occupancy and investment, favoring established guides at the expense of new entrants in the market, such as Owsichek. To grant such a special privilege based primarily on seniority runs counter to the notion of "common use."

[The court denied Owsichek damages, under the discretionary function exception of the state Tort Claims Act.]

Notes

1. Alaska has constitutionalized the antimonopoly sentiment reflected in the public trust doctrine through its common use clause. After an extensive historical overview of the trust, the court stated, "In light of this historical review we conclude that the common use clause was intended to engraft in our constitution certain trust principles guaranteeing access to the fish, wildlife and water resources of the state." What is the significance of a constitutional basis for the doctrine, as opposed to a common law or statutory basis? Given the historical underpinnings of the public trust and its description by multiple courts as an "attribute of government" (or attribute of sovereignty, as in *Geer*), could the doctrine be implied as "engrafted" in all federal and state constitutions, even those without common use clauses? The *Owsichek* court noted that "cases applying the public trust doctrine in navigable waters have frequently struck down state actions in violation of the trust without any reference to either federal or state constitutions."

2. Note that the court described the trust as an outgrowth of "popular sovereignty," emphasizing *Geer's* statement that the trust must be managed "not as a prerogative for the advantage of the government as distinct from the people, or for the benefit of private individuals as distinguished from the public good." Do you think that government

agencies today managing natural resources, pursuant to statutory authority, carry out the spirit of popular sovereignty, or do they tend towards monopolistic outcomes? Consider again the subject of drinking water aquifers discussed in the last chapter. Would a grant of a permit to a bottling company present a monopoly that violates the principles set forth in the *Owsichek* decision? Does the public trust add a dimension of duty missing in statutory law?

3. Notice that the Alaska Supreme Court is confident that *Geer v. Connecticut* survived *Hughes v. Oklahoma* in terms of state ownership of wildlife. Virtually all states claim sovereign ownership of the wildlife within their borders. *See* Oliver A. Houck, *Why Do We Protect Endangered Species, and What Does that Say About Whether Restrictions on Private Property to Protect Them Constitute "Takings"?*, 80 Iowa L. Rev. 297, 309–11, n.76 (1995); Michael C. Blumm & Aurora Paulsen, *The Public Trust in Wildlife*, 2013 Utah L. Rev. 1437, 1488–1504 (listing constitutional and statutory declarations of sovereign ownership of wildlife in 47 states).

Center for Biological Diversity, Inc. v. FPL Group, Inc.
California Court of Appeal
83 Cal. Rptr. 3d 588 (2008)

POLLAK, J.:

Plaintiffs, the Center for Biological Diversity, Inc. and Peter Galvin (collectively CBD), appeal from the dismissal of their cause of action, which alleged that defendant owners and operators of wind turbine electric generators in the Altamont Pass Wind Resource Area in Alameda and Contra Costa Counties are, by the operation of their wind turbines, responsible for killing and injuring raptors and other birds in violation of the public trust doctrine. The trial court dismissed their action ... on the ground that private parties are not entitled to bring an action for the violation of the public trust doctrine arising from the destruction of wildlife. We conclude that the trial court properly dismissed this particular action, although we qualify its broad holding and reject even broader assertions advanced by defendants in support of its ruling. Wildlife, including birds, is considered to be a public trust resource of all the people of the state, and private parties have the right to bring an action to enforce the public trust. Nonetheless, in other proceedings of which we take judicial notice, the public agencies responsible for protecting these trust resources have taken action to do so. The proper means to challenge the adequacy of those measures is by petition for a writ of mandate or request for other appropriate relief brought against those agencies. Permitting the action to proceed as presented would require the court to make complex and delicate balancing judgments without the benefit of the expertise of the agencies responsible for protecting the trust resources and would threaten redundancy at best and inconsistency at worst.

Background

In 1980, in response to federal legislation intended to encourage the development of alternative energy sources, the State Energy Resources Conservation and Development Commission (California Energy Commission) created the Altamont Pass Wind Resource Area.... Alameda County issued 46 use permits to operate private wind energy generation facilities in the approximately 40,000-acre Alameda County portion of this area. Plaintiffs' amended complaint alleges that there are currently more than 5,000 wind turbine generators operating in Altamont Pass. The amended complaint alleges that ..."Since the 1980's, the ... generators ... have killed tens of thousands of birds, including between 17,000 and 26,000 raptors...."

Plaintiffs allege that defendants' conduct violates various provisions of California law and of federal law. [In addition to these statutory claims, plaintiffs'] tenth cause of action alleges that defendants' "destruction of California wildlife is a violation of the public trust" and prays for declaratory and injunctive relief.... The appeal is directed solely to the propriety of the court's ruling dismissing the tenth cause of action on the ground that "[n]o statutory or common law authority supports a cause of action by a private party for violation of the public trust doctrine arising from the destruction of wild animals."

... When these pleadings were filed, administrative proceedings were underway in Alameda County in which consideration was being given to applications to extend (and consolidate) the existing 20-year conditional use permits to operate the wind turbines in the Alameda County portion of Altamont Pass. Public hearings on applications for conditional use permits were first held in November 2003 before the East County Board of Zoning Adjustments. Plaintiffs and other environmental groups appeared at the hearing and subsequent rehearings, voiced their objections to the applications, and participated in the appeal process before the Alameda County Board of Supervisors.

[The administrative proceedings on the use permit applications included recommendations from a "Wind Power Working Group" consisting of representatives of the California Department of Fish and Game, the United States Fish and Wildlife Service, the applicants, property owners, CBD, and other objectors. The Group's objective was "to assist the County in addressing operational issues and identifying appropriate measures to reduce avian mortality."]

[O]n September 22, 2005, the Alameda County Board of Supervisors adopted a resolution granting the conditional use permits subject to nine new conditions on wind turbine use aimed at mitigating avian mortality....

Shortly thereafter an organization named Californians for Renewable Energy (CARE) and several chapters of the National Audubon Society filed two separate superior court actions seeking writs of mandate to set aside the Alameda County Board of Supervisors resolution.... Although CBD had participated actively in all phases of the proceedings before the East County Board of Zoning Adjustments and the Board of Supervisors, it did not join in either of these actions or institute any other action to set aside the approval of the conditional use permits.

* * *

Discussion

The public trust doctrine applies to wildlife, including raptors and other birds

Defendants' first line of defense is that the public trust doctrine applies only to tidelands and navigable waters, and has no application to wildlife. While the public trust doctrine has evolved primarily around the rights of the public with respect to tidelands and navigable waters, the doctrine is not so limited. "[T]he public trust doctrine is not just a set of rules about tidelands, a restraint on alienation by the government or an historical inquiry into the circumstances of long-forgotten grants." Joseph L. Sax, *Liberating the Public Trust Doctrine from Its Historical Shackles*, 14 U.C. Davis L. Rev. 185, 186 (1980)....

The California Supreme Court has unequivocally embraced and expanded the scope of the public trust doctrine insofar as it relates to tidal and navigable bodies of water. *E.g.*, *National Audubon Society v. Superior Court*, 658 P.2d 709 (Cal. 1983); *City of Berkeley v. Superior Court*, 606 P.2d 362 (Cal. 1980). These relatively recent cases reflect the property rights rationale that historically underlies the doctrine, reiterating that the state holds tidelands and navigable waters "not in its proprietary capacity but as trustee for the public." *City of Berkeley*, 606 P.2d at 365; *see National Audubon Society*, 658 P.2d at 718–19. Both *National Audubon Society* and *City of Berkeley* hold that the public trust ensures more expansive public use of trust property than was the case historically. "Although early cases expressed the scope of the public's right in tidelands as encompassing navigation, commerce and fishing, the permissible range of public uses is far broader, including the right to hunt, bathe or swim, and the right to preserve the tidelands in their natural state as ecological units for scientific study." *City of Berkeley*, 606 P.2d at 365.

> There is a growing public recognition that one of the most important public uses of the tidelands—a use encompassed within the tidelands trust—is the preservation of those lands in their natural state, so that they may serve as ecological units for scientific study, as open space, and as environments which provide food and habitat for birds and marine life, and which favorably affect the scenery and climate of the area.

National Audubon Society, 658 P.2d at 719 (quoting *Marks v. Whitney*, 491 P.2d 374, 380 (Cal. 1971)).

While these cases recognize that an important purpose of the public trust over bodies of water is to protect the habitat for wildlife, neither was addressing whether a public trust protects the wildlife itself.... Both cases spoke of the scope of the public trust..., but neither the holdings, analysis or dicta suggest that bird life or other wildlife are not within the scope of the public trust doctrine.

To the contrary, it has long been recognized that wildlife are protected by the public trust doctrine. "Because wildlife are generally transient and not easily confined, through the centuries and across societies they have been held to belong to no one and therefore to belong to everyone in common." James L. Huffman, *Speaking of Inconvenient Truths: A History of the Public Trust Doctrine*, 18 Duke Envtl. L & Pol'y J. 1 (2007). Older decisions articulate this concept in property terms.... In *Ex parte Maier*, 37 P. 402 (1894), ... the California Supreme Court observed,

> The wild game within a state belongs to the people in their collective, sovereign capacity; it is not the subject of private ownership, except in so far as the people may elect to make it so; and they may, if they see fit, absolutely prohibit the taking of it, or any traffic or commerce in it, if deemed necessary for its protection or preservation, or the public good.

Id. at 404. The United States Supreme Court subsequently cited this "well-considered opinion" in support of "[t]he common ownership, and its resulting responsibility in the state over game" (or, as described in the opinion, animals *ferae nature*). *Geer v. Connecticut*, 161 U.S. 519, 527, 529 (1896), *[partially] overruled [by] Hughes v. Oklahoma*, 441 U.S. 322 (1979). After reviewing the history of laws controlling the taking of game, the court observed:

> Whilst the fundamental principles upon which the common property in game rests have undergone no change, the development of free institutions has led to the recognition of the fact that the power or control lodged in the State, resulting from this common ownership, is to be exercised, like all other powers of government, as a trust for the benefit of the people, and not as a prerogative for the advantage of the government, as distinct from the people, or for the benefit of private individuals as distinguished from the public good. Therefore, for the purpose of exercising this power, the State ... represents its people, and the ownership is that of the people in their united sovereignty.

Id. at 529; *see also, e.g., Lacoste v. Department of Conservation,* 263 U.S. 545, 549 (1924) ("The wild animals within its borders are, so far as capable of ownership, owned by the State in its sovereign capacity for the common benefit of all of its people."); *People v. Truckee Lumber Co.,* 48 P. 374, 375 (Cal. 1897) ("The dominion of the state for the purposes of protecting its sovereign rights in the fish within its waters, and their preservation for the common enjoyment of its citizens, is not confined within the narrow limits suggested by defendant's argument. It is not restricted to their protection only when found within what may in strictness be held to be navigable or otherwise public waters.").

The ownership rationale employed in earlier cases has come to be recognized as a legal fiction. "The whole ownership theory ... is now generally regarded as but a fiction expressive in legal shorthand of the importance to its people that a State have power to preserve and regulate the exploitation of an important resource." *Toomer v. Witsell,* 334 U.S. 385, 402 (1948). "The 'ownership' language ... must be understood as no more than a 19th-century legal fiction expressing 'the importance to its people that a State have power to preserve and regulate the exploitation of an important resource.'" *Douglas v. Seacoast Products, Inc.,* 431 U.S. 265, 284 (1977); *see Hughes v. Oklahoma,* 441 U.S. at 334–35. But, "while the fiction of state ownership of wildlife is consigned to history, the state's responsibility to preserve the public's interest through preservation and wise use of natural resources is a current imperative. In essence, the public trust doctrine commands that the state not abdicate its duty to preserve and protect the public's interest in common natural resources."

Thus, whatever its historical derivation, it is clear that the public trust doctrine encompasses the protection of undomesticated birds and wildlife. They are natural resources of inestimable value to the community as a whole. Their protection and preservation is a public interest that is now recognized in numerous state and federal statutory provisions. Fish & Game Code, § 711.7(a) ("The fish and wildlife resources are held in trust for the people of the state by and through the department [of Fish and Game.").

In *Environmental Protection & Information Center v. State Dept. of Forestry & Fire Protection* (EPIC), 187 P.3d 888 (2008), the California Supreme Court most recently referred to "two distinct public trust doctrines"—"the common law doctrine, which involves the government's 'affirmative duty to take the public trust into account in the planning and allocation of water resources'" and "a public trust duty derived from statute, specifically Fish and Game Code section 711.7, pertaining to fish and wildlife." *Id.* at 926. The court observed that "[t]here is doubtless an overlap between the two public trust doctrines—the protection of water resources is intertwined with the protection of wildlife." *Id.* The court also stated that "the duty of government agencies to protect wildlife is primarily statutory." *Id.* For purposes of deciding the issues presented in this case, it matters not whether the obligations imposed by the public trust are considered to be derived from the common law or from statutory law, or from both. Either way, public agencies must consider the protection and preservation of wildlife although, as the Supreme Court indicates, the contours of that obligation are, "[g]enerally speaking" defined by statute. *Id.* What must be determined here is whether members of the public have the right to enforce that obligation and, if so, whether they may do so in an action against private parties who are adversely affecting trust property.

CL v. St. PTP

Members of the public may enforce the public trust.

In an oft-cited footnote in *National Audubon Society,* the Supreme Court reiterated that "any member of the general public ... has standing to raise a claim of harm to the public trust." 658 P.2d at 718 n.11. Nonetheless, defendants argue and the trial court held that the standing recognized by the Supreme Court applies only to actions to enforce "the traditional public trust interest in navigable and tidal waters and tidelands." ... As the defendants argue and the trial court acknowledged, most of the cases recognizing wildlife as public trust property are actions brought by governmental agencies in the exercise of their police powers. In *People v. Truckee Lumber Co.*, for example, the court upheld an injunction obtained by the Attorney General, "in the name of the people," prohibiting a lumber company from polluting a nonnavigable stream and destroying the fish within it. *People v. Stafford Packing Co.*, which recognized the "necessity and importance of conserving the wild game and fish of this state for the benefit of the people of the state," was an action brought by the Attorney General to enforce statutory provisions limiting the amount of sardines that canning companies could use for reduction purposes. *See also, e.g., Viva! Internal. Voice for Animals v. Adidas Promotional Retail Operations, Inc.*, 162 P.3d 569, 572–573 & n.4 (2007); *People v. Perez*, 59 Cal. Rptr. 2d 596, 601 (1996).

While the trial court and defendants may be correct that the public trust over wildlife thus far has been enforced only in actions brought by public entities, there is no reason in principle why members of the public should be denied standing to maintain an appropriate action. The statement in *National Audubon Society* recognizing the standing of members of the public applied without qualification to "a claim of harm to the public trust." In *EPIC*, the Supreme Court assumed the standing of two environmental organizations to challenge, under the public trust doctrine, the issuance by the Department of Fish and Game of a permit authorizing the incidental take of two bird species.

The concept of a public trust over natural resources unquestionably supports exercise of the police power by public agencies. But the public trust doctrine also places a *duty* upon the government to protect those resources. "The heart of the public trust doctrine, however it may be articulated, is that it imposes limits and obligations on governments." Charles F. Wilkinson, *The Public Trust Doctrine in Public Land Law*, 14 U.C. Davis L. Rev. 269, 284 (1980). "[T]he public trust is more than an affirmation of state power to use public property for public purposes. It is an affirmation of the duty of the state to protect the people's common heritage of streams, lakes, marshlands and tidelands...." *National Audubon Society*, 658 P.2d at 724. "The state has an affirmative duty to take the public trust into account in the planning and allocation of water resources, and to protect public trust uses whenever feasible." *Id.* at 728. In *National Audubon Society*, the court acknowledged that by statute this duty was placed upon the Division of Water Resources with respect to the allocation of water rights, but explicitly observed that

> [t]hese enactments do not render the judicially fashioned public trust doctrine superfluous. Aside from the possibility that statutory protections can be repealed, the noncodified public trust doctrine remains important both to confirm the state's sovereign supervision and to require consideration of public trust uses in cases filed directly in the courts without prior proceedings before [the Division of Water Resources].

Id. at 728 n.27.

The interests encompassed by the public trust undoubtedly are protected by public agencies acting pursuant to their police power and explicit statutory authorization. Nonetheless, the public retains the right to bring actions to enforce the trust when the public agencies fail to discharge their duties. Many of the cases establishing the public trust doctrine in this country and in California have been brought by private parties to prevent agencies of government from abandoning or neglecting the rights of the public with respect to resources subject to the public trust. *E.g., Illinois v. Illinois Central Railroad*, 146 U.S. 387 (1892); *City of Berkeley*, 606 P.2d 362. The facts involved in *National Audubon*

Society illustrate that public agencies do not always strike an appropriate balance between protecting trust resources and accommodating other legitimate public interests; indeed, as in that case, the protection of the trust resources may be entirely ignored. The suggestion that members of the public have no right to object if the agencies entrusted with preservation of wildlife fail to discharge their responsibilities is contrary to the holding in *National Audubon Society* and to the entire tenor of the cases recognizing the public trust doctrine.

A claim for breach of the public trust must be brought against the responsible public agencies.

We thus reject the conclusion of the trial court that private parties may not invoke the public trust doctrine "beyond the traditional public trust interest in navigable and tidal waters and tidelands." That is not to say, however, that plaintiffs are entitled to maintain this action in the manner they have framed it. The defect in the present complaint is not that it seeks to enforce the public trust, but that it is brought against the wrong parties. Plaintiffs have brought this action against the windmill operators whose actions they allege are destroying natural resources protected by the public trust. Plaintiffs have not proceeded against the County of Alameda, which has authorized the use of the wind turbine generators, or against any agency such as the California Department of Fish and Game that has been given the statutory responsibility of protecting the affected natural resources....

Under traditional trust concepts, plaintiffs, viewed as beneficiaries of the public trust, are not entitled to bring an action against those whom they allege are harming trust property. The trustee charged with the responsibility to implement and preserve the trust alone has the right to bring such an action.

> [W]here a trustee cannot or will not enforce a valid cause of action that the trustee ought to bring against a third person, a trust beneficiary may seek judicial compulsion against the trustee. In order to prevent loss of or prejudice to a claim, the beneficiary may bring an action in equity joining the third person and the trustee.

Saks v. Damon Raike & Co., 8 Cal. Rptr 2d 869, 875 (1992). Thus, analogizing this action to the enforcement of a traditional trust agreement, the action must be brought against the appropriate representative of the state as the trustee of the public trust.

The necessity for proceeding against the appropriate public agencies is supported by more than analogy. As many of the references to the public trust doctrine cited above make clear, the doctrine places on the state the responsibility to enforce the trust. If the appropriate state agencies fail to do so, members of the public may seek to compel the agency to perform its duties, but neither members of the public nor the court may assume the task of administering the trust. When the Supreme Court decided in *National Audubon Society* that the Department of Water and Power of the City of Los Angeles had been permitted by the state Division of Water Resources to appropriate waters from the Mono Basin without regard to adverse impacts on Mono Lake and related environmental concerns, the remedy prescribed was not an injunction against the department's use of the water, nor was it an award of restitution or a declaratory judgment establishing an acceptable level of water appropriation. The court held that "some responsible body" should reconsider the allocation of the water rights involved, taking into account both the need for use of the water in Los Angeles and "the impact of water diversion on the Mono Lake environment." *National Audubon Society*, 658 P.2d 729. Because of the complexities of water law and water policy, and the need for expertise to appropriately balance the conflicting needs for use of the water, the court considered whether exclusive primary jurisdiction to make such a determination should be deemed conferred on the Division of Water Resources. However, the court read the particular statutory provisions relating to water rights to confer concurrent original jurisdiction on the courts to determine those rights. The Supreme Court ruled that

> [t]he court, however, need not proceed in ignorance, nor need it invest the time required to acquire the skills and knowledge the board already possesses. When the case raises issues which should be considered by the board, the court may refer the case to the board. Thus the courts, through the exercise of sound discretion and the use of their reference powers, can substantially eliminate the danger that litigation will bypass the board's expert knowledge and frustrate its duty of comprehensive planning.

Id. at 731–32.

The amended complaint in this case is just such an attempt to "bypass" the expertise that has been brought to bear on the subject in the permit proceedings before the Alameda County authorities....

* * *

Notes

1. Notice that the state sovereign ownership of wildlife in California was laid down long ago in *Ex parte Maier*, 37 P. 402, 404 (Cal. 1894) (explaining that "wild game ... belongs to the people in their collective, sovereign capacity ... [and] is not subject to private ownership except in so far as the people may elect to make it so....").

2. The court cited *Environmental Protection & Information Center v. Dept of Forestry & Fire Protection*, 187 P.3d 888 (Cal. 2008), for the notion that there exist both statutory and common law public trust doctrines in California. Is the trust doctrine involved in this case the former or the latter—due to the statutory language instructing that "[t]he fish and wildlife resources are held in trust for the people of the state"? Would it matter if the action violated one trust or the other?

3. Are violations of statutes using trust language any different from other statutory violations? Are allegations of the former given closer scrutiny by courts than the latter? Should they be?

4. The court's decision on standing is puzzling: the court instructed the environmentalists to sue the government trustees (the state or the county), not the permitted wind turbine operators. The court made no mention of *Marks v. Whitney* (p. 132), in which the California Supreme Court ruled that one neighbor had the right to invoke the public trust doctrine against his neighbor's plan to fill coastal tidelands. The *Mono Lake* court (p. 173) also assumed public standing to challenge a water diversion, although the water rights holder in that case was a public entity. Perhaps the dichotomy lies in the distinction between the statutory and common law public trust doctrines that exist in California; in other words, the statutory public trust may authorize actions only against the government, while the common law public trust may authorize simultaneous actions against both governments and private landowners.

In cases in which citizens alleged that a governmental entity violated the public trust doctrine, California courts have cited *CBD v. FPL* for the proposition that members of the public have standing to bring actions against government trustees. *E.g., Center for Biological Diversity, Inc. v. California Department of Forestry and Fire Protection*, 182 Cal. Rptr. 3d

1, 19 (2014) (citing *CBD v. FPL* for the proposition that "members of the public may have standing to bring actions against public agencies to prevent those agencies from abandoning or neglecting the public's rights with respect to resources subject to the public trust").

However, in a non-public trust case, a California district court cited *CBD v. FPL* to support its conclusion that private citizens could not bring an action against a federal agency to enforce state substantive environmental standards protective of wild birds and bats. In *Desert Protective Council v. U.S. Department of Interior*, 927 F. Supp. 2d 949 (S.D. Cal. 2013), plaintiffs sued the federal Bureau of Land Management (BLM) alleging that the agency violated Federal Land Policy and Management Act (FLPMA) by failing to comply with more stringent state standards codified in the California Fish and Game Code when BLM granted a right-of-way for a wind-power project. *Id.* at 971. The court explained that the California Department of Fish and Game is the agency responsible for interpreting and enforcing the California Fish and Game Code. *Id.* at 973. The Department not only did not object to the project, but it cooperated with BLM to create a mitigation plan to reduce the project's effects on birds and bats. The court quoted *CBD v. FPL* as follows: "The trustee charged with the responsibility to implement and preserve the trust alone has the right to bring such an action." *Id.* Thus, the court concluded that "it is the state agency that is charged with bringing [an action to enforce the state substantive standards]," and therefore the plaintiffs were unable to show that BLM had violated FLPMA. *Id.*

Does this case mean that to enforce the state standards, CBD would have had to bring an action against the California Department of Fish and Game? If the court were to rule in favor of CBD, what kind of remedy would be effective given that the BLM is the agency that granted the right-of-way for the wind project?

5. The *CBD v. FPL* court invoked the *Mono Lake* decision for the propositions that the state, as trustee, has an affirmative duty to "consciously supervis[e]" wildlife and wildlife habitat by protecting the wildlife and habitat subject to the trust "whenever feasible," and that no vested property rights bar such state protection. As in the case of water, the state may approve a use despite unavoidable harm to trust resources, but it may not do so without consideration of those resources and must avoid any "unnecessary or unjustified harm to trust interests."

An application of this "feasibility" standard may be *Texas Eastern Transmission Corp. v. Wildlife Preserve, Inc.*, 225 A.2d 130 (N.J. 1966), involving a utility seeking to condemn a right-of-way across a wildlife preserve. The New Jersey Supreme Court held that, upon a showing by the preserve owner of serious damage from the right-of-way and reasonably available alternate routes, the utility was required to show that its route was "reasonable and not capricious," after considering a variety of factors, not just that it was the cheapest route available.

6. A prescient article calling for recognition of wildlife as a public trust resource is Gary D. Meyers, *Variation on a Theme: Expanding the Public Trust Doctrine to Include Protection of Wildlife*, 19 Envtl. L. 723 (1989). *See also* Deborah G. Musiker, Tom France & Lisa A. Hallenbeck, *The Public Trust and* Parens Patriae *Doctrines: Protecting Wildlife in Uncertain Political Times*, 16 Pub. Land L. Rev. 87 (1995); Blake Hudson, *The Public and Wildlife Trust Doctrines and the Untold Story of the* Lucas *Remand*, 34 Colum. J. Envtl. L. 99 (2009) (detailing the history and similarities between the public and wildlife trust doctrines and explaining how the state of South Carolina failed to claim the public trust doctrine as a background principle in the remand in *Lucas v. South Carolina Coastal Council*, despite an invitation of the South Carolina Supreme Court

to do so). Commentators have urged public trust protection for specific species such as wolves. *See* Edward A. Fitzgerald, *The Alaskan Wolf War: The Public Trust Doctrine Missing in Action*, 15 Animal L. 193 (2009) (arguing that the public trust doctrine should be used to stop Alaskan wolf kills because it prevents a state from granting preferences to hunting and trapping interests); Jeremy T. Bruskotter, Sherry A. Enzler, & Adrian Treves, *Rescuing Wolves from Politics: Wildlife as a Public Trust Resource*, 333 Sci. 1828 (2011).

Increasingly, harm to wildlife originates from multiple sources under the jurisdiction of various sovereigns. The excerpt below draws upon the public trust doctrine to suggest correlative sovereign trust obligations towards a shared wildlife asset.

Advancing the Sovereign Trust of Government to Safeguard the Environment for Present and Future Generations (Part I): Ecological Realism and the Need for a Paradigm Shift
Mary Christina Wood
39 Environmental Law 43 (2009)

I. Introduction

The ecological crisis of today is largely a result of government's failure to protect natural resources on behalf of its citizens. Under the system of environmental statutory laws enacted in the United States over the past three decades, agencies at every jurisdictional level have gained nearly unlimited authority to manage natural resources and allow their destruction by private interests through permit systems. Although environmental statutes were designed to protect natural resources, most agencies have used permit provisions to allow continual destruction of natural resources. Though permits often contain mitigation conditions, the overall cumulative effect of agency-permitted damage pursuant to statutory authority is staggering. Nearly every natural resource—including the atmosphere, water, air, wetlands, wildlife, fisheries, soils, marine systems, grasslands, and forests—is seriously degraded, and many are at the brink of collapse. Without a fundamental paradigm shift in the way government manages the environment, government will continue to impoverish natural capital until society will no longer be able to sustain itself.

This paper draws upon the public trust doctrine as the most compelling beacon for a fundamental and rapid paradigm shift towards sustainability....

* * *

VI. The Role of Sovereigns as Cotenant Trustees over Shared Assets

A. The Sovereign Cotenancy

Some assets, like oceans, air, some rivers, and many types of wildlife, are transboundary in nature, crossing several jurisdictions. An inherent limitation of statutory law is its confinement to jurisdictional boundaries. A notable strength of the trust doctrine's property framework is that it creates logical rights to shared assets that are not confined within any one jurisdictional border. It is well established that, with respect to transboundary trust assets, all sovereigns with jurisdiction over the natural territory of the asset have legitimate property claims to the resource.[6] States that share a waterway, for example, have

---

6. See Idaho ex rel. Evans v. Oregon, 462 U.S. 1017, 1031 n.1 (1983) (O'Connor, J., dissenting) (noting "recognition by the international community that each sovereign whose territory temporarily shelters [migratory] wildlife has a legitimate and protectible interest in that wildlife").

correlative rights to the water.[7] Similarly, states and tribes have coexisting property rights to share in the harvest of fish passing through their borders.[8]

Such shared interests are best described as a sovereign cotenancy. A cotenancy is "a tenancy under more than one distinct title, but with unity of possession."[9] The Ninth Circuit Court of Appeals has invoked the cotenancy model to describe shared sovereign rights to migrating salmon.[10]

Within the United States, layered sovereign interests in natural resources arise from the constitutional configuration of states and the federal government. Where the federal government has a national interest in the resource, it is a cotrustee along with the states.[11] The concurrence of federal and state trust interests is reflected in statutory provisions that provide natural resource damages to both sovereign trustees. As one court has made clear in the context of streambed ownership, the federal government and states are held to identical trust obligations, but must carry them out in accordance with their unique constitutional roles:

> This formulation recognizes the division of sovereignty between the state and federal governments.... [T]hose aspects of the public interest ... that relate to the commerce and other powers delegated to the federal government are administered by Congress in its capacity as trustee of the *jus publicum*, while those aspects of the public interest in this property that relate to nonpreempted subjects reserved to local regulation by the states are administered by state legislatures in their capacity as co-trustee of the *jus publicum*.[12]

B. The Cotenant's Duty Not to Waste the Asset

Cotenants have duties toward the asset and towards one another. One tenant cannot appropriate the property of the other tenant by destroying the property to which both are equally entitled. They stand in a fiduciary relationship towards one another and share the obligation not to waste the common asset. Waste is the impairment of property so as to destroy permanently its value to the detriment of the cotenants.[13] Whether applied to

---

7. See, e.g., Arizona v. California, 373 U.S. 546, 601 (1963).

8. See Washington v. Wash. State Commercial Passenger Fishing Vessel Ass'n, 443 U.S. 658, 676–79 (1979); Minnesota v. Mille Lacs Band of Chippewa Indians, 526 U.S. 172, 208 (1999).

9. 20 Am. Jur. 2d Cotenancy and Joint Ownership § 1 (2005).

10. Puget Sound Gillnetters Ass'n v. U.S. Dist. Court (Gillnetters), 573 F.2d 1123, 1126 (9th Cir. 1978) ("We held that [the treaty] established something analogous to a cotenancy, with the tribes as one cotenant and all citizens of the Territory (and later of the state) as the other."); id. at 1128 n.3 ("The primary point is that the state and the tribes stand in similar positions as holders of quasi-sovereign rights in the fishery...."); United States v. Washington, 520 F.2d 685, 685–90 (9th Cir. 1975) (applying cotenancy construct, by analogy, to Indian fishing rights). Of course, a cotenancy framework for sovereign management of natural resources differs in significant ways from a private cotenancy in land among individuals. For example, a sovereign cotenancy in natural resources may not be capable of partitioning. See Gillnetters, 573 F.2d at 1134–35 (Kennedy, J., concurring). Nevertheless, the basic cotenancy construct is instructive in the sovereign context. See id. at 1128 n.3 (stating, in the treaty fisheries context: "We refer to the cotenancy analogy only because it is helpful in explaining the rights of the parties, not because all the rights and incidents of a common law cotenancy necessarily follow.... Obviously, not all the rules of cotenancy in land can apply to an interest of the nature of a profit.").

11. For an extensive discussion of these cotrustee interests, see 1.58 Acres of Land, 523 F. Supp. 120, 124 (D. Mass. 1981) (discussing tidelands: "Since the trust impressed upon this property is governmental and administered jointly by the state and federal governments by virtue of their sovereignty, neither sovereign may alienate this land free and clear of the public trust.").

12. 1.58 Acres of Land, 523 F.Supp. at 123.

13. Earl P. Hopkins, Handbook on the Law of Real Property § 214, at 342 (1896); William F. Walsh, 2 Commentaries on the Law of Real Property § 131, at 69, 72 (1947).

a shared fishery, a transboundary waterway, or the Earth's atmosphere, the prohibition against waste is an important footing in the foundation of organized society.

United States case law clearly prioritizes the duty to prevent waste over the economic ambition of individual sovereigns. The Ninth Circuit declared the sovereign cotenant duty in a treaty fishing dispute between states and tribes:

> Cotenants stand in a fiduciary relationship one to the other. Each has the right to full enjoyment of the property, but must use it as a reasonable property owner. A cotenant is liable for waste if he destroys the property or abuses it so as to permanently impair its value.... By analogy, neither the treaty Indians nor the state on behalf of its citizens may permit the subject matter of these treaties to be destroyed.[14]

In addition to the duty against waste, a corollary duty requires each tenant to pay his share of the expenses proportionate to his interest in the property. These principles form a conceptual framework for assigning ecological responsibility to sovereigns sharing a natural resource. They have potentially forceful bearing in the international context, because they imply an organic obligation incumbent on each government that shares in the natural asset.

Notes

1. In the United States, tribes have recognized sovereign property rights to wildlife on their reservations as well as off-reservation wildlife protected by treaty rights or (in some cases) executive orders. *See Muckleshoot v. Hall*, 698 F. Supp. 1504, 1510–12 (W.D. Wash. 1988); *Whitefoot v. United States*, 293 F.2d 658, 663 (Ct. Cl. 1961). The Tenth Circuit has described such rights as trust interests in wildlife populations. *Mescalero Apache Tribe v. New Mexico*, 630 F.2d 724, 734 (10th Cir. 1980) (referring to "the trusteeship duty imposed on all sovereigns" and noting its application to the Mescalero Tribe's management of wildlife on its reservation). As the article above notes, courts construing tribal treaty rights in the Pacific Northwest have characterized tribes as similar to states in their property rights to salmon migrating between borders. *See Puget Sound Gillnetters Ass'n v. U.S. Dist. Court*, 573 F.2d 1123, 1128 n.3 (9th Cir. 1978) (noting that states and tribes "stand in similar positions as holders of quasi-sovereign rights in the [salmon] fishery....").

2. In addition to the waste doctrine applicable to co-tenants of a resource, tribal sovereigns have two other property-based sets of rights that have been invoked to protect the species they rely on. One derives from treaty rights, which in the Pacific Northwest have been interpreted as safeguarding water flows and migratory conditions to protect fisheries. The other derives from a federal trust obligation to protect tribal property. This federal trust duty is in some ways analogous to, but in other ways fundamentally distinguishable from, a public trust obligation (because the beneficiaries are the tribe and its future generations rather than present and future generations of citizens that comprise the general public). These property-based tribal rights fit into the overall sovereign trust (and statutory) frameworks pertaining to water and wildlife. For discussion, see Michael C. Blumm & Brett M. Swift, *The Indian Treaty Piscary Profit and Habitat Protection in the Pacific Northwest: A Property Rights Approach*, 69 U. Col. L. Rev. 407 (1998); Mary Christina Wood, *The Tribal Property Right to Wildlife Capital (Part I): Applying Principles of Sovereignty to Protect Imperiled Wildlife Populations*, 37 Idaho L. Rev. 1 (2000). *See*

---

14. Washington, 520 F.2d at 685.

generally Judith V. Royster et al., Native American Natural Resources Law: Cases and Materials 277–309 (3d ed. 2013) (federal trust obligation); *id.* at 459–548 (treaty usufructuary rights).

3. In the last four decades the federal government has assumed a primary role in wildlife regulation under the Endangered Species Act (ESA) and other federal statutes. Federal agency decisions have been notorious for their politicized discretion that works injury to imperiled species in contravention of the spirit of the ESA. Oliver A. Houck, *The Endangered Species Act and Its Implementation by the U.S. Departments of Interior and Commerce*, 64 U. Colo. L. Rev. 277, 317 (1993) ("[T]he number of projects actually arrested by the ESA is nearly nonexistent."); Daniel J. Rohlf, *Jeopardy Under the Endangered Species Act: Playing a Game Protected Species Can't Win*, 41 Washburn L.J. 114 (2001). In some cases, federal statutory regimes that have been in effect for decades have failed systematically in their protection purpose; one example lies in regulation to protect the Columbia River Basin salmon. *See* Michael C. Blumm, Sacrificing the Salmon: A Legal and Policy History of the Decline of Columbia Basin Salmon (2002). Against the backdrop of extensive federal involvement in wildlife regulation, do public trust principles apply to ESA implementation? For an argument that they do, see Mary Christina Wood, *Protecting the Wildlife Trust: A Reinterpretation of Section 7 of the Endangered Species Act*, 34 Envtl. L. 605, 614–16 (2004):

> The wildlife trust doctrine has rich expression in state court decisions and statutes, likely reflecting the traditional primacy of state government in wildlife regulation. As yet, there is scant case law imposing the wildlife trust doctrine on the federal government, but cases make clear that the wildlife trust arises as an attribute of sovereignty—a rationale that suggests its application to any sovereign, including the federal government.

As the national interest in wildlife regulation expands and the federal government increasingly usurps traditional state functions, trust principles that inhere in the wildlife regulatory function should gain more force at the federal level. The listing of species under the ESA amounts to a federal assertion of general wildlife regulatory authority over those species and should activate, at the federal level, those longstanding trust principles that have always formed a backdrop for state wildlife regulation. Though Congress did not use the term "trust" in the language of the ESA, the statute creates an implied trust over the imperiled wildlife assets and imposes a public trustee's duty of care on the federal agencies implementing the Act.

Chapter 7

Beaches

Some of the most contentious disputes in natural resources law concern the intersection of lands and waters, especially ocean lands. As ocean access is limited and public demand is considerable, it is not surprising that many high-profile resource conflicts concern access to, or development of, ocean beaches. *See, e.g., Kaiser Aetna v. United States*, 444 U.S. 164 (1979) (concluding that the Army Corps of Engineers cannot demand public access to a marina as a permit condition); *Palazzolo v. Rhode Island*, 533 U.S. 606 (2001) (p. 156) (holding that a denial of a wetlands fill permit was not a constitutional taking because of the landowner's remaining economically viable upland uses); *Lucas v. South Carolina Coastal Council*, 505 U.S. 1003 (1992) (concerning a takings challenge to coastal protection regulation that precluded residential development); *Nollan v. California Coastal Comm'n*, 483 U.S. 825 (1987) (explaining that to avoid a taking, land use exactions from land developers must have a "nexus" to the problem created by the development); *Stop the Beach Renourishment v. Florida Dep't of Envtl. Prot.*, 560 U.S. 720 (2010) (concluding that a beach restoration project did not cause a taking).

The public trust doctrine's effect on beach access has been most pronounced in New Jersey, as the following cases illustrate.

Borough of Neptune City v. Borough of Avon-by-the-Sea

New Jersey Supreme Court
294 A.2d 47 (1972)

[One municipality, Neptune City, sued another, Avon-by-the-Sea, for amending an ordinance in 1970 that restricted the issuance of seasonal beach use permits solely to Avon residents and raised the daily rate for non-residents. Neptune City claimed that the ordinance amounted to a discriminatory application of beach access fees by effectively restricting the public's right to access ocean beaches.]

HALL, J.:

The question presented by this case is whether an oceanfront municipality may charge non-residents higher fees than residents for the use of its beach area....

* * *

Plaintiffs attacked the ordinance on several grounds, including the claim of a common law right of access to the ocean in all citizens of the state. This in essence amounts to reliance upon the public trust doctrine, although not denominated by plaintiffs as such. Avon, although inferentially recognizing some such right, defended its amendatory ordinance on the thesis, accepted by the trial court, that its property taxpayers should nevertheless not be called upon to bear the expense, above non-discriminating beach user fees received, of the cost of operating and maintaining the beachfront, claimed to result from use by non-residents and that consequently the discrimination in fees was not irrational or invidious. All recognized that an oceanfront municipality may not absolutely exclude non-residents from the use of its dedicated beach, including, of course, land seaward of the mean high water mark. *Bindley v. Lavallette*, 110 A.2d 157 (N.J. Super. Ct. Law Div. 1954)....

* * *

We prefer ... to approach [this case] from the more fundamental viewpoint of the modern meaning and application of the public trust doctrine.

That broad doctrine derives from the ancient principle of English law that land covered by tidal waters belonged to the sovereign, but for the common use of all the people. Such lands passed to the respective states as a result of the American Revolution....

A succinct statement of the principle is found in the leading case of *Illinois Central Railroad Co. v. Illinois*:

> It is the settled law of this country that the ownership of and dominion and sovereignty over lands covered by tide waters, within the limits of the several states, belong to the respective states within which they are found, with the consequent right to use or dispose of any portion thereof, when that can be done without substantial impairment of the interest of the public in the waters....

146 U.S. 387, 435 (1972).

The original purpose of the doctrine was to preserve for the use of all the public natural water resources for navigation and commerce, waterways being the principal transportation arteries of early days, and for fishing, an important source of food. This is also well pointed up in *Illinois Central*:

> It is a title held in trust for the people of the state, that they may enjoy the navigation of the waters, carry on commerce over them, and have liberty of fishing therein, freed from the obstruction or interference of private parties. The interest of the people in the navigation of the waters and in commerce over them may be improved in many instances by the erection of wharves, docks, and piers therein, for which purpose the state may grant parcels of the submerged lands; and, so long as their disposition is made for such purpose, no valid objections can be made to the grants. It is grants of parcels of lands under navigable waters that may afford foundation for wharves, piers, docks, and other structures in aid of commerce, and grants of parcels which, being occupied, do not substantially impair the public interest in the lands and water remaining, that are chiefly considered and sustained in the adjudged cases as a valid exercise of legislative power consistently with the trust to the public upon which such lands are held by the state.

146 U.S. at 452.

There is not the slightest doubt that New Jersey has always recognized the trust doctrine. The basic case is *Arnold v. Mundy*, 6 N.J.L. 1 (N.J. 1821), where Chief Justice Kirkpatrick spoke as follows:

> [The court explained that all non-private property is divided into two types: "the domain of the crown" and common property. Common property includes] the air, the running water, the sea, the fish, and the wild beasts. But inasmuch as the things which constitute this Common property are things in which a sort of transient usufructuary possession, only, can be had; and inasmuch as the title to them and to the soil by which they are supported, and to which they are ap-

purtenant, cannot well, according to the common law notion of title, be vested in all the people; therefore, the wisdom of that law has placed it in the hands of the sovereign power, to be held, protected, and regulated for the common use and benefit. But still, though this title, strictly speaking, is in the sovereign, yet the use is common to all the people.

* * *

And I am further of opinion, that, upon the Revolution, all these royal rights became vested in The people of New Jersey as the sovereign of the country, and are now in their hands; and that they, having, themselves, both the legal title and the usufruct, may make such disposition of them, and such regulation concerning them, as they my think fit; that this power of disposition and regulation must be exercised by them in their sovereign capacity; that the legislature is their rightful representative in this respect, and, therefore, that the legislature, in the exercise of this power, may lawfully erect ports, harbours, basins, docks, and wharves on the coasts of the sea and in the arms thereof, and in the navigable rivers; that they may bank off those waters and reclaim the land upon the shores; that they may build dams, locks, and bridges for the improvement of the navigation and the ease of passage; that they may clear and improve fishing places, to increase the product of the fishery; that they may create, enlarge, and improve oyster beds, by planting oysters therein in order to procure a more ample supply; that they may do these things, themselves, at the public expense, or they may authorize others to do it by their own labour, and at their own expense, giving them reasonable tolls, rents, profits, or exclusive and temporary enjoyments; but still this power, which may be thus exercised by the sovereignty of the state, is nothing more than what is called the *jus regium*, the right of regulating, improving, and securing for the common benefit of every individual citizen. The sovereign power itself, therefore, cannot, consistently with the principles of the law of nature and the constitution of a well ordered society, make a direct and absolute grant of the waters of the state, divesting all the citizens of their common right. It would be a grievance which never could be long borne by a free people.

Id. at 71, 78 (emphasis omitted).

* * *

Here we are not directly concerned with the extent of legislative power to alienate tidal lands because the lands seaward of the mean high water line remain in state ownership, the municipality owns the bordering land, which is dedicated to park and beach purposes, and no problem of physical access by the public to the ocean exists. The matter of legislative alienation in this state should, nonetheless, be briefly adverted to since it has a tangential bearing. As the earlier quotations indicate, it has always been assumed that the State may convey or grant rights in some tidal lands to private persons where the use to be made thereof is consistent with and in furtherance of the purposes of the doctrine, e.g., the improvement of commerce and navigation redounding to the benefit of the public. However, our cases rather early began to broadly say that the State's power to vacate or abridge public rights in tidal lands is absolute and unlimited, and our statutes dealing with state conveyances of such lands contain few, if any, limitations thereon....

* * *

We have no difficulty in finding that, in this latter half of the twentieth century, the public rights in tidal lands are not limited to the ancient prerogatives of navigation and fishing, but extend as well to recreational uses, including bathing, swimming and other shore activities. The public trust doctrine, like all common law principles, should not be considered fixed or static, but should be molded and extended to meet changing conditions and needs of the public it was created to benefit. The legislature appears to have had such an extension in mind in enacting N.J. Stat. Ann. 12:3-33, -34.... Those sections, generally speaking, authorize grants to governmental bodies of tide-flowed lands which front upon a public park extending to such lands, but only upon condition that any land so granted shall be maintained as a public park for public use, resort and recreation. *Cf. Martin v. City of Asbury Park*, 176 A. 172 (N.J. 1935).

* * *

We are convinced it has to follow that, while municipalities may validly charge reasonable fees for the use of their beaches, they may not discriminate in any respect between their residents and non-residents. The Avon amendatory ordinance of 1970 clearly does so by restricting the sale of season badges to residents, as defined in the ordinance, resulting in a lower fee to them. In addition the fee for daily badges, which would be utilized mostly by non-residents, may have been as well discriminatorily designed with respect to the amount of the charge. Since we cannot tell what fee schedule the municipality would have adopted when it passed this ordinance in 1970 if it had to do so on the basis of equal treatment for all, we see no other course but to set aside the entire amendatory enactment.

* * *

The judgment of the Law Division is reversed and the cause is remanded to that tribunal for the entry of a judgment consistent with this opinion. No costs.

FRANCIS, J.: (dissenting) (opinion omitted).

Notes

1. *Neptune City* might be considered the modern rebirth of the public trust doctrine in New Jersey. Of course, the origins of the doctrine in that state date to the 1821 decision of *Arnold v. Mundy* (p. 57). One hundred and fifty years later, the *Neptune City* court developed an anti-discrimination application of the doctrine that prohibits discriminatory beach access fees. The court subsequently clarified that a municipality may charge non-residents higher fees to the extent that residents finance beach facilities through local property taxes. *Hyland v. Borough of Allenhurst*, 393 A.2d 579 (N.J. 1978) (also prohibiting municipalities from reserving toilet facilities exclusively for residents).

2. By extending the public trust doctrine to include "recreational uses, including bathing, swimming, and other shore activities," the case also might have been interpreted to move the scope of the doctrine landward, above the high water mark. But the issue wasn't clarified until the court decided *Van Ness v. Borough of Deal*, 393 A.2d 571 (N.J. 1978), ruling that the borough violated the public trust doctrine by restricting membership in a municipally-owned beach resort and casino to residents. The court rejected the borough's argument that the public trust doctrine was limited to below the high water mark and that it only applied to beaches dedicated to the public. The *Van Ness* majority also rejected the dissent's claim that public access to beaches should be left to the legislature, reasoning that the limited availability of beach access required judicial attention. *Id.* at 574, 576. On the landward movement of the public trust doctrine, see Scott W. Reed, *The Public Trust Doctrine: Is It Amphibious?*, 1 J. Envtl. L. & Litig. 107 (1986).

3. The Avon beach involved in *Neptune City* was publicly owned. The New Jersey courts would soon consider whether the public trust doctrine also burdened beaches that were not publicly owned.

Matthews v. Bay Head Improvement Ass'n
New Jersey Supreme Court
471 A.2d 355 (1984)

SCHREIBER, J.:

The public trust doctrine acknowledges that the ownership, dominion and sovereignty over land flowed by tidal waters, which extend to the mean high water mark, is vested in the State in trust for the people. The public's right to use the tidal lands and water encompasses navigation, fishing and recreational uses, including bathing, swimming and other shore activities. *Borough of Neptune City v. Borough of Avon-by-the-Sea*, 294 A.2d 47 (N.J. 1972). In *Avon* we held that the public trust applied to the municipally-owned dry sand beach immediately landward of the high water mark. The major issue in this case is whether, ancillary to the public's right to enjoy the tidal lands, the public has a right to gain access through and to use the dry sand area not owned by a municipality but by a quasi-public body.

The Borough of Point Pleasant instituted this suit against the Borough of Bay Head and the Bay Head Improvement Association (Association), generally asserting that the defendants prevented Point Pleasant inhabitants from gaining access to the Atlantic Ocean and the beachfront in Bay Head. The proceeding was dismissed as to the Borough of Bay Head because it did not own or control the beach. Subsequently ... Stanley Van Ness, as Public Advocate, joined as plaintiff-intervenor. When the Borough of Point Pleasant ceased pursuing the litigation, the Public Advocate became the primary moving party. The Public Advocate asserted that the defendants had denied the general public its right of access during the summer bathing season to public trust lands along the beaches in Bay Head and its right to use private property fronting on the ocean incidental to the public's right under the public trust doctrine. The complaint was amended on several occasions, eliminating the Borough of Point Pleasant as plaintiff and adding more than 100 individuals, who were owners or had interests in properties located on the oceanfront in Bay Head, as defendants.

* * *

I. Facts

[The beach of Bay Head at issue was about a mile-and-a-quarter long, consisting of 76 separate parcels, all but six of which were privately owned. The remaining six were owned by the non-profit Bay Head Improvement Association, which also had leases to manage many of the private parcels. The Association supervised beach use in the summer, employing about 40 people as lifeguards, beach police, and beach cleaners. Membership in the association was limited to residents of Bay Head Borough, including non-owners. No non-members could use the beach above the high tide line, except for fishermen, who were permitted to access the foreshore.]

II. The Public Trust

[After discussing *Neptune City*, *Arnold*, and *Van Ness*, the court turned to the issue of whether the public trust doctrine burdened privately owned beaches.

One New Jersey case explained that] "[h]ealth, recreation and sports are encompassed in and intimately related to the general welfare of a well-balanced state." *N.J. Sports &*

Exposition Authority v. McCrane, 292 A.2d 580, 598 (N.J. Super. Ct. Law Div. 1971). Extension of the public trust doctrine to include bathing, swimming and other shore activities is consonant with and furthers the general welfare. The public's right to enjoy these privileges must be respected.

* * *

III. Public Rights in Privately-Owned Dry Sand Beaches

In *Avon* and [*Van Ness*] our finding of public rights in dry sand areas was specifically and appropriately limited to those beaches owned by a municipality. We now address the extent of the public's interest in privately-owned dry sand beaches. This interest may take one of two forms. First, the public may have a right to cross privately owned dry sand beaches in order to gain access to the foreshore. Second, this interest may be of the sort enjoyed by the public in municipal beaches under *Avon* and [*Van Ness*], namely, the right to sunbathe and generally enjoy recreational activities.

Beaches are a unique resource and are irreplaceable. The public demand for beaches has increased with the growth of population and improvement of transportation facilities. Furthermore, the projected demand for salt water swimming will not be met "unless the existing swimming capacities of the four coastal counties are expanded." New Jersey Department of Environmental Protection, *Statewide Comprehensive Outdoor Recreation Plan* 200 (1977)....

Exercise of the public's right to swim and bathe below the mean high water mark may depend upon a right to pass across the upland beach. Without some means of access the public right to use the foreshore would be meaningless. To say that the public trust doctrine entitles the public to swim in the ocean and to use the foreshore in connection therewith without assuring the public of a feasible access route would seriously impinge on, if not effectively eliminate, the rights of the public trust doctrine. This does not mean the public has an unrestricted right to cross at will over any and all property bordering on the common property. The public interest is satisfied so long as there is reasonable access to the sea.

* * *

The bather's right in the upland sands is not limited to passage. Reasonable enjoyment of the foreshore and the sea cannot be realized unless some enjoyment of the dry sand area is also allowed. The complete pleasure of swimming must be accompanied by intermittent periods of rest and relaxation beyond the water's edge. *See State ex rel. Thornton v. Hay*, 462 P.2d 671, 678–79 (Or. 1969) (Denecke, J., concurring). The unavailability of the physical situs for such rest and relaxation would seriously curtail and in many situations eliminate the right to the recreational use of the ocean. This was a principal reason why in *Avon* and [*Van Ness*] we held that municipally-owned dry sand beaches "must be open to all on equal terms...." *Avon*, 294 A.2d at 54. We see no reason why rights under the public trust doctrine to use of the upland dry sand area should be limited to municipally-owned property. It is true that the private owner's interest in the upland dry sand area is not identical to that of a municipality. Nonetheless, where use of dry sand is essential or reasonably necessary for enjoyment of the ocean, the doctrine warrants the public's use of the upland dry sand area subject to an accommodation of the interests of the owner.

* * *

Precisely what privately-owned upland sand area will be available and required to satisfy the public's rights under the public trust doctrine will depend on the circumstances. Location of the dry sand area in relation to the foreshore, extent and availability of publicly-owned upland sand area, nature and extent of the public demand, and usage of the upland sand land by the owner are all factors to be weighed and considered in fixing the contours of the usage of the upper sand.

Today, recognizing the increasing demand for our State's beaches and the dynamic nature of the public trust doctrine, we find that the public must be given both access to and use of privately-owned dry sand areas as reasonably necessary. While the public's rights in private beaches are not co-extensive with the rights enjoyed in municipal beaches, private landowners may not in all instances prevent the public from exercising its rights under the public trust doctrine. The public must be afforded reasonable access to the foreshore as well as a suitable area for recreation on the dry sand.

* * *

The Public Advocate has urged that all the privately-owned beachfront property likewise must be opened to the public. Nothing has been developed on this record to justify that conclusion. We have decided that the Association's membership and thereby its beach must be open to the public. That area might reasonably satisfy the public need at this time. We are aware that the Association possessed, as of the initiation of this litigation, about 42 upland sand lots under leases revocable on 30 days' notice. If any of these leases have been or are to be terminated, or if the Association were to sell all or part of its property, it may necessitate further adjudication of the public's claims in favor of the public trust on part or all of these or other privately-owned upland dry sand lands depending upon the circumstances....

... It is not necessary for us to determine under what circumstances and to what extent there will be a need to use the dry sand of private owners who either now or in the future may have no leases with the Association. Resolution of the competing interests, private ownership and the public trust, may in some cases be simple, but in many it may be most complex. In any event, resolution would depend upon the specific facts in controversy.

* * *

We realize that considerable uncertainty will continue to surround the question of the public's right to cross private land and to use a portion of the dry sand as discussed above....

* * *

... Judgment is entered for the plaintiff against the Association. Judgment of dismissal against the individual property owners is affirmed without prejudice. No costs.

Notes

1. The *Matthews* court extended the public trust doctrine to "quasi-public" beaches, recognizing that the public demands for beach access had greatly expanded. Could one argue, however, that providing beach access was a task best left to the legislature? The court in *Van Ness*, a case on which the *Matthews* court relied, rejected this argument. Underscoring the immediate public need for beach access, the *Van Ness* majority stated:

> The dissent herein, expressing uncertainty as to the extent of the Public Trust Doctrine, would not, at this time, hold that it applied to municipally owned dry sand beaches. However, this State is rapidly approaching a crisis as to the availability to the public of its priceless beach areas. The situation will not be helped by restrained judicial pronouncements. Prompt and decisive action by the Court is needed.

393 A.2d at 574.

Often, legislatures simply fail to take affirmative action in response to public environmental need. If courts can recognize urgency with respect to recreational interests, might they also be able to respond to climate crises caused by legislative neglect of atmospheric pollution? Isn't the human stake in atmospheric health and climate function even more pronounced than the human interests in recreation?

2. Note that, in recognizing recreation as a public trust use, the court emphasized, "[h]ealth, recreation and sports are encompassed in and intimately related to the general welfare of a well-balanced state." Does this language provide some parameters as to what public uses will be protected by the trust? Must every conceivable public use or frivolity be protected? Does the language trace back to the underlying sovereign interests of the state as emphasized in early cases such as *Illinois Central*? Can you think of public uses that would not be protected because they do not carry ample importance?

3. The *Matthews* decision set forth two distinct public rights associated with, and "ancillary to," the existing public ownership of tidelands. One is the right of access across non-public property to the tidelands. The other is the use of the dry sand area adjacent to the tidelands. Addressing the first, the right of access, the court recognized that the lack of a "feasible access route would seriously impinge on, if not effectively eliminate, the rights of the public trust doctrine." Indeed, if a shoreline were held in nearly total private ownership, wouldn't access be limited to boaters, absent a public access right? But in many states, navigable waterways and beaches are privately owned. Does the state have the duty as trustee to determine "feasible" access routes for the public? Under *Matthews*, may the public cross all private areas to access the tidelands? If not, what limitations did the court impose?

4. The second right affirmed by *Matthews* is "some enjoyment of the dry sand area." Note that the court characterized this use as necessary to full enjoyment of the public's right to recreate in the ocean, finding a public right where use of dry sand is "essential or reasonably necessary" for enjoyment of the ocean. However, the court also noted that the public's rights in private beaches are not "co-extensive with the rights enjoyed in municipal beaches" and emphasized that there must be an "accommodation" to the interests of the private owner. The approach aptly characterizes the public trust doctrine, which operates as an accommodation between private and public property ownership. *See* Michael C. Blumm, *The Public Trust Doctrine and Private Property: The Accommodation Principle*, 27 Pace Envtl. L. Rev. 649 (2010). Chapter 9 explores the accommodation in greater depth.

5. By recognizing public rights on private land to allow full beneficial use of tidelands, the *Matthews* court showed the limits of survey boundaries in delineating the public and private ownership interface. Can you think of other instances in which courts effectuate the beneficial use of one owner by jumping boundaries and implying easements or rights on a neighboring property? Are rights of access implied under special circumstances as between two private property owners? Are courts performing a similar task here? What are the differences in context? In both, the rights of one private property owner suffer to some degree.

6. Note that the right of public use of private dry sand beaches had not been previously announced, yet the *Matthews* court seemed to assume that public trust rights had always encumbered private dry sand beaches. Does the case imply that *jus publicum* implicitly co-exists with private title (not just on parcels below the high water mark) and can remain dormant until public needs demand activating the public rights? Stated somewhat differently, is *jus publicum* available as a basis for recognizing and effectuating public rights on pri-

vate land when "reasonably necessary" to protect beneficial use of public trust assets wholly owned by the public? Is this roughly the approach taken in the area of wildlife law (explored in chapter 6) where courts seem to imply a trust right of habitat protection on private land to protect the public's wildlife trust asset? While the modern conception of private property tends to fixate on boundaries, are boundaries necessarily determinative of public rights? Consider the famous statement of the U.S. Supreme Court in *Georgia v. Tennessee Copper Co.*: "[T]he state has an interest independent of and behind the titles of its citizens, in all the earth and air within its domain." 206 U.S. 230, 237 (1907).

7. The New Jersey Public Advocate was a department in the executive branch of state government that acted as a voice on behalf of the people, to make government more accountable through legal advocacy, policy research, and legislative outreach. It was created by the government in 1974, abolished in 1994, revived by legislation in 2005, and abolished again in 2010, and yet to be reinstated. Does the public need such an advocate? Why wouldn't an Attorney General be suitable? Who does the Attorney General represent?

8. The court established the so-called four "*Matthews* factors" to decide the extent of the public's right of access to and use of private beaches. Application of these factors decided the following case.

Raleigh Avenue Beach Ass'n v. Atlantis Beach Club, Inc.

Supreme Court of New Jersey
879 A.2d 112 (2005)

PORITZ, C.J.:

This case raises a question about the right of the public to use a 480-foot wide stretch of upland sand beach in Lower Township, Cape May County, owned by respondent Atlantis Beach Club, Inc., and operated as a private club. We hold today that, in the circumstances presented here, and on application of the factors set forth in *Matthews v. Bay Head Improvement Ass'n*, the public trust doctrine requires the Atlantis property to be open to the general public at a reasonable fee for services provided by the owner and approved by the Department of Environmental Protection.

[The trial court limited the public rights of access to a three-foot wide strip of land across the beach to access tidelands. The court of appeals expanded the public's right by instructing Atlantis Beach Club that it could not interfere with the public right "to free use of the dry sand for intermittent recreational purposes connected with the ocean and wet sand." The court also ruled that Atlantis could charge fees to the public reasonably related to beach services that were approved by the state department of environmental protection. The New Jersey Supreme Court, after discussing *Arnold* and *Neptune City*, turned to the application of the *Matthews* factors.]

* * *

We turn now to an application of the *Matthews* factors to the circumstances of this case in order to determine "what privately-owned upland sand area will be available and required to satisfy the public's rights under the public trust doctrine."

"*Location of the dry sand area in relation to the foreshore*":

The dry sand beach at the center of this controversy extends horizontally 480 feet from the Coast Guard property south of Atlantis to the Seapointe property north of Atlantis, and vertically, from three feet landward of the mean high water line about 339 feet to the dunes adjacent to the bulkhead and the Raleigh Avenue extension. It is easily reached by pedestrians using the path bisecting the Raleigh Avenue extension from the end of the paved roadway to the bulkhead.

"[E]xtent and availability of publicly-owned upland sand area":

There is no publicly-owned beach area in Lower Township, although it was represented to us at oral argument that there are public beaches in the "Wildwoods" north of Lower Township. The Borough of Wildwood Crest, immediately north of Lower Township, owns dry sand beach that is used by the public. Seapointe, a private entity, as required by its 1987 CAFRA [Coastal Area Facility Review Act] permit, has made its upland sands available to the public for a "reasonable" fee, approved by the DEP [Department of Environmental Protection] at a level comparable to fees charged by nearby town beaches (in 1987, Cape May City, Avalon, and Stone Harbor beaches). The Coast Guard beach to the south of Atlantis is closed to the public for the better part of the summer season (April 1 through August 15) to protect the endangered piping plover.

"[N]ature and extent of the public demand":

The Diamond Beach section of Lower Township is not large (three blocks by nine blocks), and parking is limited but available along the area streets. Local residents whose homes are within easy walking distance of Atlantis are members of the plaintiff Association, through which they have expressed their individual concerns about access and use. That there is enormous public interest in the New Jersey shore is well-known; tourism associated with New Jersey's beaches is a $16 billion annual industry.

"[U]sage of the upland sand land by the owner":

The more or less rectangular area of dry sand that constitutes the Atlantis beach has been closed to non-members of Atlantis from the summer of 1996 to May 4, 2004. On May 4, the Appellate Division required open access and use by the public to the entirety of the beach area and permitted reasonable and comparable fees to be approved by the DEP on application by Atlantis. As for the period prior to 1996, the general public used the beach without limitation or fee during the ten years between 1986 and 1996 and, it appears, enjoyed the same open access and use prior to 1986 (although the record is sparse on the issue of prior use). The La Vida condominiums, situated directly to the west of Atlantis, were constructed in 1986....

* * *

From the summer of 1996 to May 4, 2004, Atlantis charged unregulated membership fees in varying amounts for access to and use of its beach. During the 2003 season, new members (and members who joined in 2002) paid $700 and received eight beach tags per household. In violation of the La Vida CAFRA permit, in the summer of 2003 Atlantis removed the public beach access sign at the western end of the Raleigh Avenue pathway extension and replaced it with a sign that read *"Free access to gate only."* The gate was located at the end of the pathway at the bulkhead. Later that summer, contradictory signs at the gate read *"Public beach access"* and *"Public access ends here/membership available at gate."* ...

* * *

The private beach property held by Atlantis is an area of undeveloped upland sand and dunes at the end of a street in a town that does not have public beaches. The owner, after years of public access and use, ... decided in 1996 to engage in a commercial enterprise — a private beach club — that kept the public from the beach. Atlantis recognizes that as a "place of public accommodation," N.J. Stat. Ann. 10:5-5l, under the Law Against Discrimination, N.J. Stat. Ann. 10:5-1 to -42, it must provide membership opportunities to the general public without regard to race, creed, or color, *Clover Hill Swimming Club v. Goldsboro*, 219 A.2d 161 (1966). *See* N.J. Admin. Code 7:7E-8:11(b)(5) (requiring "establishments ... [that] control access to tidal waters [to] comply with the Law Against Discrimination"). The Beach Club nonetheless asserts that it will lose one of the "sticks" in its bundle of property rights if it cannot charge whatever the market will bear, and, in setting fees for membership, decide who can come onto its property and use its beach and other services (lifeguards, trash removal, organized activities, etc.). But exclusivity of use, in the context here, has long been subject to the strictures of the public trust doctrine.

In sum, based on the circumstances in this case and on application of the Matthews factors, we hold that the Atlantis upland sands must be available for use by the general public under the public trust doctrine....

[The court concluded that DEP had jurisdiction to review fees proposed by Atlantis for use of its beach. The court stated that it expects DEP to disapprove fees if they operate to "'[l]imit access by placing an unreasonable economic burden on the public.'" *Raleigh Ave.*, 879 A.2d at 125, quoting *Raleigh Avenue*, 851 A.2d 19, 33 (N.J. Super. Ct. App. Div. 2004). The court also stated that Atlantis could charge for expenses actually incurred for reasonable management services (in addition to reimbursement for other costs) in the fee calculation. It may also charge for cabana rental and other profit-making business enterprises.]

For the reasons expressed in this opinion, the decision of the Appellate Division is affirmed.

WALLACE, JR., J.: (dissenting) (opinion omitted).

Notes

1. In applying the *Matthews* factors to find a public trust easement, the court noted that the beach club was a place of public accommodation under New Jersey law and that it was already subject to anti-discrimination laws. What relevance did that have to the decision? What factors in the four-part test invite that analysis? In the wake of the *Raleigh Beach* case, the New Jersey Department of Environmental Protection promulgated "Public Access Rules" that implement the decision. *See* 7 N.J. ADMIN. CODE § 7E-8.11.

2. Suppose a case arises in which the New Jersey DEP seeks public access across a parcel that is privately owned by a single household. But the agency decides not to make a claim access against a neighboring parcel owned by a private yacht club. Faced with a challenge by the private landowner, how should the court apply the four factors? Do any of the four factors permit the court to distinguish between family or individual ownership from club ownership? What property interests are at stake in each context? As a matter of policy, how should a court rule? Why would the state choose to burden a household lot instead of a private yacht club?

3. Public access litigation has continued in New Jersey. In *Chiesa v. D. Lobi Enters.*, No. A-6070-09T3, 2012 N.J. Super. LEXIS 2218 (N.J. Super. Ct. App. Div. Sept. 28, 2012), the state sought access across property owned by Sea Bright Beach Clubs. Prior to the *Raleigh* decision, in 1993, the state signed agreements with the clubs agreeing to limit public access on replenished beaches. Following an extensive discussion of the public trust, the appellate panel affirmed the trial court's finding that such limited access provisions are "void against public policy." *Id.* at *18. The court explained:

As recounted in this opinion, the public policy of this State declares there shall be public access to tidal lands, access to the ocean, and the attendant pleasures of dry beaches by the public. Moreover, even privately-owned oceanfront properties may be required to provide access to the public to dry upland beach areas to facilitate full enjoyment of the ocean. When fashioned and executed in 1993, the law governing public access to tidal property was well-established. Certainly, after the *Raleigh Avenue* ruling, both parties to the 1993 Agreement should have recognized that the limited public access to the 80 feet of oceanfront tidal property the Club owned might be questionable and the limited public access to the remainder was wholly untenable.

Id.

For a contrary decision that rejected public beach access rights above high water, see *Opinion of the Justices*, 649 A.2d 604 (N.H. 1994). Also note that the Maine Supreme Court allowed public access to intertidal areas, even though privately owned (in Maine, landowners own to the low water mark). *McGarvey v. Whittredge*, 28 A.3d 620 (Me. 2011).

4. Other states have premised public beach access rights on grounds related to the public trust doctrine but not in name. For example, the Oregon courts have relied on the doctrine of custom, as expressed in the following decisions.

State *ex rel.* Thornton v. Hay
Supreme Court of Oregon
462 P.2d 671 (1969)

GOODWIN, J.:

William and Georgianna Hay, the owners of a tourist facility at Cannon Beach, appeal from a decree which enjoins them from constructing fences or other improvements in the dry-sand area between the sixteen-foot elevation contour line and the ordinary high-tide line of the Pacific Ocean.

The issue is whether the state has the power to prevent the defendant landowners from enclosing the dry-sand area contained within the legal description of their ocean-front property.

* * *

The defendant landowners concede that ... all tideland lying seaward of the ordinary or mean high-tide line is a state recreation area as defined in Or. Rev. Stat. 390.720.[1]

* * *

The land area in dispute will be called the dry-sand area. This will be assumed to be the land lying between the line of mean high tide and the visible line of vegetation.

The vegetation line is the seaward edge of vegetation where the upland supports vegetation. It falls generally in the vicinity of the sixteen-foot-elevation contour line....

* * *

---

1. Or Rev. Stat. 390.720 provides:
    Ownership of the shore of the Pacific Ocean between ordinary high tide and extreme low tide, and from the Oregon and Washington state line on the north to the Oregon and California state line on the south, excepting such portions as may have been disposed of by the state prior to July 5, 1947, is vested in the State of Oregon, and is declared to be a state recreation area. No portion of such ocean shore shall be alienated by any of the agencies of the state except as provided by law.

Below, or seaward of, the mean high-tide line, is the state-owned foreshore, or wet-sand area, in which the landowners in this case concede the public's paramount right, and concerning which there is no justiciable controversy.

The only issue in this case, as noted, is the power of the state to limit the record owner's use and enjoyment of the dry-sand area, by whatever boundaries the area may be described.

The trial court found that the public had acquired, over the years, an easement for recreational purposes to go upon and enjoy the dry-sand area, and that this easement was appurtenant to the wet-sand portion of the beach which is admittedly owned by the state and designated as a "state recreation area."

Because we hold that the trial court correctly found in favor of the state on the rights of the public in the dry-sand area, it follows that the state has an equitable right to protect the public in the enjoyment of those rights by causing the removal of fences and other obstacles.

* * *

In order to explain our reasons for affirming the trial court's decree, it is necessary to set out in some detail the historical facts which lead to our conclusion.

The dry-sand area in Oregon has been enjoyed by the general public as a recreational adjunct of the wet-sand or foreshore area since the beginning of the state's political history. The first European settlers on these shores found the aboriginal inhabitants using the foreshore for clam-digging and the dry-sand area for their cooking fires. The newcomers continued these customs after statehood. Thus, from the time of the earliest settlement to the present day, the general public has assumed that the dry-sand area was a part of the public beach, and the public has used the dry-sand area for picnics, gathering wood, building warming fires, and generally as a headquarters from which to supervise children or to range out over the foreshore as the tides advance and recede. In the Cannon Beach vicinity, state and local officers have policed the dry sand, and municipal sanitary crews have attempted to keep the area reasonably free from man-made litter.

Perhaps one explanation for the evolution of the custom of the public to use the dry-sand area for recreational purposes is that the area could not be used conveniently by its owners for any other purpose. The dry-sand area is unstable in its seaward boundaries, unsafe during winter storms, and for the most part unfit for the construction of permanent structures. While the vegetation line remains relatively fixed, the western edge of the dry-sand area is subject to dramatic moves eastward or westward in response to erosion and accretion. For example, evidence in the trial below indicated that between April 1966 and August 1967 the seaward edge of the dry-sand area involved in this litigation moved westward 180 feet. At other points along the shore, the evidence showed, the seaward edge of the dry-sand area could move an equal distance to the east in a similar period of time.

Until very recently, no question concerning the right of the public to enjoy the dry-sand area appears to have been brought before the courts of this state. The public's assumption that the dry sand as well as the foreshore was "public property" had been reinforced by early judicial decisions. *See Shively v. Bowlby*, 152 U.S. 1 (1894), which affirmed *Bowlby v. Shively*, 30 P. 154 (Or. 1892). These cases held that landowners claiming under federal patents owned seaward only to the "high-water" line, a line that was then assumed to be the vegetation line.

In 1935, the United States Supreme Court held that a federal patent conveyed title to land farther seaward, to the mean hightide line. *Borax Consolidated, Ltd. v. Los Angeles*, 296 U.S. 10 (1935)....

Recently, however, the scarcity of oceanfront building sites has attracted substantial private investments in resort facilities. Resort owners like these defendants now desire to reserve for their paying guests the recreational advantages that accrue to the dry-sand portions of their deeded property. Consequently, in 1967, public debate and political activity resulted in legislative attempts to resolve conflicts between public and private interests in the dry-sand area:

> (1) The Legislative Assembly hereby declares it is the public policy of the State of Oregon to forever preserve and maintain the sovereignty of the state heretofore existing over the seashore and ocean beaches of the state from the Columbia River on the North to the Oregon-California line on the South so that the public may have the free and uninterrupted use thereof.

> (2) The Legislative Assembly recognizes that over the years the public has made frequent and uninterrupted use of lands abutting, adjacent and contiguous to the public highways and state recreation areas and recognizes, further, that where such use has been sufficient to create easements in the public through dedication, prescription, grant or otherwise, that it is in the public interest to protect and preserve such public easements as a permanent part of Oregon's recreational resources.

> (3) Accordingly, the Legislative Assembly hereby declares that all public rights and easements in those lands described in subsection (2) of this section are confirmed and declared vested exclusively in the State of Oregon and shall be held and administered in the same manner as those lands described in Or. Rev. Stat. 390.720.

Or. Rev. Stat. 390.610

The state concedes that such legislation cannot divest a person of his rights in land, *Hughes v. Washington*, 389 U.S. 290 (1967), and that the defendants' record title, which includes the dry-sand area, extends seaward to the ordinary or mean high-tide line. *Borax Consolidated Ltd. v. Los Angeles*, 296 U.S. 10.

The landowners likewise concede that since 1899 the public's rights in the foreshore have been confirmed by law as well as by custom and usage. [The 1899 law] provided: "That the shore of the Pacific ocean, between ordinary high and extreme low tides, and from the Columbia river on the north to the south boundary line of Clatsop county on the south, is hereby declared a public highway, and shall forever remain open as such to the public." 1899 Or. Laws 3.

The disputed area is *sui generis*. While the foreshore is "owned" by the state, and the upland is "owned" by the patentee or record-title holder, neither can be said to "own" the full bundle of rights normally connoted by the term "estate in fee simple." 1 Richard R. Powell, Powell on Real Property § 163, at 661 (1949).

In addition to the *sui generis* nature of the land itself, a multitude of complex and sometimes overlapping precedents in the law confronted the trial court. Several early Oregon decisions generally support the trial court's decision, i.e., that the public can acquire easements in private land by long-continued user that is inconsistent with the owner's exclusive possession and enjoyment of his land. A citation of the cases could end the discussion at this point. But because the early cases do not agree on the legal theories by which the results are reached, and because this is an important case affecting valuable rights in land, it is appropriate to review some of the law applicable to this case.

One group of precedents relied upon in part by the state and by the trial court can be called the "implied-dedication" cases. The doctrine of implied dedication is well known to the law in this state and elsewhere. See cases collected in Sheldon W. Parks, *The Law of Dedication in Oregon*, 20 Or. L. Rev. 111 (1941). Dedication, however, whether express or implied, rests upon an intent to dedicate. In the case at bar, it is unlikely that the landowners thought they had anything to dedicate, until 1967, when the notoriety of legislative debates about the public's rights in the dry-sand area sent a number of ocean-front landowners to the offices of their legal advisers.

A second group of cases relied upon by the state, but rejected by the trial court, deals with the possibility of a landowner's losing the exclusive possession and enjoyment of his land through the development of prescriptive easements in the public.

In Oregon, as in most common-law jurisdictions, an easement can be created in favor of one person in the land of another by uninterrupted use and enjoyment of the land in a particular manner for the statutory period, so long as the user is open, adverse, under claim of right, but without authority of law or consent of the owner. *Feldman v. Knapp*, 250 P.2d 92 (Or. 1952); *Coventon v. Seufert*, 32 P. 508 (Or. 1893). In Oregon, the prescriptive period is ten years. Or. Rev. Stat. 12.050. The public use of the disputed land in the case at bar is admitted to be continuous for more than sixty years. There is no suggestion in the record that anyone's permission was sought or given; rather, the public used the land under a claim of right. Therefore, if the public can acquire an easement by prescription, the requirements for such an acquisition have been met in connection with the specific tract of land involved in this case.

The owners argue, however, that the general public, not being subject to actions in trespass or ejectment, cannot acquire rights by prescription, because the statute of limitations is irrelevant when an action does not lie.

While it may not be feasible for a landowner to sue the general public, it is nonetheless possible by means of signs and fences to prevent or minimize public invasions of private land for recreational purposes. In Oregon, moreover, the courts and the Legislative Assembly have both recognized that the public can acquire prescriptive easements in private land, at least for roads and highways. *See, e.g., Huggett v. Moran*, 266 P.2d 692 (Or. 1954), in which we observed that counties could acquire public roads by prescription. And see Or. Rev. Stat. 368.405, which provides for the manner in which counties may establish roads. The statute enumerates the formal governmental actions that can be employed, and then concludes: "This section does not preclude acquiring public ways by adverse user."

Another statute codifies a policy favoring the acquisition by prescription of public recreational easements in beach lands. *See* Or. Rev. Stat. 390.610. While such a statute cannot create public rights at the expense of a private landowner the statute can, and does, express legislative approval of the common-law doctrine of prescription where the facts justify its application. Consequently, we conclude that the law in Oregon, regardless of the generalizations that may apply elsewhere, does not preclude the creation of prescriptive easements in beach land for public recreational use.

Because many elements of prescription are present in this case, the state has relied upon the doctrine in support of the decree below. We believe, however, that there is a better legal basis for affirming the decree. The most cogent basis for the decision in this case is the English doctrine of custom. Strictly construed, prescription applies only to the specific tract of land before the court, and doubtful prescription cases could fill the courts for years with tract-by-tract litigation. An established custom, on the other hand, can be proven with reference to a larger region. Ocean-front lands from the northern to the southern border of the state ought to be treated uniformly.

The other reason which commends the doctrine of custom over that of prescription as the principal basis for the decision in this case is the unique nature of the lands in question. This case deals solely with the dry-sand area along the Pacific shore, and this land has been used by the public as public recreational land according to an unbroken custom running back in time as long as the land has been inhabited.

A custom is defined in 1 Bouvier's Law Dictionary, Rawle's Third Revision 742 (8th ed. 1914) as "such a usage as by common consent and uniform practice has become the law of the place, or of the subject matter to which it relates."

In 1 William Blackstone, Commentaries, Sir William Blackstone set out the requisites of a particular custom.

Paraphrasing Blackstone, the first requirement of a custom, to be recognized as law, is that it must be ancient. It must have been used so long "that the memory of man runneth not to the contrary." Professor Cooley footnotes his edition of Blackstone with the comment that "long and general" usage is sufficient. In any event, the record in the case at bar satisfies the requirement of antiquity. So long as there has been an institutionalized system of land tenure in Oregon, the public has freely exercised the right to use the dry-sand area up and down the Oregon coast for the recreational purposes noted earlier in this opinion.

The second requirement is that the right be exercised without interruption. A customary right need not be exercised continuously, but it must be exercised without an interruption caused by anyone possessing a paramount right. In the case at bar, there was evidence that the public's use and enjoyment of the dry-sand area had never been interrupted by private landowners.

Blackstone's third requirement, that the customary use be peaceable and free from dispute, is satisfied by the evidence which related to the second requirement.

The fourth requirement that of reasonableness, is satisfied by the evidence that the public has always made use of the land in a manner appropriate to the land and to the usages of the community. There is evidence in the record that when inappropriate uses have been detected, municipal police officers have intervened to preserve order.

The fifth requirement, certainty, is satisfied by the visible boundaries of the dry-sand area and by the character of the land, which limits the use thereof to recreational uses connected with the foreshore.

The sixth requirement is that a custom must be obligatory; that is, in the case at bar, not left to the option of each landowner whether or not he will recognize the public's right to go upon the dry-sand area for recreational purposes. The record shows that the dry-sand area in question has been used, as of right, uniformly with similarly situated lands elsewhere, and that the public's use has never been questioned by an upland owner so long as the public remained on the dry sand and refrained from trespassing upon the lands above the vegetation line.

Finally, a custom must not be repugnant, or inconsistent, with other customs or with other law. The custom under consideration violates no law, and is not repugnant.

Two arguments have been arrayed against the doctrine of custom as a basis for decision in Oregon. The first argument is that custom is unprecedented in this state, and has only scant adherence elsewhere in the United States. The second argument is that because of the relative brevity of our political history it is inappropriate to rely upon an English doctrine that requires greater antiquity than a newly-settled land can muster. Neither of these arguments is persuasive.

The custom of the people of Oregon to use the dry-sand area of the beaches for public recreational purposes meets every one of Blackstone's requisites. While it is not necessary to rely upon precedent from other states, we are not the first state to recognize custom as a source of law. *See Perley v. Langley*, 7 N.H. 233 (1834).

On the score of the brevity of our political history, it is true that the Anglo-American legal system on this continent is relatively new. Its newness has made it possible for government to provide for many of our institutions by written law rather than by customary law.[2] This truism does not, however, militate against the validity of a custom when the custom does in fact exist. If antiquity were the sole test of validity of a custom, Oregonians could satisfy that requirement by recalling that the European settlers were not the first people to use the dry-sand area as public land.

Finally, in support of custom, the record shows that the custom of the inhabitants of Oregon and of visitors in the state to use the dry sand as a public recreation area is so notorious that notice of the custom on the part of persons buying land along the shore must be presumed. In the case at bar, the landowners conceded their actual knowledge of the public's long-standing use of the dry-sand area, and argued that the elements of consent present in the relationship between the landowners and the public precluded the application of the law of prescription. As noted, we are not resting this decision on prescription, and we leave open the effect upon prescription of the type of consent that may have been present in this case. Such elements of consent are, however, wholly consistent with the recognition of public rights derived from custom.

Because so much of our law is the product of legislation, we sometimes lose sight of the importance of custom as a source of law in our society. It seems particularly appropriate in the case at bar to look to an ancient and accepted custom in this state as the source of a rule of law. The rule in this case, based upon custom, is salutary in confirming a public right, and at the same time it takes from no man anything which he has had a legitimate reason to regard as exclusively his.

For the foregoing reasons, the decree of the trial court is affirmed.

DENECKE, J. (specially concurring):

I agree with the decision of the majority; however, I disagree with basing the decision upon the English doctrine of "customary rights." In my opinion the facts in this case cannot be fitted into the outlines of that ancient doctrine. 6 RICHARD R. POWELL, POWELL ON REAL PROPERTY § 934, n.5, at 362 (1968); 2 THOMPSON, THOMPSON ON REAL PROPERTY § 369, n.50 at 463 (1961); GRAY, THE RULE AGAINST PERPETUITIES, ch. 17 (4th ed. 1942); H.W. Chaplin, *The Law of Dedication and its Relation to Trust Legislation*, 16 Harv. L. Rev. 329, 332 (1903).

---

2. The English law on customary rights grew up in a small island nation at a time when most inhabitants lived and died without traveling more than a day's walk from their birthplace. Most of the customary rights recorded in English cases are local in scope. The English had many cultural and language groups which eventually merged into a nation. After these groups developed their own unique customs, the unified nation recognized some of them as law. Some American scholars, looking at the vast geography of this continent and the freshness of its civilization, have concluded that there is no need to look to English customary rights as a source of legal rights in this country. *See, e.g.*, 6 RICHARD R. POWELL, POWELL ON REAL PROPERTY § 934, n.5, at 362 (1949). Some of the generalizations drawn by the text writers from English cases would tend to limit customary rights to specific usages in English towns and villages. *See* GRAY, THE RULE AGAINST PERPETUITIES §§ 572–588 (1942). But it does not follow that a custom, established in fact, cannot have regional application and be enjoyed by a larger public than the inhabitants of a single village.

In my opinion the doctrine of "customary rights" is useful but only as an analogy. I am further of the opinion that "custom," as distinguished from "customary rights," is an important ingredient in establishing the rights of the public to the use of the dry sands.

I base the public's right upon the following factors: (1) long usage by the public of the dry sands area, not necessarily on all the Oregon beaches, but wherever the public uses the beach; (2) a universal and long held belief by the public in the public's right to such use; (3) long and universal acquiescence by the upland owners in such public use; and (4) the extreme desirability to the public of the right to the use of the dry sands. When this combination exists, as it does here, I conclude that the public has the right to use the dry sands.

Admittedly, this is a new concept as applied to use of the dry sands of a beach; however, it is not new as applied to other public usages. In *Luscher v. Reynolds*, 56 P.2d 1158 (1936), we held that regardless of who owns the bed of a lake, if it is capable of being boated, the public has the right to boat it.

> There are hundreds of similar beautiful, small inland lakes in this state well adapted for recreational purposes, but which will never be used as highways of commerce in the ordinary acceptation of such terms. As stated in *Lamprey v. State*, 53 N.W. 1139 (Minn. 1893), quoted with approval in *Guilliams v. Beaver Lake Club*, 175 P. 437 (Or. 1918), "To hand over all these lakes to private ownership, under any old or narrow test of navigability, would be a great wrong upon the public for all time, the extent of which cannot, perhaps, be now even anticipated." Regardless of the ownership of the bed, the public has the paramount right to the use of the waters of the lake for the purpose of transportation and commerce.

56 P.2d at 1162.

In *Collins v. Gerhardt*, 211 N.W. 115, 116 (Mich. 1926), the defendant was wading Pine River and fishing. The plaintiff, who owned the land on both sides and the bed of Pine River, sued defendant for trespass. The court held for the defendant:

> From this it follows that the common-law doctrine, viz., that the right of fishing in navigable waters follows the ownership of the soil, does not prevail in this state. It is immaterial who owns the soil in our navigable rivers. The trust remains. From the beginning the title was impressed with this trust for the preservation of the public right of fishing and other public rights which all citizens enjoyed in tidal waters under the common law.

Id. at 118.

These rights of the public in tidelands and in the beds of navigable streams have been called 'jus publicum' and we have consistently and recently reaffirmed their existence. *Corvallis Sand & Gravel Co. v. State Land Board*, 439 P.2d 575 (Or. 1968); *Smith Tug & Barge Co. v. Columbia-Pacific Towing Corp.*, 443 P.2d 205 (Or. 1968). The right of public use continues although title to the property passes into private ownership and nothing in the chain of title reserves or notifies anyone of this public right. *Winston Bros. Co. v. State Tax Comm'n*, 62 P.2d 7 (Or. 1936).

In a recent treatise on waters and water rights the authors state:

> The principle that the public has an interest in tidelands and banks of navigable waters and a right to use them for purposes for which there is a substantial public demand may be derived from the fact that the public won a right to passage over the shore for access to the sea for fishing when this was the area of

substantial public demand. As time goes by, opportunities for much more extensive uses of these lands become available to the public. The assertion by the public of a right to enjoy additional uses is met by the assertion that the public right is defined and limited by precedent based upon past uses and past demand. But such a limitation confuses the application of the principle under given circumstances with the principle itself.

The law regarding the public use of property held in part for the benefit of the public must change as the public need changes. The words of Justice Cardozo, expressed in a different context nearly a half-century ago are relevant today in our application of this law: "We may not suffer it to petrify at the cost of its animating principle."

1 WATERS AND WATER RIGHTS 202 (1967).

Notes

1. The public's customary right to use ocean beaches seems to derive from the acquiescence of upland landowners, who failed to stop the public from using the Oregon beach "since the beginning of the state's political history" for "picnics, gathering wood, building warming fires, and generally as a headquarters from which to supervise children...." So, a tolerance for public use led to a public right to use. Why isn't this simply a prescriptive public easement? What advantage does the court see in fashioning a customary right instead of recognizing a prescriptive easement?

2. Justice Denecke's concurrence argued that the court should have ruled that the public's right to use ocean beaches is part of the public trust doctrine. Surely, the doctrine of custom is at least a close cousin, if not a subset of the public trust, but what are their differences in terms of their origin and effect? The court noted that private landowners' actions to interrupt public use could defeat a claim for custom. Doesn't this give extraordinary power to landowners—power that runs inconsistent with the purpose of the doctrine, which is to protect the public's expectations? Would a private landowner's exclusion of the public defeat a public trust claim? For an argument endorsing Justice Denecke's view, see Michael C. Blumm & Erika Doot, *Oregon's Public Trust Doctrine: Public Rights in Waters, Wildlife, and Beaches*, 42 Envtl. L. 375, 408–10 (2012).

3. Technically, the doctrine of custom (the Blackstonian version at least) requires such longstanding public use that "the memory of man runneth not to the contrary." Isn't this asking a bit much? As the court noted, one commentator suggests that "long and general" usage may suffice to establish this factor. Professor Joseph Sax asserted that the primary purpose of the PTD is to prevent disappointment to the reasonable expectations of the public "held in common but without formal recognition such as title." Joseph L. Sax, *Liberating the Public Trust Doctrine from Its Historical Shackles*, 14 U.C. Davis L. Rev. 185 (1980). In this vein, doesn't the public build up expectations over the course of a timeframe far shorter than the one Blackstone contemplated?

4. An influential article by Professor Harrison Dunning suggested that the public trust embodies "a fundamental notion of how government is to operate with regard to common heritage natural resources." *See* Harrison C. Dunning, *The Public Trust: A Fundamental Doctrine of American Property Law*, 19 Envtl. L. 515, 523 (1989). Should courts treat the doctrine of custom as a more flexible test that can bring resources into the public trust where the public demonstrates longstanding use of the resource as part of its common heritage? The Supreme Court of California emphasized this factor when it observed in its leading *Mono Lake* public trust opinion that streams, lakes, marshlands and tidelands all

make up the state's "common heritage." *National Audubon Society v. Superior Court of Alpine County*, 658 P.2d 709, 724 (Cal. 1983) (p. 173). The *Matthews* court classified the state's dry sand beaches in this way too, stating, "[b]eaches are a unique resource and are irreplaceable." *Matthews*, 471 A.2d at 364. In the same vein, a Nevada Supreme Court Justice passionately argued that Lake Walker warrants recognition as a trust asset, reasoning, "[t]he public expects this unique natural resource to be preserved and for all of us to always be able to marvel at this massive glittering body of water lying majestically in the midst of a dry mountainous desert." *Mineral County v. State, Department of Conservation & Natural Resources*, 20 P.3d 800, 808 (Nev. 2001) (Rose, J., concurring).

5. Note that, in addition to recognizing longstanding public usage of the beach, the court also emphasized that the beach is unsuitable for permanent structures due to extreme erosion and storm potential. Was the court saying that this type of land is not suited to the standard uses associated with private ownership? Did it express the same thread of reasoning that the *Just* court provided in announcing the natural use doctrine that prevents any landowner from claiming reasonable expectations to alter the natural character of the land? *See Just*, 201 N.W.2d 761 (Wis. 1972) (p. 141).

6. The Hays subsequently sued in federal court, alleging that the state court's decision amounted to an unconstitutional taking of their property without payment of just compensation. The court denied the claim in *Hay v. Bruno*, 344 F. Supp. 286 (D. Or. 1972) (ruling that there was no unpredictable change in law as a result of the *Thornton v. Hay* decision, since the state had claimed the public's right to use the beach for at least 80 years, and the result was consistent with recognition of public rights in other states).

7. Oregon is not the only state to use a version of customary rights to declare public rights of access to beaches. The Florida Supreme Court upheld the public's customary right to access the beach in *City of Daytona Beach v. Tona-Rama, Inc.*, 294 So. 2d 73, 78 (Fla. 1974) ("The general public may continue to use the dry sand area for their usual recreational activities, not because the public has any interest in the land itself, but because of a right gained through custom to use this particular area of the beach as they have without dispute and without interruption for many years."). However, the standard for customary use has been a hard one to prove. *See Trepanier v. County of Volusia*, 965 So. 2d 276 (Fla. Dist. Ct. App. 2007) (remanding because genuine issues of material fact remained on the question of whether the public had a right by custom to use the dry sand area for driving and parking).

Hawai'i recognizes public access to beaches based on customary rights through legislation. HAW. REV. STAT. §§ 115-4 to -5 (2014) ("The right of access to Hawai'i's shorelines includes the right of transit along the shorelines."). Texas also provides public access to beaches by customary rights, *Matcha v. Mattox*, 711 S.W.2d 95 (Tex. App. 1986) (upholding a public easement to use a beach based on custom), but the Texas Supreme Court recently ruled, in *Severance v. Patterson*, 370 S.W.3d 705 (Tex. 2012), that the state does not recognize a "rolling" public easement on beaches after an avulsive event (like a hurricane) creates a new beach on what was previously unencumbered private property.

The Maine Supreme Court explicitly declined to recognize the doctrine of custom as an avenue for granting public rights to use dry sand areas of beaches owned by private parties. *Almeder v. Town of Kennebunkport*, 106 A.3d 1099, 1114 (Me. 2014) (reversing the lower court's determination that the public had an easement by custom over dry sand areas of Goose Rocks Beach because the court "refus[ed] to recognize an easement by custom").

8. *Severance v. Patterson*, discussed in the previous note, dealt with a shifting land-water boundary. Many courts have taken up the issue of who owns newly-formed land that re-

sults when this boundary shifts. The Supreme Court of Iowa was one such court. In *State v. Sorenson*, 436 N.W.2d 358 (Iowa 1989), the issue was whether the state statute of limitations barred the state's claim that 150 acres of land formed by accretion on the bank of the Missouri River was owned by the state. The lower court ruled that the state's claim was barred by the statute of limitations, and the Iowa Supreme Court reversed. An excerpt of that opinion follows.

> The State … asserts that no state claims are subject to barring under this statute. As a secondary position, the State argues that its claim may not be barred in this case, because the land is "public trust" property and may not be, in effect, lost by default. Sorensen argues that the purpose of the title standards is to add predictability and certainty in land conveyancing and that such purposes would be frustrated if any party, including the state, were to be excepted from it. It further points to the language in section 614.17 [the statute of limitations] which provides that "any interest" must be preserved in order to avoid time bar of that section.

> While we give "serious consideration" to our title standards, we stop short of holding that section 614.17 is inapplicable to any claims by the State. Because of the unique nature of the property involved here, it is only necessary to decide whether that statute may be used to bar claims to "public trust" property. We do not decide the broader question of whether section 614.17 bars all types of state claims.

> Ownership of the bed of the Missouri River was granted to the State of Iowa under the equal footing doctrine when Iowa was admitted to statehood….

> While it is said that the state owns the bed of its navigable rivers, the incidents of its "ownership" are closely circumscribed. From the time statehood was granted to Iowa, Congress has made it clear that the state's control over navigable streams is subject to certain rights of the public….

> * * *

> The public trust doctrine is said to have evolved to the point that it now has "emerged from the watery depths [of navigable waterways] to embrace the dry sand area of a beach, rural parklands, a historic battlefield, wildlife, archaeological remains, and even a downtown area." Richard J. Lazarus, *Changing Conceptions of Property and Sovereignty in Natural Resources: Questioning the Public Trust Doctrine*, 71 Iowa L. Rev. 631, 649 (1986) (citations omitted). The doctrine today, both courts and commentators have noted, "reflects the assertion of public rights that preexist any private property rights in the affected resource." *Id.* at 648–49.

> [The court went on to explain that the state has limited power to dispose of public trust land and that "mistakes of officials [in attempting to convey it] cannot deprive the state of its property" (quoting *State v. Dakota County*, 93 N.W.2d 595, 599 (Iowa 1958).]

> These general principles of public trust, we believe, bear on the ultimate question in this case: Whether our legislature intended that section 614.17 would bar the State's claim to public trust property. The purpose of statutory construction, of course, is to look to the object to be accomplished, the evil sought to be remedied, or the purpose to be subserved, and place on it a reasonable or liberal construction which will best effect its purpose rather than one which will defeat it.

> In view of the stringent limitations on the state's power to alienate such property, even by design, we cannot ascribe to the legislature an intention that it be

permitted to be lost by default. We hold that section 614.17 does not apply to bar claims of the state to public trust property. This is consistent with our case law predating the enactment of section 614.17 which uniformly held that the state could not lose title to public trust type property.

* * *

Some property, by its very nature, is incapable of private ownership and should not be included in statutes of limitations such as section 614.17.

II. Is This Public Trust Land?

Sorensen argues that, even if public trust land were to be excepted from section 614.17, this land does not qualify as public trust property. He notes that, in contrast to *Illinois Central Railroad*, in which the state had attempted to sell a part of the bed of Lake Michigan, this land is not a part of the riverbed, nor is it necessary for navigation or commerce.

The public trust doctrine, however, is not limited to navigation or commerce; it applies broadly to the public's *use* of property, such as waterways, without ironclad parameters on the types of uses to be protected. *See* Lazarus, at 649; 65 C.J.S. Navigable Waters § 92, at 289–91 (Public trust purposes include "rights of navigation, commerce, fishing, bathing, recreation, or enjoyment, and other appropriate public and useful purposes, or such other rights as are incident to public waters at common law, free from obstruction and interference by private persons....").

We do not necessarily subscribe to broad applications of the doctrine, noted by one authority to include rural parklands, historic battlefields, or archaeological remains. In fact, we are cautioned against an overextension of the doctrine. Lazarus, at 692. Nevertheless, we believe that a navigable river is unquestionably a part of the public trust. The close circumspection of the state's powers with respect to such property, as discussed above, makes that clear.

Fishing and navigation are among the expressly recognized uses protected by the public trust doctrine. Fishing and navigation, whether of a commercial or recreational nature, require means of public access to the river. This means that state-owned land adjacent to the river, as well as the land actually covered by the river, must be part of the public trust. *See Peck v. Alfred Olsen Constr.*, 245 N.W. 131, 132 (Iowa 1932) (access to lake by motor vehicle necessarily incident to navigation).

The land in question here is undoubtedly suited for use as public access to the river, as evidenced by the fact there were proposals by the litigants here to use it for construction of a marina. We do not believe it is necessary, as Sorensen suggests, to examine each tract of state-owned land in proximity to navigable waterways to determine if it is used for navigation or commerce. We take judicial notice of the expanding involvement of Iowans in recreational activities on and near navigable streams such as the Missouri River. Those uses include hiking, camping, biking, and picnicking, as well as transportation on the river itself. In fact, there was considerable evidence that the public had been using the land in question for just such purposes. We conclude that the land in question here was adequately established to be a part of the public trust and is therefore subject to exception from the application of section 614.17.

III. Evidence of Accretion

In order to prevail, the State must, of course, show that it owns the land in question. It attempted to do so by introducing evidence of accretion to the riverbed. The district court, by concluding that section 614.17 would have barred the State's claim in any event, found it unnecessary to permit the evidence of accretion. It held, in effect, that any claim would be barred by section 614.17 regardless of the source of that claim.

Because we reverse the district court on its original premise that the State's claim is barred by section 614.17, the State should be permitted to establish on retrial that it had title through accretion or other means.

We reverse on the State's appeal and remand for further proceedings.

The property in question in *Sorenson* consisted of 150 acres upland, of the high water mark, which, recall, represents the traditional boundary of historic public trust cases. The court had no hesitation holding that the land was part of the public trust, noting that the state owned the land in question. However, it did not go so far as to suggest that all state-owned property is part of the public trust (briefly distinguishing historic battlefields, archeological remains, and rural parklands). What made the property unquestionably part of the trust? Is this a significant extension of the doctrine? Can it still be said that the doctrine is confined to areas below the high water mark? Is the PTD only a doctrine of streambeds any more? Was it ever just that? Thinking back to chapters 1 and 2, which explore the origins of the PTD, what does this case and others like it say about whether the equal footing doctrine represents the origin of the public trust?

Note that the court took an expansive view of public uses protected by the doctrine, stating that "it applies broadly to the public's *use* of property, such as waterways, without ironclad parameters on the types of uses to be protected." Would a floating golf course qualify as a protected public trust use? (Lake Coeur d'Alene in Idaho has such an amenity.) Note that the court quoted Professor Lazarus who employed more qualified language, describing trust uses as "appropriate public and useful purposes, or such other rights as are incident to public waters at common law...." How would a floating golf course fare under this language?

9. For more on the public trust and beaches, see Mackenzie S. Keith, *Judicial Protection for Beaches and Parks: The Public Trust Doctrine Above the High Water Mark*, 16 Hastings W.-Nw. J. Envtl. L. & Pol'y 165 (2010); Melissa K. Scanlan, *Shifting Sands: A Meta-Theory for Public Access and Private Property Along the Coast*, 65 S.C. L. Rev. 295 (2013).

10. The Oregon Supreme Court subsequently restricted the scope of the public's customary rights to ocean beaches lying adjacent to the ocean. *McDonald v. Halvorson*, 780 P.2d 714 (Or. 1989) (deciding that public customary rights did not apply to a fresh water cove beach because it was not adjacent to the ocean, and there was no history of public use of that beach). However, in a subsequent case, the court reinforced the reasoning of *Thornton v. Hay*. In *Stevens v. City of Cannon Beach*, 854 P.2d 449 (Or. 1993), an owner of two vacant lots on Cannon Beach (the same beach as in *Thornton v. Hay*) sought a permit to build a seawall as part of a plan to develop the property for a motel or hotel. The city denied the permit, and the landowner brought a case alleging a taking of property in violation of the Fifth Amendment. The Supreme Court of Oregon issued the following decision rejecting the landowner's claim. The landowner sought *certiorari* from the U.S. Supreme Court. Although the majority denied *certiorari*, the denial induced a vigorous dissent from Justice Scalia (concurred in by Justice O'Connor). The two decisions follow below.

Stevens v. City of Cannon Beach
Supreme Court of Oregon
854 P.2d 449 (1993)

VAN HOOMISSEN, J.:

[After stating the facts, the court described the decision in *Thornton v. Hay*, 462 P.2d 671 (Or. 1969)].

[P]laintiffs argue that ... because they acquired their property before this court's 1969 decision in *Thornton*, the rule from *Thornton* may not be applied retroactively to them.[3] ...

... Defendants argue that, because under the state property law doctrine of custom, the proscribed use interests in this case were not part of plaintiffs' title, there is no taking under *Lucas*.

... *Thornton*, defendants argue, did not create a new legal principle, but merely applied an existing legal principle of easement by custom grounded in Oregon's property law. Therefore, defendants argue, application of *Thornton* in the present case is not retroactive, any more than it was in *Thornton*.

* * *

The parties recognize, and we agree, that *Thornton* is directly on point. The issue, therefore, is the viability of *Thornton's* rule of law in the light of *Lucas*. We therefore begin with a discussion of *Thornton*.

The facts in this case and in *Thornton* are remarkably similar. In each case, the landowners wished to enclose the dry sand area of their Cannon Beach properties, thereby excluding the public from that portion of the ocean shore. In *Thornton*, this court held that the state could prevent such enclosures because, throughout Oregon's history, the dry sand area customarily had been used by the public....

* * *

... We now turn to the determination of what effect the Supreme Court's opinion in *Lucas* has on Oregon's well-established policy of public access to and protection of its ocean shores....

* * *

The *Lucas* Court addressed a state's sudden elimination of all economically valuable use of land without compensation, holding that: Any limitation so severe [as to prohibit all economically beneficial use of land] cannot be newly legislated or decreed (without compensation), but must inhere in the title itself, in the restrictions that background principles *of the State's law of property* and nuisance already place upon land ownership. 505 U.S. 1003, 1029 (1992) (emphasis added).

* * *

Applying the *Lucas* analysis to this case, we conclude that the common-law doctrine of custom as applied to Oregon's ocean shores in *Thornton* is not "newly legislated or decreed"; to the contrary, to use the words of the *Lucas* court, it "inhere[s] in the title itself; in the restrictions that background principles of the State's law of property and

---

3. The date of the *Thornton* decision is not relevant. Rather, the question is when, under *Thornton's* reasoning, *the public rights came into being*. The answer is that they came into being long before plaintiffs acquired any interests in their land.

nuisance already placed upon land ownership." *Id.* at 1029. As noted in *Hay v. Bruno*, 344 F. Supp. at 289, "there was no sudden change in either the law or the policy of the State of Oregon. For at least 80 years, the State as a matter of right claimed an interest in the disputed land." Plaintiffs' argument that a "retroactive" application of the *Thornton* rule to their property is unconstitutional, is not persuasive. *Thornton* did not create a new rule of law and apply it retroactively to the land at issue in that case.... *Thornton* merely enunciated one of Oregon's "background principles of ... the law of property." *Lucas*, 505 U.S. at 1029....

When plaintiffs took title to their land, they were on notice that exclusive use of the dry sand areas was not a part of the "bundle of rights" that they acquired, because public use of dry sand areas "is so notorious that notice of the custom on the part of persons buying land along the shore must be presumed." *Thornton*, 462 P.2d at 678. We, therefore, hold that the doctrine of custom as applied to public use of Oregon's dry sand areas is one of "the restrictions that background principles of the State's law of property ... already place upon land ownership." *Lucas*, 505 U.S. at 1029. We hold that plaintiffs have never had the property interests that they claim were taken by defendants' decision and regulations.

* * *

Stevens v. City of Cannon Beach
U.S. Supreme Court
510 U.S. 1207 (1994)

On Petition For Writ of Certiorari to The Supreme Court of Oregon.

The petition for a writ of certiorari is denied.

SCALIA, Justice with whom Justice O'CONNOR joins, dissenting:

This is a suit by owners of a parcel of beachfront property against the city of Cannon Beach and the State of Oregon. Petitioners purchased the property in 1957. In 1989, they sought a building permit for construction of a seawall on the dry-sand portion of the property. When the permit was denied, they brought this inverse condemnation action against the city in the Circuit Court of Clatsop County, alleging a taking in violation of the Fifth and Fourteenth Amendments. That court dismissed the complaint for failure to state a claim pursuant to Oregon Rule of Civil Procedure 21 A(8), on the ground that under *State ex rel. Thornton v. Hay*, 462 P.2d 671 (Or. 1969), petitioners never possessed the right to obstruct public access to the dry-sand portion of the property. The Court of Appeals, 835 P.2d 940 (Or. 1992), and then the Supreme Court of Oregon, 854 P.2d 449 (Or. 1993), both relying on *Thornton*, affirmed. The landowners have petitioned this Court for writ of certiorari to the Supreme Court of Oregon. They allege an unconstitutional taking of property without just compensation, and a denial of due process of law.

In order to clarify the nature of the constitutional questions that the case presents, a brief sketch of Oregon case law involving beachfront property is necessary.

I.

In 1969, the State of Oregon brought suit to enjoin owners of certain beachfront tourist facilities from constructing improvements on the "dry-sand" portion of their properties. The trial court granted an injunction. *State ex rel. Thornton v. Hay*, 462 P.2d 671. In defending that judgment on appeal to the Supreme Court of Oregon, the State briefed and argued its case on the theory that by implied dedication or prescriptive easement the public had acquired the right to use the dry-sand area for recreational purposes, precluding development. The Supreme Court of Oregon found "a better legal basis" for affirming the decision and decided the case on an entirely different theory:

> The most cogent basis for the decision in this case is the English doctrine of custom. Strictly construed, prescription applies only to the specific tract of land before the court, and doubtful prescription cases could fill the courts for years with tract-by-tract litigation. An established custom, on the other hand, can be proven with reference to a larger region. Ocean-front lands from the northern to the southern border of the state ought to be treated uniformly.

Id. at 676.

The court set forth what it said were the seven elements of the doctrine of custom and concluded that "[t]he custom of the people of Oregon to use the dry-sand area of the beaches for public recreational purposes meets every one of Blackstone's requisites." *Id.* at 677. The court affirmed the injunction, saying that "it takes from no man anything which he has had a legitimate reason to regard as exclusively his." *Id.* at 678. Thus, *Thornton* declared as the customary law of Oregon the proposition that the public enjoys a right of recreational use of all dry-sand beach, which denies property owners development rights.

Or so it seemed until 1989. That year, the Supreme Court of Oregon revisited the issue of dry-sand beach in the case of *McDonald v. Halvorson,* 780 P.2d 714 (Or. 1989). There, the beachfront property owners who were plaintiffs sought a judicial declaration that their property included a portion of dry-sand area adjacent to a cove of the Pacific Ocean. With such a declaration in place, they hoped to gain access (under *Thornton,* as members of the public) to the remaining dry-sand area of the cove lying on property to which the defendants held record title. The State intervened to assert the public's right (under the doctrine of custom) to use the dry-sand area of the cove, and to enjoin defendants from interfering with that right. The Supreme Court of Oregon held that the public had no right to recreational use of the dry-sand portions of the cove beach. *Id.* at 724. *McDonald* noted what it called inconsistencies in *Thornton, Id.* at 723, and resolved them by stating that "nothing in [*Thornton*] fairly can be read to have established beyond dispute a public claim by virtue of 'custom' to the right to recreational use of the entire Oregon coast." *Id.* at 724. "[T]here may also be [dry-sand] areas," the court said, "to which the doctrine of custom is not applicable." The court noted that

> [t]here [was] no testimony in this record showing customary use of the narrow beach on the bank of the cove.... The doctrine of custom announced in [*Thornton*] simply does not apply to this controversy. The public has no right to recreational use of the [dry-sand beach area of the cove] because there is no factual predicate for application of the doctrine.

Id. at 724.

With *McDonald* now the leading case interpreting the law of custom, petitioners here brought their takings challenge in the Oregon state trial court. As recited above, that court dismissed for failure to state a claim upon which relief could be granted, saying that

> [*Thornton*] teaches us that ocean front owners cannot enclose or develop the dry sand beach area so as to exclude the public therefrom.... [B]ecause of the public's ancient and continued use of the dry sand area on the Oregon coast ... its future use thereof cannot be curtailed or limited.

The trial court did not cite *McDonald,* and its peremptory dismissal prevented petitioners from doing what *McDonald* clearly contemplated their doing: providing the factual predicate for their challenge through testimony of customary use showing that their property is one of those areas "to which the doctrine of custom [was] not applicable." *McDonald*, 780 P.2d at 724. Moreover, when petitioners attempted to introduce such factual material on appeal they were rebuffed on the ground that appeal was confined to the purely legal question whether the complaint stated a claim under Oregon law.

In its decision here, the Supreme Court of Oregon quoted portions of *Thornton*'s sweeping language appearing to declare the law of custom for all the Oregon shore. But it then read *Thornton* (which also originated in a dispute over property in Cannon Beach) to have said that the "historic public use *of the dry sand area of Cannon Beach* met [Blackstone's] requirements." 854 P.2d at 454 (emphasis added).[4] The court then framed the issue as the continuing validity of *Thornton* in light of *Lucas v. South Carolina Coastal Council*, 505 U.S. 1003 (1992). The court quoted our opinion in *Lucas*: "'Any limitation so severe [as to prohibit all economically beneficial use of land] cannot be newly legislated or decreed (without compensation), but must inhere in the title itself, in the restrictions that background principles *of the State's law of property* and nuisance already place upon land ownership.'" 854 P.2d at 456 (quoting *Lucas*, 505 U.S. at 1029 (emphasis added by the Oregon court)). The court held that the doctrine of custom was just such a background principle of Oregon property law, and that petitioners never had the property interests that they claim were taken by respondents' decisions and regulations. 854 P.2d at 456. It then affirmed the dismissal.

II.

As a general matter, the Constitution leaves the law of real property to the States. But just as a State may not deny rights protected under the Federal Constitution through pretextual procedural rulings, see *NAACP v. Alabama ex rel. Patterson*, 357 U.S. 449, 455–458 (1958), neither may it do so by invoking nonexistent rules of state substantive law. Our opinion in *Lucas*, for example, would be a nullity if anything that a state court chooses to denominate "background law"—regardless of whether it is really such—could eliminate property rights. "[A] State cannot be permitted to defeat the constitutional prohibition against taking property without due process of law by the simple device of asserting retroactively that the property it has taken never existed at all." *Hughes v. Washington*, 389 U.S. 290, 296–97 (1967) (Stewart, J., concurring). No more by judicial decree than by legislative fiat may a State transform private property into public property without compensation. *Webb's Fabulous Pharmacies, Inc. v. Beckwith*, 449 U.S. 155, 164 (1980). *See also Lucas*, 505 U.S. at 1031. Since opening private property to public use constitutes a taking, *see Nollan v. California Coastal Comm'n*, 483 U.S. 825, 831 (1987); *Kaiser Aetna v. United States*, 444 U.S. 164, 178 (1979), if it cannot fairly be said that an Oregon doctrine of custom deprived Cannon Beach property owners of their rights to exclude others from the dry sand, then the decision now before us has effected an uncompensated taking.

To say that this case raises a serious Fifth Amendment takings issue is an understatement. The issue is serious in the sense that it involves a holding of questionable consti-

---

4. This reading of *Thornton* is in my view unsupportable. *Thornton* did not limit itself to "the dry sand area of Cannon Beach." On the contrary, *Thornton* includes the following statements: "Oceanfront lands from the northern to the southern border of the state ought to be treated uniformly." 462 P.2d, at 676. "This case deals solely with the dry-sand area along the Pacific shore...." *Id.* "The custom of the people of Oregon to use the dry-sand area of the beaches for public recreational purposes meets every one of Blackstone's requisites." *Id.* at 677. "[T]he custom of the inhabitants of Oregon and of visitors in the state to use the dry sand as a public recreation area is so notorious that notice of the custom ... must be presumed." *Id.* at 678. The passage in which *Thornton* actually applies Blackstone's seven-factor test contains not a single mention of the city of Cannon Beach. *Id.* at 677.

tutionality; and it is serious in the sense that the landgrab (if there is one) may run the entire length of the Oregon coast.[5] It is by no means clear that the facts—either as to the entire Oregon coast, or as to the small segment at issue here—meet the requirements for the English doctrine of custom. The requirements set forth by Blackstone included, *inter alia*, that the public right of access be exercised without interruption, and that the custom be obligatory, *i.e.*, in the present context that it not be left to the option of each landowner whether he will recognize the public's right to go on the dry-sand area for recreational purposes. In *Thornton*, however, the Supreme Court of Oregon determined the historical existence of these fact-intensive criteria (as well as five others) in a discussion that took less than one full page of the Pacific Reporter. That is all the more remarkable a feat since the Supreme Court of Oregon was investigating these criteria *in the first instance*; the trial court had not rested its decision on the basis of custom and the State did not argue that theory to the Supreme Court.[6]

* * *

I would grant the petition for certiorari with regard to the due process claim.

Notes

1. Note how the doctrine of custom defeats a takings claim in precisely the same way as does the public trust doctrine. In both cases, courts find that the landowner never gained the right in his/her title to exclude the public. As the Oregon Supreme Court concluded, public customary rights are "background principles" of property law that "inhere" in private land titles and prevent private rights from vesting against public rights. *Stevens*, 844 P.2d at 456 (interpreting *Lucas*). On the "background principles" test that the U.S. Supreme Court's *Lucas* decision established, see Michael C. Blumm & Lucus Ritchie, *Lucas's Unlikely Legacy: The Rise of Background Principles in Takings Cases*, 29 Harv. Envtl. L. Rev. 329 (2005) (pointing out cases concluding that both customary rights and public trust rights are background principles). Since both public trust and customary rights are background principles of property law, is the doctrine of custom essentially a branch of the public trust doctrine?

2. Justice Scalia's claim that the state, through "the newfound 'doctrine of custom'" was engaging in a "land grab" that should require compensation be paid to the affected landowner raises the issue of judicial takings. No court has ever held that a judicial opinion could unconstitutionally take a landowner's property, but Justice Scalia—for a four-member plurality—endorsed the concept of judicial takings in a case in which the Supreme Court unanimously rejected a claim that a state beach restoration project took upland

---

5. From *Thornton* to *McDonald* to the decision below, the Supreme Court of Oregon's vacillations on the scope of the doctrine of custom make it difficult to say how much of the coast is covered. They also reinforce a sense that the court is creating the doctrine rather than describing it.

6. In *Thornton,* the Supreme Court of Oregon appears to have misread Blackstone in applying the law of custom to the entire Oregon coast. "[C]ustoms ... affect only the inhabitants of particular districts." 1 William Blackstone, Commentaries *74. *McDonald* seems to suggest that a custom may extend to all property "similarly situated" in terms of its physical characteristics, *i.e.*, all dry-sand beach abutting the ocean. 780 P.2d at 724. That does not appear to comport with Blackstone's requirement that the custom affect "inhabitants of particular districts." *See Post v. Pearsall*, 22 Wend. 425, 440 (N.Y. 1839); *see also Fitch v. Rawling*, 126 Eng. Rep. 614, 616–617 (C.P. 1795) ("Customs must in their nature be confined to individuals of a particular description [and not to all inhabitants of England], and what is common to all mankind, can never be claimed as a custom"); *Sherborn v. Bostock*, Fitzg. 51, 94 Eng. Rep. 648, 649 (K.B. 1729) ("the custom ... being general, and such a one as may extend to every subject, whether a citizen or a stranger, is void").

landowners' property. *Stop the Beach Renourishment v. Dep't of Environmental Protection*, 560 U.S. 702, 713–23 (2010). *See* Michael C. Blumm & Elizabeth B. Dawson, *The Florida Beach Case and the Road to Judicial Takings*, 35 Wm. & Mary Envtl. L. & Pol'y Rev. 713 (2011).

3. Notice that Justice Scalia seemed to over-read the *McDonald v. Halvorson* case, referring to the decision as "the leading case" on Oregon customary rights and describing its language as "sweeping" and calling into question "the continuing validity of *Thornton*" in the wake of the Supreme Court's decision in *Lucas*, authored by Justice Scalia. Isn't the *Stevens* decision now the leading case on the Oregon doctrine of custom? Isn't the Oregon Supreme Court, not the U.S. Supreme Court, the final word on the scope of that doctrine?

4. The foundational discussion of the judicial takings concept is Barton H. Thompson, Jr., *Judicial Takings*, 76 Va. L. Rev. 1449 (1990) (endorsing the concept). Professor Rose, on the other hand, suggested that public access to beaches could be justified as an example of what she called "inherently public property" that also justified the public trust doctrine's use in connection with public access to historically navigable waters and highways in order to avoid private holdouts that could create economically inefficient monopolies. As for recreational uses, like swimming, fishing and hunting, Rose admitted that it was difficult "to fit into a 'holdout' rationale" those public trust uses. For recreation, she instead advanced the rationale below.

The Comedy of the Commons:
Custom, Commerce, and Inherently Public Property
Carol M. Rose
53 U. Chi. L. Rev. 711 (1986)

[Professor Rose argued for affirming the public character of certain spaces, in order to increase returns of scale to the activities practiced there. She noted that the traditional public trust doctrines for roads and waterways overwhelmingly focused on encouraging commerce, and that commerce itself has increasing returns as markets expand. She then turned to the subject of recreation.]

... Certainly the role of recreation is a striking example of historic change in public property doctrine. If recreation now seems to support the "publicness" of some property, this undoubtedly reflects a change in our attitudes toward recreation. We might suspect that this changed attitude relates to an increasing perception of recreation as having something analogous to scale returns, and as a socializing institution.

Recreation is often carried on in a social setting, and therefore it clearly improves with scale to some degree: one must have a partner for chess, two teams for baseball, etc. But in the mid-nineteenth century, Frederick Law Olmsted argued that recreation had scale returns in a much more expansive sense: recreation can be a socializing and educative influence, particularly helpful for democratic values. Thus rich and poor would mingle in parks, and learn to treat each other as neighbors. Parks would enhance public mental health, with ultimate benefits to sociability; all could revive from the antisocial characteristics of urban life under the refining influence of the park's soothing landscape. Later recreation and park advocates, though moving away from Olmsted's more contemplative ethic, also stressed the democratic education that comes with sports and team play.

Insofar as recreation educates and socializes us, it acts as a "social glue" for everyone, not just those immediately engaged; and of course, the more people involved in any so-

cializing activity, the better. Like commerce, then, recreation has social and political overtones. The contemplation of nature elevates our minds above the workaday world, and
thus helps us to cope with that very world; recreational play trains us in the democratic
give-and-take that makes our regime function. If these arguments are true, we should
not worry that people engage in too much recreation, but too little. This again argues
that recreation should be open to all at minimal costs, or at costs to be borne by the general public, since all of us benefit from the greater sociability of our fellow citizens. If we
accept these arguments, we might believe that unique recreational sites ought not be private property; their greatest value lies in civilizing and socializing all members of the public, and this value should not be 'held up' by private owners.

These arguments support the recent decisions defending public access to the beach.
The public's recreational use arguably is the most valuable use of this property and requires an entire expanse of beach (for unobstructed walking, viewing, contemplation)
which could otherwise be blocked and "held up" by private owners. But ... [d]o people
using the beach really become more civil, or acquire the mental habits of democracy?
And even if they do, is there really a danger of holdout that necessitates inalienable public access?

Attractive as this Olmstedian view may seem, these are not always easy arguments to
support, and are extraordinarily difficult to prove. The argument that recreation or the
contemplation of nature makes us more civilized and sociable has a very long pedigree
in Western thought. Moreover, it may seem particularly attractive as our confidence has
waned (perhaps somewhat unjustifiably) in the socializing qualities of commerce. With
respect to the holdout problem, one might be skeptical and think that where waterfront
owners are numerous, they cannot really siphon off the value of expansive public uses.
But whether or not one accepts these arguments in the modern beach debate, older doctrine suggests that the "scale returns" of socialization, taken together with the possibility
of private holdout, will underlie any arguments for the inherent publicness of property.

Perhaps the chief lesson from the nineteenth-century doctrines of "inherently public
property," then, is that while we may change our minds about which activities are socializing, we always accept that the public requires access to some physical locations for
some of these activities. Our law consistently allocates that access to the public, because
public access to those locations is as important as the general privatization of property in
other spheres of our law. . . .

Notes

1. Consider the arguments that Professor Rose makes about the value of recreation to
society. Do they buttress the *Matthews* court's assertion that recreation is key to a "well-
balanced state?"

2. Although Professor Rose identified the social and educational value of recreation,
in recent times another dimension has come to light. As land has become more industrialized
and privatized, youth have fewer natural areas to explore and play in. Author Richard
Louv asserted in an influential book that the lack of exposure to natural areas can have a
damaging effect on the development and happiness of children, a problem he calls "nature deficit disorder." RICHARD LOUV, LAST CHILD IN THE WOODS: SAVING OUR CHIL-
DREN FROM NATURE-DEFICIT DISORDER (2005). The book has spawned government
initiatives to create more access to natural spaces for children. One such effort in Maryland led to a report explaining the impetus for reconnecting children with nature:

Described as "nature deficit disorder," the disassociation of children and nature has been linked to a wide range of behavioral and health issues, including childhood obesity, attention deficit disorder, and depression. While most adults over the age of 30 spent large portions of their childhood outdoors in spontaneous and unstructured play with other kids, today's youth are more likely to be inside watching television or playing video games.

Research also shows that the positive impacts of spending time in nature on a child's physical, cognitive, and social development may be significantly greater than imagined. MARYLAND PARTNERSHIP FOR CHILDREN IN NATURE, REPORT AND RECOMMENDATIONS TO GOVERNOR MARTIN O'MALLEY (2009).

Does the concern about nature deficit disorder provide an even more direct connection between public recreation and a "well-balanced state"? Does this concern elevate recreation on the scale of societal needs? Does "recreation," as a term, even describe the public need for access to address nature deficit disorder?

Chapter 8

Parks and Public Lands

Most judicial decisions enforcing the public trust doctrine involve resources that have some connection with navigable water. This is true, of course, of the landmark *Illinois Central* case (p. 68) involving Lake Michigan. Many contemporary public trust controversies concern public rights to beaches adjacent to navigable waters. Even in the *Mono Lake* case (p. 173), the California Supreme Court used the public trust doctrine to protect water levels in a navigable waterbody, Mono Lake, declaring that the trust prevented appropriated water rights in its nonnavigable tributary streams from becoming vested. But is the public trust limited to water resources? Upland resources such as public parks and public lands carry great importance to society as well. This chapter explores trust protection on these lands.

As we have seen in chapter 6, any analysis that tethers the public trust strictly to navigable waters is inaccurate. The trust follows terrestrial wildlife wherever it migrates, a category of public property recognized by the U.S. Supreme Court in the *Geer* case (p. 221), and the Institutes of Justinian (which courts almost uniformly credit as the origin of the modern trust), declared air as *res communes*. Perhaps the trust is properly defined not in a strict geographic sense but rather according to the functions certain natural resources perform in supporting society. As Professor Charles Wilkinson wrote in an influential article, "[t]he public trust doctrine is rooted in the precept that some resources are so central to the well-being of the community that they must be protected by distinctive, judge-made principles." Charles F. Wilkinson, *The Public Trust Doctrine in Public Land Law*, 14 U.C. Davis L. Rev. 269, 315 (1980).

Indeed, the statement captures the thrust of the *Illinois Central* case (p. 68) which described the shoreline as "a subject of public concern to the whole people of the State." *Illinois Cent. R.R. v. Illinois*, 146 U.S. 387, 455 (1892). At the time of that case, access to navigable waterways was indispensable to efficient transportation. The Court quoted from an early New York case, stating, "The sea and navigable rivers are natural highways, and any obstruction to the common right, or exclusive appropriation of their use, is injurious to commerce, and if permitted at the will of the sovereign, would be very likely to end in materially crippling, if not destroying it." *Id.* at 458 (quoting *People v. New York & Staten Island Ferry Co.*, 68 N.Y. 71, 76 (1877)). The *Illinois Central* Court also cited with approval *Newton v. Commissioners*, 100 U.S. 5, 18 (1879), a decision holding that one legislature cannot bind another on the question of which town was to be the seat of a county because "every succeeding legislature possesses the same jurisdiction and power as its predecessor ... [and] it is vital to the public welfare that each one should be able, at all times, to do whatever the varying circumstances and present exigencies attending the subject may require...." 146 U.S. at 459. Invoking the same rationale of protecting the prerogatives of future legislatures (a constitutional principle called the "reserved powers" doctrine), the *Illinois Central* Court found that privatizing the shoreline of Lake Michigan, a resource of paramount concern to the public, was impermissible. The Court explained:

289

[I]f this is true doctrine as to the location of a county seat it is apparent that it must apply with greater force to the control of the soils and beds of navigable waters in the great public harbors held by the people in trust for their common use and of common right as an incident to their sovereignty. The legislature could not give away nor sell the discretion of its successors in respect to matters, the government of which, from the very nature of things, must vary with varying circumstances. The legislation which may be needed one day for the harbor may be different from the legislation that may be required at another day. Every legislature must, at the time of its existence, exercise the power of the State in the execution of the trust devolved upon it.

Id. at 460–61. *See* Douglas L. Grant, *Underpinnings of the Public Trust Doctrine: Lessons from* Illinois Central Railroad, 33 Ariz. St. L.J. 849 (2001). This reserved legislative powers rationale suggests that the scope of the public trust doctrine extends beyond navigable waters to other natural resources having importance to society. And, in fact, courts have recognized that the doctrine reaches into upland and inland areas, as explored in this chapter. Some court decisions have applied the public trust doctrine to public parks and state wilderness areas unconnected with navigable waters. More recently, the public trust and the related doctrine of custom have secured public access rights to dry sand beaches, a matter taken up in the last chapter. As you read the cases in this and the following chapter, consider what concerns motivate the courts to apply the public trust to these uplands and inlands. Consider too how flexible the doctrine is in face of changing societal circumstances such as population pressure, industrialization, and ecological decline or collapse.

A. State Parklands

In one sense, the doctrine's application to parklands would seem intuitive and uncontroversial. Parks (both national and state) are indisputably owned by the public, and the government administers them for the public. Whereas the wildlife cases (from chapter 6) relied on a hefty analysis of state "ownership" of *ferae naturae*, no ownership analysis is necessary in the case of parks: They are public property. If not administered as a trust, how would public parks be administered? Could they be managed as a royal prerogative for the benefit of a president or a governor or agency heads in their private capacity? Of course not. But surprisingly, public trust cases arising in the context of parks and public lands remain few. The reason might be due, in part, to the traditional navigability emphasis of public trust cases, as discussed previously, as well as the highly statutory nature of public lands management. Most challenges in the federal context are brought under statutes governing the particular land classification. But as previous chapters show, the public trust stands as an independent source of law, not "superfluous" to statutes or codes. *See, e.g., Waiahole Ditch*, 9 P.3d 409, 444–45 (Haw. 2000) (p. 189) (concluding that the applicable statutory water code does "not override the public trust doctrine or render it superfluous" and "does not supplant the protections of the public trust doctrine").

The following case, concerning a state park in Massachusetts called the Mt. Greylock Reservation, was identified by Professor Sax in his seminal article as a significant case in the development of the public trust doctrine with "far-reaching" implications. Joseph L. Sax, *The Public Trust Doctrine in Natural Resources Law: Effective Judicial Intervention*, 68 Mich. L. Rev. 471, 492 (1970). Surprisingly, the case contains no explicit public trust language. But as Professor Sax observed, the Massachusetts Supreme Court treated the park as held in trust for the people.

The state park contained the highest mountain in western Massachusetts. The Massachusetts legislature designated the park in an 1898 statute and created a commission to manage it. In 1953, the legislature authorized an aerial tramway and established the Mount Greylock Tramway Authority to carry out the project. In 1964, after struggling to finance the project, the Authority entered into an agreement with a concessionaire ("Resort") that proposed construction of a ski resort with extensive ancillary facilities. This agreement prompted a group of local citizens to sue to invalidate it. The superior court upheld the agreement, which led to the following decision on appeal.

Gould v. Greylock Reservation Comm'n
Massachusetts Supreme Judicial Court
215 N.E.2d 114 (1966)

CUTTER, J.:

Five citizens of Berkshire County seek a writ of mandamus and declaratory relief against the Greylock Reservation Commission (the Commission) and the Mount Greylock Tramway Authority (the Authority). They ask for a declaration that two instruments are invalid, viz. a 1960 lease to the Authority of 4,000 acres in the Greylock State Reservation and a 1964 agreement between the Authority and a management corporation. They also seek to prohibit the Commission and the Authority from proceeding with a scheme for the leased area for an aerial tramway, ski lifts, and a ski resort. A judge of the Superior Court adopted a thorough auditor's report as his findings of material facts and made rulings. He ordered that the petition be dismissed. The petitioners appealed.

Mount Greylock (3,491 feet) is the highest summit of an isolated range surrounded by "lands of considerably lower elevation." Prior to 1888, this range was subject to commercial lumbering operations. About 1888, a group of citizens "became associated ... for the purpose of preserving Mount Greylock as an unspoiled natural forest."

* * *

"Through the efforts of persons interested in preserving Mount Greylock in its natural state for the ... [public] benefit," the Greylock State Reservation was established by St. 1898, c. 543. Section 1 provided for an unpaid commission appointed by the Governor. The Commission ... was given (§ 4) certain powers of the Metropolitan Park Commission....

The Authority was established as "a body politic and corporate ... [to] be deemed a public instrumentality" by St. 1953, c. 606, § 3. The Authority was empowered by c. 606, § 1, to construct and operate a toll tramway and to issue revenue bonds to pay the costs.

* * *

On October 6, 1964, the Authority entered into what is entitled a "management agreement" with Resort, employing Resort "as its agent" to manage the tramway and related facilities "under the general control and supervision and at the expense of the Authority ... in conformity with applicable statutory provisions, policies, regulations and procedures prescribed ... and plans, programs and budgets approved by the Authority." There is a comprehensive delegation to Resort of duties in respect of fiscal operations, budgets, records, accounting, annual reports, purchases, inventory controls, insurance, contracting, and various other matters.

* * *

As we read the statute, the basic feature of the authorized project is the tramway. Nothing is said about chairlifts unless they come within the term "appurtenances" or the term "ski facilities" in the enumerated special conveniences mentioned in the latter part of s 6(a) as amended. A reasonable number of ski trails, practice slopes, and the like, we assume, might come within the term "appurtenances" of a tramway to be used for skiers, but four chairlifts of a total length of 14,825 feet and eleven ski trails of a total length of 56,600 feet do not seem reasonably to be within the concepts of mere "appurtenances" of a tramway 6,165 feet long, or incidental "ski facilities." The degree of interference with the natural state and appearance (even from a distance) of the reservation becomes apparent ... particularly when it is appreciated that the creation of each cleared space not only removes trees and vegetation from its immediate limits but (as the auditor found) has "a definite effect upon the ecology for some distance back from the edge of the clearing."

2. The petitioners contend that the 1960 lease deals with a far larger part of the 8,800 acre reservation than the statutes permit.

We conclude that §7 of the 1955 act authorized the Commission to lease only those portions of the reservation which may prove to be reasonably necessary to a project of permitted scope.

* * *

We hold that the 1960 lease covered an excessive area and thus was not authorized by the statutes.

3. The 1964 management agreement constitutes substantially a complete delegation of the duties of the Authority to Resort.

* * *

The delegation of the Authority's duties seems to us broader than the type of arrangement contemplated by the power to make contracts found in [the state statutory authority of the commission].

* * *

We find in the enabling legislation, however, no suggestion that the Authority was authorized to divest itself of essentially all its statutory functions, reserving at most only general supervisory powers.

* * *

It is our duty, of course, in considering the powers granted to an unusual public authority of this character to look at the substance of what it is authorized to do, or proposes to do, to determine whether it is designed or used to accomplish proper public objectives or is, instead, being employed as an artifice to obscure some other type of activity. We recognize that in recent years much wholly proper use has been made of authorities to carry out important public projects. Nevertheless, these entities present serious risk of abuse, because they are frequently relieved of statutory restrictions and regulation appropriately applicable to other public bodies. We note one troublesome aspect of the project now before us.

* * *

This recreational scheme, in the profits of which Resort is to share, is to compete with private recreational ventures of similar character. The profit sharing feature and some aspects of the project itself strongly suggest a commercial enterprise. In addition to the absence of any clear or express statutory authorization of as broad a delegation of responsibility by the Authority as is given by the management agreement, we find no express grant to the Authority of power to permit use of public lands and of the Authority's borrowed funds for what seems, in part at least, a commercial venture for private profit. If the enabling acts have not authorized such an arrangement, the contention that equity participation by the underwriter and construction company is necessary in order to obtain revenue bond financing cannot provide a justification for the agreement. The Authority, of course, can seek further legislative authorization within proper constitutional limits.

The order for judgment is reversed. A writ of mandamus is to issue to the Commission and to the Authority commanding them to cancel the 1960 lease and the 1964 management agreement. A declaration is to be made stating that these instruments in their present form are not now authorized by the enabling acts.

Notes

1. The Massachusetts Supreme Judicial Court stated that the Greylock Reservation, as a state park, was not to "be diverted to another inconsistent use without plain and explicit legislation to that end," which the court was unable to find in the statute authorizing the tramway. Professor Sax thought the reason the court scrutinized the authorizing legislation so closely was due to the public trust doctrine. Sax, cited above, at 544–45 (suggesting that the court established a presumption that the state would not ordinarily restrict public uses of trust property in favor of commercial development). Essentially, the court used the public trust doctrine as an interpretative device. For a recent discussion of this application of the doctrine, *see* William D. Ariaza, *The Public Trust Doctrine as an Interpretive Canon*, 45 U.C. Davis L. Rev. 693 (2012); *see also* Michael C. Blumm, *Public Property and the Democratization of Western Water Law: A Modern View of the Public Trust Doctrine*, 19 Envtl. L. 573, 592 (1989) (describing the public trust doctrine as imposing the "hard look" doctrine of judicial review).

2. The court seemed particularly suspicious of using public property for "a commercial venture for private profit," noting the "serious risk of abuse" when legislatures delegate authority to private entities. Does this concern parallel the Hawai'i Supreme Court's approach in *Waiahole Ditch* (p. 189) when it stated, "Although its purpose has evolved over time, the public trust has never been understood to safeguard rights of exclusive use for private commercial gain"? Does the presumption identified by Sax seem similar to the Hawai'i Supreme Court's rule that holds private commercial use of water to a "higher level of scrutiny" so as to ensure they advance public trust purposes?

3. Preserving parkland has been a special emphasis of the public trust doctrine in New York. In *Brooklyn Park Commissioners v. Armstrong*, 45 N.Y 234, 243 (N.Y. 1871), in the course of deciding whether the Borough of Brooklyn could sell land given to it under a state statute, the New York Court of Appeals stated that "the city took the title to the lands … for the public use as a park, and held it in trust for that purpose…. Receiving the title in trust for an especial public use, it could not convey without the sanction of the [state] legislature."

In *Williams v. Gallatin*, 128 N.E.2d 121 (N.Y. 1920), New York's Court of Appeals invalidated a ten-year lease of the Arsenal Building in Central Park to establish a safety and sanitary museum, noting that parks "facilitate free public means of pleasure, recreation, and amusement, and thus provide for the welfare of the community" and ruling that the lease impermissibly diverted park resources without explicit approval of the legislature.

New York courts have also ordered the removal of city sanitation equipment from Cunningham Park in New York City, *Ackerman v. Steisel*, 104 A.D.2d 940 (N.Y. App. Div. 1984); and prohibited the reconveyance of parkland for residential development, *Ellington Construction Co. v. Zoning Bd. of Appeals*, 152 A.D.2d 365, 378–79 (N.Y. App. Div. 1989) (observing that "[d]edicated park areas in New York are impressed with a public trust, and their use for other than park purposes, either for a period of years or permanently, requires the direct and specific approval of the Legislature, plainly conferred"). On the other hand, New York courts have upheld a conveyance of parkland for construction of low-income housing by finding specific legislative approval, construing the applicable statute liberally in light of the public purpose in fostering development of low-income housing. *Grayson v. Town of Huntington*, 160 A.D.2d 835 (N.Y. App. Div. 1990). For discussion of the New York public trust doctrine's protection of parklands, see Gregory Berck, *Public Trust Doctrine Should Protect Public's Interest in State Parkland*, N.Y. St. B. J. 44 (Jan. 2012).

4. An important aspect of the *Gould* case concerned the delegation of authority over trust resources. Massachusetts has developed a rule requiring that only the legislature or an "entity to which the Legislature properly has delegated authority" may administer the public trust. *Alliance to Protect Nantucket Sound, Inc. v. Energy Facilities Siting Bd.*, 932 N.E.2d 787, 799 (Mass. 2010) (citation omitted). In a controversial case involving wind energy development in the scenic Nantucket Sound, the Supreme Judicial Court of Massachusetts determined that an energy siting board gained properly delegated authority to administer the public trust so as to permit transmission lines passing through the tidelands, which were indisputably held in public trust. *Id.* at 799. The dissent argued that "the siting board has purported to act as the protector of the public's long-standing rights under the public trust doctrine without the necessary express legislative authority to do so" and that its action amounted to a "usurpation of the Commonwealth's fiduciary responsibility to the people...." *Id.* at 824 (Marshall, C.J., dissenting).

Big Sur Properties v. Mott

California Court of Appeal
62 Cal. App. 3d 99 (1976)

CALDECOTT, P.J.:

[Big Sur Properties applied to the California Department of Parks and Recreation for a right-of-way permit to cross a state park to access private land. Public Resources Code Section 5003.5 provides authority to grant such rights of way. The department rejected the permit because of restrictions contained in the gift deed of the park, and Big Sur appealed.]

Helen Hooper Brown donated the real property to the State of California in 1962. The deed was recorded the same year. Paragraph 1 of the deed provides: "Said real property shall be used in perpetuity as a public park and for all lawful uses incidental thereto, except those uses, whether or not incidental thereto, which are expressly prohibited by the terms, covenants and conditions hereinafter set forth."

Paragraph 9, the restriction giving rise to the instant action, provides: "Notwithstanding the provisions of Public Resources Code Section 5003.5, or any germane amendment thereof or similar statute, no private right of way for vehicular travel or for the purpose of transporting, hauling or conveying timber, logs, tanbark or any other product produced by logging operations on privately-owned land shall ever be granted to any person, firm or corporation upon or across any portion of the property conveyed to Grantee by this deed. This provision shall not impair or affect Grantee's authority under said Section 5003.5 to provide means of ingress to and egress from said real property to provide ready access thereto by the public."

Appellant's principal contention, and the focus of the trial court's decision, is that the restriction in the gift deed is invalid and void. However, we need not consider the validity of the specific restrictive provision contained in paragraph 9 of the deed. We hold that the public trust upon which the state holds such land prohibits private access rights-of-way (authorized by Pub. Resources Code, § 5003.5) across property acquired by gift, when such property is dedicated exclusively to public park purposes and uses incidental thereto. On this ground, we affirm the judgment.

The gift deed provides, in paragraph 1 thereof, that the property is to "be used in perpetuity as a public park and for all lawful uses incidental thereto...." This is an explicit statement of the exclusive purpose of the dedication. Thus, the trial court in its findings concluded that the "property ... is owned in fee by the State of California as trustee of a public trust for use in perpetuity as a public park for the benefit of the public."

* * *

In determining what is a park purpose we do not look to the type of structure erected, but rather, to the use of that structure in relation to the park. It seems fundamental that a right-of-way for private access across park land to private property beyond the borders of the park cannot possibly be incidental to its use as a public park.

* * *

Nor does application of the public trust doctrine, restricting the property exclusively to the public park purposes for which it was donated, make acceptance of the gift deed "an agreement to waive" the provisions of section 5003.5. Rather, the section must be applied consistently with the public trust under which the state holds the property. If the Legislature intended to alter the doctrine's application, it could have done so explicitly.

* * *

In the present case, a private right-of-way across a dedicated public park cannot be considered as a use of the same class as a public park. Nor can a reservation in a deed, prohibiting the granting of a right-of-way to a private person across a public park, be said to render the dedication ineffectual or destroy its character. In fact, the very opposite is true.

* * *

Appellant argues from this case the proposition that contracts entered contrary to express statutory authority are null and void. However, as observed earlier, section 5005 expressly authorizes acceptance by the Department of gifts of real property, as undertaken here. Application of the public trust doctrine thereupon mandates the use of such property exclusively for the purposes of the dedication, and the Legislature cannot be presumed to have implicitly altered this result. The cited case is thus inapposite, as no statutory authority is abrogated by acceptance of the gift deed.

The judgment is affirmed.

Notes

1. How did this property get into the public trust? It was not trust property before the conveyance by Brown. The court seems to assume that, once conveyed to a state entity

for public use, the land became part of the public trust *res*. Once it became part of the public trust, private uses (such as private access rights-of-way) are disfavored. Does this assumption make sense? If it were not part of the public trust, how would the property be held? Recall the *Owsichek* case (p. 239), with its emphasis on popular sovereignty as a concept infusing the public trust. Recall too that America departed from England's monarchal tendencies in property ownership.

2. Does the court's assumption of a trust over public parkland apply to other state properties? Would it apply to all other parks? Would it apply to state road maintenance facilities? To state mental institutions? Can you distinguish these properties from parks? Are these built facilities owned in more a proprietary sense and for different purposes?

3. Did this court employ the public trust as an interpretive canon, as suggested by Professor Sax and discussed in note 1 following the *Greylock* decision excerpted above? Note the court's conclusion in *Big Sur Properties* that the statute must be applied consistent with the trust: "[T]he section must be applied consistently with the public trust under which the state holds the property. If the Legislature intended to alter the doctrine's application, it could have done so explicitly." Is this the same presumption against development applied by the *Greylock* court?

County of Solano v. Handlery

California Court of Appeal
155 Cal. App. 4th 566 (2007)

HORNER, J.:

[The Handlerys conveyed land to Solano County in 1946 to use for a county fair, prohibited the county from conveying the property, and retained a possibility of reverter that would work a forfeiture to their estate upon breach of any conditions. The following year, the Handlerys executed a quitclaim deed to the county containing similar restrictions but omitted the possibility of reverter language. The county filed suit in 2004, seeking a declaration that it was the sole owner of the property in fee. The trial court found for the county on a variety of grounds, and the Handlerys' son appealed.]

This appeal arises out of an action by respondent County of Solano (County) to quiet title to certain real property it received as a gift from appellant Paul Handlery's parents, Rose and Harry Handlery, in 1946 (the property). Below, County sought a judicial determination that it owned the property free of certain restrictions on its use that were contained in the grant deed executed by Harry and Rose Handlery in 1946, and reiterated in a quitclaim deed executed by Harry and Rose Handlery in 1947. Appellant Paul Handlery (Handlery), in turn, filed a cross-complaint seeking a judicial declaration of the parties' respective rights and obligations with respect to the property. The trial court granted summary judgment on both the complaint and cross-complaint in County's favor. For reasons set forth below, we reverse the trial court's grant of summary judgment.

Discussion

* * *

Here, we note as an initial matter the deeds subject to our interpretation, the 1946 grant deed and, in particular, the 1947 quitclaim deed, contain clear language of Grantors' intention at the time of conveyance to restrict use of the property to a specific purpose — "only for a county fair or exposition for Solano County and purposes incident thereto, which may include public parks, playground and/or recreational areas, and for such other purposes for which county fairgrounds may be used."

* * *

Our inquiry, however, does not end here. For, while acknowledging its acceptance in 1947 of the property subject to the use restrictions set forth in the quitclaim deed, County contends those use restrictions are no longer enforceable, either because Grantors quitclaimed their power of termination in the 1947 deed, or because Grantors have since died. We disagree.

Under circumstances similar to those existing here, California courts have been loathe to cast aside use restrictions on property contained in deeds: "It is well settled that where a grant deed is for a specified, limited and definite purpose, the subject of the grant cannot be used for another and different purpose."

* * *

Likewise, California courts have often held that "[w]here a tract of land is donated to a city with a restriction upon its use—as, for instance, when it is donated or dedicated solely for a park—the city cannot legally divert the use of such property."

* * *

Further, where, as here, property is acquired by a public entity through private dedication, the deed is strictly construed.

* * *

County claims this so-called public trust doctrine applies only to property, unlike the property at issue here that contains tidelands. We conclude a line of California appellate decisions proves otherwise. For example, in *Welwood Murray*, the desert city of Palm Springs acquired property by two grant deeds executed by private donors that restricted use of the property in perpetuity to a public library. *Save the Welwood Murray Mem'l Library Com. v. City Council*, 215 Cal. App. 3d 1003, 1006–07 (Cal. Ct. App. 1989). In affirming an order enjoining the City from using the property for purposes other than those related to a public library, the Court of Appeal ... applied the public trust doctrine: Osego

> A public trust is created when property is held by a public entity for the benefit of the general public. ... *Big Sur Properties v. Mott*, 62 Cal. App. 3d 99, 104 (Cal. Ct. App. 1976). Here, title to the library property is held by City to be used by City for the benefit of the general public as a public library. Any attempt to divert the use of the property from its dedicated purposes or uses incidental thereto would constitute an ultra vires act. Thus, it would be proper not only to issue an injunction to enforce the obligation arising from the existence of the public trust, i.e., to enforce City's obligation to use the property as a public library, but also to prevent an ultra vires, and hence nonlegislative, act.

Welwood Murray, 215 Cal. App. 3d at 1017.

* * *

Moreover, although we are not concerned here with tidelands, we conclude these public policy concerns are indeed implicated in this case. First, were we to allow County to avoid the use restrictions on the property set forth in the 1947 quitclaim deed—despite having expressly agreed to those restrictions upon accepting the property gift—we would no doubt discourage future such gifts from other donors. Second, we would permit County to accept a benefit without the corresponding burden, in clear violation of its duty as a public entity to "exemplify equitable conduct." *City of Palm Springs v.*

Living Desert Reserve, 70 Cal. App. 4th 613, 630 (Cal. Ct. App. 1999). To avoid these results, we thus rely on the loosely-termed public trust doctrine in adopting a reasonable interpretation of the 1947 quitclaim deed that precludes County from unilaterally casting aside the use restrictions contained in that deed that it expressly agreed to in the June 13, 1947 resolution. *See Big Sur Properties*, 62 Cal. App. 3d at 105 (declining to interpret regulations in a manner that would "defeat the public trust doctrine" where "another construction is possible").

* * *

Accordingly, for the reasons stated, we conclude triable issues of material fact exist regarding the parties' interests, rights and obligations with respect to the property dedicated by Grantors for the exclusive use by the public as a county fair or exposition.

The order granting summary judgment in County's favor is reversed.

Notes

1. In *Save the Welwood Murray Mem'l Library Comm. v. City Council*, 215 Cal. App. 3d 1003 (Cal. Ct. App. 1989), cited by the *Solano* court, the court of appeal used the public trust doctrine to enjoin the city of Palm Springs from allowing a developer to use part of a property dedicated for a public library to improve access to nearby commercial areas and to provide a restaurant patio. The court ruled that the city held the land subject to a public trust and could not use the land other than for its dedicated library purposes.

2. Pennsylvania courts have also protected public parks through trust principles. In *Bd. of Trustees of Philadelphia Museum v. Trustees of the Univ. of Penn.*, 96 A. 123 (Pa. 1915), the state supreme court upheld a lower court decision setting aside a conveyance of dedicated parklands by the city of Philadelphia to the University of Pennsylvania. The court decided the city held the parkland as a public trust and lacked the authority to convey it to a private university. The Pennsylvania Supreme Court also upheld an injunction on trust grounds against a sale of a public square to a private developer in Pittsburgh. *Hoffman v. City of Pittsburgh*, 75 A.2d 649 (Pa. 1950).

3. For an overview of the public trust doctrine and public parklands, see Mackenzie Keith, *Judicial Protection For Beaches and Parks: The Public Trust Above the High Water Mark*, 14 Hastings W.-NW. J. Envtl. L & Pol'y 165 (2010).

The decision below was mentioned in chapter 3 (p. 129), discussing the evolution of navigability. Does the decision also reflect the evolution of the purposes of the public trust to include parkland protection?

Raritan Baykeeper v. City of New York

New York Supreme Court
984 N.Y.S.2d 634 (2013)

GRAHAM, J.:

* * *

The subject of these motions [is] the solid waste management facility referred to as the Spring Creek Park Composting Facility ("Spring Creek Facility" or "Facility") for which a permit has been issued for operation by the New York State Department of Environmental Conservation ("DEC").

* * *

For the reasons set forth below, this Court finds that Raritan Baykeeper is entitled to summary judgment against the Municipal Respondents and declaring that the use of the Spring Creek Facility violates the Public Trust Doctrine.

* * *

Background

Spring Creek Park is a municipal park located in the Old Mill Creek/New Lots section of Brooklyn, New York. The Spring Creek Facility is located on approximately 20 acres of Spring Creek Park [which] is primarily undeveloped land and includes salt marshes. The petitioners allege that the Park is environmentally significant as the salt marshes are alleged to act as a natural filtration system which prevents pollution from contaminating Jamaica Bay.

Beginning in 2001, the Spring Creek Facility was constructed and operated pursuant to a Memorandum of Understanding ("MOU") entered into on August 27, 2001 between the New York City Parks Commissioner and the Commissioner of the Department of Sanitation. The Department of Sanitation ("DSNY") applied to the DEC for a permit to operate a solid waste facility in October, 2001 under Title 6, NYCRR Part 360 to compost 15,000 tons of organic waste consisting of leaves, manure, branches and stumps. The permit application met with opposition by Raritan Baykeeper and others from the adjacent community.

* * *

1. Parkland Alienation/Non-Permissible Use of Parkland

The petition brought by Raritan Baykeeper in 2006, (the instant matter) challenges the decision of the Municipal Respondents to authorize and use approximately 20 acres of parkland in the park known as Spring Creek Park as an alleged violation of the "Public Trust Doctrine". Municipal Respondents argue that the City of New York is advancing the City mandate of recycling and composting by using the Facility to compost leaves, branches, manure and stumps and, as such, the use of the Facility is a permissible park use which does not violate the public trust doctrine.

Raritan Baykeeper adamantly opposes the position of the Municipal Respondents on the grounds that no solid waste management facility can be considered a traditional or legitimate park use; that the public is deprived of any and all recreational access to the subject area; and that the Facility is an eyesore and has created unbearable nuisance conditions.

* * *

Discussion

* * *

The long recognized "Public Trust Doctrine" prohibits the diversion of parkland to any use which is not consistent with public use and enjoyment of a park unless the use has been authorized by the State Legislature. In one of the earliest cases the Court of Appeals addressed the doctrine by first describing a park as "a pleasure ground set apart for recreation of the public to promote its health and enjoyment." *Williams v. Gallatin*, 128 N.E. 121 (1920). Judge Pound further stated that the park need not be open space but "no objects, however worthy, such as court houses and school houses which have no connection with park purposes should be permitted to encroach upon it without legislative authority plainly conferred." *Id. at* 121.

There is a formidable body of case law which stands for the proposition that any "non-park use" of a park requires legislative approval.

It is immediately evident from the evidence submitted to this Court that the operation of the Spring Creek Facility precludes the use of the 20 acre portion of the Park for recreational enjoyment by the public. The subject area is fenced in and operated as a solid waste management facility and there is no real dispute between the parties that the composting facility is set aside and unavailable for use by the public.

The Municipal Respondents contend that it is integral to the operation of the New York City Parks that there be a solid waste composting facility located on parkland to process the large volume of organic matter collected by the Department of Sanitation.

* * *

The Municipal Respondents assert that the use of the Facility to compost leaves and branches is a "park use" and is needed to generate compost for the various New York City parks, including Spring Creek Park. The composting of leaves is said to reduce soil compaction and increase water retention, minimizing erosion and storm water runoff. The composting material also adds nutrients to park soil and is used in planting, horticultural projects and capital projects, among other uses. Furthermore, the testimony offered on behalf of the Municipal Respondents explained that the New York City Parks Department does not have the financial capability to relocate a similar composting facility on a non-park location.

There are many New York State cases which have addressed the question of which uses of park land are permissible park uses and which are not. On one end of the spectrum are cases in which restaurants were proposed to be located within parks. In Central Park a restaurant was permitted to be located in the park with the court describing the proposed restaurant as "well-designed" and "harmonious with the Park" and there was found no violation of the public trust doctrine. In a recent case, the proposal to place a restaurant and a "holiday market" in Union Square Park was initially found by the trial court to violate the public trust doctrine. However, on appeal the [court] reversed and, in a brief decision, stated that the proposed restaurant and holiday market do not violate the public trust doctrine since they are permissible park uses. *See Union Square Park Comm'y Coalition, Inc. v. New York City Dep't of Parks & Recreation*, 107 A.D.3d 525 (N.Y. App. Div. 2013).

At least as to restaurants, there is an apparent judicial tolerance for allowing a portion of a park to be used for a private enterprise.

On the other hand, cases which involve the use of parkland for uses such as a solid waste disposal sites and landfills are deemed to be unacceptable park uses, and consequently, require Legislature approval.

As part of their supporting documentation, the Raritan Bay Petitioners have included evidence that the operation of Spring Creek Park presents an unsightly, industrial operation in Spring Creek Park which generates noise and odors to the surrounding residential community. In photos annexed to the motion for summary judgment ... the Spring Creek Facility is shown with a mountain of garbage bags containing unknown materials which are moved by the use of front end loaders or other heavy equipment. The initial motivation for creating the Spring Creek facility may be premised on a worthy goal of composting leaves and branches, yet in practice the evidence shows that it is more accurately characterized as a working garbage dump.

In reviewing the supporting evidence for the motion and cross-motion, the Court finds that the actual use of the Spring Creek Facility is a large scale solid waste facility, which is inaccessible to the public and provides no typical benefits that are expected of a park.

The scope of the Facility also makes clear to the Court that the Department of Sanitation is using Spring Creek Park as a central location to collect all types of organic waste from locations including and beyond Spring Creek Park. The reality is that the Parks Department has burdened Spring Creek Park with serving as a solid waste processing facility for the general area at the expense of its local residents.

* * *

It is impossible to consider the recycling and composting being performed at Spring Creek Park, to be an acceptable park use. The public is denied the use of the 20 acres of Spring Creek Park and the type of solid waste processing that is being undertaken is a use that presents no aesthetic or enjoyable appearance or activity typically associated with leisure and recreation. The use of Spring Creek Park as a composting facility does not add to the enjoyment of visiting the park or enhance the experience in the manner that a restaurant or café may achieve. The attempt by the Parks Department staff to describe the use of the Spring Creek Facility as a well intentioned effort to compost leaves and branches is belied by the actual industrial scale processing of waste that can not (and should not) be permitted without legislative approval.

* * *

Accordingly, Raritan Baykeepers' motion for summary judgment is granted....

Notes

1. What test did the court use to determine whether the proposed use violated the public trust? Would the case have turned out differently if the scale of the proposed compost facility was much smaller and designed to serve solely the park (i.e., as soil enhancement for the park vegetation)?

2. Why have some courts found restaurants compatible with public trust uses? How did the court distinguish those uses from the compost facility? Other state courts have also developed tests to evaluate proposed uses of trust parklands. For example, in *In re Conveyance of 1.2 Acres of Bangor Mem'l Park to Bangor Area School Dist.*, 567 A.2d 86 (Pa. Commw. Ct. 1989), the Pennsylvania Commonwealth Court upheld the denial of a local government's petition to transfer dedicated parkland for construction of an elementary school. The court concluded that the transfer failed to satisfy the public trust doctrine because the property would not be used as a park, and the local government did not show that the land was no longer practical for use for park purposes. On the other hand, the state supreme court upheld the construction of an amphitheater on public parkland in Pittsburgh on the ground that the use was consistent with park purposes which include "aesthetic recreation and mental and cultural entertainment." *Bernstein v. City of Pittsburgh*, 77 A.2d 452, 455 (Pa. 1951).

In *Paepcke v. Public Building Comm'n of Chicago*, 263 N.E.2d 11 (Ill. 1970), the Illinois Supreme Court ruled that Illinois state statutes authorized the diversion of about two percent of Washington Park to build a middle school and recreational facilities that would be leased to the Chicago Park District. After deciding that citizens had standing to challenge the proposal on public trust grounds, the court upheld the proposal under a five-factor test adapted from Wisconsin courts: 1) public bodies would control the use of the area; 2) the area would be devoted to public use and open to the public; 3) the diminution of the original use would be small compared to the entire park; 4) the park uses would not be destroyed or greatly impaired; and 5) the disappointment of those wanting to use the area for park purposes was negligible compared to the advantages of the importance to the public of the educational and recreational uses. *Id.* at 19 (citing *City of Madison v. Wisconsin*, 83 N.W.2d 674 (Wisc. 1957); *Wisconsin v. Public Service Comm'n*, 81 N.W.2d 71 (Wis. 1957)).

The Illinois Supreme Court proceeded to apply *Paepcke* to a challenge to the renovation of Soldier Field, trust property within Burnham Park, rejecting a public trust challenge in the following words:

> The rationale we used in *Paepcke* is equally applicable here. Further, we note that Soldier Field will continue to be used as a stadium for athletic, artistic, and cultural events. With improved parking, the public will gain better access to the stadium, the museums, and the lakefront generally. The public will now enjoy a fully renovated, multiuse stadium, instead of a deteriorating 78-year-old facility. These results do not violate the public trust doctrine even though the Bears will also benefit from the completed project.

Friends of Parks v. Chicago Park Dist., 786 N.E.2d 161, 170 (Ill. 2003).

3. *Raritan Baykeeper* involved land clearly designated as a municipal park to which the PTD applied. Sometimes, however, the question of whether land is designated parkland is less clear. For example, in *Glick v. Harvey*, 2014 WL 96413 (N.Y. Sup. Ct., Jan. 7, 2014), *judgment modified by* 121 A.D.3d 498 (N.Y. App. Div. 2014), New York courts were confronted with the question of whether a city-owned area (called two "super blocks" in Greenwich Village) amounted to a park to which the PTD applied. The area had been developed but contained some open space and gardens used by the public. The lower court concluded that the land had been impliedly dedicated as parkland, thus giving rise to the PTD. The court explained:

> Although the law governing what is necessary to establish parkland by implication is less than crystal clear, a number of cases suggest that the long continued use of a property as a park can, itself, establish the property as parkland by implication.... It is the view of this court that long-continued use of the land for park purposes may be sufficient to establish dedication by implication, despite the fact that the property is still mapped for long-abandoned street use. To rule otherwise would effectively eliminate the distinction between express and implied dedication of parkland.
>
> Here, petitioners have certainly shown long continuous [use] of the four parcels as parks. Such long continuous use of land as parks by the public, at least in part, triggers the notion of a "public trust."

2014 WL 96413, at *15–16. Although the Appellate Division affirmed a portion of the lower court's judgment, it disagreed with the court's factual conclusion that parkland had been established by implication:

> [P]etitioners have failed to meet their burden of showing that the City's acts and declarations manifested a present, fixed, and unequivocal intent to dedicate any of the parcels at issue as public parkland. While the City has allowed for the long-term continuous use of parts of the parcels for park-like purposes, such use was not exclusive, as some of the parcels (like LaGuardia Park) have also been used as pedestrian thoroughfares.... Further, any management of the parcels by the Department of Parks and Recreation was understood to be temporary and provisional, pursuant to revocable permits or licenses. Moreover, the parcels have been mapped as streets since they were acquired by the City, and the City has refused various requests to have the streets de-mapped and re-dedicated as parkland.

Glick v. Harvey, 121 A.D.3d at 499. The Appellate Division did, however, firmly state that parkland *could* be established by implication: "Where, as here, there is no formal dedication of land for public use, an implied dedication may exist when the municipality's acts and declarations manifest a present, fixed, and unequivocal intent to dedicate. In determining whether a parcel has become a park by implication, a court should consider the owner's acts and declarations and the circumstances surrounding the use of the land."

4. Note that the *Handlery* court (p. 296), like many other courts, decided that "[a] public trust is created when property is held by a public entity for the benefit of the general public." If the public trust applies to parklands at the state level, doesn't the very same rationale apply to the federal public lands? Aren't they held in trust as well? Interestingly, many assume, perhaps too quickly, that because the trust has been litigated primarily on the state level, it is exclusively a state doctrine. Consider, for example, the passing statement of Justice Kennedy in *PPL Montana, LLC v. Montana*, 132 S. Ct. 1215, 1234–35 (2012) (p. 94) that "[t]he public trust remains a matter of state law." Justice Kennedy's dicta contained no analysis, as there was no federal public trust issue in that case. The most extensive modern judicial inquiry to date on the federal trust is found in an opinion by the federal district court of Massachusetts in *U.S. v. 1.58 Acres of Land* (excerpted on p. 367). After an extensive review of the history and applications of the PTD, the court found the trust applicable to both the federal government and the states as an inalienable attribute of sovereignty. *1.58 Acres of Land*, 523 F. Supp. 120, 124 (D. Mass. 1981) (p. 367) (holding that "[t]he trust is of such a nature that it can be held only by the sovereign, and can only be destroyed by the destruction of the sovereign," and also stating, "the trust impressed upon this property is governmental and administered jointly by the state and federal governments by virtue of their sovereignty...."). For additional discussion of the federal public trust in the context of other resources, see the *Alec L.* case and notes following in chapter 11 (p. 389).

After passage of major land management statutes in the 1970s, most challenges to federal land management took the form of statutory claims. Consequently, modern PTD precedent is sparse concerning federal lands. Does the paucity of precedent in this area mean that federal trust claims are foreclosed? Should the lack of recent case law impede the evolution of the law to meet the felt necessities of the times? The discussion below and the cases that follow explore the application of the trust to federal public lands.

B. Federal Parks and Public Lands

In several early cases, the U.S. Supreme Court definitively announced a federal trust over public lands. *See, e.g., United States v. Trinidad Coal & Coking Co.*, 137 U.S. 160, 170 (1890) (deciding that the public coal lands are "held in trust for all the people"); *Light v. United States*, 220 U.S. 523, 537 (1911) (recognizing that "[a]ll the public lands of the nation are held in trust for the people of the whole country"). In an analysis of the federal trust obligation, Professor Casey Jarmen discussed what she described as the "upland public land trust," explaining that "[a]pproximately one-third of the land in the United States is owned by the federal government. These public lands and the natural resources within them are held by the government for the benefit of its citizens. Over the past 100 years, a common law public trust doctrine, separate from the tidelands trust, has developed with regard to these public lands." Casey Jarman, *The Public Trust Doctrine in the Exclusive Economic Zone*, 65 Or. L. Rev. 1, 11 (1986). Nevertheless, some commentators maintain that the trust does not apply to federal public lands. *See, e.g.*, Eric Pearson, *The Public Trust Doctrine in Federal Law*, 24 J. Land Resources & Envtl. L. 173 (2004).

The existence of a public trust over federal lands seems irrefutable on one basis alone: if the lands were not held in trust to be managed for the American people as beneficiaries, how would they be held? Recall the cases in the first part of this chapter in which courts assumed that parklands managed by state agencies were held in trust. In two other important sovereign contexts, one dealing with state grant lands ownership and the other concerning Indian land ownership, federal courts have implied a trust construct of title. For commentary, see Jon A. Souder & Sally K. Fairfax, State Trust Lands: History, Management, and Sustainable Use 33–36 (1996); Mary Christina Wood, *Indian Land and the Promise of Native Sovereignty: The Trust Doctrine Revisited*, 1994 Utah L. Rev. 1471, 1497–1501 (1994).

The alternative to trust ownership is private property ownership, a situation in which the entity having control over the property can use such property to serve its own singular interests. As the Court in *Light* made clear, "[T]he 'United States do not and cannot hold property as a monarch may for private or personal purposes.'" *Light*, 220 U.S. at 536 (quoting *Van Brocklin v. Tennessee*, 117 U.S. 158 (1886)). While some early cases describe Congress as a "proprietor" over public lands, the term does not imply any lack of trust obligation to the public. A careful reading of these cases reveals that the Court used the term "proprietor" to describe the powers of federal agencies, acting as owners of public property, to prosecute trespassers. Federal land managers have all of the powers of an ordinary property owner to protect the property even without explicit statutory authorization to eject trespassers. As the Court in *Camfield v. United States* said when upholding a law preventing enclosure of public lands, "the government has, with respect to its own lands, the rights of an ordinary proprietor, to maintain its possession and to prosecute trespassers." 167 U.S. 518, 524 (1897); *see also Light*, 220 U.S. at 536 (quoting *Camfield*).

Courts have repeatedly emphasized that government, as a proprietor, must manage trust property in the interest of the public beneficiaries, not as a private owner who is free to manage property for exclusive benefit. *See Geer v. Connecticut*, 161 U.S. 519, 529 (1896) ("[T]he power or control lodged in the State, resulting from this common ownership, is to be exercised, like all other powers of government, as a trust for the benefit of the people, and not as a prerogative for the advantage of the government as distinct from the people, or for the benefit of private individuals as distinguished from the public good."); *State v. Rodman*, 59 N.W. 1098, 1099 (Minn. 1894) ("We take it to be the correct doctrine in this country that the ownership of wild animals, so far as they are capable of ownership, is in the state, not as proprietor, but in its sovereign capacity, as the representative, and for the benefit, of all its people in common."); *Waiahole Ditch*, 9 P.3d 409, 448 (Haw. 2000) (p. 189) ("In *Illinois Central*, the United States Supreme Court described the state's interest in its navigable waters as 'title,' not in a proprietary sense, but 'title held in trust for the people of the State....'") (citation omitted).

At times the Court has expressed extreme deference to Congress's management choices regarding public lands. As Professor Jarmen noted, in the 19th century, the public lands trust was administered so as to promote public purposes of family settlement on lands in the West: "Accordingly, the courts gave Congress broad deference in decisions that made these lands available for homesteading and mineral claimstaking. Unlike the tidelands trust, the public land trust was not burdened with severe restrictions on alienation.... Public land law ... was aimed primarily at opening the frontier for individual families to set up small farms." Jarmen, cited above, at 11. In the beginning of the 20th century, Congress changed its policy to retain the remaining public lands. *See generally* George

C. Coggins & Robert L. Glicksman, 1 Public Natural Resources Law § 2:10–15 (2d ed. 2014). The *Light* court, in particular, underscored the latitude given to Congress in making these choices. *See Light*, 220 U.S. at 537 ("[I]t is not for the courts to say how that trust shall be administered. That is for Congress to determine. The courts cannot compel it to set aside lands for settlement, or to suffer them to be used for agricultural or grazing purposes, nor interfere when, in the exercise of its discretion, Congress establishes a forest reserve for what it decides to be national and public purposes.").

Such statements have led some to conclude that the trust does not pose a restraint on federal land management. But those cases never tested the issue of federal choices in land management (they instead concerned the federal government's ability to protect public lands from trespassers), and their statements surely did not remove all constraints of a trust. Both the *Light* and *Camfield* courts emphasized that such lands must be administered in the public's interest. Was this deferential judicial approach much different than, say, the California Supreme Court's approach in the *Mono Lake* case (p. 173) where the court refused to force a precise allocation of water but left to the water agency the matter of deciding between conflicting uses after taking into consideration trust values? The *Camfield* Court made clear that the anti-monopoly restrictions of trust management impose a firm constraint on Congress: "[Congress] may sell or withhold [public lands] from sale. It may grant them in aid of railways or other public enterprises. It may open them to preemption or homestead settlement; but it would be recreant to its duties as trustee for the people of the United States to permit any individual or private corporation to monopolize them for private gain, and thereby practically drive intending settlers from the market." *Camfield*, 167 U.S. at 524. *See also Trinidad Coal & Coking Co.*, 137 U.S. at 170 ("In the matter of disposing of the vacant coal lands of the United States, the government should not be regarded as occupying the attitude of a mere seller of real estate for its market value.... They were held in trust for all the people."); *Alabama v. Texas*, 347 U.S. 272, 273 (1954) ("The United States holds [such] resources ... in trust for its citizens in one sense, but not in the sense that a private trustee holds for [a beneficiary]. The responsibility of Congress is to utilize the assets that come into its hands as sovereign in the way that it decides is best for the future of the nation."). Might a court in modern times be far less deferential than it might have been in the past if now faced with a trust challenge to a federal agency land management? Consider the following case.

Sierra Club v. Department of Interior

U.S. District Court, Northern District of California
376 F. Supp. 90 (1974)

[Federal national parks are administered pursuant to the National Park Service Organic Act of 1916, 16 U.S.C. § 1: That Act provides:

> [The National Park Service shall] promote and regulate the use of Federal areas known as national parks, monuments, and reservations ... by such means and measures as conform to the fundamental purpose of said parks, monuments, and reservations, which purpose is to conserve the scenery and the natural and historic objects and the wild life therein and to provide for the enjoyment of the same in such manner and by such means as will leave them unimpaired for the enjoyment of future generations.

Although Congress established the Redwood National Park in 1968 "to preserve significant examples of the primeval coast redwood forests and the streams and seashores with which they are associated for the purposes of public inspiration, enjoyment, and scientific study," 16 U.S.C. § 79a, little of the park was in federal ownership. Coastal redwoods are the tallest, and some of the oldest, trees on earth and are also prized as building material because they are straight, strong, and rot-resistant. At the time of the park designation, much of the area was being logged, supplying jobs to a depressed economy along California's rural north coast. Since the designated park was quite small, logging continued on private lands on higher elevation private hands around the park.

The Sierra Club petitioned the Secretary of the Interior to stop the logging, but the Secretary took no action except to ask for the voluntary cooperation of the logging companies. The Sierra Club proceeded to sue, claiming that logging on steep slopes upstream of the park endangered the park's resources, particularly leaving the park exposed to high winds, landslides, mudslides, and stream siltation threatening tree roots and aquatic life.

The court ruled that the Secretary had a trust responsibility to the park and its resources, using the language below.]

SWEIGERT, J.:

* * *

The responsibilities of the Secretary of the Interior concerning public lands have been stated in *Knight v. United Land Association*, 142 U.S. 161 (1891) as follows:

> The secretary (of the Department of the Interior) is the guardian of the people of United States over the public lands. The obligations of his oath of office oblige him to see that the law is carried out, and that none of the public domain is wasted or is disposed of to a party not entitled to it.

Id. at 181. *See also Utah Power & Light v. United States*, 243 U.S. 389, 409; *Davis v. Morton*, 469 F.2d 593, 597 (10th Cir. 1972).

In addition to these general fiduciary obligations of the Secretary of the Interior, the Secretary has been invested with certain specific powers and obligations in connection with the unique situation of the Redwood National Park.

The Redwood National Park was created on October 2, 1968 by the Redwood National Park Act, 16 U.S.C. §§ 79a–79j, to preserve significant examples of the primeval coastal redwood (*Sequoia sempervirens*) forests and the streams and seashores with which they are associated for purposes of public inspiration, enjoyment, and scientific study, 16 U.S.C. § 79a.

Congress limited the park to an area of 58,000 acres; appropriated $92 million to implement the Act, of which $20 million remain unspent; and conferred upon the Secretary specific powers expressly designed to prevent damage to the park by logging on peripheral areas.

Title 16 U.S.C. § 79c(e) provides:

> In order to afford as full protection as is reasonably possible to the timber, soil, and streams within the boundaries of the park, the Secretary is authorized, by any of the means set out in subsection (a) and (c) of this section, to acquire interests in land from, and to enter into contracts and cooperative agreements with, the owners of land on the periphery of the park and on watershed tributary to streams within the park designed to assure that the consequences of forestry management, timbering, land use, and soil conservation practices conducted thereon, or of the lack of such practices, will not adversely affect the timber, soil, and streams within the park as aforesaid.

A House Committee Report concerning this subdivision, after explaining that financial limitations prevented inclusion of the entire watershed in the Redwood National Park, states that the Committee:

> recognizes, however, that damage may be caused to the margins of every park, however large or small it may be, by acts performed on land outside those boundaries and that the streams within a park, whatever its boundaries, may likewise by damaged if the land on the watershed above them is permitted to erode. The trees along the margin, for instance, may be subject to blowdown if clear cutting occurs right up to the property line, and the streams within the park may be heavily silted if proper soil conservation practices are not maintained upstream. It is for such reasons as these that the Committee wrote into its amendment a new section authorizing the Secretary of the Interior to negotiate agreements with the owners of adjacent lands and of lands on watersheds tributary to the park and, if necessary, to acquire interests in their lands which, while allowing selective logging, for instance, to go forward will require the land owner to follow practices that will, as far as possible, protect the trees, soil and streams within the park.

H.R. Rep. No. 90-1630, at 6 (1968).

* * *

We are of the opinion that the terms of the statute, especially § 79c(e), authorizing the Secretary "in order to afford as full protection as is reasonably possible to the timber, soil, and streams within the boundaries of the park" — "to acquire interests in land from, and to enter into contracts and cooperative agreements with, the owners of land on the periphery of the park and on the watersheds tributary to streams within the park" — impose a legal duty on the Secretary to utilize the specific powers given to him whenever reasonably necessary for the protection of the park and that any discretion vested in the Secretary concerning time, place and specifics of the exercise of such powers is subordinate to his paramount legal duty imposed, not only under his trust obligation but by the statute itself, to protect the park.

* * *

Although the inquiry into the facts is to be searching and careful, the ultimate standard of review is a narrow one that stops short of substitution of the court's judgment for that of the Secretary.

* * *

Accordingly, defendants' motion to dismiss and defendants' motion for summary judgment should be, and hereby are, denied.

Notes

1. The federal district court denied the government's motion to dismiss, deciding that both the National Park Service Organic Act and the Redwood Act imposed a judicially enforceable duty for the agency to take measures to protect the park from logging. The judge also recognized the trust as a separate basis imposing a duty to protect the parkland, noting the "general fiduciary obligations" associated with a trust and stating that the Secretary's management discretion "is subordinate to his paramount legal duty imposed, not only under his trust obligation but by the statute itself, to protect the park." The case is not at all unusual in its reliance on both the general trust obligation and also statutory expressions of the trust. Recall the many cases dealing with water

and wildlife trust assets in which courts emphasized the trust as a separate obligation, not superfluous to statutes or codes. *See, e.g., Waiahole Ditch,* 9 P.3d 409, 444–45 (Haw. 2000); *Ctr. for Biological Diversity v. FPL Group, Inc.,* 83 Cal. Rptr. 3d 588, 600–01 (Cal. Ct. App. 2008).

2. When the Interior Department failed to implement most of the recommendations in the studies it commissioned in the wake of the first case—except for voluntary cooperative agreements with timber companies—the Sierra Club filed suit again, maintaining that the agency failed to meet its trust obligation. The following opinion ensued.

Sierra Club v. Department of Interior II

United States District Court, Northern District of California
398 F. Supp. 84 (1975)

SWEIGERT, J.:

* * *

[T]he issue for decision is whether the Secretary, since the establishment of the Park, has taken reasonable steps to protect the resources of the Park and, if not, whether his failure to do so has been under the circumstances arbitrary, capricious, or an abuse of discretion.

* * *

In the pending case the conduct of the Secretary must be considered in the light of a very unique statute—a statute which did more than establish a national park; it also expressly vested the Secretary with authority to take certain specifically stated steps designed to protect the Park from damage caused by logging operations on the surrounding privately owned lands.

As the legislative history shows, these specific provisions were put into the statute because the Park boundaries authorized by Congress represented a compromise and did not include certain lands within the Redwood Creek Watershed upslope and upstream from the southernmost portion of the Park. Out of its concern that continued logging operations on those privately owned lands could cause damage within the Park, the Congress expressly invested the Secretary with these specific powers to take administrative action designed to protect it.

* * *

As pointed out in this court's previous decision, there is, in addition to these specific powers, a general trust duty imposed upon the National Park Service, Department of the Interior, by the National Park System Act, 16 U.S.C. § 1 et seq., to conserve scenery and natural and historic objects and wildlife (in the National Parks, Monuments and reservations) and to provide for the enjoyment of the same in such manner and by such means as will leave them unimpaired for the enjoyment of future generations.

* * *

The Evidence

The evidence in the pending case shows that, beginning in April of 1969, the Secretary has conducted a series of five consecutive studies of damage and threats of damage to the Park caused by the logging operations of certain timber companies on adjacent lands. These studies have resulted in many specific recommendations for steps to be taken by the Secretary, pursuant to his various powers set forth in the statute, to prevent or minimize such damage.

* * *

The evidence shows, and the court finds, that to date the Secretary has not implemented any of the recommendations made by or on behalf of his own agency in the above mentioned studies except (1) to enter into so-called 'cooperative agreements' with the timber companies who own and operate on the lands surrounding the Park and (2) to conduct further studies.

* * *

The Court also finds that ... the restraints placed upon the companies by the so-called cooperative agreements are unreasonably inadequate to prevent or reasonably minimize damage to the resources of the Park resulting from timber harvesting operations; that there is substantial on-going damage presently occurring to the timber, soil, streams, and aesthetics within the Park downslope from and as a result of clear-cutting within the so-called buffer zone, even as such clear-cutting is done in conformity with the so-called cooperative agreements.

With respect to the defendants' contentions concerning unavailability of funds, the Court further finds that it is the Congress which must make the ultimate determination whether additional sums should be authorized or appropriated and also the ultimate determinations concerning the items to which such funds should be applied; that the Secretary has never yet gone to the Congress, through the executive or otherwise, either to request the appropriation of the balance of money authorized by the statute, or to obtain whatever additional sums of money may be necessary to implement the specific powers of the statute designed for the protection of the Park.

Finally, the Court finds that in light of the emphasis in each of the Secretary's own studies that time is of the essence, the Secretary has taken (to the detriment of the Park) an unreasonably long period of time to negotiate the proposed cooperative agreements.

* * *

With all due respect for the narrow limits of judicial intervention in matters entrusted primarily to executive agencies, the Court concludes that, in light of the foregoing findings, the defendants unreasonably, arbitrarily and in abuse of discretion have failed, refused and neglected to take steps to exercise and perform duties imposed upon them by the National Park System Act, 16 U.S.C. § 1, and the Redwood National Park Act, 16 U.S.C. § 79a, and duties otherwise imposed upon them by law; and/or that defendants have unreasonably and unlawfully delayed taking such steps.

Therefore ... it is hereby ordered:

That defendants Secretary of the Interior and Assistant Secretary for Fish, Wildlife and Parks, take reasonable steps within a reasonable time to exercise the powers vested in them by law (particularly 16 U.S.C. §§. 79c(e), 79c(d) and 79b(a)),[1] and to perform the duties imposed upon them by law (particularly 16 U.S.C. § 1), in order to afford as full protection as is reasonably possible to the timber, soil and streams within the boundaries of the Redwood National Park from adverse consequences of timbering and land use practices on lands located in the periphery of the Park and on watershed tributaries to streams which flow into the Park; that such action shall include, if reasonably necessary, acqui-

---

1. The latter two provisions authorized the Secretary to 1) acquire lands or interests in lands to screen logging operations from motorists on an adjacent public highway, and 2) modify the park's boundaries to 'minimiz[e] siltation of streams, damage to timber, and ... preserv[e] the scenery' of the park.

sition of interests in land and/or execution of contracts or cooperative agreements with the owners of land on the periphery or watershed, as authorized in 16 U.S.C. § 79c(e); that such action shall include, if reasonably necessary, modification of the boundaries of the Park, as authorized in 16 U.S.C. § 79b(a); and that such action shall include, if reasonably necessary, resort to the Congress for a determination whether further authorization and/or appropriation of funds will be made for the taking of the foregoing steps, and whether the powers and duties of defendants, as herein found, are to remain or should be modified.

Defendants are further ordered to file herein, and serve upon plaintiff [within a specified time] … a progress report upon their compliance with the foregoing order, or, in lieu of compliance, a report, showing cause why compliance has not been made, is not being or will not be made with the foregoing order.

* * *

Notes

1. Note that the court emphasized again the "general trust duty" in addition to statutory obligations. Does either the National Park Service Organic Act or the Redwood Park Act direct or authorize the Secretary of Interior to regulate non-federal areas adjacent to national parks?

2. After the second decision in this litigation, the Interior Department was largely unsuccessful in a number of initiatives aimed at complying with the court's directive, including 1) not being able to convince the Ford Administration to ask Congress for funding to acquire additional funds or new statutory authority to regulate non-federal activities; 2) not being able to convince the timber companies to comply with voluntary restrictions; 3) not being able to convince the state of California to regulate the timber harvesting; and 4) not being able to convince the Justice Department to file suit against the timber companies. When the Sierra Club returned to court for a third time, the district court decided that the Interior Department had made a good faith attempt to perform its statutory duties, concluding that protection of the park required new federal legislation or new federal funding to acquire additional lands for the park. *Sierra Club v. Dep't of Interior III*, 424 F. Supp. 172 (N.D. Cal. 1976).

Did this result represent a failure of the court to design an adequate remedy that would ensure the performance of fiduciary obligations? Could the court have been more aggressive in ensuring that the agency would take "all reasonable steps within a reasonable time," as required in the opinion? It is often more difficult for a court to force action to fulfill a duty than to halt action that violates the law, yet the task remains necessary in order to give effect to the trust duty of protection. What tools are available for courts to force action? Is mandamus a remedy in face of a trust violation? Contempt of court? In protracted litigation to force a proper accounting of Indian trust funds, a federal district court resorted to contempt of court and additional injunctive measures, including shutting down the U.S. Department of Interior's internet capability and website for a period of years. *See Cobell v. Kempthorne*, 532 F. Supp. 2d 37, 40 (D.D.C. 2008) (summarizing contempt measures from prior litigation). For a discussion of the *Cobell* decision, see JUDITH ROYSTER ET AL., NATIVE AMERICAN NATURAL RESOURCES LAW: CASES AND MATERIALS 308–09 (3rd ed. 2013). For a discussion of judicial tools useful to force compliance with affirmative fiduciary duties in the public trust context, see MARY CHRISTINA WOOD, NATURE'S TRUST: ENVIRONMENTAL LAW FOR A NEW ECOLOGICAL AGE, chap. 13 (2013).

3. The litigation finally prompted congressional action in the form of the Redwood Expansion Act of 1978, 92 Stat. 163 (1978), which authorized purchase of an additional 48,000 acres for the park and also provided extensive economic benefits for timber workers whose jobs would be affected by the park expansion. So, the litigation seemed to have played a role in getting Congress to act to expand the park, thereby limiting the liquidation of redwood old growth. Thus, the litigation can hardly be described as a failure.

4. Does the Redwood Park litigation saga suggest that only the National Park Service is bound by the federal trust obligation? Consider other federal agencies that manage public lands. They include the U.S. Bureau of Land Management, the U.S. Forest Service, and the U.S. Fish and Wildlife Service, for example. Do the broad statements in *Light, Camfield,* and *Trinidad Coal & Coking Co.,* above, declaring all federal lands in trust, apply to these agencies as well? The Fish and Wildlife Service manages wildlife refuge lands, thus implicating the wildlife trust as well as public lands concerns. In 1997, Congress enacted a foundational statute for refuge management, as amendments to the 1966 Refuge Administration Act. The statute established an overriding directive to "administer a national network of lands and waters for conservation, management, and where appropriate, restoration of the fish, wildlife, and plant resources and their habitats within the United States for the benefit of present and future generations of Americans." 16 U.S.C. § 666dd(a)(2). In mandatory language, the act directed the Fish and Wildlife Service to "ensure that the biological, integrity, diversity, and environmental health of the System are maintained for the benefit of present and future generations of Americans" and directs the agency to acquire water rights needed for refuge purposes. 16 U.S.C. § 668dd(a)(4). Could you imagine a *Sierra Club*-type suit concerning refuge management that invoked a combination of general federal trust obligation and specific statutory directives? For commentary, see Robert L. Fischman, *The National Wildlife Refuge System & the Hallmarks of Modern Organic Legislation,* 29 Ecology L.Q. 457, 581 (2002) ("The mandate to make affirmative contributions toward the System mission provides a statutory basis for application of the public trust doctrine.").

5. Federal reserved areas such as national parks, refuges, national forests, and national monuments have reserved water rights to unappropriated water in a quantity necessary to fulfill the purposes of the reservation. Such rights carry a priority date matching the date the reservation was formed and are superior to the rights of future appropriators. *See Cappaert v. United States,* 426 U.S. 128, 138 (1976) (citing *Winters v. United States,* 207 U.S. 564 (1908)). Are such rights public trust assets appurtenant to the trust lands to which they attach? To what extent must federal officials protect these legal rights held on behalf of the public? In *High Country Citizen's Alliance v. Norton,* 448 F. Supp. 2d 1235 (D. Colo. 2006), the federal government during the George W. Bush Administration entered into an agreement with the state of Colorado in which it relinquished a portion of the federal reserved rights to Black Canyon of the Gunnison National Park (part of which was designated wilderness). The relinquished rights had a priority date of 1933, leaving the government to seek rights having a priority date of 2003. This, in effect, would have subordinated the federal claims to all appropriations acquired between 1933 and 2003 (making the federal reserved right's early priority date meaningless). Recognizing that "the value of this property is its priority," the federal district court invalidated the agreement on the basis that the federal defendants had "unlawfully disposed of federal property without Congressional authorization." *Id.* at 1248. The court explained:

> [A] federal reserved water right constitutes property, not just from the time the right is quantified, but from the time the reservation is created. The right arises on the date of the reservation and continues to exist even if it has not been as-

serted.... The right to a volume of water necessary to serve the canyon's purpose arose when the United States established the Black Canyon of the Gunnison National Monument in 1933. There is consensus that the Black Canyon
requires a greater quantity than the federal Defendants proposed in the 2003
amended quantification application. Accordingly, the decision to seek adjudication of a smaller amount than needed represents a disposition of federal property. Only Congress, and not an executive branch agency, can authorize the
disposition of federal property.

Id. The court also concluded that the government had violated "nondiscretionary duties
to protect the Black Canyon's resources," noting that "the National Park Service has a legal
obligation to protect the resources of the national parks." *Id.*

The court cited the National Park Service Organic Act of 1916 and the Wilderness Act
of 1964 as imposing an affirmative duty of protection without mentioning the public
trust. But the results are comparable to what a federal PTD would accomplish, in the
court's findings that 1) the settlement unlawfully delegated federal decision-making authority to the state; 2) the government unlawfully disposed of federal property (reserved
water rights) without congressional authorization; and 3) the government violated nondiscretionary duties. In its view of water rights as public property carrying an affirmative duty
of protection, could this case be a public trust case in substance although not in name?
Recall that Professor Sax in his landmark article identified the *Gould* case (p. 291), involving the Mt. Greylock Reservation in Massachusetts, as a significant development in
the evolution of the public trust doctrine, even though it contained no trust language.
What would have happened if Congress had approved the relinquishment of a reserved
water right for the Black Canyon of the Gunnison? Could that congressional action be challenged under the public trust?

6. For additional analysis of the federal public lands trust duty, see Charles F. Wilkinson, *The Public Trust Doctrine in Public Land Law*, 14 U.C. Davis L. Rev. 269, 315 (1980);
Robert L. Glicksman, *Sustainable Federal Land Management: Protecting Ecological Integrity
& Preserving Environmental Principal*, 44 Tulsa L. Rev. 147 (2008). For an interesting interpretation invoking the trust to protect federal public forests as carbon sinks to stem
global warming, see Paul A. Barresi, *Mobilizing the Public Trust Doctrine in Support of
Publicly Owned Forests as Carbon Dioxide Sinks in India & the United States*, 23 Colo. J.
Int'l Envtl. L. & Pol'y 39 (2012). See also chapter 11's discussion of the federal public
trust apart from the federal lands context (pp. 365–75, 389–95).

Chapter 9

Private Property and the Public Trust Doctrine

A. The Public Trust Doctrine's Accommodation of Private Property

The public trust doctrine is thought by some to be a kind of anti-property doctrine which can eviscerate private property rights through evasion of the constitutional right to just compensation for takings of private property for public use. *See, e.g.,* James L. Huffman, *Trusting the Public Interest to Judges: A Comment on the Public Trust Writings of Professors Sax, Wilkinson, Dunning and Johnson,* 63 Denv. U. L. Rev. 565 (1986); James L. Huffman, *Avoiding the Takings Clause Through the Myth of Public Rights: The Public Trust and Reserved Rights Doctrines at Work,* 3 J. Land Use & Envtl. L. 171 (1987); George P. Smith II & Michael W. Sweeney, *The Public Trust Doctrine and Natural Law: Emanations Within a Penumbra,* 33 B.C. Envtl. Aff. L. Rev. 307 (2006); Randy T. Simmons, *Property and the Public Trust Doctrine,* 39 Prop. & Env't Res. Center Pol'y Series 1 (2007). But according to the following account, the interaction among the public trust doctrine, recognizing public property rights, and private property is much more nuanced.

The Public Trust Doctrine and Private Property: The Accommodation Principle
Michael C. Blumm
27 Pace Envtl. L. Rev. 649 (2010)

The public trust doctrine has been attacked by libertarian property rights advocates for being grounded on shaky history, inefficient, a threat to private property, and inconsistent with the rule of law. Some libertarians see application of the public trust doctrine as an evisceration of private property rights. In reality, such claims are hyperbolic. The doctrine actually functions to mediate between public and private rights, and thus is hardly the antithesis of private property; instead, it functions to transform, not eradicate, private property rights.

This mediating function was well described over a quarter-century ago by the California Supreme Court in its famous *Mono Lake* decision as an effort to accommodate both private property and public concerns through continuous state supervision of trust resources, regardless of whether they were in public or private ownership. Courts applying the *Mono Lake* doctrine demand all feasible accommodations to preserve and protect trust assets, but they do not attempt to eliminate private property. In fact, virtually all applications of the public trust doctrine leave possession of private property unchanged.

The doctrine does, however, often alter development rights, but those rights are only one stick in the property bundle. Equating diminished development rights with a loss of all private property rights is a categorical mistake, one that perhaps serves the libertarian project of erecting the just compensation clause of the Fifth Amendment as a bulwark against continued efforts to modernize property law, but it also overlooks the many dimensions of property rights and obligations.

The public trust doctrine has a special role to play in moderating development rights because it is, as suggested by Justice Scalia's majority opinion in *Lucas v. South Carolina Coastal Commission*, a background principle of property law. Given the antiquity of the doctrine, the public trust is well suited to its role as a background principle. A number of post-*Lucas* decisions have confirmed Justice Scalia's insight that the public trust serves to limit property owners' reasonable expectations to such an extent that loss of their development rights does not give rise to constitutional compensation. In fact, the trust doctrine as a background principle has had a considerably larger effect on regulatory takings jurisprudence than the *Lucas* holding that regulations causing complete economic wipeouts are categorical takings.

This result has been disturbing to some libertarian property advocates because they assume that the public trust doctrine is the antithesis of property rights, an assumption that dovetails with their fixation on the just compensation clause as the sine qua non of property. But property rights also include the rights of possession, use, and alienation and are limited by the non-injury rule to neighbors and the community. So, a loss of the right to constitutional compensation would hardly produce a complete loss of all property rights. Thus, even where it functions to deny landowner compensation claims, the operation of the public trust doctrine should not be viewed as the equivalent of a permanent physical occupation of property, which is a categorical taking.

[The article proceeded to characterize decisions like *Arnold v. Mundy* (p. 57); *Phillips Petroleum Co. v. Mississippi* (p. 97); and *Arkansas River Rights Comm. v. Echubby Lake Hunting Club* (p. 116) as marking a "lineal division" between public and private property as one example of public/private accommodation. Decisions emphasizing a more abstract division between the *jus publicum* and *jus privatum* estates, like *Marks v. Whitney* (p. 132); *McQueen v. South Carolina Coastal Council* (p. 159); and *Glass v. Goeckel* (p. 119), were described as establishing a "conceptual division" of public and private rights, another alleged accommodation. The article then turned to a third type of accommodation by noting the Supreme Court's lodestar case of *Illinois Central Railroad v. Illinois* (p. 68), which established two exceptions for its preference for public ownership of the beds of navigable waters: 1) when a conveyance to a private party furthered public purposes; and 2) when private ownership of trust resources worked no "substantial impairment" to remaining trust use. These exceptions seem to ratify the coexistence of public and private uses.]

In this regard, consider the following decision, which applies the substantial impairment test.

Boone v. Kingsbury

Supreme Court of California (en banc)
273 P. 797 (1928)

[In this case, oil drillers appealed denial of their prospecting permits on tidal and submerged lands near a small cove of the Pacific Ocean in Ventura County. The state land office denied the applications on grounds that drilling would interfere with navigation and fishing and challenged the legislature's authority to establish a permit system on public trust doctrine grounds. In reversing the state, the California Supreme Court ruled as follows.]

SEAWELL, J.

* * *

With full knowledge of the subject, the Legislature found that there was nothing in the drilling and operation of oil wells conducted in the manner provided by the statute that would substantially impair the paramount public interest in the lands and water remaining, and upon a consideration of the case we find nothing that would justify us in holding that the finding of the Legislature, which is conclusive in such matters (*People v. California Fish Co.,* 138 P. 79 (Cal. 1913)), is not fully supported by the facts. To justify an interference by courts with the right of the Legislature to alienate tide or submerged lands it must appear that such grants do or will impair the power of succeeding Legislatures to regulate, protect, improve, or develop the public rights of navigation and fishing. *Oakland v. Oakland Water Front Co.,* 50 P. 277 (Cal. 1897). It cannot be seen that the legislation in the instant case will embarrass immediate or remote legislation.

By the provisions of the act the state reserves a supervisory control over the entire subject matter and ample provision is made for a cancellation of the lease or privilege upon a violation of any of its numerous terms designed for the protection of the state. But aside from the precautionary steps taken by the state to safeguard the public's interests, the law vouchsafes ample protection to the paramount rights of the public in the absence of express statutory provisions on the subject.

* * *

The rule to be kept in mind, and which is recognized by every case bearing on the subject, including *Illinois Central R.R. v. Illinois,* the case chiefly relied upon by the surveyor general, and from which we freely quote, is that the state has the unquestionable right to alienate its tide and submerged lands subject to the "trust in which they are held for the people of the state that they may enjoy the navigation of the waters, carry on commerce over them, and have liberty of fishing therein free from the obstruction or interference of private parties."

* * *

The state cannot abdicate its trust over property in which the whole people are interested, like navigable waters and soils under them, so as to leave them entirely under the use and control of private parties, except in the case of parcels used in promoting the interest of the public therein, or when parcels can be disposed of without impairment of the public interest in what remains.

Nothing is said in *Illinois Central R.R. v. Illinois* that would indicate that the uses to be made of the tide lands in the instant case by the agents or permittees of the state in extracting oil minerals from the ocean beds under its control and regulation would substantially impair the public interest in or use of the vast remaining area of the ocean.

The trust in which tide and submerged lands are held does not prevent the state from reclaiming tide and submerged lands from the sea where it can be done without prejudice to the public right of navigation and applying them to other purposes and uses. As said in *Ward v. Mulford,* 32 Cal. 365 (1867):

> There are large tracts of salt marsh lands, of which the land in suit is an example, which are covered and uncovered by the flow and ebb of the neap tides, and

therefore belong to the state by virtue of her sovereignty, which are of no possible use for the purposes of navigation, but may be valuable for agricultural or other purposes if reclaimed from the tides. Such lands the state may undoubtedly grant in private ownership for the purposes of reclamation and use, for by such a course no right of the public to their use for the purposes of navigation would be prejudiced. On the contrary, the right of navigation, in many cases, might be subserved by such reclamation.

* * *

The [*Shively v. Bowlby*] court [stated]:

In the yet more recent case of *Illinois Central Railroad v. Illinois,* which also arose in Illinois, it was recognized as the settled law of this country that the ownership of and dominion and sovereignty over lands covered by tide waters, or navigable lakes, within the limits of the several states, belong to the respective states within which they are found, with the consequent right to use or dispose of any portion thereof, when that can be done without substantial impairment of the interest of the public in such waters, and subject to the paramount right of congress to control their navigation so far as may be necessary for the regulation of commerce. 146 U.S. 387, 435–37, 465, 474 (1892).

* * *

[I]n *Oakland v. Oakland Water Front Co.,* 50 P. 277 (Cal. 1897) [, i]t was held ... that as a general proposition the state has full power to alienate lands into private ownership which are covered by the daily flux and reflux of the tides, subject only to the paramount public rights where capable of reclamation without detriment to the public right, but that the town of Oakland had no power to alienate its entire water front into private ownership unless such power was conferred by the Legislature, and that the act of the Legislature ratifying and confirming the ordinances of the town of Oakland applied exclusively to the local laws of the town and not to ordinances which were mere grants or attempted grants of the lands of the corporation, which were in effect attempted conveyances of the property interest of the town in its waterfront lands. In other words, the intent to alienate did not appear. The right of the state to alienate its tide and submerged lands by statute where the intent of the statute is clearly expressed or necessarily implied was again reaffirmed by this court in *People v. California Fish Co.,* 138 P. 79, 88 (Cal. 1913), wherein it is said:

> When the state, in the exercise of its discretion as trustee, has decided that portions of the tide lands should be thus excluded from navigation and sold to private use, its determination is conclusive upon the courts; but statutes purporting to authorize an abandonment of such public use will be carefully scanned to ascertain whether or not such was the legislative intention, and that intent must be clearly expressed or necessarily implied. It will not be implied if any other inference is reasonably possible. And if any interpretation of the statute is reasonably possible which would not involve a destruction of the public use or an intention to terminate it in violation of the trust, the courts will give the statute such interpretation.

Upon an examination of the numerous decisions of the American courts holding that lands covered by navigable waters are held in aid of and for the promotion of commerce, navigation, and fishing, it will be found that superadded to the uses of commerce, navigation, and fishing, when the uses in the case at hand to which the lands are to be devoted are not strictly within the narrow definition of any or all of said terms, said decisions employ such phrases as uses for the "public welfare," "parcels of land as are used in promoting the interests of the public," suggesting that when great public interest may be subserved by the alienation of parcels of tide and submerged lands the state's determination of the question in favor of alienation will not be disturbed by the courts.

In the instant case the state does not part with title to its lands, but withholds them from sale and also reserves an interest in said minerals mined on shares. No part of the lands from which said minerals are extracted is alienated into private ownership, nor is any legal right of the littoral owner invaded. No harm can come to fisheries under the protective provisions of the act, as it must be presumed that the provisions of the act will be observed, and, if not observed, the general laws enacted for the protection of fish and sea life against the pollution of waters by penalizing persons or corporations, who cause or are responsible for deleterious substances escaping into the public waters of the state, are amply sufficient to protect sea life against serious injury or destruction.

Nor is there any substantial cause of alarm lest the 1200 miles of our sea coast will be barricaded by "a forest of oil derricks," which will interfere with commerce or navigation....

* * *

We are satisfied that the state act under consideration is a valid exercise of a right which inheres in the state by virtue of its sovereign power. It does not impinge upon the state or federal Constitutions and is not in conflict with any act of Congress or the state of California.

* * *

SHENK, J., dissenting.

* * *

In ... *Ward v. Mulford*, this court said:

> ... The right of the state is subservient to the public rights of navigation and fishery and theoretically, at least, the state can make no disposition of them prejudicial to the right of the public to use them for the purposes of navigation and fishery, and whatever disposition she does make of them, her grantee takes them upon the same terms upon which she holds them, and of course subject to the public rights above mentioned.

This doctrine was again declared and emphasized in the case of *People v. California Fish Co.*, 138 P. 79, and the series of cases in the same volume dealing with the subject. In *People v. California Fish Co.*, this court quoted with approval from *Illinois Central Railroad Co. v. Illinois*, 146 U.S. 452, defining the title held by the state in trust, as follows:

> It is a title held in trust for the people of the state that they may enjoy the navigation of the waters, carry on commerce over them, and have liberty of fishing therein freed from the obstruction or interference of private parties.... The control of the state for the purposes of the trust can never be lost, except as to such parcels as are used in promoting the interests of the public therein, or can be disposed of without any substantial impairment of the public interest in the lands and waters remaining.

* * *

The tide and submerged lands of the state constitute a great public highway, whose use for navigation and fishery is analogous to that of the ordinary vehicular highway for public travel. The use of the latter is open to all with well-known guaranties against obstruction for private purposes. The former should be equally available to all for navigation and fishery, excepting, of course, that where not useful for the public purpose it may be altered to meet changing conditions and in a way not inconsistent with the trust. As to the right of fishery, no one may successfully maintain that the tidal waters will not be contaminated by the proposed operations and the fish be driven to deeper channels. The statute does not contemplate that the waters of the ocean will not be so despoiled. The act only requires that the permittees and lessees "use all reasonable precautions to prevent waste of oil or gas developed in the land." It is argued that the necessary structures to be built upon the trust property will not prevent reasonable access to the leased lands by those members of the public who may desire to navigate the waters over the leased lands or to fish therein. If this be true, it is so from a theoretical standpoint only. From a practical standpoint I believe that the occupation of lands under such a lease and operations thereunder would effect a substantial deprivation of the public right of navigation and fishery, just as an obstruction in a public highway would impede public travel.

* * *

Notes

1. The exceptions to *Illinois Central* seem to suggest that the public trust doctrine does not demand universal public ownership of trust resources so long as the purposes of the trust remain intact. In this respect, the operation of the public trust doctrine seems to resemble riparian rights in water law, which allow small diversions if there is no substantial interference with the rights of neighbors or the flow of the stream. *See* Carol M. Rose, *Joseph Sax and the Idea of the Public Trust*, 25 Ecology L.Q. 351, 360–61 (1989).

2. An early application of the exceptions announced in *Illinois Central* was demonstrated in *People ex rel. Attorney General v. Kirk*, 45 N.E. 830 (Ill. 1896), where the Illinois Supreme Court upheld a legislative grant of submerged lands abutting Lake Michigan to private parties to create Lake Shore Drive because it did not "substantially impair" public rights of commerce and navigation, since those lands were not well-suited for navigation, fishing, and commerce, and were rarely used for those purposes.

3. Another accommodation of the public trust doctrine and private property was in *Friends of the Parks v. Chicago Park Dist.*, 786 N.E.2d 161 (Ill. 2003) (upholding the state legislature's approval of a new football stadium for the Chicago Bears in Burnham Park because it involved a lease in which the state did not abdicate public control of trust resources).

4. An alternative way to view *Boone v. Kingsbury* is to interpret the California Supreme Court as allowing the state considerable leeway to choose among trust purposes if the oil wells are viewed as permissible water-based commerce. *See also Wade v. Kramer*, 459 N.E.2d 1025 (Ill. App. Ct. 1984) (upholding construction of a highway bridge over the Illinois River to connect the cities of Quincy and Springfield, despite adverse effects on a conservation area and an archaeological site).

5. The Supreme Court of Idaho construed the exceptions of *Illinois Central* as a "two part test" for alienation of public trust lands. *Kootenai Envtl. Alliance, Inc. v. Panhandle Yacht Club, Inc.*, 671 P.2d 1085, 1089 (Idaho 1983) ("[A] two part test emerges to determine the validity of the grant of public trust property. One, is the grant in aid of navigation, commerce, or other trust purposes, and two, does it substantially impair the public interest in the lands and waters remaining?"). Applying the test to the state's lease of lake shore to a private club for docking facilities, the court found the encroachment did not violate the public trust doctrine, but emphasized that "the grant remains subject to" the public trust. *Id.* at 1096. The opinion included an extensive survey of approaches of other state courts towards alienation of trust resources using the *Illinois Central* test.

6. The *Boone* court found no substantial impairment from oil drilling, noting that "[n]o harm can come to fisheries under the protective provisions of the act...." But the case was decided in a much different era. What about today's deep sea drilling practices in treacherous offshore waters? Doesn't the Deepwater Horizon oil spill in the Gulf of Mexico in 2010 show that the harm from modern drilling is in a different league than drilling contemplated by the court over 80 years ago? How should the substantial impairment test apply to the federal government leases of the outer continental shelf for deep sea drilling that could prove catastrophic to marine life in the event of a blowout or other accident? And what about the effect of oil development on the atmosphere and climate change? Should the public trust provide an old-but-new ground for checking federal leases for offshore oil development?

7. The public trust doctrine and private property rights may also be reconciled through interpreting private land titles burdened with the trust to be less than fee simple absolutes. For example, in *Boston Waterfront Development Corp. v. Commonwealth of Massachusetts*, 393 N.E.2d 356 (Mass. 1979), the Supreme Judicial Court of Massachusetts ruled that nineteenth century state statutes authorizing fills in Boston Harbor (for wharfing) granted to landowners only fee simples subject to a condition subsequent that the lands be used only for the public purpose of maritime commerce. Thus, the filled lands were subject to forfeiture if converted to private condominiums. That decision influenced the following opinion by the Vermont Supreme Court.

Vermont v. Central Vermont Railway

Supreme Court of Vermont
571 A.2d 1128 (1989)

PECK, J.

* * *

In 1827, legislation was enacted that granted littoral owners on Lake Champlain the right to erect wharves by adding fill to submerged lands along the lakeshore. The 1827 Act provided that persons complying with the statute would have, with their heirs and assigns, the exclusive privilege of the use, benefit, and control of the wharves forever. The purpose of this legislation was to increase commerce and trade without an expenditure of public funds.

In 1849, the Vermont Central Railroad, a predecessor of CVR [Central Vermont Railway], used condemnation proceedings to obtain a strip of land along the lakeshore and began filling a substantial area lakeward from this strip. By 1851, this area had been used to bring a railroad line to the waterfront. Filling operations, first by Vermont Central and later by CVR, continued until 1972. CVR also purchased contiguous lands that had been filled by others. The railroad has paid property taxes on certain portions of the lands and has sold other portions to the City [of Burlington] and the federal government.

By the late 1970s, CVR's use of the area at issue had declined significantly. At the time of trial, the railroad had only one active customer on the waterfront.

CVR has pursued three major plans over the last decade for selling and/or developing its land along the lake, which now consists of the previously mentioned 1.1 mile strip centrally located on the City's waterfront. The first two of these plans failed to materialize, but, on December 10, 1986, the railroad entered into a purchase and sale agreement in which it agreed to sell or lease a large portion of the filled lands to a real estate developer.

The City and the State petitioned the Chittenden Superior Court for a declaratory judgment, challenging CVR's title on public trust grounds. After trial, the superior court concluded that CVR "holds the filled lands ... in fee simple impressed with the public trust doctrine. This means that the railroad is free to convey such lands to any party, and those parties to any other parties, so long as such land is used for a public purpose." The court retained jurisdiction to resolve any dispute as to whether a proposed use of the property complies with the public purpose condition.

CVR brought the instant appeal, claiming that the trial court erred in concluding that its title is held subject to public trust limitations. CVR also argues that plaintiffs' claims are barred by estoppel and laches. The City and the State cross-appealed, urging: (1) that the trial court erred in holding that CVR has a fee simple interest in the filled lands; (2) that, even if CVR has such an interest, it is a fee simple determinable; (3) that, in any event, the legislature may revoke CVR's interest in the filled lands; (4) that only the state can act as public trustee; and (5) that allowing a private corporation to determine the uses of public trust property represents an unlawful delegation of legislative authority.

I.

Under the public trust doctrine, the lands submerged beneath navigable waters are "held by the people in their character as sovereign in trust for public uses for which they are adapted." *Hazen v. Perkins,* 105 A. 249, 251 (Vt. 1918). Title to these lands is deemed to be "held in trust for the people of the State that they may enjoy the navigation of the waters, carry on commerce over them, and have liberty of fishing therein freed from the obstruction or interference of private parties." *Illinois Central Railroad v. Illinois,* 146 U.S. 387, 452 (1892). The character of this title is distinctive as compared to state-held title in other lands, and different legal rules therefore apply. *Boston Waterfront Development Corp. v. Commonwealth,* 393 N.E.2d 356, 358 (Mass. 1979).

The public trust doctrine is an ancient one, having its roots in the Justinian Institutes of Roman law. *Id.* As one court has observed:

> For centuries, land below the low water mark has been recognized as having a peculiar nature, subject to varying degrees of public demand for rights of navigation, passage, portage, commerce, fishing, recreation, conservation and aesthetics. Historically, no developed western civilization has recognized absolute rights of private ownership in such land as a means of allocating this scarce and precious resource among the competing public demands. Though private ownership was permitted in the Dark Ages, neither Roman Law nor the English common law as it developed after the signing of the Magna Charta would permit it.

United States v. 1.58 Acres of Land, 523 F. Supp. 120, 122–23 (D. Mass. 1981) (citations omitted). After the American Revolution, the people of each state acquired the "absolute right to all ... navigable waters and the soils under them for their own common use." *Martin v. Waddell,* 41 U.S. 367, 410 (1842).

Despite its antediluvian nature, however, the public trust doctrine retains an undiminished vitality. The doctrine is not "'fixed or static,' but one to 'be molded and extended to meet changing conditions and needs of the public it was created to benefit.'" *Matthews v. Bay Head Improvement Ass'n,* 471 A.2d 355, 365 (N.J. 1984) (quoting *Borough of Neptune City v. Borough of Avon-by-the-Sea,* 294 A.2d 47, 54 (N.J. 1972)). The very purposes of the public trust have "evolved in tandem with the changing public perception of the values and uses of waterways." *National Audubon Society v. Superior Court of Alpine County,* 658 P.2d 709, 719 (Cal. 1983) (en banc). Nor is the doctrine fixed in its form among jurisdictions, as "there is no universal and uniform law upon the subject." *Shively v. Bowlby,* 152 U.S. 1, 26 (1894).

II.

In Vermont, the critical importance of public trust concerns is reflected both in case law and in the state constitution. Chapter II, §67 of the Vermont Constitution provides that:

> *The inhabitants of this State shall have liberty* in seasonable times, to hunt and fowl on the lands they hold, and on other lands not inclosed, and in like manner *to fish in all boatable and other waters* (not private property) under proper regulations, to be made and provided by the General Assembly (emphasis added) ...

* * *

We begin by observing that the public trust doctrine, particularly as it has developed in Vermont, raises significant doubts regarding legislative power to grant title to the lakebed free of the trust. As the Supreme Court of California has stated:

> [T]he core of the public trust doctrine is the state's authority as sovereign to exercise a continuous supervision and control over the navigable waters of the state and the lands underlying those waters.... The corollary rule which evolved in tideland and lakeshore cases bar[s] conveyance of rights free of the trust except to serve trust purposes.... [P]arties acquiring rights in trust property generally hold those rights subject to the trust, and can assert no vested right to use those rights in a manner harmful to the trust.

National Audubon Society, 658 P.2d at 712, 721. This rule obtains because the state's power to supervise trust property in perpetuity is coupled with the ineluctable duty to exercise this power. *See id.* at 721. In the landmark case of *Illinois Central Railroad,* 146 U.S. 387, the United States Supreme Court declared:

> The State can no more abdicate its trust over property in which the whole people are interested, like navigable waters and the soils under them, so as to leave them entirely under the use and control of private parties, ... than it can abdicate its police powers in the administration of government and the preservation of the peace. In the administration of government the use of such powers may for a limited period be delegated to a municipality or other body, but there always remains with the State the right to revoke those powers and exercise them in a more direct manner, and one more conformable to its wishes. So with trusts connected with public property, or property of a special character, like lands under navigable waters, they cannot be placed entirely beyond the direction and control of the State.

Id. at 453–54.

Citing dicta in *Illinois Central,* CVR argues that there are limited exceptions to the rule against alienation of trust property. *Illinois Central* involved a legislative grant to a railroad company, purportedly transferring title to the entire lakebed underlying the city of Chicago's harbor. The Court held that the grant was void on delegation grounds, observing that:

> The legislature could not give away nor sell the discretion of its successors in respect to matters, the government of which, from the very nature of things, must vary with varying circumstances. The legislation which may be needed one day for the harbor may be different from the legislation that may be required at another day. Every legislature must, at the time of its existence, exercise the power of the State in the execution of the trust devolved upon it.

Id. at 460.

In a preliminary discussion of the public trust doctrine, the Court noted the existence in "the adjudged cases" of two exceptions to the general rule against legislative alienation of trust property: grants of submerged parcels for purposes of aiding commerce or promoting the public interest and "grants of parcels which, being occupied, do not substantially impair the public interest in the lands and waters remaining." *Id.* at 452. The first of these exceptions—which have never been espoused by this Court—does not provide guidance in situations where a grantee later seeks to abandon the public purpose for which the grant was made. CVR urges that the second exception establishes that grants of public trust property can sometimes be made totally free of the trust; the State, on the other hand, argues that an unqualified grant of the lands at issue here would substantially impair the public interest in the lands and waters remaining.

We need not resolve this fundamental question of legislative power, however, because we hold that the legislature did not intend to grant the lands at issue free from the public trust. "[S]tatutes purporting to abandon the public trust are to be strictly construed; the intent to abandon must be clearly expressed or necessarily implied; and if any interpretation of the statute is reasonably possible which would retain the public's interest in tidelands, the court must give the statute such an interpretation." *City of Berkeley v. Superior Court of Alameda County,* 606 P.2d 362, 369 (Cal. 1980), *cert. denied,* 449 U.S. 840 (1980)....

* * *

Nor do we find that an intention to abandon the public trust is necessarily implicit in either of the acts before us. The 1827 Act can be read as a simple grant of wharfing rights and privileges, while the 1874 Act actually employs the language of trust law. Neither of these enactments is inconsistent with a continuing adherence to public trust responsibilities on the part of the legislature.

The Supreme Judicial Court of Massachusetts was recently confronted with a strikingly similar factual situation. *See Boston Waterfront,* 393 N.E.2d at 357–61. There, a series of early nineteenth-century wharfing statutes had granted a wharf company the right to construct wharves into Boston Harbor and to hold them in fee simple. In recent years, a development corporation obtained the rights to these wharves and sought to register and confirm title to the lands beneath them. After an exhaustive review of the public trust doctrine, the court held that the development corporation had title to the property in fee simple, "but subject to the condition subsequent that it be used for the public purpose for which it was granted." *Id.* at 367. In discussing the legislative intent underlying the wharfing statutes, the court observed that:

> At that time, it was probably inconceivable to the men who sat in the Legislature ... that the harbor would ever cease to be much used for commercial shipping, or that a wharf might be more profitable as a foundation for private condominiums and pleasure boats than as a facility serving public needs of commerce and trade. They did not speculate on what should become of the land granted to private proprietors to further development of maritime commerce if that very commerce should cease, because they did not envision it.

Id. at 366. It is unlikely that the drafters of Vermont's 1827 Act were any more farsighted than Massachusetts' nineteenth-century legislators in this regard. With respect to the subsequent 1874 Act, which related to wharfs built for railroads, it seems equally improbable that the lawmakers of that era could have imagined that the newly-laid rails would ever fall into disuse.

We are bound to interpret these enactments, if reasonably possible, to preserve the public's rights in the trust property. *See City of Berkeley,* 606 P.2d at 369. Therefore, we conclude that the legislature did not intend, through the provisions of either act, to grant a fee simple absolute in the lands at issue.

IV.

The exact nature of CVR's interest in the filled lands must still be determined. The State argues that the railroad's predecessors were granted only a franchise or an easement in the lands and that the grant was for an indefinite period of time. In support of this contention, the State cites *State v. Forehand,* 312 S.E.2d 247, 249 (N.C. Ct. App. 1984), in which the court held that a grant of submerged lands for wharf purposes "merely conveyed an appurtenant easement to erect wharves to the riparian owner."

Given the language of the two acts here, however, a similar interpretation cannot be sustained. First, the 1827 Act expressly states that the subject rights were granted "forever." While this word does not render the grant unconditional, it surely makes its duration something more than indefinite. Second, although the 1874 Act's confirmation of "legal title" to the filled lands would not necessarily be inconsistent with the grant of a franchise or an easement, it appears to connote some greater right.

Nor does this Court's obligation to construe the acts to preserve the public trust mean that we are required to characterize them as grants of easements or franchises. As we have already observed, after considering the similar grants at issue in *Boston Waterfront,* the Supreme Judicial Court of Massachusetts concluded that they were intended by that state's legislature to convey fee simple title, but subject to the condition subsequent that the property be used for the public purpose for which it was granted. *Boston Waterfront,* 393 N.E.2d at 367. We believe that such an interpretation here gives full effect to the words of the legislature while ensuring that its underlying intent to preserve the public trust is uncompromised.

Accordingly, we hold that CVR has a fee simple in the filled lands subject to the condition subsequent that the lands be used for railroad, wharf, or storage purposes. This means that the State has the right of reentry in the event that the condition is breached by the railroad. *See Collette v. Town of Charlotte,* 45 A.2d 203, 205 (Vt. 1946).

CVR notes that, under 12 V.S.A. §4983, a condition must be clearly implied by the nature of the grant it qualifies in order to support forfeiture for nonperformance of that condition. As the foregoing discussion suggests, we conclude that a condition subsequent regarding use of the property is clearly implied by the nature and the subject matter of the two acts. Although conditions subsequent are not favored in the law, *Queen City Park Ass'n v. Gale,* 3 A.2d 529, 531 (Vt. 1938), the public's sui generis interest in trust property "transcends the ordinary rules of property law." *Boston Waterfront,* 393 N.E.2d at 367. Because we must interpret the acts reasonably to preserve the public's rights in the trust property, we do not hesitate to infer a condition subsequent here.

V.

Thus, the trial court was correct in concluding that the railroad's title is impressed with the public trust. The court prefaced this conclusion, however, by citing a number of cases from other jurisdictions that, in the aggregate, endorsed a wide variety of uses for land held under the public trust. The court stated that all of these uses — including restaurants, hotels, and shopping malls — were "examples of appropriate public uses that are encompassed by the contemporary public trust doctrine." Although the court retained jurisdiction to resolve disputes over proposed uses of the filled lands, it effectively gave CVR and its successors the right to choose among the listed uses for the property. On cross-appeal, the State and the City argue that this was erroneous, and we agree.

Lands held subject to the public trust may be used only for purposes approved by the legislature as public uses. *See Boston Waterfront,* 393 N.E.2d at 366–67. Any substantial change in the filled lands must therefore be consistent with a legislative grant or mandate, subject to judicial review, and this legislative control cannot be delegated to others. *See Vermont Department of Public Service v. Massachusetts Municipal Wholesale Electric Co.,* 558 A.2d 215, 220 (Vt. 1988).

VI.

Because the railroad and its predecessors have occupied the lands at issue for 140 years and because the City has taxed portions of these lands, CVR maintains that the trial court erred by refusing to invoke the doctrine of laches as a bar to the claims made by the City and the State. CVR also argue[s] that the railroad has relied to its detriment on the past acts and statements of the State and that the State should therefore be estopped from asserting any interest in the property. We disagree on both counts.

Laches arises where a claimant fails to assert a right for an unreasonable and unexplained period of time and where the delay has been prejudicial to the adverse party; under these circumstances, enforcement of the right is held to be inequitable. *Stamato v. Quazzo,* 423 A.2d 1201, 1203 (Vt. 1980). The doctrine of equitable estoppel has a similar foundation in principles of fair play: the purpose of the doctrine is to prevent a party "'from asserting rights which may have existed against another party who in good faith has changed his or her position in reliance upon earlier representations.'" *Burlington Fire Fighter's Ass'n v. City of Burlington,* 543 A.2d 686, 690 (Vt. 1988) (quoting *Fisher v. Poole,* 453 A.2d 408, 411 (Vt. 1982)).

We hold that the claims asserted here cannot be barred through either laches or estoppel. As the Supreme Court of California has observed, the state acts as administrator of the public trust and has a continuing power that "extends to the revocation of previously granted rights or to the enforcement of the trust against lands long thought free of the trust." *National Audubon Society,* 658 P.2d at 723 (citation omitted). In *Thomas v. Sanders,* 413 N.E.2d 1224 (Ohio Ct. App. 1979), the court considered a claim that a railroad's continued payment of property taxes evinced state recognition of its ownership of trust property. The court rejected the contention, opining that "the state or city cannot relinquish [the public trust property] by acquiescence and estoppel does not apply." *Id.* at 1231.

* * *

Notes

1. Suppose the state had decided not to enforce its right of entry against the railroad. Would the public have standing to enforce it?

2. The court interpreted the railroad's title as a fee simple subject to condition subsequent. This allowed the state a right of reentry if the railroad violated the condition that the property be used for its original intended purposes to benefit the public. In so holding, the court created a title that gave effect to the *Illinois Central* rule on alienation. Is this, in fact, what the *Illinois Central* Court was trying to accomplish, even though it never used the words "fee simple subject to condition subsequent"? Doesn't the right of reentry exactly parallel the revocation authority emphasized in *Illinois Central*?

3. The transformation of trust-burdened private property into defeasible fees is a fairly unusual means of accommodating public and private property rights. More commonplace is the interpretation of the public trust doctrine as imposing a public easement on private land titles, as the New Jersey Supreme Court ruled in *Matthews v. Bay Head Improvement Ass'n* (p. 261) and *Raleigh Ave. Beach Ass'n v. Atlantis Beach Club* (p. 265). The Oregon doctrine of customary rights, expressed in *Thornton v. Hay* (p. 268) and *Stevens v. Cannon Beach* (p. 280) also fit into the public easement category.

4. Another public-trust-like easement is the right to roam over privately owned undeveloped, "open" lands recognized in England and Wales as a result of the Countryside and Rights of Way Act of 2000. On "open lands," including mountains, moors, heaths, and downlands, private landowners must allow the public to roam freely on foot, subject to several standards of reasonable behavior, not including commercial activity or camping; swimming in non-tidal areas; or fishing, hunting, or other activities that threaten wildlife. The purpose of the statute includes improving public health, reducing social divisions, and establishing "social equity." *See* Jerry Anderson, *Britain's Right to Roam: Redefining the Landowner's Bundle of Sticks*, 19 Geo. Int'l Envtl. L. Rev. 375 (2007). This right to roam was once commonplace on unfenced lands in pre-Civil War America, *see* ERIC T. FREYFOGLE, ON PRIVATE PROPERTY 29 (2007), and seems embedded in section 67 of the Vermont Constitution.

5. One interpretation of the cases discussed above is that the public trust functions "not so much [as] an anti-privatization concept as a vehicle for mediating between public and private rights in important natural resources." According to this view,

> [c]ourts have accomplished this accommodation of public and private rights sometimes through a geographical division, sometimes through a conceptual division, sometimes through allowing small privatizations of public resources, and sometimes through recognition of a public easement on private property. In none of these cases have the courts eliminated private property, but they have employed the public trust doctrine to recognize public rights in private property. Recognition of the nature of the accommodation between public and private rights that is accomplished by application of the public trust doctrine will no doubt not assuage its libertarian critics, but it might lead to more constructive conversations about the nature of public rights in privately owned land.

Michael C. Blumm, *The Public Trust Doctrine and Private Property: The Accommodation Principle*, 27 Pace Envtl. L. Rev. 649, 666–67 (2010).

B. The Public Trust Doctrine as a Background Principle of Property Law

In *Lucas v. South Carolina Coastal Council*, 505 U.S. 1003 (1992), the Supreme Court declared that a state statute forbidding development on a protected beach could amount to an unconstitutional taking of a landowner's property that would require payment of just compensation. The Court's opinion, per Justice Scalia, announced a categorical, *per se* takings rule promising landowners compensation when regulations work a complete loss of economic value. But Justice Scalia's opinion also contained an exception for regulations that merely prohibited uses that would not be permitted by "background principles of the State's law of property and nuisance." *Id.* at 1029. This exception provided government defendants a powerful defense in takings litigation, for the Supreme Court made inquiry into "background principles" a prerequisite for any successful takings claim, referring to it as "the logically antecedent inquiry." *Id.* at 1027.

Since the *Lucas* decision, numerous lower courts have rejected takings claims based on background principles of property and nuisance law. For example, *Esplanade Properties v. City of Seattle* (p. 164), *McQueen v. South Carolina Coastal Council* (p. 159), and the decision of the trial court on remand in *Palazzolo v. Rhode Island* (p. 156) all rejected landowner takings claims on the basis that the public trust doctrine was a background principle of state property law. And even before the *Lucas* decision, the Wisconsin Supreme Court in *Just v. Marinette County* (p. 141) rejected a takings claim concerning a proposed wetlands fill because it was an unnatural use of the land. For discussion of these cases, *see, e.g.*, Michael C. Blumm & Lucus Ritchie, *Lucas's Unlikely Legacy: The Rise of Background Principles as Categorical Takings Defenses*, 29 Harv. Envtl. L. Rev. 321 (2005); John D. Echeverria, *The Public Trust Doctrine as a Background Principles Defense in Takings Litigation*, 45 U.C. Davis L. Rev. 931 (2012).

Consider also the following cases concerning the public trust doctrine as a background principle of state property law.

National Association of Home Builders v. New Jersey Department of Environmental Protection

U.S. District Court, New Jersey
64 F. Supp. 2d 354 (1999)

[A coalition of land developers challenged the Hudson River Waterfront Development rule, a state statute that required the construction and maintenance of a 30-foot-wide walkway along the waterfront of the Hudson River between the George Washington and Bayonne Bridges — over 17 miles — along with an accompanying conservation and public access easements. Over eighty-eight percent of the shorelands involved were once submerged and were then filled. The court addressed the land developers' takings claim in the following opinion.]

BROWN, J.

* * *

Initially, the first category of property, which constitutes 88.7% of the property at issue in this dispute, shall be referred to as "public trust property" because this land was submerged beneath the Hudson River until such time as it was filled in artificially. This specific and very important characteristic of the first category of the property at issue is not disputed by the parties. It is clear that title to such "public trust property" is subject to the public's right to use and enjoy the property, even if such property is alienated to private owners. Neither side disputes this as well. This right of the public to use and enjoy such "public trust lands" does not disappear simply because the land that was once submerged is filled in. *See Matthews v. Bay Head Improvement Ass'n*, 471 A.2d 355 (N.J. 1984) (noting that "[t]he seashore was not private property, but 'subject to the same law as the sea itself, and the sand or ground beneath it.'") (citation omitted), *cert. denied*, 469 U.S. 821 (1984). Therefore, with respect to the 88.7% of the property at issue that was once submerged beneath the Hudson River, as correctly noted by the Defendant-Intervenors, "the public already owns rights in the land the Walkway is built on." Therefore, Plaintiffs do not have the right to exclude public access to this portion of the property. Thus, with respect to 88.7% of the property at issue, i.e. the "public trust" portion of the property,

Plaintiffs' motion is denied and the cross-motions of Defendants and Defendant-Intervenors are granted because Plaintiffs' bundle of rights is limited by the public's right to use and enjoy this portion of the property under the public trust doctrine.[1]

* * *

[The court therefore denied the takings claim for the filled lands. It also denied the takings claim for the non-filled lands, using the public access factors established by the New Jersey Supreme Court in *Matthews v. Bay Head Improvement Ass'n* (p. 261).]

Coastal Petroleum v. Chiles
District Court of Appeal of Florida
701 So. 2d 619 (1997)
Review denied, 707 So. 2d 1123 (1998)

[An offshore royalty interest owner challenged a state statute prohibiting the exploration and drilling of certain areas off the coast of Florida as a taking of its royalties. The court rejected the argument using the following reasoning.]

WOLF, J.

* * *

The public trust doctrine is embodied in article X, section 11 of the Florida Constitution:

> The title to lands under navigable waters, within the boundaries of the state, which have not been alienated, including beaches below mean high water lines, is held by the state, by virtue of its sovereignty, in trust for all the people. Sale of such lands may be authorized by law, but only when in the public interest. Private use of portions of such lands may be authorized by law, but only when not contrary to the public interest.

* * *

In regard to the public trust doctrine, the trial court specifically found as follows:

> Under the reservation of the public trust doctrine, the state has an affirmative obligation to restrict or eliminate private activity on sovereign lands when such activity becomes contrary to the public interest. Article X, section 11, Florida Constitution confirms this obligation. The present situation is a clear example of action taken by the state pursuant to the public trust doctrine. The Florida Legislature determined in 1990 that future oil and gas drilling on sovereign lands in the near shore waters of the state would be detrimental and contrary to the public interest.... *By enacting the law [90-73] the Florida Legislature was merely exercising its constitutional authority to protect the lands held in trust for all the people* (emphasis added).

In addition, ... there is support in this case for the proposition that the parties understood that the trustees had the discretion to lease or not lease the land during the terms of the agreement. The public trust doctrine as well as the responsibility of the state to exercise their police powers for the good of the public support this position. The language

---

1. Moreover, the Rule's requirement that individuals grant the State a conservation easement for the "public trust property" upon which the Walkway is constructed merely memorializes the State's role in protecting the public's right to use and enjoy the property under the public trust doctrine. Therefore, Plaintiffs' argument that the conservation easement somehow demonstrates that the property at issue was not public trust property within the State's control is without merit.

of the agreement itself acknowledges the state's rights to control the use of the land in question....

The appellant argues, however, that even though the state may have been acting in the public trust in enacting chapter 90-72, Laws of Florida, any private property taken for public use, even under the public trust, is protected by the constitution and requires compensation. *See* Art. X, § 6(a), Fla. Const. The appellant relies on *Askew v. Gables-by-the-Sea, Inc.*, 333 So. 2d 56 (Fla. Dist. Ct. App. 1976), *cert. denied*, 345 So. 2d 420 (Fla. 1977), and *Zabel v. Pinellas County Water & Navigation Control Auth.*, 171 So. 2d 376 (Fla. 1965), for this proposition. Although appellant correctly argues that the public trust doctrine does not preclude a party from asserting that state regulation has resulted in a compensable taking of an interest in property obtained from the state, not all interests obtained from the state are entitled to the same constitutional protections.

In *Askew* and *Zabel*, parties that had obtained fee title to sovereign submerged lands from the state were found to have a private property right which would be protected by the constitutional takings provision if the state precluded all reasonable use of the land. Similarly, in *State v. Leavins*, 599 So. 2d 1326 (Fla. Dist. Ct. App. 1992), this court held that a lease which provided for the immediate taking of oysters from Apalachicola Bay was a valid property right entitled to protection. Those cases are distinguishable, however, in that the interest in the instant case is not a fee interest as in *Askew* and *Zabel*, nor does this case involve an immediate right to remove presently existing resources as in *Leavins*.

In *Marine One, Inc. v. Manatee County*, 898 F.2d 1490 (11th Cir. 1990), the court ruled that certain interests in property obtained from the state are not sufficient to rise to the level of a protectable property interest under the law of inverse condemnation. In *Marine One*, the court found that a mere license or permit to use land was not a protected property right which could be taken where the interest was obtained subject to the public trust doctrine. *See id.* at 1492–93. The interest in this case is more nebulous than the one identified in *Marine One*. In the instant case, Coastal retained a right to a royalty only if someone in the future decided to mine resources which may or may not exist in the area in question. In fact, during the 15-year period prior to the enactment of the law in question, no one had requested an oil lease in this area. In addition, in the period prior to the 1976 settlement, none of the numerous test oil wells drilled in this area had yielded any oil. The trial court therefore made the factual finding that this area was not prospective for oil. As previously mentioned, the state retained the right to control land uses over the area in question. Under all the circumstances existing in this case, we conclude that the trial court was correct in determining the mixed question of law and fact that the interest of Coastal Petroleum in the land in question was too speculative to be protected through the means of inverse condemnation.

AFFIRMED.

Notes

1. The offshore royalty interest at issue in *Coastal Petroleum* was created by a 1941 "exploration contract and option to lease" with state trustees giving Coastal Petroleum's predecessor the right to search for and produce oil and other minerals in the state-owned lands in the Gulf of Mexico near Naples and in Lake Okeechobee and other fresh water bodies. Although the 1941 rights were apparently not temporally limited, in a 1976 settlement agreement Coastal surrendered a substantial portion of the areas covered by the lease, but retained a "royalty interest" in any oil and gas developed in any nearshore waters until 2016. It was that "residual royalty interest" that was at issue in this case.

2. The court ruled that the public trust doctrine did not preclude a private landowner from prevailing in a takings claim, where a regulation precluded all "reasonable use of the land," apparently misreading the *Lucas v. South Carolina Coastal Council* decision (discussed at p. 325). Why, then, didn't the state statute forbidding offshore development amount to a taking of the company's royalty interest?

R.W. Docks & Slips v. State
Supreme Court of Wisconsin
628 N.W.2d 781 (2001)

[A marina developer challenged the state's Department of Natural Resources' denial of a permit to dredge to construct the remaining 71 boat slips of its planned 272-boat marina. The lower courts rejected the developer's takings claim, and the developer appealed. The Supreme Court affirmed, ruling that the permit denial did not deny the developer all economically beneficial use, and then addressed the relationship between the marina owner's riparian rights and the public trust doctrine.]

SYKES, J.

This case pits a small emergent weedbed along the shores of Lake Superior in Bayfield, Wisconsin, against the developer of a private marina on those same shores. The Wisconsin Department of Natural Resources [DNR] sided with the weedbed, and denied the developer a dredging permit needed to complete the final phase of the marina development. The case has an ironic twist: the small emergent weedbed would not have "emerged" at all were it not for the calming effect of a breakwater the developer had built in the early stages of the project. The presence of the emergent weedbed prompted the DNR to block the developer's construction of the last set of boat slips in the marina, 71 out of a total of 272 slips.

* * *

But first there is a threshold question, and that is the nature and extent of the private property interest at stake here. This case involves riparian rights, which are subject to and limited by the public trust doctrine. The State argues that the bed and waters of Lake Superior belong to the public, not Docks, and so no taking of private property occurred. Indeed, the Supreme Court has stated that:

> [t]he hallmark of a protected property interest is the right to exclude others. That is "one of the most essential sticks in the bundle of rights that are commonly characterized as property." *Kaiser Aetna v. United States*, 444 U.S. 164, 176 (1979). That is why the right that we all possess to use the public lands is not the "property" right of anyone—hence the sardonic maxim, explaining what economists call the "tragedy of the commons," *res publica, res nullius*.

College Sav. Bank v. Florida Prepaid Postsecondary Educ. Expense Bd., 527 U.S. 666, 673 (1999). If Docks had no private property right to place boat slips on the lakebed at the marina, it cannot have suffered an unconstitutional taking.

The public trust doctrine originated in the Northwest Ordinance of 1787 and the Wisconsin Constitution, Article IX, Section 1. See *Gillen v. City of Neenah*, 580 N.W.2d 628 (Wisc. 1998). The state holds title to the beds of lakes, ponds, and rivers as follows:

> The title to the beds of all lakes and ponds, and of rivers navigable in fact as well, *up to the* line of ordinary high-water mark, within the boundaries of the state, became vested in [the state] at the instant of its admission into the Union, in

trust to hold the same so as to preserve to the people forever the enjoyment of the waters of such lakes, ponds, and rivers, to the same extent that the public are entitled to enjoy tidal waters at the common law.

State v. Trudeau, 408 N.W.2d 337, 341 (Wisc. 1987) (quoting *Illinois Steel Co. v. Bilot*, 84 N.W. 855, 856 (Wisc. 1901)). This includes the beds of the Great Lakes as well as lesser inland waters. Public ownership of the bed of a lake applies whether the water is deep or shallow, and extends to areas covered with aquatic vegetation within the ordinary high water mark of the body of water in question. Although the public trust doctrine originally existed to protect commercial navigation, it has been expansively interpreted to safeguard the public's use of navigable waters for purely recreational purposes such as boating, swimming, fishing, hunting, recreation, and to preserve scenic beauty. *See State v. Bleck*, 338 N.W.2d 492 (Wisc. 1983); *see also Gillen*, 580 N.W.2d 628.

The legislature administers the trust for the protection of the public's rights, and it may use the power of regulation to effectuate the intent of the trust. In this regard, as applicable here, the legislature has declared it to be unlawful to place a structure on the bed of a navigable waterway unless a permit has been granted by the DNR, or unless the structure is otherwise authorized by statute....

However, subject to the requirements of the public trust doctrine, "Wisconsin has ... recognized the existence of certain common law rights that are incidents of riparian ownership of property adjacent to a body of water." *Bleck*, 338 N.W.2d at 498. These include:

> [t]he right to reasonable use of the waters for domestic, agricultural and recreational purposes; the right to use the shoreline and have access to the waters; the right to any lands formed by accretion or reliction; the right to have water flow to the land without artificial obstruction; the limited right to intrude onto the lakebed to construct devices for protection from erosion; and the right, now conditioned by statute, to construct a pier or similar structure in aid of navigation.

Cassidy v. DNR, 390 N.W.2d 81, 84 (Wis. Ct. App. 1986) (footnotes omitted).

The rights of riparian owners, however, are qualified, subordinate, and subject to the paramount interest of the state and the paramount rights of the public in navigable waters. *Bleck*, 338 N.W.2d at 498–99. The common law only requires that riparian owners be allowed reasonable access and use....

The public trust doctrine as an encumbrance on riparian rights is established "by judicial authority so long acquiesced in as to become a rule of property." *Franzini v. Layland*, 97 N.W. 499, 502 (Wisc. 1903). It is part of the organic law of the state, and is to be broadly and beneficially construed. *Diana Shooting Club v. Husting*, 145 N.W. 816 (Wisc. 1914).

The DNR's denial of the dredging permit affected only Docks' ability to construct the final 71 boat slips on the bed and in the waters of Lake Superior, and, as such, implicated only Docks' riparian rights, which are subject to the public trust doctrine. Assuming that riparian rights, subordinate as they are to the rights of the public, are included in the "bundle of rights" recognized as private property for purposes of Fifth Amendment takings analysis, Docks has failed to demonstrate a compensable regulatory taking under *Penn Central* and *Zealy*.

* * *

The DNR acted primarily to protect an emergent weedbed on behalf of the public, and secondarily, to prevent interference with the rights of neighboring riparian owners. Reasonable minds can differ about whether governmental protection of weedbeds is of such a character as to outweigh private property interests. But the state, not Docks, holds title to the lakebed, and therefore, to the extent that a private property interest is implicated here, it is riparian only and therefore qualified in nature, encumbered by the public trust doctrine. We have "jealously guarded the navigable waters of this state and the rights of the public to use and enjoy them." *Delta Fish and Fur Farms v. Pierce*, 234 N.W. 881, 883 (Wisc. 1931). The character of the governmental action in this case, therefore, weighs against a finding that Docks has suffered a compensable regulatory taking.

Similarly, our evaluation of the severity of the economic impact of the DNR's action, and the extent to which it interfered with Docks' investment-backed expectations, is strongly influenced by the fact that the development of this private marina on the bed and waters of Lake Superior was encumbered by the public trust doctrine and heavily regulated from the get-go. A riparian owner may apply to the DNR for a permit to remove material from or erect a structure on the bed of a navigable waterway in order to facilitate reasonable access and use. But the riparian owner does not have a right to the issuance of a permit if it is detrimental to the public interest. *See* Wis. Stat. §§ 30.12, 30.13 and 30.20.

Docks alleges that the revenue from the sale of the 201 existing boat slips was insufficient to cover the cost of developing the marina and that it has to date lost in excess of $1 million. It claims that the final 71 boat slips would have a combined value of approximately $1.5 million, enough to cover its losses and make a small profit. But the fact that the marina development has thus far yielded a loss does not make out a takings case, and Docks never possessed an unfettered "right" to a particular number of boat slips in the first place. Under the circumstances of this case, the DNR's action cannot be said to have "gone too far" to cause the sort of negative economic impact or substantial interference with investment expectations as to amount to a regulatory taking.

* * *

The decision of the court of appeals is affirmed.

Notes

1. In *Wilson v. Commonwealth*, 583 N.E.2d 894 (Mass. Ct. App. 1992), the Appeals Court of Massachusetts remanded to the trial court to decide a takings claim by landowners who were prevented from constructing seawalls (by the state's Wetlands Protection Act) and suffered storm damage. But in doing so, the court commented:

> Additionally, the facts as developed at trial might establish that the coastal areas in question are impressed with a public trust. *See* Lahey, *Waterfront Development and the Public Trust Doctrine*, 70 Mass. L. Rev. 55 (1985). If so, the plaintiffs, from the outset, have had only qualified rights to their shoreland and have no reasonable investment-backed expectations under which to mount a taking challenge.

Id. at 901.

2. Notice that in the *Nat'l Ass'n of Home Builders* decision, the court had no difficulty in ruling that filled former wetlands remained impressed with a public trust, furnishing another example of how the public trust doctrine can reach uplands. *See also Vermont v. Central Vermont Ry.* (p. 319), concerning shorelands along Lake Champlain.

3. In *American Pelagic Fishing Co. v. United States*, 379 F.3d 1363 (Fed. Cir. 2004), the Federal Circuit rejected a takings claim by a commercial fishing operation that had obtained federal permits to fish in the ocean from the National Marine Fisheries Service, but which were subsequently revoked by an Act of Congress, because a fishing permit under the federal Magnuson Fishery Act did "not equate to a cognizable property interest for purposes of a takings analysis." *Id.* at 1377. This was because the Magnuson Act provided a background principle defeating a takings claim—even though it also provided a revocable license to fish. Thus, according to the Federal Circuit, background principles can be found in statutes and well as the common law. As Professor Alexandra Klass has shown in *Modern Public Trust Principles: Recognizing Rights and Integrating Standards*, 82 Notre Dame L. Rev. 699 (2006), the public trust can be imposed by statutes as well as through the common law. *See also Environmental Protection Information Center v. Dep't of Forestry & Fire Protection*, 187 P.3d 888, 895 (Cal. 2008) (discussing a statutory dimension of the California public trust doctrine).

4. Applying the background principles defense has proved particularly challenging to U.S. Court of Federal Claims Judge John Paul Wiese. In *Tulare Lake Basin Water Storage Dist. v. United States,* 49 Fed. Cl. 313 (2001), Judge Wiese awarded compensation to several water districts and water users due to Endangered Species Act restrictions on water deliveries in the Sacramento-San Joaquin Delta, despite arguments that the California public trust doctrine barred the compensation claims. He rejected the public trust defense on the theory that only a California court or the state water board has the authority to enforce the California public trust doctrine as a limitation on a California water right, and therefore he, as a federal judge, lacked authority to consider the defense. In an ensuing case, *Casitas Municipal Water Dist. v. United States*, 76 Fed. Cl. 100 (2007), *aff'd in part and rev'd in part*, 543 F.3d 1276 (Fed. Cir. 2008), *dismissed on remand on ripeness grounds*, 102 Fed. Cl. 443 (2011), he again refused to rule that the public trust doctrine supplied a defense to the takings claim, but for slightly different reasons. This time, the judge ruled that only the State of California, not the federal government, can raise the California public trust defense as a defense to a takings claim; alternatively, he ruled that if he had authority to consider the defense, it would require a "balancing" of public and private interests, and in this instance the United States failed to show that the public interest in protecting endangered fish outweighed the private interests in unregulated water development. Does this square with the California Supreme Court's interpretation of the public trust doctrine in the Mono Lake case? *See National Audubon Society* (p. 173) (private parties acquire no vested right in water permits). Neither ruling was subjected to appellate review because the parties reached a settlement in *Tulare Lake*, and the federal appeals court in *Casitas* ultimately ordered dismissal of the takings claim on ripeness grounds without addressing the public trust defense. For detailed criticism of both *Tulare Lake* and *Casitas*, see John D. Echeverria, *The Public Trust Doctrine as a Background Principles Defense in Takings Litigation*, 45 U.C. Davis L. Rev. 931 (2012).

Chapter 10

The Public Trust Doctrine Abroad

Because the origins of the public trust doctrine lie in Roman and English law, it is perhaps not surprising that the doctrine has taken hold internationally. In countries as diverse as India, the Philippines, Kenya, and Canada, the doctrine seems poised to play a major role in natural resources law. The scope of the doctrine in these countries, however, has expanded considerably beyond the scope recognized by courts in the United States to include uplands (such as forests) and to broadly demand environmental protection, sustainable development, and intergenerational equity. Moreover, in the two countries whose courts have given the public trust the most careful consideration—India and the Philippines—the courts have located the source of the public trust doctrine in natural law, meaning that ensuing codifications in constitutions and statutes merely reflected pre-existing law. It is no exaggeration to suggest that a considerable part of the public trust doctrine's future lies beyond the shores of the United States.

M.C. Mehta v. Kamal Nath
Supreme Court of India
1 S.C.C. 388 (1997)

[Span Resort proposed to dredge, blast, and reconstruct the riverbed of the Beas River in order to redirect the river to avoid flooding. The resort possessed a 99-year lease of government land and built its club in 1990 by encroaching on neighboring public forestland, an encroachment subsequently approved by the Minister of Environment and Forests in 1994. The encroachment led to a swelling of the river, which changed the river's course, engulfed the club and prompted the project to redirect the river again. The minister who approved the project, the defendant, Kamal Nath, had family ties to Span Resort. M.C. Mehta, an activist lawyer, filed suit after a newspaper article exposed the project, with some encouragement from the Supreme Court. (Apparently, it is not unusual in India for judges to encourage litigants to take up issues of interest to them.) The Supreme Court took the case under its original jurisdiction and issued the following opinion.]

* * *

KULDIP, SINGH, J.

This Court took notice of the news item appearing in the Indian Express dated 25-2-1996 under the caption—"Kamal Nath dares the mighty Beas to keep his dreams afloat"[:]

Kamal Nath's family has direct links with a private company, Span Motels Private Limited, which owns a resort—Span Resorts—for tourists in Kullu-Manali Valley. The problem is with another ambitious venture floated by the same company—Span Club. The club represents Kamal Nath'[s] dream of having a house on the bank of the Beas in the shadow of the snow-chapped Zanskar Range. The club was built after encroaching upon 27.12 bighas of land,[1] including substantial forest land, in 1990. The land was later regularised and leased out to the company on 11-4-1994. The regularisation was done when Mr. Kamal Nath was Minister of Environment and Forests.... The swollen Beas changed its course and engulfed the Span Club and the adjoining lawns, washing it away. For almost five months now, the Span Resorts management has been moving bulldozers and earth-movers to turn the course of the Beas for a second time.

The heavy earth-mover has been used to block the flow of the river just 500 metres upstream. The bulldozers are creating a new channel to divert the river to at least one kilometre downstream. The tractor-trolleys move earth and boulders to shore up the embankment surrounding Span Resorts for laying a lawn. According to the Span Resorts management, the entire reclaiming operation should be over by March 31....

Admitting that the Nath family had "business interests" in the company since 1981, he said, "the company is managed by a team of professional managers and Mr. Kamal Nath is not involved in the management activity of the company."

* * *

The forest lands which have been given on lease to the Motel by the State Government are situated at the bank of River Beas. Beas is a young and dynamic river. It runs through Kullu Valley between the mountain ranges of the Dhauladhar in the right bank and the Chandrakheni in the left. The river is fast-flowing, carrying large boulders, at the times of flood. When water velocity is not sufficient to carry the boulders, those are deposited in the channel, often blocking the flow of water. Under such circumstances the river stream changes its course, remaining within the valley but swinging from one bank to the other. The right bank of River Beas where the Motel is located mostly comes under forest, the left bank consists of plateaus, having steep bank facing the river, where fruit orchards and cereal cultivation are predominant. The area being ecologically fragile and full of scenic beauty should not have been permitted to be converted into private ownership and for commercial gains.

The notion that the public has a right to expect certain lands and natural areas to retain their natural characteristic is finding its way into the law of the land. The need to protect the environment and ecology has been summed up by David B. Hunter ... in the following words:

> Another major ecological tenet is that the world is finite. The earth can support only so many people and only so much human activity before limits are reached. This lesson was driven home by the oil crisis of the 1970s as well as by the pesticide scare of the 1960s. The current deterioration of the ozone layer is another vivid example of the complex, unpredictable and potentially catastrophic effects posed by our disregard of the environmental limits to economic growth. The absolute finiteness of the environment, when coupled with human dependency on the environment, leads to the unquestionable result that human activities will at some point be constrained. [H]uman activity finds in the natural world its external limits. In short, the environment imposes constraints on our freedom;

---

1. *Ed.'s note*: The bigha land measurement unit varies in size, but a single bigha generally ranges from 1,500 to 6,771 square meters (less than half an acre). The 27.12 bighas here, then, included between 10 and 12 acres.

these constraints are not the product of value choices but of the scientific imperative of the environment's limitations. Reliance on improving technology can delay temporarily, but not forever, the inevitable constraints. There is a limit to the capacity of the environment to service ... growth, both in providing raw materials and in assimilating by-product wastes due to consumption. The largesse of technology can only postpone or disguise the inevitable.

* * *

There is a commonly-recognized link between laws and social values, but to ecologists a balance between laws and values is not alone sufficient to ensure a stable relationship between humans and their environment. Laws and values must also contend with the constraints imposed by the outside environment. Unfortunately, current legal doctrine rarely accounts for such constraints, and thus environmental stability is threatened.

Historically, we have changed the environment to fit our conceptions of property. We have fenced, plowed and paved. The environment has proven malleable and to a large extent still is. But there is a limit to this malleability and certain types of ecologically important resources—for example, wetlands and riparian forests—can no longer be destroyed without enormous long-term effects on environmental and therefore social stability. To ecologists, the need for preserving sensitive resources does not reflect value choices but rather is the necessary result of objective observations of the laws of nature.

In sum, ecologists view the environmental sciences as providing us with certain laws of nature. These laws, just like our own laws, restrict our freedom of conduct and choice. Unlike our laws, nature cannot be changed by legislative fiat; they are imposed on us by the natural world. An understanding of the laws of nature must therefore inform all of our social institutions.

[David B. Hunter, *An Ecological Perspective on Property: A Call for Judicial Protection of the Public's Interest in Environmentally Critical Resources*, 12 Harv. Envtl. L. Rev. 311 (1988).]

The ancient Roman Empire developed a legal theory known as the "Doctrine of the Public Trust." It was founded on the ideas that certain common properties such as rivers, seashore, forests and the air were held by government in trusteeship for the free and unimpeded use of the general public. Our contemporary concern about "the environment" bears a very close conceptual relationship to this legal doctrine. Under the Roman law these resources were either owned by no one (*res nullius*) or by everyone in common (*res communes*). Under the English common law, however, the sovereign could own these resources, but the ownership was limited in nature; the Crown could not grant these properties to private owners if the effect was to interfere with the public interests in navigation or fishing. Resources that were suitable for these uses were deemed to be held in trust by the Crown for the benefit of the public. Joseph L. Sax, Professor of Law, University of Michigan—proponent of the modern public trust doctrine—in an erudite article *Public Trust Doctrine in Natural Resource Law: Effective Judicial Intervention*, 68 Mich. L. Rev. 473 (1970), has given the historical background of the Public Trust Doctrine as [follows]:

The source of modern public trust law is found in a concept that received much attention in Roman and English law—the nature of property rights in rivers, the sea, and the seashore. That history has been given considerable attention in the legal literature, need not be repeated in detail here. But two points should be emphasized. First, certain interests, such as navigation and fishing, were sought to be preserved for the benefit of the public; accordingly, property used for those purposes was distinguished from general public property which the sovereign could routinely grant to private owners. Second, while it was understood that in certain common properties — such as the seashore, highways, and running water — "perpetual use was dedicated to the public," it has never been clear whether the public had an enforceable right to prevent infringement of those interests. Although the State apparently did protect public uses, no evidence is available that public rights could be legally asserted against a recalcitrant government.

The public trust doctrine primarily rests on the principle that certain resources like air, sea, waters and the forests have such a great importance to the people as a whole that it would be wholly unjustified to make them a subject of private ownership. The said resources being a gift of nature, they should be made freely available to everyone irrespective of the status in life. The doctrine enjoins upon the government to protect the resources for the enjoyment of the general public rather than to permit their use for private ownership or commercial purposes. According to Professor Sax the public trust doctrine imposes the following restrictions on governmental authority:

> These types of restrictions on governmental authority are often thought to be imposed by the public trust: first, the property subject to the trust must not only be used for a public purpose, but it must be held available for use by the general public; second, the property may not be sold, even for a fair cash equivalent; and third the property must be maintained for particular types of uses.

The American law on the subject is primarily based on the decision of the United States Supreme Court in *Illinois Central Railroad Co. v. Illinois*. In the year 1869 the Illinois Legislature made a substantial grant of submerged lands — a mile strip along the shores of Lake Michigan extending one mile out from the shoreline — to the Illinois Central Railroad. In 1873, the legislature changed its mind and repealed the 1869 grant. The State of Illinois sued to quit title. The Court while accepting the stand of the State of Illinois held that the title of the state in the land in dispute was a title different in character from that which the state held in lands intended for sale. It was different from the title which the United States held in public lands which were open to pre-emption and sale. It was a title held in trust — for the people of the state that they may enjoy the navigation of the water, carry on commerce over them and have liberty of fishing therein free from obstruction or interference of private parties. The abdication of the general control of the state over lands in dispute was not consistent with the exercise of the trust which required the government of the state to preserve such waters for the use of the public. According to Professor Sax the Court in *Illinois Central* "articulated a principle that has become the central substantive thought in public trust litigation. When a state holds a resource which is available for the free use of the general public, a court will look with considerable skepticism upon any governmental conduct which is calculated either to relocate that resource to more restricted uses or to subject public uses to the self-interest of private parties."

* * *

[The court proceeded to discuss Professor Sax's article and the case law he examined as well as the California Supreme Court's decision in *Mono Lake* (p. 173).]

* * *

It is no doubt correct that the public trust doctrine under the English common law extended only to certain traditional uses such as navigation, commerce and fishing. But the American Courts in recent cases have expanded the concept of the public trust doctrine. The observations of the Supreme Court of California in *Mono Lake* case clearly show the judicial concern in protecting all ecologically important lands, for example fresh water, wetlands or riparian forests. The observations of the Court in *Mono Lake* case to the effect that the protection of ecological values is among the purposes of public trust, may give rise to an argument that the ecology and the environment protection is a relevant factor to determine which lands, waters or airs are protected by the public trust doctrine. The Courts in United States are finally beginning to adopt this reasoning and are expanding the public trust to encompass new types of lands and waters. In *Phillips Petroleum Co. v. Mississippi* the United States Supreme Court upheld Mississippi's extension of public trust doctrine to lands underlying non-navigable tidal areas. The majority judgment adopted ecological concepts to determine which lands can be considered tide lands. *Phillips Petroleum* assumes importance because the Supreme Court expanded the public trust doctrine to identify the tide lands not on commercial considerations but on ecological concepts. We see no reason why the public trust doctrine should not be expanded to include all ecosystems operating in our natural resources.

Our legal system—based on English common law—includes the public trust doctrine as part of its jurisprudence. The State is the trustee of all natural resources which are by nature meant for public use and enjoyment. Public at large is the beneficiary of the seashore, running waters, airs, forests and ecologically fragile lands. The State as a trustee is under a legal duty to protect the natural resources. These resources meant for public use cannot be converted into private ownership.

We are fully aware that the issues presented in this case illustrate the classic struggle between those members of the public who would preserve our rivers, forests, parks and open lands in their pristine purity and those charged with administrative responsibilities who, under the pressures of the changing needs of an increasingly complex society, find it necessary to encroach to some extent upon open lands heretofore considered inviolate to change. The resolution of this conflict in any given case is for the legislature and not the courts. If there is a law made by Parliament or the State Legislatures the courts can serve as an instrument of determining legislative intent in the exercise of its powers of judicial review under the Constitution. But in the absence of any legislation, the executive acting under the doctrine of public trust cannot abdicate the natural resources and convert them into private ownership, or for commercial use. The aesthetic use and the pristine glory of the natural resources, the environment and the ecosystems of our country cannot be permitted to be eroded for private, commercial or any other use unless the courts find it necessary, in good faith, for the public good and in public interest to encroach upon the said resources.

Coming to the facts of the present case, large area of the bank of River Beas which is part of protected forest has been given on a lease purely for commercial purposes to the Motels. We have no hesitation in holding that the Himachal Pradesh Government committed patent breach of public trust by leasing the ecologically fragile land to the Motel management. Both the lease transactions are in patent breach of the trust held by the State Government. The second lease granted in the year 1994 was virtually of the land which is a part of the riverbed. Even the Board in its report has recommended de-leasing of the said area.

This Court in *Vellore Citizens' Welfare Forum v. Union of India*, 5 S.C.C. 647 (1996), explained the "Precautionary Principle" and "Polluters Pays Principle" as [follows]:

Some of the salient principles of "Sustainable Development", as culled out from Brundtland Report and other international documents, and Inter-Generational

Equity. Use and Conservation of Natural Resources, Environmental Protection, the Precautionary Principle, Polluter Pays Principle, Obligation to Assist and Cooperate, Eradication of Poverty and Financial Assistance to the developing countries. We are, however, of the view that "the Precautionary Principle" and "the Polluter Pays Principle" are essential features of "Sustainable Development". The "Precautionary Principle"—in the context of the municipal law—means:

(i) Environmental measures—by the State Government and the statutory authorities—must anticipate, prevent and attack the causes of environmental degradation.

(ii) Where there are threats of serious and irreversible damage, lack of scientific certainty should not be used as reason for postponing measures to prevent environmental degradation.

(iii) The "onus of proof" is on the actor or the developer/industrialist to show that his action is environmentally benign.

"The Polluter Pays Principle" has been held to be a sound principle by this Court in *Indian Council for Enviro-Legal Action v. Union of India*, 3 S.C.C. 212 (1996). The Court observed: "[W]e are of the opinion that any principle evolved in this behalf should be simple, practical and suited to the conditions obtaining in this country." The Court ruled that: "Once the activity carried on is hazardous or inherently dangerous, the person carrying on such activity is liable to make good the loss caused to any other person by his activity irrespective of the fact whether he took reasonable care while carrying on his activity. The rule is premised upon the very nature of the activity carried on."

Consequently, the polluting industries are "absolutely liable to compensate for the harm caused by them to villagers in the affected area, to the soil and to the underground water and hence, they are bound to take all necessary measures to remove sludge and other pollutants lying in the affected areas." The "Polluter Pays Principle" as interpreted by this Court means that the absolute liability for harm to the environment extends not only to compensate the victims of pollution but also the cost of restoring the environmental degradation. Remediation of the damaged environment is part of the process of "sustainable development" and as such polluter is liable to pay the cost to the individual sufferers as well as the cost of reversing the damaged ecology.

The precautionary principle and the polluter pays principle have been accepted as part of the law of the land.

[*Vellore Citizens' Welfare Forum v. Union of India*, 5 S.C.C. 647 (1996).]

It is thus settled by this Court that one who pollutes the environment must pay to reverse the damage caused by his acts.

We, therefore, order and direct as [follows]:

1. The public trust doctrine, as discussed by in this judgment is a part of the law of the land.

2. The prior approval granted by the Government of India, Ministry of Environment and Forest by the letter dated 24-11-1993 and the lease deed dated 11-4-1994 in favour of the Motel are quashed. The lease granted to the motel by the said lease deed in respect of 27 bighas and 12 biswas of area, is cancelled and set aside. The Himachal Pradesh Government shall take over the area and restore it to its original-natural conditions.

3. The Motel shall pay compensation by way of cost for the restitution of the environment and ecology of the area. The pollution caused by various constructions made by the Motel in the riverbed and the banks of River Beas has to be removed and reversed. We direct NEERI [National Environmental Engineering Research Institute] through its Director to inspect the area, if necessary, and give an assessment of the cost which is likely to be incurred for reversing the damage caused by the Motel to the environment and ecology of the area. NEERI may take into consideration the report by the Board in this respect.

4. The Motel through its management shall show cause why pollution fine in addition be not imposed on the Motel.

5. The Motel shall construct a boundary wall at a distance of not more than 4 metres from the cluster of rooms (main building of the Motel) towards the river basin. The boundary wall shall be on the area of the Motel which is covered by the lease dated 29-9-1981. The Motel shall not encroach/cover/utilise any part of the river basin. The boundary wall shall separate the motel building from the river basin. The river bank and the river basin shall be left open for the public use.

6. The Motel shall not discharge untreated effluents into the river. We direct the Himachal Pradesh Pollution Control Board to inspect the pollution control devices/treatment plants set up by the Motel. If the effluent/waste discharged by the motel is not conforming to the prescribed standards, action in accordance with law be taken against the Motel.

7. The Himachal Pradesh Pollution Control Board shall not permit the discharge of untreated effluent into River Beas. The Board shall inspect all the hotels/institutions/factories in Kullu-Manali area and in the board shall take action in accordance with law.

8. The Motel shall show cause on 18-12-1996 why pollution fine and damages be not imposed as directed by us. NEERI shall send its report by 17-12-1996. To be listed on 18-12-1996.

The writ petition is disposed of except for limited purpose indicated above.

Notes

1. Notice that the Indian Supreme Court found the public trust doctrine in natural law, declaring that "[an] understanding of the laws of nature must therefore inform all of our social institution[s]." What is the effect of finding the public trust doctrine embedded in natural law?

2. Like the California Supreme Court in its *Mono Lake* decision, the India Supreme Court described the Beas River case as involving a "classic struggle between those members of the public who would preserve our rivers, forests, parks, and open lands in their pristine purity and those charged with administrative responsibilities who, under pressures of the changing needs of an increasingly complex society, find it necessary to encroach to some extent upon open lands heretofore considered inviolate to change." On the use of U.S. cases by courts in India, see Rajeev Dhaven, *Borrowed Ideas: On the Impact of American Scholarship on Indian Law*, 33 Am. J. Int'l L. 505 (2006); Adam M. Smith, *Making Itself At Home: Understanding Foreign Law in Domestic Jurisprudence: The Indian Case*, 24 Berkeley J. Int'l L. 218 (2006). In addition to Professor Sax's article, the Indian Supreme Court also relied heavily on David Hunter, *An Ecological Perspective on Property: A Call for Judicial Protection*, 12 Harv. Envtl. L. Rev. 311 (1988).

Might U.S. courts consider the reasoning of India's courts (and others around the world) persuasive as to its PTD interpretation?

3. Two years after the principal case, the India Supreme Court located the public trust doctrine in the Indian Constitution. In *M.I. Builders Private, Ltd. v. Radhey Shayam Sahu*, (1999) 6 S.C.C. 464 (India), the Court enjoined construction of an underground shopping center complex approved by a local development authority within a public park. The Court ordered restoration of the park by the builder and ruled that the park was protected by Article 21 of the Constitution, which declares that "[n]o person shall be deprived of his life or personal liberty except according to procedure established by law." *Id.* at 466 (citing Professor Sax again, for the proposition that "a court will look with considerable skepticism on any government conduct which is calculated either to reallocate [a resource available for free public use] to a more restricted use or to subject public uses to the self-interest of private parties").

4. In *Fomento Resorts & Hotels v. Minguel Martins*, 1 N.S.C. 100 (India 2009), the Supreme Court ruled that a resort violated the public trust doctrine by constructing recreational facilities that obstructed a traditional footpath to a public beach. The Indian Supreme Court clarified that, although the trust doctrine was constitutionally enshrined, its common law and natural law origins had not been superseded:

> The Indian society has, since time immemorial, been conscious of the necessity of protecting the environment and ecology. The main [motto] of social life has been "to live in harmony with nature." [The] preachings [of sages and saints of India] ... are ample evidence of the society's respect for plants, trees, earth, sky, air, water and every form of life. It was ... a sacred duty of every one to protect them ... people worshipped trees, rivers, and sea which were treated as belonging to all living creatures. The children were educated ... about the necessity of keeping the environment clean and protecting earth, rivers, sea, forests, trees, flora[], fona [sic] and every species of life.

Lower Indian courts continue to emphasize the "time immemorial," natural law origin of the Indian public trust doctrine, and the Supreme Court has even traced its foundation to the Chen Dynasty. *See* Michael C. Blumm & Rachel D. Guthrie, *Internationalizing the Public Trust Doctrine: Natural Law and Constitutional and Statutory Approaches to Fulfilling the Saxion Vision*, 45 U.C. Davis L. Rev. 741, 763 (2012) [hereafter cited as *Internationalizing the Public Trust Doctrine*].

The *Fomento Resorts* Court applied the public trust duty to all citizens: "Today, every person exercising his or her right to use the air, water, or land and associated natural ecosystems has the obligation to secure for the rest of us the right to live or otherwise use that same resource or property for the long term and enjoyment by future generations." Generally the public trust is asserted by citizens against government trustees, but this language also suggests a duty incumbent on all land and resource users. Does the obligation form an encumbrance on all property rights to land and natural resources?

5. The Supreme Court of India has also applied the PTD to natural gas deposits. *Reliance Natural Res. Ltd. v. Reliance Indus. Ltd.*, 7 S.C.C. 129 pt. I, ¶ 11 (India 2010). On the scope, purposes, public standing, and remedies available under India's public trust doctrine, see *Internationalizing the Public Trust Doctrine,* cited above, 45 U.C. Davis L. Rev. at 763–65. For an overview of the public trust doctrine in Pakistan, see *id.* at 766–70. *See also* David Takacs, *The Public Trust Doctrine, Environmental Human Rights, and the Future of Private Property*, 16 N.Y.U. Envtl. L. J. 711, 735–40 (2008) (discussing the Indian public trust cases).

Juan Antonio Oposa et al. v.
The Honorable Fulgencio S. Factoran, Jr., G.R.
Supreme Court of the Philippines
No. 101083, 224 S.C.R.A. 792 (July 30, 1993)

DAVIDE, JR., J.:

[Schoolchildren brought a class action suit challenging timber licenses issued by the Department of Environment and Natural Resources, authorizing the harvest of virtually all of the forest in the Philippines. The Supreme Court reversed a lower court dismissal of the suit (without reaching the merits), using sweeping language in interpreting the Constitution's right to a healthy environment, which states "[t]he State shall protect and advance the right of the people to a balanced and healthful ecology in accord with the rhythm and harmony of nature." Const. (1987), art. II, sec. 16 (Phil.), *available at* http://lawphil.net/consti/cons1987.html. The Constitution in turn implements the 1977 Environmental Policy, which requires the nation to "recognize, discharge, and fulfill the responsibilities of each generation as trustee and guardian of the environment for succeeding generations." Philippine Environmental Policy, Pres. Dec. No. 1151, sec. 2 (1977).]

[T]his petition bears upon the right of Filipinos to a balanced and healthful ecology which the petitioners dramatically associate with the twin concepts of "inter-generational responsibility" and "inter-generational justice." Specifically, it touches on the issue of whether the said petitioners have a cause of action to "prevent the misappropriation or impairment" of Philippine rainforests and "arrest the unabated hemorrhage of the country's vital life-support systems...."

The principal plaintiffs ... are all minors duly represented and joined by their respective parents.... The complaint ... alleges that the plaintiffs "are all citizens of the Republic of the Philippines, taxpayers, and entitled to the full benefit, use and enjoyment of the natural resource treasure that is the country's virgin tropical rainforests."...The minors further asseverate that they "represent their generation as well as generations yet unborn." Consequently, it is prayed for that judgment be rendered [to]:

"(1) Cancel all existing timber license agreements in this country; [and]

(2) Cease and desist from receiving, accepting, processing, renewing or approving new timber license agreements."...

The complaint starts off with the general averments that the Philippine archipelago of 7,100 islands has a land area of thirty million (30,000,000) hectares and is endowed with rich, lush and verdant rainforests in which varied, rare and unique species of flora and fauna may be found; these rainforests contain a genetic, biological and chemical pool which is irreplaceable; they are also the habitat of indigenous Philippine cultures which have existed, endured and flourished since time immemorial; scientific evidence reveals that in order to maintain a balanced and healthful ecology, the country's land area should be utilized on the basis of a ratio of fifty-four per cent (54%) for forest cover and forty-six per cent (46%) for agricultural, residential, industrial, commercial and other uses; the distortion and disturbance of this balance as a consequence of deforestation have resulted in a host of environmental tragedies, such as (a) water shortages, ... (c) massive erosion and the consequential loss of soil fertility and agricultural productivity, ... (d) the endangering and extinction of the country's unique, rare and varied flora and fauna, (e) the disturbance and dislocation of cultural communities, including the disappearance of the Filipino's indigenous cultures, ... and (k) the reduction of the earth's capacity to process carbon dioxide gases which has led to perplexing and catastrophic climatic changes such as the phenomenon of global warming, otherwise known as the "greenhouse effect."

... As their cause of action, they specifically allege that:...

8. Twenty-five (25) years ago, the Philippines had some sixteen (16) million hectares of rainforests constituting roughly 53% of the country's land mass....

10. More recent surveys reveal that a mere 850,000 hectares of virgin old-growth rainforests are left, barely 2.8% of the entire land mass of the Philippine archipelago and about 3.0 million hectares of immature and uneconomical secondary growth forests....

12. At the present rate of deforestation, i.e. about 200,000 hectares per annum or 25 hectares per hour (nighttime, Saturdays, Sundays and holidays included) the Philippines will be bereft of forest resources after the end of this ensuing decade, if not earlier.

* * *

[T]he respondents aver that the petitioners failed to allege in their complaint a specific legal right violated by the respondent Secretary for which any relief is provided by law. They see nothing in the complaint but vague and nebulous allegations concerning an "environmental right" which supposedly entitles the petitioners to the "protection by the state in its capacity as parens patriae." Such allegations, according to them, do not reveal a valid cause of action. They then reiterate the theory that the question of whether logging should be permitted in the country is a political question which should be properly addressed to the executive or legislative branches of Government. They therefore assert that the petitioners' recourse is not to file an action in court, but to lobby before Congress for the passage of a bill that would ban logging totally....

This case ... has a special and novel element. Petitioners minors assert that they represent their generation as well as generations yet unborn. We find no difficulty in ruling that they can, for themselves, for others of their generation and for the succeeding generations, file a class suit. Their personality to sue in behalf of the succeeding generations can only be based on the concept of intergenerational responsibility insofar as the right to a balanced and healthful ecology is concerned. Such a right, as hereinafter expounded, considers the "rhythm and harmony of nature." Nature means the created world in its entirety....

Needless to say, every generation has a responsibility to the next to preserve that rhythm and harmony for the full enjoyment of a balanced and healthful ecology. Put a little differently, the minors' assertion of their right to a sound environment constitutes, at the same time, the performance of their obligation to ensure the protection of that right for the generations to come....

We do not hesitate to find for the petitioners[.] ... The complaint focuses on one specific fundamental legal right—the right to a balanced and healthful ecology which, for the first time in our nation's constitutional history, is solemnly incorporated in the fundamental law. Section 16, Article II of the 1987 Constitution explicitly provides:

"SEC. 16. The State shall protect and advance the right of the people to a balanced and healthful ecology in accord with the rhythm and harmony of nature."

This right unites with the right to health....

"SEC. 15. The State shall protect and promote the right to health of the people and instill health consciousness among them."

While the right to a balanced and healthful ecology is to be found, under the Declaration of Principles and State Policies and not under the Bill of Rights, it does not follow that it is less important than any of the civil and political rights enumerated in the latter. Such a right belongs to a different category of rights altogether for it concerns nothing less than self-preservation and self-perpetuation—aptly and fittingly stressed by the petitioners—the advancement of which may even be said to predate all governments and constitutions.

As a matter of fact, these basic rights need not even be written in the Constitution for they are assumed to exist from the inception of humankind. If they are now explicitly mentioned in the fundamental charter, it is because of the well-founded fear of its framers that unless the right to a balanced and healthful ecology and to health are mandated as state policies by the Constitution itself, thereby highlighting their continuing importance and imposing upon the state a solemn obligation to preserve the first and protect and advance the second, the day would not be too far when all else would be lost not only for the present generation, but also for those to come—generations which stand to inherit nothing but parched earth incapable of sustaining life.

The right to a balanced and healthful ecology carries with it the correlative duty to refrain from impairing the environment.... A denial or violation of that right by the other who has the correlative duty or obligation to respect or protect the same gives rise to a cause of action. Petitioners maintain that the granting of the [timber license agreements], which they claim was done with grave abuse of discretion, violated their right to a balanced and healthful ecology; hence, the full protection thereof requires that no further [timber license agreements] should be renewed or granted....

The foregoing considered, Civil Case No. 90-777 cannot be said to raise a political question. Policy formulation or determination by the executive or legislative branches of Government is not squarely put in issue. What is principally involved is the enforcement of a right vis-à-vis policies already formulated and expressed in legislation....

[The] Petition is hereby [granted].

Notes

1. Note that the government defendants cast the case as more appropriate for legislative resolution, saying the clear-cutting raised a "political question." The federal government has raised the same sort of defense in cases brought in the United States. *See, e.g., Alec L. v. Jackson*, 863 F. Supp. 2d 11 (D.D.C. 2012), *aff'd sub nom. Loorz ex rel. Alec L. v. McCarthy*, 561 F. App'x 7 (D.C. Cir. 2014) (p. 389) (atmospheric trust litigation). How did the *Oposa* Court respond to the government's position? Is the political question doctrine inapplicable in the trust context? Wouldn't application of that doctrine leave the matter of trust management entirely to the trustee, thereby removing the essential element of judicial enforcement from the trust? How does the public trust context differ from other contexts in which the political question defense applies to shield government behavior?

2. The ringing endorsement of the public trust doctrine as both inherent in the Philippines Constitution and in pre-constitutional natural law had remarkably little effect on timber harvesting, however, as the Court's decision did not cancel the licenses or even enjoin the issuance of new licenses. *See* Dante B. Gatmaytan, *The Illusion of Intergenerational Equity:* Oposa v. Factoran *as a Pyrrhic Victory*, 18 Geo. Int'l Envtl. L. Rev. 457 (2003) (explaining that commercial logging continued largely unabated). These results emphasize the importance of a remedy to enforce public trust obligations. The next case represents another landmark trust ruling by the Supreme Court of the Philippines, but this time the Court developed a far-reaching remedy.

Metropolitan Manila Development Authority v. Concerned Residents of Manila Bay

Supreme Court of the Philippines
574 S.C.R.A 661 (2008)

VELASCO, JR., J.:

The need to address environmental pollution, as a cause of climate change, has of late gained the attention of the international community. Media have finally trained their sights on the ill effects of pollution, the destruction of forests and other critical habitats, oil spills, and the unabated improper disposal of garbage. And rightly so, for the magnitude of environmental destruction is now on a scale few ever foresaw and the wound no longer simply heals by itself. But amidst hard evidence and clear signs of a climate crisis that needs bold action, the voice of cynicism, naysayers, and procrastinators can still be heard.

This case turns on government agencies and their officers who, by the nature of their respective offices or by direct statutory command, are tasked to protect and preserve, at the first instance, our internal waters, rivers, shores, and seas polluted by human activities. To most of these agencies and their official complement, the pollution menace does not seem to carry the high national priority it deserves, if their track records are to be the norm. Their cavalier attitude towards solving, if not mitigating, the environmental pollution problem, is a sad commentary on bureaucratic efficiency and commitment.

At the core of the case is the Manila Bay, a place with a proud historic past, once brimming with marine life and, for so many decades in the past, a spot for different contact recreation activities, but now a dirty and slowly dying expanse mainly because of the abject official indifference of people and institutions that could have otherwise made a difference.

This case started when, on January 29, 1999, respondents Concerned Residents of Manila Bay filed a complaint before the Regional Trial Court (RTC) in Imus, Cavite against several government agencies, among them the petitioners, for the cleanup, rehabilitation, and protection of the Manila Bay.... [T]he complaint alleged that the water quality of the Manila Bay had fallen way below the allowable standards set by law, specifically Presidential Decree No. (PD) 1152 or the Philippine Environment Code. This environmental aberration, the complaint stated, stemmed from:

> [The] reckless, wholesale, accumulated and ongoing acts of omission or commission [of the defendants] resulting in the clear and present danger to public health and in the depletion and contamination of the marine life of Manila Bay, [for which reason] ALL defendants must be held jointly and/or solidarily liable and be collectively ordered to clean up Manila Bay and to restore its water quality to class B waters fit for swimming, skin-diving, and other forms of contact recreation.

* * *

[The trial court found for the Concerned Residents and directed the government to undertake a comprehensive plan to clean up and rehabilitate Manila Bay, ordering a variety of specific actions to prevent pollution within six months. The court of appeals affirmed, and the government appealed to the Supreme Court, which affirmed on statutory grounds, and then turned to the public trust claim.]

* * *

In the light of the ongoing environmental degradation, the Court wishes to emphasize the extreme necessity for all concerned executive departments and agencies to immediately act and discharge their respective official duties and obligations. Indeed, time is of the essence; hence, there is a need to set timetables for the performance and completion of the tasks, some of them as defined for them by law and the nature of their respective offices and mandates.

The importance of the Manila Bay as a sea resource, playground, and as a historical landmark cannot be over-emphasized. It is not yet too late in the day to restore the Manila Bay to its former splendor and bring back the plants and sea life that once thrived in its blue waters. But the tasks ahead, daunting as they may be, could only be accomplished if those mandated, with the help and cooperation of all civic-minded individuals, would put their minds to these tasks and take responsibility. This means that the State, through petitioners, has to take the lead in the preservation and protection of the Manila Bay.

The era of delays, procrastination, and *ad hoc* measures is over. Petitioners must transcend their limitations, real or imaginary, and buckle down to work before the problem at hand becomes unmanageable. Thus, we must reiterate that different government agencies and instrumentalities cannot shirk from their mandates; they must perform their basic functions in cleaning up and rehabilitating the Manila Bay. We are disturbed by petitioners' hiding behind two untenable claims: (1) that there ought to be a specific pollution incident before they are required to act; and (2) that the cleanup of the bay is a discretionary duty.

RA 9003 [the Ecological Solid Waste Management Act] is a sweeping piece of legislation enacted to radically transform and improve waste management. It implements Art. II, § 18 of the 1987 Constitution, which explicitly provides that the state shall protect and advance the right of the people to a balanced and healthful ecology in accord with the rhythm and harmony of nature.

So it was that in *Oposa v. Factoran, Jr.* the Court stated that the right to a balanced and healthful ecology need not even be written in the Constitution for it is assumed, like other civil and political rights guaranteed in the Bill of Rights, to exist from the inception of mankind and it is an issue of transcendental importance with intergenerational implications. Even assuming the absence of a categorical legal provision specifically prodding petitioners to clean up the bay, they and the men and women representing them cannot escape their obligation to future generations of Filipinos to keep the waters of the Manila Bay clean and clear as humanly as possible. Anything less would be a betrayal of the trust reposed in them.

[The court ordered the government agencies to "clean up, rehabilitate and preserve Manila Bay, and restore and maintain its waters ... to make them fit for swimming, skin-diving, and other forms of contact recreation."]

Notes

1. The injunction ordered by the *Metro Manila* decision extended to a dozen agencies that had shirked their duties under statutory law. It included directives to construct sewage treatment plants, restock Manila Bay with indigenous fish, and "inculcate in the minds and hearts of the people" the importance of the environment through education. To implement the injunction, the Court ordered the trial court to maintain continuing jurisdiction to oversee the cleanup. *See* Presbitero J. Velasco, Jr., *Manila Bay: A Daunting Challenge in Environmental Rehabilitation and Protection*, 11 Or. Rev. Int'l L. 441 (2009)

(Associate Justice of the Supreme Court of the Philippines and author of the *Metro Manila* decision, describing the remedy the Court ordered); *see also* Arturo Iluminado C. de Castro, *Cleaning Up Manila Bay: Mandamus as a Tool for Environmental Protection*, 37 Ecology L.Q. 791 (2010). For analysis of the *Manila Bay* remedy and its usefulness as a model for other public trust lawsuits, see Mary Christina Wood, Nature's Trust: Environmental Law for a New Ecological Age, ch. 11 (2013).

2. The *Metro Manila* case arose from widespread agency disregard of statutory duties. The agencies claimed that the Bay cleanup was a discretionary duty, despite a multitude of statutory provisions providing resource protection. The Supreme Court effectively found such duties obligatory, issuing a writ of mandamus to force compliance with the statute. Did the trust obligation, in effect, transform statutory discretion into statutory obligation? Could the same approach work in the United States against agencies that routinely claim discretion to ignore statutory goals?

3. In 2014, Antonio Oposa, Jr., with the support of Our Children's Trust (see p. 389, below, in chapter 11), filed a petition in the Philippines Supreme Court on behalf of a group of young people and the 98% of Filipinos who do not have cars, asserting the right of present and future generations to a livable atmosphere. *Segovia et al. v. Climate Change Comm'n*, Petition for Writ of Kalikasan & Continuing Mandamus, *available at* http://ourchildrens trust.org/sites/ default/files/Philippines%20Petition%20.pdf. Oposa's petition sought to have half of the nation's roads set aside for those citizens. The petition sought a "writ of kalikasan," a Filipino legal instrument that provides a remedy for citizens seeking redress for violations of their environmental rights. The petition describes this unique remedy as follows:

> *Kalikasan* means "Nature" in Filipino. The Writ of *Kalikasan* is an innovation in the Rules of Court in Philippine Law. The writ is a remedy available to a natural or juridical person, entity authorized by law, people's organization, non-governmental organization, or any public interest group accredited by or registered with any government agency, on behalf of persons whose constitutional right to a balanced and healthful ecology is violated, or threatened with violation by an unlawful act or omission of a public official or employee, or private individual or entity, involving environmental damage of such magnitude as to prejudice the life, health or property of inhabitants in two or more cities or provinces.

Segovia, Petition at 5 n.2. The *Segovia* petition for a writ of kalikasan asserted that the atmosphere is a "thing held in trust" as "a vital life-support system." *Id.* at 24. The petition represents one of the more recent filings in a global Atmospheric Trust Litigation campaign brought on behalf of youth and future generations, discussed more fully below in chapter 11. *See also* http://ourchildrenstrust.org/legal/inter national/Philippines (last visited Feb. 21, 2015).

For more on the scope, purposes, public standing, and remedies available under the Philippines' public trust doctrine, see *Internationalizing the Public Trust Doctrine*, cited above, 45 U.C. Davis L. Rev. at 774–76.

Advocates Coalition for Development and Environment (ACODE) v. Attorney General
High Court of Uganda
Misc. Cause No. 0100 (2004)

[Under a longstanding lease, Kakira Sugar Works had the right to take firewood from the neighboring Butamira Forest Reserve for its sugar refinery. Kakira then applied for a

50-year permit from the federal government to transform the forest into plantation lands. The government granted the permit, and ACODE challenged its issuance on public trust grounds, inducing the following opinion from the High Court.]

* * *

In very brief terms the essence of the [case concerns] the legal right of the public to use certain land and waters. It governs the use of property where a given authority in trust holds title for citizens. Citizens have two co-existing interests in trust land; the *jus publicum*, which is the public right to use and enjoy trust land, and the *jus privatum*, which is the private property right that may exist in the use, and possession of trust lands. The state may convey the *jus privatum* to private owners, but this interest is subservient to the *jus publicum*, which is the state's inalienable interest that it continues to hold in trust land or water.

In Uganda, the above doctrine has been enshrined in the 1995 Constitution in its National Objectives and Directive Principles of State Policy as follows:

> The state shall protect important natural resources, including land, water, wetlands, minerals, oil, fauna and flora on behalf of the people of Uganda.

The doctrine is restated in Article 237(2)(b) of the Constitution which states:

> The Government or a Local Government as determined by parliament by law, shall hold in trust for the people and protect, natural lakes, rivers, wetlands, forest reserves, game reserves, national parks, and any land to be reserved for ecological and tourist purposes for the common good of all citizens.

The above provisions were operationalized by section 44 of the Land Act in the following terms:

44 *Control of Environmentally Sensitive Areas*

(1) The Government or a local government shall hold in trust for the people and protect natural lakes, rivers, ground water, natural ponds, natural streams, wetlands, forest reserves, national parks and any other land reserved for ecological and tourist purposes for the common good of all citizens.

* * *

(4) The government or a local government shall not lease out or otherwise alienate any natural resources referred to in this section.

(5) The government or a local government may grant concessions or licenses or permits in respect of any natural resources referred to in this section subject to any law.

(6) Parliament or any other authority empowered by parliament may from time to time review any land held in trust by the government or a local government whenever the community in the area or district where the reserved land is situated so demands.

Article 237(2)(b) should be read together with section 44(4) of the Land Act. The same should apply to Article 237(2)(a) and section 42 of the Land Act. The two provisions allow Government or a Local government to acquire land in public interest subject to Article 26 of the Constitution and conditions set by parliament.

It is clear from the above expositions that Butamira Forest Reserve is land which government of Uganda holds in trust for the people of Uganda to be protected for the common good of the citizens. Government has no authority to lease out or otherwise alienate it. However, Government or a local government may grant concessions or licenses or permits in respect of land held under trust with authority from parliament and with consent from the local community in the area or district where the reserved land is situated.

In the instant case there was evidence that the permit was granted to Kakira Sugar Works amidst protests from local communities which raised up a pressure group of over 1500 members who depended on the reserve for their livelihood through agro-forestry, and source of water, fuel and other forms of sustenance. There was therefore breach of public doctrine. I must add that this doctrine was applied by the principle forest officer when he rejected the demands to alienate to Reserve to Kakira Sugar Works Ltd. in 1956.

Notes

1. The Ugandan court had no trouble concluding that the public trust doctrine applies to uplands, reading the doctrine into the Ugandan constitutional provision that announced that the government "shall protect important natural resources, including land, water, wetlands, mineral, oil, fauna and flora on behalf of the people of Uganda." CONST. OF THE REPUBLIC OF UGANDA, art. 13.

2. The expansive scope of the public trust doctrine in Uganda includes "intellectual, moral, cultural, spiritual, political, and social well-being." For a discussion of the scope, purposes, public standing and remedies available under the Ugandan public trust doctrine, see *Internationalizing the Public Trust Doctrine*, cited above, 45 U.C. Davis L. Rev. at 779–81.

3. Perhaps the most remarkable aspect of this decision is the Court's reading of the public trust doctrine to require local consent to the conversion of forest preserve lands to plantation lands, suggesting that development projects need both national and local support.

4. A pending case in Uganda courts seeks to force carbon reduction to stem global warming. Filed by the environmental organization, Greenwatch, on behalf of local youth plaintiffs against the Ugandan government on September 20, 2012, the complaint invokes a governmental public trust duty under Articles 39 and 237 of the Uganda Constitution to protect the country's atmospheric resources from climate change. Detailing deaths to Ugandan children caused by extreme climate conditions and attributing political unrest over rise in food and fuel prices to government inaction on climate change, the youth plaintiffs seek court orders to compel Ugandan agencies to enforce international climate treaties, conduct an accounting of carbon emissions, develop a climate change mitigation plan, and protect Ugandan youth and children from the harmful impacts of climate change. The suit is part of the international "hatch" of Atmospheric Trust Litigation cases around the world described above in note 3 following the *Metropolitan Manila Development Authority* case. For the complaint and updates, consult http://ourchildrenstrust.org/legal/international/uganda. For further discussion of atmospheric trust litigation, see p. 382.

Waweru v. Republic

High Court at Nairobi, Kenya
1 K.L.R. 677 (2006)

[Appealing a criminal conviction for discharging raw sewage into the Kiserian River, a public water source, in violation of the Public Health Act, Waweru claimed that the prosecution violated his fundamental rights and freedoms because, among other things, the prosecution was discriminatory, and the government gave improper notice, sought sanctions against fewer than one-quarter of the approximately one-hundred dischargers, and the cost of compliance with the waste water requirements was prohibitive. Discussing the environmental obligations of both the residents and the government, the Court agreed that the prosecution failed to give adequate notice and was discriminatory; the Court then took up the public trust doctrine on its own motion.]

* * *

It has been contended by the applicants that they cannot comply with the health requirements concerning the waste water and that the cost of having treatment works in their perspective plots would be out of reach of the individual property owners—and that the costs would be prohibitive. We have been unable to accept this agreement, firstly, because sustainable development has a cost element which must be met by the developers, and secondly, because they have not stated that they have thought of other alternatives which could be more environmentally friendly to deal with the problem.

* * *

As a Court we cannot therefore escape from touching on the law of sustainable development although counsel from both sides chose not to touch on it although to goes to the heart of the matter before us.

* * *

The four principles which we consider directly relevant to the matter at hand are: [(1) sustainable development, (2) the precautionary principle, (3) the polluter pays principle, and (4) the public trust doctrine.]

We shall shortly turn to each of the above principles when we consider the relevance and impact of each on the subject matter of this constitutional matter.

Klaus Topfer, the Executive Director of the United Nation's Environment Programme (UNEP), which is in turn located in our great country, stated in his message to the UNEP Global Judge's Programme 2005, in South Africa:

"The judiciary is also a crucial partner in promoting environmental governance, upholding the rule of law and in ensuring a fair balance between environmental, social and developmental consideration through its judgments and declarations."

Sustainable Development

The Rio Declaration on Environment and Development 1992 adopted the following:

"In order to achieve sustainable development environmental protection shall constitute an integral part of the development process and cannot be considered in isolation from it."

[The] Precautionary Principle

The Rio Declaration adopted this principle in these words:

"In order to protect the environment, the precautionary approach shall be widely applied by States according to their capabilities. Where there are threats of serious or irreversible damage, lack of full scientific certainty shall not be used as a reason for postponing cost-effective measures to prevent environmental degradation."

Under Principle 16, the internationalization of environmental costs and polluter pays principle was adopted as follows:

"National authorities should endeavor to promote the internalization of environmental costs and the use of economic instruments, taking into account the application that the polluter should in principle bear the cost of pollution with due regard to the public interest and without distorting international trade and investment."

Nothing summarizes the concept of sustainable development better than the United Nations World Commission on Environment and Development's 1987 published report *Our Common Future* at 44:

"Development that meets the needs of the present without compromising the ability of future generations to meet their needs."

[The] Public Trust [Doctrine]

The essence of the public trust is that the state, as trustee, is under a fiduciary duty to deal with the trust property, being the common natural resources, in a manner that is in the interests of the general public.

The best example of the application of the principle is in the Pakistan case of *General Secretary West Pakistan Salt Miners Labour Union v. The Director of Industries and Mineral Development*, 1994 s CMR 2061. The case involved residents who were concerned that salt mining in their area would result in the contamination of the local watercourse, reservoir and pipeline. The residents petitioned the Supreme Court of Pakistan to enforce their right to have clean and unpolluted water and filed their claim as a human rights case under Article 184(1) of the Pakistan Constitution.

The Supreme Court held that as Article 9 of the Constitution provided that "no person shall be deprived of life or liberty, save in accordance with the law"; the word "life" should be given expansive definition: the right to have unpolluted water was a right to life itself.

In *Zia v. Wapda PLD*, 1994 SC 693, Justice Saleem Akhtar [of the Rabistan Supreme Court] held as follows:

> The Constitution guarantees dignity of man and also right to "life" under Article 9 and, if both are read together, question will arise whether a person can be said to have dignity of man if his right to life is below bare necessity line without proper food, clothing shelter education, healthcare, clean atmosphere and unpolluted environment.

The Court went on to establish a Commission to supervise and report on the activities of the salt mining for the purpose of protecting the watercourse and reservoirs, hence illustrating the public trust doctrine implicit in the decision.

Definition of life

Concise Oxford English Dictionary, 11th Edition, defines life as ..."the condition that distinguishes animals and plants from inorganic matter, including the capacity for growth, functional activity and continual change preceding death — living things and their activity."

The Kenyan Constitutional provision on the right to life is section 71(1) of the Constitution states[:] "No person shall be deprived of his life intentionally save in execution of the sentence of a court in respect of a criminal offence under the law of Kenya of which he has been convicted."

Whereas the literal meaning of life under section 71 means absence of physical elimination, the dictionary covers the activity of living. That activity takes place in some environment and therefore the denial of wholesome environment is a deprivation of life.

* * *

Summary of Remedies

1. Statutory Remedies and the Public Trust. We accept the applicant's counsel argument that the responsibility to provide a safe sewerage treatment works under the Water Act and the Local Government Act respectively falls on the Water Ministry (i.e., The relevant water services board) and the county council under which the township falls. There is mention of a treatment site having been identified and subsequently suspiciously acquired for private use. To this we find that both the Ministry of Water and the Olkejuado County Council are under statutory duties to find a suitable site for the sewage treatment work for the township. The idea of the Council having been constitutionally mandated to handle trust land and also having the responsibility to deal with matters of public health in its jurisdiction places the Council in a position of public trust to manage the land resources in the township so as to ensure that adequate land is available for treatment works.

We further declare that the government itself is both under a statutory obligation by virtue of the Water Act the Local Government Act and the Environment Management and Coordination Act and also under a public trust to provide adequate land for the establishment of treatment works. We further declare that both the government, through the Water Ministry and under the Local Government Act, is under a statutory obligation to establish the necessary treatment works and since the development of the township has been going on with Government and the Local County Council approval and since the development poses a threat to life we order that a *mandamus* issue under § 84 of the Constitution to compel them to establish and maintain the treatment works. In the case of land resources, forests, wetlands and waterways to give some examples, the government and its agencies are under a public trust to manage them in a way that maintains a proper balance between the economic benefits of development with the needs of a clean environment.

* * *

[The Court proceeded to endorse the concepts of sustainable development and environmental justice.]

* * *

Conclusion

For the above reasons ... the charges [should be] quashed and we further reiterate that an order of *mandamus* shall immediately issue to compel the Ministry of Water — i.e., the Nairobi Water Services Board and the Olkejuado County Council to construct Sewerage Treatment Works.

Notes

1. Notice that the Court read the constitutional right to life (like the Supreme Courts of India and the Philippines) to be a natural law right: "The right to a clean environment is primary to all creatures, including man. It is inherent from the act of creation, the recent restatement in the Statutes and Constitutions of the world notwithstanding." *Waweru v. Republic*, (2006) 1 K.L.R. 677, 687 (Kenya).

2. Although the Court seemed to commingle the public trust doctrine with several environmental principles, including sustainable development, the polluter pays principle, and the precautionary principle, the Court distinguished the trust doctrine in terms of remedies by ruling that both the national and local governments were "also under a public trust to provide adequate land for the establishment of [water] treatment works." The

Court also declared that "[i]n the case of land resources, forests, wetlands, and water-way[s], to give some examples[,] the government and its agencies are under a public trust to manage them in a way that maintains a proper balance between the economic bene-fits of development with the needs of a clean environment."

3. After this decision, Kenya adopted a new constitution in 2010, which expressly in-corporated the public trust doctrine. The constitution retained the "right to life" in Ar-ticle 21 and added a new right to a clean and healthy environment in Article 42, including the right "to have the environment protected for the benefit of present and future gener-ations through legislative and other measures. . . ." Article 69 requires the government "to ensure sustainable exploitation, utilization, management, and conservation of the envi-ronment and natural resources, and ensure the equitable sharing of the accruing bene-fits" for the people of Kenya. Article 62 declares that the national government owns public lands "in trust for the people of Kenya and [they] shall be administered on their behalf by the National Land Commission." Article 69 declares that "[a]ll land in Kenya belongs to the people of Kenya collectively as a nation, as communities and as individuals." Arti-cle 69 also requires the state to eliminate activities likely to endanger the environment, to protect genetic resources and biological diversity, and to maintain tree cover on at least ten percent of the land.

4. On the scope, purposes, public standing, and remedies available under the Kenyan public trust doctrine, see *Internationalizing the Public Trust Doctrine*, cited above, 45 U.C. Davis L. Rev. at 784–86. The Pakistani cases discussed by the *Waweru* Court are exam-ined in *id.* at 766–70. For an overview of the public trust doctrine in countries that have no judicial interpretations but strong constitutional or statutory provisions—including Nigeria, South Africa, Brazil, and Ecuador—see *id.* at 786–801. See also the discussion of Norway's recent constitutional amendment discussed below (p. 359).

5. In Indonesia, the fourth most populous country in the world in 2014, the Consti-tution incorporates the public trust doctrine in two provisions: (1) Article 33(3) ("the land, the waters and the natural resources within shall be under the control of the State and shall be used for the greatest welfare of the people"), adopted in 1945; and (2) Arti-cle 28H(1) ("everyone shall have the right to live prosperous physically and spiritually, settle and enjoy an environment that is sound and healthy"), adopted in 2002. Indone-sia's Constitutional Court has been aggressively interpreting these provisions to preserve public trust rights. For example, in 2004 the court declared the country's Electricity Act unconstitutional largely for authorizing an "unbundling" scheme allowing significant electric privatization because it violated Article 33(3)'s requirement of "state control," which the court interpreted to require "regulating, administering, managing and super-vising to ensure that [the resource] is being used truly for the greatest prosperity of the people." *In re Electrical Power* (Indonesian Const. Ct., Judicial Review of Law Number 20 Year 2002, Case No. 001-021-022/PUU-I/2003, Dec. 15, 2004).

In 2005, the Indonesian court ruled that the 2004 Water Resources Law was only "con-ditionally constitutional" (meaning the statute was constitutional only if implemented consistently with its opinion). The court referred to water as "*res commune*" (common property), interpreting the constitution to impose a trust duty on the government to pre-serve water as a human right and the requirement of "state control" to require government balancing of the primary individual right to water for domestic and small farm uses with secondary purposes, such as for agriculture, energy, and industrial uses. This duty re-quires "active intervention" on the part of the state to ensure a just distribution of water, including preserving water for conservation, developing public drinking water systems, and imposing limits on the amount of water private entities may control. *In re Water Re-*

sources (Indonesian Const. Ct., Judicial Review of Law Number 7 Year 2004, Case Nos. 058-059-060-063/PUU-II/2004 and 008/PUU-III/2005, July 19, 2005).

The court also reviewed two versions of the Indonesian Oil and Gas Act in 2005, striking down provisions of the 2001 Oil and Gas Act giving authority to private enterprises to conduct oil and gas exploration and production and setting a maximum allocation for the domestic market. These clauses violated the constitutional duty of maintaining "state control," and the maximum allocation without a minimum for domestic use also violated the constitution's promise of providing for the "greatest prosperity of the people." *In re Oil & Natural Gas* (Indonesian Const. Ct., Judicial Review of Law Number 22 Year 2001, Case No. 002/PUU-I/2003, Dec. 21, 2004). Then, in 2012, a second decision of the constitutional court invalidated revisions to the Oil and Gas Act which sought to establish a quasi-state authority—BP Migas—to manage oil and gas operations because the constitution demanded "direct state management" of oil and gas, and the scheme would degrade state control through the contracts of BP Migas that the state would be bound to honor. *In re Oil & Natural Gas* (Indonesian Const. Ct., Judicial Review of Law Number 22 Year 2001, Case No. 36/PUU-X/2012, Nov. 13, 2012). For English translations of decisions of the Constitutional Court of the Republic of Indonesia, see http://www.mahkamahkonstitusi.go.id/index.php?page=web.Putusan&id=1 &kat=1 (last visited Feb. 23, 2015; click on "English" in the drop-down list under "Language").

Another interpretation of the Indonesian constitutional public trust doctrine was handed down by a Samarindan trial court in 2014 in a citizen suit filed against the Ministries of Environment and Energy and Mineral Resources and the city Samarinda, challenging a permit to mine coal. The court agreed with the citizens that the coal permit's failure to require reclamation and protect green spaces, farms, and water supplies was a failure to perform the constitutional duty to create a sound and healthy environment. The court ordered a review of all coal mining permits to ensure reclamation and post-mining operations and to protect community farms and fisheries from coal mining pollution. *Komari v. Mayor of Samarinda*, Samarinda Trial Ct. (Putusan No. 55/Ptd.G/2013/PN.Smda., July 24, 2014).

The Public Trust Doctrine, Environmental Human Rights, and the Future of Private Property

David Takacs

16 N.Y.U. Envtl. L.J. 711 (2008)

...Who owns the Earth and its resources? To what extent may the general public claim the pure water, clean air, rich soil, and the myriad services Earth provides to sustain human life? Across continents and spanning centuries, a dynamic tension continues between those who would circumscribe the Earth's bounty for private use and those who would carefully allot Earth's riches to satisfy human needs....

The Public Trust Doctrine perseveres as a value system and an ethic as its expression in law mutates and evolves. More recently, scholars, activists, and lawyers have begun discussing the rights of people to access and enjoy various essential resources and services the Earth so generously yields. The spreading notion of "Environmental Human Rights" expresses the same persistent notion that sometimes, for some resources and in some places, it is immoral and illegal for private parties to arrogate what the Earth provides freely and what is necessary for human health and happiness.

Yet the "Public Trust Doctrine" and "Environmental Human Rights" do not convey precisely the same idea and do not carry the same legal weight in the United States or abroad....I explore how the notion of "Environmental Human Rights" complements and expands the Public Trust Doctrine's legal connotations, which, for 1,500 years, have constrained how Earth's resources can be used and have guided who must bear responsibility for stewarding resources for the public good.

When employed individually, ... the Public Trust Doctrine and Environmental Human Rights may constrain what government officials and private property owners may do. When working together in synergism—as they do in South Africa, India, and elsewhere, as I shall investigate here—they impose new responsibilities on governments to steward the Earth for the benefit of citizens, and they put powerful constraints on what counts as "private," "property," and "ownership"—calling into question what "owners" can do with "their" land.

I. The Public Trust Doctrine

Occasionally law review articles change the world. As one scholar puts it, Joseph Sax's article, *The Public Trust Doctrine in Natural Resource Law: Effective Judicial Intervention*, "represents every law professor's dream: a law review article that not only revived a dormant area of the law but continues to be relied upon by courts some two decades later." This still holds true more than three decades later, including, as I describe below, in India and South Africa. Sax found in the Public Trust Doctrine a legal tool that any citizen could use to fight exploitation of resources that should rightfully be protected common property. [S]ax elucidates the Public Trust Doctrine and lays out a vision for how the doctrine has worked and should work in American jurisprudence.

Three conceptual principles justify the Public Trust Doctrine. First, "certain interests are so intrinsically important to every citizen that their free availability tends to mark the society as one of citizens rather than of serfs." Thus no small subset of individuals should ever be allowed to control these interests. Second, "certain interests are so particularly the gifts of nature's bounty that they ought to be reserved for the whole of the populace." Finally, "certain uses have a peculiarly public nature that makes their adaptation to private use inappropriate."

From these philosophical underpinnings derive further fundamental principles inherent in the Public Trust Doctrine. First, citizens have legally enforceable rights equal in dignity to private property owners. When people talk of a "right to a decent environment," it implies that people have rights "simply by virtue of their status as members of the public and that those rights should be phrased in a way to put them on a plane with traditional private property rights." Sax evokes the Public Trust Doctrine to make what has previously been considered valueless—i.e., resources held for the public good—accrue economic value comparable to that accorded private property....

B. Environmental Human Rights

...I believe recognition of global Environmental Human Rights is trending towards the kind of fundamental rights implied in the Public Trust Doctrine and various constitutions. If this momentum continues—as, I believe, is likely as humans continue to undercut Earth's life support systems—Environmental Human Rights may become absolute rights that create non-derogable duties for all private and public actors....

When the United Nations Sub-Commission on the Promotion and Protection of Human Rights passed a resolution on "Promotion of the realization of the right to drinking water and sanitation," it declared that the right to water is both a separate human right, and is also a necessary corollary to other human rights. Sounding much like a modern day, expanded formulation of the Public Trust Doctrine, the resolution averred that because access to clean water is a fundamental human right, neither public nor private entities could restrict access to drinking water, and public authorities had an affirmative duty to maintain access to drinking water for all citizens.

As in the Public Trust Doctrine, this approach to environmental protection is not about rights of the environment, but rights of humans to various environmental protections. This may include provisions for future generations to enjoy certain rights, or even to ensure the very survival of future generations.... While some biocentric or ecocentric environmental activists may use either the Public Trust Doctrine or Environmental Human Rights to protect ecological assets themselves from human despoliation, both doctrines are fundamentally homocentric....

III. Synthesis and Synergy Between the Public Trust Doctrine and Environmental Human Rights

The Public Trust Doctrine is a forerunner of the movement to guarantee certain environmental rights as fundamental human rights. The Public Trust Doctrine is both an appealing idea that lays the groundwork for Environmental Human Rights, and a venerable legal doctrine that has historically managed to protect certain resources for public use, and may still be called upon to protect those resources in the name of Environmental Human Rights. Justinian's intuition about where the sovereign fit in the relationship between his citizens and his Empire's natural resources finds new, cogent, urgent expression in Environmental Human Rights. In Sax's justification of the Public Trust Doctrine, some public interests in the environment are intrinsically important, the gifts of nature's bounty ought not be constrained for private use, and some uses of nature are intrinsically inappropriate. Those who advocate for Environmental Human Rights cite these same justifications, too. Clean water or clean air or functioning ecosystems are rights because human life cannot exist without them; these gifts of nature's bounty ought not be traded away for the use of private entities at the expense of what is essential to every single human's life.

But I believe that Environmental Human Rights is more than just putting old Public Trust Doctrine wine in gleaming new bottles. Once we label something as a fundamental right or an inviolable right, it is much less likely to come up short in a balancing test. Sax indicates that Public Trust Doctrine "rights" can be traded away, and even constitutionally based rights sometimes can be lost. The more fundamental the right is considered, the more nonderogable are duties to protect those rights, and the heavier the weight of international shaming falls upon the violator. Fulfillment of these rights supervenes any legislation that conflicts with such fulfillment.

Environmental Human Rights create more duties of each individual and the sovereigns who serve them not only not to usurp resources that are the object of these rights, but to affirmatively protect the natural objects and processes that form the basis of the rights. This means greater legislative and executive impetus to protect and advance these rights, and heightened judicial scrutiny when fundamental rights are violated. And Environmental Human Rights dramatically expand the body of plaintiffs, defendants, and intervenors who may vindicate the right or be charged with abridging the right. While the Public Trust Doctrine's reach tends to be limited to the boundaries of a state or nation, Environmental Human Rights reach across national boundaries in terms of who may bring claims against which violators, who may intervene to vindicate those rights, and who can have jurisdiction to hear violations of fundamental rights....

B. South Africa

The constitution of the Republic of South Africa, ratified in 1996 after a long era of brutal, systemic racial oppression, is perhaps the most progressive constitution in the world today in terms of guaranteeing an expansive set of fundamental human rights, and in naming affirmative duties of a government to advance those rights.... [T]he Bill of Rights includes Section 24's explicit, fundamental environmental rights:

> Everyone has the right: a) to an environment that is not harmful to their health or well-being; and b) to have the environment protected, for the benefit of present and future generations, through reasonable legislative and other measures that: i) prevent pollution and ecological degradation; ii) promote conservation; and iii) secure ecologically sustainable development and use of natural resources while promoting justifiable economic and social development.

The constitution further guarantees the right to "sufficient food and water." Just as Supreme Court Justices did in India, South Africa's legislators have reintroduced the Public Trust Doctrine as part of national law, and as such have expanded dramatically the Environmental Human Rights of the public at the expense of individual rights of private property owners.

As separate rights, but also rights used to access other fundamental rights, all South Africans have the rights of "access to information," "just administrative action," and "access to courts." The constitution gives broad standing to anyone to stake a claim when their constitutionally codified rights have been violated....

The case *The Government of the Republic of South Africa v. Irene Grootboom* illustrates the broad reach of these fundamental rights. Desperately poor citizens were able directly to appeal their lack of housing, food, and water — which resulted in a "land invasion" by those attempting to secure basic needs — and the government's abdication of its fundamental duties to provide them with these fundamental rights. The court begins by noting the "harsh reality that the Constitution's promise of dignity and equality for all remains for many a distant dream." Noting that Section 7(2) of the constitution "requires the state 'to respect, protect, promote and fulfill the rights in the Bill of Rights' and the courts are constitutionally bound to ensure that they are protected and fulfilled," the court rules that it is beyond question that all the rights of the constitution are justiciable, and the only question remaining is "how to enforce them in a given case." The court explores "the concept of minimum core obligation" where "each right has a 'minimum essential level' that must be satisfied by the states parties."

The government's obligations to fulfill these rights are manifold. Legislation alone is not enough and must be "supported by appropriate, well-directed policies and programmes," which themselves "must also be reasonably implemented."... The court holds that the government is obliged "to provide access to housing, health-care, sufficient food and water, and social security to those unable to support themselves and their dependants. The state must also foster conditions to enable citizens to gain access to land on an equitable basis." The court appoints the Human Rights Commission, an amicus in the case, to monitor progress in meeting these goals, and to report back on results. While the court acknowledges the "extremely difficult task for the state to meet these obligations in the conditions that prevail in our country," the judge concludes: "I stress, however, that despite all these qualifications, these are rights, and the Constitution obliges the state to give effect to them."...

In 1998, to fulfill its constitutionally mandated affirmative duties to secure the right to water, supported here by the constitutionally mandated rights of "access to information," "just administrative action," and "access to courts," South Africa passed a National Water Act. Decades of racial apartheid left over 10 million South Africans without access to clean, safe water and over 20 million South Africans without adequate sanitation. The National Water Act requires distribution of basic water supplies to fulfill the constitutionally mandated right to water, but also requires the government to fulfill the constitutionally mandated duties to promote conservation and prevent ecological degradation through the mechanism of an environmental "reserve," which conserves water for future human and current nonhuman use.

As part of the National Water Act, in the same year that India's Supreme Court mandated its Public Trust Doctrine, the South African government disinterred its own moribund Public Trust Doctrine, which had been buried through decades of apartheid regimes whose leaders felt no need to act to preserve resources for the majority of the public. The National Government is "the public trustee of the nation's water sources" and must "ensure that water is protected, used, developed, conserved, managed and controlled in a sustainable and equitable manner, for the benefit of all persons and in accordance with its constitutional mandate."

The White Paper that led to the National Water Law prepared the foundation for re-instituting the Public Trust Doctrine. As background, the Paper recites that:

> In Roman law (on which South African law is based) rivers were seen as being resources which belonged to the nation as a whole and were available for common use by all citizens, but which were controlled by the state in the public interest. These principles fitted in well with African customary law which saw water as a common good used in the interest of the community.

The White Paper further proclaims that:

> The recognition of Government's role as custodian of the "public trust" in managing, protecting and determining the proper use of South Africa's water resources ... is a central part of the new approach to water management. As such it will be the foundation of the new water law. The main idea of the public trust is that the national Government has a duty to regulate water use for the benefit of all South Africans, in a way which takes into account the public nature of water resources and the need to make sure that there is fair access to these resources. The central part of this is to make sure that these scarce resources are beneficially used in the public interest.

The White Paper refers to United States court precedents overturning private water rights "on the grounds that water remains subject to the public trust," confirming the development of the public trust as including "the state's duty to protect the people's common heritage of rivers, streams, lakes, marshlands, tidelands and the sea-shore." The authors nonetheless state that "the idea of water as a public good will be redeveloped into a doctrine of public trust which is uniquely South African...." This means, among other things, that riparian allocations will not carry permanent property rights, but will be "time limited" to allow for both the ebbs and flows of natural processes and the "evolving socio-economic demands placed on them." That is to say, the Public Trust Doctrine continues to allow reasonable use by riparians, but that use is always subject to government redistribution schemes. Furthermore, "claims, allocations and uses which are not beneficial in the public interest, have no basis in the common law, nor will they be recognized under the new law." New allocations may be "redressing the results of past racial discrimination."

Thus riparian rights will be reallotted to emphasize uses that help fulfill constitutional mandates for fundamental human rights, serve the public interest, and ameliorate allotments unjustly given during apartheid. When combined with the "Just Administration," expanded standing, and other procedural rights codified in the constitution, the Public Trust Doctrine's "uniquely South African" twist comes close to marrying Joseph Sax's vision of intertwined substantive and procedural rights while curtailing certain property "rights" in water.

The policy adopted by South Africa to deliver "Free Basic Water" to all its citizens is not without problems: allocated amounts are low (25 liters/day), the system is underfinanced, some local governments turn to profit-making corporations to deliver basic services, and despite the fact that local authorities are supposed to be guided by "compassion" in assessing rates, some poor families cannot afford the price. Nonetheless, between the time the constitution was implemented in 1996 and 2002, South Africa managed to provide free basic water supplies to 27 million (of its approximately 44 million) people, and plans to achieve full compliance with their constitutionally mandated duty by providing free basic water to the entire population by 2009.

* * *

Conclusion: The Public Trust Doctrine, Environmental Human Rights, and the Future of Takings and Private Property

While some of our founding fathers saw private property as the key to freedom, the Public Trust Doctrine and Environmental Human Rights suggest freedom requires access to a wide range of ecological assets that ought always to have been in the public realm. They further suggest that property rights spring not from natural law but from positive law, rooted in the will of the people, which allow temporary loans of property "rights" from the sovereign acting in the name of the public good. Benjamin Franklin believed that "Property ... is a Creature of Society, and is subject to the Calls of that Society, whenever its Necessities shall require it...." What the sovereign gives in the name of the people, the sovereign can redefine or revoke when the people's needs change....

Environmental Human Rights, the further they are towards the inviolable rights end of the spectrum, suggest that it does not matter what property owners' expectations were: they have nonderogable duties now that are supreme to any expectations they might have had or laws that might have facilitated those expectations. World consensus—as reflected in national constitutions, international agreements, and the work of legal scholars—is nudging this notion of Environmental Human Rights towards status of fundamental rights, or even inviolable rights....

The Public Trust Doctrine has always reflected a value preference for public over private access to environmental assets. Invoking environmental rights as human rights amplifies the public's right, now and in the future, to share in ecological gifts fundamental to human health and wellbeing. By linking the hoary Public Trust Doctrine to the modern Environmental Human Rights movement, citizens, scholars, and lawyers can promote a world of deeper equity for individuals, communities, and the natural world.

Notes

1. In Professor Takacs' view, how does the human rights approach augment the public trust? Does it help in conceptualizing a priority scheme for water uses? Would it bring a more tangible focus to the rule of *Waiahole Ditch* (a water appropriation case) requiring the trustees to maximize the value of the water asset for the beneficial use of the people? *See Waiahole Ditch* (p. 189) (stating that "the water resources trust also encompasses a duty to promote the reasonable and beneficial use of water resources in order to maximize their social and economic benefits to the people of this state.").

2. Although a modern environmental movement is gaining momentum around the concept of human rights, hasn't human rights always been at the core of the public trust? Wasn't the initial expression of public property rights in Roman times propelled by the people's need to access certain resources for their survival?

3. Does a human rights focus make it easier to portray the public trust doctrine as an attribute of sovereignty embedded in all constitutions that presuppose a government derived from the people? Would the people, as part of the sovereign contract, ever give the power to government to put resources crucial to their survival (such as water) in the hands of private parties who could exploit them with abandon? In South Africa, as Professor Takacs points out, the public trust right to water was enshrined in the nation's constitution. Could courts in other nations find it embedded in constitutions that do not provide specific protection of public water access?

4. As Professor Takacs noted, both Sax's landmark article and a white paper (prepared by the Department of Water Affairs & Forestry) proved quite influential in laying the legal groundwork and providing a vision for how the public trust would apply to water access in South Africa. Sax's article also proved compelling to Indian courts in establishing a public trust doctrine in that country. *See M.C. Mehta v. Kamal Nath*, cited above, p. 333. The white paper is accessible on the web. *See* Dep't of Water Affairs & Forestry, S. Afr., White Paper on a National Water Policy for South Africa ß 2.2.3 (1997), *available at* http://www.dwaf.gov.za/Documents/Policies/nwpwp.pdf.

5. How does a human rights approach respond to the framing of water as a commodity, a problem that Professor Arnold identified in his article excerpted in chapter 5 (p. 208)? Does it respond both on a legal and cultural level? Water expert Maude Barlow has argued for a pairing of the public trust doctrine and human rights thinking to advance the water justice movement world-wide. *See* Maude Barlow, *Advice for Water Warriors*, YES! Magazine (Nov. 8, 2010), http://www.yesmagazine.org/planet/advice-for-water-warriors.

6. In addition to the human rights convergence with the public trust, two other rights-based approaches increasingly intersect with the public trust. One focuses on intergenerational justice, that is, the right of future generations to inherit a sustainable planet. *See* Burns H. Weston, *Climate Change and Intergenerational Justice: Foundational Reflections*, 9 Vt. J. Envtl. L. 375 (2007). This focus is distinguishable from a human rights approach which concentrates on present citizens and their needs.

In 2014, Norway amended its constitution to include the public trust principles of intergenerational justice. The amendment includes the right to a healthful environment for every person, and it extends that right to future generations: "Natural resources should be made use of on the basis of comprehensive long-term considerations whereby this right will be safeguarded for future generations as well." Norway Const., art. 112. Professor Beate Sjåfjell at the University of Oslo has observed, "[t]he provision now clearly stipulates that the state [must] ensure our right and the rights of future generations to a liveable climate and environment." Beate Sjåfjell, *Article 112 of the Constitution Demands Action, Not Words*, Concerned Scientists Norway (Sept. 2014), *available at* http://cs-n.org/2014/09/article-112-of-the-constitution-demands-action-not-words/#more-1058.

The second rights-based approach focuses on Rights of Nature, recognizing the rights of ecosystems to survive and thrive in ecological balance. A growing body of thinking called Earth Jurisprudence develops this approach. *See* Judith E. Koons, *What is Earth Jurisprudence?: Key Principles to Transform Law for the Health of the Planet*, 18 Penn. St. Envtl. L. Rev. 247 (2009). In 2008, Ecuador amended its constitution to provide for nature's rights, declaring, "Natural communities and ecosystems possess the unalienable right to exist, flourish and evolve within Ecuador." *See* Clare Kendall, *A New Law of Nature*, The Guardian (Sept. 24, 2008) (citing the new constitution).

7. Professor Takacs emphasized the central importance of the right to access environmental assets in securing freedoms promised by the public trust doctrine and environmental human rights. He further suggests that the sovereign can redefine or revoke private property rights in the name of the people when need or necessity so requires, those rights having stemmed from the temporary loan of private property "rights" from the sovereign in the first instance.

Consider, in light of this argument, the European "right to wander." In 2000, Britain somewhat surprisingly renounced the absolutism of Blackstonian property (that claimed "sole and despotic" landowner control) and the associated private right to exclude by enacting the Countryside and Rights of Way Act which allowed public access to hike on millions of acres of private "open country," including mountains, moors, and downlands. Private landowners received no compensation for this loss of the right to exclude, which seemed to reverse the effects of three centuries of the enclosure movement of 18th century that resulted in the privatization of a considerable amount of common property and fenced out the public to many areas previously accessible. The new statutory right of public access did not include rights to hunt, log, build fires, or use off-road vehicles. As explained by Professor Anderson,

> The loss of these "roaming" rights seems to have been chafing at Britons ever since [the enclosure movement]. Public discontent with lack of access resulted in celebrated protests, to which Parliament responded with a gradual shift back to greater access. Rather than a radical nationalization of private property rights, then, [the Countryside and Rights of Way Act] can be viewed as an attempt to regain a balance between public and private rights to land that was upset during the enclosure period.

Jerry L. Anderson, *Britain's Right to Roam: Redefining the Landowner's Bundle of Sticks*, 19 Geo. Int'l Envtl. L. Rev. 375, 379 (2007). For a review of the public trust in England and a discussion of the right to wander as a "sister doctrine" of the public trust, see Bradley Freedman & Emily Shirley, *England and the Public Trust Doctrine*, 8 J. Planning & Envtl. L. 839–48 (2014).

In Nordic nations, the right to roam seems well established if not universally codified. In Norway, for example, the public has an historic right of access to uncultivated land in the countryside, including wild-berry foraging, that was eventually codified in 1957 in the Outdoor Recreation Act. Building on coastal land is prohibited within 100 meters of the sea, although exceptions have been made by local authorities, but landowners may not restrict the public's access to the shore. The public has rights to non-motorized recreation on all waters, but hunting and fishing are within the discretion of the freshwater landowner. All activities are subject to government regulation.

In Sweden, the Constitution recognizes a common right to have access to nature, as an "everyman's right" that trumps the private right to exclude, absent crimes, damaging activities, or being otherwise prohibited. The Swedish right to roam also includes a responsibility to preserve the countryside under the maxim of "do not disturb, do not destroy." The "everyman's right" includes rights to access, walk, cycle, ride, ski, camp, and pick wild fauna on any land (but not hunt), including beaches and shorelines—with the exception of private gardens, the immediate vicinity of a dwelling house, land under cultivation, and nature reserves and other protected areas. Swimming in any lake and using an unpowered boat on any waterbody is within the public right unless explicitly forbidden. Fishing, however, is essentially subject to private landowner discretion, except for the biggest five lakes and the seacoast, including the Baltic Sea. *See generally* Swedish Environmental Protection Agency, *The Right of Public Access, available at* http://www.swedish epa.se/Enjoying-nature/The-Right-of-Public-Access/ (last visited Feb. 23, 2015).

Finland recognizes similar public rights: the public may walk, ski, or cycle in the countryside where not harming either the natural environment or the landowner—except in gardens or in the immediate vicinity of private homes. The public has rights to camp temporarily in the countryside (a reasonable distance from homes), pick mineral samples, wild berries, mushrooms and flowers (not protected species). Public waterway rights include the right to fish, recreate, even use a motorboat on waterways (subject to restrictions), as well as to swim or bathe in both inland waters and the sea. The public has the right to walk, ski, and ice fish on frozen lakes, rivers, and the sea. But the public right does not include the right to damage private property; disturb breeding birds, reindeer, or game animals; cut living trees; light fires; or camp in a way that disturbs landowner privacy. The public right is subject to government regulation, especially in natural preserves. *See* Pekka Tuunanen (ed.), *Everyman's Right in Finland, Public Access to the Countryside: Rights & Responsibilities*, Finnish Ministry of the Environment (1999), *available at* http://www.ymparisto.fi/fi-FI.

British Columbia v. Canadian Forest Products Ltd.
Canadian Supreme Court
2 S.C.R. 74 (2004)

[In the wake of the Stone Fire in 1992, which destroyed some 1500 hectares of Crown forest land located in northern British Columbia, including trees in an environmentally sensitive area reserved from logging to protect drinking water and fish habitat and control floods and erosion, the province sued Canadian Forest Products (Canfor), the licensee, in negligence for starting the fire. A lower court held Canfor and the province equally liable, the former for starting the fire, the latter for failing to adequately fight it. The Court of Appeal upheld the finding of contributory negligence on the province's part, but reduced provincial liability to thirty percent. Before the Supreme Court, the province argued that it should be able to recover both for the trees that were in harvestable locations and for trees in the environmental reserve. The Supreme Court agreed with damages for the former, but a majority of the Court refused to award damages for the latter because the province had failed to put forth a coherent theory of damages and had not argued a sovereign (*parens patriae*) claim at the trial. Nevertheless, the Court signaled it was willing to award such damages in a properly pleaded case and discussed the public trust doctrine in the course of its decision on damages.]

The notion that there are public rights in the environment that reside in the Crown has deep roots in the common law: *see, e.g.,* J. C. Maguire, *Fashioning an Equitable Vision for Public Resource Protection and Development in Canada: The Public Trust Doctrine Revisited and Reconceptualized*, 7 J.E.L.P. 1 (1997). Indeed, the notion of "public rights" existed in Roman law:

> By the law of nature these things are common to mankind—the air, running water, the sea. . . .

The Institutes of Justinian (1876), Book II, Title I, at p. 158.

A similar notion persisted in European legal systems. According to the French *Civil Code*, art. 538, there was common property in navigable rivers and streams, beaches, ports, and harbours. A similar set of ideas was put forward by H. de Bracton in his treatise on English law in the mid-13th century:

By natural law these are common to all: running water, air, the sea and the shores of the sea.... No one therefore is forbidden access to the seashore.... All rivers and ports are public, so that the right to fish therein is common to all persons. The use of river banks, as of the river itself, is also public by the *jus gentium*....

Bracton on the Laws and Customs of England (1968), vol. 2, at pp. 39–40.

By legal convention, ownership of such public rights was vested in the Crown, as too did authority to enforce public rights of use. According to de Bracton, cited above, at pp. 166–67:

[It is the lord king] himself who has ordinary jurisdiction and power over all who are within his realm.... He also has, in preference to all others in his realm, privileges by virtue of the *jus gentium*. (By the *jus gentium*) things are his ... which by natural law ought to be common to all.... Those concerned with jurisdiction and the peace ... belong to no one save the crown alone and the royal dignity, nor can they be separated from the crown, since they constitute the crown.

Since the time of de Bracton it has been the case that public rights and jurisdiction over these cannot be separated from the Crown. This notion of the Crown as holder of inalienable "public rights" in the environment and certain common resources was accompanied by the procedural right of the Attorney General to sue for their protection representing the Crown as *parens patriae*. This is an important jurisdiction that should not be attenuated by a narrow judicial construction.

* * *

The American law has also developed the notion that the states hold a "public trust." Thus, in *Illinois Central Railroad Co. v. Illinois*, 146 U.S. 387 (1892), the Supreme Court of the United States upheld Illinois' claim to have a land grant declared invalid. The state had granted to the railroad in fee simple all land extending out one mile from Lake Michigan's shoreline, including one mile of shoreline through Chicago's central business district. It was held that this land was impressed with a public trust. The State's title to this land was

different in character from that which the State holds in lands intended for sale ... It is a title held in trust for the people of the State that they may enjoy the navigation of the waters, carry on commerce over them, and have liberty of fishing therein freed from the obstruction or interference of private parties.

Id. at 452. The deed to the railway was therefore set aside.

The *parens patriae* and "public trust" doctrines have led in the United States to successful claims for monetary compensation. Thus, in *New Jersey, Department of Environmental Protection v. Jersey Central Power & Light Co.*, 336 A.2d 750, 759 (N.J. Super. Ct. App. Div. 1975), the state sued a power plant operator for a fish kill in tidal waters caused by negligent pumping that caused a temperature variation in the fish habitat. The state sought compensatory damages for the harm to public resources. The court concluded that the state had the "right and the fiduciary duty to seek damages for the destruction of wildlife which are part of the public trust" in "compensation for any diminution in that [public] trust corpus," noting that:

It seems to us that absent some special interest in some private citizen, it is questionable whether anyone but the state can be considered the proper party to sue for recovery of damages to the environment.[2]

---

2. *Ed.'s note*: This decision of the New Jersey Court of Appeals was overruled by the New Jersey Supreme Court because the plaintiffs had failed to establish causation in their claim for damages for fish kills due to the discharge of high temperature water by the power company. *State Dep't of Envtl. Prot. v. Jersey Cent. Power & Light Co.*, 351 A.2d 337 (1976). The state supreme court also held that

See also State of Washington, Department of Fisheries v. Gillette, 621 P.2d 764 (Wash. Ct. App. 1980), and *State of California, Department of Fish & Game v. S.S. Bournemouth*, 307 F. Supp. 922 (C.D. Cal. 1969). The potential availability of damages in *parens patriae* and "public trust" environmental actions has also been affirmed in *State of Maine v. M/V Tamano*, 357 F. Supp. 1097 (D. Me. 1973), and *Maryland Department of Natural Resources v. Amerada Hess Corp.*, 350 F. Supp. 1060 (D. Md. 1972). These were all cases decided under the common law, not *CERCLA*.

Notes

1. The Court used the public trust doctrine to rule that the provincial Attorney General has the authority to sue for damages to public trust resources, like forests. The Court did not address the rights of the public to take action against inaction on the part of the Attorney General. But see note 3, below.

2. In *Labrador Inuit Ass'n v. Newfoundland*, 155 Nfld. & P.E.I.R. 93 (Can. 1997), the Newfoundland Court of Appeal reversed a lower court decision and required an environmental assessment on a government approval of a mining project. The court indicated that trust principles would inform its review of the implementation of the assessment requirements:

> If the rights of future generations to the protection of the present integrity of the natural world are to be taken seriously, and not to be regarded as mere empty rhetoric, care must be taken in the interpretation and application. Environmental laws must be construed against their commitment to future generations and against a recognition that, in addressing environmental issues, we often have imperfect knowledge as to the potential impact of activities on the environment.

Id. at para. 11.

3. In 2005, a Prince Edward Island trial court refused to dismiss a breach of public trust claim brought by the province against the federal Minister of Fisheries and Oceans concerning a failure to maintain a common right to fish in Atlantic fisheries. The court cited the Supreme Court's *Canfor* decision and explained that if the government can sue "as guardian of the public interest to claim against party causing damage to that public interest, then it would seem in another case [that] a beneficiary of the public interest ought to be able to claim against the government for a failure to properly protect the public interest … [because] a right gives a corresponding duty." *Prince Edward Island v. Canada Minister of Fisheries & Oceans*, 256 Nfld. & P.E.I.R 343 (Can. 2005) para. 6.

4. On the scope, purposes, public standing and remedies available under the Canadian public trust doctrine, see *Internationalizing the Public Trust Doctrine*, 45 U.C. Davis L. Rev. at 805–07. For more detail on the Canadian public trust doctrine, see the following articles, all by Andrew Gage: *Highways, Parks, and the Public Trust Doctrine*, 18 J. Envtl. L. & Prac. 1 (2007); *Public Rights and the Lost Principle of Statutory Construction*, 15 J. Envtl. L. & Prac. 107 (2005); and *Public Environmental Rights: A New Environmental Paradigm for Environmental Law?*, Continuing Legal Educ. Soc'y of B.C. 1 (2007).

---

the state could not seek damages because the federal statute preempted claims under both *parens patriae* and the public trust. *Id.* at 342 ("[A] finding of nonliability for Jersey Central is also dictated because of federal preemption.... [T]he assertion of damages by the State either as Parens patriae or public trustee are not permissible under the circumstances because of infringement upon and conflict with a subject matter over which Congress has vested exclusive jurisdiction in the [Atomic Energy Commission].").

5. The public trust finds expression in the laws of other countries beyond those explored in this chapter. For discussion, see Ved P. Nanda & William K. Ris, Jr., *The Public Trust Doctrine: A Viable Approach to International Environmental Protection*, 5 Ecology L. Q. 291, 304–06 (1976) (describing public use protections over resources in France, Mexico, Canada, England, some African nations, and New Zealand, and contrasting the nature of wildlife ownership between Eastern and Western European countries); Mary Turnipseed et al., *Reinvigorating the Public Trust Doctrine: Expert Opinion on the Potential of a Public Trust Mandate in U.S. and International Environmental Law*, Env't Mag. 6 (Sept.–Oct. 2010) (observing that public trust protections exist in Ecuador, Mexico, Australia, Eritrea, Sri Lanka, and Tanzania, in addition to the nations discussed above throughout this chapter).

Chapter 11

The Global Public Trust and Co-Trustee Management

Most of the American cases litigated under the public trust concern resources within one sovereign's jurisdiction. Assets like tidelands, wetlands, and parks typically fall under the jurisdiction of one state. But many public trust assets are trans-boundary in nature, with multiple sovereigns both managing them and claiming beneficial use rights to them. Consider the Columbia River salmon fishery, which migrates between three inland states, as well as several Indian reservations, and travels to ocean waters off the coasts of Alaska and Canada. And consider the Great Lakes, which border several U.S. states as well as Canada; and the Amazon Basin, spanning several nations in South America. What about the Earth's atmosphere, shared among all nations across the globe? As a fundamental doctrine of property law, does the public trust provide a framework for assigning reciprocal responsibilities towards shared assets that cross boundaries?

Many of the most urgent global issues, such as climate crisis, ocean acidification, and species extinction remain unresolved by international treaty processes. Can such planetary assets be subject to the public trust? Given that so many nations in the world recognize a public trust (see chapter 10), can a fiduciary obligation towards these assets find enforcement in domestic courts throughout the world? Many scholars are asking these questions and developing trust models of international obligation. This chapter explores the PTD as it can apply to shared sovereign assets. It begins with an analysis of co-trustees, then turns to scholarship characterizing a planetary trust. The last two sections explore the trust as applied to climate crisis and ocean health.

A. Co-Tenant Trustees

Advancing the Sovereign Trust of Government to Safeguard the Environment for Present and Future Generations (Part I): Ecological Realism and the Need for a Paradigm Shift
Mary Christina Wood
39 Envtl. L. 43 (2009)

* * *

VI. The Role of Sovereigns as Cotenant Trustees over Shared Assets

A. The Sovereign Cotenancy

Some assets, like oceans, air, some rivers, and many types of wildlife, are transboundary in nature, crossing several jurisdictions. An inherent limitation of statutory law is its confinement to jurisdictional boundaries. A notable strength of the trust doctrine's property framework is that it creates logical rights to shared assets that are not confined within any one jurisdictional border. It is well established that, with respect to transboundary trust assets, all sovereigns with jurisdiction over the natural territory of the asset have legitimate property claims to the resource. States that share a waterway, for example, have correlative rights to the water. Similarly, states and tribes have coexisting property rights to share in the harvest of fish passing through their borders.

Such shared interests are best described as a sovereign cotenancy. A cotenancy is "a tenancy under more than one distinct title, but with unity of possession." The Ninth Circuit Court of Appeals has invoked the cotenancy model to describe shared sovereign rights to migrating salmon. *Puget Sound Gillnetters Ass'n v. U.S. Dist. Court*, 573 F.2d 1123 (9th Cir. 1978).

Within the United States, layered sovereign interests in natural resources arise from the constitutional configuration of states and the federal government. Where the federal government has a national interest in the resource, it is a cotrustee along with the states. The concurrence of federal and state trust interests is reflected in statutory provisions that provide natural resource damages to both sovereign trustees. As one court has made clear in the context of streambed ownership, the federal government and states are held to identical trust obligations, but must carry them out in accordance with their unique constitutional roles. *United States v. 1.58 Acres of Land*, 523 F. Supp. 120, 123 (1981).

B. The Cotenant's Duty Not to Waste the Asset

Cotenants have duties toward the asset and towards one another. One tenant cannot appropriate the property of the other tenant by destroying the property to which both are equally entitled. They stand in a fiduciary relationship towards one another and share the obligation not to waste the common asset. Waste is the impairment of property so as to destroy permanently its value to the detriment of the cotenants. Whether applied to a shared fishery, a transboundary waterway, or the Earth's atmosphere, the prohibition against waste is an important footing in the foundation of organized society.

United States case law clearly prioritizes the duty to prevent waste over the economic ambition of individual sovereigns. The Ninth Circuit declared the sovereign cotenant duty in a treaty fishing dispute between states and tribes:

> Cotenants stand in a fiduciary relationship one to the other. Each has the right to full enjoyment of the property, but must use it as a reasonable property owner. A cotenant is liable for waste if he destroys the property or abuses it so as to permanently impair its value.... By analogy, neither the treaty Indians nor the state on behalf of its citizens may permit the subject matter of these treaties to be destroyed. *United States v. Washington*, 520 F.2d 676, 685 (9th Cir. 1975).

In addition to the duty against waste, a corollary duty requires each tenant to pay his share of the expenses proportionate to his interest in the property. These principles form a conceptual framework for assigning ecological responsibility to sovereigns sharing a natural resource. They have potentially forceful bearing in the international context, because they imply an organic obligation incumbent on each government that shares in the natural asset.

C. The Global Atmospheric Trust

Extrapolating from classic principles of sovereign trust law, the atmosphere can be characterized as a global asset belonging to all nations on Earth. The trust construct positions all such nations as sovereign cotenant trustees of this shared atmosphere. In addition to a fiduciary obligation owed to their own citizens to protect the atmosphere, all nations have duties to prevent waste arising from their cotenancy relationship with one another. Citizens and courts are positioned to define these duties by tying them directly to scientific prescriptions for carbon reduction. This approach is quite opposite from the diplomatic stance taken by the United States in the climate arena—namely, that carbon reduction is a political choice.

Notes

1. Note that the article suggested three reinforcing duties and roles for sovereigns vis-à-vis transboundary assets. First, the sovereign acts as a trustee of resources with fiduciary duties towards its own citizens. Second, the sovereign is a co-tenant with other sovereigns that share the asset; each has a duty to prevent "waste" to the shared asset, which equates to a duty of protection. And third, shared interests in a trust position the sovereigns as co-trustees as well, sharing fiduciary duties towards the asset as a whole.

2. How can a property-based framework of sovereign co-tenant trusteeship add to existing international law? Does it provide an enforcement lever that international law lacks because there is no super-jurisdiction on the global level? Could courts draw normative standards of care (the duty of protection and the duty against waste) towards a global asset and enforce them domestically as a matter of property law? Could such domestic enforcement of global fiduciary standards provide the missing link in international law? Will any international treaty promises of protection be worth anything without such domestic enforcement? What factors currently impair courts in the enforcement of international treaties?

3. The article identified three sovereigns in the U.S. that stand as co-tenant trustees of shared resources: states, tribes, and the federal government. Note that the federal role ranks paramount in global disputes. The case below defines that role within the framework of the public trust.

United States v. 1.58 Acres of Land

U.S. District Court, Massachusetts
523 F. Supp. 120 (1981)

[The federal government condemned state-owned submerged land in Boston Harbor to redevelop a Coast Guard support center. The state challenged the taking on grounds that the federal government could thereafter convey the trust land to private parties, and thereby destroy the trust.]

GARRITY, J.:

The issue is whether or not the United States may take a full fee simple title to land below the low water mark without destroying the perpetual public trust impressed upon that land. If it cannot, then serious constitutional and statutory questions are raised concerning the power of the federal government to destroy forever an important aspect of the Commonwealth's sovereignty. We hold, however, that the United States may obtain full fee simple title to land below the low water mark without destroying the public trust which is administered by both the federal and state sovereigns.

Public trust theory has its roots in the Roman law. For centuries, land below the low water mark has been recognized as having a peculiar nature, subject to varying degrees of public demand for rights of navigation, passage, portage, commerce, fishing, recreation, conservation and aesthetics. *See* Note, *The Public Trust in Tidal Areas: A Sometime Submerged Traditional Doctrine*, 79 Yale L.J. 762, 777–78 (1970). Historically, no developed western civilization has recognized absolute rights of private ownership in such land as a means of allocating this scarce and precious resource among the competing public demands. Though private ownership was permitted in the Dark Ages, neither Roman Law nor the English common law as it developed after the signing of the Magna Carta would permit it. *Bost. Waterfront Dev. Corp. v. Commonwealth*, 393 N.E.2d 356 (Mass. 1979); Note, *supra*, at 772–74. The common law held that rights to property below the high water mark were divided into two categories: "a proprietary *jus privatum*, or ownership interest, and a governmental *jus publicum*, by which the king held the land in his sovereign capacity as a representative of all the people." *Bost. Waterfront Dev. Corp.*, 393 N.E. at 358; *see Shively v. Bowlby*, 152 U.S. 1, 11–14 (1894). The king could convey the *jus privatum*, but could not convey the *jus publicum* because this interest was held in trust for all the people. Since Parliament eventually took control of the *jus publicum*, while the king retained the *jus privatum*, neither could convey a free and clear title to a private individual. *Bost. Waterfront Dev. Corp.*, 393 N.E. at 358; *see Martin v. Waddell*, 41 U.S. (16 Pet.) 367, 410 (1842).

The division of public rights and private rights in tideland and land below the low water mark continued in this country by virtue of the adoption of the English common law. However, our federal system of dual sovereignty has required a number of modifications of the common law public trust theory. In 1892, the United States Supreme Court explained the status of the doctrine:

> It is the settled law of this country that the ownership of and dominion and sovereignty over lands covered by tide waters, within the limits of the several States, belong to the respective States within which they are found, with the consequent right to use or dispose of any portion thereof when that can be done without substantial impairment of the interest of the public in the waters, and subject always to the paramount right of Congress to control their navigation so far as may be necessary for the regulation of commerce with foreign nations and among the States.

Ill. Cent. R.R. v. Illinois, 146 U.S. 387, 435 (1892). This formulation recognizes the division of sovereignty between the state and federal governments [of] those aspects of the public interest in the tideland and the land below the low water mark that relate to the commerce and other powers delegated to the federal government [and] are administered by Congress in its capacity as trustee of the *jus publicum*,[1] while those aspects of the public interest in this property that relate to nonpreempted subjects reserved to local regulation by the states are administered by state legislatures in their capacity as co-trustee of the *jus publicum*.

The problems that have arisen by the administration of the *jus publicum* in our system of dual sovereignty must further account for the supremacy of the federal government over those matters within its powers.[2]

---

1. "The United States holds (such) resources ... in trust for its citizens in one sense, but not in the sense that a private trustee holds for a *cestui que* trust. The responsibility of Congress is to utilize the assets that come into the hands of the sovereign in the way that it decides is best for the Nation." *Alabama v. Texas*, 347 U.S. 272, 277 (1953) (Black, J., dissenting).

2. An explicit power of the federal government found in the commerce clause of the Constitution is its dominant navigational servitude. "The power to regulate commerce comprehends the control for that purpose, and to the extent necessary, of all the navigable waters of the United States.... For this purpose they are the public property of the nation, and subject to all the requisite legislation by Congress." *United States v. Rands*, 389 U.S. 121, 122–23 (1967) *citing Gilman v. Philadelphia*, 3 Wall. 713, 724–25 (1866).

* * *

Neither the federal government nor the state may convey land below the low water mark to private individuals free of the sovereign's *jus publicum*. Moreover, the state's administration of the public trust is subject to the paramount rights of the federal government to administer its trust with respect to matters within the federal power. The trust is of such a nature that it can be held only by the sovereign, and can only be destroyed by the destruction of the sovereign.

> The trust devolving upon the State (or the federal government) for the public, and which can only be discharged by the management and control of the property in which the public has an interest, cannot be relinquished by a transfer of the property. The control of the State for the purposes of the trust can never be lost.... The State can no more abdicate its trust over property in which the whole people are interested, like navigable waters and soils under them, so as to leave them entirely under the use and control of private parties.... than it can abdicate its police powers in the administration of government and the preservation of the peace.

Ill. Cent. R.R., 146 U.S. at 452–53. Since the trust impressed upon this property is governmental and administered jointly by the state and federal governments by virtue of their sovereignty, neither sovereign may alienate this land free and clear of the public trust. When the federal government takes such property by eminent domain, however, the federal government obtains the fullest fee that may be had in land of this peculiar nature: the jus privatum and the federal government's paramount jus publicum.

Therefore we hold that the federal government may take property below the low water mark in "full fee simple" insofar as no other principal may hold a greater right to such land. It must be recognized, however, that the federal government is as restricted as the Commonwealth in its ability to abdicate to private individuals its sovereign *jus publicum* in the land. So restricted, neither the Commonwealth's nor the federal government's trust responsibilities are destroyed by virtue of this taking, since neither government has the power to destroy the trust or to destroy the other sovereign.

Notes

1. The case above represents, to date, the most considered analysis of the federal co-trustee obligation. Where does it locate the federal public trust obligation? Is this duty lodged in the constitution? Does it pre-date the federal constitution? Revisit the *Robinson Township* plurality opinion (p. 82). Recall that Justice Castille lodged the trust in the basic rights retained by citizens. Wouldn't these rights hold against the federal government as well as the state governments?

In *United States v. 11.037 Acres of Land*, 685 F. Supp. 214 (N.D. Cal. 1988), a federal district court held that when the federal government condemned state tidelands held in trust, it extinguished California's public trust easement. The court declined to follow *1.58 Acres of Land* because it reasoned that the state's public trust easement could not bind the federal government under the Supremacy Clause of the Constitution. But didn't the *1.58 Acres of Land* court acknowledge the Supremacy Clause and describe the public trust in the context of federalism? Rather than holding that the federal government was subservient to the state, it held that the federal government was, as a sovereign, bound by its own public trust obligation.

2. The Department of Justice, representing the federal government, resists mightily any public trust duty in litigation. Why? One of the cases frequently cited in federal briefs is *District of Columbia v. Air Florida, Inc.*, 750 F.2d 1077 (D.C. Cir. 1984), where the court refused to address the question of a federal trust. In that case, the District of Columbia sued an airline for response costs necessitated by the crash of an airline into the Potomac River. On appeal, the District asserted a new theory of recovery based on the public trust, asserting that the federal government's trust duty had been delegated to the District, and that "Air Florida owed the city a duty of care regarding the river which was breached by the crash." *Id.* at 1078. The court refused to address the viability of the District's theory, stating:

> We decline to consider in this case whether the public trust doctrine provides a basis for Air Florida's liability. The District neither made any allegations in its complaint that it was surrogate trustee for the Potomac or that the public trust doctrine was in any way implicated in this case, nor did it raise this theory in its memoranda or arguments before the District Court.... [T]he trial judge surely had no obligation to create, unaided by the plaintiff, a new legal theory in order to support the city's complaint.... Our decision not to consider the District's public trust claim is reinforced by our belief that the argument that public trust duties pertain to federal navigable waters, such as the section of the Potomac River at issue here, raises a number of very difficult issues concerning the rights and obligations of the United States (which is not a party here), the creation of federal common law, and the delegation of trust duties to the District. We would prefer to have the benefit of a complete trial record, including the District Court's thinking on these questions, before reaching such novel issues on appeal; we therefore leave the resolution of these issues to another day and another case.

Id. at 1078–79. In another part of the opinion, the court provided background on the PTD, noting that it has developed "almost exclusively as a matter of state law" without "parallel development of the doctrine as it pertains to federally-owned waterbeds, such as the portion of the Potomac...." *Id.* at 1082–83. Accordingly, it concluded:

> We emphasize that we imply no opinion regarding either the applicability of the public trust doctrine to the federal government or the appropriateness of using the doctrine to afford trustees a means for recovering from tortfeasors the cost of restoring public waters to their pre-injury condition. Our point is simply that, given the paucity of relevant precedent and the lack of pleadings referring to the doctrine, the District Court could not have been expected to ponder *sua sponte*: 1) whether common-law public trust duties apply to the federal government; 2) whether these duties regarding the Potomac have been implicitly delegated by Congress to the District; and 3) whether the public trust doctrine provides a trustee in the District's position with a basis for recovery.

Id. at 1084.

Given the clear refusal of the court to address the applicability of the public trust to the federal government, can this case be taken as precedent that there is no federal duty? Wasn't the court taking pains to say it did not decide the issue?

3. In an atmospheric trust litigation case against the federal government, *Alec L.* ex rel. *Loorz v. McCarthy*, 561 Fed. App'x 7 (D.C. Cir. 2014), *cert denied* No. 14-405, 2014 WL 6860603 (discussed more in section C, below, p. 389), the D.C. Circuit held that there was no constitutionally based federal public trust. For this proposition it cited Justice Kennedy's dicta in *PPL Montana v. Montana*, 132 S. Ct. 1215 (2012) (p. 82), in which

Justice Kennedy referred to the doctrine as a state law doctrine. Justice Kennedy did not explain his conclusory statement, as the case did not present the question of whether there was a federal trust. Couldn't there be both a state-based doctrine (or actually, 50 such doctrines), and also a federal doctrine? Don't other countries recognize trust principles limiting the power of their national governments? See chapter 10. For an analysis calling for a rejection of the D.C. Circuit's interpretation of Justice Kennedy's statement, see Michael C. Blumm & Lynn Schaffer, *The Federal Public Trust Doctrine: Misinterpreting Justice Kennedy and* Illinois Central Railroad, 45 Envtl. L. (forthcoming 2015), *available at* http://ssrn.com/abstract=2554614.

4. Interestingly, in the past, attorneys for the federal government clearly recognized a universal trust obligation to protect global assets. At the end of the 19th century, U.S. officials asserted the trust obligation in a dispute over seal hunting brought before an international tribunal of arbitration. Condemning the overconsumption of Earth's resources, the legal brief of the United States to an international arbitration panel stated:

> The earth was designed as the permanent abode of man through ceaseless generations. Each generation, as it appears upon the scene, is entitled only to use the fair inheritance. It is against the law of nature that any waste should be committed to the disadvantage of the succeeding tenants.... That one generation may not only consume or destroy the annual increase of the products of the earth, but the stock also, thus leaving an inadequate provision for the multitude of successors which it brings into life, is a notion so repugnant to reason as scarcely to need formal refutation.

Argument of the United States, *Fur Seal Arbitration* (U.S. v. Gr. Brit. 1893), *reprinted in* 9 Fur Seal Arbitration: Proceedings of the Tribunal of Arbitration (Gov't Printing Office 1895); also reprinted in 1 John Bassett Moore, History & Digest of the International Arbitrations to Which the United States Has Been a Party 755, 813–14 (1898).

5. Do statehood acts represent a potential federal law basis for enforcing the public trust? Many of these state enabling acts explicitly declared protections for public access to waterways. States formed out of the former Northwest Territory apparently remain subject to the Northwest Ordinance of 1787, which provided that navigable waterways flowing into either the Mississippi or St. Lawrence Rivers, together with portage routes between such rivers, "shall be common highways, and forever free." 1 Stat. 51, 52 note (1789), *re-enacted at* 1 Stat. 51 (1789). According to the chief interpretive decision, *Economy Light & Power Co. v. United States*, 256 U.S. 113, 122 (1921), the Northwest Ordinance remains valid and in effect to the extent that "it established public rights of highway in navigable waters." Supreme Court rulings from the 1880s and early 1890s curtailed the Ordinance to the extent needed for states to authorize bridges and waterway improvements, but with respect to the public rights of highway in navigable waters, the Ordinance remained supreme: the Court declared the Ordinance was "no more capable of repeal by one of the states than any other regulation of interstate commerce enacted by the Congress." *Id.*

Can federal statutes also provide a legal basis for enforcement of the federal public trust? For example, the Rivers & Harbors Act, 33 U.S.C. §403, banned all obstructions of navigable waters except those permitted by federal law. Doesn't this statute reflect a legislative embodiment of the promise of public highways? What about other modern statutes that expressly recognize the trust responsibility of the federal government? For example, the National Environmental Policy Act (NEPA) declares a federal duty to "fulfill the responsibilities of each generation as trustee of the environment for succeeding generations." 42 U.S.C. §4331(b)(1).

Assuming the continued existence of a federal public trust that protects public access to navigable waters, how should clashes between state and federal interpretations be resolved? Two contemporaneous rulings from Georgia illustrate such a divergence. Under Georgia state law, only the largest waterways, capable of floating large commercial barges, are available for public use under Georgia law. See *Givens v. Ichauway*, 493 S.E.2d 148 (Ga. 1997). But according to a federal court, a whitewater river in Georgia with rapids, rocks, and shifting currents usable by kayaks after rains was open to the public as a matter of federal law under the navigation servitude. *Atlanta Sch. of Kayaking, Inc. v. Douglasville-Douglas-County Water & Sewer Auth.*, 981 F. Supp. 1469 (N.D. Ga. 1997).

In re Steuart Transportation Company
U.S. District Court, Eastern District of Virginia
495 F. Supp. 38 (1980)

CLARKE, DISTRICT J.

This matter is before the Court on the motion for summary judgment filed by Steuart Transportation Company (hereinafter referred to as "Steuart"). The Commonwealth of Virginia (hereinafter "the Commonwealth") and the Federal Government have each filed claims for damage to migratory waterfowl, statutory penalties, and cleanup costs against Steuart, all arising from an oil spill in the Chesapeake Bay on February 2, 1976. Approximately 30,000 migratory birds allegedly were destroyed as a result of the oil spill. The sole issue to be determined on this motion for summary judgment is whether the Commonwealth and/or the Federal Government have a right to sue for the loss of migratory waterfowl.

Steuart contends that neither government can maintain the action because they do not "own" the birds. Essentially, Steuart argues that to recover money damages for the loss of property one must establish an ownership interest, and that the Supreme Court of the United States, over the years, has concluded that neither the state nor the Federal Government has an ownership interest in migratory waterfowl. The seminal case is *Missouri v. Holland*, 252 U.S. 416 (1920), in which Justice Holmes, writing for the Court, rejected the State of Missouri's attack on the Migratory Bird Treaty Act. The State contended that the Act interfered with the State's control over wild animals within its boundaries.

The Commonwealth and the United States, on the other hand, maintain that their right to recover for the loss of migratory waterfowl does not depend upon ownership, as Steuart contends, but upon the sovereign right to protect the public interest in preserving wildlife resources. This sovereign right derives from two theories: (1) the public trust doctrine, and/or (2) the doctrine of *parens patria*.

This Court agrees with Steuart's position that the State of Virginia does not "own" the migratory waterfowl in question. The authority in support of this position is clear and voluminous. *See, e.g., Baldwin v. Fish & Game Comm'n of Mont.*, 436 U.S. 371 (1978); *Douglas v. Seacoast Products, Inc.*, 431 U.S. 265 (1977); *Toomer v. Witsell*, 334 U.S. 385 (1948); *Missouri v. Holland*, 252 U.S. 416 (1920). However, many of the cases refuting a state's claim to ownership of resources turned upon principles of federalism and pre-emption by federal legislation of state control measures. Neither of these principles is applicable to the current issue before this Court.

Rather, the State of Virginia and the United States do not seek recovery for the value of the waterfowl based upon a claimed ownership interest. These governments seek recovery under either, or both, the public trust doctrine and the doctrine of *parens patria*. This Court is of the opinion that both of these doctrines are viable and support the State and the Federal claims for the waterfowl.

Under the public trust doctrine, the State of Virginia and the United States have the right and the duty to protect and preserve the public's interest in natural wildlife resources. Such right does not derive from ownership of the resources but from a duty owing to the people. *See, e.g., Toomer v. Witsell*, 334 U.S. 385, 408 (1948) (upholding state's right "to conserve or utilize its resources on behalf of its own citizens"). Likewise, under the doctrine of *parens patria*, the state acts to protect a quasi-sovereign interest where no individual cause of action would lie. *See, e.g., Hawaii v. Standard Oil Co.*, 301 F. Supp. 982 (D. Haw. 1969), *rev'd on other grounds*, 431 F.2d 1282 (9th Cir. 1970), *aff'd*, 405 U.S. 251 (1972). In the case currently before this Court, no individual citizen could seek recovery for the waterfowl, and the state certainly has a sovereign interest in preserving wildlife resources.

Accordingly, the Court DENIES Steuart's motion for summary judgment.

Notes

1. The decision upheld a right of the U.S. federal government, acting as a public trustee, to recover for damages to the wildlife asset. Since the state also has a trust responsibility for wildlife and can recover for damages, what role does the federal government have? In 1989, the federal district court of Nebraska similarly concluded that the federal government has a responsibility to protect natural resources on public lands, citing both *Steuart Transportation* and *1.58 Acres of Land*. In a federal action to recover damages for wildlife destroyed in a fire on public lands, the district court held that the United States could maintain an action to recover for damages to its resources under the public trust doctrine, recognizing that the trust extends beyond its traditional applications:

> [A]lthough the defendant correctly notes that the public trust doctrine has traditionally been asserted by the States, the doctrine has also been applied to the Federal Government.... Although the public trust doctrine traditionally applied to tidalwaters and the land submerged beneath them, the concept of the United States holding its land in trust for the general population has been extant for quite some time. For example, in *United States v. Beebe*, 127 U.S. 338 (1888), in an action to set aside and cancel certain land patents, the Supreme Court noted that the "public domain is held by the Government as part of its trust. The Government is charged with the duty and clothed with the power to protect it from trespass and unlawful appropriation...."

United States v. Burlington N.R. Co., 710 F. Supp. 1286, 1287 (D. Neb. 1989).

Does the federal sovereign trust interest outweigh the states' interest on the international level for wildlife that migrate between national boundaries? In these international settings, the states cannot play any role, due to the supremacy of the federal government in the international realm. U.S. Const. art. II, § 2 (conferring treaty power on the federal government). Is this what the court in *1.58 Acres of Land* was observing when it said, "the administration of the *jus publicum* in our system of dual sovereignty must further account for the supremacy of the federal government over those matters within its powers"? Without a recognized federal sovereign interest in global trust assets, would the U.S. government be able to assert any interest on behalf of its citizens in species that migrate between borders, or in international waterways, or in the atmosphere itself? Without a national property interest, would the federal government have any standing in international treaty negotiations? Without such an interest, would the federal government be acting *ultra vires* in conducting such negotiations?

2. The co-trustee role of the federal and state governments in the context of wildlife was explained in Mary Christina Wood, *The Tribal Property Right to Wildlife Capital (Part*

I): Applying Principles of Sovereignty to Protect Imperiled Wildlife Populations, 37 Idaho L. Rev. 1, 73–76 (2000):

> [T]he trusteeship is shaped by the form of the government that holds it. Within the United States, the federal, tribal, and state sovereigns seemingly all enjoy a sovereign trusteeship in wildlife, yet the manifestations of the trusteeship differ according to the characteristics of the particular sovereign. Because three types of sovereigns co-exist within one nation, the federal, tribal and state governments must exercise governmental prerogatives in a manner compatible with the sovereign relationships established by the Constitution.
>
> * * *
>
> While the states certainly enjoy a general trust interest in wildlife as a result of the federal transfer of land to them, the vital importance of wildlife to national interests seemingly assures a residuary supreme federal trust interest. Certainly the federal government asserts a national property interest in wildlife on the international level when negotiating treaties allocating rights to transitory wildlife shared between foreign nations.

3. *Steuart Transportation* was decided several months before Congress enacted the Comprehensive Environmental Response, Compensation, and Liability Act (CERCLA). In that law, Congress expressly recognized the role of the federal government, as well as states, to act as trustees with the authority to seek natural resource damages to trust assets such as water and wildlife. *See* 42 U.S.C. § 9607(f)(1) (2004). The Oil Pollution Act of 1990 similarly recognizes the role of the federal government to act as trustee for national resources. 33 U.S.C. § 2706(a) (2004). For a discussion suggesting statutes such as CERCLA implicitly delegate the federal trust authority to executive agencies, see Susan D. Baer, *The Public Trust Doctrine—A Tool to Make Federal Administrative Agencies Increase Protection of Public Land and Its Resources*, 15 B.C. Envtl. Aff. L. Rev. 385, 426 (1988) (analyzing various laws as examples of where Congress "implicitly delegated" public trust protection authority to agencies, including: Wild Free-Roaming Horses and Burros Act, 16 U.S.C. §§ 1331–1340, the Federal Land Policy & Management Act, 43 U.S.C. §§ 1701–1784, the National Park Service Act, 16 U.S.C. §§ 1–460, and CERCLA, 42 U.S.C. §§ 9601–9657).

4. The Oil Pollution Act and CERCLA also both contain provisions allowing tribal governments (along with the federal government and state sovereigns) to recover natural resource damages (NRDs) for injury to tribal resources. CERCLA, 42 U.S.C. § 9607(f)(1) (1980); Oil Pollution Act of 1990 (OPA), 33 U.S.C. § 2706(a) (1990) (similar). Tribes are recognized as domestic dependent nations with sovereignty pre-existing the United States. *See* Felix S. Cohen, Handbook of Federal Indian Law 231–32 (1982). For an analysis of the potential role of tribes as co-trustees in climate crisis, see Mary Christina Wood, *Tribal Trustees in Climate Crisis*, 2 Am. Indian L. Rev. 518 (2014).

5. In one case involving a natural resource damages action brought under CERCLA, the federal district court of Idaho found a tribe to be a co-trustee, along with the state of Idaho and federal government, of certain natural resources. *Coeur d'Alene Tribe v. Asarco, Inc.*, 280 F. Supp. 2d 1094 (D. Idaho 2003). Endorsing a co-trustee framework, the court stated:

> [I]n many instances, co-trustees are the norm and not the exception.... The evidence has not shown nor have counsel provided legal authority that would prohibit or suggest that there cannot be co-trustees of our natural resources. In fact, the law clearly anticipates the same because in practice that is the only feasible

way it could work. The migration of birds and fish from one area to another and the use of habitat as they move demonstrate that our natural resources are not static to one area.

The court decided to allocate natural resource damages among the sovereign co-trustees according to "the ratio or percentage of actual management and control that is exercised by each of the various co-trustees." *Id.* at 1106. But a later decision modified that result after finding out that the tribe had agreed to allow the federal government to represent its interests (pursuant to the federal Indian trust responsibility), and that the state was not a party to the litigation, which left just one trustee (the federal government) to pursue natural resource damages. *United States v. Asarco, Inc.*, 471 F. Supp. 2d 1063 (D. Idaho 2005). The court thus recognized the federal government as trustee for "the federal and tribal land as well as the migratory natural resources of: fish, wildlife, birds, biota, water and groundwater." *Id.* at 1069. The court justified the federal trusteeship role under CERCLA "based on [its] involvement in the management and control of such natural resources and applicable federal statutes [that] give the United States trusteeship duties over fish, wildlife and birds [and the] United States' jurisdiction over navigable waters [as discussed in the prior opinion]." *Id.* at 1069–70. The court crafted a general rule to guide CERCLA natural resource damage actions:

> The language of the statute dictates that a co-trustee acting individually or collectively with the other co-trustees may go after the responsible party or parties for the full amount of the damage, less any amount that has already been paid as a result of a settlement to another trustee by a responsible party. If there is a later disagreement between the co-trustees, that disagreement would have to be resolved by successive litigation between the trustees, but it could in no way affect the liability of the responsible party or parties.

Id. at 1068.

6. For an argument that fossil fuel companies should be liable for natural resource damages to the atmosphere, and fund restoration projects designed to extract atmospheric carbon dioxide through soil sequestration and reforestation, see Mary Christina Wood & Dan Galpern, *Making the Fossil Fuel Industry Pay: Recovering Damages to the Atmosphere from Carbon Emissions*, 45 Envtl. L. (forthcoming 2015).

B. The PTD on a Global Level

This section explores whether the co-trustee concepts from above can be extrapolated to a planetary level. The dominant paradigm for managing resources with global importance is the negotiated treaty framework. There are over 500 international treaties dealing with the global environment. But just as statutes have largely failed to protect the environment on the domestic level, so have international treaties failed to protect it on the global level. A United Nations report cast doubt on their effectiveness, pointing out that, of 90 internationally agreed goals and objectives assessed, significant progress could only be shown for four. United Nations Environment Programme, Global Environmental Outlook 5: Environment for the Future We Want, Preface xvii (2012). *See also* John Vidal, *Many Treaties to Save the Earth, but Where's the Will to Implement Them?*, The Guardian (June 7, 2012) (analyzing the report and concluding that the international treaty system is in "semi chaos"). As the world struggles with governance mechanisms, the UN has warned:

The scale, spread, and rate of change of global drivers are without precedent. Burgeoning populations and growing economies are pushing environmental systems to destabilizing limits. The idea that the perturbation of a complex ecological system can trigger sudden feedbacks is not new: significant scientific research has explored thresholds and tipping points that the planetary system may face if humanity does not control carbon emissions. Understanding feedbacks from the perspective of drivers reveals that many of them interact in unpredictable ways. Generally, the rates of change in these drivers are not monitored or managed, and so it is not possible to predict or even perceive dangerous thresholds as they approach. Critically, the bulk of research has been on understanding the effects of drivers on ecosystems, not on the effects of changed ecosystems on the drivers—the feedback loop.

GLOBAL ENVIRONMENTAL OUTLOOK 5, cited above, at Part I, at 4.

Notably, the real acceleration of ecological damage has taken place between 1970 and present—during the modern era of environmental law. Overall, Earth's natural ecosystems have declined by 33 percent during the last 30 years, according to a comprehensive report issued in 2000 by the World Wildlife Fund (WWF). WWF, LIVING PLANET REPORT 2000 1 (Jonathan Loh ed., 2000) (also concluding that "the ecological pressure of humanity on the Earth has increased by about 50 percent over the same [thirty-year] period"). In June 2012, a team of 22 scientists published an article in the prestigious journal, *Nature*, warning that humans are now causing "state shifts" in biological systems—"planetary-scale critical transition[s] ... with the potential to transform Earth rapidly and irreversibly into a state unknown in human experience." Anthony D. Barnosky et al., *Approaching a State Shift in Earth's Biosphere*, 486 Nature 52 (2012), *available at* http://www.ecoearth.info/shared/docfeed/biosphere_state_ shift_nature.pdf.

International frameworks share a basic weakness: no global super-jurisdiction exists to force nations to agree to protective standards in treaties, and there is no sure mechanism to enforce even those treaties agreed to. In that sense, international "law" lacks the force of law, and its success rests on voluntary compliance. Nations often prioritize their own economic self-interest over the more generalized interest of sustaining global ecology. Why is this? Could it be that the failure of international treaties traces back to the failure of domestic political will to confront environmental problems and the reluctance of state and federal agencies to regulate powerful industries? *See generally* JAMES GUSTAVE SPETH, THE BRIDGE AT THE EDGE OF THE WORLD: CAPITALISM, THE ENVIRONMENT, & CROSSING FROM CRISIS TO SUSTAINABILITY 85 (2008) (describing politically captured environmental agencies); MARY CHRISTINA WOOD, NATURE'S TRUST: ENVIRONMENTAL LAW FOR A NEW ECOLOGICAL AGE, Part I (2013) (describing politicized nature and dysfunction of present regulatory regime).

Could a public trust doctrine provide both standards of care for planetary assets and new models for enforcing such standards? In an influential article, Professor Peter Sand posited, "A transfer of the public trust concept from the national to the global level is conceivable, feasible, and tolerable." Peter H. Sand, *Sovereignty Bounded: Public Trusteeship for Common Pool Resources*, 4 Global Envtl. Pol. 47, 57 (2004). Fundamental questions arise in this transference of the doctrine from a national to a global level. How does one define the global trust assets to be protected? Who are the beneficiaries? How would such a trust be enforced? Could judges enforce a planetary trust obligation in domestic courts? How would a general trust approach add to the multitude of already existing expressions of trust in international instruments (such as the Stockholm Declaration of 1972, which calls for safeguarding the "natural resources of the earth ... for the benefit of present and future generations....")? Principle 2, Declaration adopted by the United Nations Conference on the Human Environment (Stockholm, 16 June 1972), UN Doc. A/Conf.48/14; *International Legal Materials* 11:1416. The following materials consider these questions.

The Public Trust Doctrine: A Viable Approach to International Environmental Protection
Ved P. Nanda & William K. Ris, Jr.
5 Ecology L.Q. 291 (1975–1976)

To achieve even minimal prevention of environmental degradation and restoration of a damaged environment requires common enforcement among national, bilateral, and regional governments. That achievement is still more difficult on an international level.... Given the decentralized structure of the world community, securing international compromise and consensus often requires adopting vague declarations and ineffective institutional arrangements, thereby avoiding establishment of the strong enforcement mechanisms needed. An example is adoption of the United Nations General Assembly resolution declaring oceans and their resources to be the "common heritage of mankind." No means are suggested by which to secure that heritage or to define its parameters. Nations will only enter agreements for the regulation of international environmental problems on their own terms.... Accordingly, there is a critical need to explore new international legal strategies to protect the global ecosystem.

One new approach would be to apply on an international level the doctrine of public trust. The analysis which follows shows that the doctrine contains two important features that make it a viable approach to the problem. First, its roots exist both in the civil and common law systems. Thus, the basic concepts, if not the precise formulation, are familiar within a broad spectrum of legal systems. Second, as it has evolved in recent years, the doctrine has qualities of breadth and flexibility that make it particularly useful to the solution of complex international environmental problems....

The doctrine of public trust, as it has evolved in the United States, recognizes that certain defined property is held by the sovereign in trust for the public. Specifically, the state and federal governments serve as "public guardian[s] of those valuable natural resources which are not capable of self-regeneration and for which substitutes cannot be made by man."[3] ...

[The authors inventory various expressions of trust duty in international instruments.]

An explicit acknowledgment of the doctrine, however, would provide an authoritative basis for encouraging and promoting a wider acceptance of the notion that states are responsible not only to their own nationals, but also to all humankind for the maintenance, preservation, and conservation of selected uses and resources that fall into two categories. The first category consists of uses and resources of the commons, while the second consists of uses and resources of global importance lying within exclusive jurisdiction of nation states. A United Nations declaration adopted by the General Assembly, followed by an international convention establishing a public trust doctrine, would be an appropriate medium for such an acknowledgment. This proposed United Nations acknowledgment of the public trust doctrine is designed to deal with transnational environmental

---

3. Bernard S. Cohen, *The Constitution, the Public Trust Doctrine, and the Environment*, 1970 Utah L. Rev. 388 (1970).

problems and should include four essential features: (1) a recognition that nation states with resources of unique importance lying within their exclusive jurisdiction should hold them in trust for all mankind; (2) an international agency to serve as a trustee over areas and resources of commons outside national jurisdictions; (3) a method of identifying resources anywhere in the world that should be subject to the public trust; and (4) strong incentives for states to identify and submit areas and resources within their individual jurisdictions to the public trust....

For areas and resources outside any national jurisdiction, an international agency affiliated with the United Nations system should be established.... The mandate of [the] newly established agency should include the authority to license or dispose of trust property, to acquire trust property, to regulate activities of states, multinational enterprises, and individuals pertaining to the trust property, and to prevent damages to and seek damages for diminution of the trust corpus. [T]he proposed agency would discharge its functions pertaining to the uses of both living and nonliving resources in ocean space, air space, such other common areas as Antarctica, and the uses and potential resources of outer space....

An important feature of the proposal presented here is that incentives, instead of sanctions, should be used to induce states to comply with the agency decisions.... This proposal prefers incentives over coercion and enforcement mechanisms. The reasons for this choice are inherent in the present system. As already mentioned, the Security Council is the only United Nations organ authorized to take enforcement measures against a nation state; authority to do so is limited to three enumerated situations: threats to the peace, breaches of the peace, and acts of aggression.... Thus, it is advisable to opt for persuasion, encouragement, assistance, and incentives, especially in areas pertaining to uses and resources.

Notes

1. The authors recognized that some resources lying within a nation's exclusive jurisdiction should be treated as global trust assets. In the article that follows, Peter Sand agreed, positing with respect to such resources: "The message is simple: The sovereign rights of nation states over certain environmental resources are not proprietary, but *fiduciary*." What assets carry such significant planetary importance as to be considered global trust assets? Could some assets be considered the common heritage of humankind such that a planetary obligation is owed for their protection? Are the elephants and tigers, both perilously close to extinction, part of a planetary wildlife trust? The 1992 Convention on Biological Diversity (CBD) proclaimed that "the conservation of biological diversity is a common concern of humankind," and that "States are responsible for conserving their biological diversity and for using their biological resources in a sustainable manner." Convention on Biological Diversity, preamble, June 5, 1992, 1760 U.N.T.S. 79. What about major ecosystems such as the Amazon Forest, often described as the lungs of the planet? What about sites of outstanding scenic value? Consider the World Heritage Convention (WHC), which recognizes (in its preamble) that "cultural or natural heritage [sites] are of outstanding interest and therefore need to be preserved as part of the world heritage of mankind as a whole." Convention Concerning the Protection of the World Cultural and Natural Heritage, Nov. 16, 1972, 1037 U.N.T.S. 151. For commentary on the WHC as an expression of a public trust, see Mary Christina Wood et al., *Securing Planetary Life Sources for Future Generations: Legal Actions Deriving from the Ancient Sovereign Trust Obligation, in* THREATENED ISLAND NATIONS (Michael B. Gerrard & Gregory E. Wan-

nier, eds., 2013) (contending that the WHC "establishes, on the international level, what is best characterized as a global trusteeship over designated sites with duties incumbent on nations as co-trustees of the heritage.").

2. As to enforcement, the authors acknowledged that international protection for domestic assets runs up against a norm of international law that recognizes national sovereignty over domestic natural resources. *See* Nanda & Ris, above (quoting Resolution 1803 of the United Nations General Assembly that acknowledges "the right of peoples and nations to permanent sovereignty over their natural wealth and resources must be exercised in the interest of their national development and the well-being of the people of the state concerned."). As to the "commons" (oceans and atmosphere, for example), the authors argued for an incentive-based system. Do you think that is likely to work, given the huge monetary stakes in exploiting resources?

3. Even recognizing a planetary trust, doesn't the main challenge come down to enforcement? Given the lack of any international enforcement mechanisms, is the best solution to seek enforcement of trust obligations from courts on the domestic level? Couldn't domestic courts enforce planetary fiduciary obligations on the basis of property law that applies to all co-tenant trustees of the asset? That, indeed, is the approach sought by Atmospheric Trust Litigation explored in section C, below.

Sovereignty Bounded:
Public Trusteeship for Common Pool Resources?

Peter H. Sand
4 Global Envtl. Pol. 47–71 (MIT Press 2004)

∗ ∗ ∗

Environmental Trusteeship in International Law

...Proposals to make use of the public trust doctrine in an international context date back to the 1893 Bering Sea Fur Seal Arbitration. They re-surfaced during preparations for the 1972 UN Stockholm Declaration and the UNESCO World Heritage Convention, and have since been taken up by a number of international publicists, especially in the legal debate on intergenerational equity....

[T]he legal structure of international public trusteeship is not a bilateral one, but typically *trilateral*.... [The article shows a diagram depicting the Community as the trustor/settlor, the States (nations) as trustees, and the People as beneficiaries.] Admittedly, this oversimplified model leaves a number of questions open for debate—starting with the definitions of the community concerned as *trustor/settlor* (the global community? or the community of members of specific international regimes; e.g., contracting parties to a multilateral convention?); of the sovereign entity concerned as *trustee* (states only? or also intergovernmental institutions acting in areas outside national jurisdiction; e.g., the UN International Seabed Authority?); of the people concerned as *beneficiaries* (present *and* future civil society? individuals *and* groups?); and of the *corpus* of the trust (designated resources only? or the global commons? or the whole environment?).

There are essentially three options for the creation of an international environmental trust:

(a) by a specific trust "deed" (*affectation*) designating a particular resource to be conserved for a beneficial purpose; e.g., the "listing" of protected areas under the UNESCO World Heritage Convention, through a process of formal nomination (by a host state) and conditioned acceptance (by a committee representing the member states), based on agreed criteria;

(b) by a treaty designating an entire category of trust resources to be so conserved in all member states; e.g., the genetic resources included in Annex I of the FAO Plant Gene Treaty, subject to ratification by the *in situ* states concerned; or

(c) arguably, by customary law or "objective" extension of a conventional trust regime to all states (*erga omnes*) regardless of their membership in the treaty, on the basis of objective natural criteria of the resource (*par nature*)—which would presumably in turn require some kind of declaratory or customary specification of the international community's "common concern"—e.g., for the deep seabed under the UN Law of the Sea Convention: common heritage "as a form of international trusteeship."

Save for the last-mentioned hypothesis of an "objective regime" (which remains controversial), the majority of international environmental trusts are likely to arise in one of the consensual forms described under options (a) and (b); hence, their legal effects will normally be limited to relations between parties to the multilateral regimes concerned....

Notes

1. Professor Sand offered three structures that could support a trust. The third, as he noted, is a free-standing "objective" regime that could apply to all nations regardless of participation in a treaty. Who could enforce objective trust standards?

2. Could domestic courts of nations draw such standards from the public trust? Atmospheric Trust Litigation, explored below, represents perhaps such an approach.

The Planetary Trust: Conservation and Intergenerational Equity

Edith Brown Weiss
11 Ecology L.Q. 495 (1984)

...Our capacity to harm the environment globally forces us for the first time to be concerned at a global level with survival of the natural and cultural heritage that we pass to future generations. We have only begun to act on this concern. To date, our responses have been limited by a lack of appropriate conceptual and institutional tools. This article suggests a normative framework which, if adopted and internalized by our political, economic, and social institutions, might enable them to serve as vehicles for ensuring that future generations will inherit their just share of our global heritage. Its thesis is that the human species holds the natural and cultural resources of the planet in trust for all generations of the human species....

This planetary trust obligates each generation to preserve the diversity of the resource base and to pass the planet to future generations in no worse condition than it receives it. Thus, the present generation serves both as a trustee for future generations and as a beneficiary of the trust. In fulfilling our role as planetary trustees, we can draw on the law of trusts, a body of distilled teachings concerning intergenerational cooperation and conflict, to help resolve the challenges confronting our global heritage....

II. A Planetary Trust

...Each generation has a deep moral obligation, which may be associated with notions of natural justice, to conserve the planet for future generations. To confer the force of law upon this fiduciary relationship, however, the trust must create legally enforceable duties.... Thus, the members of each generation must confer legal status on the trust by enacting and enforcing positive laws affirming their obligation to future generations.

A. Trustees and Beneficiaries

Under the planetary trust, each generation acts as trustee for beneficiaries in succeeding generations, just as past generations served as trustees for it. In this sense, the trust is analogous to a charitable trust, in that the trustee usually does not stand in a fiduciary relationship to any specific person. Each generation serves as trustee not only for adjacent generations, but for all future generations as beneficiaries under the trust....

B. Purposes of the Trust

Before addressing our obligations as trustees in administering the planetary trust, the purposes for which we hold the earth's resources in trust must be identified. The basic purpose of the trust is to sustain the welfare of future generations. This purpose can be broken down into three sub-purposes: to sustain the life-support systems of the planet; to sustain the ecological processes and environmental conditions necessary for the survival of the human species; and to sustain a healthy and decent environment....

a. Preservation of Resources

The doctrine of preservation requires parties to maintain a resource in approximately the same condition it was in when they assumed responsibility. The object is to preserve features of the natural or cultural heritage which people now value or may come to value in the future.

b. Responsible Use: The Prohibition of Waste

The law against waste emerged in the common law system to limit the power of the life tenant over property, in order to protect the remainderman. Under this view, the preservation and waste doctrines were essentially equivalent....

IV. Implementing Our Fiduciary Obligation to Future Generations

[In this section, Professor Weiss turns to a strategy for enforcing the trust through representation of future generations in decision-making processes at the international, regional, national, and local levels.]

A. Representation of Future Generations

We can take at least a small step towards ensuring that the interests of future generations are respected by granting standing to a representative of future generations in judicial or administrative proceedings or by appointing and publicly financing ombudsmen charged with ensuring compliance with the proposed trust principles once they are embodied in positive law.

1. Standing for Future Generations

A representative of future generations should be granted standing to intervene in proceedings of domestic, regional, and international courts and administrative bodies. In United States courts, a guardian ad litem could be designated to present claims on behalf of future generations. Historical evidence suggests that the Framers intended the United States Constitution to protect future generations.... If members of future generations constitute a constitutionally protected class, a guardian should be appointed to represent their interests in judicial proceedings, since they cannot themselves assert the protection.

When both immediate and long-range harm to the environment is threatened, as by nuclear testing in the atmosphere, the interests of present and future generations may coincide. In these cases, courts may authorize parties to represent a class including both present and future generations. In the United States, there is already judicial precedent for such treatment. In other cases, where the interests of future generations differ from those of the present, a separate representative will be needed to present their claims.

Charitable trust law also offers guidance regarding how to provide representation for future generations. The power to enforce a charitable trust lies primarily with the attorney general as protector of the public for whom the trust is established. Similarly, in enforcing the planetary trust, the attorney general or some other official could serve as a protector of future generations and designate guardians ad to represent their interests....

An alternative to granting standing to a representative of future generations, is to grant standing to the co-trustees of any trustees who allegedly breach their fiduciary duties. Co-trustees and persons with a "special interest" share with the attorney general the power to seek equitable relief to enforce a charitable trust. Under the planetary trust, members of the present generation as co-trustees could file suit for breach of a fiduciary obligation.... Suits by co-trustees could facilitate enforcement of the planetary trust and ensure against the possibility that an attorney general might fail to appoint a guardian ad litem to represent future generations in meritorious cases....

Countries should grant each other's representatives of future generations reciprocal access to their national courts and administrative bodies....

2. An Ombudsman For Future Generations

Establishing an ombudsman for future generations is, perhaps, the most promising approach to representing future generations in present day local, national, regional, and international decision making processes. Ombudsmen would be responsible for ensuring that the trust principles, as developed in detail by positive law, were observed, for responding to complaints, and for alerting communities to threats to the conservation of our planetary heritage.... Ombudsmen now exist all over the world....

Ombudsmen for future generations should be responsible for ensuring that the proposed principles for administering the planetary trust are observed. They could oversee enforcement of relevant laws, respond to specific complaints of citizens or non-governmental institutions, and act as watchdogs to alert communities to threats to the wellbeing of future generations. In performing these tasks ombudsmen may act as mediators, communicators, and public educators — roles which existing ombudsmen often play....

C. The Atmospheric Trust and the Climate Crisis

As the following article explains, climate change due to greenhouse gas emissions is perhaps the most crucial environmental issue of the 21st century. Yet on the federal level, Congress has been unable to confront it in even the most abstract way. On the international level, nations of the world expressed a fiduciary obligation towards the atmosphere in the UNFCCC, which declares the duty to "protect the climate system for the benefit of present and future generations of humankind" and prevent "dangerous anthropogenic heating" to the planet. United Nations Framework Convention on Climate Change, S. Treaty Doc. No. 102–38, art. 2 & 3 (1992). Yet, despite such sweeping language, treaties have persistently failed to arrive at binding carbon reduction measures adequate to thwart climate crisis. *See Theatre of the Absurd: After Three Failures, This Year's UN Climate Summit Has Only Modest Aims*, The Economist (Dec. 1, 2012) (noting failures of climate negotiations in Copenhagen, Denmark, 2009; Cancun, Mexico, 2010; and Durban, South Africa, 2011).

Is there a role for the public trust doctrine to impose trust responsibilities concerning the health of the atmosphere? Over a decade ago, Professor Gerald Torres suggested, "Properly understood ... the traditional rationale for the public trust doctrine provides a necessary legal cornerstone ... to protect the public interest in the sky." Gerald Torres, *Who Owns the Sky?*, 19 Pace Envtl. L. Rev. 515, 533 (2002). The following excerpt explores the possibility of applying the public trust to the modern climate crisis and explains how domestic courts could use their authority to force carbon reduction in countries worldwide.

Atmospheric Trust Litigation Across the World

Mary Christina Wood
in Fiduciary Duty and the Atmospheric Trust, chap. 6
Ken Coghill, Charles Sampford & Tim Smith, eds. (Ashgate Publishing 2012)

Leading climate scientists warn that Earth is in "imminent peril," on the verge of runaway climate heating that will impose catastrophic conditions on generations to come. In their words, continued carbon pollution will cause a "transformed planet"—an Earth obliterated of its major fixtures including the polar ice sheets, Greenland, the coral reefs, and the Amazon forest. The annihilatory trajectory of civilization over the past century threatens to trigger the planet's sixth mass extinction—the kind that hasn't occurred on Earth for 65 million years. Should business as usual continue even for a few more years, future humanity for untold generations will be pummeled by floods, hurricanes, heat waves, fires, disease, crop losses, food shortages, and droughts as part of a hellish struggle to survive in deadly greenhouse conditions.

In a world of runaway climate heating, these unrelenting disasters would force massive human migrations and cause staggering numbers of deaths—culminating in, as more and more analysts predict, humanity's own "self-destruction." As author Fred Pearce states: "Humanity faces a genuinely new situation ... a crisis for the entire life-support system of our civilization and our species."

In order to stem global warming, the law must recognize and calibrate to the physical, chemical, and biological requirements for achieving climate equilibrium. Such requirements are set by nature, not politicians. Stated another way, averting climate disaster is a matter of carbon math, not carbon politics. Scientists warn that the world has only a short time to begin reversing global emissions of carbon before the planet passes a "tipping point"—a point at which dangerous feedback loops will unravel the planet's climate system despite any subsequent carbon reductions achieved by humanity. While just recently scientists believed the "tipping point" would be triggered at 450 parts per million (ppm) of atmospheric carbon dioxide, the dangerous threshold is now thought to be at, or even well under, 350 ppm. Present levels are at 387 ppm and climbing by 2 ppm a year. Leading scientists warn that, if humanity follows business as usual for even another few years, it will "lock in" future catastrophic global heating.

These circumstances have hurled the Earth into a state of planetary emergency. In 2007, the head of the United Nation's climate panel told the world: "What we do in the next two to three years will determine our future. This is the defining moment." Immediate and decisive action to slash carbon pollution is imperative. Yet, despite this planetary crisis, there has been little action at either the international and national levels. This may well be due to the fossil fuel industry's strangulating hold on political leaders, economies, and governmental systems world-wide. Exclusive reliance on the political branches for climate response now seems ill-advised.

This chapter explains a legal strategy called Atmospheric Trust Litigation (ATL) that calls upon the judicial branches of governments world-wide to force carbon reduction. ATL seeks to accomplish, though decentralized domestic litigation in countries across the globe, what has thus far eluded the centralized, international diplomatic treaty-making process. The strategy draws upon fundamental principles of sovereign trust obligation to provide a framework that holds governments accountable for forcing carbon reduction within their own countries. The ATL approach is consistent with, and gives meaning to, the principles declared in the United Nations Framework Convention on Climate Change (UNFCCC), agreed to in 1992 by 192 nations, representing "near universal" international membership. Notably, in the United States, the UNFCCC still exists as a ratified treaty— which gives it Constitutional rank as the "supreme law of the land." The ATL approach neither hinders nor forecloses any possibility for future international frameworks to address climate crisis, but rather, if successful, would infuse a strong fiduciary obligation into what has so far been a wholly discretionary diplomatic process....

I. Governmental Inaction

In December 2009, nations of the world gathered in Copenhagen, Denmark for the United Nations Conference on Climate Change. Although the Conference resulted in a resolution that has been joined by many industrialized nations (including most of the major greenhouse gas emitters such as the United States, China, India, Brazil, Australia, and members of the European Union), the Copenhagen Accord is widely regarded as a failure. It is not legally binding, and many pledges are contingent on action taken by other nations. A UN analysis showed that, even if the various national pledges were fulfilled, the total combined carbon reduction would still bring about a 3°C temperature rise, capable of triggering catastrophic climate change. Notably, the United States remains a recalcitrant global polluter, having offered only a meager reduction proposal at the Copenhagen Conference....

On the domestic level within various nations, one could hope for national legislation. There have been enormous efforts to pass such legislation within the United States, which produces a lion's share of the globe's pollution and has the most extensive set of environmental laws in the world. But the reality is that Congress remains beholden to the fossil fuel industry, which spent a whopping $514 million over eighteen months lobbying against a climate bill, until prospects for legislation came to a "crashing demise" in summer, 2010. Leading climate advocates admit that "hope for any sweeping or comprehensive measure is probably gone." Even if a bill emerges, it is not likely to be adequate. The bills proposed thus far have fallen far short of providing sufficient reduction.

The judicial branch should hold government to its legal responsibilities. So far, however, though many lawsuits have been filed, none have forced the carbon reduction needed to curb runaway atmospheric heating. Most lawsuits are structured around statutory mandates; in the United States, for example, plaintiffs have sued under the Clean Air Act, NEPA, the Endangered Species Act, and other statutes. So far, these claims have not delivered any meaningful aggregate relief. In general, this may be because environmental statutory law (at least in the United States and perhaps in many other countries as well) has degenerated into an embrace of administrative political discretion. The vast majority of agencies use their discretion to allow projects that cause significant environmental damage. The statutes themselves are a major engine of environmental destruction: two-thirds of the greenhouse gas pollution in the United States is emitted pursuant to government-issued permits. Even where a statutory lawsuit is successful, it often fails to deliver meaningful relief. Remedies usually take the form of procedural remands to the agency, returning the matter to the same highly political process that produced the case in the first place. Moreover, statutes, which are typically narrow in scope, fracture government's overall climate responsibility into isolated, disjointed parts. Statute-based strategies — while nevertheless important in many respects — tend to diffuse the climate litigation effort and drain it of practical force in addressing the magnitude of climate crisis.

Climate crisis demands broad, system-changing solutions and doctrines. The judiciary is potentially a crucial player in forcing carbon reduction, because it tends to be a less politicized branch of government (in most, though certainly not all, countries) with power to order swift and decisive relief. But, for litigation to have any meaningful effect before the planet slips over irrevocable climate thresholds, litigators must present courts with macro-level claims that address government's full obligation to protect the atmosphere. Moreover, such claims must find their premise in government obligation, not discretion, which is readily hijacked by politically powerful interests. Finally, such claims must be linked to a premise that has global reach and transcends different legal systems and cultures.

The legal foothold for [ATL] is the ancient public trust doctrine, which imposes a strict fiduciary obligation on government to protect natural resources in trust for the citizens. The ATL strategy presents a macro-level approach to climate crisis by focusing on the atmosphere as a single asset in its entirety. It characterizes all nations on Earth as co-tenant sovereign trustees of that asset, bound together in a property-based framework of corollary and mutual responsibilities. The seeds of the public trust are evident in legal systems world-wide and accessible by lawyers across the globe....

B. The Atmospheric Trust

While traditionally applied to water-based resources, the public trust doctrine has expanded its reach over time, and commentators increasingly point out the logic of a trust approach to climate crisis.... At the time of the *Illinois Central* case, lakebeds served a vital function in supporting fishing, navigation and commerce. Describing the lakebed as property in which "the whole people are interested," the Court reasoned: "The trust with which they are held, therefore, is governmental ... follow[ing] necessarily from the *public character of the property*."

As a legal doctrine, the public trust compels protection of those ecological assets necessary for public survival and community welfare. Courts have recognized an increasing variety of assets held in public trust on the rationale that such assets are necessary to meet society's changing needs....

The essential doctrinal purpose expressed by courts in these public trust cases compels recognition of the atmosphere as one of the crucial assets of the public trust. The public interests at stake in climate crisis are unfathomable leagues beyond the traditional fishing, navigation and commerce interests at the forefront of *Illinois Central*. Atmospheric health is essential to all civilizations and to human survival across the globe. As one climate analyst put it, carbon reduction is necessary for averting "the end of life as we know it." Given the essential nature of air, it is unsurprising that numerous state constitutions and codes recognize air as part of the *res* of the public trust. Moreover, federal statutory law includes air as a trust asset for which the federal government, states, and tribes can gain recovery of natural resource damages.

The Roman origins of the public trust doctrine classified air — along with water, wildlife and the sea — as "*res communes*." In a landmark public trust decision, *Geer v. Connecticut*, the United States Supreme Court relied on this ancient Roman classification of "*res communes*" to find the public trust doctrine applicable to wildlife. Just a few years later, the Court explicitly recognized the states' sovereign property interests in air and found such interests supreme to private title. In *Georgia v. Tennessee*, the Court upheld an action brought by the state of Georgia against Tennessee copper companies for discharging noxious gases that drifted across state lines. The Court declared: "[T]he state has an interest independent of and behind the titles of its citizens, in all the earth and air within its domain." Though the Court did not use the word "trust," the decision essentially proclaimed air as the people's sovereign property.

... This is a time in human history when lawyers world-wide must draw upon timeless principles and extrapolate them in logical fashion to new circumstances. Throughout history, courts have found themselves in the position of declaring new law in response to unforeseeable, often urgent, circumstances. The same principles that have informed all of the historic public trust cases apply with even greater force to the atmosphere....

Though conditions change with time, the basic task and the principles that guide courts remain constant. While air has not yet been the subject of trust litigation, modern courts have a solid legal rationale from which to draw in designating the atmosphere as a public trust asset....

D. The Public Trust and Shared Assets: A Sovereign Co-Tenancy

... [The public trust property framework creates a cotenancy with duties] readily extrapolated to the atmosphere, a natural asset that (like a migratory fishery) transcends sovereign borders. Within a sovereign property framework, all nations on Earth are co-tenant trustees of the global atmosphere. This conception is reinforced by the UNFCCC, which essentially declares a commonly held atmospheric trust obligation. From this property framework, two separate duties arise. First is the sovereign duty that each government, as trustee, has towards its own citizens to protect the atmospheric asset and prohibit waste of their natural inheritance. Second is the duty owed by each nation towards all other nations, arising from the sovereign co-tenancy relationship, to prevent waste to their common asset, the atmosphere. The two duties merge into a uniform obligation, incumbent on all governments, to reduce atmospheric emissions.

III. Atmospheric Trust Litigation

By characterizing the atmosphere in its entirety as a defined trust asset, ATL is designed as a macro-level legal strategy to enforce scientifically based prescriptions for carbon reduction. It seeks to impose concrete, quantitative carbon reduction requirements on governments worldwide. As co-trustees of the world's atmosphere, all sovereign nations are bound by the fiduciary obligation to ensure overall health of the asset. The various agencies and sub-jurisdictions of government, as agents of the trustees, are similarly bound. Fiduciary standards are defined by objective, not political, criteria. Scientific prescriptions for achieving climate equilibrium form the yardstick for the atmospheric fiduciary obligation. The judicial role is to compel the political branches to meet their fiduciary obligation through whatever measures and policies they choose, as long as such measures sufficiently reduce carbon emissions within the required time frame. The courts' role is not to supplant a judge's wisdom for a legislature's approach, but rather to police the other branches to ensure fulfillment of their trust responsibility in accordance with the climate imperatives of nature. By linking to scientific prescriptions as the measure of fiduciary responsibility, the ATL approach is aimed at divesting the world's political leaders of their assumed prerogative to take action only according to their political objectives....

In May 2011, Dr. Hansen and other leading scientists issued a path-breaking paper that set forth a trajectory of global carbon reduction that could return the atmosphere to equilibrium at 350 ppm. They presented projections showing that a global decline of 6 percent in fossil fuel emissions, beginning in year 2013, would lower the atmospheric concentration of CO2 to 350 ppm by the end of the century, assuming a corresponding major effort to extract roughly 100 Gigatons of CO_2 (GtC) from the atmosphere through reforestation and improved forestry and agricultural practices (they deemed 100 GtC the "largest practical extraction")....Courts should adopt the recently developed 350 ppm scientific prescription ... as a general atmospheric fiduciary obligation shared by all co-trustee sovereigns on Earth. *This global trajectory is the marker to which courts around the world may calibrate in assigning carbon reduction pathways to sovereign trustees in their own jurisdictions.*

In the big picture, this planetary carbon reduction can only be met by every nation taking responsibility for the problem. Stated another way, the necessary global emissions reductions will be achieved only if reductions among all nations add up so as to satisfy the required "carbon math." Each industrialized nation must carry out its proportion of the overall planetary carbon reduction....

[Professor Wood explains how a global scientific prescription can be tailored to the individual circumstances of each nation under the waste principle, while still meeting the overall global trajectory.]

Relying on a judicially created property law framework to give meaning to treaty obligations is not unprecedented. In the United States, there is a rich history of courts interpreting and enforcing broad treaty obligations as to natural resources shared between sovereigns. The landmark Indian fishing cases, originating out of fish allocation disputes between states and tribes, gave rise to a vast and much celebrated body of case law that gave detailed interpretation to basic treaty language. The language was sparse, reserving Indian rights to take fish "*in common with*" with the non-Indian settlers. Without the willingness of courts to define, in practical terms, the rights and responsibilities arising from this basic treaty obligation, Indian fishing that had endured 10,000 years surely would have been crushed in the juggernaut of industrialization....Even as some courts today hesitate to confront climate change, it is worth remembering that, based on just three key words lodged in the Indian treaties, U.S. courts constructed a co-tenancy framework, declared a waste principle, and created detailed, practical remedial structures to give force and effect to sovereign property rights. Today, courts confront basically the same task. In order to save the planet from catastrophic heating, they must give force to the public trust responsibility towards the atmosphere, which finds elucidation in the principled language of the UNFCCC.

While the suggested analysis may seem over-simplified in response to multifarious policy concerns and complex science, the urgency in launching planet-saving efforts requires a decisive and straightforward approach that the judicial branches of government can spearhead across the planet through atmospheric trust decrees. The fact that any one court cannot enforce a global reduction scheme—because its jurisdiction is domestic—should not dissuade courts of any nation. As the U.S. Supreme Court recognized in *Massachusetts v. EPA*, the climate problem can be tackled on the domestic level despite the lack of jurisdiction over other nations: "Nor is it dispositive that developing countries such as China and India are poised to increase greenhouse gas emissions substantially over the next century: A reduction in domestic emissions would slow the pace of global emissions increases, no matter what happens elsewhere."

In this manner, atmospheric trust litigation invokes a decentralized judicial strategy to achieve what has long eluded the centralized (and thus far ineffectual) diplomatic system of treaty negotiation. Of course, any decentralized strategy opens the door for inconsistent results across jurisdictions. This may cause some legal thinkers to recoil, as the law has always valued uniformity, sometimes even elevating it over other concerns. But inconsistency may be neither an outrageous nor unwelcome prospect. While legal traditions favoring consistency certainly carry some weight, it is perhaps time to recognize that choosing consistency for the sake of consistency may not be a useful strategy for the present era, which is marked by urgency and crisis. The singular quest for consistency has, if anything caused a dangerous stagnation in climate response and threatens to draw standards down to the lowest common denominator. While uniformity is well-suited to times of stability, times of crisis eras might be met best by innovation and experimentation. Atmospheric trust litigation breaks the mold by inviting judicial innovation, and its partner, inconsistency....

[Professor Wood offers a judicial remedy consisting of carbon reduction plans subject to the continued supervision and enforcement of the court.]

Although courts will not be able to enforce every minute detail of a carbon reduction plan, many courts have it well within their power to force carbon reduction through discrete injunctive measures tailored towards obvious carbon sources. An injunction may contain "backstops" that consist of measures the court will mandate if the budget is not carried out. The broad realm of environmental and land use litigation provides precedent for many measures that may serve as effective backstops. Such measures might include, for example, injunctions prohibiting new coal-fired plants, large-scale logging, recreational vehicle use on public lands, airport expansions, sewer hook-ups, issuance of air pollution permits, and a myriad other activities. It is within the traditional province of courts of equity to devise relief to remedy the harm. Of course, the ultimate enforcement mechanism is to hold government officials personally in contempt of court for failure to carry out court-ordered fiduciary duties.

Notes

1. Professor Wood's article drew on property law concepts in applying the public trust to the problem of greenhouse gas emissions. Notice that she described the *jus publicum* as a cotenancy. Why? With what effect? The Ninth Circuit's treaty fishing rights opinion making an analogy to cotenancy law featured a concurrence by then Judge Anthony Kennedy, now at the center of the U.S. Supreme Court. *Puget Sound Gillnetters Ass'n v. District Court*, 573 P.2d 1123, 1134 (9th Cir. 1978) (Kennedy, J., concurring). The concept of joint trustees of the global atmosphere is also discussed in Evan Fox-Decent, *From Fiduciary States to Joint Trusteeship of the Atmosphere: The Right to a Healthy Environment through a Fiduciary Prism, in* FIDUCIARY DUTY AND THE ATMOSPHERIC TRUST 253 (Ken Coghill, Charles Sampford & Tim Smith eds., 2012).

2. How did Professor Wood suggest the public trust doctrine would lead a court to fashion a judicially enforceable remedy for greenhouse gas emissions to avoid "irrevocable climate thresholds"? In the article, she tied the sovereign fiduciary obligation to language in the UNFCCC that called upon all nations to prevent "dangerous anthropogenic heating," and drew upon a scientific prescription developed by one of the world's leading climate scientists, Dr. James Hansen, head of NASA's Goddard Institute for Space Studies. This prescription set forth a global trajectory of carbon reduction of 6% a year beginning in 2013. *See* James Hansen et al., *Scientific Case for Avoiding Dangerous Climate Change to Protect Young People and Nature* (Mar. 2012), *available at* http://pubs.giss.nasa.gov/abs/ha08510t.html.

3. The theory and strategy presented in the article has been used in a global Atmospheric Trust Litigation campaign consisting of lawsuits and petitions covering every state in the United States. At the time this text went to press, the campaign included one federal lawsuit against the Obama Administration, lawsuits against 15 state governments, and petitions for rulemaking covering all remaining states in the United States. Although some of these actions have concluded, many remain pending. The ATL campaign has also produced lawsuits in other countries (e.g., Uganda, Ukraine, Philippines, Indonesia), with more planned by the coordinating organization, Our Children's Trust. All of the legal actions have been brought on behalf of youth plaintiffs, similar to the Philippines cases, *Oposa* and *Manila Bay* (pp. 341, 344), and all call for enforceable climate recovery plans to implement the scientific prescription described above as the state's fiduciary obligation. The decisions excerpted below resulted from the campaign.

Alec L. et al. v. Jackson

United States District Court, District of Columbia

863 F. Supp. 2d 11 (2012), *aff'd* 561 Fed. Appx. 7 (D.C. Cir. 2014) (mem.)

WILKINS, J.:

Five young citizens and two organizations, Kids vs. Global Warming and Wildearth Guardians, bring this action seeking declaratory and injunctive relief for Defendants alleged failure to reduce greenhouse gas emissions. The Plaintiffs allege that Defendants have violated their fiduciary duties to preserve and protect the atmosphere as a commonly shared public trust resource under the public trust doctrine. Plaintiffs' one-count complaint does not allege that the defendants violated any specific federal law or constitutional provision, but instead alleges violations of the federal public trust doctrine.

* * *

I. Background

A. Public Trust Doctrine

The public trust doctrine can be traced back to Roman civil law, but its principles are grounded in English common law on public navigation and fishing rights over tidal lands. *PLL Montana, LLC v. Montana*, 132 S. Ct. 1213, 1234 (2012). "At common law, the title and dominion in lands flowed by the tide water were in the King for the benefit of the nation.... Upon the American Revolution, these rights, charged with a like trust, were vested in the original States within their respective borders." *Phillips Petroleum v. Mississippi*, 484 U.S. 469, 473 (1988) (quoting *Shively v. Bowlby*, 152 U.S. 1 (1894)). Upon entry into the Union, the states received ownership of all lands under waters subject to the ebb and flow of the tide. *Id.* at 476. The states' right to use or dispose of such lands, however, is limited to the extent that it would cause "substantial impairment of the interest of the public in the waters," and the states' right to the water is subject to "the paramount right of [C]ongress to control their navigation so far as may be necessary for the regulation of commerce with foreign nations and among the states." *Ill. Cent. R.R. Co. v. Illinois*, 146 U.S. 387, 435 (1892). Thus, traditionally, the doctrine has functioned as a restraint on the states' ability to alienate submerged lands in favor of public access to and enjoyment of the waters above those lands.

More recently, courts have applied the public trust doctrine in a variety of contexts. See e.g. *District of Columbia v. Air Fla., Inc.*, 750 F.2d 1077, 1083 (D.C. Cir. 1984) (noting that "the doctrine has been expanded to protect additional water-related uses such as swimming and similar recreation, aesthetic enjoyment of rivers and lakes, and preservation of flora and fauna"). And while Plaintiffs have cited authority for the application of the doctrine in numerous natural resources, including groundwater, wetlands, dry sand beaches, non-navigable tributaries, and wildlife, they have cited no cases, and the Court is aware of none, that have expanded the doctrine to protect the atmosphere or impose duties on the federal government. Therefore, the manner in which Plaintiffs seek to have the public trust doctrine applied in this case represents a significant departure from the doctrine as it has been traditionally applied.

B. The Relief Requested by Plaintiffs

Plaintiffs seek a variety of declaratory and injunctive relief for their public trust claim. First, Plaintiffs ask the Court to declare that the atmosphere is a public trust resource and that the United States government, as a trustee, has a fiduciary duty to refrain from taking actions that waste or damage this asset. Plaintiffs also ask the Court to declare that, to date, Defendants have violated their fiduciary duties by contributing to and allowing unsafe amounts of greenhouse gas emissions into the atmosphere. In addition, Plaintiffs ask the Court to further define Defendants' fiduciary duties under the public trust by declaring that the six Defendant federal agencies have a duty to reduce global atmospheric carbon dioxide levels to less than 350 parts per million during this century.

With respect to injunctive relief, Plaintiffs have asked this Court to issue an injunction directing the six federal agencies to take all necessary actions to enable carbon dioxide emissions to peak by December 2012 and decline by at least six percent per year beginning in 2013. Plaintiffs also ask the Court to order Defendants to submit for this Court's approval: annual reports setting forth an accounting of greenhouse gas emissions originated by the United States and its citizens; annual carbon budgets that are consistent with the goal of capping carbon dioxide emissions and reducing emissions by six percent per year; and a climate recovery plan to achieve Plaintiffs' carbon dioxide emission reduction goals.

* * *

II. Analysis

The central premise upon which Plaintiffs rely to invoke the Court's jurisdiction is misplaced. Plaintiffs contend that the public trust doctrine presents a federal question because it "is not in any way exclusively a state law doctrine." The Supreme Court's recent decision in *PPL Montana, LLC v. Montana*, 132 S. Ct. 1215, 1235 (2012), appears to have foreclosed this argument. In that case, the Court while distinguishing the public trust doctrine from the equal footing doctrine, stated that "the public trust doctrine *remains a matter of state law*" and its "contours ... *do not depend upon the Constitution.*" *Id.* (emphasis added). The Court went on to state that the public trust doctrine, as a matter of state law, was "subject as well to the federal power to regulate vessels and navigation under the Commerce Clause and admiralty power." *Id.*

The parties disagree as to whether the Supreme Court's declaration regarding the public trust doctrine is part of the holding or, as Plaintiffs urge, merely dictum. The Court, however, need not resolve this issue because "'carefully considered language of the Supreme Court, even if technically dictum, generally must be treated as authoritative.'" *Overby v. Nat'l Ass'n of Letter Carriers*, 595 F.3d 1290, 1295 (D.C. Cir. 2010) (quoting *United States v. Dorcely*, 454 F.3d 366, 375 (D.C. Cir. 2006). Thus, dicta or not, the Court's statements regarding the public trust doctrine would nonetheless be binding on this Court.

Even if the Supreme Court's declaration was not binding, the Court finds it persuasive. Likewise, dictum from this Circuit is also persuasive. The D.C. Circuit has had occasion to state, albeit in dictum, that "[i]n this country the public trust doctrine has developed *almost exclusively as a matter of state law*" and that "the doctrine has functioned as a constraint on states' ability to alienate public trust lands." *District of Columbia v. Air Fla., Inc.*, 750 F.2d 1077, 1082 (D.C. Cir. 1984) (emphasis added). The Court also expressed its concerns that a *federal* common-law public trust doctrine would possibly be displaced by federal statutes. *Id.* at 1085 n.43.

Thus, it appears that Plaintiffs have not raised a federal question to invoke this Court's jurisdiction....

Alternatively, even if the public trust doctrine had been a federal common law claim at one time, it has subsequently been displaced by federal regulation, specifically the Clean Air Act. In *American Electric Power Company v. Connecticut* [hereinafter *AEP*], the Supreme Court held that: "the Clean Air Act and the EPA actions it authorizes displace *any* federal common law right to seek abatement of carbon-dioxide emissions from fossil-fuel fired power plants." 131 S. Ct. 2527, 2537 (2011) (emphasis added).

The Plaintiffs attempt to escape the holding in [*AEP*] by arguing that its holding should be limited to common law nuisance claims, while Plaintiffs are proceeding here under a common law public trust theory. Plaintiffs also attempt to distinguish the *AEP* case because that case was brought against four private companies and the Tennessee Valley Authority, a federally owned corporation, as opposed to the federal agency defendants in this case. Plaintiffs argue that this distinction is significant because, in Plaintiffs' view, the fiduciary duties of the public trust doctrine can only be imposed on the states and the federal government. According to Plaintiffs, because the plaintiffs in the *AEP* case could not bring a public trust claim against the defendants in that case, the holding in that case should be limited to those facts.

The Court views these as distinctions without a difference. The particular contours of the public nuisance doctrine did not in any way affect the Supreme Court's analysis in *AEP*. Indeed, the Court's holding makes no mention of the public nuisance doctrine at all, as the Court clearly stated that *any* federal common law right was displaced. *Id.* Further, there is nothing in the Court's holding to indicate that it should be limited to suits against private entities. Indeed, the Court described in great detail the process under which federal courts may review the action, or inaction, of federal agencies with respect to their statutory obligations under the Clean Air Act. *Id.* at 2539.

Moreover, the question at issue in the *AEP* case is not appreciably different from the question presented here—whether a federal court may make determinations regarding to what extent carbon-dioxide emissions should be reduced, and thereafter order federal agencies to effectuate a policy of its own making. The *AEP* opinion expressed concern that the plaintiffs in that case were seeking to have federal courts, in the first instance, determine what amount of carbon-dioxide emissions is unreasonable and what level of reduction is practical, feasible and economically viable. *Id.* at 2540. The Court explained that "the judgments the plaintiffs would commit to federal judges ... cannot be reconciled with the decisionmaking scheme Congress enacted." *Id.* The Court further explained that Congress designated the EPA as an agency expert to "serve as primary regulator of greenhouse gas emissions" and that this expert agency "is surely better equipped to do the job than individual district judges issuing ad hoc, case-by-case injunctions." *Id.* at 2539. The Court, in holding that the federal common law cause of action was displaced by the Clean Air Act, concluded that federal judges may not set limits on greenhouse gas emissions "in the face of a law empowering EPA to set the same limits, subject to judicial review only to ensure against action arbitrary, capricious, ... or otherwise not in accordance with the law." *Id.*

In the present case, Plaintiffs are asking the Court to make similar determinations regarding carbon dioxide emissions. First, in order to find that there is a violation of the public trust — at least as the Plaintiffs have pled it — the Court must make an initial determination that current levels of carbon dioxide are too high and, therefore, the federal defendants have violated their fiduciary duties under the public trust. Then, the Court must make specific determinations as to the appropriate level of atmospheric carbon dioxide, as determine whether the climate recovery plan sought as relief will effectively attain that goal. Finally, the Court must not only retain jurisdiction of the matter, but also review and approve the Defendants' proposals for reducing greenhouse gas emissions. Ultimately, Plaintiffs are effectively seeking to have the Court mandate that federal agencies undertake specific regulatory activity, even if such regulatory activity is not required by any statute enacted by Congress.

These are determinations that are best left to the federal agencies that are better equipped, and that have a Congressional mandate, to serve as the "primary regulator of greenhouse gas emissions." *Id.* at 2539. The emissions of greenhouse gases, and specifically carbon dioxide, are subject to regulation under the Clean Air Act. *Massachusetts v. E.P.A.*, 549 U.S. 497, 528–29 (2007). Thus, a federal common law claim directed to the reduction or regulation of carbon dioxide emissions is displaced by the Act. *AEP*, 131 S. Ct. at 2537 (noting that the test for legislative displacement is whether the statute "speaks directly to the question at issue"). Therefore, even if Plaintiffs allege a public trust claim that could be construed as sounding in federal common law, the Court finds that that cause of action is displaced by the Clean Air Act.

IV. Conclusion

Ultimately, this case is about the fundamental nature of our government and our constitutional system, just as much — if not more so — than it is about emissions, the atmosphere or the climate. Throughout history, the federal courts have served a role both essential and consequential in our form of government by resolving disputes that individual citizens and their elected representatives could not resolve without intervention. And in doing so, federal courts have occasionally been called upon to craft remedies that were seen by some as drastic to redress those seemingly insoluble disputes. But that reality does not mean that every dispute is one for the federal courts to resolve, nor does it mean that a sweeping court-imposed remedy is the appropriate medicine for every intractable problem. While the issues presented in this case are not ones that this Court can resolve by way of this lawsuit, that circumstance does not mean that the parties involved in this litigation — the plaintiffs, the Defendant federal agencies and the Defendant-Intervenors — have to stop talking to each other once this Order hits the docket. All of the parties seem to agree that protecting and preserving the environment is a more than laudable goal, and the Court urges everyone involved to seek (and perhaps even seize) as much common ground as courage, goodwill and wisdom might allow to be discovered.

For the foregoing reasons, the Defendants' and Defendant-Intervenors' motions to dismiss are granted. The Plaintiffs' First Amended Complaint is hereby dismissed.

Notes

1. The district judge refused to find a federal public trust obligation, citing the U.S. Supreme Court's unanimous decision in *PPL Montana v. Montana* (authored by Justice Kennedy

and discussed earlier at p. 94). But the Supreme Court's decision did not discuss the question of a federal public trust, as it dealt exclusively with an equal footing issue involving state title to riverbeds. Did the district court judge err by making too much of the Court's passing statement that the public trust "remains a matter of state law," when in fact that Court did not say that the trust was exclusively a matter of state law and offered no analysis of the trust doctrine? Did it also err in relying on *District of Columbia v. Air Florida, Inc.*, when that court took great pains to emphasize that it was not deciding the matter of a federal public trust? Is it troublesome that the district judge cited these two cases but failed to mention the two federal cases that have imposed, after considered analysis, a trust obligation on the federal government, *1.58 Acres of Land* and *Steuart Transportation, Inc.* (pp. 367, 372)?

2. The plaintiffs appealed the district court's decision to the D.C. Circuit. *Alec L.* ex rel. *Loorz v. McCarthy*, 561 Fed. Appx. 7 (2014) (mem.). That court cancelled oral argument in the case and summarily issued a conclusory, unpublished opinion affirming the district court's judgment. With almost no analysis, the opinion held that there was no federal question sufficient to invoke federal jurisdiction under 28 U.S.C. § 1331. The court rejected the youth plaintiffs' argument (supported by 33 amicus law professors) that there exists a federal trust obligation arising under the Constitution and laws of the United States. Instead, just as the district court did, the D.C. Circuit interpreted Justice Kennedy's dicta in *PPL Montana v. Montana* to indicate that there is no federal public trust obligation: "[T]he Supreme Court recently reaffirmed that 'the public trust doctrine remains a matter of state law' and that 'the contours of that public trust do not depend upon the Constitution.'" *Alec L.*, 561 Fed. Appx. at 8 (quoting *PPL Montana, LLC v. Montana*, 132 S. Ct. 1215, 1235 (2012)). Why would the D.C. Circuit cancel oral argument in such an important climate case, and why would it refuse to publish its opinion? Are these indications of judicial reluctance to play any role in climate crisis? Is it appropriate for the third branch of government to stay out of the fray when the habitability of the nation may well be at stake, putting the welfare of youth and all foreseeable generations in jeopardy?

The plaintiffs proceeded to file a petition for certiorari before the Supreme Court, but the Justices decided not to grant certiorari in the case. *See* Petition for a Writ of Certiorari, Alec L. *ex rel.* Loorz v. McCarthy, 2014 WL 5017962 (No. 14-405) and Alec L. *ex rel.* Loorz v. McCarthy, 135 S. Ct. 774 (mem.) (2014) (denying certiorari). The issue of whether the federal government owes a trust obligation to the people has not been finally resolved, however. Consider the following argument rejecting the District Court's interpretation of Justice Kennedy's language:

> [T]he D.C. courts misinterpreted the scope of the public trust doctrine in the *Alec L.* case by failing to understand the limited nature of Justice Kennedy's dicta in his *PPL Montana* opinion.... The mistake of the D.C. courts was, in part, their failure to carefully examine [*Illinois Central Railroad*]. A close look at *Illinois Central* reveals that the decision had no state law basis, despite the unreasoning dicta in later Supreme Court cases, which claimed that it did. If, as we maintain, the Supreme Court grounded its *Illinois Central* decision in federal law, the D.C. courts' rationale in *Alec L.* is flawed and should not prevail in other circuits or in the Supreme Court.... The erroneous interpretation of *Illinois Central* began with *Appleby v. City of New York*, a 1926 decision that actually did not involve the public trust doctrine, in which the Court, in dicta, erroneously suggested that "the extent of the power of the State and city to part with property under the navigable waters ... is a state question." ... Unfortunately, ensuing Supreme Court de-

cisions lifted without close analysis the *Appleby* dictum about state law governing the public trust doctrine.

Michael C. Blumm & Lynn S. Schaffer, *The Federal Public Trust Doctrine: Misinterpreting Justice Kennedy & Illinois Central Railroad*, 45 Environmental Law __ (forthcoming 2015), *available at* http://ssrn.com/abstract=2554614 (describing also the federal public trust obligations recognized in numerous longstanding federal court decisions as well as federal statutes). The article excerpted above reflects a substantial adaptation of the arguments made in an amicus curiae brief submitted to the Supreme Court in support of the youth plaintiffs in *Alec L. See* Amicus Curiae Brief of Law Professors in Support of Granting Writ of Certiorari, Alec L. *ex rel.* Loorz v. McCarthy, 2014 WL 5841697 (No. 14-405), *available at* http://papers.ssrn.com/sol3/papers.cfm?abstract_ id=2518260. More than 50 law professors, collectively sharing more than 1,100 years of teaching experience, supported the plaintiffs' petition for certiorari. Additional amicus briefs filed in the case included the support of numerous non-profit organizations, prominent economists and national security experts, cities, and faith organizations representing literally millions of people. *See* Press Release, *Prominent* Amicus *Groups File Supreme Court Briefs In Support Of Climate Change Case Brought By Young Americans* (Nov. 6, 2014), *available at* http://ourchildrenstrust.org/sites/default/files/14.11.06SupremeCourtAmicusBriefPR.pdf. Assume the legislature and agencies continue to sit idle on climate crisis, and courts continue to reject claims based on procedural defenses such as the displacement doctrine. What result for humanity? Is this a situation where another legal forum has a chance of working in time to prevent climate tipping points of which scientists warn? Are these run-of-the-mill environmental cases? Given the potential result of judicial abstinence in the face of climate change, does this case reflect an issue of exceptional "national importance" that the Supreme Court ought to decide?

3. Did the district court appropriately find that the Supreme Court's decision in *American Electric Power Co. v. Connecticut (AEP)*, 131 S. Ct. 2527 (2011), precluded a federal atmospheric trust claim? In *AEP*, states and other plaintiffs brought a federal common law public nuisance claim against major carbon-dioxide emitters (four private power companies and the federal Tennessee Valley Authority, together the five largest carbon dioxide emitters in the United States). The Court held that the federal nuisance action was displaced by the federal Clean Air Act (CAA), which authorizes EPA to regulate carbon-dioxide emissions. Was the district court correct in holding that the same CAA displacement applies to public trust claims? Aren't public trust claims against government agencies fundamentally different than nuisance claims against polluters? As the *AEP* Court explained, the test for whether a statute displaces common law is "simply whether the statute 'speak[s] directly to [the] question' at issue." *Id.* at 2537. Although the CAA directly speaks to the pollution emitted by the defendants in the nuisance case, does it speak to whether the government has fulfilled its duties to the citizen beneficiaries in regulating that pollution? Doesn't the public trust demand that government prove that its regulation is adequate to meet fiduciary duties of asset protection? Can a statute that must be judged for adequacy under a fiduciary obligation displace the very trust basis that demands such judgment?

Moreover, is it proper to equate the trust with standard common law that can be displaced by statute? Characterized by many courts as an attribute of sovereignty, can the trust be displaced by statute? Doesn't judicial review of legislative action under the trust strike at the heart of the constitutional separation of powers between the three branches of government? *See Ariz. Ctr. for Law in the Pub. Interest v. Hassell*, 837 P.2d 158, 169 (Ariz. Ct. App. 1991) ("The check and balance of judicial review provides a level of protection against improvident dissipation of an irreplaceable res."). For arguments that the *AEP* case does not support displacement in public trust claims, see Mary Christina Wood et al., *Securing Planetary Life Sources for Future Generations: Legal Actions Deriving from the Ancient Sovereign Trust Obligation, in* THREATENED ISLAND NATIONS (2013) and Lynn S. Schaffer, *Pulled From Thin Air: The (Mis)Application of Statutory Displacement to a Public Trust Claim in* Alec L. v. Jackson, 19 Lewis & Clark L. Rev. 169 (2015).

4. The *Alec L.* court noted that the proper remedy for carbon pollution lies against the federal agencies. But in this case the agencies have remained idle in face of a grave planetary threat. In the private trust context, would a court excuse a recalcitrant trustee that allowed ongoing damage to the trust assets on the basis that the trustee, not the court, has the duty to protect the assets? What is the court's role in the private trust context? Without judicial enforcement, is a trust really a trust at all, or does it represent unbridled power held by the trustee? The *Alec L.* court concluded that "this case is about the fundamental nature of our government and our constitutional system." How do these concerns fit into the American constitutional democracy?

5. Dr. James Hansen, a leading climate scientist and former head of NASA's Goddard Institute of Space Studies, wrote in an amicus brief submitted in support of the youth plaintiffs in the *Alec L. v. Jackson* litigation before the D.C. Circuit Court: "[F]ailure to act with all deliberate speed, so as to dial back the thermostat within the short remaining time, risks eliminating the option of preserving a habitable climate system." Brief of Climate Scientists as Amici Curiae Supporting Petitioners, 2014 WL 5841696 (No. 14-405). For an argument that the judiciary should play a central role in climate crisis through enforcement of public trust obligations, *see* Mary Christina Wood, *The Planet on the Docket: Atmospheric Trust Litigation to Protect Earth's Climate System and Habitability*, 9 Fla. A&M U. L. Rev. 401 (2015).

6. The complaint filed in *Alec L.* was part of a wave of lawsuits filed throughout the country concerning the application of the public trust doctrine to greenhouse gas emissions; most of the cases continue to work their way through state courts. The following is a judgment from Texas endorsing the concept of an atmospheric trust.

Bonser-Lain *ex rel.* TVH, et al. v. Texas Commission on Environmental Quality

No. D-1-GN-11-002194 (Aug. 2 2012)
201st Judicial District Court of Travis Co., Tx.
2012 WL 3164561, *vacated* 438 S.W.3d 887, 895 (Tex. App. 2014)

TRIANA, J.:

On the 14th day of June, 2012, came to be heard Defendant Texas Commission on Environmental Quality's First Plea to the Jurisdiction and the merits of the above-reference cause.... The Court finds that the Defendant's Plea to the Jurisdiction should be denied.

On the merits of the suit, the Court finds that Defendant's conclusion that the public trust doctrine in Texas is exclusively limited to the conservation of the State's waters and does not extend to the conservation of the air and atmosphere is legally invalid. Rather, the public trust doctrine includes all natural resources of the State including the air and atmosphere. The public trust doctrine is not simply a common law doctrine but was incorporated into the Texas Constitution at Article XVI, Section 59, which states: "The conservation and development of all of the natural resources of the State, ... and the preservation and conservation of all such natural resources of the State are each and all hereby declared public rights and duties; and the Legislature shall pass all such laws as my be appropriate there to."

The Court further finds that the protection of air quality has been mandated by the Texas Legislature in the Texas Clean Air Act (TCAA), which states, "The policy of this state and the purpose of this chapter are to safeguard the state's air resources from pollution by controlling or abating air pollution and emissions of air contaminants.... (b) It is intended that this chapter be vigorously enforced and that violations of this chapter ... result in expeditious initiation of enforcement actions as provided by this chapter." *See* Health and Safety Code § 382.002. The Texas Legislature had been provided Defendant with statutory authority to protect the air quality by stating: "Consistent with applicable federal law, the commission by rule may control air contaminants as necessary to protect against adverse effects related to: (1) acid deposition; (2) stratospheric changes, including depletion of ozone; and (3) climatic changes, including global warming." *See id.* § 382.0205.

The Court also finds that Defendant's conclusion that it is prohibited from protecting the air quality because of the federal requirements of the Federal Clean Air Act (FCAA), Section 109 is legally invalid. Defendant relies upon a preemption argument that the State of Texas may not enact stronger requirements than is mandated by federal law. The Court finds that the FCAA requirement is a floor, not a ceiling, for the protection of air quality, and therefore Defendant's ruling on this point is not supported by law....

However, in light of other state and federal litigation, the Court finds that it is a reasonable exercise of Defendant's rulemaking discretion not to proceed with the requested petition for rulemaking at this time.

Notes

1. Although the court ruled in favor of the plaintiffs on the substantive public trust issues, it denied relief because of pending litigation involving the state of Texas regarding the applicability of greenhouse gas regulations under both the Texas Clean Air Act and the Federal Clean Air Act. The result demonstrates that while the public trust imposes obligations independent of statutory and regulatory law, courts are often inclined to defer a trust remedy in light of ongoing regulatory processes. Is such an outcome justifiable?

On review, the Texas Court of Appeals vacated the district court's decision on the grounds that neither the state Administrative Procedure Act nor the Water Code provided for judicial review, and dismissed the case for lack of subject matter jurisdiction. *Bonser-Lain ex rel. TVH v. Tex. Comm'n on Envtl. Quality*, 438 S.W.3d 887, 895 (Tex. App. 2014). The Court of Appeals did not reach Judge Triana's declarations with respect to the public trust doctrine. *Id.*

2. Notice that Judge Triana indicated that the public trust doctrine applied not only to air but to all natural resources of the state, and that it was grounded on the Texas Constitution's declaration of rights and duties to include the conservation, preservation, and development of the state's natural resources. The judge also decided, contrary to the District of Columbia District Court, that the federal Clean Air Act did not displace the public trust doctrine, since it established only a floor, not a ceiling, for air quality.

3. Cases are proceeding in other states. In New Mexico, a district court judge initially denied the state's motion to dismiss and forced a decision on the merits as to whether the state has complied with its public trust obligation to protect the atmosphere. *Wild Earth Guardians v. Martinez*, No. D-101-CV-2011-1514 (Jul. 14, 2012). However, the court ultimately ruled that the public trust doctrine did not apply to the case because the state agency,

the New Mexico Environmental Improvement Board, "made findings that there was no need to regulate the State's greenhouse gas emissions, because that would have no effect on the issue of global warming or climate change." *Reed v. Martinez*, No. D-101-CV-2011-01514, 2012 WL 8466121 (N.M. Dist. Ct. July 14, 2012). The case currently awaits decision from the New Mexico Court of Appeals. Do you agree that a decision at the state level has "no impact" on the issue of global warming or climate change? What implications arise if the federal government refuses to recognize its trust obligations over the atmosphere? *See* Jordan M. Ellis, Comment, *The Sky's the Limit: Applying the Public Trust Doctrine to the Atmosphere*, 86 Temp. L. Rev. 807, 819 (2014) (arguing that state application of the public trust can protect the atmosphere from future harm, but asserting that the public trust doctrine "is a creature of state law"); *cf.* Michael C. Blumm & Lynn Schaffer, *The Federal Public Trust Doctrine: Misinterpreting Justice Kennedy &* Illinois Central Railroad, 45 Environmental Law (forthcoming 2015), *available at* http://ssrn.com/abstract=2554614.

In an Iowa case, the Iowa Court of Appeals declined to extend the public trust to the atmosphere, but a concurring opinion issued by Judge Doyle indicated that it was the role of the state supreme court to do so. *Glori dei Filippone v. Iowa Dep't of Natural Res.*, No. 2-1005/12-0444 (Iowa Ct. App., Mar. 13, 2013). Citing statutes expressing the "policy of the state of Iowa to protect its natural resource heritage of *air*, soils, waters, and wildlife for the benefit of present and future citizens," he stated:

> I agree there is no Iowa case law for extending the public trust doctrine to include the atmosphere. But, I believe there is a sound public policy basis for doing so.... The legislature, the voice of the people, has spoken in terms as clear as a crisp, cloudless, autumn Iowa sky. Nevertheless, in view of our supreme court's stated reluctance to extend the public trust doctrine beyond rivers, lakes, and the lands adjacent thereto, I do not feel it is appropriate for a three-judge panel of this court to take on the task of expanding the doctrine to include air.

Id.

4. In Oregon, a lower court dismissed the ATL case against the state, finding that it was not the court's role to interfere with legislative policy choices affecting climate. The ruling implicated the political question doctrine discussed in chapter 2. The Oregon Court of Appeals reversed, allowing the litigation to move forward. It squarely rejected the state's argument that its obligations are grounded only in statutes and the constitution and dismissed the state's argument that an order enforcing trust duties against the state would violate separation of powers principles. The court stated:

> [I]f the doctrine itself imposes specific affirmative obligations on defendants (like requiring defendants to take the particular actions that plaintiffs request), a judgment declaring that defendants have breached those obligations or ordering defendants to take the requested actions might not unduly burden the other branches of government or result in the judiciary impermissibly performing duties or making policy determinations that are reserved to those other branches.

Chernaik v. Kitzhaber, 263 Or. App. 463 (2014). For press on the opinion, *see* http://registerguard.com/rg/news/local/31714161-75/court-state-judge-trust-public.html.csp.

5. Will nature's climate tipping points wait for protracted judicial appeals in these atmospheric trust cases? In two federal cases, courts have recognized the urgency associated with tipping points. *See Ctr. for Biological Diversity v. Nat'l Highway Traffic Safety Admin.*, 508 F.3d 508, 523 (9th Cir. 2008) ("Several studies also show that climate change may be non-linear, meaning that there are positive feedback mechanisms that may push global warming past a dangerous threshold (the 'tipping point').")); *Green Mountain Chrysler v.*

Crombie, 508 F. Supp. 2d 295, 313–17 (D. Vt. 2007) (finding reliable the "tipping point" theory of non-linear climate change advanced by NASA scientist James Hansen and stating: "[The] 'tipping point' theory posits that at a certain point the changes associated with global warming will become dramatically more rapid and out of control.... [D]rastic consequences, including rapid sea level rise, extinctions, and other regional effects, would be inevitable with a two to three degrees Celsius warming expected if no limits are imposed and emissions continue at their current rate. Such changes could happen quickly once a tipping point is passed."). Should appeal courts use expedited review processes for climate cases? In Montana, the plaintiffs sought original jurisdiction in the Montana Supreme Court on the basis that the case presented an urgent matter. But the court declined to exercise original jurisdiction, agreeing with the state that the case presented no emergency requiring its immediate attention and declaring that it was "ill-equipped to resolve the factual assertions" presented by the petitioners. *See Barhaugh v. Montana*, OP-11-0258 (June 15, 2011).

6. Some state ATL suits have drawn amicus briefs from government officials, tribes, and the faith community in support of the youth plaintiffs. Updated information on the ATL litigation is available at Our Children's Trust, http://ourchildrenstrust.org/. The litigation is accompanied by an outreach campaign featuring short documentaries on the youth plaintiffs, produced by the WITNESS organization, available at http://ourchildrenstrust.org/trust-films. What is the role of such outreach in the overall success of litigation? Could climate litigation succeed in prompting societal change without such outreach? For an intriguing look at the celebrated public trust litigation involving Mono Lake in California and an argument that the conservationists' "persistent activism and efforts at both public education and problem solving were at least as critical to their success at saving Mono Lake as their legal victories were," *see* Craig Anthony (Tony) Arnold, *Working Out an Environmental Ethic: Anniversary Lessons from Mono Lake*, 4 Wyo. L. Rev. 1, 18 (2004).

7. The climate litigation campaign is now moving forward in other countries as well. ATL proceedings have been brought in Uganda and Ukraine, the Philippines, and the Netherlands. For updates, *see* http://www.ourchildrenstrust.org/ legal/international. The Netherlands litigation represents the first "macro" approach to forcing carbon emissions reduction in Europe. For materials, see http://www.wijwillenactie.nl/?page_id=1097. *See also* ROGER COX, REVOLUTION JUSTIFIED (2013) (arguing for emergency judicial action worldwide to stem catastrophic climate change from uncontrolled carbon emissions).

8. The ATL campaign seeks to force carbon emissions reduction sufficient to implement a prescription set by an international team of scientists led by Dr. James Hansen. The prescription calls for a global reduction of 6% emissions beginning in 2013. *See* James Hansen et al., *Assessing "Dangerous Climate Change": Required Reduction of Carbon Emissions to Protect Young People, Future Generations and Nature*, PLOS ONE (Dec. 3, 2013), http://www.plosone.org/article/info%3Adoi%2F10.1371%2Fjournal.pone.0081648. For commentary, *see* Mary Christina Wood, *The Planet on the Docket: Atmospheric Trust Litigation to Protect Earth's Climate System and Habitability*, 9 Fla. A&M L. Rev. 401 (2015), *available at* http://papers.ssrn.com/sol3/papers.cfm?abstract_id=2446689.

In Eugene, Oregon, the birthplace of ATL, the City Council passed an historic public trust climate ordinance on July 28, 2014, forcing carbon emissions reduction of 6% a year to implement the city's public trust responsibility. For the press release issued by Our Children's Trust, *see* http://ourchildrenstrust.org/sites/default/files/14.07.29Eugene AdoptsClimateRecoveryOrdinance.pdf. Could such an ordinance serve as a model for other cities? Could it influence courts that have pending ATL cases?

9. For more on the potential role of the public trust doctrine to combat climate change, *see* Karl S. Coplan, *Public Trust Limits on Greenhouse Gas Trading Schemes: A Sustainable Middle Ground?*, 35 Colum. J. Envtl. L. 287 (2010); Robin Kundis Craig, *Adapting to Climate Change: The Potential Role of State Common-Law Public Trust Doctrines*, 34 Vt. L. Rev. 781 (2010); Margaret E. Peloso & Margaret R. Caldwell, *Dynamic Property Rights: The Public Trust Doctrine and Takings in a Changing Climate*, 30 Stan. Envtl. L. Rev. 51 (2011). ATL has spawned articles examining its potential in particular states. *See* Kylie Wha Kyung Wager, *In Common Law We Trust: How Hawai'i's Public Trust Doctrine Can Support Atmospheric Trust Litigation to Address Climate Change*, 20 Hastings W.-N.W. J. Envtl. L. & Pol'y 55 (2014) and Gregory S. Munro, *The Public Trust Doctrine & the Montana Constitution as Legal Bases for Climate Change Litigation in Montana*, 73 Mont. L. Rev. 123 (2012).

D. The Ocean Trust

Oceans are a classic transboundary resource degraded from the polluting activities of multiple sovereigns. Oceans now suffer from extreme acidification, fisheries collapse, pollution, coral reef bleaching, and a host of other problems. Over the years, nations have "enclosed" more areas of the oceans near their coastlines, asserting sovereignty to allow activities that affect other nations and the planet ecosystem as a whole. Does the trust obligation apply to the federal government when it exercises sovereignty affecting the oceans and coastlines? Justice Douglas famously declared in *Alabama v. Texas*, 347 U.S. 272, 277–82 (1954):

> The marginal sea is not an oil well; it is more than a mass of water; it is a protective belt for the entire Nation over which the United States must exercise exclusive and paramount authority. The authority over it can no more be abdicated than any of the other great powers of the Federal Government. It is to be exercised for the benefit of the whole.... [W]e are dealing here with incidents of national sovereignty. Could Congress cede the great Columbia River or the mighty Mississippi to a State or a power company? I should think not. For they are arteries of commerce that attach to the national sovereignty and remain there until and unless the Constitution is changed. What is true of a great river would seem to be even more obviously true of the marginal sea.

In the materials below, several commentators suggest a federal public trust obligation to hold the U.S. government accountable in managing the ocean and seabed resources. Yet this area has not produced litigation, as has been the case with the atmosphere. As you read the materials below, consider what management standards would derive from a trust obligation and how it would be enforced.

The Public Trust Doctrine in the Exclusive Economic Zone
Casey Jarman
65 Or. L. Rev. 1 (1986)

On March 10, 1983, President Reagan issued a Proclamation establishing an "exclusive economic zone" (EEZ) extending 200 nautical miles from the baseline from which the territorial sea is measured. The Proclamation claims for the United States "sovereign rights for the purpose of exploring, exploiting, conserving, and managing natural resources, both living and nonliving, of the seabed and subsoil and the superjacent waters," as well as for the protection of the marine environment. As a result, the United States is asserting jurisdiction over ocean resources covering an area of over six million square miles, an area representing approximately one and a half times the total land mass of the United States....

Resources claimed under the Proclamation are public resources which the government holds in trust for the people of the United States.... To ensure that these trust resources are adequately protected, the courts should adopt the public trust doctrine, thereby creating a judicially enforceable public trust override in their management....

[O]cean areas outside the limited territorial seas of coastal nations generally were considered high seas until the advent of the EEZ concept. Within this area, resources were regarded as common property to which all nations had equal rights. Although a specific international public trust as such has not been acknowledged over these resources, the customary doctrine of freedom of the high seas is based upon the same commons concepts from which the public trust doctrine developed. The rights secured on the high seas are the same as those traditionally protected by the public trust—fisheries, navigation, and commerce. Present application of the public trust doctrine therefore is consistent with historic treatment of EEZ resources.

Under the Proclamation, the federal government now owns the living and nonliving resources of the EEZ in trust for the people of the United States. In addition, the government is obligated to preserve certain high seas common rights for the world community. This dual responsibility supports the need for an increased role of public stewardship beyond that provided under the current statutory regime. The tidelands public trust is an appropriate legal tool for exercising this stewardship. Because the rationale behind the existence of such a trust for tideland resources is equally applicable to the EEZ, it is arguable that the sovereign rights asserted over EEZ resources are burdened with a judicially enforceable trust obligation to protect the public's interest in these common resources....

(b) Scope of the Trust

...Certain common principles can be derived from a review of state cases. First, as stated by the Supreme Court in *Illinois Central*, no absolute prohibition exists against the disposition of public trust properties. Tidal resources can be allocated to private entities so long as the government does not divest itself of its ability to control a "whole area" of submerged lands. Courts enforcing the public trust look closely at reallocations favoring narrow constituencies. Second, the disposition cannot substantially impair the public interest in remaining areas. Third, the resource must be maintained and held available for uses that benefit the public. This holding is tempered by some courts which provide a limited exception for statutorily authorized conveyances that promote the general interests of the public. Fourth, conveyances of public trust lands to private parties do not extinguish the trust; i.e., a new landowner cannot prohibit the public from exercising, in a reasonable manner, common rights such as fishing and navigation. Finally, there are no definitive sets of priorities among trust uses....

Central to the above principles is the existence of a government duty to manage trust resources so as not to extinguish the public's right to use them.... Congress, then, can pass legislation managing EEZ public trust resources, but if such laws impair the trust, the courts have the authority to review the legislation or the administrative action taken pursuant to the law. This right of action, available to private citizens as well as governmental entities, should be separate from and in addition to any remedies available in the statutes themselves or the Administrative Procedures Act....

Oil and gas activities which would interfere with traditional public uses should be subject to intense scrutiny under the public trust rationale for several reasons. First, one agenda of the OCSLA [Outer Continental Shelf Lands Act] is to expedite the leasing of OCS lands. At least one recent Secretary of the Interior has interpreted this as giving him a broad mandate to open the entire OCS of the United States for oil and gas leasing and exploration at a rapid pace. Such large scale divestiture of public resources into private hands is a contemporary example of the type of abrogation of the public trust that the court in *Illinois Central* attempted to guard against.

Second, pollution associated with oil and gas development can pose a significant risk to other public trust uses. The OCSLA recognizes this potential conflict, but also seems to reflect an optimistic attitude that the two uses are not mutually exclusive. *** Compatible with the presumption that the government does not ordinarily intend to permit a utilization of trust property that lessens public uses and promotes private profits, a court would take a close look at the extent to which the decision would interfere with the public trust obligation....

Fisheries are a renewable resource which, if managed properly, can provide a perpetual source of both food and economic wealth.... Protection of the marine environment therefore is an important component of management. Oil and gas, on the other hand, are nonrenewable resources, development and management of which are dependent primarily upon the state of the art of technology for discovery, extraction, transportation, and processing.... In situations where scientific information bearing on the effect of oil and gas development on the marine environment is conflicting, decisions based on such information should be resolved in favor of protecting the fisheries resource. Such a result could be reached under a public trust rationale....

The Public Trust Doctrine: What a Tall Tale They Tell
Hope M. Babcock
61 S.C. L. Rev. 393 (2009)

... One function of common law in a statutory legal regime is to fill gaps left in the legal framework....

The gap-filling function of common law is particularly important when applied to natural resources of communal value that are under siege by private commercial interests because these resources are inadequately protected by positive law....

The failure to develop a comprehensive regulatory structure for the EEZ has caused wild fish stocks to plummet from overfishing, leaving the fish that remain vulnerable to the adverse effects of an array of nonfishing commercial activities, such as fish and wind farms and deep seabed mining. Despite the apparent recovery of four badly depleted wild fish stocks, the persistent possibility of a "global collapse of fish stocks" if current fishing trends continue illustrates the seriousness of this problem and magnifies the impact of additional disturbances on these stocks.

Application of the public trust doctrine to fill the regulatory gap on the EEZ might avert this environmental crisis and the resulting economic destabilization that would occur from the global collapse of the world's fisheries. According to Professor Sax, averting such crises is one function of the public trust doctrine....

B. Providing Normative Standards and Other Management Tools

The public trust doctrine, with its emphasis on preserving trust resources for future generations, offers normative management standards that can guide resource managers.

The doctrine's ability to "constrain the natural tendency of governmental officials to exhaust resources in the present generation" acts like "a normative anchor ... geared towards sustaining society for generations to come."

For example, the public trust standard of nonimpairment is similar to preserving the sustainability of a given natural resource. Professor Wood suggests that this is nothing more than "the basic fiduciary duty ... to maintain [an] asset's ability to provide a steady abundance of environmental services for future generations." A sustainability standard could inform the levels at which and circumstances under which fish are harvested or other natural resources are depleted. Such a standard means, for example, that wild fish stocks must be left in a sustainable state after harvesting—in other words, development of the resource to satisfy present needs cannot be at the expense of "the ability of future generations to satisfy their ... needs." The management standards put in place as a result of the application of the public trust doctrine could then inform whatever regulatory regime the federal government develops.

... [The] doctrine's emphasis on preserving trust resources for present and future generations requires the nonexclusive uses and " 'reversible commitments' " of these resources. Therefore, consistent with public trust principles, a resource manager cannot allow any single user of trust resources to consume the entire resource....

To help with the process of choosing between uses of trust resources, the public trust doctrine also offers a balancing mechanism under which the public's interest in maintaining stocks of wild fish can be balanced against other nontrust uses of the area that are proposed. In doing this, a decision maker who is presented with an application for a fish or wind farm must carefully consider the activity's impact on trust resources and assure herself that the conversion of trust resources serves a public interest and that the use "does not substantially impair the public interest in the lands and waters remaining." ...

The Silver Anniversary of the United States' Exclusive Economic Zone: Twenty-Five Years of Ocean Use and Abuse and the Possibility of a Blue Water Public Trust Doctrine

Mary Turnipseed et al.
36 Ecology L.Q. 1 (2009)

... The failure of the 1976 Magnuson-Stevens Act and 1996 Sustainable Fisheries Act to ensure sustainable fisheries management in the United States can be traced, at least in part, to the lack of a firm public trust responsibilities in federal ocean waters. Both of these statutory authorities developed to govern sustainable fisheries management neglected to incorporate explicit public trust principles. As a result, NMFS has lacked a clear public trust authority, which would have provided an organizing mission—to manage fisheries resources in the best interest of current and future citizens—as well as a valuable backstop when setting catch limits and other fishing regulations.

... In introducing the public trust doctrine as a mechanism for environmental protection, Professor Sax had hoped that it would enable the judiciary to rein in "rather dubious projects" that "clear all the legislative and administrative hurdles which have been set up to protect the public interest." However, when the Magnuson-Stevens and the Sustainable Fisheries Acts failed to impose a clear public trust burden on NMFS, they short-circuited the ability of courts to participate in ensuring U.S. fisheries management was sustainable. As a result, the judiciary has tended to override federal fishery management decisions in only the most egregious situations....

A public trust doctrine-infused oceans management regime would realign the horizon of current fisheries management with long-term considerations. It would also give U.S. oceans agencies the legal bedrock on which to build ecosystem-based management—a radically different approach to ocean governance that will require a comprehensive legal underpinning to implement....

Generally, an ecosystem-based approach seeks to protect the "structure, functioning, and key processes" of ecosystems to sustain the services that humans want and need. Managing complex systems like ocean ecosystems in this fashion is a relatively new concept that has yet to be widely implemented.

Fortunately, the vast majority of services provided by the oceans originate in relatively cohesive continental shelf ecosystems, which typically fall within coastal nations' EEZs. For example, at last estimate, 90 to 95 percent of fish and shellfish captured by marine fisheries are from continental shelf ecosystems. The fact that most services provided by oceans stem from processes that occur within continental shelf ecosystems is not insignificant—governance institutions already exist in most, if not all, coastal nations' EEZs. Thus, protecting the ecosystem services provided by continental shelf ecosystems will not require new governance institutions, but simply a new mandate for existing institutions to implement ecosystem-based management....

In the United States, this new mandate to manage for the resilience of marine ecosystem services can be located in the public trust doctrine. Professors J.B. Ruhl and James Salzman assert that the doctrine can be employed even under the strictest utilitarian interpretation of its scope. Protecting ecosystem services essentially preserves the traditional triad of public trust uses, i.e., fishing, commerce, and navigation. Since the historical raison d'etre for the public trust doctrine is to promote these public uses of trust resources, even a conservatively interpreted public trust doctrine can be applied to protect ecosystem services....

Because resources in state waters are coextensive with resources in federal waters, state governments cannot protect them if the federal government does not also adequately protect those resources within its jurisdiction. Fish populations don't heed lines on maps, and many commercially important species inhabit both state and federal waters over the course of their life histories. State governments cannot protect their citizens' right to fish, for example, if the federal government does not also adequately protect fish in federal waters.

It is apparent that the cohesive nature of continental shelf ecosystems is well suited for a coherent management regime. By establishing a duty to conserve entire continental shelf ecosystems—not just those components with economic value, or those that fall under the aegis of state public trust doctrines—a federal public trust doctrine could unify federal ocean agencies with state efforts under a common ecosystem-based vision....

New Discourses on Ocean Governance: Understanding Property Rights and the Public Trust
Gail Oshrenko
21 J. Envtl. L. & Litig. 317 (2006)

* * *

[The article reviews the public trust and suggests its applicability to ocean resources.]

As demands for new or expanded uses of public trust resources lead to conflict, the trustee must weigh current-use value against the interest of future beneficiaries to determine the appropriate trade-off between current profits and long-term provision of goods and services from the public trust property. Unlike a private foundation trust invested in monetary instruments, the corpus of a trust in the ocean cannot be converted to monetary instruments and invested solely for profit. The ocean, or more aptly, ocean ecosystems, must be protected so that they may continue to produce ecosystem services (food, medicine, climate stabilization, recreation, aesthetic enjoyment, as well as navigation and commerce). We now recognize the important role of the oceans in moderating and stabilizing the earth's climate as well as the vital role of the oceans in providing seafood (wild and cultivated). Along many coastlines, the economic value of tourism, recreation, and the associated services related to these industries far outstrip revenues from commercial fishing.... Courts have emphasized the flexibility of the public trust doctrine. The allowed uses are not fixed, but the principles are. Thus, water-dependent activities usually are allowed by the public trust doctrine, but commercial and residential developments are not allowed except as incidental to water-dependent structures.

New uses, such as offshore renewable-energy development; open-water aquaculture; offshore, floating, LNG terminals; and mining of deep-sea vents would present a challenge for government trustees as each would entail closure of some areas to public access. In a private trust, the trustee may be given instructions to invest conservatively and thus might be reluctant to allocate trust assets to new ventures. By analogy, government policy sets the terms for exercise of public trust obligations, and implementing agencies must exercise their trust responsibility in accord with current (and changing) policy. Many scholars consider the principle of intergenerational equity to be a part of the public trust doctrine....

In my judgment, the public trust doctrine naturally extended from navigable waters and the territorial sea to the EEZ with the expansion of U.S. sovereign rights over this area. The public trust doctrine applies to common property over which the U.S. government exercises control but not ownership, including resources within the EEZ.... While the federal government may use leases, permits, dedicated-access privileges, and other legal instruments to determine the appropriate uses of the EEZ, it may not fully privatize the commons or undermine the interests of the wider public expressed in numerous court cases, federal laws, and other authoritative writings regarding the public trust doctrine....

On the high seas, which under the UNCLOS are "the common heritage of mankind," the members of the community include all peoples, and states exercise a common role as trustees for the beneficiaries, including future generations. Under the 1982 Convention, the International Sea-bed Authority is given the formal role of trustee over mineral resources of the seabed in areas beyond coastal-state jurisdiction....

Both treaty obligation and customary law confirm that the trusteeship concept does not cease at the territorial sea. The oceans retain their status as common property, and the public trust concept as articulated in Roman Law and carried out throughout domestic and international law applies to governments exercising jurisdiction over ocean commons....

In the United States, we are likely to see the evolution of the public trust doctrine for governing ocean commons throughout the territorial sea and EEZ. As pressures for use expand, so does the need to apply public trust principles, both geographically and functionally.... The language of "ownership" and private property rights has little place in the current order of the oceans. The concepts of public trust responsibilities, intergenerational equity, ecosystem-based management, marine spatial planning, and comprehen-

sive ocean zoning have emerged in a twenty-first century discourse that is reshaping social institutions for the sea.

Notes

1. All of the commentators above suggest a federal public trust over the EEZ. What is
the benefit of the public trust in that context? How does it change judicial review? How
does it differ with current statutory standards? How can it protect ecosystems?

2. Increasingly, as the above articles point out, the EEZ is subject to a host of conflicting uses, ranging from wind farms to oil drilling to fishing to recreation. How should
federal trustees balance such uses? Does the public trust doctrine provide normative standards by which to prioritize certain uses over others? Does the doctrine altogether preclude certain uses?

3. As some of the commentators mention, one of the major purposes of the PTD is
to prevent alienation of trust property where doing so would create substantial impairment to the remaining trust assets. Modern deep-sea drilling involves unprecedented hazards, manifest in the 2010 Deepwater Horizon spill in the Gulf of Mexico that discharged
4.9 million barrels of oil over the course of 84 days. *See* Jonathan L. Ramseur, Cong. Research Serv., R42942, Congressional Research Service, *Deepwater Horizon Oil Spill: Recent Activities and Ongoing Developments*, Summary (2013). Do leases allowing dangerous
drilling violate the federal government's fiduciary duty to protect ocean waters and marine life under the public trust doctrine?

4. Climate crisis and ocean acidification are closely related. The oceans absorb carbon
pollution, which in turn leads to acidification of water that puts shellfish at risk. *See* Juliet
Eilperin, *Ocean Acidification Emerges as New Climate Threat*, Wash. Post (Sept. 30, 2012).
Given the severe threat to ocean life caused by continued burning of oil, are federal trustees
violating the "substantial impairment" standard by continuing to allow ocean oil drilling?

5. Should the "substantial impairment" standard apply to ocean drilling that can irrev-
ocably damage the atmosphere and the planet's climate system? Dr. James Hansen warns
in no uncertain terms that the carbon dioxide emissions resulting from burning all of the
remaining reserves of petroleum would send the world beyond climate tipping points into
catastrophic heating that would leave a "devastated, sweltering Earth purged of life." *See* JAMES
HANSEN, STORMS OF MY GRANDCHILDREN: THE TRUTH ABOUT THE COMING CLIMATE
CATASTROPHE AND OUR LAST CHANCE TO SAVE HUMANITY 260, 269 (2009). Shouldn't
federal trustees take this into account in deciding whether to continue leasing the Outer
Continental Shelf for oil drilling? Would this be a reason to switch public trust uses to renewable energy ventures such as wind and wave energy? For a detailed description of the
heating projected by burning the remaining fossil fuels in the known reserves, see Bill
McKibben, *Global Warming's Terrifying New Math*, Rolling Stone Mag. (July 19, 2012).

Chapter 12

Frontiers of the Public Trust

The future of the public trust doctrine is in many different hands, as judges and legislators in numerous jurisdictions have the authority to shape the doctrine. So, in many respects, the doctrine is a quintessential example of common law-like decision making, adapted to the felt necessities of the time by local decision makers. Predicting the future, therefore, is difficult. But nonetheless, there are logical opportunities for future growth of the doctrine in constitutions and judicial decisions, both in the United States and other nations. This chapter considers frontier issues of the public trust doctrine. The following article suggests an approach called "Nature's Trust" that offers ways in which the doctrine should expand to meet a new ecological age. For a comprehensive description of the paradigm, see MARY CHRISTINA WOOD, NATURE'S TRUST: ENVIRONMENTAL LAW FOR A NEW ECOLOGICAL AGE (Cambridge U. Press 2013).

"You Can't Negotiate with a Beetle":
Environmental Law for a New Ecological Age
Mary Christina Wood
50 Nat. Res. J. 167 (2010)

* * *

Though the public trust doctrine is embedded in scores of judicial decisions over the past century, it has been all but lost in the administrative jungle that has choked the field of environmental law over the last three decades. Modern-day bureaucrats and politicians no longer see themselves as trustees of public property and resources. They view their roles as political decision-makers, vested with statutory discretion to allow damage to natural assets belonging to the public. Indeed, the vast body of statutes and regulations essentially gives government at all levels the power to privatize ecology by handing out permits to destroy and exploit natural resources. The present legal system fails to impose a corresponding duty adequate to temper this enormous power.

Revived to apply to modern bureaucracy, public trust principles would introduce an old-but-new limitation on government acting through modern statutory law. The trust interjects a fiduciary duty into every government action involving the environment....

A Nature's Trust paradigm has the potential to create an organizing framework responsive to the new ecological era. But to do so, it must push beyond the current boundaries of the public trust doctrine. The doctrine has been the subject of considerable legal scholarship beginning with a landmark work by Joseph Sax in 1970, but, perhaps focusing too much on the existing cases rather than on the inherent potential of the doctrine, it has never been articulated as a cohesive paradigm for managing natural resources. Courts have repeatedly invited expansion of the doctrine by emphasizing its flexibility to accommodate emerging societal needs. Nature's Trust invites a re-conceptualization of the public trust doctrine in at least nine different respects.

First, the public trust doctrine is assumed to be primarily applicable to states, probably because most of the historic cases have involved state action. But the taproot of the public trust lies in sovereign understandings that are equally applicable to the federal government and local governments—both of which play key roles in environmental management. The Nature's Trust approach defines government's duty in natural resources management as obligatory and organic to governmental power. It suggests a trust limitation as an attribute of government itself. Properly cast as intrinsic to government, and reaching back to fundamental understandings that are part of sovereign duty, the Nature's Trust framework logically applies to any local, state, regional, or national government. All forms of government are either sovereign themselves or agents of a sovereign. They are thus either trustees themselves or agents of the trustees. Broadening the jurisdictional reach of the doctrine is essential to arrest the hemorrhage of nature's destruction currently taking place through the instrument of environmental law at all levels of government.

Second, the traditional public trust scholarship has never fully illuminated the constitutional basis of the public trust doctrine. Cast as a constitutional doctrine, the courts have significant authority to rein in legislative abuses of the trust. In a careful analysis of the *Illinois Central* opinion, Professor Douglas Grant ties Justice Field's holding and rationale to the reserved power doctrine, a constitutional doctrine that was particularly prominent in Contract Clause cases at the time.[1] [Under this reserved powers doctrine,] any one legislature could not act to compromise a future legislature's ability to exercise sovereignty on behalf of the people. Because of the crucial nature of submerged lands, Justice Field determined they were a "subject of concern to the whole people" and, as such, were clothed with sovereign interests. The lakebed at issue in *Illinois Central*, along with other navigable waterways, thus served such paramount public interests that the Supreme Court classified them as reserved assets of the people's sovereignty that could not be conveyed away by any one legislature....

Third, the public trust doctrine has not been folded into the modern context of environmental bureaucracy. Indeed, Sax's landmark delineation of the doctrine pre-dated most of the major environmental statutes. For the trust duty to be of use in contemporary contexts, much work remains to be done to import the fiduciary principles into the statutory and administrative framework. Within this framework, Nature's Trust is aimed directly at agency discretion, which is the magnet for political influence across nearly all agencies and the major source of dysfunction in the field of environmental law. To this end, the trust obligation is best thought of as an interstitial legal duty that finds expression through the statutory procedural edifice of current environmental law.

Two facets of the doctrine are key to curbing agency discretion. The first is agencies' substantive fiduciary obligation to protect natural resources. Fiduciary standards can be applied to rivers, species, forests, or even to broad ecological assets, including the atmosphere. They can be expressed as species recovery targets, sustainable logging rates, instream flows, carbon pollution reduction goals, and so forth, all calibrated toward replenishing nature's assets. Yardsticks of fiduciary performance and asset health must draw from nature's own laws and, as such, are best offered by scientists that operate outside the spheres of political influence. Second, a duty of loyalty toward public beneficiaries—and

---

1. Douglas L. Grant, *Underpinnings of the Public Trust Doctrine: Lessons from* Illinois Central Railroad, 33 Ariz. St. L.J. 849, 856 (2001).

not toward singular private interests—must bridle agency actors in their decisions regarding public ecological resources. A robust set of safeguards must be developed to ensure that such a duty of loyalty is carried out. By imposing a duty of protection and loyalty on the administrative discretion that is generic to nearly all agencies, the Nature's Trust approach is intended to create a holistic and uniform principle that is transformative across the modern environmental bureaucracy.

As a fourth matter, the historic interpretation of the public trust has unduly limited its geographic reach to streambeds and water-related areas. This limitation is superficial and at odds with the overriding truth of nature that all ecological resources are interconnected and interdependent. While the public trust has been characterized as a doctrine primarily related to water and wildlife, the core rationale for the trust clearly extends to all vital natural resources needed by society. The essential doctrinal purposes underlying the public trust doctrine would extend government's fiduciary duty of protection in a holistic manner to all natural assets, including air, atmosphere, forests, wildlife, wetlands, aquifers, and soils. Indeed, the Nature's Trust framework would extend fiduciary protection to the full ecological *res* needed by the citizenry.

Fifth, the public trust has characteristically been portrayed as a creature of U.S. law, though a few have attempted to explore its iterations in other countries. In fact, trust principles are manifest in many other legal systems of the world including, for example, India and the Philippines. As Charles Wilkinson has put it: "The real headwaters of the public trust doctrine ... arise in rivulets from all reaches of the basin that holds the societies of the world."[2] If the basic premise of the doctrine—the duty to protect vital natural resources for all generations of citizens—is cast as an inherent attribute of sovereignty, the doctrine holds tremendous potential to protect citizens of other nations against government abuse or corruption in natural resources management....

Sixth, the public trust doctrine is most often cast as a one-dimensional doctrinal tool, used to constrain the actions of one single sovereign, usually a state government or agency. It has far greater potential as a medium in which to allocate inter-sovereign rights to shared resources. Because trust principles are grounded in property law, they suggest trans-border responsibilities for shared resources such as major waterways, oceans, wildlife, and the atmosphere. The trust ownership of such shared natural resources can be expressed as co-tenancies in which each nation or state serves as a co-trustee. As co-tenant trustees, each has the duty to not waste, or destroy, the common asset. The duty against waste arises both from the trust doctrine and ancient rules pertaining to co-tenancy....

A seventh area in which the public trust doctrine still falls short is at the interface between public property rights and private property ownership. The fact is that much of the ecology needing paramount protection—such as forests and soils—exists on private land. Courts have yet to explain how private property ownership must adjust to a new era of natural scarcity and uncertainty. A handful of cases relating to streambeds and shorelines recognize the ecological obligations of landowners by presenting the trust as a public encumbrance on title that thwarts Fifth Amendment takings claims. In this corner of public trust jurisprudence, courts have created a structure of accommodation by defining a *jus publicum/jus privatum* interface in the title to land. This concept should stretch to a far broader realm of land and resources in order to fully reconcile the doctrine with private property ownership....

---

2. Charles F. Wilkinson, *The Headwaters of the Public Trust: Some Thoughts on the Source and Scope of the Traditional Doctrine*, 19 Envtl. L. 425, 431 (1989).

An eighth limitation is that the public trust scholarship has, for the most part, failed to create judicial enforcement mechanisms that are adequate for the multi-sovereign, procedurally complex situations that arise time and time again. To be effective, a Nature's Trust framework must construct a robust role for the judiciary, one that does not fall easily to traditional defenses. Defenses related to standing, the political question doctrine, and preemption all present a different twist when viewed through a trust frame (as opposed to a statutory frame), yet these have not been fully explored in the trust scholarship. A related challenge is creating tangible ways in which to equip the judicial branch with the power to enforce the people's trust. While past eras saw active judicial innovation of common law remedies, these are rare in the modern statutory era, as judges typically remand matters to the agency for further proceedings. Many existing hybrid judicial/administrative tools offer mechanisms for enforcing common law public rights but few have been explored in the public trust context.

Finally, because the public trust has always been thought of as a creature of the law, scholarship has never tapped the broader potential of the doctrine to galvanize a political, social, and economic transformation—one that would reinforce legal initiatives. To be at all effective, any legal crusade must be part of an overall cultural and economic movement that spans many levels and human institutions. Legal principles that do not resonate with culturally and spiritually rooted human values will be short-lived and destructive. Over the course of four decades, U.S. environmental law became unmoored from the deeply shared ethic reflecting the sanctity of human survival, local economic security, and natural abundance. The passionate calls for environmental democracy heard in the 1970s are now muffled by thousands of acronyms and garbled techno-jargon, deafening the legal system to core environmental values. Not surprisingly, the law now fails to inspire broad environmental protection, and some have announced the death of environmentalism as we know it.

Trust principles, however, tap the deep inclination of human beings to secure natural abundance for children and society at large. These principles harness powerful concepts of intergenerational equity. They harmonize with many religious and spiritual understandings that view humans as Earth's stewards, and thereby dovetail with worldwide religious movements toward sustainability. Furthermore, a trust approach has extraordinary synergy with economic proposals of natural capitalism that have potential to jumpstart a sagging economy with green jobs. The prohibition against waste of public resources can help kindle a business revolution and spur cradle-to-cradle design of all products to eliminate environmental hazards. In short, the trust has deeply inspiring applications when viewed as a political concept, an ethical mooring, and an economic principle as well. By reflecting many of the fundamental civic expectations in a democratic society, the Nature's Trust discourse could greatly strengthen legal initiatives toward environmental restoration.

* * *

A. An Expanding *Res*

Expanding the scope of the public trust doctrine has been an ongoing process for a century and a half, as these materials repeatedly have indicated. Two resources that the trust doctrine might expand to include are the atmosphere and groundwater. As far back as Justinian, the Institutes declared, "[b]y the law of nature these things are common to

mankind—the air, running water, the sea and, consequently, the shores of the sea." IN-
STITUTES OF JUSTINIAN, Book II, Part I: Of the Different Kinds of Things. "Air" would
certainly seem to include the atmosphere, and while "running water" might be interpreted
to include only surface water, modern hydrological science has revealed that where surface and groundwater are interconnected, they are functionally the same resource. However, the characterization of the trust as a concept related to streambeds and navigable waters
has impeded the logical progression of the doctrine to address modern circumstances.
Yet judge-made law is known for its adaptability to new exigencies. As the Oregon Supreme
Court once declared:

> The very essence of the common law is flexibility and adaptability.... If the com-
> mon law should become ... crystallized..., it would cease to be the common law
> of history, and would be an inelastic and arbitrary code. It is one of the estab-
> lished principles of the common law, which has been carried along with its growth,
> that precedents must yield to the reason of different or modified conditions.

In re Hood River, 227 P. 1065, 1086–87 (Or. 1924).

As chapter 11 discussed, court rulings granting trust protection to air and atmosphere
could perhaps supply an antidote to the political gridlock over controlling greenhouse
gas emissions which threaten the ecological integrity of the planet itself. In the Atmospheric Trust Litigation campaign, two state trial courts have found air as part of the public trust. *Bonser-Lain v. Tex. Comm'n on Envtl. Quality*, No. D-1-GN-11-002194, 2012
WL 3164561 (Tex. Dist. Ct. Aug. 2 2012) (p. 395) (but denying relief due to other pending litigation involving air pollution regulation); *Reed v. Martinez*, No. D-101-CV-2011-
01514, 2012 WL 8466121 (N.M. Dist. Ct. July 14, 2012) (p. 397) (allowing case to proceed
and denying government's motion to dismiss). In an Arizona Court of Appeals memorandum decision, the court assumed without deciding that the public trust included air
and atmosphere, stating, "Without deciding the issue, we understand that the argument
for including the atmosphere within the public trust is based on a definition of the public trust as applying to a resource for which all citizens depend and share and which cannot be divided for purposes of private ownership." *Butler ex rel. Peshlakai v. Brewer*, No.
1 CA-CV 12-0347, 2013 WL 1091209, at *6 (Ariz. Ct. App. Mar. 14, 2013). The court
addressed the role of precedent, stating:

> While public trust jurisprudence in Arizona has developed in the context of the
> state's interest in land under its waters, we reject Defendants' argument that such
> jurisprudence limits the Doctrine to water-related issues. The Defendants over-
> state the importance of the substance of the precedent discussed above, or mis-
> construe it, by arguing that "[i]n Arizona, the public trust doctrine applies *only*
> to Arizona's navigable streambeds" (emphasis added). Arizona courts have never
> made such a pronouncement nor have the courts determined that the atmos-
> phere, or any other particular resource, is *not* a part of the public trust. *See* Danielle
> Spiegel, *Can the Public Trust Doctrine Save Western Groundwater?*, 18 N.Y.U. Envtl.
> L.J. 412, 441 (2010) ("Arizona courts have not issued any ... holdings that ex-
> plicitly reject the application of the public trust doctrine to the protection of a given
> area or interest."). The fact that the only Arizona cases directly addressing the
> Doctrine did so in the context of lands underlying navigable watercourses does
> not mean that the Doctrine in Arizona is limited to such lands. Any determina-
> tion of the scope of the Doctrine depends on the facts presented in a specific case.

> As a consequence, our precedent does not address the measures by which a re-
> source may be determined to be a part of the public trust or a framework for

analyzing such contentions as Butler's that the public trust applies to the atmosphere with respect to GHG emissions and climate change. For purposes of our analysis, we assume without deciding that the atmosphere is a part of the public trust subject to the Doctrine.

In a footnote, the court added, "[t]hat no Arizona court has had the occasion to apply the Doctrine in other contexts or to other resources such as the atmosphere, however, does not persuade us that Butler's claim is foreclosed under Arizona law or that the scope of the Doctrine is limited to navigable streambeds as the Defendants argue." *Id.* at *6 n.4 (citing *San Carlos Apache Tribe v. Superior Court of Ariz.*, 972 P.2d 179, 199 (Ariz. 1999) ("It is for the courts to decide whether the public trust doctrine is applicable to the facts.")). The decision, however, was unpublished, and court rules prevent it from being treated as precedent or freely cited in legal proceedings. Why would a court fail to publish a decision having such important consequences? The court rejected the youth plaintiff's claim on the basis that she had not identified a constitutional provision justifying the relief sought. *Id.* at *7.

Groundwater represents another logical extension of the trust. Here too, the precedent is mixed. The Hawaiian Supreme Court, in the *Waiahole Ditch* case (p. 189), had no difficulty in ruling that groundwater was subject to that state's public trust doctrine. But the California Court of Appeal, in *Golden Feather Community Ass'n v. Thermalito Irrigation Dist.*, 257 Cal. Rptr. 836 (Cal. Ct. App. 1989), and the Washington Supreme Court, in *Rettkowski v. Dep't of Ecology*, 858 P.2d 232 (Wash. 1993), ruled against applying the public trust doctrine to groundwater, in the California case because of a lack of connection to a navigable water, and in the Washington case because of a lack of legislative intent. Great Lakes states also generally have rejected application of the trust to groundwater on a lack of link to navigability. *See, e.g., Mich. Citizens for Water Conservation v. Nestle Waters North America*, 709 N.W.2d 174, 218–20 (Mich. Ct. App. 2005), *aff'd in part, rev'd in part*, 737 N.W.2d 447 (Mich. 2007), *reh'g denied*, 739 N.W.2d 332 (Mich. 2007); *Bott v. Natural Resources Comm'n*, 327 N.W.2d 838, 846 (Mich. 1982). However, as noted in chapter 3 (p. 124), the Great Lakes Compact considers groundwater to be a public trust resource, although it also declares that it is not aimed at changing state common law rules.

In 2008, the Vermont legislature became one of the leading jurisdictions to include groundwater among public trust resources, 10 V.S.A. § 1390(5) (declaring "the groundwater resources of the state are held in trust for the public"). The Environmental Division of the Vermont Superior Court ruled that the statutory change meant the state Agency of Natural Resources could not authorize disposal of tailings into a lined disposal facility under rules existing prior to the statutory change in 2008 because the agency performed no separate public trust analysis. *In re Omya Solid Waste Facility Final Certificate*, No. 96-6-10 Vtec (Vt. Super. Ct. May 16, 2011) (clarifying an earlier order). In the decision below, the Supreme Court of Wisconsin extended public trust consideration to groundwater wells that affect navigable waters.

Lake Beulah Management District v. State of Wisconsin Department of Natural Resources
Supreme Court of Wisconsin
799 N.W.2d 73 (2011)

CROOKS, J.

This is a review of a published decision of the court of appeals involving the Wisconsin Department of Natural Resources' (DNR) decision to issue a permit to the Village of

East Troy (the Village) for a municipal well, Well No. 7, on September 6, 2005. Well No. 7 was constructed and began operating on August 1, 2008. The Lake Beulah Management District (LBMD) and the Lake Beulah Protective and Improvement Association (LBPIA), referred to collectively as the conservancies, challenged the DNR's decision to issue the 2005 permit without considering the well's potential impact on nearby Lake Beulah, a navigable water. The [circuit court] denied the petition for review, concluding that, while the DNR had some duty to consider the impact of proposed wells on waters of the state, the DNR did not violate its obligations by issuing the 2005 permit because there was no evidence that the well would harm Lake Beulah. The conservancies appealed.

The court of appeals held that the DNR has the authority and duty to consider the environmental impact of a proposed high capacity well if presented with sufficient scientific evidence suggesting potential harm to waters of the state. The court of appeals concluded that the DNR was presented with such evidence in this case and remanded to the circuit court to order the DNR to consider the impact of Well No. 7 on Lake Beulah.

We conclude that, pursuant to Wis. Stat. § 281.11, § 281.12, § 281.34, and § 281.35 (2005–06), along with the legislature's delegation of the State's public trust duties, the DNR has the authority and a general duty to consider whether a proposed high capacity well may harm waters of the state. Upon what evidence, and under what circumstances, the DNR's general duty is implicated by a proposed high capacity well is a highly fact specific matter that depends upon what information is presented to the DNR decision makers by the well owner in the well permit application and by citizens and other entities regarding that permit application while it is under review by the DNR.

We further hold that to comply with this general duty, the DNR must consider the environmental impact of a proposed high capacity well when presented with sufficient concrete, scientific evidence of potential harm to waters of the state. The DNR should use both its expertise in water resources management and its discretion to determine whether its duty as trustee of public trust resources is implicated by a proposed high capacity well permit application, such that it must consider the environmental impact of the well or in some cases deny a permit application or include conditions in a well permit.

* * *

A. The Scope of the DNR's Authority and Duty

The focus of the conservancies' challenge to the 2005 permit is their assertion that the DNR has both the authority and duty to consider the impact of a proposed high capacity well on waters of the state. To a certain extent, the DNR agrees. The DNR asserts that it has the authority and a general duty to consider the impacts of a proposed well on waters of the state when deciding whether to issue a permit though it asserts that this duty did not require the DNR to undertake its own environmental analysis or to deny the permit in this case. The DNR and the conservancies agree that this authority and duty derives from both the public trust doctrine and Wis. Stat. ch. 281.

Regarding the public trust doctrine, they argue that the State has delegated its duties as trustee of public trust resources to the DNR, and that this imposes a duty on the DNR to protect navigable waters. Further, they assert that the DNR's authority and duty is also derived from Wis. Stat. § 281.11 setting forth the purposes and policies of that subchapter, and in Wis. Stat. § 281.12, outlining the DNR's duties under that subchapter to protect and preserve waters of the state. They assert that nothing in the more specific statutory standards for high capacity wells in Wis. Stat. § 281.34 and § 281.35 revokes this broad grant of authority or limits the DNR's duty under the public trust doctrine. They note that the Village's narrow interpretation of the DNR's authority would lead to an absurd result where the DNR knew a proposed high capacity well would cause harm to waters of the state but had to issue the permit and wait to pursue remedies until after the harm occurred. The DNR asserts that after-the-fact remedies would not be sufficient to protect public trust resources. Finally, the DNR adds, in response to the Village's argument to the contrary, that the DNR's long history of conducting public trust analyses provides sufficient standards and guidance for permittees.

The Village argues that the DNR does not have the authority to consider the effect of a proposed high capacity well on waters of the state or to reject a well permit application because of such concerns. The Village asserts that the specific statutory scheme set forth in Wis. Stat. § 281.34 and § 281.35 circumscribes the DNR's authority to conduct environmental reviews and limits it to only those proposed high capacity wells specifically enumerated in the statute (which do not include Well No. 7): certain wells with a capacity of between 100,000 and 2,000,000 gpd [gallons per day] and all wells with a capacity of over 2,000,000 gpd. The Village argues that the legislative history of Wis. Stat. § 281.34 and § 281.35 indicates that this statutory scheme evinces a deliberate legislative choice to limit the DNR's authority. The Village asserts that this specific, limited grant of authority cannot be superseded by the public trust doctrine or the general policy provisions in Wis. Stat. § 281.11 and § 281.12. The Village argues that interpreting the DNR's authority so broadly would create a permit system without clear standards and would provide no guidance for permit applicants. The Village notes that concerns about the environmental impacts of high capacity wells may be addressed through (1) the DNR's enforcement authority under ch. 30, (2) the State's authority to address nuisance conditions caused by excessive water withdrawals, and (3) citizen nuisance actions.

It is undisputed that Lake Beulah is a navigable water. Thus, we begin our analysis with the applicability of the public trust doctrine to the DNR's regulation of high capacity wells because "[w]hen considering actions that affect navigable waters in the state, one must start with the public trust doctrine, rooted in Article IX, Section 1 of the Wisconsin Constitution." *Hilton v. Dep't of Natural Res.*, 717 N.W.2d 166 (Wis. 2006). While originally derived from the Northwest Ordinance, the public trust doctrine emanates from the following provision of the Wisconsin Constitution: "[T]he river Mississippi and the navigable waters leading into the Mississippi and St. Lawrence, and the carrying places between the same, shall be common highways and forever free." Wis. Const. art. IX, § 1.

This court has long confirmed the ongoing strength and vitality of the State's duty under the public trust doctrine to protect our valuable water resources. In *Diana Shooting Club v. Husting*, we explained the importance of a broad interpretation and vigorous enforcement of the public trust doctrine:

> The wisdom of the policy which, in the organic laws of our state, steadfastly and carefully preserved to the people the full and free use of public waters cannot be questioned. Nor should it be limited or curtailed by narrow constructions. It should be interpreted in the broad and beneficent spirit that gave rise to it in order that the people may fully enjoy the intended benefits. Navigable waters are public waters, and as such they should inure to the benefit of the public.

145 N.W. 816, 820 (Wis. 1914). We reaffirmed this maxim in *Muench v. Public Service Commission* in our examination of the history and evolution of the public trust doctrine, which indicated a "trend to extend and protect the rights of the public to the recreational enjoyment of the navigable waters of the state." 53 N.W.2d 514, 521 (Wis. 1952). We have further explained, "The trust doctrine is not a narrow or crabbed concept of lakes and streams.

It appreciates such bodies of water as more than arteries for waterborne traffic." *Menzer v. Vill. of Elkhart Lake*, 186 N.W.2d 290, 296 (Wis. 1971).

From this fundamental tenet of our constitution, the State holds the navigable waters and the beds underlying those waters in trust for the public. *Hilton*, 717 N.W.2d 166; *ABKA Ltd. P'ship v. Wis. Dep't of Natural Res.*, 648 N.W.2d 854 (Wis. 2002); *Wis. Envtl. Decade, Inc. v. Dep't of Natural Res. (DNR)*, 271 N.W.2d 69 (Wis. 1978). "This 'public trust' duty requires the state not only to promote navigation but also to protect and preserve its waters for fishing, hunting, recreation, and scenic beauty. The state's responsibility in the area has long been acknowledged." *Wis. Envtl. Decade v. DNR*, 271 N.W.2d at 72–73 (internal citations omitted).

While it is primarily the State's duty to protect and preserve these resources, "[i]n furtherance of the state's affirmative obligations as trustee of navigable waters, the legislature has delegated substantial authority over water management matters to the DNR. The duties of the DNR are comprehensive, and its role in protecting state waters is clearly dominant." *Id.* at 73; *see also Hilton*, 717 N.W.2d 166; *ABKA Ltd. P'ship*, 648 N.W.2d 854, 858 ("The legislature has delegated to the DNR broad authority to regulate under the public trust doctrine and to administer ch. 30.").

... Similarly, we conclude that, through Wis. Stat. § 281.11 and § 281.12, the legislature has delegated the State's public trust duties to the DNR in the context of its regulation of high capacity wells and their potential effect on navigable waters such as Lake Beulah. After examining the role of the public trust doctrine, we turn to the language of the relevant statutes.

The statutory scheme governing high capacity wells, in subchapter II of Wis. Stat. ch. 281, combines the DNR's overarching authority and duty to manage and preserve waters of the state with certain specific, minimum statutory requirements.... Wisconsin Stat. § 281.12(1) further sets forth the DNR's powers and duties under subsection II of Wis. Stat. ch. 281, "The department shall have general supervision and control over the waters of the state. It shall carry out the planning, management and regulatory programs necessary for implementing the policy and purpose of this chapter."

In subchapter II of Wis. Stat. ch. 281, the legislature has further directed the DNR to regulate high capacity wells. Wis. Stat. §§ 281.34–281.35. A high capacity well is one that "has a capacity of more than 100,000 [gpd]." Wis. Stat. § 281.34(1)(b). The owner of a proposed high capacity well must "apply to the [DNR] for approval before construction of a high capacity well begins." Wis. Stat. § 281.34(2). While the statutes refer to the DNR's "approval" of a proposed high capacity well, the DNR's "approval" of a well is actually its decision to issue a permit, and we refer to it as such herein.

For wells with a capacity of between 100,000 and 2,000,000 gpd, the DNR must review the well permit application using the formal environmental review process in Wis. Stat. § 1.11 for those wells (1) "located in a groundwater protection area," (2) "with a water loss of more than 95 percent of the amount of water withdrawn," or (3) "that may have a significant environmental impact on a spring." Wis. Stat. § 281.34(4)(a). For certain wells in the above categories, depending upon the DNR's conclusions in the environmental review process, the DNR may issue a permit, may deny a permit, or may issue a permit with conditions to "ensure that the ... well does not cause significant environmental impact," or, in the case of a public utility well, to "ensure that the environmental impact of the well is balanced by the public benefit of the well related to public health and safety." *See* Wis. Stat. § 281.34(5)(b)–(d).

For wells with a capacity of more than 2,000,000 gpd, the legislature has imposed significant additional requirements. Wis. Stat. § 281.35(4)(b), (5). Before issuing a permit for such a well, the DNR must determine, among other things, that "no public water rights in navigable waters will be adversely affected[,] ... the proposed withdrawal and uses will not have a significant adverse impact on the environment and ecosystem[,] ... [or] a significant detrimental effect on the quantity and quality of the waters of the state." Wis. Stat. § 281.35(5)(d).

We conclude that, through Wis. Stat. ch. 281, the legislature has explicitly provided the DNR with the broad authority and a general duty, in part through its delegation of the State's public trust obligations, to manage, protect, and maintain waters of the state. Wis. Stat. §§ 281.11, 281.12; *see also Wis. Envtl. Decade v. DNR*, 271 N.W.2d at 73. Specifically, for all proposed high capacity wells, the legislature has expressly granted the DNR the authority and a general duty to review all permit applications and to decide whether to issue the permit, to issue the permit with conditions, or to deny the application. Wis. Stat. §§ 281.34(2), (4)–(5), 281.35(4)(b), (5). The high capacity well permitting framework along with the DNR's authority and general duty to preserve waters of the state provides the DNR with the discretion to undertake the review it deems necessary for all proposed high capacity wells, including the authority and a general duty to consider the environmental impact of a proposed high capacity well on waters of the state.

The parties agree that there is no requirement either for the formal environmental review in Wis. Stat. § 281.34(4) nor for the detailed environmental findings in Wis. Stat. § 281.35(5) for Well No. 7 because it has a capacity of 1,400,000 gpd and does not fall into any of the special categories in Wis. Stat. § 281.34(4) for which formal environmental review is required. However, the Village argues that the "graduated permit framework" in Wis. Stat. § 281.34 and § 281.35 limits the DNR's authority to consider environmental concerns to only those wells for which minimum review standards are prescribed. The Village's interpretation of the high capacity well statutes would require the DNR to issue a permit when the minimum statutory requirements are met.

To the contrary, there is nothing in either Wis. Stat. § 281.34 or § 281.35 that limits the DNR's authority to consider the environmental impacts of a proposed high capacity well, nor is there any language in subchapter II of Wis. Stat. ch. 281 that requires the DNR to issue a permit for a well if the statutory requirements are met and no formal review or findings are required.

Indeed, the Village's interpretation conflicts with the permissive language in the statutes, which allow the DNR to exercise its discretion when deciding whether to issue a permit. The legislature can, and in other contexts does, mandate that the DNR issue a permit when certain requirements are met, but the legislature has not done so for high capacity well permits. Finding no language expressly revoking or limiting the DNR's authority and general duty to protect and manage waters of the state, we conclude that the DNR retains such authority and general duty to consider whether a proposed high capacity well may impact waters of the state. This interpretation best harmonizes all of the high capacity well statutes and avoids potential conflicts between the statutes and with the State's delegation of its public trust duties.

Contrary to the Village's argument, this does not create a permit system without standards. The Village's argument ignores the reality of how the DNR exercises its authority and complies with its duty within the statutory standards. As with many other environmental statutes, within the general statutory framework, the DNR utilizes its expertise and exercises its discretion to make what, by necessity, are fact-specific determinations. General standards are common in environmental statutes and are included elsewhere in the high capacity well statutes. The fact that these are broad standards does not make them non-existent ones.

We conclude that the meaning of these provisions is clear: the DNR has the authority and a general duty to consider potential environmental harm to waters of the state when reviewing a high capacity well permit application.

The DNR's general duty certainly does not require the DNR to investigate the potential environmental harm of every high capacity well permit application or to undertake a formal environmental review for every application. Such an interpretation would be inconsistent with the legislature's decision to mandate that level of environmental review for only certain high capacity wells. Wis. Stat. §§ 281.34(4), (5), 281.35(5); *see also Rusk Cnty. Citizen Action Group v. Dep't of Natural Res.*, 552 N.W.2d 110 (Wis. Ct. App. 1996).

However, given its general duty, the DNR is required to consider the environmental impact of a proposed high capacity well when presented with sufficient concrete, scientific evidence of potential harm to waters of the state. Upon what evidence, and under what circumstances, that duty is triggered is a highly fact-specific matter that depends upon the information submitted by the well owner in the well permit application and any other information submitted to the DNR decision makers while they are reviewing that permit application. The DNR should use both its expertise in water resources management and its discretion to determine whether its duty as trustee of public trust resources is implicated by a proposed high capacity well permit application such that it has an obligation to consider environmental concerns. This is consistent with the fact-specific determinations that the DNR often must make to comply with its obligations under other environmental statutes.

The limited review available to those who wish to challenge the DNR's discretionary permitting decisions provides an additional restriction that limits when a court will hold that the DNR's duty required it to take further action when considering a particular high capacity well permit application. As outlined in greater detail below, a legal challenge to the DNR's decision under ch. 227 is limited to the record on review and is deferential to the DNR's expertise in this area. Thus, citizens must present any evidence of potential harm to the agency *before* the decision is made or risk losing the ability to challenge the DNR's discretionary decision based on such evidence.

B. Application to This Case

The conservancies argue that the DNR had a duty to consider potential harm to waters of the state in this case because the conservancies provided the DNR with concrete, scientific evidence showing potential harm to Lake Beulah. The conservancies assert that they triggered the DNR's duty by submitting the Nauta affidavit, which they argue contained such evidence, to the DNR while it was making its decision regarding the 2005 permit, and that the DNR violated its duty by not considering it....

* * *

The Nauta affidavit is not in the record on review in this case. The conservancies assert that the DNR actually had this information while making its decision regarding the 2005 permit because they served the Nauta affidavit on the DNR's attorney related to the 2003 permit challenge while the DNR was reviewing the Village's 2005 permit application. At this stage in the proceedings, this argument is of no avail. Instead, before the circuit court, the conservancies could have asserted this argument in support of proper motions to correct or supplement the record on review. *See* Wis. Stat. §§ 227.55, 227.56(1). The conservancies did not make such motions in regard to the Nauta affidavit, and therefore it was not included as part of the record on review.

* * *

We conclude that the DNR properly exercised its discretion and complied with the law in issuing the 2005 permit. Its decision is supported by the evidence in the record on review of the 2005 permit, specifically the documents submitted in the Village's application including Layne-Northwest's conclusion that Well No. 7, pumping at its full capacity, "would avoid any serious disruption of groundwater discharge to Lake Beulah." There is no concrete, scientific evidence in the record on review that would trigger the DNR's duty to consider the impact of Well No. 7 on waters of the state....

* * *

Notes

1. The Wisconsin Supreme Court upheld the permit on the basis that the conservancies had failed to present concrete evidence during the permit proceeding of a harmful impact on navigable waters. Although the conservancies had presented an expert affidavit to the attorney representing the DNR that showed harm, the affidavit did not become part of the administrative record. Consequently, the court refused to consider it. Did the court err in its approach to the evidence in this case? Isn't it the duty of the trustee, not the beneficiaries, to vigilantly explore all possibilities of serious damage to the trust? Did the court turn the duty inside out when it placed the burden on the citizens? *Lake Beulah Mgmt. District*, 799 N.W.2d at 90 ("[W]e conclude that to trigger the DNR's duty to consider the impact of a well on waters of the state, citizens must present sufficient concrete, scientific evidence of potential harm to waters of the state directly to the DNR decision makers while they are considering the well permit application."). Do citizens usually have the capacity, time, and expertise to monitor the trustees of their property when management involves highly technical issues? And in that case, do you think the conservancies assumed that, by submitting the affidavit to the attorney, they had submitted it to the agency represented by the attorney? As a related matter, should trust cases be confined to an administrative record? Because the trust duty stands independent of statutory schemes, shouldn't courts accept evidence of damage to the trust even if such evidence is not contained in the administrative record?

2. Groundwater is on the frontier of the public trust. As discussed in chapter 5, some states now consider groundwater to be a trust resource. *See In re Water Use Permit Applications* (*Waiahole Ditch*), 9 P.3d 409 (Haw. 2000) (p. 189); *Robinson Twp. v. Pennsylvania*, 83 A.3d 901 (Pa. 2013) (p. 82); *In re Omya Solid Waste Facility Final Certification*, No. 96-6-10 Vtec, (Vt. Super Ct. May 16, 2011), interpreting Vt. Stat. Ann. tit 10, § 1390(5) (West 2009). However, this is still a minority perspective, which reflects how strongly water as a trust resource remains tethered to navigability. Given the widespread reliance on groundwater for drinking water supplies, do you predict courts in more states will extend the trust to groundwater in the future?

An alternative approach to groundwater is to subject it to the PTD only where it demonstrably affects navigable waters, as groundwater often does. *See Envtl. Law Found. v. State Water Res. Control Bd.*, No. 34-2010-80000583 (Cal. Super. Ct. July 15, 2014) (p. 184).

3. As the public trust expands to meet new societal needs, some people have explored application of the PTD to the electromagnetic spectrum. Like the beds of navigable waters and other trust natural resource resources, radio and television franchises are conveyances of public, common property to private licensees, so the trust doctrine could apply by analogy. The following article discusses the possibilities, which, so far, have not been seriously considered by Congress or the courts.

Application of the Public-Trust Doctrine and Principles of Natural Resource Management to Electromagnetic Spectrum

Patrick S. Ryan

10 Mich. Telecomm. & Tech. L. Rev. 285, 335–44, 347 (2004)

* * *

The public-trust doctrine relates to the ownership, protection, and use of essential natural and cultural resources, and acts as a sort of common-law check-and-balance against governmental allocation mistakes with regard to public natural resources. The public-trust doctrine has proved useful in the past to correct government misallocations, and it can also do so with the regulation of the electromagnetic spectrum. The public-trust doctrine can — and has — "reached back" and corrected governmental natural-resources-allocation mistakes made long ago (not unlike the spectrum giveaways). For example, the 1983 California Supreme Court decision *Mono Lake*[3] reached back to state water allocation decisions made over forty years before and reversed them, holding that California's government has an "affirmative duty to take the public trust into account" when it makes decisions affecting natural resources, and that it also has a duty of continuing supervision over these resources which allows and may require modification of such decisions whenever they were made.[4] In other states, courts have held that the public-trust doctrine has "emerged from the watery depths [of navigable waterways] to embrace the dry sand area of a beach, rural parklands, a historic battlefield, wildlife, archeological remains, and even a downtown area."[5] Courts have done this by relying on academic opinions and recommendations for extension of the public trust to natural resources, and this Article hopes to make a first step in a similar extension of the public-trust doctrine to the electromagnetic spectrum.

The public-trust doctrine has been used both to prevent government from conveying public resources to private enterprises,[6] and to guarantee the public access to natural resources *after* the resources have been conveyed to private interests[7] (particularly for purposes of "fishing, fowling and navigation").[8] ...

If the doctrine, which already affords people access to certain natural resources, is to be applied to electromagnetic spectrum, then the first question must be whether the spectrum is legally a natural resource. Supporting the conclusion that it is, the United States Supreme Court has stated that electromagnetic spectrum is a "scarce"[9] "natural resource."[10]

---

3. *Nat'l Audubon Soc'y v. Superior Court of Alpine Cnty.*, 658 P.2d 709 (Cal. 1983).

4. *Id.* at 728.

5. *State v. Sorensen*, 436 N.W.2d 358, 362 (Iowa 1989).

6. *See Illinois Cent. R.R. v. Illinois*, 146 U.S. 387 (1892).

7. *Commonwealth v. Alger*, 61 Mass. 53, 67–68 (1851) (holding that intertidal waters are impressed with public rights via the Public-Trust Doctrine — even if the property owner's title reaches to the low-tide line — preserving the public's right to "fishing, fowling and navigation").

8. *Arnold v. Mundy*, 6 N.J.L. 1, 9 (N.J. 1821) (involving oysters, but also applying to fishing, fowling and navigation rights, this was the first United States public-trust-doctrine case).

9. *See Red Lion Broad. Co. v. F.C.C.*, 395 U.S 367, 376 (1969) (calling electromagnetic spectrum a "scarce resource"); *F.C.C. v. League of Women Voters*, 468 U.S. 364, 377 (1984) ("The fundamental distinguishing characteristic of the new medium of broadcasting ... is that [b]roadcast frequencies are a scarce resource.").

10. *See Columbia Broad. Sys., Inc. v. Democratic Nat'l. Comm'n.*, 412 U.S. 94, 173–74 (1973) (making a direct link between electromagnetic spectrum and natural resources: "At the outset, it should be noted that both radio and television broadcasting utilize a natural resource — electromagnetic spectrum ... [a]nd, although broadcasters are granted the temporary use of this valuable resource for terminable three-year periods, 'ownership' and ultimate control remain vested in the people of the United States.").

President Bush has also told us that the electromagnetic spectrum is "a vital and limited national resource."

Given that the electromagnetic spectrum is a natural resource—the easy part—the next question is whether the public-trust doctrine should be applied to it. Commentators have argued convincingly that the public-trust doctrine should be extended to *all* natural resources, and a few wise advocates have suggested that electromagnetic spectrum should be included in the public trust as a subset of "all natural resources." A smaller number of authorities have flirted with the direct possibility of marrying electromagnetic spectrum and the public-trust doctrine. The New America Foundation, for example, has argued in a creative *amicus* brief (filed in connection with a Federal Communications Commission Notice of Inquiry related to spectrum policies) that the public-trust doctrine deprives Congress of the authority to sell off the public airwaves:

> The more fundamental underpinning for common ownership and democratic control of the airwaves is that like other natural systems—including the oceans, navigable waterways and the atmosphere—spectrum is inherently a common asset.... Throughout history, both law and tradition have recognized that certain assets are inherently public and not subject to ownership—not by private parties, or even by the state. The classic examples from Roman law were roads, harbors, ports and navigable waterways. The Romans called this third category of property, *res publicae,* which has been ... incorporated into ... American law as the "public-trust doctrine." The doctrine holds that, because of their unique characteristics, certain natural resources and systems are held in trust by the sovereign on behalf of all citizens.

This reasoning is in line with the public-trust doctrine's history, but it addresses only about half the doctrine's potential. For the public-trust doctrine operates as a superior right guaranteeing qualified access to *all* kinds of property, whether it is owned privately, held by the state, or *unownable,* like the air and the sea. So the New America Foundation has combined a powerful common-law doctrine with a relatively new idea, but it has only considered the doctrine's application to the government's selling of public property to private interests, while ignoring one of the doctrine's most powerful (and often controversial) aspects: its ability to preserve certain rights in a natural resource for the public *even if* the government has conveyed the resource to a private party.

Thus, applying the public-trust doctrine to the spectrum has been proposed before, but only to remedy one of the spectrum's problems (namely, the problem of much of it being essentially privately owned through exclusive licenses to large broadcasting companies). And it has been proposed to utilize only one characteristic of the public-trust doctrine, namely, its ability to defeat private ownership of natural resources. We will now look at how the doctrine's *other capability* (that is, its ability to place restrictions on the private ownership of a resource) can be used to address the *other problems* that the spectrum has.

1. The "Prohibition on Conveyance" and Illinois Central

There is a rich body of literature describing the public-trust doctrine's long history in Roman law, but that writing is only of general interest, because to understand the doctrine as it is employed today, one must note the contemporary distinction between the two different characteristics of the public-trust doctrine as it has developed in the past century. One category of doctrine, most often propounded by the "high-tide states," asserts that public-trust property may not be conveyed to private ownership. Another set of doctrines, usually emanating from the "low-tide states," says that the public trust lets the state make certain private conveyances, but the property remains *impressed* with certain reservations that are held for the public trust. I will call the first interpretation of the public-trust doctrine "prohibition on conveyance," and the second "conveyance with impression." These categories can be seen as two different paradigms: states that allow property ownership to the high-tide line, which lean towards prohibition on conveyance; and the minority of coastal states, which extend property ownership all the way to the low-tide line and which follow the conveyance-with-impression model.

The most cited United States case for the prohibition-on-conveyance interpretation of the public-trust doctrine is *Illinois Central Railroad v. Illinois*.[11] In that decision, the state legislature had transferred ownership of the submerged area of nearly the entire waterfront of Chicago (over 1,000 acres) to the railroad, and four years later a new legislature sought to revoke the transfer but the railroad challenged the revocation. The United States Supreme Court upheld the revocation and returned the waterfront to the state, famously describing title to the land as:

> *different in character* from that which the state holds in lands intended for sale.
> It is different from the title which the United States holds in public lands which
> are open to preemption and sale. *It is a title held in trust for the people of the State*
> that they may enjoy the navigation of the waters, carry on commerce over them,
> and have the liberty of fishing therein freed from the obstruction or interference
> of private parties.

Submerged lands, therefore, possess a *different character* than other forms of property, and they carry with them an implied trust for the public's benefit. Here the presence of water altered the character of the land, so the state's use and disposition of that land had to be consistent with a different standard.

The public-trust doctrine does not mean that a state may *never* convey submerged lands to a private party. To the contrary, the Supreme Court in *Illinois Central* noted that conveyance is permissible, so long as it furthers the public trust interest, and so long as

> [t]he control of the State for the purposes of the trust can never be lost, except
> as to such parcels as are used in promoting the interests of the public therein, or
> can be disposed of without any substantial impairment of the public interest in
> the lands and waters remaining.

The problem in *Illinois Central* was that the state gave away *too much* land with *too little* public purpose. It was a matter of degree: the court weighed the public's interest in the waterfront against the public gain from conveying title to private parties. The outcome is not surprising, because even if the railroad had built certain facilities from which the public had benefited, it is doubtful that the railroad would have needed the entire waterfront.

* * *

Illinois Central is a good example of a prohibition-on-conveyance case: conveyance was revoked, or prohibited, under the public-trust doctrine. We will now turn to the other interpretation of the doctrine, in which conveyance of natural resources to private parties is permitted but the grantee takes the land subject to certain restrictions.

---

11. 146 U.S. 387 (1892). Professor Sax called *Illinois Central* "the Lodestar in American public trust law." Joseph L. Sax, *The Public-Trust Doctrine in Natural Resource Law: Effective Judicial Intervention*, 68 Mich. L. Rev. 471, 489 (1970).

2. The Conveyance-with-Impression Cases and the Jus Privatum Versus Jus Publicum Dichotomy

The conveyance-with-impression cases are also well known within the *jus publicum/ jus privatum* dichotomy, which is simply the clash between private interests and public interests that has been seen not only in public-trust cases but also in more "traditional" property cases (where it is well settled that superior public interests can supersede private-property interests). Public interests' superiority to private ones can be seen in the deference that has been given to the public's environmental interests,[12] aesthetic tastes,[13] administrative ease in delivering public services,[14] and zoning.[15] The phenomenon is apparent in both general property-rights cases and public-trust cases. In the early Massachusetts public-trust decision of *Commonwealth v. Alger*,[16] Justice Shaw declared:

> [I]t is a settled principle, growing out of the nature of well ordered civil society, that every holder of property, however absolute and unqualified may be his title, holds it under the implied liability that his use of it may be so regulated, that it shall not be injurious to the equal enjoyment of others having an equal right to the enjoyment of their property, nor injurious to the rights of the community.

While Shaw's opinion imposed restrictions upon private-property rights through the public-trust doctrine, he also embraced private property in general by calling upon the common law for an established principle, the *sic utere* doctrine, and then distinguishing it. The *jus publicum/jus privatum* principle underlies many traditional property-law (i.e. non-public trust) cases, particularly in zoning matters.

Compare Justice Shaw's declaration in the public-trust case *Alger* with that of Justice Owen in the Wisconsin zoning case, *Carter v. Harper*.[17] Justice Owen used language inspired by the United States Supreme Court in *Chicago, B. & Q. v. People of State of Illinois*,[18] which has since become a cornerstone of California law through its integration into *Miller v. Board of Public Works*[19] and at least a half dozen subsequent cases.[20] Justice Owen observed:

> It is thoroughly established in this country that the rights preserved to the individual by these constitutional protections are held in subordination to the rights

---

12. *See, e.g., Aspen Wilderness Workshop, Inc. v. Colo. Water Conserv. Bd.*, 901 P.2d 1251, 1257 (Colo. 1995) (restricting a ski resort's use of its private property so that the court could protect instream flows); *Selkirk-Priest Basin Ass'n v. Idaho ex rel. Andrus*, 899 P.2d 949, 953 (Idaho 1995) (granting standing to an environmental group to challenge the sale of timber on state forest lands, which, allegedly, harmed fish in an adjacent creek).

13. For example, signs on private property are a protected form of free speech, but the state may regulate signs' physical characteristics because they take up space and may sometimes obstruct views, distract motorists, displace alternative uses of land, and pose other problems that justify state regulation under municipal police powers. *See City of Ladue v. Gilleo*, 512 U.S. 43 (1994).

14. *See Chicago B. & Q. Ry. Co. v. Illinois*, 200 U.S. 561, 587 (1906) (noting that public utilities are "quasi-public" organizations that may take property (with compensation) under eminent domain for the greater public interest).

15. *Miller v. Bd. of Public Works*, 234 P. 381 (1925), *appeal dismissed*, 273 U.S 781 (1926).

16. 61 Mass. 53 (1851).

17. 196 N.W. 451 (Wis. 1923).

18. *Id.* at 453 (citing *Chicago B. & Q. Ry. Co. v. Illinois*, 200 U.S. 561 (1906)).

19. 234 P. 381, 385 (Cal. 1925), *appeal dismissed*, 273 U.S. 781 (1926).

20. *See Kelly v. Mahoney*, 8 Cal. Rptr. 521, 523 (Cal. Ct. App. 1960); *HFH, Ltd. v. Superior Court*, 542 P.2d 237, 242 (Cal. 1975); *Agric. Labor Relations Bd. v. Superior Court*, 546 P.2d 687, 694 (Cal. 1976); *Robins v. Pruneyard Shopping Ctr.*, 592 P.2d 341, 344–45 (Cal. 1979); *Viso v. California*, 154 Cal. Rptr. 580, 583 (Cal. Ct. App. 1979); *Judlo, Inc. v. Vons Cos.*, 259 Cal. Rptr. 624, 626 (Cal. Ct. App. 1989).

of society. Although one owns property, he may not do with it as he pleases, any more that he may act in accordance with his personal desires. As the interest of society justifies restraints upon individual conduct, so also does it justify restraints upon the uses to which property may be devoted. It was not intended by these constitutional provisions to so far protect the individual in the use of his property as to enable him to use it to the detriment of society. By thus protecting individual rights, society did not part with the power to protect itself or to promote its general well-being. Where the interest of the individual conflicts with the interest of society, such individual interest is subordinated to the general welfare.

In a sense, the public-trust doctrine does the same thing as the principle outlined in *Miller:* it affirms that private ownership and rights reserved for the general public are compatible with each other, but it holds that private rights are subordinate to public rights. This has tremendous upside potential for spectrum advocates, even if it may repulse absolutist property-rights proponents, because it could mean that regulators do not have to decide today whether privatization or the commons is the better model, i.e. whether spectrum should be allowed to be owned and traded like property, or whether (as this Article advocates) it should instead be open to all, like other natural resources. If the *jus privatum/jus publicum* dichotomy is applied to electromagnetic spectrum, the conveyance-with-impression interpretation of the public-trust doctrine will make it possible to reserve certain rights for the public and apply them to both the privatization and the commons models. Specifically, this could manifest itself in the right of UWB [Ultra Wideband] and SDR [Software Defined Radio] users to navigate within the spectrum of others, as long as they do not interfere with the principal use of the spectrum.

* * *

The public-trust argument has found its way into many different areas of law and policy, including the preservation of culture, where the American Association of Museums has declared that the country's museums "are organized as public trusts, holding their collections and information as a benefit for those they were established to serve." And in New York, courts have held that state parks are "impressed with a public trust."[21] Although an effort to extend public-trust thinking to copyright was not successful, the attempt was indicative of the applicability of the concept to additional areas.

Notes

1. What characteristics do airwaves share with natural resources like navigable waters and highways? What effect would application of the public trust doctrine have on the issuance and operation of broadcast licensees? Would application of the trust doctrine to airwaves be inconsistent with the First Amendment rights articulated by the Supreme Court's decision in *Citizens United v. Federal Election Comm'n,* 558 U.S. 310 (2010) (ruling that the First Amendment prohibited the government from restricting independent political expenditures by corporations and unions)?

2. Notice that applying the public trust doctrine to the electromagnetic spectrum would require overcoming the perception that the federal government is not bound by the public trust doctrine. This perception has also surfaced in the context of federal public lands, atmosphere, and ocean waters. Chapters 8 and 11 explored the federal trust obligation in

---

21. *Grayson v. Town of Huntington,* 160 A.D.2d 835, 837 (N.Y. App. Div. 1990).

these contexts. Is it time now to rid the doctrine of the widespread (but dubious) characterization as an exclusively state law doctrine?

3. On the *jus publicum* versus *jus privatum* dichotomy, note the article's reliance on Judge Lemuel Shaw's decision in *Commonwealth v. Alger,* a case discussed earlier (p. 38), as well as the Wisconsin case of *State ex rel. Carter v. Harper,* 196 N.W. 451 (Wis. 1923). Of what relevance are these vintage decisions to modern concerns about the allocation of rights to the electromagnetic spectrum?

4. The electromagnetic spectrum has always existed, but it has no mention in the Institutes of Justinian, the Magna Carta, or the foundational public trust opinions of the United States. The reason, of course, is that technology had not yet developed to recognize its importance. Part of the expansion of the trust doctrine entails expanding the interests which it protects. As we have seen, courts have greatly broadened the societal interests from their nineteenth-century focus on fishing, navigation, and commerce to include aesthetics, ecological function, wildlife habitat, and recreation, among other interests. What about society's interest in its cultural or religious protection? The following articles advance these as interests that should be protected by the trust. However, the two suggested approaches differ in one important aspect. The first argues that the trust should protect religious freedom to sacred sites on public lands. Because such lands already exist in public trust, as chapter 8 explained, this approach simply expands the interests protected by the trust to include indigenous religious freedom. The second article suggests expanding the trust *res* to include human-made objects of cultural significance. This represents an expansion of the trust well beyond its traditional realm of nature's bounty. As you read these articles, consider what reasons justify, or work against, expansion of the trust, both as to the assets in the *res* and as to the interests protected.

A Property Rights Approach to Sacred Sites Cases: Asserting a Place for Indians as Nonowners
Kristen A. Carpenter
52 UCLA L. Rev. 1061 (2005)

For practitioners of religions throughout the world, certain places are sacred. Well-known examples include Mecca, Jerusalem, and Mt. Calvary, places where religious adherents come to pray, sacrifice, heal, and contemplate. These are locations in the physical world where humans revere, recognize, and experience the supernatural, and try to understand its meaning in their lives. Indigenous peoples, too, have sacred places that are essential to their religions and cultures. For them, the sacred is often part of the natural landscape. Tribal cultures, from the time of their creation, have been formed, shaped, and renewed in relationship with mountains, mesas, lakes, rivers, and other places that are imbued with the spirituality, history, knowledge, and identity of the people. Today, at numerous sacred sites in the United States, American Indians conduct ceremonies that revitalize their communities and keep their world in balance.

This Article is about a special problem that American Indians face in practicing their religious and cultural activities at sacred sites—many Indian sacred sites are now located on lands owned by the federal government and the government has the legal power to destroy them. In the major case of *Lyng v. Northwest Indian Cemetery Protective Ass'n,*[22]

22. 485 U.S. 439, 442–43 (1988).

for instance, the United States Forest Service decided to build a road and harvest timber on sacred lands where tribal people conducted ceremonies. Northern California Indians challenged the project, but the Supreme Court held that the federal government's project did not violate the First Amendment's Free Exercise Clause, even though the construction and logging would "virtually destroy the Indians'... religion."[23]

Lyng presents a formidable bar to the legal protection of American Indian religious freedoms.... While the free exercise implications of this case have been well-studied by scholars, this Article contends that a deeper understanding of property law is also essential to understanding *Lyng*. Indeed, the Supreme Court treated *Lyng* as a case about both religion and property.... [T]he Court held: "Whatever rights the Indians may have to the use of the area, ... those rights do not divest the Government of its right to use what is, after all, *its* land."

This second prong of *Lyng* is a property law holding—it provides that the federal government's rights *as an owner* trump any interests that the Indians have in using their sacred sites. Despite this very robust, or even extreme, formulation of the government's ownership rights, this holding has gone largely unchallenged....

This Article takes a different approach. It argues that Indian nations can use property law to challenge the absolutist version of ownership espoused by the Court in *Lyng*. Indian nations can assert that even as nonowners, they may have enforceable rights at sacred sites located on federal public lands. And they can argue that despite the government's status as the owner, it may have enforceable obligations at sacred sites....

* * *

Sacred site cases typically concern the federal government's management of sacred sites located on federal public lands. These lands include national parks and forests, monuments, and historic sites, owned by the federal government and managed through agencies such as the National Park Service and United States Forest Service. The development of natural resources on these lands, such as timber harvesting and energy projects, has long threatened the physical and spiritual integrity of the sites, as well as Indians' abilities to practice their religions....

* * *

2. The Federal Indian Trust Doctrine

[Professor Carpenter provided background on the Indian trust doctrine.]

Like [other resources protected by the Indian trust doctrine], sacred sites located off the reservation are essential to community vitality and the wellbeing of Indian nations. For this reason, the federal government's trust responsibility should encompass a duty to protect the physical integrity of sacred sites and American Indians' meaningful access to them....

* * *

C. The Public Lands Context

* * *

---

23. *Id.* at 447–51.

2. Citizens' Rights in Public Lands: The Public Trust

The Anglo American public trust doctrine is traceable to Roman law recognizing property rights in rivers, oceans, and coastlines, and to later English law prohibiting the monarch from denying commoners' rights to natural resources. Growing out of the Magna Carta, the English public trust doctrine held that the monarch owned common lands for the benefit of the public, thus giving rise to the concept of "sovereign property" and the "inescapable duty of state stewardship." African, Muslim, Spanish, Mexican, French, and American Indian legal traditions also historically protected certain natural resources for public, instead of private, welfare.

The American public trust doctrine has evolved over time, with both state and federal versions. The underlying idea is that citizens have protectable interests—usually economic or environmental—in certain lands....

* * *

3. Applying the Public Trust to Sacred Sites Cases

The public trust doctrine has been used to protect citizens' commercial, subsistence, and environmental interests in public lands. Or, to put it another way, the public trust doctrine allows citizens to express their values—in favor of economic growth, living off the land, and natural resources protection. Because individual citizens may not be able to devote their own private land to these uses for economic or other reasons, the doctrine enables citizens to effectuate their values through use of the public lands.

The public trust doctrine similarly could be used to express collective values in favor of religious freedoms on public lands. The freedom of religion is a clearly entrenched American value. It serves, along with freedom of speech and other fundamental rights, as a marker of a free society. In a pluralistic society, people generally agree that all citizens deserve the freedom of religion. Despite a history of suppressing Indian religions, most Americans would, if asked today, probably agree that Indians should enjoy the right to practice their religions....

... The public trust doctrine allows the government to effectuate our common interest in religious freedom by accommodating spiritual practices, including Indian spiritual practices, on public lands.

If we can agree that the public trust doctrine in theory should be used to effectuate the value of religious freedom, the next question is how. Under a robust view of the doctrine, advocates could seek federal judicial review of agency action, claiming that an administrative agency has an affirmative public trust *duty* to accommodate religious uses of public land. In sacred sites cases, this might include a duty to provide access to practitioners and to maintain the physical integrity of the land in question....

* * *

Some might point out that this application of the public trust doctrine is rather novel. The doctrine has more often been used to protect non-Indian citizens' economic and environmental interests. But the doctrine is broad and flexible. As Carol Rose has argued, "Given the possibility of historical change in our attitudes about what are and what are not valuable socializing institutions, we might expect that our views of inherently public property should change over time."[24] Respect for freedom of religion

---

24. Carol M. Rose, *The Comedy of the Commons: Custom, Commerce, and Inherently Public Property*, in PROPERTY AND PERSUASION 148 (1994).

is a form of "social glue" that holds our society together. Our common interest in freedom of religion applies to Indians, and it can be expressed through the public trust doctrine.

* * *

Notes

1. The article argued for an expansion of the interests protected by the public trust doctrine, rather than the expansion of the *res*. As chapter 8 suggested, federal lands are already held in public trust. Courts, however, have tended to defer to congressional priorities in managing such land. As the public trust doctrine modernizes to adapt to emerging societal interests, can the interest in religious freedom create an enforceable substantive standard of protection for sacred sites? Recall that in the New Jersey beach cases, the courts found that recreation was key to a "well-balanced state." *Matthews v. Bay Head Improvement Ass'n.*, 471 A.2d 355, 363 (N.J. 1984) (p. 261). Is religious freedom for native practitioners also key to a "well-balanced state"? How should this interest square with consumptive uses such as logging and mining? Can courts determine that one interest should prevail over the other? Recall the cases stating that private economic development is not an interest protected by the trust. *In re Water Use Permit Applications*, 9 P.3d 409, 450 (Haw. 2000) (p. 189) ("[T]he public trust has never been understood to safeguard rights of exclusive use for private commercial gain. Such an interpretation, indeed, eviscerates the trust's basic purpose of reserving the resource for use and access by the general public without preference or restriction.").

2. In another, non-excerpted portion of the article, the author discussed Indian-based property doctrines, including the federal Indian trust doctrine, that provide grounds for protection of sacred sites. The Indian trust obligation is, like the public trust, a sovereign obligation, but it inures to the benefit of tribes rather than the general public. The author suggested that the Indian trust and public trust are mutually reinforcing in the context of sacred sites. Can you see conflicts around access issues, however?

3. How far should the trust extend? Should it apply to all cultural resources? Consider the argument of Edith Brown Weiss in *The Planetary Trust: Conservation and Intergenerational Equity*, 11 Ecology L.Q. 495, 502–03 (1984):

> The corpus of the planetary trust includes both the natural heritage of the planet and the cultural heritage of the human species. Our cultural heritage — the intellectual, artistic, social and historical record — is important because it represents our contribution as a species to the planet. Moreover, it is a crucial resource for future generations to draw upon in their temporary habitation of the earth. It is the source of ideas, knowledge, and skills that future generations may use in their efforts to provide for their own well-being. As our capacity to exploit our natural heritage grows, and with it our ability to harm the global environment, our cultural heritage will become an increasingly valuable resource for managing the complex interactions between the human species and the natural environment.

Consider how such cultural property would be protected. How would the trust assets be defined? Who are the beneficiaries and who are the trustees? How would courts derive a fiduciary duty of protection? The following article advocates for protection of cultural property under the public trust. In a non-excerpted portion of the article, the author suggested a model statute that incorporates trust principles.

Identity and Cultural Property:
The Protection of Cultural Property in the United States
Patty Gerstenblith
75 B.U. L. Rev. 559 (1995)

* * *

Culture is, on the one hand, the very expression of our soul both individually and collectively, and on the other, the source of criticism, confrontation and discontent....

[C]ulture, to the anthropologist, the folklorist and the archeologist, is part of the immutable web of what a society is and does. It is the tribal dance, the sacred ground, the strain of rice, the herbal remedy, the architecture, the folk wisdom, the flora and the fauna and the oral tradition. In short, it is the best manifestation of what a society has created, what a society values and what a society believes. These activities and objects come alive only in the context of the whole society.

A second view is that culture can be defined as what is collected by a country's museums and libraries. It includes what prior generations have prized enough to preserve and honor, so by this definition, United States culture would include Greek vases, Klikitat masks and bronzes from the Chi'n dynasty. It is derivative and collective.

A third view contends that our culture resides in those commodities that we are able to buy and sell, and the greater the price, the more prized the item.

* * *

... This Article posits that cultural property is a finite, depletable, and nonrenewable resource that requires uniformity of protection throughout the United States....

* * *

2. Public Trust Doctrine and Group Ownership of Cultural Property

Under the Anglo-American legal system, archaeological resources that are not religious or that are not associated with human remains are subject to ownership....

The public trust doctrine is the most appropriate legal doctrine for explaining the public interest and for protecting the rights of a cultural group in its cultural property....

* * *

Both before and after the publication of Sax's article, courts expanded the public trust doctrine's application to cover other natural resources, such as wildlife, public lands, marine life, and rural parklands. Of importance for this Article is the question of whether the doctrine extends its protection to archaeological resources. In *Wade v. Kramer*,[25] an Illinois appellate court accepted the plaintiff's contention that the public trust doctrine protects archaeological resources,[26] although in that circumstance, the court found that the state had not violated the trust.[27] A California appellate court differed in its approach when it held that the public trust doctrine does not extend to archaeological resources lo-

---

25. 459 N.E.2d 1025 (Ill. App. Ct. 1984).
26. *Id.* at 1027.
27. *Id.* at 1028 (holding that when balancing the construction of a public highway against the public trust doctrine, "the Legislature may reallocate property from one public purpose to another without violating the public trust doctrine").

cated on private land because the state had never owned the objects.[28] The California Supreme Court rejected this reasoning in *City of Los Angeles v. Venice Peninsula Properties*[29] and found that the public trust doctrine can apply to private property that the public has never owned. Furthermore, in *Pennsylvania v. National Gettysburg Battlefield Tower, Inc.*,[30] the Pennsylvania Supreme Court noted that, according to the state constitution, Pennsylvania served as trustee of public natural resources. In the absence of specific legislation defining the contours of the public trust, however, the court did not prohibit construction on private land that would interfere with an historic battlefield and cemetery.

The development of the public trust doctrine from a narrow application to protect specific natural resources to a more expansive use to protect the environment parallels the development of our society's consciousness of, and appreciation for, first, scenic beauty, and then later, the broader environment. The growing recognition that archaeological resources are also finite, nonrenewable, and depletable makes protection of archaeological resources the next logical step for the public trust doctrine to take.

In its application to the protection of cultural property, the public trust doctrine provides the basis for a state's authority to legislate protection of these resources. As a corollary to this function, the doctrine explains why archaeological resource protection that applies to cultural property found on private land does not trigger a takings challenge. Furthermore, the doctrine defines a trust standard for evaluating the conduct of both the government and any private owner of cultural property. It thus imbues the protection of cultural property with the doctrine's trust relationship and imposes a fiduciary standard upon that relationship.

* * *

A protective scheme premised on the public trust doctrine requires identification of a trustee who is charged with responsibility for protection of the cultural property in question. For cultural property belonging to the politically dominant, Western European-derived culture in the United States, both federal and state governments stand as the representative of the cultural group. When government possesses cultural property, it acts as trustee on behalf of the relevant cultural group for protecting and utilizing the object for the benefit of the group. The government may convey possession, either temporary or permanent, or ownership, either subject to the trust or free of the trust, to individuals or various types of public institutions....

Cultural property is not, by definition, inalienable. The problem of alienability lies in obtaining consent of the relevant "owners"—the cultural group. Although one may posit that the government or group representative, as trustee, may alienate cultural property, the problem is representation of future generations, which are also beneficiaries of the trust. Limited alienability is therefore possible, subject, as appropriate, to such restrictions as maintenance of public access for study or display purposes or to a requirement to remain in a particular geographic area....

* * *

28. *San Diego Cnty. Archaeological Soc'y, Inc. v. Compadres*, 146 Cal. Rptr. 786, 788 (Ct. App. 1978) ("[T]he public trust doctrine ... does not involve private property except where the state has conveyed the land into private hands. It does not cover artifacts located on private property.").
29. 644 P.2d 792 (Cal. 1982), *rev'd sub nom. Summa Corp. v. California ex rel. State Lands Comm'n*, 466 U.S. 198 (1984).
30. 311 A.2d 588 (Pa. 1973).

Notes

1. There is little doubt that protection of culture is an important societal interest. But does that necessarily mean it should be protected under the public trust? Isn't human-made property fundamentally different than natural bounty? What are the distinctions between nature's bounty and human-made property that might prove problematic in extending trust protection?

2. What types of cultural property would warrant trust protection? Historic objects? Religious objects? Works of art? Rare books? Cartoons? Children's drawings? Where does one draw the line? Is this an area more appropriate for statutory resolution, particularly since the private property interests in fungible goods and real property (land) involve very different property traditions? For an inquiry into the dilemmas of private property ownership of important cultural objects, see JOSEPH L. SAX, PLAYING DARTS WITH A REMBRANDT (2001).

3. In the case of natural bounty, one can derive a specific duty of protection through reference to nature's own laws. For example, in the *Just* case (p. 141), the Supreme Court of Wisconsin referred to the natural state of land to arrive at a trust obligation. Similarly, the Supreme Court of Hawai'i emphasized in *Waiahole Ditch* that the trust demands "maintenance of ecological balance." *In re Water Use Permit Applications*, 9 P.3d at 458 (p. 189). But what is the baseline of protection for cultural property? Must all of it be protected and in the same way?

4. Would extending the trust to human-made objects stretch the doctrine so far as to cause courts to reject it altogether? Is there a danger of bringing too much under the jurisprudential umbrella?

5. One unconventional application of the public trust doctrine was the effort to extend the doctrine to copyrights, specifically a challenge to Congress's extension of copyright protection to existing rights-holders' monopoly power (for 75 years). The challengers' arguments paralleled those of Professor Richard Epstein in the following article, in which he argued that the public trust doctrine should restrain this alleged giveaway by Congress, analogizing to the attempted giveaway in the nineteenth-century *Illinois Central Railroad* case involving Chicago Harbor (p. 68).

Congress's Copyright Giveaway

Richard A. Epstein
Wall St. J., December 21, 1998

* * *

In this holiday season, we are reminded that it is better to give than to receive. But it is even better to give what you own — not what belongs to other people.

Yet that's precisely what Congress and the president did when it presented Disney shareholders with an early Christmas present this year by passing the Copyright Term Extension Act. This measure, which the president signed in October, extends the period of copyright protection on existing copyrightable material by 20 years. For a grateful Disney, which led the lobbying for the legislation, this was no Mickey Mouse extension but a gift of billions of dollars in future revenues. Thanks to Congress's giveaway, its happy gang of cartoon characters — Mickey, Donald, Goofy and Snow White — won't soon slip into the public domain.

Our legal system recognizes no natural, perpetual right to copyright. Copyright's constitutional pedigree allows Congress to make take-it-or-leave it deals with authors. To promote their literary and scientific efforts, authors get the exclusive use of their work for a limited period of time.

In return, everyone gains the right to use the copyrighted material once its protected period is over. The limited period knocks out the monopoly restrictions on the dissemination of the work by allowing its free use to everyone else, including other authors. It also has the added virtue of keeping the government forever out of the business of controlling literary works forever.

This copyright bargain, however, only makes sense going forward. The works covered under the new law were produced with the incentives available under then existing law. The public gets no new quid pro quo from extending copyright protection for works already created. Removing these works from the public domain works a huge uncompensated wealth transfer from ordinary citizens to Disney, Time Warner and other holders, corporate and individual, of preexisting copyrighted material. It also produces a net social loss by restricting overall level of use of this material.

In other words, Congress's political conniving will cost the public billions. It may be unconstitutional to boot. Here's why.

When Congress takes property from a private individual for public use, it must compensate the holder of that property for the loss. One function of that protection is to prevent government from singling out an individual or group to bear exclusive burdens for benefits obtained by the public at large. A second function is to improve the odds that Congress only takes property with greater value in public than private hands, which won't often happen if it can snap up property for nothing, or even for less than it is worth.

The Constitution does a worse job with government givings than with government takings. But the applicable principles are the mirror image of those that govern moving assets from private to public hands.

Suppose the Disney board transferred Mickey's copyright to Michael Eisner's family without charge. Disney shareholders could recover the copyright from the Eisners just like they could recover transferred cash, land or Goofy's portrait. Similarly, Congress cannot transfer literary works in the public domain unless it receives a quid pro quo, conspicuously absent here, for the benefit of all in exchange.

More than 100 years ago, under what's known as the public trust doctrine, the Supreme Court set aside an Illinois grant of land to the Illinois Railroad as an improper disposition of public assets for private benefit. Similarly, the public trust doctrine ought to apply to the new grant of intangibles under the Copyright Extension Act. If anything, the mechanics for setting aside a transfer of intangible property are easy to work out, for no reconveyance of specific land has to be made to the government. Ordinary citizens can simply resist copyright infringement suits brought by holders of expired copyrights.

Defenders of the act have urged that the extension was necessary to allow U.S. firms to take advantage in the European Union of the 20 additional years of copyright protection available there. The applicable legal rule protects U.S. copyrights in the EU, and vice versa, only for the shorter period in either place.

Before the Copyright Term Extension Act, the shorter U.S. standard applied both here and abroad for cross-national copyrights. The act therefore benefits U.S. firms by allowing them to continue to charge for copyright use overseas. By the same token, it protects EU copyrights in the U.S. for another 20 years, and thus harms American consumers twice, once for domestic and once for European works.

Some readers might find it odd that I take so dim a view of the copyright holders' new claim in light of my nonstop condemnation of the paltry protection offered private property under the Constitution's takings clause. But the real-estate cases that sparked my criticism are very different; the individual owner has perpetual title in his own property while here the copyright holder's term had run out.

My position, moreover, does protect some copyright holders against a second provision of the new law—the Sensenbrenner Amendment, which flatly exempts small restaurants, bars and shops from paying license fees for the right to broadcast copyrighted music. Congress's ad hoc pruning of existing property rights works no better for copyrights than for land: It is as unconstitutional as a hypothetical statute that allows only stamp clubs to use an owner's land free of charge while preserving to the owner the right to exclude all others.

Two wrongs don't make a right, in copyright law or anywhere else. Congress has the power to tinker with the length and scope of copyright protection for new works. But once rights have been created under an existing system, both sides of the bargain, public and private, should be respected.

The stability of property rights in the face of government intrigue is as important for literary work as it is for land or water. It is as necessary for rights in the public domain as for those in private hands. The Supreme Court shouldn't tolerate the copyright shenanigans of Congress on this or any other Christmas.

Notes

1. Professor Epstein, a well-known private rights enthusiast, *see, e.g.,* RICHARD A. EPSTEIN, TAKINGS: PRIVATE PROPERTY AND THE POWER OF EMINENT DOMAIN (1985), might seem to be an unlikely proponent of the public trust doctrine. But this was not his only endorsement of the doctrine. *See* Richard A. Epstein, *The Public Trust Doctrine*, 7 Cato J. 411, 426 (1987) (maintaining that the public trust doctrine is the "mirror image" of the Constitution's eminent domain clause, since "[b]oth doctrines derive from a strong sense of equity that condemns ... uncompensated transfers as a genteel form of theft, regardless of whether the original holdings are public or private").

2. The effort to use the public trust doctrine to challenge the extension of copyright terms in the Sonny Bono Copyright Term Extension Act, Pub. L. No. 95-298, 112 Stat. 2827 (1998), was unsuccessful in *Eldred v. Reno,* 74 F. Supp. 2d 1, 4 (D.D.C. 1999) ("Insofar as the public trust doctrine applies to navigable waters and not copyrights, the retroactive extension of copyright protection does not violate the public trust doctrine."). Both the D.C. Circuit, 239 F.3d 372 (D.C. Cir. 2001), and the Supreme Court, *sub. nom. Eldred v. Ashcroft,* 537 U.S. 186 (2003), affirmed without reaching the public trust doctrine.

3. As to copyrights and other human creations, would a more generalized commons approach fare better, and carry more legitimacy, than a public trust approach? A trust creates a specific trustee, designates beneficiaries, and gives rise to strict, enforceable fiduciary obligations. By contrast, the "commons" characterization simply treats particular items as belonging to everyone, but without necessarily a trust construct. Whereas the public trust remains a bounded property concept, the commons rejects formal property designations. Professor Burns H. Weston and David Bollier explain the commons approach in their book, GREEN GOVERNANCE: ECOLOGICAL SURVIVAL, HUMAN RIGHTS, AND THE LAW OF THE COMMONS 124–25 (2013):

[T]he Commons … may be understood less as an ideology than as an intellectual scaffolding that can be used to develop innovative legal and policy norms, institutions, and procedures relative to a given resource or set of resources. These new structures, however, do not evolve of themselves, nor are they State-directed. Instead, they are animated by commoners who have the authority to act as stewards in the management of the given resource. A commons constitutes a kind of social and moral economy. It is also a matrix of perception and discourse — a worldview — that can loosely unify diverse fields of action now seen as largely isolated from one another.

* * *

… Typically, a commons consists of non-State resources controlled and managed by a defined community of commoners, directly or by delegation of authority. Where appropriate or needed, the State may act as a trustee for a commons or formally facilitate specific commons, much as the State chartering of corporations facilitates Market activity. A commons, however, generally operates independent of State control and need not be State sanctioned to be effective or functional.

The authors distinguish a public trust, stating:

To be clear, the public trust doctrine is not the same as the commons paradigm. It is a venerable principle of State Law that can reinforce the Commons by recognizing the importance of commonly held use rights. [The p]ublic trust doctrine can be invoked as an antidote to the "tragedy of the commons" by requiring the State to uphold its responsibilities to protect resources that belong to the citizenry at large — or, in the case of transboundary resources such as oceans or mountain ranges, to act as a "tenant in common" (with other jurisdictions) to protect those resources. As an attribute of State sovereignty, the public trust doctrine provides a legal framework for the State to define common ownership of natural resources and authorizes State action to protect them. That State sovereignty, however, is based on people's original grant of authority to the State to protect earthly resources that are essential to their survival....

Id. at 240–41.

Already, a vibrant commons has developed, quite outside the formal public trust, regarding Internet materials and scholarly works. *See* David Bollier, Viral Spiral: How the Commoners Built a Digital Republic of Their Own (2009). Could Congress simply recognize public rights in human-created materials and reject private rights?

B. New Enforcement Approaches

Clearly, a trust is only a trust if it can be enforced judicially. Without judicial enforcement, what purports to be a trust amounts to unchecked power exercised by the trustee. Enforcement, then, remains a paramount concern. The following article examines how state constitutions might augment enforcement of public trust obligations on the domestic level in the United States. Following the article is a proposal to create an Oregon Office of Legal Guardian to represent future interests. Legal guardians have also been proposed to represent future generations in the context of planetary resources, as explored in chapter 11.

Democracy, Distrust, and the Public Trust: Process-Based Constitutional Theory, the Public Trust Doctrine, and the Search for a Substantive Environmental Value

William D. Araiza
45 UCLA L. Rev. 385 (1997)

* * *

IV. The Public Trust Doctrine and State Constitutions

[S]tate constitutional provisions dealing with the environment can furnish the substantive commitment to resource conservation that, in turn, justifies judicial application of the public trust doctrine. The constitutions of approximately two-thirds of the fifty states include provisions that, in some way or another, aim at the protection of natural resources. While these provisions vary widely in the scope and type of protection they provide, none has formed the basis for serious judicial protection of public trust resources. This Article suggests the possibility of a symbiotic relationship between these provisions and the process-based public trust doctrine sketched above: while the former provide the substantive political value justifying special judicial solicitude for public trust resources, the latter provides an analytical method, and a justification for that method, that allows courts to engage in this review while respecting the technical and ultimately political nature of the challenged decisions....

A. State Constitutional Provisions and Their Treatment by the Courts

Courts have consistently refused to interpret the [federal] Constitution as providing protection to natural resources or a general right to a clean environment. However, approximately two-thirds of state constitutions do speak in some way to environmental concerns. Although these provisions vary widely, they can be described as falling into seven types, presented here in rough order from the weakest to the strongest protection afforded the environment: (1) authorizations for legislative action (normally for preservation activities or the contracting of indebtedness to pay for preservation); (2) creation of a decision-making body charged with resource preservation; (3) creation of a trust fund or other funding mechanism for preservation purposes; (4) broad statements of a state's pro-preservation policy or directions to the legislature to protect certain resources; (5) restrictions on the legislature's power to alienate certain resources; (6) establishment of certain resources as the public domain; and (7) conferrals of a right to a clean environment on individuals.

The record thus far is not encouraging to those who had hoped that state constitutions could be used to provide significant environmental protection. When confronted with legal challenges alleging violations of these provisions, courts have generally either held that the provisions are not self-executing, or, if self-executing, that they embody such a lenient standard of review of the challenged action as to provide no legally independent grounds for scrutinizing the challenged action. Nevertheless, the remainder of this Article suggests that several categories of these provisions can be reasonably read so as to provide a basis for judicial application of [a] process-based public trust doctrine....

* * *

3. Limits on Government Authority

A number of state constitutional provisions impose a substantive limit on governmental action affecting the environment. These provisions vary in form from grants of individual rights to a clean environment, to the denomination of some or all of the state's natural resources as property vested with some sort of public trust, to explicit restrictions on the government's authority to alienate certain resources. However worded, the provisions all share the characteristic of establishing an explicit limit on governmental discretion to act in ways affecting the environment, by establishing a new relationship between the government and either the people of the state (as with the granting of rights to individuals) or the resource itself (as with restrictions on the legislature's power to alienate certain resources).

These provisions seem to be prime candidates for interpretation based on…process-based principles…. Such provisions alter the legal relationship between the government and the resource, or between the government and the people of the state (third-party beneficiaries of the resource preservation). For example, in *Payne v. Kassab*,[31] the Pennsylvania Supreme Court held that a provision of the Pennsylvania Constitution that declared the state's public natural resources to be a public trust of which the state was a trustee created legal relationships that the court had the power to defend. Moreover, because such provisions limit the government's authority to act, they do not present the same separation of powers obstacles to judicial enforcement as those provisions directing the government to act.

Nevertheless, the conclusion that such provisions can be judicially enforced does not end the inquiry. Instead, it only raises the next question—that of the level of scrutiny courts will employ. For example, in *Payne*, the court, after determining that the constitutional provision at issue was capable of judicial enforcement, went on to interpret it as requiring judicial review exactly co-extensive with a Pennsylvania statute establishing procedure with which the state had to comply before it could proceed with that type of project. To the extent that future cases might deal with factual situations in which those statutory safeguards might not apply, the state supreme court's opinion is unclear as to whether those considerations would apply as constitutional requirements. Lower Pennsylvania courts, however, have held that the constitutional provision does not authorize an agency to take into consideration factors that its authorizing statute does not mention.

Even if the constitutional provision did include its own requirements, the lower appellate court's statement of these requirements makes clear that the requirements do not encompass particularly careful judicial scrutiny of administrative action. The intermediate appellate court in *Payne* crafted a three-party test, examining whether: (1) there was compliance with statutory and administrative law relevant to environmental protection; (2) the record demonstrated "a reasonable effort to reduce the environmental incursion to a minimum;" and (3) the environmental harm so outweighed the benefit from the action as to constitute an abuse of discretion. The state supreme court noted this test with apparent approval. It is hard to disagree with the commentator who concluded that the *Payne* test "strips the [Pennsylvania constitutional] provision of much substantive impact."

Payne reflects the problem courts will inevitably face if they attempt to engage in a substantive review of agency action in areas as complex as natural resource use…. However, [a process-based] test would not seek to second-guess the substantive decisions. Instead, this test contemplates a remand to the agency as the appropriate response. Thus, the constitutional commitment to government solicitude for the environment would take the form of heightened judicial scrutiny of the process by which decisions affecting the environment were made, with the remand remedy avail-

---

31. 361 A.2d 263, 272 (Pa. 1976) (holding that the state constitutional provision dealing with the environment "creates a public trust of public natural resources for the benefit of all the people (including future generations as yet unborn)").

able for agency procedures that failed the test. This test has the effect of keeping the courts out of the business of deciding the appropriate balance between environmental protection and competing values — a balance the courts are ill-equipped to draw — while nevertheless giving effect to unquestionable, if vague, political commitments to resource preservation.

B. Does the Analysis Make Any Difference?

Two objections may be made at this point. First, it could be argued that this analysis adds nothing to state statutory law, specifically, the "little NEPA" state-law analogues to NEPA, which impose many of the requirements that this analysis would impose as a matter of state constitutional law. Second, it could be argued that only a few states have the types of constitutional provisions that may be susceptible to an interpretation allowing this sort of process review. These objections must be met: the analysis will have little practical impact if most states have statutes that yield the same effect as this analysis or if few state constitutions contain the provisions to which this analysis can apply.

1. Does this Analysis Add Anything to the Little NEPAs?

Sixteen states, the District of Columbia, and Puerto Rico have environmental policy acts modeled on NEPA. NEPA requires that the federal government consider the environmental consequences of any action it might take that would have a significant effect on the environment, and that it disclose those consequences. NEPA imposes essentially procedural requirements on the government; it does not require particular outcomes, nor does it authorize courts reviewing government compliance with NEPA to second-guess agencies' ultimate decisions to proceed with an action. Most little NEPAs are similarly procedural.

The requirements that little NEPAs impose on state governments appear at first glance quite similar to those this Article suggests can be derived from state constitutions. This should not be surprising: just as NEPA and the little NEPAs reflect a governmental policy of environmental conservation coupled with an acknowledgment of the need for economic development, so too the constitutional provisions discussed in this Article enunciate or reflect a broad, but not absolute, policy in favor of environmental conservation. Indeed, the little NEPAs may be viewed as legislatures' implementation of the environmental conservation policies embodied in their state constitutions. On the other hand, a number of states whose constitutions establish such a policy do not have a little NEPA. In these states, the constitutional policy would have to be effectuated by the courts, without the benefit of implementing legislation.

Even in states with little NEPAs, the analysis suggested in this Article may play an independent role. This analysis suggests a methodology by which a court can determine which governmental decisions should arouse judicial suspicion and thus receive heightened scrutiny. This methodology is analogous to Rose's analysis of judicial decisions that found some ostensibly private property to be "inherently public," and is illustrated by the questions Sax suggests courts should ask when determining whether a particular resource-use decision was inappropriate. This methodology allows a court somewhat more flexibility in reviewing governmental action, by allowing it to tailor that review to circumstances that may change over time or that differ with the particular governmental action at issue. The flexibility in turn makes this methodology particularly appropriate for constitutionalization, as it allows for a dynamic adaptation of a fundamental social value implemented by a governmental branch relatively more insulated from day-to-day political pressures.

Equally importantly, it is significant that constitutional provisions are part of a state's fundamental law. As such, they are beyond legislative overruling in the normal course of legislative business and thus are less susceptible to legislative tinkering in the face of particular actions the legislature may wish to authorize or prohibit. Such tinkering can assume various forms, such as amendments to the statute itself, subsequent limitation of the statute's scope, "interpretation" of the statute by means of subsequent legislation, or enactment of legislation explicitly authorizing or prohibiting certain action notwithstanding the requirements of more general laws. To the extent such tinkering occurs exactly when consideration of environmental values may be most unpopular (and thus most important), the unique status of a constitutional provision as fundamental law enforceable by the courts becomes most useful.

2. The Lack of Constitutional Provisions

The constitutions of at least twenty states, plus Puerto Rico, include provisions that embody the fundamental commitment to environmental preservation that can, in turn, serve as the source for this Article's proposed analysis. At least fifteen constitutions either claim some type of natural resource as the public domain, for reasons other than pure reservation of exploitation rights, or restrict or qualify the government's power to alienate such resources. At least ten constitutions include a pro-conservation policy statement. Finally, at least six confer upon their residents some form of a right to a clean environment.

Thus, there appears to be significant potential for this Article's analysis to find a basis in American state law. Moreover, the trend toward adopting such provisions is quite pronounced, and suggests an even greater potential. For example, every state constitution enacted since 1959 has included some sort of environmental protection provision. Adoption of this Article's proposed analysis may well assist in this trend by increasing the possibility that a state polity's adoption of such a provision would in fact have concrete effects, and would not be merely a symbolic gesture. At the very least, basing a public trust analysis on such a provision increases the legitimacy of such decisions given the classic public trust doctrine's substantive haziness and unclear legal foundation.

Conclusion

This Article has attempted to determine whether the public trust doctrine may be justified as another expression of the political-process model of American constitutional law, whereby heightened judicial scrutiny of some governmental action is justified as a judicial check on a malfunctioning political process. The same objection that attends this model in its original equal protection context—namely, that close judicial scrutiny of certain governmental actions requires an embrace of some substantive value—applies equally to the public trust context. Thus, while at some level of abstraction it might make sense to conceive of public trust resources as "discrete and insular minorities," that conclusion only postpones the question of why courts should care that such resources in fact are not fully "represented" in the political process.

The reason courts should care is that state polities have expressed a desire to protect such resources through the adoption of state constitutional provisions reflecting this value. Because resource decision making is inherently a technical process that requires the balancing of competing goals, judicial enforcement of these constitutional provisions must refrain from second-guessing those value balances. Instead, courts must restrict themselves to ensuring that the government understood and implemented the polity's concern with environmental conservation, a methodology quite at home with this Article's advocacy of not just a process *justification* for judicial review, but also a process-based methodology for *implementing* such review.

Notes

1. Notice the layers of constitutional analysis: (a) does the provision embody the public trust doctrine? (b) is it judicially enforceable? (c) what level of judicial scrutiny is appropriate? (d) does the provision require more than existing statutes? (e) does the provision impose only procedural requirements on the state, or does it impose substantive obligations? Most state courts have yet to interpret state constitutional provisions to impose substantive duties to implement the public trust doctrine. A notable recent exception is *Robinson Township v. Pennsylvania*, 83 A.3d 901 (Pa. 2013) (p. 82), which interpreted Pennsylvania's Environmental Rights Amendment to provide both substantive and procedural fiduciary responsibilities on both the legislature and agencies. The plurality also found a basis for substantive governmental limits in the rights reserved by citizens as part of the social compact with government.

2. Professor Araiza argued for a process-based approach on the assumption that it would be inappropriate for courts to make judgments balancing substantive trust interests, and he accordingly recommends remands to the agencies. But does this solve the balancing problem? Environmental agencies are notoriously politicized and often serve those with the most political power, as Sax's landmark article pointed out. Isn't it the function of courts to protect the property of the people? Should public property rights to the *res* of a trust be left to the discretion of the trustee or its agents? Would that defeat the very purpose of the trust construct? And do remands to agencies protect the interests of future generations, who are also the beneficiaries of the trust?

3. Could some of the deficiencies in existing state constitutions be remedied through the amendment process? The Climate Legacy Initiative (CLI) developed a model state constitution (with commentary) to implement an environmental right for present and future generations. *See* Burns H. Weston & Tracy Bach, *Recalibrating the Law of Humans with the Laws of Nature: Climate Change, Human Rights, and Intergenerational Justice*, CLI Recommendation No. 2, at 65 (2009), *available at* http://www.area-net.org/fileadmin/user_upload/Maja/Future_Justice_Library/Library_2.pdf.

4. Montana has one of the strongest state constitutions, providing for a "clean and healthful environment" as one of the "inalienable rights" held by citizens of the state. Mont. Const. art. II, §3. In an extensive analysis, Professor Gregory Munro has argued that Montana's public trust doctrine and state constitution should provide the basis for a judicial remedy to curb greenhouse gas pollution causing climate change that harms the state and its citizens. *See* Gregory S. Munro, *The Public Trust Doctrine and the Montana Constitution as Legal Bases for Climate Change Litigation in Montana*, 73 Mont. L. Rev. 123 (2012). Although the Montana Supreme Court dismissed one atmospheric trust case on procedural grounds, the opinion did not foreclose future litigation brought in the district court. *Barhaugh v. State*, 264 P.3d 518 (Table) (Mont. 2011). Professor Munro concluded:

> The Montana Constitution and Montana Supreme Court decisions recognizing the public trust doctrine constitute the foundational underpinnings for climate change jurisprudence in this state. Montana law is particularly poised to allow application of the public trust doctrine for the protection of the atmosphere. Two things are necessary, however, for Montana to lead the way in climate change

litigation. First, the Court needs to clarify that the fundamental right to a clean and healthful environment found in the Montana Constitution is self-executing, so as to provide a legal basis to protect the air from harmful greenhouse gases. The right to a clean and healthful environment is the first of the fundamental rights mentioned in our Constitution. It becomes meaningless if it exists only insofar as the legislature sees fit to effectuate it.... Second, Montana Courts should apply the public trust doctrine to the air under Article II, § 3 and Article IX, which are in accord with such an expansion. By their nature, common-law doctrines in general and the public trust doctrine in particular are flexible enough to accommodate extensions of the law to fit the needs of society. There can be no more pressing need than the protection of the air that sustains the biosphere.

By virtue of its strong common-law recognition of the public trust doctrine and the environmental provisions of its 1972 Constitution, Montana is a uniquely suited forum for climate-change lawsuits in the civil justice system. Montana jurisprudence includes ample precedent that recognizes and applies the public trust doctrine in protection of navigational and recreational waters. There appears to be no sound theoretical basis for a government to impose a trust on navigable waters and not navigable air and airways. Moreover, the Montana Constitution provides the underpinnings for using public trust doctrine for protection of the atmosphere and airways.

By its nature, common law has historically been flexible and subject to extension. One would be hard-pressed to cite a situation in human history that makes a more compelling argument to extend the law to protect the public than climate change resulting from global warming. If resort to the judicial branch of government is to have any effect on the climate crisis, those litigating the cases will have to move quickly and seek remedies with the highest impact and most visibility. The public trust doctrine and the environmental provisions of the Montana Constitution may be the most effective tools in the litigation arsenal.

Munro, at 159–60.

What would be the effect of one state supreme court ruling creating a judicial remedy for carbon pollution? Would the rationale spread to other states and inspire similar judicial rulings in pending atmospheric trust cases in a kind of domino effect? Is it partly a matter of judicial courage? Given the recalcitrance of state legislatures and agencies, as well as the federal government, to control carbon pollution, is there any legal recourse left other than the courts? For background on air as a public trust asset and the legal campaign known as Atmospheric Trust Litigation, see chapter 11 (p. 382).

5. For a list of state constitutional provisions arguably incorporating the public trust doctrine in water law, see Michael C. Blumm, *Public Property and the Democratization of Western Water Law: A Modern View of the Public Trust Doctrine*, 19 Envtl. L. 573, 576, n.12 (1989) (listing provisions from the Alaska, California, Colorado, Idaho, Montana, Nebraska, New Mexico, North Dakota, Texas, and Wyoming Constitutions, surveying only the constitutions of the western states). For a more broad-ranging analysis, see Matthew Thor Kirsch, *Upholding the Public Trust Doctrine in State Constitutions*, 46 Duke L.J. 1169 (1997).

6. The trust is unique among laws and doctrines in that it internalizes protection for future generations by expressly treating them as beneficiaries. But a question remains: who can present their interests in legal proceedings? Legal protection without representation will prove ineffective. In this regard, consider the draft rule/executive order proposed by a study group of the Oregon State Bar's Sustainable Futures Section.

Office of Legal Guardian for Future Generations

[DRAFT 6-26-12, To be created by Administrative Rule or Executive Order]

1. CREATION OF OFFICE OF LEGAL GUARDIAN

1.1 OFFICE. There is created an Office of Legal Guardian for Future Generations (the "Office") within the Department of Administrative Services.

1.2 LEGAL GUARDIAN. The Office shall be comprised of a Legal Guardian (the "Legal Guardian") appointed by the Governor. The Legal Guardian shall have the following qualifications:

(a) A background in ecology and of the dependence of living beings on healthy, functioning ecological systems, an understanding of sustainability, and familiarity with the precautionary principle and decision-making in the face of scientific uncertainty;

(b) A background in financial and budgetary matters and role of economics in public policy;

(c) An understanding of the State's governmental structure, political system and finances;

(d) An understanding of the needs and interests of future generations and how governmental action and public policy can impact such needs and interests; and

(e) The general absence of any ownership interest or membership in any business, industry or occupation or any personal relationship that would be reasonably likely to (i) affect or create the appearance of affecting the exercise of independent judgment relating to actions or decisions in an official capacity, (ii) influence or create the appearance of influencing the outcome of actions or decisions in an official capacity or (iii) generate a private pecuniary benefit or detriment for the Legal Guardian or his or her relative arising from actions or decisions in an official capacity.

2. PURPOSE.

The Office is created to fulfill the responsibility of the State to serve as a trustee of the environment to ensure that a clean, healthful, ecologically balanced, and sustainable environment is passed on to future generations.

3. POWERS AND DUTIES OF LEGAL GUARDIAN

3.1 DEFINITIONS. The following definitions shall apply to Sections 1 to 4:

(a) "Ecological health and sustainability of the environment" is the capacity for self-renewal and self-maintenance of the soils, water, air[,] people, plants, animals and other species that collectively comprise the environment.

(b) The "environment" is the totality within the State of physical substances, conditions and processes (including all living organisms in the biotic community, air, water, land, natural resources and climate) that affect the ability of all life forms to grow, survive and reproduce. The "environment" includes both natural and human-created substances, conditions and processes.

(c) "Future generations" means all people descended from the current generation.

(d) "Future Generations Impact Statement" has the meaning set forth in Section 4.1.

(e) "Inventory of Significant State Resources" has the meaning set forth in Section 3.2(a).

(f) "Legal Guardian Response" has the meaning set forth in Section 4.3.

(g) "Ombudsperson" means a person appointed by an agency of the State to protect the interests of future generations with respect to actions or decisions of such agency.

(h) "Response to Impact Findings" has the meaning set forth in Section 4.2.

(i) "State" means the State of Oregon.

3.2 Functions. The Legal Guardian shall:

(a) Prepare an inventory (the "**Inventory of Significant State Resources**") that identifies all resources of significant ecological or cultural importance located in the State, whether owned by the State, the Federal government, Native American tribes, private parties or otherwise, within one year of the date of this [Administrative Rule or Executive Order] and thereafter update the Inventory of Significant State Resources not less frequently than every five years, identifying additional resources and any change in the status or condition of previously identified resources;

(b) Identify and assess all material threats presented by decisions and actions of the State, including all executive agencies, to the ecological health and sustainability of the environment for future generations, including, without limitation, material threats to the resources on the Inventory of Significant State Resources;

(c) Evaluate alternatives to all governmental decisions and actions of the State, including all executive agencies, that may present a material threat to the ecological health and sustainability of the environment for future generations and identify those that provide the least threat and those that improve the ecological health and sustainability of the environment for future generations;

(d) Propose goals and actions that can be taken by the State, including all executive agencies, that to the extent allowed by law will best protect and improve the ecological health and sustainability of the environment for future generations;

(e) Review, in the exercise of the Legal Guardian's discretion or at the request of a legislator, proposed legislation in the State to identify and assess all material threats to the ecological health and sustainability of the environment for future generations;

(f) Review, in the exercise of the Legal Guardian's discretion, proposed administrative rules in the State to identify and assess all material threats to the ecological health and sustainability of the environment for future generations;

(g) Issue a Future Generations Impact Statement for any proposed legislation or proposed administrative rule in the State that the Legal Guardian reviews and believes may or could pose a material threat to the ecological health and sustainability of the environment for future generations in accordance with Section 4.1;

(h) Whether or not a Future Generations Impact Statement is issued, evaluate alternatives to proposed legislation and proposed administrative rules that may present a material threat to the ecological health and sustainability of the environment for future generations and identify those alternatives that provide the least threat and those alternatives that improve the ecological health and sustainability of the environment for future generations and disclose such matters to the Legislative Assembly (or committees or members thereof) or to agencies, as the Legal Guardian determines is appropriate;

(i) Issue a Legal Guardian Response, as the Legal Guardian determines is appropriate, in accordance with Section 4.3;

(j) Act, in the Legal Guardian's discretion and upon such terms and conditions as the Legal Guardian deems appropriate, in the capacity of a mediator or arbitrator in any dispute that involves a material threat to the ecological health and sustainability of the environment for future generations, but only if all necessary parties to the resolution of such dispute request in writing that the Legal Guardian act in the capacity of a mediator or arbitrator.

(k) Consult with the State, the Legislative Assembly (or committees or members thereof), agencies, Ombudspersons or any other person on any matters relating to the Legal Guardian's functions and furnish such assistance in the performance of the Legal Guardian's functions as may be reasonably requested;

(l) Testify in legislative, administrative, judicial, or other hearings that relate to the Legal Guardian's functions, as the Legal Guardian determines is appropriate, or intervene in any judicial proceeding that relates to the Legal Guardian's functions, as the Legal Guardian determines is appropriate;

(m) Serve in pending litigation, at the request of a state or federal judge in Oregon, as: a special master, expert witness, or settlement judge.

(n) Ensure, together with Ombudspersons, that to the extent allowed by law, the State, including all executive agencies, carries out the proposed actions and achieves the proposed goals identified by the Legal Guardian for best protecting and improving the ecological health and sustainability of the environment for future generations;

(o) Enter into contracts to carry out the functions of the Legal Guardian;

(p) Seek appropriate legal relief to enforce the power and authority of the Legal Guardian; and

(q) Maintain a website for the purposes of educating the public regarding the Legal Guardian's responsibilities and actions, and publishing the Inventory of Significant State Resources, the Annual Report and all Future Generations Impact Statements.

[Sections 3.3, 3.4, and 3.5 provide for professional staff, funding, and annual reporting.]

3.6 NO PRIVATE RIGHT OF ACTION. The creation of Office of Legal Guardian, and the Legal Guardian's powers and duties are not intended to create any private right of action, and nothing herein shall be interpreted to imply any private right of action.

4. FUTURE GENERATIONS IMPACT STATEMENT

4.1 PREPARATION OF FUTURE GENERATIONS IMPACT STATEMENT. In the exercise of the Legal Guardian's discretion or at the request of a legislator, the Legal Guardian shall prepare a Future Generations Impact Statement, containing such information as the Legal Guardian deems advisable consistent with this Section 4.1, on a legislative measure reported out of a committee of the Legislative Assembly if the Legal Guardian determines that the legislative measure poses a material threat to the ecological health and sustainability of the environment for future generations. In the exercise of the Legal Guardian's discretion, the Legal Guardian shall prepare a Future Generations Impact Statement, containing such information as the Legal Guardian deems advisable consistent with this Section 4.1, on a proposed administrative rule, whether permanent or temporary, for which a notice of rulemaking procedure is noticed if the Legal Guardian determines that the proposed administrative rule may or could pose a material threat to the ecological health and sustainability of the environment for future generations. The Future Generations Impact Statement shall provide a written explanation of how the legislative measure or proposed administrative rule poses a material threat to the ecological health and sustainability of the environment for future generations and, if appropriate, identify those alternatives that provide the least threat and those alternatives that improve the ecological health and sustainability of the environment for future generations. The Legal Guardian shall review or withdraw the Future Generations Impact Statement, as the Legal Guardian determines is appropriate, if the legislative measure or proposed administrative rule is amended.

4.2 RESPONSE TO ISSUANCE OF FUTURE GENERATIONS IMPACT STATEMENT. If the Legal Guardian issues a Future Generations Impact Statement with respect to a legislative measure, the committee of the Legislative Assembly out of which the legislative measure was reported, within ten days (or such longer period to which the Legal Guardian agrees) after the Future Generations Impact Statement was issued, shall prepare a written response (a "Response to Impact Findings") to each finding in the Future Generations Impact Statement, which response shall accept or deny such finding and shall provide a written explanation of the denial of any such finding, as the committee determines is appropriate. If the Legal Guardian issues a Future Generations Impact Statement with respect to a proposed administrative rule, the agency which proposed the administrative rule, within ten days (or such longer period to which the Legal Guardian agrees) after the Future Generations Impact Statement was issued, shall prepare a written response (a "Response to Impact Findings") to each finding in the Future Generations Impact Statement, which response shall accept or deny such finding and shall provide a written explanation of the denial of any such finding, as the agency determines is appropriate. The Legal Guardian may extend the time period for the preparation of the Response to Impact Findings as the Legal Guardian determines is reasonably appropriate.

4.3 RESPONSE BY LEGAL GUARDIAN. Within ten days after a Response to Impact Findings is issued by a committee of the Legislative Assembly or an agency pursuant to Section 4.2, the Legal Guardian may prepare a written response (a "Legal Guardian Response") with respect to each finding in the Future Generations Impact Statement that the committee or agency has denied. The Legal Guardian Response shall provide such written explanation as the Legal Guardian determines is appropriate.

4.4 DISCLOSURE. If the Legal Guardian issues a Future Generations Impact Statement with respect to a legislative measure, the Speaker of the House of Representatives and the President of the Senate shall cause the Future Generations Impact Statement, the Response to Impact Findings (when issued), and the Legal Guardian Response (if and when issued) to be set forth on any print or electronic version of the legislative measure to which it relates. If the Legal Guardian issues a Future Generations Impact Statement with respect to a proposed administrative rule, the agency proposing the administrative rule shall cause the Future Generations Impact Statement, the Response to Impact Findings (when issued), and the Legal Guardian Response (if and when issued) to be set forth on any print or electronic version of the proposed administrative rule to which it relates.

4.5 CONSIDERATION OF LEGAL GUARDIAN'S CONCLUSIONS. If the Legal Guardian issues a Future Generations Impact Statement with respect to a legislative measure, the Legislative Assembly shall consider the Future Generations Impact Statement and the Legal Guardian Response (if and when issued) in acting on the legislative measure to which it relates. The Legislative Assembly shall provide a written explanation with respect to any legislative measure that is passed by the Legislative Assembly that is inconsistent with the Future Generations Impact Statement or the Legal Guardian Response (if and when issued) before the legislative measure is submitted to the Governor for action, which explanation shall be set forth on any print or electronic version of the legislative measure to which it relates. If the Legal Guardian issues a Future Generations Impact Statement with respect to a proposed administrative rule, the agency shall consider the Future Generations Impact Statement and the Legal Guardian Response (if and when issued) in acting on the proposed administrative rule to which it relates. The agency shall provide a written explanation with respect to any administrative rule that is promulgated that is inconsistent with the Future Generations Impact Statement or the Legal Guardian Response (if and when issued) before the administrative rule becomes effective, which explanation shall be set forth on any print or electronic version of the administrative rule to which it relates.

* * *

Notes

1. Section 3.6 of the Oregon proposal stipulated that it would create "no private right of action." What does this mean in terms of enforcing the proposal's provisions?

2. What authority exists to direct a legislative committee to respond to a Future Generations Impact Statement (§ 4.2)? Or to direct the legislature to provide a written explanation of action inconsistent with such a statement (§ 4.5)? What would happen if the legislation enacted a law without complying with these provisions?

3. In an ambitious project to delineate legal mechanisms for the protection of future generations against climate impacts, the Climate Legacy Initiative (comprising a group of leading scholars) recommended a model executive order establishing an Office of Legal Guardian for Future Generations that could be adopted at the state and federal levels. The Initiative also recommended that courts rely on special masters and expert witnesses to discern the interests of future generations in cases that affect them. *See* Burns H. Weston & Tracy Bach, *Recalibrating the Law of Humans with the Laws of Nature: Climate Change, Human Rights, and Intergenerational Justice,* CLI Recommendation Nos. 10, 12, at 81–82, 84 (2009), *available at* http://www.area-net.org/fileadmin/user_upload/Maja/Future_Justice_Library/Library_2.pdf.

4. In public trust cases, should courts allow present generations to also represent the interests of future generations? In the Philippines *Oposa* case (p. 341), children sued the national government to halt clear-cut logging that was eliminating the nation's forests. They asserted a role to "represent their generation as well as generations yet unborn." The Supreme Court of the Philippines held in favor of the youth plaintiffs, stating:

> This case ... has a special and novel element. Petitioners minors assert that they represent their generation as well as generations yet unborn. We find no difficulty in ruling that they can, for themselves, for others of their generation and for the succeeding generations, file a class suit. Their personality to sue in behalf of the succeeding generations can only be based on the concept of intergenerational responsibility insofar as the right to a balanced and healthful ecology is concerned. Such a right, as hereinafter expounded, considers the 'rhythm and harmony of nature.' ...

> Needless to say, every generation has a responsibility to the next to preserve that rhythm and harmony for the full enjoyment of a balanced and healthful ecology. Put a little differently, the minors' assertion of their right to a sound environment constitutes, at the same time, the performance of their obligation to ensure the protection of that right for the generations to come.

Oposa v. Factoran, 224 S.C.R.A. 792 (1993) (p. 341). In *The Planetary Trust: Conservation and Intergenerational Equity,* 11 Ecology L.Q. 495, 499 (1984), Professor Edith Brown Weiss suggested the same approach to intergenerational standing ("This planetary trust obligates each generation to preserve the diversity of the resource base and to pass the planet to future generations in no worse condition than it receives it. Thus, the present generation serves both as a trustee for future generations and as a beneficiary of the trust.").

The Public Trust Doctrine in Motion
David C. Slade
(2008)

[T]he Public Trust Doctrine continues to evolve. It is a doctrine in motion, as it has been since Justinian times. Courts may, and should, strictly scrutinize every lawyer's argument to expand the scope of the Public Trust Doctrine. But, without recognizing the Doctrine's inherent flexibility to evolve as the mores and needs of society evolve, as our scientific understanding advances, and as our natural resources suffer the weight of modern society, courts could, as Tom Jefferson foresaw, force modern society "to wear still the coat which fitted him when a boy" and "civilized society to remain ever under the regimen of their barbarous ancestors."

[Case law] show[s] that the Public Trust Doctrine is being actively litigated all around the country. Of the 50 states, 40 are represented in this study—25 coastal and 15 inland states. And litigation is just the proverbial tip of the iceberg. Actual utilization of the doctrine in resource management and permitting actions is undoubtedly a constant across the Nation. Of the 284 disputes that made it all the way to court, thousands upon thousands of Public Trust Doctrine issues must have been resolved at the agency or neighbor level. The doctrine is firmly embedded in state property, resource and environmental protection law....

* * *

Also of importance is what the [case law does not] show. As noted, most of the states are represented in the 284 cases, but not all. This is to be understood. Not every state in the Union must have Public Trust Doctrine court cases. One reason is that trust issues may well be resolved at the agency or neighbor level. But sadly, another reason is that in some states, the Trustees are not only asleep on the job. Worse. In some states the Public Trust Doctrine has never once been invoked since Statehood. Maryland, conspicuously absent from the [s]tudy [c]ases, is one such state. One of the original 13 states, Maryland possesses the Nation's largest estuary, Chesapeake Bay. Despite the great heraldry and fanfare from the politicians about the millions of dollars spent on trying to improve Chesapeake Bay, the fact remains that it is dying. Every summer, vast areas of oxygen depleted "dead zones" cover the main body of the Bay. The Chesapeake Bay Foundation [CBF] recently graded that Bay's health at 28, where 100 is the benchmark for the pristine health of the Bay when Captain John Smith first sailed its waters in 1600s. The CBF affirms that, in...spite of some success such as the return of the rockbass, the overall health of the Bay continues to decline. The need is clear: leaders at every level must do much more if we are to rescue the Bay from a slow asphyxiation and death. One thing the state Trustees—the Governor, Attorney General and the Legislature—could do is wake up and invoke the Trust Power. The fact that they never have [done so] is a sad, yet clear, breach of their trust duty to the citizens of Maryland.

The Public Trust Doctrine is by no means a panacea. But, with the Doctrine's inherent flexibility to evolve as the mores and needs of society evolve, as our scientific understanding advances, and as we recognize more every day that our natural resources are suffering under the weight of modern society, the Doctrine's essential place in resource stewardship is abundantly clear. The Public Trust Doctrine had evolved in our own time from an ancient code, designed to keep the seas, shorelands and fish open to the public, to a modern doctrine of environmental stewardship. Although it remains pegged to "navigable" waters in most states, it is clear that the principles inherent in the Public Trust Doctrine can be, perhaps should be, applied to all publicly-held resources.... It is a doctrine in motion.

Index